Library of
Davidson College

Anthropology in the Development Process

Anthropology in the Development Process

Edited by
Hari Mohan Mathur

With the collaboration of
Christoph von Fürer-Haimendorf

VIKAS PUBLISHING HOUSE PVT LTD
New Delhi Bombay Bangalore Calcutta Kanpur

VIKAS PUBLISHING HOUSE PVT LTD
5 Ansari Road, New Delhi 110002
Savoy Chambers, 5 Wallace Street, Bombay 400001
10 First Main Road, Gandhi Nagar, Bangalore 560009
8/1-B Chowringhee Lane, Calcutta 700016
80 Canning Road, Kanpur 208004

301.2
A6286

COPYRIGHT © HARI MOHAN MATHUR, 1977

ISBN 0 7069 0541 5

1V02M4401

82-4287

Printed at Dhawan Printing Works, 26-A Mayapuri, New Delhi 110064

Acknowledgements

Grateful acknowledgement is made to the authors, publishers, and copyright holders for granting us permission to reprint material that originally appeared in various books and journals, as indicated below:

Chapter 1   *Finance and Development*, vol. 11, no. 2, June 1974, pp. 20-23.
Chapter 2   *International Social Science Journal*, vol. 24, no. 1, pp. 80-94.
Chapter 3   *The Crisis of Indian Planning*, edited by Paul Streeten and Michael Lipton. London: Oxford University Press, 1968, pp. 271-89.
Chapter 4   *Human Organization*, vol. 12, no. 3, 1953, pp. 4-12.
Chapter 6   *Development Administration: Concepts and Problems*, edited by Irvig Swerdlow. Syracuse: Syracuse University Press, 1963, pp. 66-84.
Chapter 8   *The Journal of Asian Studies*, vol. 16, no. 1, November 1956, pp. 19-30.
Chapter 9   *Human Organization*, vol. 22, no. 1, 1963, pp. 95-104.
Chapter 10 *Economic Development and Cultural Change*, vol. 1, December, 1952, pp. 261-72.
Chapter 11 *Fact and Theory in Social Science*, edited by Earl Count and Gordon T. Bowles. Syracuse: Syracuse University Press, 1964, pp. 201-21.
Chapter 12 *Culture and Population: A Collection of Current Studies*, edited by Steven Polgar. Chapel Hill, N.C.: Carolina Population Center, 1972, pp. 160-66.
Chapter 13 *India: A Survey Compiled from the Times*. London: The Times Publishing Co., 1962, pp. 35-38.
Chapter 14 *Economic and Political Weekly*, vol. 29, no. 29-31, July 1970, pp. 1-9.
Chapter 15 *Journal of British Association for the Advancement of Science*, vol. 23, December 1966, pp. 399-409.
Chapter 16 *Pacific Affairs*, vol. 29, no. 1, March 1956, pp. 37-45.

Chapter 17	*Communication and Change in the Developing Countries,* edited by Wilbur Schramm and Daniel Lerner. Honolulu: East-West Center Press, 1967, pp. 129-67.
Chapter 18	*Eastern Anthropologist,* vol. 8, nos. 3 and 4, March-August 1955, pp. 215-28.
Chapter 19	*Human Organization,* vol. 22, no. 1, Spring 1963, pp. 66-74.
Chapter 20	*Economic and Political Weekly,* vol. 9, nos. 6, 7 and 8, February 1974.
Chapters 21 and 22	*Health, Culture, and Community,* edited by Benjamin D. Paul. New York: Russell Sage Foundation, 1955, pp. 107-34 and 239-68.
Chapter 23	*Research Previews,* vol. 19, no. 1. 1972, pp. 24-29.
Chapter 24	*The Adivasis.* Delhi: The Publications Division, Government of India.
Chapter 25	*The Tribal World of Verrier Elwin.* Delhi: Oxford University Press, 1964, pp. 287-303.
Chapter 26	*Report of the Scheduled Areas and Scheduled Tribes Commission,* vol. 1. Delhi: Government of India Press, 1961, pp. 487-99.
Chapter 27	*India and Ceylon: Unity and Diversity,* edited by Philip Mason. London: Oxford University Press, 1967, pp. 182-222.

Contributors

CYRIL S. BELSHAW
Professor of Anthropology, **University** *of British Columbia, Vancouver, Canada.*

AGEHANANDA BHARATI
Professor of Anthropology, Syracuse University, Syracuse, New York, U.S.A.

F.G. BAILEY
Professor of Anthropology, University of California, San Diego, U.S.A.

G. MORRIS CARSTAIRS
Vice-Chancellor, University of New York, England.

GLYNN COCHRANE
Professor of Anthropology, Syracuse University, Syracuse, New York, U.S.A.

S.C. DUBE
Director, Indian Institute of Advanced Study, Simla, India.

VERRIER ELWIN
Late Advisor on Tribal Affairs to the Governor of Assam, India.

T. SCARLETT EPSTEIN
Fellow, Institute of Development Studies, University of Sussex, Brighton, England.

THOMAS M. FRASER, Jr.
University of Massachusetts, Amherst, Massachusetts, U.S.A.

CHRISTOPH VON FURER-HAIMENDORF
Director, School of Oriental and African Studies, University of London, London, England.

MILDRED S. LUSCHINSKY
Department of Anthropology, Cornell University, Ithaca, New York, U.S.A.

DAVID G. MANDELBAUM
Professor of Anthropology, University of California, Berkeley, U.S.A.

McKIM MARRIOTT
Professor of Anthropology, University of Chicago, Chicago, U.S.A.

JOHN F. MARSHALL
Scientist, Human Reproduction Unit, W.H.O. Geneva, Switzerland.

HARI MOHAN MATHUR
Director, State Institute of Public Administration, Jaipur, India.

ADRIAN C. MAYER
Professor of Asian Anthropology, School of Oriental and African Studies, University of London, London, England.

JOAN P. MENCHER
Professor of Anthropology, City University of New York, U.S.A.

KUSUM NAIR
East-West Center, University of Hawaii, Honolulu, U.S.A.

JAWAHARLAL NEHRU
Late Prime Minister of India.

MORRIS E. OPLER
Professor of Anthropology, University of Oklahoma, U.S.A.

D.F. POCOCK
Dean, School of African and Asian Studies, University of Sussex, Brighton, England.

M.N. SRINIVAS
Senior Fellow, Institute of Economic and Social Change, Bangalore, India.

Preface

Until recently, the study of village life in the less developed countries of Asia, Africa and elsewhere was the subject of exclusive professional interest to the anthropologists. The development of these societies is now increasingly gaining the attention of the governments of these countries, many international development agencies and a wide variety of development specialists.

The growing current interest of the planners in the rural problems of the Third World nations is quite understandable. A vast majority of the poor in these countries lives in the villages and, as the evidence from several recent studies shows, these are the groups of people whom the development efforts of the past quarter century have failed to benefit in any significant manner. Equity, which is being so much talked about these days everywhere, requires that the struggle against poverty be intensified, more particularly in the areas of its greatest concentration.

With their knowledge of the problems of the poor the societies around the world, anthropologists can surely help in designing more realistic development plans and programmes for them, and also assist the planners and administrators in their effort to see that the benefits of economic growth do indeed reach down to the target populations. Development planners and administrators are themselves beginning to realize that they need the assistance of anthropologists in their work in several important ways. But this understanding is as yet very limited. It needs to be more widely diffused to be able to contribute to development effectively.

Development planners and administrators engaged in various programmes aimed at improving the quality of life of the people living in poverty will find this reader useful to them. An effort has been made here to include only such writings as would particularly contribute to a better appreciation of the socio-cultural context in which all development occurs. The authors in this book offer no "solutions" to the human problems which confront the planners and administrators, but they do point to the several socio-cultural factors which must be taken into account if development is to really succeed among the rural people whose lives are still largely governed by tradition.

On the anthropology of development, the existing literature is not very abundant. It is also not easily accessible; scientific journals, specialist studies, conference papers and such materials usually have a rather restricted circulation. This volume brings together a selection of writings on the subject in the hope that it will overcome the problem of inaccessibility, introduce the planners and administrators to a core of anthropological writings relevant to their development work, and help promote a more systematic study of the anthropological contribution to development problems.

An anthropological approach to planning and development which these writings make explicit is valid for all Third World countries. However, the book is focused on India chiefly for two reasons. One, within the broad field of anthropological studies, anthropology in India is an area of particular interest to us. In fact, this happens to be true of nearly all the contributors to this volume who are internationally renowned anthropologists mainly from India, England, and the U.S.A. They have lived and done anthropological fieldwork in India's villages for a longer or shorter period. Their writings reflect their deep interest in and an insightful understanding of India's many complex, pressing development problems. Two, India happens to be the only country for which there perhaps exists sufficient documentation exemplifying an anthropological approach to the problems of development planning and administration.

What merit this volume has, owes a great deal to many colleagues who have been so generous with their help. The

Preface

idea for the production of this reader on development anthropology really sparked a great deal of enthusiasm. Permission to reprint their writings was granted by almost all the authors most willingly. Their cooperation and assistance are very much appreciated. Grateful thanks are due to the following for the helpful and encouraging comments they offered on the plan of this book: Irma Adelman, Yogesh Atal, Glynn Cochrane, George Dalton, Ishwar Dayal, Nitish R. De, S.C. Dube, T. Scarlett Epstein, R.N. Haldipur, David G. Mandelbaum, McKim Marriott, K.S. Mathur, Adrian C. Mayer, Joan P. Mencher, J.P. Naik, Morris E. Opler and L.P. Vidyarthi.

T. Scarlett Epstein's paper is appearing in this volume for the first time. Presented to the 1973 Annual Conference of the Association of Social Anthropologists held at Oxford, this has been revised specially for this volume. Some changes have been made by David F. Pocock in his article. A few minor changes were suggested by David G. Mandelbaum and McKim Marriott in their papers and these have been incorporated.

Perhaps we can speak for the authors in expressing the hope that this book will be useful both to the anthropologists who are gradually becoming interested in development problems and to the development specialists engaged in fighting a fearsome battle against poverty in the Third World.

HARI MOHAN MATHUR
CHRISTOPH VON FURER-HAIMENDORF

Contents

HARI MOHAN MATHUR *Introduction* 1

PART I: ANTHROPOLOGY AND DEVELOPMENT

1 GLYNN COCHRANE *What Can Anthropology Do for Development?* 17
2 CYRIL S. BELSHAW *The Contribution of Anthropology to Development* 27
3 DAVID POCOCK *Social Anthropology: Its Contribution to Planning* 48
4 DAVID G. MANDELBAUM *Planning and Social Change in India* 70
5 T. SCARLETT EPSTEIN *The Role of Social Anthropology in Development Studies* 88
6 AGEHANANDA BHARATI *Cultural Hurdles in Development Administration* 104
7 HARI MOHAN MATHUR *Anthropology, Government, and Developmental Planning in India* 121

PART II: SOCIO-CULTURAL DIMENSIONS OF PLANNED DEVELOPMENT

8 S. C. DUBE *Cultural Factors in Rural Community Development* 139
9 THOMAS M. FRASER, Jr. *Socio-cultural Parameters in Directed Change* 156

10	McKim Marriott	Technological Change in Overdeveloped Rural Areas 183
11	Morris E. Opler	Cultural Context of Population Control Programmes in Village India 201
12	John F. Marshall	Topics and Networks in Intravillage Communication 226
13	Kusum Nair	Human Element in Indian Planning 234

PART III: PROGRAMME ADMINISTRATORS AND THE PEOPLE

14	Joan P. Mencher	Change Agents and Villager 241
15	F. G. Bailey	The Peasant View of Bad Life 270
16	Adrian C. Mayer	Development Projects in an Indian Village 292
17	S. C. Dube	Communication, Innovation, and Planned Change in India 304

PART IV : RURAL COMMUNITIES AND CHANGE

18	M. N. Srinivas	Village Studies and their Significance 329
19	Mildred S. Luschinsky	Problems of Culture Change in the Indian Village 346
20	Joan P. Mencher	Conflicts and Contradictions in the "Green Revolution" 370
21	G. Morris Carstairs	Medicine and Faith in Rural Rajasthan 394
22	McKim Marriott	Western Medicine in a Village of North India 421
23	John F. Marshall	Some "Meanings" of Family Planning to an Indian Villager 451

PART V: DEVELOPMENT ADMINISTRATION IN TRIBAL AREAS

24	Jawaharlal Nehru	An Approach to Tribal Problems 461

25 VERRIER ELWIN — *Growth of a "Philosophy"* 468
26 Report of the Scheduled Areas and Scheduled Tribes Commission — *A New Deal for Tribal India* 485
27 CHRISTOPH VON FURER-HAIMENDORF — *The Position of Tribal Population in Modern India* 503

Bibliography 545

Index 555

Hari Mohan Mathur

Introduction

Planners are now becoming more and more concerned with improving the income levels of the small farmers, the landless labourers, the tribal pastoralists, the traditional craftsmen and other poorer segments of the population living mostly in the rural communities of the Third World. This heightened interest in the problems of these people stems chiefly from the realization that while the development policies pursued in the past quarter century did succeed in achieving a higher economic growth rate, their failure to secure adequate participation of the poor in the development process has tended to sharpen the inequalities, and has in many cases only made things worse for them (Adelman and Morris, 1973; Chenery et al., 1974; Elliott, 1975). About the growth pattern of a Latin American country it was recently remarked that that country was doing well but its people were not.[1] To the planners, whose current development efforts are largely focussed towards the people particularly the poorer groups, this surely cannot be an acceptable development model.

The broad elements of a global policy to attack poverty of these approximately 900 million poor people—comprising roughly 40 per cent of the population of around one hundred less developed countries in Asia, Africa and Latin America—were outlined by the President of the World Bank, Robert S. McNamara

---

[1]Quoted in Stefan H. Robock, 1976. "Are There Development Lessons from Brazil?", *International Development Review*, Vol. XVIII, No. 1, p. 16.

(1973) while addressing the Meeting of the Board of Governors of the World Bank Group in Nairobi, Kenya in 1973. The Bank has since taken several quick steps to implement this new development strategy.[2] A drastic shift in its pattern of lending has occurred in recent years. Much larger share of Bank lending is now going into projects with clear social dimensions (agriculture, population, education, health, nutrition, etc.) than into purely infrastructural projects (power plants, communications, etc.).[3]

It is simply not possible to neglect the poor and more. They are loudly demanding their share in the economic progress. Most governments of the less developed countries have themselves begun trying to improve the conditions of the poor to ensure that development truly benefits all segments of the population. In India, where development and welfare programmes for the very poor have always been accorded the highest priority, the one overriding objective of all major government socioeconomic plans and programmes today is only to alleviate the widespread, grinding poverty.[4]

As the emphasis in planning comes increasingly to be laid on rural development, employment creation, income distribution and the removal of poverty, and as projects with explicit social dimensions get started on a wider scale, the need in development agencies for experts most familiar with the

---

[2] Just two years after Robert S. McNamara had enunciated the World Bank Policy towards the poor in his Address at Nairobi, Kenya, in 1973, he was able to report substantial progress in this direction in his Address to the 1975 Meeting of the Board of Governors. He stated emphatically: "We have not only elaborated policy. We have moved ahead with an expanded lending program in rural development and we now lend more in this sector than in any other. This is a clear change in emphasis: 50% of all rural development lending in the history of the Bank has occurred in the last year. We expect to commit $ 7 million more in this field over the next five years." (Robert McNamara, *Address to the Board of Governors*, World Bank, Washington D.C., 1975.)

[3] See J.H. Adler, 1972. "The World Bank's Concept of Development-An In-House *Dogmengeschichte*," in Jagdish N. Bhagwati and Richard S. Eckaus, eds., *Development and Planning: Essays in Honour of Paul Resenstein Rodan*. London: George Allen & Unwin Ltd.

[4] The Prime Minister's Twenty Point Programme announced on 1 July 1975 seeks to direct all efforts for the rapid socioeconomic development of poorer segments of the population.

problems of the rural poor is certain to grow. Anthropologists, who alone over the years have been concerned with micro-level studies of the rural poor communities and whose knowledge of the processes and problems of sociocultural change in the traditional societies of the Third World is unsurpassable, certainly seem best equipped to help planners in dealing with the development problems of the very poor. In the changed context, the traditional skills and ways of handling the problems of the poor that have all along been in exclusive use are increasingly believed to be inadequate. But what, in actual fact, has been happening in the development agencies to enlist the assistance of the experts who can really help? Is the need for the participation of anthropologists in the development programmes being felt? And are the anthropologists there to work for the development agencies and to assist the planners in their task of involving the poor in the development process?

There is certainly a growing appreciation today of the role of anthropology in the field of development studies and action. David H. Penny (1972:5), an economist, writes: "From certain points of view, social anthropologists appear, from their training, to be well qualified to study the development process—they learn the language of the people they are studying, they stay long enough in the field to get to know at least some people well, and to see development in process, and they know that they must study a society in all its aspects." Some development specialists with practical experience of work in the Third World countries now regard the association of anthropologists and other social scientists in the new development projects as of critical significance. Recently Anthony Bottrall (1974) even went to the extent of arguing that development programmes were unlikely to succeed unless the skills of the people forming the traditional core of the development profession (namely, the technical experts and the economists) were supplemented by those of the skills with a specialized interest in the sociocultural characteristics of the rural communities (meaning anthropologists and other social scientists).

But while the need for anthropological and other social science input in the planning process is beginning to be fairly widely recognized, what has been done so far to incorporate these skills in the development profession remains clearly inadequate. Why, then, are the skills so urgently needed for development work not being utilized? The conservatism of the development agencies is partly the answer. But there are several other reasons as well.

In 1972, the World Bank invited Glynn Cochrane to advise on what could be done to make greater use of anthropolgy in the Bank operations. Reviewing the Bank experience with anthropologists, Glynn Cochrane found that sporadic use of anthropologists in the Bank work was mainly attributable to three main reasons: (*a*) lack of familiarity of the Bank staff with anthropology and the attendant problems of how to recruit anthropologists and how to interpret and use their recommendations, (*b*) lack of an institutional basis for use of anthropologists, and (*c*) absence of in-hose capacity.[5] These same reasons would also seem to hold good for the limited use of anthropologists in other development agencies as well.

Economists have exclusively been in the business of making development plans all these years. And the confidence they seem to have acquired in their planning ability is enormous. Gunnar Myrdal (1971:20) says of this confidence:

> Place any economist in the capital city of an underdeveloped country and give him the necessary assistance and he will in no time make a Plan. In this regard we are unique among the social scientists. No sociologist, psychologist, or anthropologist would ever think of trying to do such a thing.

For the economist the task of making development plans is made easier by the fact that he usually limits his study to measurable economic phenomena. Then use of highly sophisticated statistical techniques permits him to study a larger universe. This in turn helps him to think in broader terms and make plans for the entire country.[6]

---

[5]Quoted in Tariq Husain, *The Use of Anthropologists in Project Appraisal by World Bank*. Paper presented to the IXth International Congress of Anthropological and Ethnological Sciences, Chicago, 1973.

[6]The economist is also greatly helped by the fact that there is an institutional support to his work, which in the case of other social scientists is completely lacking. Donald V.M. Granahan observes: ''A major

As a basis for planning development, this macro-analysis in purely "economic" terms might perhaps be a valid procedure for countries in the West. Tradition and attitudes there are basically in conformity with the goals of development. But in most of the Third World, where forces favouring the status quo are stronger than the forces favouring change, this approach may not be the most appropriate one.

Often macro-analysis in purely "economic" terms overlooks the role of social factors which in these countries so importantly determine the outcome of all development effort. From a distance it really is not possible to appreciate the significance of all the minutest features of life in the far-flung villages. An observation by Peter Worsley (1971: 26) in this regard is very pertinent: "In peasant society, differences in social status which are invisible to the airport sociologist loom very large under the anthropologist's microscope." The implications of seemingly small matters in planning change in traditional societies come to the fore only when some project failures are analyzed.

While the anthropologist is able to see the interconnections between economic and social variables and the effect on different aspects of social life produced by these variables operating together, he cannot make generalizations valid for wide geographic regions. He is hindered by the simple fact that his universe is small, comprising a tribal group, a village, or one small segment of a big city. On the basis of his micro-level studies, he is surely in a position to say that a development plan that fails to take account of certain social factors is unlikely to yield the anticipated results, but making a national plan is clearly not the job which the anthropologist in the present state of anthropological knowledge would even think of attempting. And for this reason the anthropologist is rather modest about his role as a planner. T. Scarlett Epstein (1973:2) says:

---

difficulty in building up an integrated discipline of development is the fact that the social sciences such as sociology, anthropology and social psychology have no recognised operational outlet in an organ of government unlike economics, which has ministries, departments or councils of economics in the government." In "Notes on Development Research by International Organisations," *International Social Science Journal*, Vol. XXVI, No. 3, 1974, p. 524.

As yet our understanding of social processes is too limited to allow for general socio-economic theories to be developed on a macro-level. We are only beginning to appreciate the heterogenous nature of different societies, of sections within them and of individuals within each group. It is relatively easy for social anthropologists, or other social scientists to prick holes in the economists' development bubbles and burst them, but it is much more difficult, in fact it seems still impossible, to suggest all-embracing development theories which may be universally applicable. Social anthropologists realize much more clearly than do economists the severe limitations the vast scope and range of human societies sets to their research.

Development, continuing to be largely designed by the economists on a purely "economic" basis, cannot hope to fully realize the goals now set by the planners. Nobody, however, would suggest that the planning be abandoned simply because social science is not yet ready with an all-embracing theory of socioeconomic development. All that the anthropologists would urge is that the knowledge about different societies that they have assiduously gathered should not be excluded from planning considerations. As T. Scarlett Epstein (1973:4) makes the point further:

> It would be foolish to suggest that development planning should wait until social anthropologists have gathered sufficient knowledge to help produce a general growth model applicable to even only one particular country, let alone to suit at large. It is only to be hoped that in the meantime planners in underdeveloped countries...try and learn as much as possible at grass roots level about the problems and difficulties of the people for whom they plan development .... Planners in particular and development economists in general will have to acquaint themselves with many social anthropological and other micro-studies relating to the underdeveloped regions of the world.

To be more realistic, planning will have to increasingly

concern itself with the facts of life of the people it aims to change.

But this need to take the human factor into account, self-evident to anthropologists, is still not felt by all development specialists. Reports by development administrators operating at ground level in various Third World countries have in recent years been persistently pointing to the failure on the part of the planning agencies to give to the human factor the importance due to it.[7] While a large number of development economists readily admit the importance of non-economic factors in development, those who actually take these factors into account in their analysis are still very few.[8]

Planners are usually so busy in their offices with endless data collecting, computing, report writing and other similar work that they finally end up losing all touch with the grass-roots reality.[9] Commenting on this lack of contact between planners and the people in rural areas, Gilbert Etienne (1968: 285) observes:

> A number of young Indians have thus become as much a foreigner in the villages as a Westerner. Being without first hand experiences, they tend to indulge in abstract analysis of the peasant's needs.

This separation of planners from the people for whose development they work naturally gives rise to erroneous ideas concerning behaviour, values, attitudes, and motivations of the

---

[7]See Herbert H. Hyman *et al.*, 1967. *Inducing Social Change in Developing Communities: An International Survey of Expert Advice.* Geneva: UN Research Institute for Social Development.

[8]Gunnar Myrdal is a leading economist who thinks that social variables cannot be excluded from the planning process of countries like India. Gunnar Myrdal, 1971 *The Challenge of World Poverty: A World Anti-Poverty Programme in Outline.* London: Allen Lane, The Penguin Press.

[9]Michael Lipton finds "urban bias" in India's planning which largely accounts for the slow development of agriculture. See Michael Lipton, 1968. "Strategy for Agriculture: Urban Bias and Rural Planning," in Paul Streeten and Michael Lipton, eds., *The Crisis of Indian Planning.* Bombay: Oxford University Press.

rural poor.[10] There is, for example, the popular notion that peasants resist all change. This belief is, however, not supported by the mirco-level studies which have accumulated evidence to show that the farmer does not blindly adhere to the tradition if the need for change is convincingly demonstrated to him.[11]

If the farmers decide not to adopt new agricultural practices, they often have valid reasons. To show that the decision-making of the farmers is a rational process, Beals (1962: 79) cites the following case from Gopalpur:

> To purchase improved agricultural equipment, the farmer must sever his traditional relationship with the Blacksmith and Carpenter. This is more than an economic relationship. Not only are the Carpenter and Blacksmith neighbours and friends, but they have religious functions that make their presence essential on such occasions as birth, marriage, and death. The Carpenter and Blacksmith offer an integrated set of tools and guarantee repairs. Under these circumstances, the purchase of a moldboard plow, or any improved equipment, becomes a tricky and difficult business. On their side, the Carpenter and Blacksmith receive a fixed quantity of grain at harvest time. If they were to improve their product, they would find it difficult to raise their prices to cover its greatest cost. The benefits of improved agricultural techniques have not been demonstrated, and their use is attended by great economic and social risk. In refusing to adopt new methods, the farmer of Gopalpur shows common sense, not conservatism.

---

[10]Polly Hill, an economist who made an essentially anthropological study of Cacao farmers in Ghana, came to the conclusion that many of the ideas concerning the peasants held by economists are simply untenable. See Polly Hill, 1963. *The Migrant. Cacao Farmers of Ghana.* New York: Cambridge University Press.

[11]Prawl thinks that stereotype generalizations cannot be accepted in the face of new evidence. He says, "Many development field workers confess that they find farmers more receptive to change than the agents of change and the administrators with whom they worked. I agree with them, both as a result of personal experience and from research I have conducted on this subject." Warren L. Prawl, 1969. "It is the Agents of Change Who don't like Change," *CERES FAO Review on Development,* Vol. 2, No. 4, July/August.

Introduction

In the given circumstances, the options that the farmer chooses are indeed quite rational. Policies designed to effect changes in the lifestyle of the people which are not based on a proper sociocultural understanding of these communities are unlikely to succeed. Potter (1971: 361) cautions: "Unless rural development planners have an intimate knowledge of all aspects of a culture, unnecessary difficulties will occur for both the planning agency and the people involved."

The obvious way to see that social factors receive consideration in the planning of development programmes would then seem to be to secure the involvement of anthropologists in this process on a scale significantly larger than has been the case until now. It is true that anthropologists, like other social scientists, still are "short on theory and long on cliches," but their exclusion from the multi-disciplinary planning teams would only mean the continued neglect of knowledge of the social factors in the planning process. Not putting to use this existing knowledge when that can surely be helpful in getting development going in the right direction would be most unwise. Anthony Bottrall (1975:74) argues: "The rudimentary state of rural institutional theory offers no real excuse for denying social scientists a more prominent role in decision-making: the essential nature of the problem is well enough understood and a substantial improvement in theory will be virtually impossible unless they are given more opportunity for field experience and experiment."

To some extent, anthropologists are themselves responsible for their limited involvement in the development programmes. Not many of them really believe that the skills they possess are what the development agencies are eagerly looking for. Also, they generally do not take the initiative to suggest that their knowledge can have practical uses for several development jobs. On the contrary, it is the economists and others who have been showing an interest in collaborating with the anthropologists in development work which is essentially interdisciplinary in character. Addressing a gathering of anthropologists recently, Gunnar Myrdal (1975: 331) observed:

> For the time being the situation is that while, on the one hand, we economists, who monopolize national planning for development, are on the verge of coming to see the necessity

of a much broader approach to this planning, our colleagues in the other social sciences and, in the first place, the anthropologists, are not providing us with the information we need. Even in the fields where relevant studies have been made, the findings are seldom organized to be suitable for our purposes, as they have been prepared by scientists who have not worked under the planning perspective.

They can raise a warning finger urging the economist planner not to forget this or that. But not being themselves accustomed to think in terms of planning for development, they are not equipped effectively to challenge our planning. When economists now, very belatedly, are gradually coming to see the need for a "unified" approach, this has on the whole not been caused by systematic criticism from our colleagues in the other social sciences, responsible for what we call the "noneconomic" factors. It has mainly been some of the economists themselves, and some politicians and administrators, who have been finding out the need for a broader knowledge for planning.

There are some anthropologists, then, who genuinely think that they need not concern themselves with practical problems at all. They stoutly believe that they are students of change, not agents of change. In actual fact, they usually lack the necessary training and experience to be directly useful to the planning agencies. Glynn Cochrane (1974: 20) says:

The discipline, of course, has been university based, and the academic orientation has meant that anthropologists as a class have not yet had sufficient opportunity to develop and accumulate the kind of institutional experience which would enable them to contribute to the integrated framework of policies and practices that characterize modern development. Part of the problem has been training in modern schools of anthropology, which pays insufficient attention to development work.

Surely, it will be necessary for anthropologists wanting to work in the field of development to be trained differently from the way the university departments traditionally have been producing the bulk of their graduates.[12]

On a few rare occasions in the past when anthropological advice was sought, it did not always live up to the expectations of the development agencies which sought the advice. And many began doubting the usefulness of the anthropological contribution to development matters. But anthropologists cannot here be entirely blamed for their limited use to the agencies seeking their assistance. More often than not, anthropological consultants are called, if at all, when it is too late. At that stage they obviously cannot do much to find solutions to the problems which arise from the initial deficiencies in the planning process. Unless planning agencies begin associating anthropologists at all stages of planning, like other members of the interdisciplinary development teams, they will not be able to make any significant impact on the outcome of development effort. Anthony Bottrall (1975: 50) observes in this connection:

> So long as sociologists or anthropologists are assigned at the best only a peripheral role in decision-making, it is predictable that most of them will be inclined to remain introvertedly academic, muttering disgruntled comments from the sidelines. Before judgement is passed on their practical capabilities, they should surely be given enough responsibility to be consulted about critical questions before most of the options have been closed and enough opportunity for regular association with technical people and economists to develop a fruitful working relationships with them. Only then might it be possible to decide whether their basic intellectual training inevitably breeds an outlook which makes most of them fundamentally unsuited to collaborative development work or whether the shortcomings they are accused of are mainly the result of inadequate access to the world of practical decision-making.

[12]Some suggestions on what needs to be done to make anthropology courses more oriented to the requirements of development planning will be found in the following: Glynn Cochrane, 1971. *Development Anthropology*. New York: Oxford University Press. Cyril S. Belshaw, 1972. "The Contribution of Anthropology to Development," *International Social Science Journal*, Vol. XXIV, No. 1, pp. 80-94.

Another factor working against the employment of anthropologists in the planning agencies is the persisting common belief that they are opposed to all change and development. Analyzing reasons for the anthropologists' failure to contribute to development significantly, Solo (1972: XII) says: "One explanation for this is his vested interest in preserving traditional structures of tribal societies re-enforced by a long standing moral commitment to protect tribal cultures from the disintegrative force and mindless disruption of imperialism and industrialization." It is true that anthropologists have been cautioning against introducing change without preparing the people for it and with no regard to its consequences on different aspects of life. In fact, anthropologists would always prefer change to be introduced in such a way that the target population is protected from the traumas which development surely brings with it. But this cannot be taken to mean that anthropologists do not want the societies in the Third World to proceed on the path of development. If anything, with their knowledge of the people involved, they can be very helpful in furthering rapid development.

An impression that needs to be dispelled is that anthropologists are committed to gradualism in introducing change under all circumstances. Nowhere does anthropological research indicate that rapid change is in itself a bad thing. Margaret Mead's study of a Manus community in the Admirality Islands suggests that rapid change is not necessarily destructive. According to Mead (1956: 372), this experience suggests "that rapid change is not only possible, but may actually be very desirable, that instead of advocating slow partial changes, we should advocate that a people who choose to practice a new technology or enter into drastically new kinds of economic relationships will do this more easily if they live in different houses, wear different clothes, and eat different, or differently cooked food." This view has also been confirmed by other studies. Farmer (1974: 277) observes: "The experience of some Indian tribal peoples, notably the Khasis of Assam, endorses these conclusions."

Poverty-focused development strategies can work only if planners try and understand the people for whom they plan development. It is not enough to produce plans which look excellent on paper. Plans designed to assist the development of poor people must take account of their needs, and their capacity to absorb the benefits from the development process. In the final analysis, most plan failures can be attributed not to the technical imperfections in their formulation, but usually to the lack of understanding of the sociocultural realities on the part of both planners and project administrators.

With their understanding of sociocultural matters, anthropologists can certainly help planners in both the designing and implementation of development. But to be able to do so, effectively anthropologists need to broaden their own understanding of the development process. The concern with development has not yet evoked much enthusiasm among anthropologists (Schneider, 1975). By and large they lack the training and experience needed for working with development agencies. The discipline must now consciously prepare itself to meet the development challenge.

An awareness of, and sensitivity to, human problems, it is often argued, is not the monopoly of the anthropologists alone. Many technical experts and economists do acquire an understanding of the social implications of their development efforts. But it is doubtful if, in addition to their technical job, they can also be expected to do social research, and do it as competently as trained anthropologists. The professional preparation of anthropologists obliges them to live close to the people whom they study. This greatly helps them in developing a perspective on human relationships. And there certainly must be someone in the interdisciplinary development team who has a scientific understanding of the life of the people experiencing development and change. It is important that an effective team approach is fostered so that all the needed skills contribute to the development process. Indeed, the planners' task of seeing that the benefits of development reach down to the very poor is so complex that it can hardly be confined to one single discipline or to a number of disciplines acting independently of each other.

REFERENCES

Adelman, Irma and Cynthia Taft Morris, 1973. *Economic Growth and Social Equity in Developing Countries.* Stanford: Stanford University Press.

Beals, Allan R., 1962. *Gopalpur: A South Indian Village.* New York: Holt, Rinehart and Winston, Inc.

Bottrall, Anthony F., 1974. "The McNamara Strategy: Putting Precept into Practice," *ODI Review* 1-74, p. 80.

———, 1975. "Rural Development: The Gaps in Expertise," *ODI Review* 1-75.

Chenery, Hollis et al., 1974. *Redistribution with Growth.* London: Oxford University Press.

Cochrane, Glynn, 1974. "What Can Anthropology do for Development ?", *Finance and Development*, Vol. 11, No. 2, June.

Elliott, Charles, 1975. *Patterns of Poverty in the Third World.* New York: Praeger Publishers.

Epstein, T. Scarlett, 1973. *South India: Yesterday Today and Tomorrow.* London: Macmillan.

Etienne, Gilbert, 1968. *Studies in Indian Agriculture: The Art of the Possible.* Berkeley: University of California Press. Translated from the French by Megan Mothersole.

Farmer, B.H., 1974. *Agricultural Colonization in India since Independence.* London: Oxford University Press.

McNamara, Robert S., 1973. *Address to the Board of Governors.* Washington D.C.: World Bank.

Mead, Margaret, 1956. *New Lives for Old: Cultural Transformation-Manus, 1928-1953.* New York: Mentor.

Myrdal, Gunnar, 1971. *The Challenge of World Poverty: A World Anti-Poverty Program in Outline.* London: Allen Lane. The Penguin Press.

———, 1975. "The Unity of the Social Sciences," *Human Organisation*, Vol. 34, No. 4, Winter.

Penny, David H., 1972. "Development Studies: Some Reflections," in T. Scarlett Epstein and D.H. Penny, eds., *Opportunity and Response: Case Studies in Economic Development.* London: C. Hurst & Co.

Potter, Jack M., 1971. "Modernization Processes and Rural Development in Developing Countries: An Anthropological View," in Raanan Weitz, ed., *Rural Development in a Changing World.* Cambridge: The MIT Press.

Schneider, Harold K., 1975. "Economic Development and Anthropology," in Bernard J. Siegel et al., eds., *Annual Review of Anthropology*, Vol. 4. Palo Alto, California: Annual Reviews Inc.

Solo, Robert A., 1972. "Introduction: Sociologist, Anthropologist, Economist," in Robert A. Solo and Everett M. Rogers, eds., *Inducing Technological Change for Economic Growth and Development.* East Lansing: Michigan State University.

Worsley, Peter, ed., 1971. *Two Blades of Grass: Rural Cooperatives in Agricultural Modernization.* Manchester University Press.

Part One

Anthropology and Development

Glynn Cochrane

1 What Can Anthropology Do for Development?

Over fifty years ago, Bronislaw Malinowski, one of the intellectual progenitors of modern anthropology, undertook an anthropological analysis of the accumulation and distribution of a few hundred dollars of shell wealth in the remote Trobriand Islands group of the Western Pacific. His purpose was to explain to the developed world that Trobriand islanders were only primitive insofar as their technology was concerned, and that there was nothing rudimentary about their mental processes.

Today, it is still a problem to convince sophisticated people about the value of anthropological analysis, and even among the staff of the biggest development assistance agencies, such as the World Bank, serious reservations remain.

Modern anthropology is hard for many people to appreciate because it is so diverse; its practitioners often seem to go, in one mind-boggling jump, from paleontology and Neanderthal man, to Margaret Mead writing in popular magazines about the problems of women. Such diversity can be more easily understood if one keeps in mind that an anthropologist's choice of what to study is a personal matter, virtually uninfluenced by scientific considerations. It is the difference between anthropologists as people which accounts for diversity. How the study is carried out, in terms of the collection and analysis of data, will conform to common standards and procedures that are the hallmark of modern anthropology.

Social anthropology usually involves mapping out the nature and types of social relationship in a community. The manner of their arrangement delineates social structure. The reasons for change or maintenance of those relationships yield an account of the system of beliefs and values which may be unique to that community. Anthropological analysis is not an abstruse discipline. It merely aims to ask the right questions of the right people, so as to account for and explain behaviour which, though perfectly rational when viewed against the underlying and interlocking system of beliefs and values of a particular society, may be very different from our experience. An anthropologist concerned with development is basically interested in studying behaviour with a view to the prediction and production of social change.

The discipline, of course, has been university based, and this academic orientation has meant that anthropologists as a class have not yet had sufficient opportunity to develop and accumulate the kind of institutional experience which would enable them to contribute to the integrated framework of policies and practices that characterize modern development. Part of the problem has been the training in modern schools of anthropology, which pays insufficient attention to development work: the counterpart has been a lack of institutional leadership in the sense of large public enterprises provided incentives through creation of a demand for adequately trained anthropologists.

Changes in Bank Lending

In early 1970 the World Bank presented an opportunity to test the belief that adequately trained development anthropologists had something useful to contribute. The bank was then moving from a pattern of lending in the fields of power, communications, etc., where the risk factor was perhaps reasonably calculable, to increased lending for agriculture, population, and education where behavioural assessments, from an anthropological view, might be both more important and more difficult to make. It was hoped, that anthropology, in view of its accumulation of experience and data on poor communities all over the world, would be well equipped to assist in the syste-

What Can Anthropology Do for Development?

matic treatment of social issues—the problems of jobs, income distribution, and very poor people.

A development project ought to have an effect quite out of proportion to mere immediate financial and institutional inputs. But little attention is now paid to considering how the spread of demonstration effects of a project are achieved. Spread effects tend to be regarded as a by-product of projects rather than as something that ought to be planned and worked for in phase with the project itself. Some projects have a better cultural "fit" and hence a better potential for spread effect than others. How is demonstration achieved, i. e., should particular status groups be involved, should media be used in promotion, what are the institutional constraints on spread effects? The contribution of a project to the broader scene is important but not yet precisely measured. Anthropologists can help with such matters.

It is important that institutions develop a policy on anthropology rather than relying on a series of *ad hoc* and *ad hominem* contacts between anthropologists and staff members. In the case of the World Bank, before 1970, individual anthropologists had acted as consultants on projects and had worked on Bank studies, but these spasmodic contacts had not led to the adoption of a comprehensive policy on anthropology. In addition, without anthropologists on the permanent staff it seemed likely that there would be problems in briefing and evaluating the work of consultants.

It seemed desirable, therefore, that the utility of the discipline should be demonstrated to the satisfaction of staff members within the context of existing operations, that the potential work load should then be made to the Bank. An overview of the institution's work would be crucial to this endeavour. Equally crucial would be the demonstration—doing anthropology instead of writing about it—because as time passed there was no evidence to show that anthropologists and the Bank would establish an effective relationship of things continued as they were. The Bank's operations were not well-known to anthropologists: the writings of anthropologists did not seem to be getting through to very busy staff members, anthropologists were not sensitized to the problem of development.

The Research Proposal

In 1971 I submitted a research proposal calling for a fifteen-month analysis of the Bank's project operations to see where anthropology might be useful and what methods could be employed to make this contribution available. Upon its approval, Raymond Noronha, a recent graduate of Syracuse University, was also engaged in work on the study.

The first requirement when research commenced at the Bank in June 1972 was to learn as much as possible about how the institution actually functioned—how problems were approached, how they were tackled, what the constraints were, what the time frame was, and the makeup of the staff. We tried to understand the Bank as a system in which there were well-defined roles, hierarchical levels of authority, a distinct set of values on how things should be done—all complicated by a very heavy work programme.

A factor that quickly emerged in this study was the importance of the loan officer, he or she was in a sense the lynchpin between the concerns of projects operations staff and the concerns of regional departments. It was clearly important to assess the willingness of loan officers to innovate by using anthropology. What would encourage them to do so, and what might discourage them? Did incentives and disincentives vary with different geographical areas and different types of projects? What was to be learned from recent experience with other innovations? How accurate and realistic were staff members' perceptions of what the discipline could do?

Answers to such wide-ranging questions were not easy to obtain, and the pursuit involved talking to several hundred staff members. There were some five hundred projects that might have been looked at, though in practice it was clearly impossible to consider so many. Instead it was decided to draw up a sample of projects from all sectors, covering the widest possible geographical distribution. The objective was to analyze projects that were representative of a type of problem commonly experienced or of a particular sector. It was hoped the result would show that the discipline really needed to be considered a normal and necessary part of project work.

What Can Anthropology Do for Development? 21

It is impossible to give here details of the individual projects examined. It may, however, be useful to provide a brief list of some common anthropological assumptions about development work. It is obvious that all projects affect social relationships in terms of the acquisition and distribution of power, wealth, and status in the societies in which they are located. These are broad sociological concepts always made locally meaningful in analysis of particular cases.

The Problems of Change

People in developing countries want some of the benefits of modernization but, inevitably, they also want to enjoy those benefits in a societal framework and within a traditional culture and rhythm of life. It is one of the tasks of the anthropologist interested in development to find out what that framework is: the beliefs, values, and attitudes that generate structural alignments in the society, the potentialities for change, and what harm may come from the change.

Methods of Evaluation

Many people believe that the usual methods of evaluation for development involving gross national product and per capita growth have not proved entirely adequate. There has been an obvious need to increase the range of quantifiable measures. Now variables to be considered include the availability and quality of health services, nutrition levels, housing, clean water, electric power, and sewage facilities. They must obviously be regarded as something more than social overhead capital. They can be regarded as necessary though not sufficient variables.

Nor are the difficulties in isolating what is thought to be responsible for growth entirely overcome through the use of shadow prices to correct for undervaluation of capital and foreign exchange and for the overpricing of unskilled labour represented by market wage rates. The use of shadow prices is a step toward converting the private rate of return to a social rate of return. But this is not enough. Shadow prices are not, for example, useful in dealing with income distribution since that problem, not being a factor of production, will not enter into the rate of return calculation. Econometric approaches have widely acknowledged limitations unless there is some input from the other social sciences.

A number of issues could be seen in a new light if there were clear conceptual recognition that a project might be a financial success and yet fail to meet social equity or social development goals. Such recognition would make it easier to adopt an appropriate organizational response.

How can these social issues be avoided in situations where governments help a small number of farmers to increase their incomes through provision of low-cost finance while those on the edge of the project pay usurious rates for their capital? Anthropology can often help in such cases by working on the local subjective image of poverty and so establishing what those people would be prepared to accept as reasonable. This kind of information can illuminate the problem of distribution, many economists' data seem on the other hand to be about income averaging. There is no "scientific" way to achieve the best distribution of benefits. I believe all one can, and should, do is to take off the rough edges. This, of course, must be a matter for collaboration because it is fully appreciated that the World Bank is dealing with sovereign governments. In many cases these governments have little enthusiasm for tackling what outsiders consider to be important social issues.

Staff in development assistance agencies at present are encouraged to view projects in specific countries against a background of universal behavioural characteristics. Thus they inquire how a project conforms to general expectations. On the other hand, anthropologists prefer to ask what it is that makes a country special and unique. Thus they ask how a project departs from general considerations. Examples are not hard to find.

Problem Projects

A "problem" project in many development assistance agencies is usually considered to be one that has failed to live up to standards deemed necessary in financial calculations. But from the anthropological point of view, problems are often strangely attributed to broad and culturally meaningless categories seldom anchored by empirical material. An "administrative" or "organizational" problem in one culture may have no parallel in another culture. For example, there is no agricultural scheme anywhere whose failure could not be broadly attributed to one of the criteria used in the project cycle, such as organization or management. Yet how far can such a labelling process take us in determining exactly why a project encountered problems?

It is necessary to know why this project in this society has problems or is likely to have problems at this time. Here is where an anthropologist can frequently help.

Development assistance agencies operate under considerable constraints beyond the great increase in the volume of demand for aid in recent years. There is, as the Pearson Report pointed out, the continuing need to guard the reputation of development agencies in their home countries. Unfortunately, in my opinion, the Pearson Report was not well informed about the capability of the non-economic social sciences.

Often, appraisal in bilateral and multilateral agency project work seems to have concentrated almost exclusively on the official side in a developing country while paying insufficient attention to the very poorest people—non-government people—whose support is essential if a project is to achieve its goals. Their support often tends to be assumed. Therefore, it is not surprising that when an explanation is attempted for projects which have "human" problems, one sometimes hears that "models do not show..." or that certain statistics are not adequate. But many of these post-mortems might have been avoided had there been contact with people at the village level in the initial stages of the project.

When a project is at or near completion of the project cycle stage, it is too late for anthropologists to produce data that would have been produced had an anthropologist with the appropriate facility and experience been associated with the project from the identification stage. This is why participation at the identification stage is often necessary to prove the benefit and utility of the approach. However, it is possible to investigate a project in retrospect from two points of view.

First, by an examination of the premises on which the project was based to see if they were socially feasible. What were the possible effects of change? Finding the answer to this question requires professional digging since the unanticipated consequence of social change is extremely complex and difficult to determine. One could then decide if it would have been desirable to engage an anthropologist as a consultant, and what he or she should have been asked to look at.

Second, by looking at the project in terms of wider objectives. Did it conform to what people in that society considered reasonable? What kinds of mechanism were there in that society for diffusion of the kinds of innovation represented by the project? Could anthropological knowledge have helped to ensure that the project had a demonstration effect? Which groups were likely to benefit at the expense of what other groups? In this way one could even in retrospect get a grip on intangibles and, at the same time, pay some attention to social issues.

Dealing with Non-economic Issues

The sociological and economic aspects of this problem are especially important—more so in the immediate future than are the purely technical aspects. . . . It is true to say that the adoption in the field of any major practical improvement for the cattle industry or agriculture depends . . . on social and administrative influences. . . . Our observations of conditions in the field lead to the conclusion that nontechnical aspects of development are a matter for the district administration.

This paragraph from an old World Bank economic report on a livestock improvement scheme exposes a common development agency attitude toward the treatment of social issues. Why write a report if what has been identified as a crucial problem is without any advice, analysis, or recommendation and is simply left with the local administration? Of course, it is all too easy to be wise, and wrong, after the event. It is easy to appreciate the weakness involved in trying to go to the

What Can Anthropology Do for Development? 25

past. But it does have the value of highlighting a number of substantive points for contemporary discussion and analysis.

It is prudent, in dealing with projects where there is a substantial human element, to begin by assuming that the local reaction will be special and unique until there is evidence to the contrary. The present tendency is to assume that if the means are provided, then people in a different culture will react in what Euro-Americans consider would be a rational manner.

OVERVIEW VERSUS COMMUNITY KNOWLEDGE

Anthropologists feel that bilateral and multilateral agencies should appoint anthropologists to their permanent staff, despite some obvious difficulties. Institutions with global responsibilities need their staff to have an overview and a geographical and cultural flexibility that make it difficult for anthropologists to operate in terms of their real strength and community knowledge. But it is possible to envisage a system where a permanent cadre of anthropologists based in regions would be able to deal with policy matters, the initial monitoring of projects, and the selection and briefing of specialist consultants when required.

Clearly anthropologists are not the only social scientists who now play little or no institutional role. Geographers, psychologists, political scientists and many others also have much to give. There are sound reasons for deeper exploration of the possibilities of the non-economic social sciences and for developing in-house capacity in these disciplines. It cannot be assumed that the pool of manpower skills developed by development agencies in the past is now sufficient to deal adequately with the very poorest people. It is not enough to give the old players new jerseys, to call economists rural development specialists and so on. There is an urgent need for new inputs.

Another reason is the need to provide leadership in dealing with social development issues. Often this leadership is easy to see in research efforts where anthropological insights are frequently involved. But there is usually no clear relationship between the resources devoted by development agencies to research and the resources devoted to their own manpower development. Consequently there is no adequate assurance that the results of research can be applied on the ground in a meaningful way.

Still another reason is the matter of public relations. It makes little sense for agencies to talk about the plight of the poorest people and then to have a staffing pattern which excludes and ignores those disciplines that have dealt with such people in other cultures for over half a century.

A good case for the permanent appointment of anthropologists in development agencies can be made. Only by working in a community of staff members that go to make up a development institution can anthropologists provide their best input— a view based on the classic procedures of Malinowski who felt, half a century ago, that the only way to get his point across was to go and work in the Trobriands. Malinowski's work became the model and inspiration for many similar studies and it is to be hoped that, on a much more modest level, the approach to anthropology as policy worked out at the Bank will stimulate interest in similar studies being carried out at other institutions with bilateral and multilateral responsibilities. Certainly my own more recent experience at the U.S. Agency for International Development, where I have just completed a similar study, confirms this opinion.

Cyril S. Belshaw

2 The Contribution of Anthropology to Development

This article is written exclusively from the point of view of a social and cultural anthropologist. Nevertheless, this should not be taken to imply that archaeology or physical anthropology lack relevance for the questions being considered. For example, there are circumstances in which archaeological investigation is crucial to the growth of a cultural heritage, on the one hand contributing to national pride and confidence, and on the other stimulating artistic forms of expression. Thus it may add to the stock of ideas and the range of satisfactions which are part of the development objective. Again, physical anthropology, when linked explicitly to the behavioural sciences, can show the bearing of medical, nutritional, demographic and anatomical factors upon such diverse topics as the actions of a labour force or the culture of poverty.

THE SCOPE OF CULTURAL AND SOCIAL ANTHROPOLOGY

Anthropology is the discipline primarily concerned with the intensive, holistic and comparative analysis of culture, including the movement of culture over time, and the influence of cultures upon each other. Volumes have been written defining culture, but a concise statement would be that culture consists of all those material things and non-material ideas which man has produced and which he continues to value. Central to the analysis of culture is the identification of a symbol, since without symbolization there can be no recognition, identification, communication, or valuation. Valuation is a most important element in the analysis of cultural processes, since it is central to choice and decision-making, which in turn are the essential elements of social action. Thus the study of symbols, values, communication, and choice are crucial to the questions that lie before us.

Anthropologists also study social relations, linking up with the work of other social scientists. Perhaps the keys to the anthropological orientation here are that social relations are (*a*) placed in a cultural context that is related to values, communication, and choice; (*b*) studied from a cross-cultural perspective; (*c*) studied with the objective of cross-cultural comparison; and (*d*) analyzed in a cross-disciplinary manner. By the last point, I mean that anthropologists traditionally draw theoretical perspectives from their neighbouring social sciences, and hence apply the theories of, for example, psychology, economics, game theory, ecology, political science, and sociology to their materials. Not all anthropologists place equal weight on all theories and perspectives, but it is taken as a matter of course that such varieties of approach are legitimate, that there will be cross-fertilization and rivalry between them. In its approach to society, therefore, anthropology as a whole tends towards the synthesis of knowledge. However, it should be noted that I do not claim, and no anthropologist can claim, that by this fact anthropology subsumes the other disciplines.

In studying social relations, two broad perspectives currently stand out. One is structural, that is with an emphasis upon normative regularities or systems which are characteristic of given cultural groups. This approach tends towards typological classifications and the identification of continuous working systems, from which behaviour and predication can be derived in somewhat conservative terms. The other begins with individual decision-making in an environmental context and derives norms, structures, and social organization from such decisions and their interactions. Some anthropologists argue that this approach, though not yet firmly established, offers greater potential for the study of change, for systems analysis,

The Contribution of Anthropology to Development

and for mathematical and computer treatment, as well as being closer to the realities of action.

The points mentioned above must be stated, at perhaps greater length than for other disciplines, since there is a curious view in the general public and among some colleagues that anthropology is an antiquarian subject, concerned with the primitive and archaic. If this were so, then anthropology's role in development would be rather like that of archaeology, except that our fossils would be living. Or anthropologists would be limited to bringing archaic, lost tribes into the modern world.

The point must be stressed that the characteristics I have mentioned above are general ones. They are not limited to particular classes of society. It is true that in the past some anthropologists (the majority in some countries) have concentrated on problems of cultural origin and evolution; but this has not been a majority occupation for anthropologists for half a century. It is more true that anthropologists have sought out other cultures and that most of these have been primitive. This, however, has not been an end in itself. It has been part of an unconscious research strategy, making it mandatory for anthropologists to cross-cultural boundaries, to start from scratch in the analysis rather than being moulded by a literature, and it has enabled them to handle issues in what appeared to be, at least at first sight, simple forms.

Anthropologists tend to avoid the term "primitive," and think rather in some such term as "non-literate," which has a functionally operational definition. It should be noted that until recently the majority of the world's cultures were non-literate, another reason for anthropological concentration.

But it should also be noted that anthropologists are giving specific attention, on a large scale, to the study of peasant societies, to urban studies (particularly in Africa, Asia and Latin America), to market phenomena. They are bringing the perspectives I have listed above to the study of kinship in Western society, to multiracial interaction whether it be in Africa, Belgium or the United States, to the study of the culture of poverty. In addition, anthropologists are applying some of the lessons they have learned in the analysis of peasant and non-literate economies to the investigation of entrepreneurial and market behaviour in the capitalist firm, and to the choices of migrant individuals and groups. These are but a few exampels of the predominant interest of modern anthropology in non-archaic conditions.

ANTHROPOLOGY AND THE APPROACH TO DEVELOPMENT

In considering the anthropological approach to development, three terms and two spheres of scholarly activity must be distinguished. The terms are "growth," "performance" and "development." The spheres of activity are anthropological contributions to the macro-analysis of social processes, and the implications of empirical field studies for development theory and interpretations.

Usually the words "growth," "performance" and "development" are preceded by the word "economic." This implies that the indicators used to judge movement, or used in comparison, are derived from data about the formal system which provides for the exchange of goods and services, as recognized by economic statisticians. Where it is desirable to recognize that there are other elements in growth, performance, and development, the adjective "socioeconomic" tends to be used. The ambiguities and misconceptions which flow from this distinction are extremely important to the future contribution of anthropological analysis. Only a few of them can be summarized here.

It is analytically unsatisfactory to apply the term "social" to a "social service" or "social welfare" sector, since such sectors may be treated either from the point of view of economic analysis, or an anthropological socio-cultural analysis. Similarly the so-called "economic" sector can be treated in terms of cultural components and social relations.

For similar reasons, movements in the economy of such organizations as households, subsistence production, religious groups, voluntary organizations; and non-measured elements in socio-economic processes, such as the ideological influence of business executives upon each other, are frequently ignored, or fail to be integrated into an analysis. In some

The Contribution of Anthropology to Development

contexts this is unimportant, but in others it may make all the difference between a successful or unsuccessful prediction about the significance or outcome of a developmental measure.

An anthropologist must use the broad approach to data and analysis. He must recognize that religion can be thought of in the context of applying scarce resources of competing ends, and that a production decision by a board of management may be influenced by cultural judgements and external relationships.

"Growth" implies a change in the volume of goods and services produced, of purchasing power, or similar general and usually value-neutral indicators.

While indicators are value-neutral in themselves, they are not value-neutral vis-a-vis the society to which they are applied. "Performance" implies the degree to which events, actions, and processes maximize the satisfactions or the objectives of the people in the society in question. Growth is not synonymous with an increase in performance. It is quite feasible to have tremendous growth according to all the current indicators, yet to argue that performance decreased. The destruction of valued institutions, the channelling of effort by authoritarian measures, are cases in point. Or a simple society may just not wish to grow or develop. Growth and development would thus represent a loss of performance.

"Development" represents an increase in the capacities of a society to organize for its own objectives, and to carry out its programme more effectively. The essential element here is *organization*. When, anthropologically speaking, one society is developed and another undeveloped, the former is, by comparison with the latter, able to make much more complicated decisions and to do more complicated things. This has nothing to do with the direct presence or absence of physical resources. New Guinea has vast resources but little complexity and sophistication of organization: Japan, Hong Kong, and Switzerland use the complexity and sophistication of their organization to control and use resources which are initially not within their boundaries. The former is relatively undeveloped, the latter are relatively developed.

Nor has "development" per se anything to do with satisfaction. It is widely assumed in the literature that an improvement in development (and/or growth) implies an improvement in satisfaction or welfare. The fact is that some forms of development under some circumstances improve performance: other forms of development do not. Anthropologists are perhaps in a better position than any other social scientist to understand this, but their understanding has not yet been matched to an explicit and clear statement, in general terms, of the differences in satisfaction that correlate with the various types and circumstances of development. This is a major challenge to anthropology: until it is taken up, anthropological reservations about some forms of development will be interpreted as, and indeed may be, sentimental or politically biased rather than scientifically objective. On the other hand, other social scientists and, even more, political decision-makers, are just as naive in a more dangerous form when they imply that development (and/or growth) inherently means increased performance. (As an aside, it might be noted that a new element in protest movements is essentially anti-developmental and pro-simplicity.)

Anthropologists find themselves uncomfortable in the movement back and forth between micro field studies and the macro interpretations that are increasingly necessary. More than any other social scientist, except perhaps historians, they are aware of the gap between general theory and broad interpretation on the one hand, and empirical, down-to-earth interpretation on the other. Almost every general statement turns out to be simplistic when the fate of human communities is in the balance. A great part of the applied role of field studies has in fact been to show that theoretical or commonsense prescriptions just do not work like that, and that what appears to be most sensible and normal in a regional or national office is thought of as most insensible and abnormal by the people whose fate is being influenced. Yet to leave matters there is insufficient. Any broad theory, and any practical policy, is and must be an approximation. A major task of anthropology is to come to terms with such approximations. The best way to do this is to attempt to formulate alternate or modified general theories and policies, a task that anthropology has tended to ignore. A concomitant is that the often irritating field criticisms of anthropologists should be taken constructively, and collated and used in the modification of the theories and policies of others. This indeed might be a good time for a stocktaking of that kind, i.e., a consideration of the theories of other social sciences, and of general developmental policies, in the light of anthropological field reports.

With these considerations in mind, let us for a moment examine certain development propositions which would receive general currency today:

1. It is certain that development implies change involving new objectives, ideas, methods, forms of relationship. It can sometimes happen that such change may take place as part of a regrouping of social forces which may have the effect of reducing the growth in national income for a short or long period as a means of providing a foundation for self-sustained growth. This poses serious problems in judging development effects, particularly between a short- and long-term view. It also poses problems in the judgement as to whether a particular form of development is desirable or undesirable in the eyes of the population, particularly in relation to its political philosophy.
2. While stress is placed on the ability of particular countries to guide their own destiny and generate their own growth and development, this is becoming less and less realistic. Note two points. Nationalism may be a most useful driving force to overcome the effects of cultural segmentation, and to ensure that goals are in accord with the world-view of a country, but (*a*) nationalism may also provoke regional hostility and stamp out local initiatives; and (*b*) nationalism may prevent the movement of ideas across national boundaries. Further it may be the case that international, para-national and supra-national organizations (economic, cultural and political) are at the point of having a determining effect on the abilities of national governments to make decisions. Thus both the internal and external relations of governments need to be studied for their effects on development.

3. That the structure of developed countries may affect the position of developing countries needs great stress. One needs only point to such factors as: (*a*) the attitudes of people from developed countries creating reactions in developing countries, both during personal visits and as communicated in the media; (*b*) the fragmented structure of government organization in developed countries has imposed a fragmented structure on international organization and on the administration of aid in developing countries; (*c*) philosophies related to the value of work and the nature of organization may not mesh the development needs of particular countries.
4. There is a considerable danger of ethnocentrism as Western scholars and advisers make assumptions about the nature of society in developing countries and talk of the way in which parts of that society must change prior to a development take-off. For example, one hoary fallacy which is still heard today despite tremendous contrary evidence, is that the destruction of extended kinship systems and of complex ceremonial is a prerequisite to development. This is only true if the development model being reached for is that of Western society in its detail: but as other cultures (e.g., Japan, Taiwan) develop we know that much more variation is possible than we thought before. This is not just a philosophical issue. Government measures directed towards such destructions may indeed hold up development if they have been poorly judged.
5. We do not yet know about the conditions under which speedy development can take place with minimal counter-effects and with an optimal effect upon the creation of solid and enduring foundations for permanent development. It is probably not sound to categorize crash programmes of rapid change as "development" and slow process of movement as "non-development." They are simply two different speeds of change. Furthermore, while many crash programmes or revolutionary movements may be both desirable and necessary, under some circumstances they can set back the time-table very seriously. See paragraph 1 above.

6. The anthropologist is very deeply aware that self-consciousness, awareness, coordination and planned analysis are optimally desirable, one should hasten and substantiate the foundations of development—provided those who are directing matters know what they are doing. The holistic bias in anthropological field studies inevitably leads to this conclusion, and it was this kind of philosophy which led to the original notions of community development (in its substantive rather than its group dynamic form).

But there are some very serious qualifications to this proposition. First, the anthropologist, because he endeavours to work from the point of view of the people he studies, becomes more aware than most outsiders of the fact that almost all plans and projects are imposed, even where the philosophy is one of consultation. This raises questions of justice and of technical effectiveness.

Second, it is almost impossible, given current techniques, to provide overall planning and smaller-scale project designing which is a hundred per cent effective within, and only within, the terms of the designers. The primary reason for this is that social science analysis (other than economics) is not included in the planning technique, or is not appropriately adapted to that technique. Even if it were there would inherently be a large measure of discrepancy. Thus, the effects of a plan or a project, particularly in terms of spinoff effects in related areas, are largely unpredicted, unexpected, unanalyzed and unnoticed. Some observers believe that these unplanned effects are often the major reasons for the success of a project and that most development, historically and currently, even where planning is sophisticated, is of this order.

If this were to be true, the function of planning might be more modest and at the same time more subtle. It would be to find crucial points in the socioeconomic system which could be influenced for maximum derived and multiplying effects. There is a great deal in the anthropological materials which bears upon such linkages, but at the moment this has resulted in little by way of clear theoretical conclusions couched in terms useful to the development planner.

Educational Policy

The quantity of work directed by anthropologists to the study of formal education is relatively small, although it has a long history. Much of it has been carried out in contexts in which alien or national educational philosophies and systems have been applied to cultural groups which do not share the philosophy or have sympathy with or understanding of the system. The immediate problems have therefore been of ethics and of educational content as it affects the ability of a child to effectively learn those matters which help him take his place in changing society, yet with a respect for the values which he derives from his own culture.

From this point of view, the severe contradictions and ethical problems involved in educational action can hardly be resolved by reference to a general a priori theory, but only through a very intimate analysis of the total context in which the school system finds itself. It could be argued, for example, that some of the most rapid and enduring changes in personal skills and viewpoints have occurred where children have been removed from the family at an early age, and hence from contact with their basic culture, and subjected to intensive education elsewhere. But this must be in terms of the destruction of the pre-existing culture, since it either means the removal of all its future carriers, or the removal of those judged to be the most alert and responsive to teaching. And it creates severe stresses and counter-frustrations if the children in effect return to their basic cultural environment following this shock treatment. Hence such processes have been thoroughly discredited and the problems that remain are ones of relatively modest and constrained influence aiming at a congruence with and a bridging of cultures, and thus dependent on the goodwill and understanding of parents and the training of teachers to understand and recognize the challenge of cross-cultural education.

This latter point is crucial and gives great cause for worry among anthropologists. We are aware that many anthropological materials are in use in the training of teachers for such purposes, but that they are often misused to over-simplify or to reinforce prejudices. Many systems of teacher training

The Contribution of Anthropology to Development

fail to communicate the most basic information about processes which relate to the function and operation of the school within a societal context. Much is made of the role of the school to create change, which sometimes gives a messianic or reforming role to teachers for which they are not given a mandate by local and familial authority, and which they are not trained to understand. Often teachers overcome this deficiency by personal sensitivity, dedication, modesty and example: but others run head-on into cultural resistance and become discouraged and defeated.

Anthropological knowledge can be and has been used to influence the curriculum to make it more meaningful and relevant for developmental transition. This work has been thin on the ground, patchy in its applications, and uncertain in its results. A critical and positive appraisal is urgently required.

A second contribution which anthropology has made is a result of field studies which have cast light on the general processes of socialization, the ways in which values tend to be formed, and the influence of institutions such as age-grade initiation on the formation of loyalties. There is some impact of these studies upon teacher training. But a wider implication has not, to the same extent, made its more general impact. While many of the detailed studies have little relevance for development, the underlying problem has. It is that formal education is not the only, and may not even be the main, influence on the creation of points of view, incentives, drives and orientations to action. Because the formal educational system is somewhat amenable to government influence, it tends perhaps to be overestimated in the total context of formative influences. While social theories pay adequate attention to other factors, development planning practices ignore them or regard them as nuisances to be overcome through action within the formal system. If too heavy a burden is placed on the formal educational system, there is a danger that it will come to be treated as an enemy or will in practice cease to be effective.

Education is both a goal and a means. A standard, a quality, and a direction of education will in any society be judged against an ideal, the judgement constituting one component in the society's estimation of its own performance. A change may improve or distort that performance. Furthermore, education creates and channels incentives, personal objectives, and occupational skills, and may be articulated with the total socioeconomic system in an instrumental or anti-instrumental way. The bearing of education upon development must be decided through a juxtaposition of all these considerations.

Here the contribution of anthropology is, potentially, to link education to the cultural goals of the society and perhaps to draw attention to some skills and incentive orientations which might be overlooked by disciplines less concerned with cross-cultural values.

There are two further points at which anthropology might join with sister disciplines. The ability of a society to move ahead in a developmental context and yet to retain and improve its satisfactions, depends to some degree upon the manner in which it can secure the solution to new problems which arise in its own terms. The presence of problem-solving skills in a form in which members of the population can tackle new questions in new contexts creatively, is thus crucial. Anthropology can sometimes reveal weaknesses in education orientation, such as dependence upon knowledge linked with the solution of *old* problems, rote learning instead of question forming, and the solution of problems in an ethnocentric manner inappropriate to the society in question (especially by outside advisers).

Further, anthropologists, among others, are aware of the lack of social science skills in many of the developing countries, lack of support for indigenous social science research, and the lack of awareness by governments of the need for social science education and support. This is perhaps less true for some disciplines than for others, but it is certainly true for anthropology. If we are considering the degree to which the educational system is structured to provide required skills, the social sciences should be included, to the relevant degree, among those skills: but, as with others, their mere existence is only part of the question.

The other part is the degree to which the institutions of society can absorb and use them.

Scientific and Technological Policies

Quite frequently, governmental and scientific establishments pose the following type of question: given the need for scientific and technological advance and given the formation of a suitable policy, how can social scientists help to render the policy palatable, and how can they soften its effects on the population? Put in this kind of way, the question alienates social scientists, who further note that the definition of what is socially relevant tends under such circumstances to be made by scientists or technicians, with the occasional help of economists. Resulting tensions have certainly occurred in developed countries. In developing countries they may be discounted by the obvious need and priority for scientific and technological development: nevertheless they are perhaps only muted by the condition that social scientists are seldom in a position to speak up.

The primary matter for concern, which is increasingly coming to be recognized, is of a different order. It includes such questions as: given the social and cultural objectives of the society, what science and technology policies meet them best? How can the inquiries of social scientists reveal these objectives and make it possible for science and technology to fit them? How can the social sciences analyze the comparative effects of alternative policies to reveal the ones with the most suitable mix? In other words, given man, how can science and technology help him; not given science and technology, how can man be made to fit?

Anthropology is better equipped now than at any other time to contribute to such questions and answers, both in theoretical perspective and in field detail. There is now a considerable accumulation of field studies delineating the effects of technological change and providing information about how choices are made when innovations appear. There are a few studies of the way in which world-view, philosophical systems and cultural preoccupations affect the work of technicians, and scientists, and the choices made about policy. The strong current interest in cultural and biological ecology puts anthropology in a position to more effectively consider the social implications of environmental change brought about by scientific and technological applications (pollution, river-basin development, growth of cities). The use of mathematical models in economic anthropology and studies of decision-making is bringing the analysis of social institutions closer to the point at which they can be analyzed in terms which more readily link with other social sciences, e.g., with cost-benefit analysis.

Anthropology can also consider the total social and cultural framework in which scientific and technical policy operates: its congruence with social values; its link with status and reward; its degree of penetration through the stratification system; the manner in which institutions require or reject experiment and innovation; and the implication of such matters for development and satisfaction.

Communication

If communication is thought of in the sense of mass media, anthropology at present has very little to say about it expect in commonsense terms. It is true that the McLuhan school of thought borrowed heavily from anthropological relativism in order to demonstrate the existence and likelihood of non-linear cultures. Most anthropologists would argue, however, that such judgements are based on an as yet undemonstrated relationship between the linguistic and symbolic apparatus of a culture and behaviour. At best, the extrapolations to contemporary society and notions such as world tribalism, represent rather crude analogies and elaborations of half-truths.

Other more controlled studies of the mass media are not normally in the anthropological domain, although it is likely that some contact will develop in the future.

On the other hand, anthropologists tend to be somewhat critical and sceptical of an over-concentration of attention to the mass media in communications studies. This has perhaps prevented them from applying some of their potential knowledge, e.g., through the analysis of the use of symbols in television programmes, of audience impact in multicultural or stratified societies, at least in any concerted manner.

In another sense, communication is at the centre of anthropological studies. Communication, despite the slogan "the medium is the message," cannot take place without symbols, that is recognized stimuli or signals which are interpreted with meaning. Symbols, meaning ideas, are at the very heart of culture and the analysis of culture is what anthropology is largely about. There is a vast corpus of studies which present hypotheses about the way in which symbol systems relate to action and reaction. Strangely enough, structural and cultural anthropology, in this sense, is often thought of as an academic philosophical exercise with few applications to the real world, and it must be admitted that most anthropologists concerned with such matters have not made the transition necessary to think of applications. The nearest we get to it is the rather vague consideration of cultural themes and values which somewhat underlie action orientations and hence govern predispositions to development—a highly debatable and not particularly rigorous set of propositions. In this whole field, anthropology is far behind psychology: yet in my view, the anthropological materials in a multicultural world are potentially more powerful, with considerable implications for their use, for good or ill, by the media manipulators.

A further potential contribution, again lying at the theoretical core of anthropology, may be termed transactional, or social exchange, analysis, social relations, it is postulated, consist of transactions between persons who exchange words, ideas, effects, power, material things and symbols. Such transactions are the raw material out of which we abstract roles, social structure, social networks and organization. Transactions are, of course, acts of communication and are essential to an anthropological understanding of communication.

The relevance of these notions for development are very direct, although since theoretical analysis is in its infancy, the refinement of applications leaves much to be desired. The importance of the approach can be indicated by two examples. Firstly, the movement of any idea or practice and the diffusion of its acceptance is dependent upon a wide range of factors. One of these consists of the network of transactional relationships, and the body of obligation, power and self-interest which affect decisions in the course of the transactions. Any development programme which is based on a false analysis of the network will be reduced in effectiveness. Secondly it can be argued that the capacity of a culture to produce innovations, other things being equal, will be a function of the size and complexity of the pool of ideas. It can be further argued that the size of this pool consists not only of, as it were the number of different ideas, but also of the velocity of their circulation. (This is somewhat on the analogy of the quantity theory of money.) If this is so, then communication must be a crucial variable in a society's capacity to innovate.

Cultural Policy

Like other matters considered here, cultural policy may be considered to be a means contributing to development, a goal of development and performance, and a factor which development programmes must take into account. It was once the case that most anthropological field studies concerned themselves with tribal or subcultural values in a context isolated from the main developmental trends of the national political entity of which the subcultures were a part: indeed it used to be said that even here the anthropologist's in-depth knowledge was of a village rather than a culture.

These points have never been wholly true. Studies of cultural change and applied anthropology have almost always been in the context of wider considerations. Further, the methods and interests of contemporary anthropologists are now such that they combine their traditional participant observation technique with sampling and statistical analysis, to handle larger cultural areas and to relate these to national and multicultural trends. Techniques and perspectives are in some respects blending with those of sociology.

It is, however, still true that most anthropology involves an intimacy of involvement with the culture being studied which is not as typical of other disciplines. Anthropologists tend to identify with the people with whom they work. Such identification has some obvious risks of losing broader perspectives, of losing sight of the fact that the anthropologist is still in some sense an outsider, of playing a role as spokesman for the culture. On the other hand, in many instances the issues and analyses presented will simply not be made unless the anthropologist makes them. It is in the very nature of anthropology that the materials be obtained at the grassroots level and that development be viewed primarily from that perspective. Since development is meant to be at the service of man, one would hope that such a perspective would be recognized and valued, even where it might lead to a modification of enthusiastic national goals.

The success or failure of anthropology here will be a response not only to the competence of anthropologists, but to the ambience of the national system within which their studies take place. Clearly, the task and success of anthropology will be much greater if national policy is based upon tolerance of cultural variation and a determination to link national development to the interests of the subcultures which make up the nation, as well as the creation of a national social system based upon a respect for interaction between members of such subcultures.

Yet it is true that the analytical techniques and interests of anthropology have seldom been clearly focused on the problem of the instrumental results of different kinds of compromise and interactions between subcultures and the national organizations, a problem which can be of major importance for development policy in many countries. This is not for lack of knowledge or technique but rather because of such matters as a lack of anthropological manpower and a failure by both anthropologists and governments to grasp the implications. Again, a few examples will have to suffice. Anthropologists have done some work, and could carry out much more, on such problems as: (*a*) the adaptation of national and commercial institutions to regional cultural differences; (*b*) the implications of cultural and linguistic variation for the effective operations of a national civil service; (*c*) increasing the visibility and understanding of cultural achievements as a contribution to a growth in regional and national pride and identity; (*d*) the identification of significant subcultural differences in order to sensitize developmental policy and render it more effective; (*e*) analysis of the significance of frictions in communication between subcultures as a factor inhibiting the operation of a social system.

The analysis of culture has many broader facets of basic

significance to the theory and practice of development, particularly if development is to be related to performance. To the anthropologist, culture consists of ideas, artefacts and symbols. Artefacts have long been recognized as an imporant element, like capital, in the resource stock which provides the tools and the mainspring for economic movement and hence development. To the anthropologist, ideas and symbols are equally important: they are part of man's heritage, the cultural stock which must be drawn upon if action is to take place. While their mere use does not cause depreciation, they contain their own systematic dynamism as old ideas give way to new. The interrelation of elements in the cultural stock is an important area of investigation for anthropology, although so far there has been little attempt to connect ideas to their instrumental functions and implications, a connection which must be made more systematically if the significance for development is to be followed through.

The way in which a cultural system operates has been traced from several distinct viewpoints. Culture is so complex, and by its very nature so difficult to measure, that most interpretations have a strong subjective, even philosophical, flavour. This is always likely to be the case, although occasionally corrected by more neutral scientific attempts. For example, culture cannot be summed, it can only be described. Thus, we could construct a behavioural profile of culture which consists of a list of those things which people in a culture actually express through behaviour. Such a profile would be somewhat similar to a level of living index, although including much broader values. We can also construct a potential profile of culture which consists of a listing of the goals and aspirations of a people, given certain conventions of analysis. The interaction over time between elements in the two profiles gives relatively controlled indications of connections within the cultural system: the relationship between the behavioural and the potential profiles gives an indication of the state of performance of the culture: and the degree of complexity exhibited in the profiles, together with the instrumental effectiveness of its elements, provides indications of the state of development.

The Promotion of Development Action

To sum up, anthropology can effectively enter into the analysis of development strategy and projects whenever the following conditions apply: (*a*) when there is a question of identifying values which are to be satisfied; (*b*) when a project implies that people will be making decisions and choices in the light of cultural values and cultural, social and economic resources; (*c*) when questions arise about the interaction of individuals within a social structure or social organization, and the ramifications of social networks for the passage of concepts, ideas, materials, goods and actions; (*d*) when it is necessary to analyze whether a strategy or project will have dynamic, ramifying effects upon the social system; (*e*) when it is necessary to analyze the valuational and cultural components in the skill-resources available for development.

Other points could be added. These five are, however, sufficient to demonstrate that any project or strategy of development involves analysis which the anthropologist regards as his field of interest. Put another way, development involves change and change involves adjustments in values, ideas and the socio-institutional system, all of which are the subject matter of anthropology.

While anthropological techniques may be used to obtain data, anthropology is essentially an analytical discipline. Its greatest use will be in the analysis of the most appropriate, or optimal, development strategy: in analyzing the consequences of alternative projects; in setting out the most effective manner of creating particular projects; and in assessing the results and ramifications of projects. In making such assessments, anthropology will tend to stress the significance of the values and goals of the persons directly affected by the projects.

Nevertheless, none of the above matters are the exclusive preserve of anthropology. We come back to the fundamental issue. No human event can be completely understood by any single social science. Yet it is surely impractical to have teams representative of each of the social sciences bearing in upon each development project.

Recommendations

I have summarized some of the contributions of anthropology and in most instances have made the point that on the particular topic at issue, anthropological knowledge has been dispersed, requires more specific concentration upon applied purposes, is in a form which requires a reorientation if it is to be most effective, or needs much more work before firm conclusions can be stated with confidence. It would be relatively simple to recommend twenty or thirty topics upon which scholars could be called to concentrate or which could be the subject of working conferences. But such action would, I suspect, not meet the basic problems. These, as I see them, are as follows:

> There is a shortage of resident indigenous anthropologists in most of the developing countries, and their status is not adequately recognized by comparison with other academic disciplines, or in relation to government action and policy. This leads to an undue dependence upon foreign anthropologists (usually more interested in academic rather than applied problems), a limit on the growth of the very complex fundamental knowledge that is needed, and a failure to integrate the resident anthropologists adequately into development planning procedures. Hence a recommendation would be that action be undertaken to improve the supply of anthropologists in developing countries, to improve their status and conditions of work, and to ensure the recognition of their contribution in universities and government service.
>
> For similar reasons, a second recommendation would be that anthropologists in developed countries be called upon, through such scholarly organizations as the International Anthropological and Ethnological Union, the Pacific Science Association, and the Congress of Americanists, to orient their work in developing countries in such a way that it provides maximum support for the growth of the science in the countries concerned. There is some reason to believe that social scientists are less concerned with this objective than with the objective of completing their own projects with minimal concern for the discipline locally.

The point of view that development is a matter of interdisciplinary concern is of major importance. This leads directly to the notion that there might be a profession of development advisers concerned with advising governments, ministries and agencies, in a completely interdisciplinary manner. The training of such a profession becomes of crucial importance. At the moment it is hampered by the complexity of each discipline and the unwillingness, in university circles, to train in an interdisciplinary way. We are all aware of the argument that an economist cannot apply economics unless he knows most if not all economics: hence he must have a completed Ph.D. in the subject. The same philosophy applies in anthropology. Yet patently it is not necessary to know all economics for most development project purposes, or to know all anthropology.

Hence an appropriate recommendation might be to enlist social scientists in the effort of devising an interdisciplinary curriculum for the training of development analysis advisers. The objective of such a curriculum would be to create a corpus of socioeconomic advisers rather than technical project administrators. If such a curriculum were successfully devised, pilot degree or training programmes could then be initiated.

David Pocock

3 Social Anthropology: Its Contributions to Planning[1]

HAVE THE PLANNERS A CONSISTENT STRATEGY?

The starting point for the social anthropologist faced with the Draft Fourth Plan is not primarily the proposals, but the planners themselves. This is difficult for a planner to swallow, insofar as he thinks of himself as standing back from his material and discussing it in an objective manner. I hope, however, to show that by considering the position of the planners in modern Indian society, we can firstly understand the document itself better, and secondly put ourselves in a position to be constructively critical.

Michael Lipton's references to urban bias[2] touch on a cleav-

[1] This paper was originally prepared for a seminar at the University of Sussex to discuss the Draft Outline of India's Fourth Plan published in 1966 and inevitably bears the stamp of its time. In the discussion which followed, the comments of the economists, both Indian and British, demonstrated a remarkable ignorance of Indian rural life and no great sense that this ignorance was incapacitating: the reader must judge for himself how much this situation has changed over ten years.

I have made a few minor clarifications, and page references are to the Draft Outline.

[2] In the original symposium Michael Lipton specified what he called "the urban bias" in Indian planning as a basis that revealed itself as much in the effective personnel as in the major preoccupations of the planning operation. See Paul Streeten and Michael Lipton, 1968, eds., *The Crisis of Indian Planning*. Oxford University Press.

age in Indian society between what can be fairly characterized by two "ideal types." On the one hand we have a minority, based on the cities, valuing change, oriented towards the nation; on the other, a majority, based on the villages, indifferent to change, oriented towards the neighbourhood. The fact of being involved in the planning process not merely places the planners in the first category, but approximates them to the purest expression of the type. They are committed to an ideology which is not shared by the majority of their compatriots, but is opposed to the ideology of the majority. The planner derives from Western models an ideal of the unified secular state; he is planning for a people who, for the most part, think in terms of the localized unities of castes, hierarchically organized according to religious values. Thus the situation is one of conflict, and the ends of the planner are revolutionary.

In a country which has accepted democratic procedures one cannot, of course, expect a planning commission to declare war on the electorate in so many words. We may be sure that in defining the situation as one of conflict we are not saying something of which many planners are unaware. But the Draft Fourth Plan shows that the implications of the conflict have not been clearly thought out. We certainly would not expect to see a clear outline of the proposed strategy, but at the same time we should hope not to find evidence that none exists.

It is, however, difficult to derive from the outline any clear picture of the future life envisaged for the rural masses of India. One thinks first of all of the effect of the Plan's proposals upon the caste system, taking that as the embodiment of traditional values. The planners have little to say directly about this. They observe:

> In spite of efforts to end the practice of untouchability the evil still persists to some extent, specially in the rural areas. Provisions in the Constitution banning the practice of untouchability and making its practice a cognizable offence have not been found adequate. ... It is clear that in this sphere there is no room for complacency and there is need for a nation-wide effort to create a sense of worth and equal dignity for every citizen in the land (p. 380).

The first comment to be made on this is a correction of the phrase "to some extent." The practice of untouchability is pervasive in the rural areas.

The Commission suggests two sorts of remedies: those which would improve the general economic condition of the scheduled castes as a result of an overall improvement in the rural economy, and those which would lift members of the scheduled castes out of the rural milieu primarily by means of education and industrialization. Since it will obviously be many years before the latter outlets are accessible to most members of scheduled castes, clearly the former remedy is supposed to be the effective one. But the hierarchy of caste is not an economic hierarchy. The link between economic standing and caste status is far from perfect. In Gujarat I have observed long-established cooperatives (founded by missions) which have raised the standard of living of untouchables above that of some purer castes without affecting relative caste status. And in the same villages landless Brahmins remain at the head of the hierarchy, while entirely dependent economically upon the local landowners. A more general theoretical point follows: the practice of untouchability flows from the basic religious principles organizing the caste hierarchy and will not be abolished until those principles have been replaced by secular ones.

Is this sociological purism, in that greater economic independence will go far to make the scheduled caste indifferent to the judgement of their neighbours? I shall later give some evidence for this view. What I am at present concerned with, however, is the small extent to which the Planning Commission appears to have any such strategy based upon an understanding of the total social situation in which untouchability is practised.

For example, the Draft Plan seeks to answer the question of decentralizing industry *both* through "small industries, especially for the production of a variety of ancillary parts and components required by large industries" *and* by the development "of some of the traditional village industries which have been languishing" (p. 240). This demonstrates a failure to distinguish between the social functions of these two kinds of small-scale industry. The first, whether it is established in a village or a town, encourages workers to move away from the village ethos, which is the ethos of caste, and creates contractual relationships between employer and employee in a labour situation to which caste is much less relevant. To this extent it gives the labourer, of whatever caste, a moral and economic independence from traditional relationships and pressures. The "traditional village industries," on the other hand, are without exception linked to caste and thus to the caste hierarchy. To revive those that are languishing is, whatever the economic benefit to the individuals concerned, to reinforce caste values, which of course include the practice of untouchability. The apparent failure to see this distinction, strengthens my suspicion that the Planning Commission has not taken the measure of the rural society that it must restructure if the Plan is to succeed.

Alternative strategies to deal with caste will be considered later. All that need be said here is that the average educated townsman in India today has little experience of untouchability. The more he moves in educated circles, the less he has to do even with lesser caste distinctions. The only experience of caste that he may have is the fact that he is almost certainly married into his caste, and to the extent that this gives stability and community to his marriage, he cannot think of it as sociologically linked with discriminations contrary to his ideology.

Is Anthropology too Small-scale to Help?

Two arguments against this general line of criticism have been advanced by defenders of the Plan. It is said that the variety in social organization from one part of the country to the other, and the differences even within one small area, make it impossible for the Planning Commission to enter into regional details. Secondly, it is argued that the primary concern of the planners is with large-scale economic phenomena, the implication being that the benefits resulting from the manipulation of these phenomena will seep down to the masses. Thus we are told:

> Since 90 per cent of the scheduled castes live in the villages and a considerable proportion among them engage in agricultural labour or in occupations of low skill and productivity, whatever measures can be taken to build up the agri-

cultural economy and to diversify the rural occupational structure, will be of benefit to the scheduled castes (p. 380).

As regards the first argument, the notorious diversity of the Indian social scene is more apparent than real. The prevalence of the caste system from one end of the country to the other might make us suspect underlying similarities permitting a remarkable degree of generalization. In fact, the detailed study of a caste or a village in south India has immediate comparative relevance for the social anthropologist working in the north. The traditional value pattern is the same throughout. The concept of the "dominant caste," first put forward by M.N. Srinivas, has universal application in India.[3] Connected with the dominant caste is the so-called "jajmani system" which, despite variations as to detail, expresses the political and economic dependence of the specialist castes (including Brahmins where these are not also dominant) and, more generally, of all inferior castes.[4] To be aware of this alone is to be chary of developing "traditional village industries."

In short, one does not ask that the planner immerse himself in all the social anthropological literature on India. There are not, nor are there ever likely to be, detailed studies of each of its 646,000 villages, but one is entitled to ask for some awareness of the degree of generalization which social anthropology has been able to achieve in India. Were this reflected in the Plan, it would be much easier for any development officer, concerned with a particular village, to appreciate in considerable detail in what way it was unique and to modify his approach accordingly. If, for example, social anthropologists have advanced the generalization that power within *panchayati raj* tends to be preserved in the hands of the dominant caste, and have described the circumstances in which this tendency is strongest, the local worker is in a better position to observe the conditions in which this is not so, or is less so, and to

---

[3]M.N. Srinivas, 1955. "The Social System of a Mysore Village," in McKim Marriott, ed., *Village India*, p.18.

[4]I have discussed this with particular reference to change in D. Pocock, 1962. "Notes on Jajmani Relationships," *Contributions to Indian Sociology*. The Hague, vi.

ponder the advisability or feasibility of encouraging these circumstances elsewhere.

The second defence of the Plan, that it is properly concerned with the manipulation of large-scale economic phenomena, is more simply dismissed. If progress depended entirely on the correct incentives and depressants properly applied at the right time, a generation of economic planning would presumably have discovered the right brand of carrot and the suitable length of stick. But the planner must also know to whom the benefits are flowing, and whatever it is in the long-term interests of planning that they should so flow. There is, for example, no evidence that a build-up of the agricultural economy would inevitably benefit the scheduled castes. On the contrary, wherever there has been an improvement in the peasant condition in India, this has been monopolized by higher landowning castes, and the condition of the landless has remained unchanged (see p. 137). In Gujarat it was not the growing prosperity of the tobacco and cotton-growing Patidar of Kaira district that after independence doubled the cost of seasonal labour: it was the competition of new, small, local industries.

Furthermore, the planners do not in fact limit themselves to large-scale economic operations. Against untouchability, for instance, they urge the provision of unsegregated housing sites in the village for scheduled caste families (p. 381). There is no indication how the ancient prejudice making for segregation is to be overcome. I shall later give an instance of just such a victory, admittedly in favourable circumstances; it is quite wrong to attribute some kind of perverse invulnerability to the "external dharma." It is true that every man has his price, but we have to find out in what currency it is to be paid. One would have, for instance, to balance the long-term benefit of integrated housing in the village against the possible ill effects of complementary benefits to families of the dominant caste, through whom this might be implemented. Because village leaders do not value the currency of liberalism and communal uplift, this does not mean that they are immune to all inducements. It simply means that the planners have proposed a desirable end and have not at all considered the ground upon which it can be achieved.

To sum up at this point: India's elite is committed to the creation of a state of affairs that does not adapt to—indeed would run entirely counter to—the established order of the mass of the population. This gulf between ideals finds demographic expression in the fact that this elite is of its nature urban in background and outlook. Entry to the Indian intellectual and governing elite is still, except in rare cases, through the town or city. But in the Draft Fourth Plan we find no such awareness of this difference, which is nothing less than a difference in world-view. On the contrary, on the grounds that planner and planned alike are all Indians, there is an *assumption* of continuity: some, many, are behind-hand; but the ideal is common to all. The said truth is that the ideal is not common to all and the planners should take this into account by making specific proposals aimed at creating the desired continuity.

Possible Changes in the Planners' Conceptual Structure

Three interconnected intellectual operations seem necessary. Firstly, the members of the Planning Commission should conceive it possible that they are themselves the products of a certain social milieu with its specific values, ideals, assumptions, and blind spots. Such a self-consciousness should be made rationally objective in a formal ideal type. Secondly, this could then be the better compared with a similarly formal construct of the traditional situation based on the findings of social anthropology. Finally, resulting from this confrontation, a model, or rather a series of models of varying degrees of complexity, could be projected as guides to planning. These models would not be planning proposals themselves, however much closer to social realities they might be than much of the Draft Fourth Plan. They would be artificial, ideal constructs derived from the confrontation of the two former models. Thus if the planners realized that they were committed to demolishing not only the branches but also the roots of the caste system, they might, for example, consider the implications of the single-caste village, served from outside by specialist castes, secular and religious, on contractual terms. An important implication is that contractual relationships are encouraged in such a situation while, conversely, common residence subordinates contract and contractual interests to status relationships. When the encouragement of small-scale industry is being considered, the social value of such development can be assessed together with its economic value. It is socially valuable to the extent that it creates a landless villager free from dependence on a status-tied occupation. A few such people in any village have exemplary value, and their presence is corrosive to the traditional system. The ideal situation is that in which the families of the dominant caste in a village are reduced to the position of the single-caste villagers, obliged to contract with their fellow villagers who are now "outsiders," or with others who in fact are residentially outside.

If such a model is erected in formal terms, then the contradictions between it and similar models emerge with clarity for more detailed consideration. For instance, when sociologists use the term "dominant caste," they know that this refers to a condition of graduality on the ground. By this I mean that within the area of dominance of one caste there will be many villages in which the families of that village can be said to be "dominant" only by association with their richer and more powerful caste-fellows in other villages. And at the fringes of the area equivocal situations are to be found.[5] Now it might be that the planners had erected, as a counter to caste stratification, an ideal of stratification by class. Clearly such a structural ideal would turn the mind more to a consideration of the possibility of exploiting the potentiality for fission in the economic disparity of the dominant caste, strengthening economic ties and equivalencies running across castes, and concentrating on village solidarities and inter-village rivalries.

It is perfectly possible that, in the making of practical decisions on the ground, the logical contradictions of models can appear to be ignored. It would, for instance, be clearly impossible (under Indian conditions of rapid population growth and scarce land) to draw off so much landless labour into local industry as to turn the village into a dormitory for the bulk of

---

[5]See, for example, D. Pocock, 1957. "Inclusion and Exclusion," *Southwestern Journal of Anthropology*, Vol. 8, No. 1.

its population, leaving the cultivation of the land in the hands of relatively few farmers, as was the economic implication of the model of the single-caste village on p. 277. But such an "ideal type" enables one the better to appreciate the more-than-economic advantages of an increase in local industries. Again, awareness of potentialities for class stratification in the rural areas could be related to the most general normative theme of the Planning Commission's charter: the socialist commitment. The controlled encouragement of a class society could be operated through the existing psychology of hierarchy. At the same time it would contradict the principles of the traditional hierarchy by substituting achieved for ascribed status. To the extent that this controlled development operated against caste, class could be used in the transition to a socialist society.

The Use of Local Industry in Moving from Caste to Achievement as the Basis of Hierarchy

I have so far been concerned chiefly with the planners themselves, since they appear to have ignored the social actualities of their own situation even more than those of the countryside. In this section I propose to describe a situation of social changes in the Okhamandal district of western Gujarat. The purpose of the description is to draw attention to likelihoods, and to suggest possibilities, for planned social action on a wider scale.

The traditional fame of the Okhamandal district derives from the temple of Dwaraka, which draws pilgrims from all over India. The area is bleak and chronically short of water. The availability of salt led to the establishment of the Tata Chemical Works, some twelve miles from Dwaraka town, and their privately-owned industrial colony, Mithapur. There are four major communities in Okhamandal. The Brahmins of Dwaraka traditionally serve in the temple and attend to the needs of pilgrims. The Lohana have been known for centuries as a trading community. These two are centred on Dwaraka town. In the surrounding district the Vagher are the dominant caste who, by their own admission, relied a great deal in the past upon brigandage, both locally on pilgrims and by making forays into the heart of Gujarat. Such cultivation as was possible in

Okhamandal was carried on by the untouchable Meghwa.
When Mithapur was first established. the great need was for
unskilled labour and simple clerical labour. For the first, both
Vagher and Meghwa appear to have been employed in equal
quantities. For the latter, Brahmins and Lohana were available. As the construction period drew to a close and the
industry became diversified, the need for unskilled labour
decreased. The Vagher pride themselves on lordly traditions
and are not suited to service, and (rightly or wrongly) personnel
officers of the factory claimed that the Meghwa were more sub-
missive and trainable. There has therefore been a decline in
Vagher employment, and today a second generation of Meghwa
is moving into the semi-skilled and skilled ranges of the daily
rated workers.

What has happened to untouchability in the colony and in
the surrounding district? The formal policy of the management
at Mithapur is more than non-discriminatory; it is not even
permissive to caste prejudice. Details of caste are no longer
collected by the time-office. Restaurants in the colony, which
operate on licence from the company, carry large notices
announcing availability of service to all regardless of caste or
religion. With the exception of a small chapel for the nuns
connected with the hospital, the management has not allowed
the construction of any temple or mosque on its property. In
the factory no concession is made to caste prejudice either in
the canteen or in nature of employment. A newly employed
Brahmin or Lohana, for instance, may well find himself
appointed "mate" to a man of lower caste, even an untouchable. This means that he has not only to work in close proximity with him, but even to fetch his tea and remove the dirty
cup when it is finished. The latter act is traditionally regarded
as particularly abhorrent.

The residential area of the colony is divided into named
sections according to the type of housing and accompanying
facilities available. There is no correlation between housing
area and caste; the correlation is rather with the wage grade.
Nor does there appear to be any "natural" tendency towards
caste segregation. My samples do not suggest it, and the company's town officers state that requests for alternative housing
are usually based on a desire for improved facilities rather than

on objections to the caste of neighbours. They point out that the acute housing shortage militates against any "natural" tendency there might be.

The housing shortage is important. The company's rents are low and, with some exceptions dating from the earlier period, the accommodation is satisfactory. Alternative accommodation exists in the surrounding villages at a price, and in Dwaraka and at Okha Port, from which some workers in fact do commute. In such alternative accommodation, especially in Dwaraka, caste rules are often observed. It is clear, however, from Mithapur's long waiting list that even locally-born workers who have ancestral accommodation in their villages prefer the relative privacy, the running water, and the main drainage of the colony to the value of caste segregation in the village.[6]

Much of the above account may appear banal to the English reader. I therefore contrast it briefly with the situation in another Gujarati industrial colony which, for obvious reasons, I shall not name. There the formal charter of company policy was as at Mithapur. Caste was not officially tolerated. It was the experience of workers, however, that the management, through the foreman, was permissive to caste regulations; in assigning kinds of work and working partners, it took caste into account. In the residential area there was as clear a segregation of the untouchables' quarters as I have ever seen in a traditional village. The apparent contradiction between this and the official policy of the company (not to speak of the government) was explained to me by the senior personnel officer. It was not that people were forced to live *apart* from others, but that people preferred to live *with* their own caste fellows. Even if we accept his statement as a faithful representation, we have here, nevertheless, an instance of wanton permissiveness. However, I observed a small shrine to Hanuman in the factory compound and asked why it should be

---

[6] The housing shortage also means that it is difficult to entertain relatives for lengthy periods in the traditional manner. Some lament this, others significantly use it as an excuse for avoiding expenses associated with kinship. I suspect that there are many vulnerable spots in the body social at which people would gladly spend more on education, for instance, if they can be given a good excuse for avoiding traditional demands.

Hanuman in particular. I was told that to move a Hanuman image required no elaborate deinstallation or reinstallation ceremony and that, therefore, if untouchables exercised their right to enter the shrine, the image could conveniently be removed into a private house.

To return to Mithapur, closer examination revealed that apart from housing, the belief in untouchability survived to a certain extent. Despite the notices in company-licensed restaurants, some restaurant-keepers were known to have given in to Vagher intimidation and discouraged Meghwa custom. The Vagher were said to shun the works canteen where the Meghwa were of sure service. This is the negative side of the affair. On the positive side we can point to what Mithapur expresses in an almost pure form—the inevitable caste neutrality of a modern urban setting.[7] The Vagher are not concerned to discriminate against untouchables in general, indeed they scarcely have any such concept. They are concerned with their "own" untouchables, the Meghwa. They do not care about people who may be regarded as untouchables from other people's point of view and who come from other areas. In general, all immigrant situations involving Indians are bound to affect caste hierarchy, whether the migration is to an industrial colony, to a city, or to a foreign country. A family, or a group of families, can take hierarchical notions with it, but these notions can only be socially operative in the particular social surround or origin. Wherever migration situations have been described, there is no recorded example of a new hierarchy having been established between newcomers.[8] Castes continue to exist as endogamous blocs but the caste *system* has gone. We have to distinguish here between the caste system and "casteism," by which we describe the phenomena of castes operating as interest groups

---

[7]The emphasis here is upon "modern." The modern urban situation co-exists very often with the traditional urban caste situation and is all too often ignored by social anthropologists. See D. Pocock, 1962. "Sociologies: Urban and Rural," *Contributions to Indian Sociology.* The Hague, iv.

[8]For a simple example see D. Pocock, 1957. "Difference in East Africa," *Southwestern Journal of Anthropology,* Vol. 8, No. 1, Albuquerque, New Mexico.

in modern political situations. The latter is possibly the price to be paid temporarily for the destruction of the former.

In the surrounding villages the reversal of economic conditions between the Vagher and the Meghwa is striking. The Meghwa quarter is immediately identifiable by the altogether superior condition of its cottages and by the cleanliness and quality of the inhabitants' clothing which reflect the benefit of regular wages. The Vagher have taken to the plough and have developed the skills of intensive horticulture in response to a predominantly vegetarian market in Mithapur.

As regards relations between the two communities, the untouchability of the Meghwa remains unchanged. It is, however, no longer supported by specialization in impure occupations or politico-economic dependence. For the majority of the Meghwa their villages have become dormitories and, as they are increasingly imbued with the secular values of the factory, they appear quite unconcerned to challenge their traditional ranking.

The Vagher have taken to horticulture, but largely preserve a subsistence psychology. A separate Tata organization, the Dorabji Trust, has been working for their economic betterment. This has largely been achieved through one man who (and this seems an essential qualification) has been working among the Vagher for several years. The guiding policy of the trust appears to be that assistance should be given in the first place to those who have, rather than to the have-nots. In accordance with Tata philosophy, assistance is in the form of interest-free loans, leniently collected, rather than grants. A Vagher farmer who already has a viable homestead and appears to be developing its resources as best as he can, is loaned not only cash but also improved grains, and is generally used as the inlet for more efficient farming techniques of all kinds. A few such selected farmers provide an experimental ground for the trust. Some years ago it was decided that the Vagher would benefit by the improvement of their poultry; White Leghorns and Rhode Island Reds were introduced. This innovation came up against Vagher traditions of hospitality, and after repeated attempts it became clear that no Vagher was willing to sacrifice the demands of hospitality or greed for the sake of a regular supply of eggs. The trust's worker then set up in the egg and poultry business in his own compound, hoping by example to demonstrate the economic possibilities of the situation.

In agriculture the trust had been, at the time of my visit, altogether more successful. There is little extreme disparity in income among the Vagher, and so the farmer used as a model to invite imitation was not already so far ahead of his fellows as to nullify the tactic. Neighbouring farmers could see the improved grain ripening on one side of the lane and the traditional grain on the other. They could see that there was no element of Stakhanovism in the situation. In potentially more prosperous areas a farmer of middle-range income would serve this end better than one from the wealthiest families.

When the evident advantage of the improved grain had been established, there was no question of a paternalistic handout, but of a repetition of the pattern. That is to say, those who were sufficiently convinced, and were in a position to make the relatively small sacrifice, were encouraged to buy the seed-grain for the following year.

Michael Lipton had made the point elsewhere (pp. 113-17), here strongly endorsed, that it is probably erroneous to look out for the "progressive farmer" whose value as a model for emulation is limited to a tiny minority of the rich. He points out that among the small farmers there are progressive ploughmen, composters, etc., but "these are not the same people." This may well be so, and we look forward to a detailed spelling out of what he has called the algorithms of particular families.[9] The issue is not, however, between wealthy "progressive" farmers on the one hand and the utter specificity of a particular family with its peculiar algorithm on the other. The wealthy farmer is useless as a model precisely because his fellow villagers are all too aware of what they do not share with him—resources of all sorts. The middle-range farmer *is* useful as such a model because his fellow villagers are aware of what they share. Any one of them may be a better rice cultivator or a better ploughman, but all cultivate rice and all plough.

[9]The original reference here was to a work which Lipton proposed to publish in 1969. This has not in fact appeared and the reader is referred to "The Theory of the Optimising Peasant," *Journal of Development Studies*. I.D.S., University of Sussex, April 1968.

The Dorabji Trust's tactics suggest that the choice of an overall successful farmer in the middle-range for the introduction of improved techniques works. An obvious reason is that the wealthiest farmers seem to lie outside the range of possible emulation. Here, attention will be drawn to three less obvious reasons for success—social reasons, pointing to the useful links that could be developed between planners and social anthropologists. The reasons are that the social respectability of agricultural experiment was guaranteed, that the diffuse associations of traditional social hierarchies were exploited to transform them, and that a sharp traditional distinction between two castes, each largely undifferentiated internally, can itself be a powerful source of rapid social and economic change.

First of all, the middle range-farmer is chosen, for help and improvement by a helping authority which may or may not guarantee the *economics* of the situation but which, by its intervening act of choice, guarantees its *social respectability*. This need seems to be well met in the overall Tata action. The Dorabji Trust is separate from Tata Chemicals but derives moral support from its association with the company. The chosen farmers, by being chosen, are invested with a certain prestige. To this extent the operation depends upon the paternalistic principle, still very active in rural society. But by making loans and not grants, by keeping up a gentle pressure for collection of phased repayments—in general by refusing to have any part of the "something for nothing" mentality that can be, and in India often has been, the corrupt accompaniment of paternalism—the Dorabji Trust seems to be successfully using a traditional principle for a revolutionary end.

A second reason for success in Okhamandal is that the tactic rests on the knowledge that status in Indian rural society is not differentiated as much as it is amongst ourselves. Once the religious qualifications are met, good economic standing connotes a diffuse prestige. This was and still is the way in which the Hinduism of the literary Brahmins and the philosophy of the sects percolate to the masses: through the assumption by wealthier families of religious practices which, because superior, are more in accordance with their economic standing. In the same way the economically advantaged family becomes, or can be made to become, the trend-setter for non-economic patterns of behaviour in the matter of hygiene, education, social morality, and so on.[10]

This modernization of a traditional hierarchy is not confined to Okhamandal. It was dramatically brought home to me in the Kaira district of Gujarat in 1964. Twelve years earlier the obsession with white-collar profession had dominated the minds of fathers thinking about their sons' education. Subsequently, in response to the opportunities open in industry for the technically trained, technical high schools had been privately founded in several of the wealthier villages. I could not have thought it possible in 1952 that the sons of men whom I then knew would be encouraged to work manually in all those trades traditionally associated with low castes like those of the ironsmith, mason, potter, and carpenter. This development had had a liberating effect upon poorer sections who now find a whole range of occupations open to them, the respectability of which is sanctioned by families whose superiority on all other matters is unquestioned.[11] I should make it clear that this development does not raise the status of the traditional artisan castes. They, if anything, suffer by the loss of a traditional monopoly as far as potential employment in industry is concerned. Even this is mitigated by the fact that the new technicians will not compete at the rural level.

The third reason for success in Okhamandal points towards further research. The degree of graduality among the Vagher is slight (i.e., most of them are similar in socioeconomic status and function). This relevance and economic feasibility of any

---

[10] A similar and related point is made by A.H. Hanson, 1966. *The Process of Planning* (O.U.P. for RIIA). Speaking of caste and community groups he says: "Could it be that those much-maligned groups which appear to press so hard against the democratic frontier are in fact one of the forces that preserve it from violation?" (p. 255). I would add the proviso that the overall strategy accepts this view as inevitable and temporary. The tactical use of caste interests is quite a different thing from the encouragement of uneconomical caste occupations under the guise of fostering village industries (see p. 273 above).

[11] Similarly, among the Patidar, a large Gujarati caste with members at many different economic levels, the custom of widow-remarriage is despised at the lower levels but admired, if not yet practiced, at higher levels because yet more sophisticated kinsmen in Baroda and Ahmedabad have allowed it.

particular demonstration of superior technique is therefore likely to be appreciated on a relatively wide scale, and quickly. Where the degree of graduality is greater (as it must almost inevitably be in a larger caste), it is clear that the social area within which such improvements will be appreciated as relevant and feasible has to be discovered by the social worker.[12] The question of graduality has wider relevance for social planning, as I have suggested above. The Vagher/Meghwa situation, like so many so-called "tribal" situations, gives simple expression to the basic purity/impurity formula of the caste system.[13] In such essentially two-caste situations, unaccompanied by graduality, untouchability may (for practical purposes if not in appearance) be drawn off, as to a large extent it has been in Okhamandal. There are already signs that the Vagher are not only obliged to cultivate their fields themselves but also to take up leather work which Meghwa are no longer available to carry out for them. Where there is a two-caste situation with graduality within the dominant caste, we may hypothesize that the near Okhamandal solution will be less likely in proportion to the degree of graduality. Usually, but not always, a dominant caste will exhibit more graduality where it comprises a high proportion of the local population.

Village Power and Planners' Attitudes

As the Okhamandal story should have made clear, it is hardly possible yet for the social anthropologist to supply "variables" with which the planning economist can adjust his models. Such relatively sophisticated collaboration is premature in relation to the Draft Fourth Plan. Only great faith in large-scale planning from which localized benefits are expected to flow, or else inexcusable ignorance, can account for the naivety of the rural

---

[12]This is neither novel nor difficult. Adrian Mayer has distinguished the "kindred of co-operation" from the "kindred of recognition" within caste. See his *Caste and Kinship in Central India*. London, 1960, Chapter 8. The kindred of cooperation will be, formally or informally, an area of affinal ties which will correspond roughly to economic parity.

[13]Compare the Kond/Pan situation in F.G Bailey, 1960. *Tribe, Caste and Nation*, Manchester, Chapter 6.

Social Anthropology

picture as presented by the Commission. The social anthropologist, trying to help the planner, must begin by recommending the monographs and theoretical studies that constitute a basic training in the subject. More creative cooperation can occur only when plans for social change are presented from a common body of shared knowledge.

If this sounds extreme, let us look at a final example of planthink. Michael Lipton has drawn attention (p. 135) to the failure to discuss the balance of power within the village. We could strengthen this observation and say that there appears to be no awareness that there is a balance of power. The Draft Outline's view of *panchayati raj* is an example of idealism so far departed from reality that it meets its opposite and is indistinguishable from cynical indifference. "With the emergence of *panchayati raj* institutions as partners of the Centre and the States in the task of national development, it is necessary that these institutions should be induced in every way to step up their resource mobilization" (p. 123). "Through *panchayati raj*, a system of rural democracy is being built up at the village, block and district level. It is essential that *panchayati raj* institutions should be fully involved in undertaking welfare programmes in these areas" (p. 364). Elsewhere (p. 382) it is recommended that such local communities and institutions should be induced to provide housing sites for untouchables, and in such a manner that the latter are not, even when adequately housed, still segregated.

The idealism springs, we may suppose, from the ideology of the nation-state. To wish that the integrated, harmonious intermeshing system suggested in the word "partners" were the established state of affairs is idealistic, but wholesome enough. To ignore all the facts presenting an alternative picture, and the factors maintaining that alternative, suggests indifference.

The relation between the centre and the parts at federal and at state level is a relation of conflict. This is most acute when we confront the two extremes, the central government and the village *panchayat*. It is by now commonplace that the political adaptability of the caste system has enabled powerful landowning castes, or factions of such castes, to turn local potentialities for power to their own gain (see pp. 136-41). One of the earliest discussions of this, which at the same time brings out the problem most simply, is Cohn's account of the attempts made by a depressed caste to enjoy those powers to which the constitution entitled them. The landowners, with considerable political cunning, withdrew their opposition and allowed the untouchables to take over the forms of power and to learn for themselves that without control of the traditional underpinnings—wealth, influence, contacts—the mere assurances of constitutional rights were not enough.[14] More recently an Indian author, Dr Beteille, writing in 1965, observes in relation to his village study in Tanjore:

> The image of the village *panchayat* as it has been visualized by the leaders of the country, is that it works through consensus and unanimity.[15]

He goes on to show how, in the village of his study, the *panchayat* is characterized more by domination and unequal participation. He describes how the formerly politically-dominant Brahmins have largely withdrawn from participation, while:

> The Adi-Dravidas [Untouchables] by and large find themselves excluded because of their low economic, social and ritual position. When they do attend meetings of the *panchayat*, they are required to sit separately. Often they are informed about a meeting only after it has been held, and their thumb impressions are later secured on the relevant documents.[16]

These and similar facts are known not only to social anthropologists, Indian and foreign, but also to local politicians. The latter, however high their ideals, know that what limited good they can achieve depends on conceding these realities. This is not to say that changes will not come, or indeed, are

---

[14]Bernard S. Cohn, 1955. "The Changing Status of a Depressed Caste," in *Village India*. American Anthropological Association, No. 83.

[15]Andre Beteille, 1965. *Caste, Class and Power*. Berkeley: University of California Press, p. 151.

[16]*Ibid.*, p.153.

not already in process. But such changes are only impeded by what appears to be an idealistic disregard for the present reality on the part of those whose business it is to draw up the blueprint for them.

This extended comment on the first of the three passages from the draft outline, cited on p. 286, sufficiently places the quality of the two following ones. They are unimpeachable as exhortations but as recommendations they fail for lack of a realistic assessment of the social facts.

I should here qualify the rather negative view of *panchayati raj* that the preoccupations of the chapter oblige me to take. The more balanced view is given by V.M. Sirskar who, while recognizing the present gulf between ideal and actuality, stresses the educative function of the ideal and describes the gradual evolution of rural political leaders able to communicate both with the Westernized elite and the peasantry.[17] Professor Adrian Mayer has suggested how the institution of *panchayati raj* has obliged power seekers to accommodate to new political forms.[18] This is not a dramatic success, but it is an encouraging beginning of a new political orientation.[19]

WHAT CAN ANTHROPOLOGISTS DO?

The literature that would furnish an altogether more informed and realistic view of likelihood is there, but the planners have not used it at all. Nevertheless, the situation is not entirely satisfactory on the sociological side. This is not the place to spell out the criticism in detail. The fact is that Indian sociologists have inherited, for the most part uncritically, an intellectual position built up in circumstances which differed

---

[17] V.M. Sirskar, 1960. "Political Role of Panchayati Raj," *Economic and Political Weekly*, November 19. See also George Rosen, 1960. *Democracy and Economic Change in India*. Berkeley: University of California Press, Chapter 5.

[18] Adrian C. Mayer, 1963. "Some Political Implications of Community Development in India," *Archiv. European Sociology*, Vol. IV, pp. 86-106.

[19] A recent work suggests, however, that at least in Maharashtra the political elite is increasingly making itself independent of the rural electorate. See Anthony Carter, 1974. *Elite Politics in Rural India*. Oxford University Press.

markedly from their own. It was no part of the academic British social anthropologist's vocation to advise the colonial government how it might better implement its notion of the colonial state. Social anthropology developed in an ambience that was at best neutral to colonial governmental interests. The contrast between the colonial and post-colonial periods could not be more marked than in the way it effects the moral stance of social anthropologists in India. By and large, however, there is little sign that academic social anthropologists have recognized that their place is with the planners. By a greater consciousness and commitment they might have prevented much of the naivety that has been criticized. The kind of commitment sought would result in a significant shift in the emphasis in the work done. Local organizations would no longer be studied only to discover their self-maintaining mechanisms and their interaction with other organizations, but rather from the point of view of their vulnerability to change and their discontinuity from other institutions. It is by no means required of the academic anthropologist that he approve the Plan or even planning as such. His precise opposition may well be as valuable as his collaboration; in my sense it is collaboration. Academic social anthropology in India is not expected to work for this or that particular end of the Plan, but it can be expected to take cognizance of it and to realize that planning is as much a part of Indian society as caste.

I would propose that apart from this moral commitment on the part of academics, they can also assist in a special way. The Draft Fourth Plan draws attention to the "gap between planning and implementation" (p. 154), and the burden of this essay has been the need for sociological knowledge at the village level. One notes with approval the allocation in the Draft Fourth Plan of forty million rupees to the Commission's Committee for Social Science Research. We must hope that this committee, with the cooperation of academic social anthropology will develop a distinctive cadre of constructive anthropologists who would be government employees working at the village level.[20] Such workers would be committed to the implementation of plan politics far more than the academics. We might hope that the latter would have assisted in the formulation of realistic propositions at the planning stage. The work of the constructive anthropologist would be implementation of these propositions in the particularities of each rural situation. In effect this is a proposal for a new kind of extension worker, altogether better trained than his predecessors, and fully conscious of his mediate role between national and local plan.

---

[20] I prefer the term "constructive" to "applied" as in "applied anthropology" because there is no simple application of social anthropology. The training of a constructive anthropologist would be directed towards problems, health, and methods of education.

David G. Mandelbaum

4 Planning and Social Change in India

The planning of social behaviour is not particularly new in human history and is an old story in India, having been practised by the earliest civilizations. From the third millennium B.C. there is evidence of quite elaborate planning as evidenced in the meticulously laid out street plan of Mohenjo-Daro and in the great granary at Harappa. Even development plans in the sense of deliberately manipulated social change for the general welfare are not new in India. In the third century B.C. the Emperor Asoka planned and carried out communication networks, water improvements and conservation measures through a great part of the subcontinent.

More recent centuries have seen no dearth of what are now called development projects. In the late eighteenth century, the East India Company introduced a new system of land tenure in Bengal and other areas. It was intended to create an Indian counterpart of those English gentry who responsibly managed the land, but it succeeded mainly in establishing a class whose chief function became the pocketing of rent. In the mid-nineteenth century, a large-scale development project was set up to expand and improve the cultivation of cotton. This project was complete with modern appurtenances such as investigating legislative committees, planning directives, and barnstorming American experts.

The history of India in the last hundred years records a number of plans for amelioration, many of which bore either small outcome or yielded results quite at variance with the good intentions of the planners. One basic factor in the failure of such plans was and is the planners' general ignorance of the life of the people for whom they are planning. Administrators in the earlier stages of British rule often sought knowledge of local culture, especially of social organization. Important administrative policies, for example, revenue collection, came to be based on what were thought to be native social systems. But the knowledge was usually fragmentary and the policies set were rarely dispassionately examined for social and cultural consequences.

Social and cultural factors may be as important to the success of an irrigation project as the strength of the dams which are designed for it. Few planners would draw up blueprints for such a project without getting expert opinion on location of dam-site, suitability of water channels, and similar matters within the technical competence of engineers. Yet most planners for countries like India cheerfully assume that no specialist knowledge is required of the most complex of all aspects of a development project—its impact on the life of the people it is designed to serve.

It should be noted at once that the advice of social scientists—whose professional interest is in such problems—will not make the solutions to vexing problems arising from refractory human habit suddenly clear. At the present stage of social science development, such advice may do no more than point out what specific information and what theoretical formulations are needed to approach a solution. But this in itself will better serve the goals of the development planners whose aims of better food and health and living conditions are frequently undermined by haphazard notions or dealing with social matters which they use in their plans.

I

The misfire of some development schemes in earlier decades is illustrated in the life of a group of villagers in south India whom I have known over a number of years. The Kota of Kolmel village in the Nilgiri Hills live in an area which has been particularly favoured by governmental interest. It was the seat of the

Madras government for part of every year when government officers and other Europeans came up to escape the heat of the plains. Because they were thus under the eyes of Europeans, the four indigenous peoples of the area, of whom the Kota are one, became the recipients of special attention and had greater opportunity to take on Western patterns than did people in most other districts of India. Not only did they have the opportunity to benefit from development projects—that term was not used in earlier days, of course, but equivalent ones were—but sometimes they were compelled to be beneficiaries.

For example, a mission school was established within sight of Kolmel village over a century ago, in 1839, and has been in continual operation since. For the last half-century there has been a government school in the village itself with attendance compulsory for all village children. While the compulsion to attend has been indifferently enforced, none the less most adults in the village have spent several childhood years in school and nearly all the men, about a hundred in number, have sat in the school house during eight or ten of their earlier years.

All these men can read and write. Not one of them reads a newspaper or any other printed material regularly, and the principal occasion for writing is when they must sign their names to get a loan. They have been given the tools of literacy but cannot use them properly because they have not acquired either the means or the incentive for such use. In this village, as in many other villages, the time and money spent in inculcating mere literacy, without consideration of the social and cultural base necessary for the proper use of this skill, bring considerably more feeble returns than those which were planned and hoped for.

Writing about Africa, Professor Meyer Fortes makes similar observations. "Literacy can be an extremely valuable tool in a previously pre-literate society. It cannot become an instrument of social transformation without the institutional matrix which gives it life and meaning; and poets and publishers are as important in this martix as schools and colleges."[1]

---

[1] Meyer Fortes, 1945. "An Anthropologist's Point of View," in Rita Hinden, ed., *Fabian Colonial Essays*. London: George Allen and Unwin, p. 231.

In agriculture also, technical advice has long been available in the Nilgiri district (the first experimental farm was established in 1830) but the Kotas have had little advantage from the seeds or the counsel of the agricultural officer. Similarly, a cooperative credit society operates under government auspices and offers loans at a much lower rate of interest than the villagers have to give to the moneylender. Nevertheless, moneylenders are much resorted to and the cooperative facilities are seldom used by Kotas because here, as in other places, the villagers find the rules and rigidity enforced by the manager of the cooperative too high a price to pay for the low interest rates.

These ameliorative measures in education, agriculture and credit have had as little impact on the pastoral Todas of the area as they have had on the Kotas, who are artisans and musicians as well as cultivators. But the agricultural Badagas, by far the most numerous of the inhabitants of the district, have taken much more readily to these and similar benefits. But even among them, the results of such acculturation have not been entirely what the governmental administration has aimed for. One outcome has been the great extension of Badaga cultivation which has markedly accelerated erosion and that, in turn, is seriously threatening the basis of livelihood for the now expanded Badaga population.

No planning officer can be expected to foresee all the major consequences of a planned innovation. By now, however, certain consequences are more foreseeable than they were when the peoples of the Nilgiris were first introduced to improvement schemes. Not all groups have been as impervious as have the Kota, but in India the total effect of such projects has generally been less fortunate than expected. There has been little in the way of happy enhancement, by which a first boost to raise the material standard of living is provided for the people, who then acquire momentum to continue of their own accord. Many factors have been involved in this, but one which is not generally recognized and which has particular pertinence at the present time is the social position of the planners.

The planners—of the past as well as the present—are hampered in their understanding of the people they are planning for by their very social status. They are officials of a governmental agency: many of them in India today are as devoted, intelligent and hard-working as comparable officers of any government. They are, and realize they are, engaged in a task vital to the nation's welfare. There is no serious question that India must plan for its future.

Frequently these civil servants fondly retain connections with their ancestral villages. But in order to qualify for the demanding duties of a government officer they necessarily have had to be divorced from the life of that village during most of their lives. They have been schooled in urban centres in a catechism far removed from the day-to-day realities of village life. Some of them have had additional, and even more remote, schooling at such places as Cambridge and California. Little wonder that the plans they devise in Lucknow or Madras—which may be revised in New Delhi and perhaps further amended in Colombo, Washington or London—sometimes bear unexpected fruit in Kishan Garhi. In this village, as in others recently studied by anthropologists, the villagers have reasons which the reason of the planners does not yet comprehend. This is true elsewhere in the world than India, but in countries like India it is a particularly dangerous pitfall for planners because there is relatively little effective upward communication from the cultivator to the higher echelons of his government.

II

A great burden of responsibility for the affairs and enrichment of the village has, in recent legislation in Uttar Pradesh and in other parts of India, been placed on the local *panchayat*—the village council—an ancient institution which still functions in very many villages. It seems reasonable to suppose that this old local institution, which the people themselves have so long maintained and which has served them well, should be the proper vehicle for those improvements the governmental administration desires to encourage. But the new, elected *panchayats* often bog down and do not produce the planned for and hoped for results. Opler has appositely discussed some of the reasons why the old institution does not fit well into the new demand.[2]

The traditional *panchayats* were and are, Opler points out, informal groups of respected villagers brought together for various purposes—to arbitrate a quarrel, to decide what was to be done about a transgression of caste or village custom, to arrange for a festival, to raise funds for some worthy purpose. It was an agency to conserve the known ways of life about which there was little dispute. There were caste *panchayats* as well as village *panchayats*, if need be there might be a clan *panchayat* or a *panchayat* of several villages. Respected place in the council was not sought by the individual but was accorded to him by the consensus of his fellows because of the general respect he had won. The task of the council was to preserve the social equilibrium of the village, to minimize dissatisfaction and dissension through compromise and arbitration.

The new, elected *panchayat* is expected to do something quite different. It is supposed to innovate on various fronts—to introduce land reform and irrigation ventures under the proper legislative authority, to distribute fertilizer and arrange for the building of roads, to foster education and to look after sanitation. Its members must electioneer for office and are sometimes obliged to exhibit the kind of extrovert behaviour in seeking office which would tend to disqualify them from selection for the old council. The new *panchayatdars*, members of the council, are supposed to act in the public interest and are so exhorted by voices from afar, whereas every local pressure is on them to act in the special interests of a particular caste or faction within the village.

The acts of legislatures occasionally bear some hallmarks of sympathetic magic. In this case the affixing of the name of the old institution to the new social form is automatically supposed to transfer the solid grassroots virtues of the traditional social agency to a newly chartered unit. And while the shortfall of plans is attributed to various causes, Opler well concludes that "What one never hears mentioned, though in my opinion it is

---

[2]Morris E. Opler, 1952. "Village Social and Political Organizations and Economic Growth in Modern India," mimeographed paper contributed to the Conference on Economic Growth in Selected Countries, Social Science Research Council, p. 11.

the most important factor involved, is the social organizational difficulty of expecting a social structure which was essentially fluid, diffuse, and conservative to implement programmes which demand decision, despatch, and an experimental frame of mind."[3]

In most villages studied by anthropologists since the new *panchayats* have been elected, the old and the new councils exist side by side. The old *panchayats* continue to function, albeit their authority is diminished by recent social and economic conditions and their deliberations are rent with more bitter factional dissent than ever. The new *panchayats* tend to operate in the shadow of the old. Some do nothing, others are used to carry out the will of the old *panchayat* or of one village faction or another. Still others are neither totally cooperative nor wholly in the hands of old power groups but try to make some headway on their own. Few seem to have gone briskly to work on village affairs as ideally they should. Quick results need not be expected from social forms enacted by legislative fiat, but there is danger that abiding discredit will fall on the new process of open deliberation by elected representatives, because they are being associated with the increasing tensions and discords of the older forms of village polity.

In a village of the Tanjore district of Madras, Kathleen Gough notes that all the members of the elected *panchayat* board are Brahmins, since they own the land of the village. The relatively modern institutions of village headman and *panchayat* board have, in fact, been welded into a much older form of administration which is still of great importance."[4] But the traditional rule, both temporal and spiritual, of the Brahmins is being vigorously challenged, especially by non-Brahmins who have settled in the village in the last fifty years. In this village the older group sanctions are still strong and the newer political forms are worn only as a front for them, but there are clear indications that breaks in the old ways and consequent trials of strength in the new forms may not be long in coming. Within the Brahmin group, litigation and dispute are kept in check by

---

[3]*Ibid.*, p. 11
[4]Kathleen Gough, 1952. "The Social Structure of a Tanjore Village," *The Economic Weekly*, Bombay, 24 May, p. 532.

the need to maintain unity and authority before the lower castes.

In Kishan Garhi, one of the Uttar Pradesh villages studied by Marriott, there has been greater political upheaval.[5] The old wielders of power were a clan of landowners who maintained economic and social paramountcy. They still have influence and, because of their background of wealth and education, they have taken over many of the new governmental and party posts. When voting during the last national elections, the villagers had to choose among candidates all of whom were of this former landlord caste.

But now there are more villagers of other castes who own land, and within the village the old supremacy of the former landlords is gone. They still retain a more tightly-knit organization than do the other village castes, as is true of the Brahmin landowners mentioned above, but there are fallings out even within their ranks. In this village the Brahmins are mainly farmers who were formerly tenants of the landowners. They constitute about one-quarter of the population of the village and hold about half the land. They are now bidding for village leadership but cannot as yet agree as to who among them shall take precedence or new various interests within their group should be represented.

The caste and clan councils of all castes have here as elsewhere, lost some of their former authority. Marriott attributes this loss of force to the increased differentiation of status within each caste, to greater knowledge of freer ways than those of the old village society, and to pervasive internal dissensions.

An elected village *panchayat* and a rural court have been established in Kishan Garhi under the new Panchayat Raj Act. As elected, the *panchayat* includes members of various castes; that *panchayat* never meets. "The group which really does what the elected panchayat is supposed to do, which discusses public issues and uses the authority of the Act, is the old informal Brahmin caste council...." The ex-landlords now abstain from overt participation in village affairs and the Brahmin council has neither the necessary unity nor the external authority to

---

[5]McKim Marriott, 1952. "Social Structure and Change in a U.P. Village," *The Economic Weekly*, Bombay, 23 August, pp. 869-74.

conduct these affairs well. Taxes and fines for village use remain largely uncollected, projects for village improvement remain undone. The new rural court, planned as a solvent of social frictions, solves little because the magistrates "do battle among themselves using the litigants as pawns."[6] Litigation increases, and competition among men and groups in the village is often played out in the expensive journeys of the higher courts.

While the changes which were intended by the legislature are thus incompletely realized, certain other changes have moved apace as the unintended results of other legislation. Joint family holdings in land are being rapidly split up as a result of agrarian reform legislation, including the recent Zamindari Abolition Act, which has brought about a considerable redistribution of land. This legislation is aimed at abolishing absentee landlords rather than at breaking up the joint family. Indeed, the proposed Hindu Code Bill, which would, among other changes, give rights of inheritance to daughters, has been bitterly fought because it was feared that such changes would imperil the solidarity of the joint family. But the cultivators themselves are less concerned about joint family unity than they are about the steep court costs which frequently plague families whose possessions must be divided. Hence they welcome the opportunity provided under the new legislation to not only acquire land but also to register ownership of newly-acquired land separately, in the names of the individual male members and even of minor children, rather than in the name of the joint family.

This undermining of the economic basis of joint family cooperation contributes to the general loosening of old bonds of village social organization. In this and in other villages, there used to be a social order within which the work and aspirations of men were directed for their own and the social welfare. That order was mirrored, reinforced, and re-established in the yearly pattern of ritual and ceremony. While that pattern and order are by no means totally gone, they are not followed as they once were and are changing under the impact of new forces. It is not to be supposed that there was no friction and dissatisfaction under the old order, or that there should be a return to

[6] *Ibid.*, p. 874.

that order. The former is not so, and the latter is neither possible nor even desirable to most villagers. The problem for villagers and planners alike is that of assimilating changes and establishing an adapted order so that food will not be less but more.

Much the same political conditions are portrayed by Carstairs for Fatehpura village in Udaipur as are depicted for Kishan Garhi.[7] Udaipur was a princely state of Rajputana and the palace of the local *jagirdars*, the lords and landlords, still towers above the village. But their absolute dominance is gone. The nominal chief authority is now the democratically-elected *panchayat*. "In fact, however, this body has not yet gained the citizens' respect and confidence." Various groups and strong men are warily trying for eminence in village affairs, while few can avoid being drawn into a major feud which has developed between two factions of traders and moneylenders.

Rivalry between factions often thwarts genuine measures for the welfare of the whole village. If one side takes the lead in sponsoring such a measure, it is interpreted by the other side as a bid for factional advantage and as a threat to their own interests. In the older village society there was factionalism in plenty, but the traditional order demanded cooperation for certain economic and ritual purposes. Hence factionalism was continually overridden in vital matters so long as the old order strongly prevailed. Nor was there at that time, as there is now, pressure from governmental sources for joint activities by the villagers, as part of a regional or a national enterprise.

Stalemate between village factions is described for a village in eastern Uttar Pradesh by M.E. Opler and R.D. Singh.[8] In this village, called Madhopur, the ruling landowners of the Thakur caste were outvoted in the village election by an alliance consisting mainly of the lower castes. But the elected council can accomplish little, because only the Thakurs have the necessary training and experience in political affairs, and they

---

[7]G. Morris Carstairs, 1952. "A Village in Rajasthan—A Study in Rapid Social Change," *The Economic Weekly*, Bombay, 26 January, pp. 75-77.

[8]Morris E. Opler and Rudra D. Singh, 1952. "Two Villages of Eastern Uttar Pradesh (U.P.), India: An Analysis of Similarities and Differences," *American Anthropologist*, Vol. 54, pp.179-90.

still control much of the land and wealth in the village as well as forming a sizable minority of the population. They will not cooperate with the rival coalition in improvement projects; proposals for water and road betterment are stymied.

In the other village discussed by Opler and Singh, "Ramapur" near Allahabad, there was no struggle for dominance at election time. Memberships in the village council were parcelled out to the main castes. At the first meeting of the *panchayat*, the agriculturalists attempted to pass ordinances which would be of special benefit to them. Non-agriculturalists interpreted these proposals as nuisance measures aimed at them. They remained uninterested in the elected *panchayat* which is as ineffective here as in the other villages from which we have recent field reports.

III

But villagers can unite as well as divide. Their lives are not always cramped by crippling factionalism. The swift impact of recent economic and social forces seems to have aggravated factional strife. More isolated communities may be more immune to it, at least so long as their isolation holds. Thus recent accounts of a secluded Himalayan village in Kulu and of villages of the Bhil tribe in Rajasthan reveal relatively little factionalism of the corrosive kind.[9]

But even when factionalism is deep and bitter, the antagonists may act in concert in certain contexts. The opposing sides of the Kota village of Kolmel dropped their in-fighting and presented united front when faced with a threat from their Badaga neighbours. Among Uttar Pradesh folk, Opler notes, "In one village where I thought factionalism was rife, I was assured that if the village were attacked or opposed from without, the people would close ranks and 'even the stones of the

---

[9]Collin Rosser, 1952. "A 'Hermit' Village in Kulu," *The Economic Weekly*, Bombay, 17 May, pp. 477-82. G. Morris Carstairs, 1952. "Bhil Villages of Western Udaipur," *The Economic Weekly*, Bombay, 1 March, pp. 231-33.

village' would resist."[10]

The nature of village unity in the community of Kodagahalli in Mysore has been discussed by M.N. Srinivas.[11] Here, too, there are factions. Caste *panchayat* are still powerful, apparently more so than in some of the examples previously mentioned, and village and caste leaders work together. But there are frequent complaints from officials and political leaders who visit the village, about the internal divisions which impair— but do not prevent—village-wide cooperation. For Srinivas tells how all participate in common ritual practices when drought threatens. When men of another village insult one's fellow villagers, all the neighbours rally in support of the aggrieved person. The villagers closed ranks on an occasion when the local government authorities proposed to auction off the fishing rights to the village tank, rights which had been held by the villagers in common. On the day of the auction, all the villagers saw to it that no one could approach to put in a bid for the fishing rights.

Similar consolidation of strength has been noted in other villages as well. While an outside threat brings about such defensive unity quickly, joint action is frequently and freely undertaken for certain constructive purposes, i.e., to build a new temple. These cases indicate that villagers will work together zealously and efficiently under certain conditions. Thus far, the conditions set up by planners and legislators have too often had the unintended effect of widening the common factional division in the villages.

It is not, of course, to be expected that so gigantic a task as that which confronts planners in India will proceed smoothly from blueprint to reality with certitude and despatch. There have been successes as well as errors in the brief period since independence, and those responsible for the progress of the

---

[10] David G. Mandelbaum, 1940. "Social Trends and Personal Pressures: The Growth of a Culture Pattern," in Leslie Spier *et al.*, eds., *Language, Culture and Personality*. Wisconsin: Menasha, p. 236. Morris E. Opler, 1952, *op. cit.*, "Village Social and Political Organization. . .," p. 1.

[11] M.N. Srinivas, 1951. "The Social Structure of a Mysore Village," *The Economic Weekly*. Bombay, 30 October, pp. 1051-56.

large power, irrigation, and industrial projects deserve commendation. Great enterprises must be set in motion before all the kinds in their planning can be straightened out. But it is to be expected that by now the danger signals in the sphere of culture and society will be noted, and that consideration will be given toward providing conditions which will encourage rather than discourage village unity. But before intelligent and effective provision of this kind can be made, the planners and administrators will have to have much better equipment in the way of social information than they now possess.

IV

Even if the presently-planned targets for production are achieved, if village output is greatly increased with the help of technical innovations, there are still other social problems that take shape. The gains of land reform acts and of increased agricultural efficiency tend to go to those who have some land. The landless labourers, and there are many millions of them, get little good from these improvements at the present time. In Malabar, as Adrian Mayer points out, agrarian reform legislation has successfully been of advantage to various classes of the population, but the landless workers still have practically no benefit from it.[12] Where other classes do profit, the economic difference between the disadvantaged and the others grows greater and is potentially explosive. Opler makes the same point in relation to a well-publicized development scheme in north India. "On the basis of increased cereal production figures the project is hailed as an example of what technical programmes can accomplish, but not long ago, when I asked the chief American consultant to the project what was in store for the hard-pressed landless labourer, and whether more problems might not be created than are being solved, he could only say that he, too, was worried about the final outcome."[13]

Those groups in a village who suffer the greatest disabilities are

---

[12]Adrian C. Mayer, 1952. *Land and Society in Malabar*. Bombay: Oxford University Press, p. 92.
[13]Opler, *op. cit.*, "The Problem of Selective Culture Changes," p. 132.

not necessarily the ones most restless for drastic change. They may be so greatly concerned with the sheer problem of keeping alive, so fearful of upsetting their slim margin of subsistence, so little aware of other social possibilities, that they are content to keep going much as they are. But those who can visualize a different and better state of affairs for themselves, who can afford to take some risks toward attaining it, or who have had broader social experience, are frequently the most restive. Thus in the Tanjore village described by Kathleen Gough, the greatest opposition to the Brahmin landowners who still control the community is not from their very poor tenants but from the better-off and more independent newcomers into the village. Supporters of the Communist party are less evident among the landless labourers, who still work for their traditional masters, than among low-caste men who have worked outside the village and have come back to find the old way no longer to their liking, and among young men of any caste who have some Western education and no land. Mayer makes the same comment concerning the latter group in Malabar where many communists are found among the young men of the higher castes who have had some Western education and have neither jobs nor land.[14]

A final social snag may be mentioned, one which arises not from the social organization in the villages but from the social relations in the bureaucracy. Officials of the regular branches of government can hardly be expected to be enthusiastic about the new echelon of development officials thrust into their territory, who are often endowed with funds and powers beyond the hope of the regular official, and full of that necessary sense of importance of their jobs which is not usually contagious across bureaucratic departments. One large project in India nearly came to grief on that score because development officers cannot operate successfully against the covert opposition of other governmental officials.

V

The general problem far transcends any one country or set of countries. It concerns the much-discussed fact of modern times,

---

[14]Gough, *op. cit.*, pp. 535-36; Mayer, *op. cit.*, p. 135.

the diffusion of power-science patterns of culture from Europe and North America to other continents and other cultures. Within Europe and America the internal spread of new patterns raises many problems of displacement and development. Special problems develop among other peoples, as in India, when recurrent waves of new techniques and concepts make an impact. The new ways are frequently welcomed as means of bettering material resources; when taken over they are found to have an effect, sometimes a most unwelcome one, on standards and values other than those material.

Increasingly, agencies of government are being given direct responsibility for controlling this diffusion, especially in relation to large-scale economic enterprises. Insofar as these enterprises are fruitful, they almost inevitably entail social change. Hence, the governmental agencies can scarcely avoid being involved with far-reaching changes in culture and society, often ramifying into areas where neither government nor change is expected to appear.

Governmental planning, if it is to fulfill its purpose, must take human factors into account, in addition to those of engineering and economics which are customarily considered. The contributions of engineers and economists are, of course, not to be dismissed; they remain as vital as before and can be accomplished only by the respective specialists. But their net accomplishment does not depend on such professional skill alone. Thus the economist's studies of formation of capital are requisite for the effective planning of development projects but given proper capital resources, development programmes can be brought to grief, as we have noted, by forces outside the professional ken of economists and engineers.

Certain general statements which can be made about these forces have been illustrated above, as well as the particular Indian phrasings of the general propositions. Thus we have noted the very simple but often overlooked consideration that culture patterns are not as interchangeable among societies as jeep wheels are among jeeps. Even so apparently easy as interchange as that of an "improved" variety of wheat seed for indigenous wheat seed, turns out to be far from easy. When there is very little surplus of subsistence, as among many of the cultivators of India, the taking over of new seeds, new tools, new techniques may appear as a possibly catastrophic gamble, with too slender resources urged by an uncomprehending outsider. New technical processes very often demand a period of experimentation by the villager before he can adapt them to his local conditions. Many in India simply cannot afford the experimental period if it threatens the yield of a single harvest. But if the new techniques are presented not as substitutes for the traditional techniques but as an addition to them which will supplement income, they may be as eagerly seized as are opportunities for brief periods of employment which do not interfere with the regular procedures of cultivation.

Considerations of social organization are frequently of high importance in these attempts to direct social change. We have noted how class stratification and the nature of communication between members of different social classes affect not only development projects but many spheres of national life. Government officials in agrarian countries, even more than elsewhere, tend to form a class apart from the village people. They are frequently both socially isolated and culturally different from them. The members of the bureaucracy have great power over the fortunes of the villagers who, in turn, determine whether and how the directives of the officials are to be carried out. Villagers may themselves be stratified by region, religion or economic interest, but vis-a-vis officialdom they often react together. Thus there is reciprocal influence without corresponding avenues for communication.

If channels of mutual communication are set up and used, there is then the possibility (although not any guarantee) that each side will modify its actions toward the other in the light of information received. When both sides manifest such self-corrective behaviour, whether consciously or not, there is greater opportunity for the realization of purposes shared by both classes. Under the British administration, the district officer was expected to maintain mutual communication by constant touring of the villages in his district. In the Soviet Union, as Inkeles has shown, the office of agitator and the practice of letters-to-the-editor purport to maintain informational contact between party and people.[15]

[15] Alex Inkeles, 1951. "Understanding a Foreign Society: A Sociologist's View," *World Politics*, pp. 272-73; also, *Public Opinion in Soviet Russia*. Harvard University Press, 1950.

In contemporary India, district officers still do some circuit riding but the administrative chores of theirs jobs give them little time for confabulation with villagers; their training or inclination does not encourage it, nor are their relations with theirs superiors such that they can pass on village information effectively even if they have it. Nor is the Soviet model a suitable one for the Indian scene. Political parties of the democratic type are still not sufficiently well established to provide such channels of communication. It might be well worth devising several communication arrangements and testing each experimentally on a small scale.

But establishing communication between bureaucracy and villagers is only one preliminary step, important as it is. Our discussion has indicated that problems appear *seriatim*; as one set is resolved, another set becomes significant. This is true both for practical problems toward a goal of higher living standards, and theoretical problems toward a goal of keener explanatory and predictive ability. Practically, we have seen that in a case when certain governmental officers established quite effective communication with village people and carried forward the development plans, the problem arose of their none-too-happy relations with other officials of the regular ministries. When those relations are smoothed over, there will later arise the serious problem of the gap between those villagers who gain from the projects and those landless labourers whose lack or gain makes them feel all the more greatly disadvantaged.

The social role of the person bearing innovations is another significant consideration. When an outsider appears in a community and offers new techniques, he is given some role by the people. That is, a set of expectations about his behaviour are attached to him. The expectations may be much modified as his behaviour is actually observed, but the role assignment may well condition the people's perception of what he does. The role assigned is usually part of the community's known repertoire of roles, which has been derived from its social system and experience.

Thus the role assigned to Western-trained doctors by some villagers is not the same as the status he usually assumes he has. Indeed the people's experience with so different a

Planning and Social Change in India

functionary as the tube-well operator may shadow their perception of the doctor as another technician whose monopoly of technical knowledge enables him to exact exorbitant tribute when that knowledge controls village livelihood.

Not all parts of development programmes depend crucially on the relations between those who bring innovations and those for whom they are intended. But many do, and in those aspects it is important to make allowance for the fact that the reception of the innovation is related to the role which is given to and taken by the innovator. If the bearer of innovations can set up as part of his role the kind of communication we have been discussing, the chances of success for his purpose are probably increased. In Indian villages it may be particularly difficult to create such a role because non-villagers who concern themselves with village affairs tend to be tagged as officials of some sort and the traditional behaviour toward those in official roles is that of passive verbal acceptance. Their exhortations are politely received, perhaps even vigorously assented to, then quickly forgotten once the presence departs. There are both social and psychological bases for this pattern of behaviour, and it differs from typical peasant behaviour toward officials in many other parts of the world only in its greater degree of nominal acquiescence and of actual imperviousness.

Villagers know other roles and have other institutions than those traditionally used as a defence against officialdom. It seems but elementary sense for planners to try to utilize for their purposes ways of social cooperation long practised by the villagers for their own purposes.

In development programmes where these two purposes have no major conflict and have the same goals of more food, better health, greater security, it is indeed but commonsense to link the new techniques and ideas to functioning social forms. As our discussion of *panchayats* indicated, such adaptation can be effectively made if there is a considerable correspondence of form and function between the traditional group and any proposed newer version, not if the correspondence is one of form, or of name, only. There are strong constructive and cooperative potentialities in Indian village life. When they can be paired with the new strength sponsored by the planners, the resultant social changes should better suit all concerned.

T. Scarlett Epstein

5 The Role of Social Anthropology in Development Studies*

Development has until very recently been generally regarded as synonymous with economic development and in turn with the growth of the total national product. This emphasis on *economic* development reflects the economists' monopoly of the development field. Their traditional worship of quantification led them to make national income accounting the pivot round which all development activities were to rotate. National income is a convenient and readily quantifiable variable, movements in which can be analyzed into changes in different categories of expenditure. All this facilitates model building. Disregarding the fact that much of the basic statistical data in developing countries had little resemblance to economic reality, most economists preached the gospel of maximizing the rate of economic growth measured in terms of per capita income. This has been regarded as the panacea for all development ills. To give but one example, Arthur Lewis wrote in his *Theory of Economic Growth*:

> First it should be noted that our subject matter is growth, and not distribution. It is possible that output may be

*This is a revised version of the paper presented to the 1973 Annual Meeting of the Association of Social Anthropologists held at Oxford. I gratefully acknowledge the many helpful comments and criticisms I received from colleagues, which helped in the redrafting of this paper.

growing and yet that the mass of the people may be becoming poorer... but our primary interest is in analysing not distribution but growth (1955: 9).

Gradually, some leading development economists began to doubt the wisdom of defining development only in narrow economic terms and challenged the belief that the rate of national output growth truly reflects economic development. Thus Seers, for example, defined the aims of development as the provision of the necessary conditions for "in the realisation of the potential of human personality" (1969: 3), i.e., to insure full employment, to reduce inequality and eliminate poverty. However, "the fulfilment of human potential requires much that cannot be specified in purely economic terms" (Seers, 1969: 5).

Yet until the 1970s most agencies and planners concerned with LDCs continued to have blind faith in the maximization of the overall rate of economic growth. A recent ILO publication specifically states that "the first development decade of the UN is now recognised as a failure despite the fact that the developing countries met the overall income objectives of 5 per cent per annum. It failed in what was the originally unstated, but more and more generally recognised, corollary objective of translating the gains from growth into rising standards of living for people and primarily for the poorest" (1972: 59). Thus, finally, the myth seems to have been exploded that a fast rate of economic expansion automatically solves the problem of poverty. In fact the contrary has been found: in many instances there is a positive correlation between the rate of economic growth and the extent of economic differentiation, with the former being the determining variable. India's "green revolution" area provides an excellent example of such development (see Frankel, 1971).

The UN motto for the present decade is "the relief of poverty." McNamara, President of the World Bank, stated in his address to the Board of Governors that all efforts should be concentrated on helping the low-income strata—roughly the poorest forty per cent—of the total population in all developing countries (1972: 9).

Some of the more radical Marxian scholars hold that it is

impossible to understand and analyze development problems without viewing them in their global context. Frank goes so far as to claim that all aid—in whatever form—that the advanced capitalist economies offer to LDCs is only an attempt to disguise their own vested interests in maintaining the status quo. Moreover, he accuses social scientists like Hoselitz and Nash of aiding and abetting the capitalistic attempt of dressing up what is basically an exploitative exercise. He asserts that they provide the "... emperor's clothes, which have served to hide his naked imperialism. Rather than fashioning a new suit, these people will have to dethrone him and clothe themselves" (Frank 1971:55). The British structural-functionalist school is referred to only en passant by Frank when he says that "they select small 'societies' in Africa and elsewhere for study and analyse them as though they had an isolated existence independent from the imperialist system of which they formed an integral part at the time of the study" (1971: 16). This seems to imply that Frank does not regard British social anthropologists with their micro-studies quite as vicious and harmful as the American sociologists with their "index and diffusionist approach."

In this paper I do not want to take up the cause of our American counterparts but rather confine myself to discussing the part British social anthropology can play in the field of development.

Development is a concept loaded with value judgements. No one generally accepted definition exists, nor do we have a convenient means by which to measure the rate of development, now that per capita income growth has been discarded as such. If development is defined in such a way that it necessitates the overall reorganization of the ownership of the means of production, as Frank obviously implies, then his insistence on the global approach to the problem makes sense. Such an approach logically leads to advocating a revolutionary restructuring of world society at large. Under these preconditions the task of the sociologist would not only be to expose the socioeconomic interdependence between advanced capitalist and underdeveloped economies, as Frank advocates, but also to investigate and analyze the socioeconomic relationships existing between the socialist countries and their underdeveloped satellites, a very important field of research which Frank completely ignores.

On the other hand, if the meaning of development is taken to be more limited, namely to relate to the process by which poverty is alleviated, inequality reduced, and the opportunities for the self-fulfilment of all individuals are increased, then British social anthropology with its emphasis on micro-research has an important role to play in this sphere of studies.

I, and I expect many of my colleagues, subscribe to this second and more restricted definition of development. This, admittedly, may imply that we prefer small short-term gains for the underdeveloped poor rather than opting for more basic long-term improvements. But to repeat a well-known cliche, which is yet appropriate in this context, "in the long run we are all dead in any case."

In what follows I discuss three fields of enquiry in which I suggest social anthropology can make a useful contribution to development studies.

Facts and Fiction about Development

Most LDCs have by now introduced legislative measures aimed at helping the poorest strata in society. Many politicians, planners and administrative officers cheerfully assume that legislation is automatically implemented and planning provisions fulfilled. The lower ranks of the administrative hierarchy usually have a vested interest in assuring their superiors that orders have been successfully executed simply because this is the only way they hope to ensure promotion for themselves. This is one of the major reasons for the fictitious development achievements so often reported. It is in this context that the social anthropologist can contribute to development. His lengthy fieldwork in one small-scale society, where he collects detailed data, much of it by participant observation, enables him not only to expose the facts of the situation but also to outline the why and wherefore of it all. There are plenty of accounts published by different social anthropologists who worked in different LDCs which I could quote here in evidence. Let one of my own experiences suffice.

In India, where economic differentiation closely coincides with ascribed caste status, paragraph 46 of the Constitution specifically states that "the State shall promote with special care the educational and economic interests of the weaker sections of the people, and, in particular, of the Scheduled Castes and the Scheduled Tribes, and shall protect them from social injustice and all forms of exploitation" (1955: 15). In line with this the government of Mysore introduced land rules according to which fifty per cent of the land available for disposal in any village should be granted to persons belonging to scheduled castes and tribes (M.L.G.R., 1969: 1057). *The Mysore Land Grant Rules*, 1969, set out the government rates for selling this land to scheduled castes: the price of one wet hectare must be less than Rs 2,500 but more than Rs 500. The maximum price of Rs 1,000 for one wet acre of government land is well below the current market rate of about Rs 7,000. Many Mysore politicians, planners and administrators seemed convinced that with these land grant rules they had done their share to help village scheduled caste households to acquire land. Moreover, their minds are likely to have been put at ease having seen entries in village land records of newly purchased land against the names of some village scheduled caste men. I actually found such a case when I returned to Wangala in 1970.

Rana, a scheduled caste man, had an entry of three irrigated acres in the village land record. He looked blank when I asked him what he was growing on his wet land and did not know what I was talking about. Slowly it dawned on him that I was referring to a land transfer three years previously in which he had been involved. Kempegowda, his peasant caste patron, had called him and told him that he would give him Rs 3,000 for the purchase of three acres of newly irrigated government land which Kempegowda would then cultivate. If Rana did as he was told, he was promised help with the forthcoming marriage of his son. Rana had been worrying how to raise money to celebrate his son's wedding but, being already heavily indebted to his patron, he had been afraid of approaching him again. Thus he was overjoyed when Kempegowda volunteered help on his own account. Rana went to the authorities in Mandya and paid over the money Kempegowda had given him. This was the first and last time that he had anything to do with this land purchase. He was not even aware that the land was still entered under his name. As far as he was concerned the land belonged to Kempegowda, who had paid for it and cultivated it. Rana could not even perceive what it would be like to own such a vast fortune as three wet acres; all he had was two dry acres. Kempegowda did keep his promise and lent Rana Rs 100 in support of the latter's son's wedding.

Kempegowda already had six irrigated acres; the additional three wet acres enabled him to extend his cashcropping, which was particularly remunerative during the prohibition period when sugarcane prices soared. Subsequently, when I talked over this land transaction with Kempegowda himself, he made it clear that he did not think he had done anything wrong. He assured me that he was in the process of getting the land put under his own name, as a number of his fellow village landowners had already done in similar transactions. He made no secret that he thought the government foolish for expecting village scheduled caste men to be able to purchase new wet land and put it under the plough. He pointed out that Rana and his like did not have the necessary assets such as iron ploughs and bullocks, let alone the required working capital. The hereditary relationship he had with Rana provided him with an avenue by which to acquire newly irrigated government land at nominal prices and he was convinced he had done the right thing by following it.

Rana, on the other hand, was keen to please his peasant master because this assured him at least a minimum of social security. Rana was fully aware that as he belonged to a scheduled caste he had special claims to loan facilities, but he also knew that to get such finance needed the signature of an administrative official who had to be bribed before he was prepared to oblige. Thus Rana was convinced that he had no chance of acquiring this land for himself.

The facts in this case differed from the fiction of development because of a number of different interdependent variables. Village scheduled caste households are too poor to take advantage of the government help offered them in acquiring land. Officials are in a strategic position and can demand bribes. Rana, like so many of his kind, sees no alternative to his continued dependency on his peasant patrons. Kempegowda has always helped when Rana found himself in extreme financial difficulties. This was a good enough reason for Rana to believe that such help would continue to be forthcoming. By contrast, government authorities have not as yet given Rana any concrete help. To try and fight for the attainment of the rights that legislation assured him, seemed far too risky compared with the minimum of social security he still enjoyed as part of the continued hereditary labour relationship he had with local landowners. He was not prepared to jeopardize this arrangement.

This case study illustrates the importance of social anthropology in exploding the myths surrounding much of development. Moreover, it can act as a bridge between high-powered decision-makers and small-scale societies where development policies have actually to be implemented. It can also point to the reasons for the often considerable discrepancies between plans and their implementation.

The Social Hinterland of Development

Much of economic theory is derived from the "Rational Economic man model" according to which man is completely individualistic and not influenced in the least by his fellow beings; moreover, maximization of profits (or material benefits) for himself is the only motive which activates him. As a concession to reality, economic man has been accepted as acting in the context of his immediate nuclear family. This model, though still bearing little relationship to real life, provided economists with a convenient base for deductive reasoning. Knight strongly asserted that "the principles of economy are known intuitively; it is not possible to discriminate the economic character of behaviour by sense observation; and the anthropologist, sociologist or historian seeking to discover or validate economic laws by inductive investigation has embarked on a wild goose chase" (1960: 512).

In view of the economic development debacle it now seems appropriate to rephrase Knight's statement and say that it is the economist who embarks on a wild goose chase when he thinks he can discern the process of development simply by way of a priori reasoning. There is a mutual interdependence and interaction between the total social framework of a society and its development process. Most economists, unable to incorporate social variables in their analyses, regard as obstacles all the non-economic social factors affecting development, and still dream of a world peopled by truly rational economic men. Alas, they have to wake up and face cruel reality, which is much more complex than their models allow for.

Some sociologists do set out to investigate the part socio-economic variables play in development. Yet their methodology of research is such that one cannot help but doubt some of their findings. For instance, one such study set out to investigate the process of agricultural innovation in Indian villages. It states that secular orientation of village leaders is one of the four major factors explaining differences among villages in adoption of improved agricultural practices. This claim is based on a questionnaire enquiry conducted among sampled village leaders who were asked eight items such as: Can evil spirits cause disease? and, If your son wanted to marry a lower caste girl would you allow it? (Fliegel, 1968: 47). It is difficult to see how much significance, if any, can be attached to these answers to casual once and for all questions when the informant is likely to have tried to provide the answer he thought was expected of him. Such sociological surveys do not attempt to crosscheck verbal answers with observable behaviour. Like so many other statistically oriented surveys, they regard individual social variables as isolable and fail to view societies as social systems, each part of which is interdependent with some, or all, other parts.

No doubt, quantitative enquiries are an important facet of development studies but they can never tell the whole story; they need to be supplemented by qualitative data to help explain the intricate independence of the different socioeconomic variables all involved in the development process. It is in this sphere of study that social anthropological micro-studies can contribute most to a better understanding of development problems. Here again I discuss examples from my own work, though of course there are innumerable other studies that could be mentioned to indicate how the social anthropologist can help to clarify the way societies adapt to developmental conditions and in turn also affect them.

Family Structure

Development economists usually regard the extended family system as a symptom of subsistence or near subsistence economies and as inimical to economic growth (e.g., Bauer, 1957: 65). Likewise, many studies of Indian society by anthropologists and sociologists have pointed to the decline of the joint family as a result of economic growth. Bailey says with reference to Bissipara, the Orissa village he studied, that "the joint family cannot survive divergent interests and disparate incomes" (1957: 92). Kaldate states that "in the process of social disorganisation the changes in family organisation tend to take the form of changes from the larger or joint family system to the small family system" (1962: 104); Lannoy remarks that "wherever there has recently been radical betterment of the economic conditions of sectors of the Indian populations, correspondingly great changes have been found in the pattern of family life. Structurally there is a change from the joint to the nuclear system" (1971: 124). My own earlier fieldwork in south India (1954) led me to pronounce the decline of the joint family system (1962:177), which I also explained in terms of basic economic changes having taken place in the villages I studied. My return visit to the same villages in 1970 made me realize the fallacy of arguing in terms of outright economic determinism. Economic changes no doubt affected family structure, but different socioeconomic strata adapted their familial organization in different ways (1973). All of the present Wangala and Dalena magnates, who were already among the wealthiest in 1955, now live in joint households. Those of the magnates of 1955 who in the meantime had to yield to their sons' requests to partition their property, have by now disappeared from the village economic scene. Those of the magnate joint households without a male descendent, in fact extended either along lateral or affinal lines. All the magnate joint families practise division of labour. Each male adult member performs specialized tasks; the oldest member usually looks after the cultivation of their lands, while the younger generation takes care of running business enterprises such as shops, flour mills or cane-crushers.

This illustrates a number of important points. In the first place, it is clear that magnates fully realize the economies of scale to be derived by living in joint families. Second, they appear to trust only their near kin as reliable partners in their economic ventures. Third, in the Indian lineally related three-generation joint family, where each son has the right to an equal share in the ancestral property, persistence of the joint family depends largely on the personality of the head of the household and the sort of relationship he establishes with his sons and their wives.

Among Wangala and Dalena middle-farmers, the conventional types of joint family where "the different kinsmen along with their spouses and children occupy the same dwelling, eat and worship together and enjoy property in common" (Driver, 1962: 112) has continued to decline. However, there are signs of new family arrangements emerging within this socioeconomic category of villagers, which provide one example of an adaptation of the conventional joint family to new economic circumstances. I call this new type of family "share family" for lack of a better name. The share family, of which I found a number in Dalena, differs from joint families insofar as the family no longer lives jointly under one roof; it differs from the elementary family because it involves a number of near kin—agnatic or affinal—who each live separately with their families but who have informally agreed to share their incomes as well as their expenditure. Such share families exist in cases where one or more male members of a family have taken up urban employment. The farming members of the family undertake to cultivate the land belonging to the urban worker and usually let him have at least part of the yield; in turn the wage-earning relative reciprocates by meeting the necessary cash requirements of his rural kin. These share arrangements are usually highly flexible, without any fixed terms laid down. So far hardly any quarrels have arisen within these share families. This new type of family organization is regarded as mutually beneficial by all concerned. It enables villagers who work in urban employment to keep their stake in the rural economy, which seems of supreme importance to them. At the same time it allows the farming members of the family to concentrate on cultivating their lands without having to worry about earning cash. This makes them prepared to keep their cash demands within manageable limits. Moreover, many men working outside their village try to provide as many modern amenities for their rural kin as they can afford. In this way they retain a foothold in the village social system and can continue to participate in the international struggle for prestige.

The share family is a suitable adaptation to new situations. Its productive integration, accompanied by only a loosely-knit living arrangement, enables elementary families participating in such a share union to have the best of both worlds: each gains from the resulting division of labour and specialization, while each is free to live its life according to its own judgement. Similar families adjustments have been discussed with reference to successful Madras industrial leaders (Singer, 1968: 445) as well as some other Indian communities (Beteille, 1964: 243).

Wangala and Dalena landless villagers and those with insignificant size landholdings have for the most part continued to live as elementary families. A new migrant labour settlement in Wangala, however, indicates that the poorest landless labourers, who have to be continuously on the move in search of work and livelihood, extend their family relations over a wide network of lineal, lateral and affinal kin. In this way they manage to spread the risk and have a better chance of survival by providing for themselves at least a minimum of social security. The activation of classificatory kin links in this instance, therefore, promotes development by relieving the extremes of poverty.

Familial changes in India exemplify the flexibility and adaptability of such a basic social institution as the family. The joint family persists among the wealthiest by providing the best conditions for them to benefit from economies of scale; the new share family offers participating units the possibility to perform different economic functions in a mutually beneficial way. The formation of large kin networks among the poorest rural transients improves their chances of survival.

From all this it emerges clearly that not only has the family organization adapted to changing economic conditions but it has in turn actively affected and influenced the pattern of development. The persistence of the joint family among the richest farmers has resulted in greater concentration of wealth in the hands of the few, and consequently increased economic differentiation. Although the magnate joint families increased the rate of overall village economic growth, they impeded development, as I defined it, by accentuating inequalities. By contrast, the new share family among middle-farmers, as well as the formation of extended kin networks among the poorest transient labourers, have helped to reduce inequalities and relieve conditions of extreme poverty.

In this section I have tried to show not only how social anthropology examines changing social institutions in their social context but also the important contribution it can make to a better understanding of development processes.

DEVELOPMENT MODELS, PREDICTION AND POLICY IMPLICATIONS

Lastly, and most important, social anthropology has a vital part to play in building realistic development models as well as outlining trends of change and their policy implications.

By their very nature, all models are abstractions from reality. Most development models construed by economists involve only economic variables and lump all sociopolitical ones under the general heading of "social constraints," thereby implying that all existing sociopolitical institutions and arrangements inevitably represent obstacles to development. This is far from true, as I have tried to illustrate with my discussion of different types of family structures. The exclusion from development models of all or most noneconomic variables, necessarily results in their being so far removed from the social system they are meant to depict that they become irrelevant and useless as planning devices. In this context it becomes essential to emphasize one of the newest branches of social anthropology, namely *development anthropology*. As yet there are only few experts in this field of enquiry which is reflected in the dearth of a general theoretical framework for the analysis of socioeconomic changes. This is an area of study which requires immediate attention; development anthropology will come of age only when it will have succeeded in replacing the outmoded "rational economic man model" with a sound socioeconomic model.

Predicting trends of societal changes and working out their policy implications is often even more difficult than building the development model in the first instance.

Prognostication is a hazardous and uncertain exercise. Economic analysis usually concentrates on securing changes in a few variables and shelters behind the clause that all other things remain equal. Social anthropology, with its emphasis on studying interdependent social variables, cannot cling to the same protective clause. Research among small communities might seem to offer a sounder basis for prediction than do many of the unreliable macro-economic or sociological surveys in LDCs. Macro-predictions necessitate adequate statistical data which is often simply not available in these LDCs. Micro-predictions are subject to rather different kinds of limitations. There is, for example, the question of "representativeness" and the problems of generalizing from a situation in which there can be no guarantee that all the relevant variables are present. There is the further and related issue that the more restricted the form of observation, the greater the likelihood of the local situation under study being affected by intrusive factors. As against this, the validity of an analysis, however interesting, cannot be established unless it is subjected to testing. Social anthropologists studying social change should be prepared to go beyond their analysis of present-day conditions and attempt extrapolating past trends into the future.

In my own recent work I have tried to do just this. I have attempted to predict what the future holds for Wangala and Dalena. I myself may not be able to test the accuracy of my prognosis twenty-five years hence, but hopefully one or other of the younger social scientists may either verify it then or where necessary expose its falseness and improve my analysis.

The pace of social change is quickening. This necessitates increasing emphasis on the study of the dynamics of the process, which in turn should result in forecasts of the likely future pattern of change. Development is usually associated with planned changes, even in the most laissez-faire capitalist economies of the present-day world. The accuracy in predicting the trend of social change is now generally regarded as one of the most important determining variables in the efficiency of development planning and its implementation. It is important that social scientists concerned with development should try to indicate the policy implications emerging from their studies. Though it is unlikely that any one researcher in the development field will be able to prescribe the panacea for all development ills, most should be in a position to suggest at least some palliative measures to help hasten the development process on its way.

As a result of my restudy of Mysore villages I put forth a number of policy suggestions which arose directly out of my findings. For instance, I established that the purchasing power of casual daily wages in Wangala has been reduced by about fifty per cent between 1955 to 1970, in a period when agricultural productivity and crop prices have considerably increased, and the quantity of crops a labourer received for one day harvesting paddy remained stable. Prior to irrigation and the introduction of cash crops individual groups in Wangala used to share in the village product according to their social status and the stake they had in the rural economy. Population growth, resulting from natural increase as well as net immigration, has upset the traditional balance between the supply of labour and its demand. The concomitant monetization of rural economies as well as inflation made it easier for farmers to reduce real wage rates. Attempts to legislate for a minimum rural wage have so far failed in south India. If rural rewards are to keep up with rising food prices it would seem sounder to try and introduce agricultural minimum wages expressed in terms of a fixed quantity of the staple crop grown in the different areas. It may be argued that to revert to barter is a retrogressive step, but "if this is retrogression, can the constant deepening of the already desperate poverty of so many millions of men, women, and children be called a progression?" (Spate, 1973: XV). This is just one example showing concrete policy implications emerging from a social anthropological micro-study.

Conclusion: Development Anthropology

I feel I should stress at this point that I am by no means advocating that *all* social anthropological studies must or even should concern themselves with social change, prediction of future trends or policy implications. There are obviously other perfectly valid and fascinating aspects of society which warrant investigation. All I am saying is that social anthropologists concerned with development, i.e., development anthropologists, should try not only to evolve general theories of social change but also to reorient their analysis with a view to prognostication and applied research.

The development of less developed societies poses a challenge not only to politicians, administrators and planners but also to social scientists which unless met by a joint effort will not only reflect on governmental inadequacies but even more so indicate the failure of social science in making a meaningful contribution to the better understanding of the development process.

REFERENCES

Bailey, F.G., 1957. *Caste and the Economic Frontier*. Manchester: Manchester University Press.

Baner, P.T. and B.S. Yamey, 1960. *The Economics of Underdeveloped Countries*. Cambridge: James Nisbet & Co. Ltd.

Beteille, A., 1964. "Family and Social Change in India and other South Asian Countries," *Economic Weekly*, Vol. XVI, Nos. 5, 6 and 7, annual number, February.

Eptstein, T.S., 1962. *Economic Development and Social Change in South India*. Manchester: Manchester University Press.

―――, 1973. *South India: Yesterday, Today and Tomorrow—Mysore Villages Re-visited*. London: Macmillan & Co. Ltd.

Fliegel, F.C., P. Sen Roy, and J.E. Kivlin, 1968. *Agricultural Innovations in Indian Villages*. Hyderabad: National Institute of Community Development.

Frank, A.G., 1971. *Sociology of Development and Underdevelopment of Sociology*. Pluto Press.

Frankel, F.R., 1971. *India's Green Revolution—Economic Gains and Political Costs*. Princeton: Princeton University Press.

Hoselitz, 1964. "Social Stratification and Economic Development," *International Social Science Journal*, Vol. 16, No. 2.

I.L.O., 1972. *Scope, Approach and Content of Research-oriented Activities*

of the World Employment Programme. Geneva: International Labour Office.
Kaldate, Sudha, 1962. "Urbanization and Disintegration of the Rural Joint Family," *Sociological Bulletin*, Vol. II, Nos. 1 and 2.
Knight, F.H., 1960. "Anthropology and Economics," in *Economic Anthropology*. New York: Alfred A. Knopf.
Lannoy, R., 1971. *The Speaking Tree: A Study of Culture and Society*. London: Oxford University Press.
Lewis, A.W., 1955. *The Theory of Economic Growth*. London: George Allen & Unwin Ltd.
McNamara, R.S., 1972. Address to the Board of Governors. Washington: World Bank.
M.L.G.R., 1969. Mysore Land Grant Rules, Bangalore.
Seers, D., 1969. *The Meaning of Development*. Communication Series No. 44, IDS.
Spate, O.H.K., 1973. "To him that has . . ." in T.S. Epstein, ed., *South India: Yesterday, Today and Tomorrow—Mysore Villages Revisited*. London: Macmillan & Co. Ltd.
The Constitution of India, 1955. Allahabad: Law Publishers.

Agehananda Bharati

6 Cultural Hurdles in Development Administration

Cultural hurdles may be defined as the traditional attitudes or customs which are part of the cultural base in a particular region and which constitute barriers to innovation. In this study "culture" is used in the narrow sense of tradition; if everything that happened in an area were viewed as part of its culture, the concept of cultural hurdles would be meaningless. Cultural hurdles must also be distinguished from what could be called "universal psychological hurdles" which are general human phenomena and do not grow out of any specific cultural base. It is the thesis of this paper that genuine cultural hurdles to development are not very numerous in any particular region.

The following sketch of cultural hurdles on the Indian scene has a general relevance in other countries where administrators seek to promote change. Indigenous patterns of thought and tradition in a region are often ignored or misunderstood not only by alien but by native administrators. A Punjabi civil servant usually knows little more about a Kerala milieu than an American guest administrator. It matters not in what area or country the administrator is operating; failure to be aware of cultural hurdles can seriously undermine efforts, whereas familiarity with and use of cultural patterns can greatly facilitate the modernizer's task. The anthropologist can offer no cut and dried methods of procedure. However, using India as our example, we can point to pitfalls and indicate lines of approach for the administrator who seeks to shape tradition and promote change.

Religious Tradition and Cultural Hurdles in India

In India and in other regions (e.g., Sri Lanka and Bangladesh) where predominant importance is given to the spiritual world, and religious tradition is the guiding reference for behaviour, people may be reluctant to cooperate when innovation seems to conflict with religious tradition. Most cultural hurdles in India derive from the strength of religious tradition. Mundane efforts are considered basically trivial—a powerful impediment to development administration on all levels.

Thailand provides an illuminating contrast to the Indian pattern. Though the Thais inherited a purely Indian set of moral doctrines through *Theravada* Buddhism, religious tradition does not pose cultural hurdles for Thai development. The Siamese enthusiastically welcome innovation. They render up to Buddha what is Buddha's—concern with nirvana, etc. But while life lasts, they reason, the best should be made of it. The painful essence of life belongs in the realm of theological definition. The idea that life can be fun is definitely not Buddha's teaching but it characterizes the Thai attitude, both clerical and lay. Hence, Siamese planners and administrators do not consider that development clashes with tradition nor is development administration considered trivial.[1]

It is obvious that cultural hurdles must be evaluated in terms of specific areas and situations. General standards for evaluation must be given situational content. The present study is directed toward actual or potential reactions of Indian (Pakistani or Ceylonese) individuals or groups in contact with native or foreign development administration. The situation is one of unprecedented effort to introduce innovation in a specific cultural milieu where novel administrative patterns cannot be or are not wholly absorbed.

In India most cultural hurdles can be related to a traditional lack of secular institutions. Historical accident, not something innate in the Indian national character or in any of the indigenous religious traditions, accounts for this lack of secular institution building. All Indian tradition distinguishes between

---

[1] See my "Saffron Robes and Joie de Vivre—A Letter from Thailand," *Quest*. Bombay, 1956.

two totally different and unconnected realms of truth and existence—the phenomenal or ephemeral world, and the absolute un- and anti-worldly universe. Individuals or groups are respected and influential because of their identification with the spiritual world. In ancient Greece and Rome, and in seventeenth and eighteenth century England and Germany, absolutist philosophers looked down upon lay commoners, minimizing their intellectual importance and even their integrity. But philosophical or religious censure never inhibited the lay European's zeal for secular activity. The lay Indian institution builder, on the other hand, has been and remains profoundly affected by the absolutists' scoffs.

There have been secular institutions in all periods of Indian history but spiritual institutions and conceptions have always been the cynosure of the Indian scene. Rulers of the state of Rajasthan call themselves *vazir*, i.e., "representatives" of the tutelary deity.[2] While in Western dynasties such titles are just ornamental, they have very direct and real importance in India. The king who renounces the throne and becomes an itinerant saint is the ideal. If a king or a ruler or a minister does not turn completely toward the spiritual world in his later days—and very few actually did—he is conscious of his omission and his people are equally conscious of it. Orthodox Hindus praise Gandhi for his spiritual, ascetic way of life, and they blame Nehru for not regarding the spiritual as the intrinsic goal of life.

Injunctions or codes of religious tradition have a direct relation to administrative efforts in India. Individuals or groups may either *believe* a novel situation to be incompatible with tradition or a situation may be objectively incompatible. Indian legislation extending educational opportunities is objectively incompatible with traditional patterns. According to the scriptures only twice-born males may study canonical literature. Recent legislation has done away with exclusion from any branch of learning because of sex, caste, or creed. All now may study the *Veda* (Hindu scriptures) and are indirectly encouraged to do so. Actually, the new legislation has left behaviour substantially

---

[2]The ruler in Travancore's epithet was the "servant of Visnu" (God preservation and wealth—Padamanabhadasa).

unchanged because very few scheduled class Hindus would embark on the study of the *Veda*. Though university students of all castes in India study Sanskrit, including the *Veda*, such texts are approached as literature, not as religious tracts.

Cases in which innovations are *believed* incompatible with religious tradition far outnumber cases of actual incompatibility. In many regions there is a wide gap between knowledge of codified tradition and the general image of the tradition. The strength of imagined incompatibility diminishes in emancipated regions. In any region, however, only theological or academic audiences would demand specific illustrations of codes which conflict with a particular development proposal. A rhetorical appeal to the spirit of a tradition is a powerful instrument. Individuals or groups central to an administrative effort may believe or claim to believe that an innovation conflicts with scriptural or oral tradition. Most political leaders assume somewhat naively that because they are inspired, they know the tradition which inspired them. The development administrator must obviously be able to cope with such flat assertions if he is to get anything accomplished.

Aside from specific religious injunctions and codes which objectively or subjectively conflict with innovation, tradition gives rise to patterns of thought which can seriously interfere with development. In some cases what might be considered universal psychological hurdles take on a peculiar manifestation in the specific cultural milieu. Take, for example, a situation in which Indian farmers or members of the *panchayat*[3] must cooperate in setting up a power station to provide electricity and water for a number of villages. Some farming land must be used and the villagers compensated; for budgetary reasons the villagers must work for nominal wages or even without compensation. The farmers are likely to argue: "you promise us advantages x, y, and z later if we give you a,b, and c, now; but how do we

---

[3]The *panchayat* is the council of five village elders of traditional India. It has been reinstated as the minimum unit of local self-government in independent India. The senior member of this council is at the same time the village headman. A rather good outline of the self-image of the *panchayat* is given in Ralph H. Retzlaff, 1962. *A Case Study of Panchayats in a North Indian Village*. Berkeley: Center for South Asia Studies, Institute of International Studies, University of California.

know that you will bring these advantages? Rulers, parties, landowners, and their clerks also promised advantages which we never enjoyed. People act as they always have. Why should we believe you are different?" Superfically, there is nothing particularly Indian about such resistance to innovation. Yet the intensity of reaction and the form which opposition takes do have a cultural basis. A cyclical world-view underlies Hindu thought on all levels of sophistication. Cyclical Hindu cosmology has even become deeply ingrained among the Muslims.[4] Everything that happens has happened before. The promises of development administrator or modernizer are no different.

Another peculiarly Indian manifestation of the universal phenomenon of resistance to change is the peasant's strong aversion to recording in secular documents anything which pertains to an individual or kin group. The Indian farmer feels that whatever is written down in an official ledger can and will later be held against him. An Indian peasant refused to sign a petition demanding diversion of an irrigation channel into an area adjacent to his village because he "did not like to appear in writing anywhere except in the book of *Vishvanath*."[5] Signing the *Vishvanath*, the ledger at the famous shrine at Banaras, brought no fear because this was a religious document pertaining to another world.

The genuine and deep-seated fear of secular documents may also explain why many villagers prefer the moneylender to a bank even though the former charges a hundred per cent or more in interest. Such discrepancy, the villager would reason, means the bank must have some ulterior motive. He derives security in the knowledge that no signature or mark must be made, no ceremony undergone at the hands of unknown people and, most important, no permanent record is kept of any debt.

Closely tied to religious tradition, with patterns of behaviour based on religious sanction, is the Indian caste and kinship

---

[4] Indian Islamic commentaries of the Ahmadiya and Khoja sects and the Muslim mystical tradition have been strongly influenced by Hindu cyclical cosmology.

[5] Personal communication from a peasant of Bhojpur. Caste Hindus have their names entered in the records at places of pilgrimage by a Panda, a Brahmin official at large shrines; this is a meritorious act and the record is of a religious deed.

structure. Such traditional patterns can pose powerful cultural hurdles. Development of radio and television educational programmes in a very traditional region such as Rajasthan, for example, might be opposed because such innovations would influence young people to abandon their respect for the old, members of the lower-caste groups to lose their deference for higher groups, or women to rebel against the traditional injunction of obedience to their husbands.

In all regions there are potential or actual hurdles which are universal phenomena, e.g., inertia, insecurity or self-defence, unrelated to the cultural base in any but the vaguest sense.[6] In some cases there may be initial resistance to change. For example, if a new kind of seed, more resistant to weather and disease, were introduced into a region confined to traditional agricultural methods, the peasants, at least temporarily, might claim that the *roti* (chappatti) made with the new wheat does not taste as good. Such situations should not impede innovation, however, for the peasants are soon won over by visible evidence of success.

Where tradition does not conflict or is not believed to conflict with programme administration, initial resistance can generally be overcome by visible evidence of success. There is seldom, if ever, continued resistance on principle to innovation, be it

---

[6] A skit presented for the students of Pilani University in Rajasthan in 1951 demonstrates such universal hurdles. In it a trouser-wearing administrator tries to persuade a villager to use a project's new methods of irrigation. The villager listens attentively and even lauds the project, but constantly reverts to the *cilkha*, an ancient water-splashing device, and refuses to see that the new scheme would make the *cilkha* redundant. The older contraption comes up repeatedly in the villager's refrain. The villager finally convinces the weary administrator that while his project is more efficient, the *cilkha* is more reliable and gives the farmer stronger muscles. This skit is representative. The villager will not adduce such quasi-sophisticated reasons for retaining his old equipment as manual labour is better for man's morality or the host of moralizing propositions which the Indian nationalist movement has brought in its wake. Nor does the villager seem to feel that the simpler devices are in any way nobler. The villager's initial objections may be stubborn and archaic but they do not stem from traditional attitudes peculiar to his culture.

administrative or technological.[7] Farmers and labourers in India and Pakistan are eager for pertinent innovations of any sort, particularly if they entail labour-saving devices. A few years ago the government of India invited a group of Japanese agricultural experts to instruct farmers in the Japanese method of rice planting by intensive soil cultivation. The method was avidly adopted by thousands of villages throughout rice-growing regions in India.

Religious tradition by no means always poses hurdles to innovations, in many cases it can be of positive benefit to modernization. Once an innovation or administrative situation is shown to be beneficial, religious teachings often encourage cooperation. Hindu scriptures, for example, speaks of *niskamakarma* (action without the desire for its fruits), a code taken up by Gandhi and most other Hindu leaders. The second in the four stages of life in the Hindu religion, *artha*, is one of keen participation in any social activities which improve material and ideal living standards among fellow men.[8]

Religious Tradition and the Development Administration in India

Knowledge of the cultural processes in a region can be of positive benefit to the development administrator. A familiarity with tradition can help the administrator refine his method of introducing and encouraging support for an innovation. Traditional patterns of thought and action can often be turned from impediments into assets. Generally the methods rather than the targets of administration determine whether cultural processes will retard or facilitate development efforts. The targets are so broad and general that they can be made palatable no matter what the cultural milieu. But an agency or adminis-

---

[7] Even in India or Pakistan, there does not seem to be much of the exasperating attitude that "my father and his father did x in fashion y; hence y and x are good enough for me." Fears of such attitudes do not seem based on much field observation but on pre-anthropological notions of the "wise, stubborn man of the land."

[8] Knowledge of such canonically supported, popular ideas will benefit administrators in non-Indian areas where there is a large Hindu audience, e.g., East Africa, the Fiji Islands, British Guiana, and Bangladesh.

trator's methods may either clash or fall in line with traditional patterns. In the Thai egalitarian tradition, for example, a charismatic figure—someone whose name is known and respected—is not required to sponsor a development effort. Government agencies could encourage development-oriented attitudes through relatively impersonal procedures. An effective hierarchy to channel information and orders from the government, ministry, or secretariat, would suffice.

In India the persuasive power of the religious or charismatic leader as the traditional authority figure is essential in mobilizing popular support. Typically, a religious leader is either a *sadhu* (wandering holy man) or *apta* (leads a professional religious life and is familiar with the codified religious tradition). In no less than five Indian movies which the author saw, a *sadhu* persuaded the people to perform necessary secular acts.[9] When Nehru's *obiter dictum*, resting is taboo (*aram haram hai*), was quoted at a community development centre meeting, the audience nodded approval. If Panditji pronounces such a rule, it must be accepted. The charismatic figure's dictum becomes law (*shruti* in Hindu India) even though it may militate against the general temperament. Nehru was a charismatic figure even though he headed a totally different government and asked support for exactly the opposite kind of policy. Since heroworship is the dominant political practice, any leader personality—religious and secular alike—would be followed no matter what his policy or ideology. "If Nehru were the Chairman of the Indian Communist Party, he would still be the idol of the masses."[10]

Fortunately, the development administrator does not need to enlist the aid of Nehru to convince the people to cooperate on the local level. The authority of a religious scholar, respected for his knowledge of tradition, is quite sufficient to persuade an apathetic or hostile audience of the need for innovation and convince doubters that there is traditional sanction for the

---

[9] *Maharshi Valmiki*, Bombay, 1947; *Jhanak Jhanak Payal Baje*, Bombay, 1955; *Jhansi ki Rani*, Bombay, 1953; *Ram Rajya*, Bombay, 1944 (this is a popular representation of the epic *Ramayana*, and was the only movie Gandhi ever saw and recommended); and *Baiju Bawra*.

[10] Personal communication from the late M.N. Roy, leader of Communist Party, 1952.

innovation. The *apta* does not *support* a governmental or any other policy. He states what is good, and if the governmental policy *happens* to coincide with what he states, it will be implemented, or at least there will be cooperation. The government policy and efforts to encourage are secondary in importance. The *apta's* statement is the primary stimulus. In other words, the Hindu audience does not conceive of the sage as supporting government policy; rather, it reasons that sage X tells us a certain type of action leading to a certain achievement is good, and the government happens to want the same action; hence let us cooperate.

Occidental administrators would not think or presume to challenge the authenticity of a reference to indigenous tradition. With the help of the religious scholar, however, the development administrator might soon find that Hindu tradition actually poses fewer barriers to modernization that most Hindus think or care to know.[11] The administrator himself cannot convince an audience that an innovation is only *believed* incompatible with tradition. For example, members of Indian Parliament recently strongly objected to a proposal that the government disseminate information on birth control on the grounds that contraception was contrary to Hindu scriptures and repugnant to the "spirit" of Hindu tradition. Here was a case of rhetorical appeal to *believed* tradition. The leader of the Communist party in the House pointedly noted: "It is regrettable that there is no Hindu scholar here who would show that Hinduism does not object to birth control.[12] Only a religious scholar could effectively challenge objectors to point out scriptural or other codes which they call "our tradition" or the "spirit" of our tradition.

An *apta* or *sadhu* could also be enlisted to demonstrate that a proposed change is compatible with tradition; scripturally uninformed yet orthodox Hindus then generally accept almost any innovation with relative ease. The Malampuzha Dam in

---

[11] See W. Norman Brown, 1961. "The Content of Cultural Continuity in India," *Journal of Asian Studies*, Vol., XXIV; also Milton Singer, 1956. "Cultural Values in India's Economic Development," *Annals of the American Academy of Political and Social Sciences*. CCCV, May. These two authors advance the thesis that Hindu tradition poses few barriers to innovation.

[12] Personal communication (New Delhi, 1955).

Kerala, for instance, was pictured by a *sadhu* as fulfilling an aspect of the Hindu *shastras* (i.e., the written canonical tradition). The *sadhu's* statement was sufficient encouragement for the initially reluctant.

In 1938 Gandhi intensified his efforts to convince Hindus that outcastes were entitled to all benefits then reserved for caste Hindus. Non-caste Hindus, like non-Hindus, were barred from worshipping at most Hindu shrines. This question of temple entry, incidentally, has not been completely settled even today. Gandhi called upon a learned *pandit* whose views were quite radically divergent from those of other orthodox scholars. Accompanying the Mahatma to a lecture before an audience of learned Brahmins, the scholar "quoted" scripture in support of Gandhi's view that Harijans (People of God, the Gandhian term for outcastes) could enter and worship in temples. The Brahmins were convinced.[13]

The savant later confined that he had quoted non-existent passages which he had composed in Vedic Sanskrit for the occasion. To most Westerners trained in an occidental ethic, this procedure might seem morally suspicious if not downright condemnable. For the orthodox Hindu, on the other hand, this action was morally unassailable because it furthered the cause of the scriptures in the long run as a *lokahitartha* ("for the benefit of the world" strategem).[14] The *lokahitartha* is well established as a scriptural vindication of a course of action directed toward a morally desirable end.

The *lokahitartha* is often used to justify compromise between tradition and the demands of modernization. For example, a large section of a valley in the south Indian state of Andhra had to be flooded to build a reservoir for irrigation. Old Buddhist and Hindu shrines were located in the area. Destruction of any Hindu or Buddhist shrine is an abomination to the Hindu. (One

---

[13] Personal communication from the late M.N. Roy (Dehra Doon, India, August 1951).

[14] See the *Bhagavadgita*, 2nd Canto, "*hato va prapsyase svargam jitva tu bhoksase mahim* . . ." ("if you are killed, you will go to heaven, if you win, you will enjoy the earth. . ." hence fight, kill your relatives and other Kinsmen.) The *Bhagavadgita* is the most important of moral codes in modern Hinduism, and almost all leaders have interpreted this book according to their light and for their purposes.

of the main reasons for the Hindu hatred of early Muslim conquerors was the desecration of Hindu shrines.) There were learned and not so learned arguments for and against flooding the temples' site. The state and national Parliaments and local and central ministers regretted the necessity of destroying the shrines. Progressively oriented *pandits* argued that the destruction was *lokahitartha*. When the flooding actually took place, there was little complaint. The archaeological survey of the central government removed virtually all the *objets d'art* to a museum erected for this purpose and a fine book of the site and treasures was published.

Cultural Hurdles and the Development Administrator's Task

It is easier to identify hurdles to development administration which derive from a specific cultural base than it is to make the concept operationally significant for administrators in any area. In this final section we shall derive several generalizations from our specific standards by which the administrators can evaluate cultural hurdles. Obviously general standards are few while specific standards are as numerous as the cultural patterns in any administrative area.

Administrators must keep in mind both quantitative and qualitative questions when locating and evaluating the significance of cultural hurdles. In any administrative area it is obviously necessary not only to determine how many people oppose the administrator or a proposed change, but also to gauge the strength of the opposition's influence. Resistance from a learned Brahmin or respected scholar is clearly more serious than that from the ordinary bureaucrat. Qualitative problems also involve determining whether a proposed innovation or administrative action conflicts with actual or believed tradition. Often the administrator, with indigenous help, can successfully demonstrate that a particular change is only an imagined conflict with tradition. Although some aspects of tradition may dictate opposition to a particular change, others may well support the innovation. In India, for example, some passages from the *Veda* could be interpreted as condemning birth control while others seem to encourage this practice. In some cases cultural hurdles can be ignored without undermining the development effort. In others the administrator can circumvent on obstacle by pointing to precedent or by persuasive discourse.

In assessing the nature of culture hurdles and determining his approach, the administrator must have a fairly refined and sophisticated knowledge of the region. While he may often be charting new courses, his approach should be conditioned by informed judgement. The need for familiarity with the region is so basic that it tends to be overlooked by authors who concentrate on structural analysis. Such understanding is vital not only for the alien but for the native administrator. The mere fact of birth or of physical presence in a region does not imply knowledge about the region.[15]

The administrator cannot hope to develop the necessary understanding of any area by reading official publications or by concentrating solely what groups say about themselves. Indian official manuals, for examples, give no indication of the contribution which the *sadhu* or Brahmin scholar can make in promoting acceptance of change. At the same time Indian government agencies deny or try to ignore the existence of caste status which significantly affects all development— economic as well as political. Equally important to remember is that one of "the people," "the man in the street," or the office worker cannot usually discern or does not speak of his own traditional attitudes or culture patterns. Members of the white collar or *babu* class[16] in India generally do not mention their predominantly non-or anti-secular attitude, their reluctance to give moral priority to any mundane matters, including their own jobs, or their distaste of career advancement of people outside their social caste. "Getting to know the people

---

[15] This is a caveat for academicians as well. Very often, a person is invited to a highly specialized Orientalist scholar's talk because "he was in India two years ago" (on a world tour, en route to elsewhere on business, etc.) Nor does an Indian student of chemical engineering know more about India than an American chemical engineer knows about America.

[16] Clerks and white collar workers of all kinds, short of executives, are called *babu* all over India. The term was first used in Bengal, the home of the first British-Indian administrative units.

as you work with them" without some previous study is a hazardous affair.

In understanding any region the administrator should first survey the salient culture patterns of the groups with which he has to deal. "Salient" here refers to what the learned or at least sophisticated opinion in a given society regards as important. It requires trained people from several disciplines who question many more than one or two "men in the street" to make relevant statements about a group. Sophisticated observers of Indian culture—non-Indian as well as Indian (e.g., Minoo Masani, M.N. Srinivas, Iravati Karve, Morris Opler, Edward Shils, Milton Singer, etc.)—have done informed and critical analyses. Such studies give the administrator a short-cut to greater efficiency through the best possible information. The social scientist, even though he may be interested in theoretical constructs and generalizations to an extent that they are not operational for the administrator, does provide instruments whereby pitfalls can be avoided. From such studies the administrator can anticipate what obstacles to innovation may arise and chart possible approaches for avoiding them. No one can dogmatize about "national character." The facts and facets of a country's traditions and the predilections of its *dramatis personae* are accidents, but they are accidents which the administrator should know.

What the administrator reads or gathers from learned opinion will have to be supplemented by large doses of practical experience and intuition. Although learned opinion about a region reveals the inhibiting factors, it cannot convey the comparative strength of these factors in a manner which will be a tool for the administrator. Stating that the average audience of area x is extremely sensitive about criticism, warns the administrator of a diffuse character trait in his region, but the term "extremely" does not add an important datum to his awareness. Another author, writing about the same region, may use, "extremely" to denote his own perception of intensity which may or may not coincide with the previous author's. There is no semantic standardization of adjectives of degree. A British ethnologist's "rather" may have just about the same meaning as a young American anthropologist's "extremely."

Next arises the thorny question of what to do when administrative expedience conflicts with cultural tradition. The question becomes complicated by the fact that the alien administrator generally subscribes to a set of moral values different from indigenous values. As pointed out above, the Westerner might well consider the Indian practice of using or manipulating the scriptures as unethical. It would probably be unethical for an administrator to attempt to impose his values on his audience or to adopt values inconsistent with his own. The anthropologist cannot say whether operational consideration should overrule ethical reflections, for this is a philosophical decision. He can point out the dilemma and suggest cultural variants affecting solutions. He is neither a moralist nor the administrator; the moralist may volunteer counsel, especially when he is not charged with making decisions. The anthropologists' task is to predict cultural reaction to administrative procedure, but the administrator is not bound by such prediction.

In most cases the administrator can reach a satisfactory solution through candid discussion with his audience. The administrator should be able to divert attention from most potential blocks. If no one raises objections, the administrator should go ahead with his business. Respect for local peculiarities which might interest the philosopher, archaeologist, or anthropologist does not justify hesitation on the part of the administrator. The anthropologist's contribution to the administration of development should not be to create problems but to indicate solutions to existing problems or to facilitate avoidance of potential hurdles.

There is another side to the cultural-hurdle coin. The administrator, himself, often has certain pre-conceived notions about individual and group attitudes in his assigned area which interfere with a correct evaluation of the cultural situation. It is understandable that the alien administrator, particularly in areas culturally remote from his own, might either fail to recognize cultural hurdles, or "see" hurdles where none exist. But pre-conceived notions such as "the Irish are...." "Indians are..." beset the path of the native as well as the alien programme administrator.[17] There is a traditional self-image expressed in propositions beginning with "we Irish are..." and "we Indians are...," and there is a pseudo-scientific alter-image of any alien milieu. A Hindu administrator entrusted with an industrial development task among the Santhals, a large aboriginal group in Bihar, assumes "we Hindus are spiritual people, hence we must go easy in creating an industrial pattern." His assumption derives from the highly eclectic modern Hindu self-image, which is based on nostalgia rather than fact.[18] This self-image is reinforced by the popular occidental image in India. But it so happens that the Santhals are not at all spiritual in any sense this particular administrator assumes. An extrovert, sensuous personality structure is considerably more common among the Santhals than among surrounding caste-Hindu groups.[19]

The objection that everyone knows it is harmful to entertain pre-conceived notions and prejudices is too general to be helpful. Pre-conceived ethnic notions are highly specific biases, and it requires directed effort and the sort of study suggested earlier to dispel such pre-conceptions. Before the administrator takes up his work, he must acquaint himself with the general cultural patterns of the society in which he will serve, be it his own or a totally alien one.

We have been discussing situations which are specific in terms of area and culture. At least one general principle emerges from our propositions. This general principle might be called "multiple configuration expectancy"; "expectancy" is "multiple" because the administrator and his audience belong

[17] A logician might call this phenomenon a "subjective counterfactual" or subjective hurdle pattern.

[18] For an excellent analysis of this problem, see E. Shils, 1961. *The Intellectual between Tradition and Modernity: The Indian Situation.* Series Comparative Studies in Society and History, Supplement No. 1. The Hague: Mouton.

[19] See N. Datta-Majumdar, 1956. *The Santal—A Study in Culture Change* Memoir No. 2, New Delhi: Department of Anthropology, Government of India. Also M. Orans, 1959. A Tribal People in an Industrial Setting," in Milton Singer, e.d., *Traditional India: Structure and Change.* "Bibliographical Series," Vol. X, Philadelphia: American Folklore Society.

to the same or to a different social milieu. The multiple configuration expectancy principle appears in four patterns:

(*a*) the cultural self-image of the audience to which the development programme is administered;
(*b*) the cultural self-image of the administrators;
(*c*) the alter-image of the audience, i.e., the image which the audience thinks the administrator has of its members;
(*d*) the alter-image of the administrator, i.e., the image the administrator thinks the audience has of him.

An Indian illustration of this general principle can be depicted:

(*a*) we, members of the *panchayat*, are experienced, traditionally and pragmatically educated, sagacious leaders of the community;
(*b*) I, Mr Banerji, ICS, am a Hindu by birth, a British administrator by training, attached to my own traditions, but intellectually committed to the values taught by such British thinkers as Tennyson, T.S. Eliot, and Harold Laski;
(*c*) that bookish, city-dwelling, trouser-wearing Bengali Brahmin *babu* thinks of us as good, simple, uneducated folk, who must be coaxed into what he thinks or says is good for us;
(*d*) these *panchayat* men are shrewd in their own way; they know our weaknesses and they may doubt the sincerity of the administration. They know that I am learned, but they think I am unpractical, peevish, etc.

Consideration of an area in the patterns of multiple configuration expectancy gives an awareness of the interplay and inter-relationships between the administrator and his audience. By constant reassessment of his acquired knowledge in terms of actual field experience and a flexible adaptation of the demands of modernization to those of tradition, the administrator can fashion his methods of introducing change to yield positive results.

What are the implications of this study for the civil servant, particularly on the administrative and executive level? The anthropologist would love to advise the administrator to study cultural anthropology and cultural hurdles; but then the sociologist would suggest that the administrator do the same with sociology, the psychologist with psychology. Clearly, such suggestions are not operational, but there are a few minimal points, rules of thumb, which can be profitably derived from this survey.

In order to create an awareness of possible cultural hurdles, the administrator should consider his area in the framework of the multiple configuration expectancy. He should be aware that cultural hurdles are mutual, that both he and the audience supply them, and that there is no such thing as one-sided cultural mischief.

He should listen with particular attention to sophisticated or learned opinion about his audience. He must strive to distinguish cultural hurdles, conditioned by peculiarities in his area's tradition, from what we have called universal psychological hurdles, e.g., fear, general poverty, insecurity, ignorance. Changes which are objectively incompatible with tradition must be distinguished from those that are only believed incompatible. Obstacles arising from cultural as distinguished from universal hurdles can often be circumvented by reference to tradition. Only by such understandings can the administrator's methods be designed to minimize friction between modernization and tradition.

Finally, failure to introduce innovation because of real or fancied cultural hurdles is the worst sort of procedure. We have noted that the administrator is not a moralist or philosopher: his job is to get things done. It is far better to act, taking actual or potential hurdles into account and adjusting to specific situations, than to dismiss desired change because it appears "culturally impossible."

Hari Mohan Mathur

7 Anthropology, Government, and Developmental Planning in India

In India, the government interest in the anthropological contribution to development problems has grown noticeably over the past few years. Delivering the chairman's address to a seminar on "The Tribal Situation in India" held at Simla recently, M.N. Srinivas (1972: 27) observed: "From the little I know of the Government of India and its functioning I find today sharply increased awareness of the importance and urgency of associating sociologists and anthropologists in the solution of the many complex and baffling problems which confront the country today." A British anthropologist, F.G. Bailey (1962: 254), finds that:

> ...at the present time anthropologists in India whether Indian or foreign are considered an asset by the Administration and their books are read and their point of view considered even by their fellow intellectuals in other disciplines. No research team is complete without someone to put the anthropological point of view, and no welfare organization feels itself properly constituted unless it has someone carrying on social research for the purpose of planning or evaluation.

This should be a matter of no small satisfaction to the anthropologists when considered alongside the fact that in many newly emerging nations, particularly in Africa, their colleagues are not as well thought of.[1] India, in fact, has had a long tradition of utilizing anthropological knowledge in administrative actions and policies directed towards improving the living conditions of its aboriginal peoples. In the pre-independence era, the administrators found anthropology of considerable use to them in implementing several government programmes. A few among them, including Risley, Dalton, Ibbetson, Crooks, Thurston, Russell, Mills and Button, even carried out extensive ethnographic research on their own. All this helps, to an extent, to enhance receptivity to anthropology on the part of today's planners and administrators.

There are also some other factors that would seem to be particularly conducive to the utilization of anthropology in government-directed developmental activity. In the first place, planning for economic growth and social change presupposes a thorough understanding of the sociocultural profile of the country. In India, with its sharply contrasting ethnic, linguistic, religious, and other sizeable heterogeneous population groups, the need for planners of these facts becomes even more urgent. Anthropologists who make these studies can evidently be relied on for providing this material to the planners. Secondly, the planning effort seeking rapid economic and socio-cultural modernization of all peoples, with special emphasis on the development of tribal areas, surely requires expertise that directly derives from anthropological research into the problems of socio-cultural dynamics. Planned development in India has also fascinated many anthropologists and the fast proliferating literature on change in India's tribal and village life should interest the planners and administrators very much. Lastly, anthropology in India has matured into a fairly well established discipline and therefore the anthropologists who could be trained to work for development are not in short supply.

What, in the face of those apparently abundant opportunities, have anthropologists contributed to the process of planned development initiated in India over two decades ago by the

---

[1] See in this connection Onwauchi, P. Chike, and Alwin W. Wolfe, "The Place of anthropology in the Future of Africa," *Human Organisation*. 25: 93-95.

government? In what ways can the contribution of anthropology to development now be made purposive? How is this participation in development viewed by the anthropologists themselves? These are questions that should interest the anthropologist as much as the planner. It would surely be worthwhile to examine them.

But there is the other aspect to this problem, the role of the government in promoting the use of anthropological knowledge in its development programmes. In order to have a clear perspective on the issues concerning anthropology's role in development it would be useful to first briefly review all that the government has been doing to involve anthropologists in this process.

RESEARCH IN AID OF PLANNING

Since the dawn of planning, development planners in India, have pursued the policy of encouraging social research. It has been hoped that the results might help in facilitating and accelerating the adjustments to new conditions arising in rural and tribal areas in the wake of changes implanted in their traditional concepts and practices of community and cooperative organization, education, nutrition, family pattern, medicine and public health. As part of this policy, they have given new directions to the activities of already existing research institutions, and set up others specifically for conducting applied research. Some of the institutions are briefly described below.

The Census of India

This is the oldest organization providing useful sociological data. It celebrated its centenary in 1971. Keeping the planner's interest in view, the Census of India has now considerably expanded its research operations. The census organization employed some anthropologically trained researchers specifically for producing a series of village studies after the last decennial census in 1961. Irma Adelman and George Dalton (1971) recently used this data in a highly sophisticated study of micro-development in India. George Dalton (1971: 7) made this comment on their utility:

We hope that the result is judged to be sufficiently promising to encourage departments of planning and statistics in Third World countries to emulate the Government of India in collecting hard data series on village communities.

The Anthropological Survey of India

Established in 1948 on a permanent basis, the Anthropological Survey of India has been functioning on and off for quite some time. The origin of this institution actually goes back to 1905 when an Ethnographic Survey was launched under the direction of Risley.[2] Today the Anthropological Survey is the largest government-supported anthropological research organization of its kind in the world. Its wide ranging publications include many of interest particularly to planners.

Tribal Research Institutes

A prerequisite to successfully executing development schemes in the tribal areas is a thorough understanding of the tribal way of life. It is the desire to sharpen this understanding for planning purposes that led, in the past fifteen years or so, to the setting up of a chain of tribal research institutes in all the states with pockets of tribal concentration. These research centres located in Assam, Bihar, Gujarat, Madhya Pradesh, Maharashtra, Nagaland, Arunachal Pradesh, Orissa, Rajasthan and West Bengal, occasionally bring out, in addition to their regular bulletins, useful research publications on various aspects of tribal life.

National Institute of Community Development

The planned programmes of change in village life which began in 1952, needed sociological research support. The National Institute of Community Development (NICD) was created to meet this need. Action-oriented research conducted here on a

---

[2] A fuller account will be found in Majumdar, N.D., "Development of Anthropology, Government of India," *American Anthropologist*. 50: 578-81.

wide range of development problems has the primary aim of discovering ways by which rural populations can be persuaded to accept recommended innovations. In recent years the institute has been bringing out useful publications on the strategy of promoting change in agricultural practices, family planning methods, and other aspects of rural life. It also publishes a quarterly journal "Behavioural Sciences and Community Development."

Research Programmes Committee

Over a period of about twenty years, this committee of the Planning Commission, Government of India has made an important contribution to valuable research by funding several research projects of anthropologists attached to universities and other institutions of higher learning. Without this financial backing, the academic centres would perhaps not have been able to undertake many of their useful research schemes.

Indian Council of Social Science Research

These functions of the Research Programmes Committee (RPC) were taken over by the Indian Council of Social Science Research (ICSSR) when it came into existence in 1968. The ICSSR has recently sponsored a large research project involving study of the development needs of tribal populations in various states. The results of these studies are expected to provide material for formulating programmes of development in the tribal areas during India's Fifth Five Year Plan period (1974-79).

UTILIZATION OF ANTHROPOLOGY

This governmental support to anthropological studies has the simple objective of planning and implementing development programmes in the light of research experience. The ways in which this objective is sought to be achieved are several and, by now, clearly identifiable.

The development administration is, firstly, well served by the results of anthropological research that the institutions created specifically for the purpose make available. The planners are additionally benefited by the research conducted (a) by the Programme Evaluation Organization (PEO) attached to the Planning Commission; and (b) by the anthropologists themselves as part of their study of the socio-cultural change process.

Sometimes, the government specially consults anthropologists for their expert advice on particular development problems. A case in point is the study by Oscar Lewis (1954) of factionalism in a north Indian village. Reports of visiting missions[3] that include anthropologists also provide useful information to the planners.

The working groups set up by the Planning Commission to recommend policy measures and plans of action for tribal areas, development of rural areas, forestry, cooperatives etc., often include anthropologists. The planning process also greatly profits from associating anthropologists with special commissions set up periodically for suggesting improvements in the implementation of particular development programmes. A committee appointed to examine the functioning of the special multi-purpose tribal blocks was headed by a noted anthropologist, Verrier Elwin (1960). He was also associated with the Scheduled Areas and Scheduled Tribes Commission which was appointed under Article 339 of the Indian Constitution.[4] Currently Dr Sachidananda, an anthropologist, is a member of the panel of sociologists attached to the Indian National Commission on Agriculture.

Anthropologists are also represented on the Central Advisory Board for Tribal Affairs which came into existence in 1958. This is a forum where their participation can and does influence governmental thinking on policy and action aspects of tribal development.

Development administration is further helped by the fact that a large number of anthropologists are employed in several

[3]An example is Adams, H.S., G.M. Foster, R.P.S.S. Taylor, 1955. "Report on Community Development Programs in India, Pakistan, and the Phillippines."

[4]This commission (1960-61) submitted its report in 1961, "Report of the Scheduled Areas and Scheduled Tribes Commission." Delhi: Manager of Publications, 1962.

training institutions and programme executing agencies. In fact the requisite qualification for jobs in several agencies, say, in the office of the Commissioner for Scheduled Castes and Scheduled Tribes, is a degree in anthropology.

IMPACT ON THE DEVELOPMENT PROCESS

It is obvious that the government has assisted the production of anthropological research and ensured its effective utilization in the development process. The question that arises now is: what impact has the anthropologists' participation had on the development process? Have they been able to help the planners and administrators speedily achieve planned socio-cultural and economic change?

This question of the eventual outcome of the anthropologists' involvement in the development endeavour has indeed much to do with the considerations that go into the decision-making. It is important to note that in determining any development goal or planning strategy, anthropology can be only one of several interacting factors. Quite obviously it is not the only determinant of the policy line or course of action. Despite this constraint, anthropology in India has been able to add some dimension to development policy and action.

ROLE IN POLICY-MAKING

On the basis of his research among the Baigas, a tribe inhabiting central India, Verrier Elwin (1939) once suggested that to ensure development of these people it was essential to temporarily insulate them against contact with outsiders, who were always exploiting them in various ways. This gave rise to a heated debate. Branding the anthropologists as a group intent on keeping the tribal people tribal for the sake of their research, many, including some social scientists,[5] then proposed that instead the tribals should be totally assimilated

---

[5] G. S. Ghurye, a sociologist, in his book *The Aborigines So-called and Their Future*, published in 1943 (Bombay: Popular Book Depot) argues for the complete assimilation of tribal groups in the Indian society. This book has now reappeared under the title *The Scheduled Tribes*.

into Indian society. Though the isolation versus assimilation controversy is now over and anthropologists are no longer accused of keeping the tribal people in a zoo, it gave anthropology a great set-back. For a long time they were not thought fit to be consulted on tribal matters.

It is to the anthropologists' credit that they have not only since regained lost ground but also made some positive advances. The government policy towards tribal people[6] that the late Prime Minister Nehru laid down was to a great extent influenced by the views of an anthropologist. Referring to the influence of Verrier Elwin on his thinking about this subject Nehru (1957) confessed that:

> I have learnt much from him, for he is both an expert on this subject with great experience of tribal life and my own views, vague as they were, have developed under the impact of certain circumstances and of Verrier Elwin's own writings.

But tribal life apart, there is no other major sphere where anthropology could very significantly be able to contribute to policy formation. With their studies of the changing rural scene, anthropologists could have been in a good position to help shape development policy for rural areas, but they do not seem to have done much.

Effect on the Implementation Side

The contribution of anthropology in the execution of development plans has not been very remarkable. It is true that many anthropologists are employed in the government, but a large number of officials who are supposed to carry out the policy at the grassroots level are not adequately equipped for the job. The critical importance of training in anthropology and social sciences is still not appreciated at all levels.

Naturally, this results in faulty implementation of otherwise wisely formulated plans. Talking of community development

---

[6]The principles that should guide development in tribal areas were spelt out by the late Prime Minister of India Nehru in the second edition to Verrier Elwin's *A Philosophy for NEFA* (Shillong: 1959).

programmes in the tribal areas, Furer-Haimendorf (1967) has pointed out how, in the absence of knowledge of local conditions, things could go away:

> ...Thus houses were built but people would not live in them, roads were built only to be washed away in the rainy season, basketry centres started where there were no bamboos, and bee-keeping established where there were no flowers.

In his opinion, the implementation of development on the whole does not receive as much attention as its planning:

> ...It would appear that the provisions for the welfare of the tribes are strong on the constitutional and planning sides, but weak on the executive side. The concern of the Government of India and of Parliament for the rights and progress of the tribes is admirable, but by the time measures decided upon at the centre have filtered down to state and district level, their impact is often weakened or outright lost. In all the reports of the Commissioner for Scheduled Castes and Scheduled Tribes, the Planning Commission and other bodies concerned with tribal affairs, there is the repeated complaint that the staff and administrative machinery provided by the states is not adequate to carry out the policy of the centre, even if the necessary funds are voted by Parliament.

In states where implementation is given importance, things have been moving as they should. Revisiting NEFA after some years Furer-Haimendorf recently found the development policy for the tribal people there to be helping them largely as intended.[7]

---

[7]Christoph von Furer-Haimendorf reporting his experiences in "Recent Developments in Nagaland and NEFA," *Asian Affairs*: Journal of the Royal Central Asian Society, Vol. 59, February 1972 says: "I should like to conclude this account of my impressions by expressing my admiration for the spirit of understanding and service which I found among all the officials engaged in the administration of these regions. It is undoubtedly due to their efforts and motivation that the solution of the people of Nagaland and NEFA as far better than that of the tribal population of any other region of India of which I have personal knowledge."

Overall, this account of the anthropological contribution to developmental planning in India does not look very impressive. It is possible that their involvement in all decisions affecting agriculture, education, population control, communications, medicare and public health may not have been thought so very vital. But the fact must be faced that anthropology, in the present stage of its development, does not have much to offer India. Anthropologists are themselves realizing that due partly to their own inadequacies they have not been able to accomplish all that they had hoped to achieve. Dr S.C. Dube (1971: 89-90), who has had a long association with governmental developmental planning machinery, is perhaps correct in his estimation that:

> As an organized profession they have done little more than pass platitudinous resolutions making claims for their discipline which were never demonstrated in the shape of concrete accomplishments. They did take up a number of sponsored research projects, some of which yielded valuable data and adequate analysis, but a large number of these exercises were carried out in a mechanical way and their results were uninspiring. The operational suggestions they contained were all too often simplistic or trite. The strategy of policy-oriented research lacked focus and coordination, and the low prestige assigned to it by the academics resulted in much inferior work. With imaginative direction there could have been much better utilization of available resources.

Needed Changes in the Government

The difficulties of implementing policies by staff which is not fully equipped are well-known. Furer-Haimendorf (1967) says:

> The Planning Commission has clearly recognised the problem of finding suitable personnel for tribal development work, and in the Third Five Year Plan the suggestion has been put forward that the Central Government and state governments should cooperate in forming a special cadre comprising technical and other personnel for work in Scheduled Areas. The most significant aspect of such a policy would be that a

body of trained persons would spend their entire period of service among the tribal people, so that their knowledge, experience and sense of identification would become a vital factor in assuring rapid and uninterrupted service.

A similar proposal was also made in the Fourth Five Year Plan. But the trouble is that such ideas do not get translated into action, as a former member of the Planning Commission, Dr V.K.R.V. Rao (1969:198), rightly thought "because of apprehensions that members of the cadre, particularly the officials may not like to be tied down to tribal areas for the entire life-time." The start in this direction, which has been long overdue, is therefore not being made. About the doubts of those to be included in this cadre, something possibly can be done. As Dr V.K.R.V. Rao (1969:198-99) himself put it:

> It should be possible to allay the fears by restricting the period of direct service in tribal areas to a limited period of five to seven years, widening the area of recruitment, and providing sufficient incentives for attracting persons of good calibre and right spirit. Since tribal development has ceased to be a more localised effort, officials who have done their tenure in tribal areas could be assigned supervisory, administrative and planning positions at the Central and State levels. This might help to offset what is felt as the hardship of service in tribal areas and promote better recruitment to the special cadre for service in tribal areas. It could also lead to better planning of tribal development at the central and state levels because of the presence of officers with first-hand knowledge and experience of having served in the tribal areas.

For the anthropologists seeking jobs in the government the career opportunities are very limited. Those who value academic freedom consequently neither feel encouraged nor prefer to join government service. Quoting from the report of the Commission for Scheduled Castes and Scheduled Tribes, Stephen Fuchs (1969: 71) says:

> The Commissioner for Scheduled Castes and Scheduled Tribes, in his Report for 1963-64, complains that "there is

a dearth of properly qualified and experienced persons for manning the newly created posts. . . ." This scarcity of trained personnel is, however, due not to the unavailability of trained anthropologists in India but, as the Commissioner himself pointed out in his Report, to the fact "that pay-scales offered are not attractive enough. . . ." Such factors deter competent anthropologists from joining these institutes, and they prefer more lucrative congenial posts elsewhere.

Surely something needs to be done to improve matters here.

Changes desired in development administration would also come about rapidly by improving the training capability of the National Institute of Community Development and the various tribal research institutes. There are two things that need to be done first in this connection. Firstly, more officials must be sensitized to the human aspects of development at these centres than has been the case so far. Secondly the quality of training must be greatly improved. Of course, the development agencies would then ensure that none of their trained staff are shifted to jobs elsewhere.

Also, the government would get higher returns from expenditure on research conducted through its own organizations if they all coordinated their efforts more meaningfully. It would indeed be futile to mount research on the same problems in all the institutes. Efforts must then also be directed towards wider dissemination of research findings amongst concerned officials and development agencies.

Finally, things would considerably improve if anthropologists were more closely associated with decision-making at the highest levels in the government.

Making Anthropology more Relevant

These suggested changes in the government would not by themselves bring about overall improvement in the situation. There have to be corresponding changes in the anthropological profession. Anthropology can genuinely help accelerate the development process only if attention is devoted to things such as action-oriented research—which need not be regarded by academics as something unworthy of their attention. At present developmental planning still seems to have little or no attraction for most of them and as Pocock (1968: 288-89) observes:

> There is little sign that academic social anthropologists have recognised that their place is with the planner... it is by no means required to the academic anthropologist that he approve the plan or even planning as such. His precise opposition may well be as valuable as his collaboration; in my case it is collaboration. Academic social anthropology in India is not expected to work for this or that particular end of the plan, but it can be expected to take cognizance of it and to realise that planning is as much a part of Indian society as caste.

Anthropologists in India tend to think of their action role only in the context of tribal affairs. Actually development must be seen to embrace all areas of human life. It is necessary to clearly identify relevant issues in development if the research effort is to proceed in the right direction. The really challenging problems today are poverty, unemployment, inequality, high rate of population growth, and generally low productivity. But not all of these problems seem to attract much attention from the anthropologists. An understanding of the socio-cultural dimensions of these problems can be helpful in planning the programmes more realistically.

Anthropologists should also try and communicate with development planners and administrators more frequently. By keeping aloof, anthropologists are only rendering them less useful. Developmental planning is basically an interdisciplinary field. Therefore, they should increasingly participate in projects involving sociologists, economists, public administration specialists, communication experts and others.

Lastly, there should be an effort to present research findings in a language that the administrators understand. If many of the books by anthropologists which are as outcome of action-research done at the government's expense are any indication, it is clear that they normally prefer to write with their own professional colleagues in view. This should change.

Collaboration with Development Planners and Administrators

The proposal to give anthropology a further applied slant is not likely to enthuse all anthropologists. There is already a strong feeling that the conduct of research through government funding not only jeopardizes academic freedom, but also makes a heavy demand on the scarce manpower available for investigating fundamental questions. M.N. Srinivas (1960) expressed his fears thus:

> ...There is a danger here which must be pointed out if sociology and social anthropology are not to take a wrong direction. The Government of India has an understandable tendency to stress the need for sociological research that is directly related to planning and development. And it is the duty of sociologists as citizens that they should take part in such research. But there is a grave risk that "pure" or "fundamental" research might be sacrificed altogether. We are not so rich in our human resources that we can afford to have our few sociologists all doing applied research.

On the other hand, development planners naturally want more applied research done to facilitate their task. For them this obviously has the greatest importance. As Elwin (1964: 143) put it:

> In India at the present time, when, as a result of the great Five-Year Plans, the tribal people are being very rapidly changed and merged into ordinary society, I believe that we should put every possible anthropologist and sociologist into the work of guiding development and training its agents.

Their duty as citizens is certainly recognized by anthropologists. In a seminar on urgent research in social anthropology, Berreman, Dube, Furer-Haimendorf, Vidyarthi, Fuchs, and Edward Jay, among others, did stress the need to take the practical aspect into account. Berreman (1969: 43) said:

Ours is the science of man; it cannot ignore human relevance. I am simply making the point that in all of our research and writing and teaching we should exercise the sociological imagination to the limit of our abilities lest we become a science of man irrelevant to man.

However, the fact remains that the research sponsored by the government for practical uses does result in the neglect of basic research on problems which for the anthropologist be of crucial importance. Furer-Haimendorf (1969: 78) stresses this point:

> For the administrator and the politician many of the most primitive populations are of comparatively little interest. Their numbers are small and they are unlikely to cause any disturbances of which governments would have to take note. In this respect they differ greatly from such substantial tribal groups as Nagas, Mizos, or Santals. Those expected to apply anthropological knowledge to the solution of contemporary problems have therefore little incentive to spend much time and energy on the study of such small tribal communities. Yet, it is just the most primitive groups which most easily lose their individuality and are absorbed within more advanced ethnic groups. Their study is hence even more urgent than that of the bigger tribes which have a better chance to maintain at least some aspects of their traditional way of life.

The conflict in the role as citizen and scientist should not, however, be altogether irreconcilable. Even in government-sponsored research there should be opportunities for the promotion of scientific objectives. The pursuit of anthropology for anthropology's sake cannot be the sole cherished goal of everybody who is attracted to the study of man. Indeed, the participation of anthropologists in the development endeavour should be useful to both them and their country.

REFERENCES

Adelman, Irma, and George Dalton, 1970. "A Factor Analysis of Modernization in Village India," in George Dalton, ed., *Economic*

Development and Social Change. New York: Natural History Press.

Bailey, F.G., 1962, "The Scope of Social Anthropology in the Study of Indian Society," in T.N. Madan and Gopala Sarana, eds., *Indian Anthropology.* Bombay: Asia Publishing House.

Berreman, Gerald D., 1969. "Urgent Anthropology in India," in Behari L. Abbi and Satish Saberwal, eds., *Urgent Research in Social Anthropology.* Simla: Indian Institute of Advanced Study.

Dalton, George, 1971. *Economic Anthropology and Development.* New York: Basic Books Inc.

Dube, S.C, 1971. *Explanation and Management of Change.* New Delhi: Tata McGraw-Hill Publishing Co.

Elwin, Verrier, 1939. *The Baiga.* London: John Murray.

———, 1960. Report of the Committee on Special Multipurpose Tribal Blocks. New Delhi: Ministry of Home Affairs.

———, 1964. *The Tribal World of Verrier Elwin.* Bombay: Oxford University Press.

Fuchs, Stephen, 1969. "Urgent Anthropological Research in Middle India," in Behari L. Abbi and Satish Saberwal, eds., *Urgent Research in Social Anthropology.* Simla: Indian Institute of Advanced Study.

Furer-Haimendorf, Christoph von, 1967. "The Position of Tribal populations in Modern India," in Philip Mason, ed, *India and Ceylon: Unity and Diversity.* New York: Oxford University Press, pp. 182-222.

———, 1969. "Fundamental Research in Indian Anthropology," in Behari L. Abbi and Satish Saberwal, eds., *Urgent Research in Social Anthropology.* Simla: Indian Institute of Advanced Study.

Lewis, Oscar, 1954. *Group Dynamics in a North Indian Village.* New Delhi: Planning Commission, Government of India.

Nehru, Jawaharlal, 1957. "Foreword," in *A Philosophy for NEFA.* Shillong.

Pocock, David, 1968. "Social Anthropology: Its Contribution to Planning," in Michael Lipton, ed., *The Crisis of Indian Planning.* London: Oxford University Press.

Rao, V.K.R.V., 1969. "Social Change and the Tribal Culture," in L.P. Vidyarthi, ed., *Conflict, Tension and Cultural Trends in India.* Calcutta: Punthi Pustak.

Srinivas, M.N., 1960. "Editor's Introduction," in *India's Villages.* Bombay: Asia Publishing House.

———, 1972. "Chairman's Address," in K. Suresh Singh, ed., *Tribal Situation in India.* Simla: Indian Institute of Advanced Study.

Part Two

Socio-cultural Dimensions of Planned Development

S.C. Dube

8 Cultural Factors in Rural Community Development

Experiments in the field of technological change and rural community development in many underdeveloped areas of the world have brought into sharp focus the importance of cultural factors in the acceptance or rejection of the programmes of directed change sponsored by external agencies. There has been a growing realization among rural extension experts and technical assistance workers that even some of the less involved technological or economic innovations have latent cultural and social dimensions that need careful consideration if the success of these programmes is to be assured. Detailed case studies of specific action programmes have revealed that secondary and tertiary ramifications of given innovations are of critical significance in determining their ultimate acceptability. With this understanding planners and their staff members no longer approach an underdeveloped community with the naive assumption that it will enthusiastically adopt superior tools and techniques when they are placed within its reach; instead, considerable emphasis is now laid on adapting modern techniques to the culture and values of the community in which the programme has to operate.

Agents of rural development projects and of programmes of technical assistance are confronted with these factors at almost every step in their work. The acceptance of the agents of change, as well as the effectiveness of the media through which they endeavour to communicate their innovations, are largely governed by the cultural predispositions, attitudes, and social organization of the community in which they operate. The acceptance of the programme itself, or of its constituent parts, is determined to a considerable extent by a variety of complex cultural factors, ranging from simple habits and accepted social practices to the intricate patterns of belief, social structure, world-view, and values and attitudes.

From our study of a community development project[1] in action in its different aspects, a number of points emerge that illustrate the range and effectiveness of cultural factors influencing such programmes.

To begin with, the habits and tastes of the people have determined the initial response of the community to a large number of innovations and programmes promoted by the community development project. The improved varieties of wheat seed promoted by the project were not very enthusiastically received by the community because of their flat taste and also largely because of the difficulties the women experienced in using the new flour to make the conventional type of unleavened bread. The superiority of the new seed in respect to its proportionately higher yield, disease- and rain-resisting qualities, and better marketability, was generally accepted, but when it came to making a choice on grounds of taste, flavour, digestibility, and general health-building qualities the preference was unmistakably for the traditional variety. In respect to sugarcane, people took the improved varieties because they brought much higher prices from the mills as a cash crop, but the old variety was still remembered with nostalgia for its superior taste and allegedly better food value. Even when the community took to these new seeds for pressing reasons of a market economy, this acceptance was not ungrudging. A large number of minor ailments and diseases such as common colds, coughs, and stomach disorders were attributed to the new products, and they were

---

[1]The community development project is located in one of the western districts of Uttar Pradesh, India. A block of 153 villages, with a population of 78, 337, has been selected for intensive development. The project, formally inaugurated in October 1953, has been working mainly in the fields of agricultural extension, rural health and sanitation, social education, youth welfare, and women's welfare.

Cultural Factors in Rural Community Development 141

believed to be responsible for a general deterioration in the health of the people.

Considerable difficulty was experienced by the extension agents in introducing improved seed for new purposes. For example, the community was familiar with peas, and had been growing a degenerate local variety of it as a fodder crop. The superior edible variety introduced by the community development project was still viewed as a fodder crop and the people, being unfamiliar with its use as a food, wondered why they should spend more on buying an improved seed for a crop to be grown primarily for consumption by cattle. Also, the success of the project in introducing new crops was hampered because the people were not sure about their utility in terms of the everyday needs of the community. Very few persons were enthusiastic about taking up vegetable growing on a reasonable scale because in their view vegetables formed a delicacy—a kind of embellishment to the diet—but were not considered a staple or a necessary part of the diet. For their novelty and prestige as an urban item of diet, some people were willing to grow vegetables on small patches of land but, because of the commonly-held views regarding the place and importance of vegetables in daily diet, the people were unwilling to extend this cultivation.

Force of habit also influences the attitude toward programmes in areas other than food production. The construction of public latrines in one of the project villages was initially welcomed as a progressive measure in the direction of urbanization, but their use was practically abandoned after a few weeks as they were not agreeable to the habits and aesthetic sense of the people. While there was general agreement that cowdung was more valuable as manure than as fuel, people still continued to burn it. They did not find any other type of fuel as good for their smoking water pipes (hubble-bubble) or for the slow heating of milk. The use of a substitute cuts down their smoking pleasure, and slow heating of milk over a cowdung fire is a necessary part in the traditional process of making *ghee* (clarified butter), which is regarded as one of the most essential and desirable parts of the diet.

Model sanitary repairs to wells were enthusiastically received in most project villages, but there was a general decline in the people's enthusiasm for them after a few weeks. They liked the appearance of these wells and could look to them with a certain sense of achievement, but it was not easy for them to adjust to the new way water had to be drawn from the reconditioned wells. For one thing there were only two to four pulleys on each well, depending on its size, and this meant that at any one time only two to four persons could draw water from them. Others had to wait their turn and many found this rather trying. Then the high parapet wall and the rope going down the well over a pulley fixed still higher, necessitated a change in the posture as well as in the motions involved in drawing water. Most people, especially women, found this inconvenient. They claimed that the method to which they were accustomed was physically less exhausting than the one which they had to adopt in the use of the new type of well.

When it comes to established social practices, neither appeals on scientific grounds nor logic can easily persuade the village people to give up their traditional life-ways. As a part of the rural sanitation programme the village level workers got compost pits dug outside the settlements in a number of project villages. In this they had, on the whole, understanding cooperation from the people: both for aesthetic reasons and for reasons of public health villagers thought it desirable to have pits for the deposit of manure and refuse outside the village, and cooperated willingly with the project authorities in digging them. The local village councils passed resolutions making it obligatory for the villagers to use these pits. Depositing refuse in the village was to be punished by the council with fines. However, most of these pits remained unused. Cultural factors explain the failure on the part of the people to use these pits. Traditionally it is the work of women to clean the house and cattle-shed and deposit refuse and dung in one corner of the house compound or in an open space near the house. While women of even the highest castes can do this kind of work at their homes, those belonging to the higher castes are not expected to be seen carrying loads from their houses all the way to compost pits on the outskirts of the village. Men could not do so, because culturally such a task is defined as "women's work." As very few families could afford to engage servants for this work, the traditional practice continues.

Cultural factors governing traditional work patterns determined the nature of public participation in many sectors of development activity. The Government's efforts to mobilize local manpower in village reconstruction and development have received wide publicity. *Shramdan*, or "gift of free, voluntary labour by the people," is viewed as an effective instrument of securing the people's cooperation in constructive activities. Observation and analysis of four *shramdan* drives in this project forcefully brought to our attention how the established work-patterns of a community can defeat the very essence of such movements. In the villages under the development project, the upper-caste groups traditionally assume supervisory roles, leaving the actual hard work to the poor lower-caste groups. It was usual for influential men in the village to use pressure—often bordering on coerion—on the lower castes to make them undertake the hard work in all communal undertakings of the village such as repairs to roads, cleaning of wells, and construction of public buildings. The *shramdan* drives, inaugurated with great fanfare and considerable speech-making, were in practice reduced to the traditional work-patterns: the rich and influential upper caste people contribute their labour in the form of supervision, advice, and encouragement; the lower castes did all the work. As no payment was made to them for the work, the low caste labourers naturally resented it. Another related factor may also be mentioned here. While in some other parts of India, women with the exception of those from high castes, join work teams engaged in community undertakings, because of their traditional seclusion in this area they cannot participate in such work.

The established social practices of the community appear to have affected the educational programmes of the project materially. The value of education is recognized, and projects in this field get considerable verbal support from the people, but practical difficulties become apparent once these projects get started. The idea of an adult education of class sounds good but few adults want to adopt the role of a school-going child and enroll in these classes. The few who do join these classes also eventually give up because of the general amusement their position arouses. It must be remembered that we are dealing here with a population which is very sensitive concerning matters of honour and unwilling to risk any ridicule. Classes for women meet with similar difficulties: a daughter-in-law is customarily not expected to leave the house frequently until she attains a comparatively responsible status within the family by becoming the mother of two or three children. When she is young her "daughter-in-law" role prevents her from joining these classes, and when she has children her "adult" role coupled with responsibilities of the household prevents her from taking advantage of them.

The ideal of ownership and management of farms by the family or close kin is so firmly established in the community, that innovations seeking even slight modifications in the pattern are resisted by the people. The programme of planting community orchards sponsored by the project was largely a failure because no one thought of it as a serious and worthwhile investment. Where people yielded to pressure and agreed to plant community orchards, they thought of the venture as a gesture of compliance with the wishes of the government and not as a serious undertaking. Partly because of the impersonal nature of their ownership and also partly because of the local tradition that the owners of fruit trees, except when they take to horticulture on a commercial scale, should allow almost anyone to take some of it, these community orchards did not receive sufficient attention from those who had planted them. The idea of cooperative ownership of tractors was received very coldly too, and no one gave any serious thought to making such a risky and uncertain investment.

Resistance can be expected when programme of change touch the sensitive area of belief. The state has been actively promoting programmes of introducing better methods of cattle breeding, but without much success. The agriculturalists recognize the importance of good draft cattle, and indeed invest large sums of money in buying animals of good breed, but locally they cannot do much to change the methods of cattle breeding because of the presence in the villages of a large number of scrub bulls. The government has distributed—free or at subsidized rates—a number of pedigree bulls in the area, but they are not much help because no effective ways can be devised to dispose of the scrub bulls. Being the mount of Lord Shiva, a bull is regarded as sacred, and many of these bulls are released for religious methods after a death or as a supplication to supernatural powers. Because of their sacred character, interference with their freedom is regarded as a sin, and plans to castrate them are viewed as unthinkable by most villagers. The artificial insemination centre started by the project appeared to be a way of countering the cultural resistance of village people, but even this method was not without its problems. First, the villagers are not used to watching for the time when cows are ready for impregnation. Often the scrub bulls impregnate them before their condition is noticed by the owners. Then, the necessity of having to take them to a distant insemination centre interferes with other activities. Finally, some people get worried about the propriety of mechanical interference with the body of the cow, and view the denial of the satisfaction of her normal bodily cravings as a sin.

Traditional practices rooted in beliefs can be obstacles to the acceptance of a wide range of programmes in the fields of rural health and hygiene, and practices connected with maternity and child care. The body image conveyed by the culture, views regarding the essentials of good health, and theories about disease and its treatment held by the village people, determine their reponse to modern ideas regarding sanitation and personal hygiene and the prevention and treatment of diseases. Notwithstanding compulsory vaccination, smallpox is still regarded as a "sacred" rather than a "secular" disease. Because they regard smallpox as the visitation of a mother-goddess, village people give more attention to the performance of the prescribed rituals and worship than to the proper isolation and care of the patient. Certain types of ailments are attributed to supernatural causes such as the evil eye, magic, and one wrath of gods and spirits. In the case of all such diseases the villagers find it hard to grasp the necessity and utility of preventive measures, and they tend to trust the traditional methods more than the modern methods. Popular beliefs embodied in prevalent theories of disease and treatment not only determine the response of the villagers to the promoters and practitioners of modern medicine and their methods of diagnosis and treatment, but are of vital significance for the success of the programmes of preventive medicine and immunization. The common belief that medicinal treatment can commence only when the presence of a disease has definitely been established through diagnosis is largely responsible for the failure of measures in the field of preventive medicine. Adoption of modern practices in maternity and child care are also governed by some deep-seated beliefs of the people. A woman is not given any milk in the latter part of her pregnancy and for a few months following confinement for fear that this will result in a child too big for normal delivery and will cause swelling and pus formation in the mother's fallopian tubes. For several months a new-born baby is not given any water to drink because this is believed to upset the delicate mechanism of the child's body with its "cold" effect. The efforts of the midwives appointed by the project had very limited success in changing the traditional practices of the community because of the strength of conventional beliefs in this area.

The interplay of factors affecting programmes of directed change in the general area of social structure is more complex. In this sphere it is necessary to take account of social segmentation and stratification, role differentiation in terms of age, sex, and types and levels of leadership, and vital factors of group dynamics and factionalism within the community.

The division of the society into castes, with their associated norms and expected standards of behaviour and overt and latent stresses and tensions in intergroup relations, posed a number of important problems to planners and development workers. With what particular group should they identify themselves in the village? Whose norms and standards of behaviour should they adopt? Identification with upper income and status groups, and acceptance of their norms, wins for the extension worker a certain measure of support from these influential groups; but at the same time it alienates the underprivileged groups and promoters of change. If they act in the reverse direction, the extension agents meet with coldness and even hostility from groups on the higher levels of the social hierarchy. Where the village level workers interacted mostly with the upper-caste groups, the lower castes looked on them with suspicion and distrust and complained that the government was seeking to make the rich groups richer and was thereby indirectly contributing to the further economic deterioration of the lower levels. Adoption of certain improved agricultural implements such as cultivators and tractors by the upper-caste agriculturalists was especially criticized by the lower castes, as it reduced employment opportunities for them. These items, promoted and often subsidized by the project, were welcomed by the upper castes because they generally reduced their dependence on the lower groups. Welfare measures among untouchables were adversely criticized by the upper castes as politically motivated steps for vote-getting that developed disturbing notions among the untouchables. The presence of women from the untouchable castes in the adult education classes started by the project in an important village of the block resulted in the boycott of the class by the women of the upper castes. It is generally agreed by persons working on action teams that the caste of an extension man materially affects his acceptance—both social and as an agent of change—by the villagers. His behaviour is closely watched, and deviations from traditional norms arouse interest and comment in the society. In her enthusiasm for adoption of progressive ideas the assistant project officer for women's welfare (an upper-caste girl with university education) accepted food from untouchables. This act won for her the sympathy and support of the untouchable group, but also created a sensation in the general community. The episode was widely discussed and its echoes were heard even at the district headquarters. The more traditionally minded people started asking whether the government was out to destroy the social system of the Hindus by letting its employees set such examples.

The effects of role differentiation in terms of sex as well as kinship status and general socioreligious status, have been mentioned earlier in anothor context. A word may be added here about age as a determinant of leadership roles. Age and experience are considered a desirable, often a necessary, attribute of positions of leadership and influence. As a consequence of this norm, measures initiated by the project always need the blessings and support of the more tradition-bound elders. Projects initiated and run by the younger age groups are viewed as temporary developments of minor significance, and rarely taken seriously by the community. This seriously affects the selection of the local agents of change and initiation of projects with long-range effects.

An understanding of the levels of leadership and of the specific roles of different types of leaders is vital for the development programmes. In the rural areas certain types of persons having urban contacts, especially contacts with administration and political leaders, occupy a strategic position. Yet it would be a mistake to single them out as local agents of change to the exclusion of persons on the other levels of leadership. As pointed out earlier in another context,[2] the elite group and individuals occupying existing positions of power, especially in elective offices, are looked upon by the common village people as a link between them and the urban world of administrators, politicians, and businessmen, and consequently they come to have a somewhat specialized role in village affairs. For reasons of local prestige the elite group identifies itself more with the officials and with city ways than with the common village people and their traditional way of life. Because of this attitude they alienate the more traditionally-minded villagers who do not accept their leadership in all spheres of life without mental reservations. For effective penetration to the grassroots the promoters of change will have to find out the key individuals who function as decision-makers on the levels of organized kin groups and castes. Village factionalism often puzzles development workers, and failure on their part to understand the group dynamics in the rural communities under their charge often leads to the ultimate failure of their desirable and technically sound projects. By narrowing down their search for "village leaders" to function as the local agents of change and community development to the rural elite, the extension agents and development workers indirectly worked to restrict the appeal and benefits of their efforts to certain sections of the village population only. As another outcome of this policy, in some villages of the development block certain sections of this favoured group developed some vested interests and tended to block those aspects of

---

[2]S.C. Dube, 1956. "Some Problems of Communication in Rural Community Development," Cornell University Indian Programme Report of 9 February.

community development activities which appeared to them to be helpful to their rivals and antagonists in village affairs.

Finally, in the area of attitudes, values, world-view, and social relations we come to grips with cultural determinants that shape the course of development projects and decide their outcome most powerfully.

In respect to attitudes, it is necessary to consider the village people's view of change. Do they consider it necessary and desirable? Then it is useful to find out their attitude towards the promoters of change. Do the people trust them? Or do they have any misgivings about their motivations? Finally, it is necessary to determine the attitude of the people to the actual action programmes and to the methods adopted for implementing it. Does the community regard the individual development projects as useful and beneficial? Do they find methods devised for their adoption by the community acceptable?

As in many other parts of rural India, the villagers in this community development project tend to idealize and glorify the past, but as a concession to the necessities of the day they also admit the inevitability and desirability of change. The traditional Hindu view of time not only admits the possibility of change but also predicts its inevitability.[3] It is true that every successive stage marks a progressive decline from the high and noble standards of the idyllic past, but the dictum that values and norms of life are situational, i.e., they are determined by the context of time and geographical location, does leave enough room for acceptance of change. Apart from this deep-rooted cultural view of change the people have been sufficiently exposed to urban contacts and have known or heard enough about some of the modern amenities of life, that there has been a decided change in their level of expectation. Persistent nationalist propaganda regarding the benefits of freedom to the village people has affected the hopes and

---

[3]According to the classical Hindu view, time is divided into four *yugas* or Ages; beginning from the ideal Age of Truth (*Satyayuga*) human society has passed through *tretayuga* and *dwaparayuga* and has now come to the present Age of Decline or *kaliyuga*. The cycle will start again when divine intervention, necessitated by the chaos and confusion of the later stages of this Age, will re-establish traditional values and inaugurate the *satyayuga*.

aspirations of a considerable section of the village population. The range of variation in the expectations of the different groups and levels of village population is very wide. Indicative of this divergence are the two extremes of thought; one hoping that a free Indian government will undo the evil influence of an alien government and will re-establish the society on its traditional foundations by recognizing and enforcing the relative statuses of different castes, and another, reflected in the thinking of the politically conscious leaders of the lower castes that the government will take active steps to eradicate the barriers separating the high caste from the low caste and the rich from the poor. The first group interprets the Gandhian concept of *Ramarajya* ("the return of the reign of Rama") to include the revival of the ancient social order in all aspects; the other group often quotes the opinions of national leaders on socioeconomic matters in support of its stand.

Thus there is expectancy of change among significant sections of village people, although there is general uncertainty about its nature and outcome. However, regarding the promoters of change and their motivations there are considerable misgivings. Indeed very few people have grasped the all-India scope and national significance of the development plans. Some people read hidden political motives in these plans. These range from the desire on the part of the Congress to ensure success in the next elections, to the secret plan of the government first to encourage more agricultural production and then to enhance taxation. To a large number of people, however, this activity is nothing more than a passing fancy of the government, not unlike many previous short-lived drives and campaigns which were promoted by the British government with great initial enthusiasm but which finally languished due to lack of continued state interest in them. The common view regarding the development workers is that they work to justify their salary, not for any higher motivation. To the average villager the aim of the development workers is to satisfy and please their official superiors, and with this understanding they always cooperate with these minor officials executing "show projects" whenever visits of political dignitaries and important officials are announced. This view is fostered by the village people's experience with government-sponsored village welfare work under the previous regime, and while there has been a good deal of talk about changing the very bases of government activities, in concrete terms people have not so far had enough evidence of it to warrant a change in their attitude. The relations between the common village people and government officials are characterized by considerable distance, reserve and distrust. This attitude projects itself into action situations which call for joint participation by officials and the people. The people have little share in determining the development targets for their villages. As they have practically no experience in planning and executing community undertakings on a cooperative and democratic basis, it would perhaps be expecting too much from them to assume that they can turn out well-formulated blueprints of village development. Externally determined targets, a rigid work schedule, and insistence on visible accomplishments by the higher levels of the development staff impose severe strains on the project officials and leave them little time or inclination to employ time-consuming educational and discussion methods to enable the village people to formulate their needs and take steps to meet them. Consequently on the village level the people themselves do not have a hand either in determining development projects or in executing them, nor do they have too much of an opportunity of learning to do so. From among the externally determined targets they choose for adoption what appears to be beneficial to them. A few more items are taken up for a variety of diverse motives or because of official pressure. And a number of others are ignored.

Values play a major role in determining the people's attitude towards programmes offered to them by the community development project. Working for the prosperity, well-being, good name, and enhancement of the prestige of the family and the immediate kin group occupies a significant place in the village people's code of family ethics. Programmes contributing towards the material prosperity of the household are therefore taken up without much resistance. Several items of the agricultural extension programme have been accepted on the basis of their possible economic rewards. However, the project has done very little to direct the expressions of family prosperity. Additional incomes earned through adoption of modern innovations and improved techniques have often been spent in putting up expensive *chaupals*[4], in providing impressive dowries, or in buying gold and silver ornaments, rather than in productive investments. Rural communities place a very high value on education, and for this reason projects for building schools for children get appreciable support from the villagers. But here we also find a series of conflicting values in operation. While the higher castes want their children to have modern education so that they may equip themselves to face the changing conditions of the modern world and by acquiring modern urban skills help their parents in maintaining their privileged status and position, there is also the fear that lower-caste children may use their education to break away from tradition and may thus bring about a disintegration of the traditional social organization. For its novelty value women's education is supported, but fears are often expressed that as a result of this education village women may take to some undesirable traits of urban women and may become misfits for traditional domestic roles. Concern for health is a dominant theme in the village people's thoughts. This predisposes them to support public health measures. But modern ideas of health and hygiene as well as modern medicine have to compete with deep-rooted traditional beliefs and in the absence of effective public health education programmes, measures in this sphere go amiss. Preserving the "good name of the village" is another important value held by the people. Several community undertakings have been motivated by the desire to maintain or enhance the prestige of the village rather than by felt needs.

It has been suggested earlier that the widening world of the villagers has had a marked influence on raising their level of expectation and aspiration. This has contributed towards their mental preparedness for some major changes. Some recent governmental measures such as *zamindari* abolition, creation of statutory elective village *panchayats*, and a constitutional ban on the public practice of untouchability have pointed towards the inevitability of change. The impact of these events on the general pattern of social relations—interpersonal as well as

---

[4]Place where men sit, smoke, and usually sleep at night.

intergroup—has indeed been significant. The emerging aspects of group alignments and changes in power equations in the village communities have a significant bearing on the problems and prospects of rural community development.

The social analyst attempting an evaluation of the role of cultural factors in economic development in the communities like the one discussed in this paper is struck by a series of paradoxes. While there is an extreme dependence on the state for welfare measures, there is a general distrust of the minor government official who represents the state on the village level. Although there is much verbal idealization of traditional patterns of village life and a general suspicion and distrust of city ways, there is an unmistakable covert desire to turn to the urban people as a model for many things and to imitate their ways. Notwithstanding the acceptance of tradition as the ideal in preference to uncertainties of change, there is a strong expectancy of change. An understanding and critical evaluation of the inner dynamics of these apparently paradoxical attitudes, values and motivations can greatly help the planner and his extension agents in the implementation of their plans.

The planners and promoters of development programmes have to take account of a number of other manifestations of cultural factors. In the first place it is not enough to look for the immediate cultural consequences of an innovation in one aspect of life; its extensions into other spheres are equally important. Then, its secondary and tertiary effects also cannot be ignored. The vital cultural linkages existing between different aspects of life in peasant communities almost immediately carry the effects of an innovation to spheres other than the one in which the change was introduced. Thus, at first sight the introduction of a new kind of seed may appear to be a simple change in traditional agricultural practices, but its effects are felt in spheres of life as diverse as food habits, beliefs about health and disease, home management, and even domestic peace. Examples of the effects of the introduction of new types of seeds on food habits and health concepts have been given earlier. Home management practices are affected by these new foods when women have to put in extra labour in grinding the grain and kneading the flour, and have to be more careful in making and storing the bread. It was repeatedly pointed out to us in the field that the new type of seed could even affect domestic peace. Unless the unleavened bread made with the flour of the new wheat seed is served hot and fresh from the oven it is not only flat and tasteless, it gets "hard like hide" and is very hard to chew. A farmer returning home tired after a hard day's work in his fields does not find this bread very satisfying, and his dissatisfaction often expresses itself in angry outbursts addressed to his wife and children. These new seeds also involve a change in the routine to which the agriculturalists are accustomed. With the old seed the threshing of one lot took about three days; the same operation for the new seed takes about five days. The cattle found the straw and chaff of the local variety of wheat more agreeable; the "hard and dry" straw of the new variety is not as good as fodder and is believed to be less nourishing to the animals. Thus, the introduction of a new seed also requires devising new techniques of making and storing bread, introducing a new method of threshing and finding alternative sources of fodder supply for the cattle.

It is also essential to watch the extreme selectivity and differential acceptance of the items of change offered by the development projects at different levels of the community. Closely allied to this factor is the tendency in cultures to reinterpret the proffered innovations in terms of the dominant themes and existing needs of the society. Case studies done in connection with this research are illustrative of the selective trends in the acceptance of projects seeking to bring about modifications and changes in the society. Certain items of the development programme are accepted for reasons totally different from those which motivated the planners. The programmes of renovation of wells, paving of village lanes, and construction of soakage and compost pits have been accepted in a number of villages, but there is as yet very little understanding of their significance for the health of the community. Their acceptance has been motivated by such diverse factors as "they look new and good," and "with them our village will look like a town," "we must do what the government asks us to do," "that is all that we can show the important visitors from outside," and "other villages are doing it and so we must also do it." Education has come to acquire a special value with the upper castes because, among other things, it is one of the factors that can enable them to maintain their traditionally higher social position. The lower castes value it because their achievements in this field promise the possibility of breaking down some of the harsh ascriptive aspects of the traditional social organization. Organization of democratically elected village *panchayats* was expected to provide a machinery for cooperative village self-government, and they were also expected to reduce internal village tensions. In many instances, the village people did not grasp the purpose for which these new *panchayats* are created. Many viewed them as modern counterparts of traditional village councils, which functioned wholly as arbitrating and mediating bodies in village disputes. Far from reducing internal tensions, in the first instance they were instrumental in creating more tensions: those in existing positions of power sought to confirm it through popular vote, and those who were aspiring to rise found in the elections an outlet to make their challenge public.

In conclusion it may be said that in devising action programmes of community development, especially in their educational aspects, it is necessary to keep in mind the cultural factors that vitally influence their acceptance or rejection by the people. Many programmes are rejected not because the people are traditionally minded, conservative, or "primitive," but because the innovations, in all their ramifications, do not fit into the total cultural setting of the community. A balanced and critical evaluation of the motivations and mechanism of change in these societies, together with the analysis of the cultural determinants of acceptance and rejection, can provide fruitful insights toward better planning and execution of development programmes.

Thomas M. Fraser, Jr.

9 Socio-cultural Parameters in Directed Change

The charge has been made that the methodological tools and theoretical models available to anthropologists are insufficiently precise to enable accurate prediction in the field of directed social and cultural change. It has further been charged that in their ex post facto analyses of the dynamics involved in such situations, anthropologists as well as other social scientists tend to give far more attention to attempted innovations that "didn't work" than to those areas where change has been successful. While the second charge is belied by many studies such as those included in the volumes edited by Spicer and Paul and the special issue of *Applied Anthropology*,[1] anthropologists have, for the most part, been hesitant to extend their generalizations, based on the analysis of change, to the task of more or less concretely specifying the conditions favouring or inhibiting social and cultural change. Thus, in spite of a growing theoretical corpus, there appears to be reluctance to put it to the practical test of prediction or planning.

While the conclusions presented in the present paper have also been reached in retrospective analysis, the attempt is made to present them in such a way that they may be tested

[1]Edward H. Spicer, ed., 1952. *Human Problems in Technological Change*. New York: Russell Sage Foundation; Benjamin D. Paul, ed., 1955. *Health, Culture and Community*. New York: Russell Sage Foundation; *Applied Anthropology*. Vol. III, No. 2, June 1943, Special Issue: Five Case Studies of Successful experiments in Increasing Food Production.

as predictive tools. Both the data and their analysis are based on a larger study by the author of a programme of directed change conducted by the American Friends Service Committee in the Sambalpur district of Orissa, India.[2] The material for analysis will be presented below as a series of paired cases, where one change-directed programme in each pair was a success and the other a failure. Data not pertinent to the present analysis will not be included in the cases. An attempt will then be made to "factor out" those aspects of the innovative situation which on the one hand fostered or permitted the desired change, and on the other inhibited it. Further general consideration will be given to the possibilities of developing a predictive methodology on the basis of this analysis.

The Setting

The programme of directed change to be discussed below were all undertaken at Barpali Village Service, a small community development project operated by the American Friends Service Committee in the plains area of Sambalpur district, Orissa. Barpali *thana*, or police district, consists of seventy-seven villages with a population of somewhat more than sixty thousand. The main village of the *thana*, Barpali (population about six thousand), lies just north of the centre of the *thana* at the junction of two highways. One of these is the paved road connecting Sambalpur, some forty miles to the north, and Bolangir, headquarters of the adjacent district. A frequent bus service along this road provides easy communication between Barpali and the administrative and commercial facilities of Sambalpur. While of less significance in regard to modern transportation, the east-west road passing through Barpali is also of importance to the community. Not only does this road link together a number of weekly markets within the *thana* and beyond, but it also forms part of the ancient highway and pilgrimage route joining the religious centres of Banaras on the Ganges river with Puri on the

---

[2]Thomas M. Fraser, Jr., *Barpali: Case Studies in Community Development*, forthcoming.

coast of Orissa. During the dry season thousands of pilgrims pass over this route through Barpali. Thus there is not only easy communication with the relatively urban centre of Sambalpur and beyond that with Calcutta, but also contact with two of the traditional centres of Hinduism and with the religious devotees journeying to and from them.

Originally, and in large part still today, the area has been devoted to a single, monsoon-irrigated crop of rice. In addition to the single rice crop, small quantities of winter vegetables have been traditionally grown by the Mali caste of cultivators, while other cultivators have grown a few peanuts and pulses on the dry uplands as well as a very limited quantity of irrigated sugarcane for sale. In 1957, canal irrigation from the Hirakud Dam on the Mahanadi river first reached Barpali *thana*, allowing a second and even a third crop of rice for those cultivators desiring it, and facilitating the production of supplemental or cash crops. In addition to agriculture and the usual complement of occupations in an Indian rural area, a significant minority of the population has long been engaged in the production of cotton and *tussah* cloth. The cotton weavers, in particular, are renowned throughout a large area for their colourful saris employing a variety of intricate woven and *ikat* designs.

Barpali *thana* had been chosen for the establishment of Barpali Village Service in 1952 because of its agricultural and economic backwardness, and because of the potential for growth which would be provided by the introduction of irrigation facilities and eventually electric power from the Hirakud Dam. Although the staffing pattern of the project has varied over its ten years because of the difficulties of obtaining suitable personnel, it had aimed at maintaining one Indian and one Western technician in the fields of agriculture, public health and sanitation, village industries and cooperatives, and education, as well as an Indian rural life analyst and a Western director. In addition to the technical staff, the project has trained and assigned to villages a number of multipurpose village level workers recruited from within the state of Orissa. This pattern is essentially the same as that which had been in use at Allahabad Agricultural Institute and at

Socio-cultural Parameters in Directed Change 159

the Etawah project[3] and which was subsequently adopted by the community projects scheme of the government of India. The aim of the Barpali project has been to improve the economic standards and living conditions of the area by enlisting the efforts of the members of the community and, wherever possible, by letting the direction of the programme be guided by community needs, either explicitly recognized or developed by antecedent work of the project.

Although most of the programme undertaken by Barpali Village Service have resulted in neither complete success or acceptance nor in complete failure or rejection, the programme discussed in the following analysis all tend to approach one of the extremes of success of failure. These extreme cases have been chosen to facilitate the isolation of socio-cultural factors influencing their acceptance or rejection. Once such factors are identified, situations in which a large number are involved or in which a balance between opposing factors is approached should yield more readily to both retrospective and predictive analysis.

PAIR 1—PROTECTED WATER SUPPLIES AND SANITARY LATRINES

Early in its efforts to improve health conditions in Barpali *thana* Barpali Village Service undertook to tackle the two greatest problems in the control of disease germ transmission: unprotected drinking water supplies and unsanitary disposal of human excreta. The general practice in the villages was to collect drinking water from large open catchment tanks or ponds which served for bathing, laundering, and stock watering as well. Villagers defecated in the open fields just outside the villages or, frequently, along the banks of the tanks before bathing.

The programme to provide protected water in the villages had two phases. During the early years of the project no reliable, economical pump appeared to be available, so project

[3]See Allahabad Agricultural Institute, 1956. *Gaon Sathi, Experiment in Education.* Bombay: Oxford University Press, pp. 32-62, and Albert Mayer, 1958. *Pilot Project, India.* Berkeley: University of California Press, pp. 63-86.

technicians attempted to organize entire village populations to decide upon and contribute labour and materials for the construction of open wells for common village use. Money was made available by the state government for material not obtainable locally (mainly cement) and for specialized labour. During the first year of the programme four wells were started, one of which was completed during the dry digging season. In the next and final season of the open well programme fifteen wells were started, seven of which were completed that year and five more during subsequent seasons. By the third year of working on the problem of protected water, Barpali Village Service technicians, cooperating with pump manufacturers in Calcutta, developed a mechanically simple hand pump which could be installed over a well having half the diameter of the previous open wells at a substantial saving in *total* cost.[4] By the close of the 1961 well-digging season, 154 pump wells had been installed in the villages of Barpali *thana*, and nearly one hundred had been installed outside of the *thana* by project personnel. The figure of 154 represents an average of exactly two wells for each of the seventy-seven villages of the *thana* and, while not *every* village had in fact installed such a well, the goal of a protected water supply was largely realized.

A programme to introduce sanitary water-seal latrines to the villagers was launched at the same time as the first phase of the well programme. A molded concrete latrine was developed which could be manufactured at the project and sold to the villagers at an extremely low cost. While the purchase and use of a latrine was essentially an individual decision in contrast to the group or total village decision involved in the construction of a well, Barpali Village Service attempted to create group opinion and pressure in favour of

[4] These wells comprise a covered reservoir made of three precast concrete rings, and a concrete slab, set at the bottom of the pit (approximately thirty feet). From the reservoir a chimney of six-inch diameter precast concrete pipe, through which the water pipe is inserted, leads to the surface and is sealed at the pump platform. Earth is then filled in over the reservoir and around the chimney. This arrangement not only reduces digging labour, but obviates the necessity of a costly masonry lining for the entire pit.

Socio-cultural Parameters in Directed Change 161

latrines by holding village meetings, demonstrations, and eventually a two-week intensive village-wide campaign in one village in which the active participation of most of the village leaders was obtained. However, by the end of 1960, only about three hundred latrines had been sold within the *thana*, and of these only 120 were in even irregular use. On the other hand, there was a relatively great demand for "Barpali latrines" from towns, particularly Sambalpur, and from government installations.

Neither of these programmes was based on an explicit felt need of the villagers, but they were undertaken by the project in view of the enormity of the problem of water-borne diseases in the area. In the interpretation of Barpali Village Service, both programmes were directed at the same set of village problems; the need for the acceptance of one was approximately equal to the need for the acceptance of the other. Why did one programme achieve a large measure of success, while the other was almost a total failure in the villages of Barpali *thana*?

The factors operating to cause the differential reaction to these two programmes are perhaps the most direct and striking of any encountered in the work of Barpali village Service. As will be seen from the following discussion and from Table 1, the great majority of cultural linkages in the areas affected by wells and latrines would point to the failure of *both* programmes. However, one aspect of the situation was of sufficient importance to outweigh the inhibiting factors in the case of the well programme. During the hot dry months, water was in very scarce supply in many of the villages of Barpali *thana*. The women, who carried all the water for household needs from the village tank, often half a mile to a mile from their homes, frequently found the tanks dried up altogether, requiring an even longer trek to an adequate source of water such as a dry river bed where water could be collected in holes dug in the sand. The significance of this factor in causing acceptance of the well programme can be judged by comparing these villages with the few where pre-existing water supplies had been entirely adequate. In these latter villages little or no progress could be made in introducing improved (from the sanitary point of view) wells. In addition to the acute need for an adequate supply of water was the convenience of having it located right in the village and, of course, the fact that much of the cost of these wells was borne by the government.

In the case of the latrine programme there was no such significant objective or situational reason or set of reasons fostering acceptance. On the contrary, all factors of this type, except the low cost of the latrines, militated against acceptance. While wells were a convenience to life in these villages, latrines were a decided inconvenience. In order to flush these latrines properly at least one quart of water was required each time one was used and in a large family, the mere provision of flushing and cleaning water would add a considerable water-carrying burden to the woman or women of the household who had little interest in the latrines or their use anyway. A further significant fact was that in the villages of Barpali *thana* almost all of the men are cultivators whose work is in their fields. These men could hardly be expected to leave their agricultural work and return home, often a considerable distance, simply to make use of a latrine. It was pointed out earlier that there has been a relatively good demand for latrines in large towns such as Sambalpur; similarly the acceptance of latrines in Barpali *thana* has been greatest in those villages which have the largest population (and thus greater average distances from the homes to the open fields used for nocturnal defecation) and where there was a greater proportion of individuals carrying on sedentary occupations such as priests, teachers, weavers, and smiths. While problems of initial cost were not great either in the case of wells, which were largely subsidized, or in the case of latrines which could be bought for as little as five rupees (about $1.05), subsequent maintenance and care were resented by the villagers. Proper installation of a latrine required the digging of a pit and the erection of some sort of fencing for privacy. In roughly half the cases of newly installed latrines, the cause for discontinuation of use has been that the fencing fell into disrepair and was not mended or replaced. Pump and well maintenance has been under the supervision of the technicians of Barpali Village Service and they have attempted to build up a cadre of mechanically trained men in the villages and also to organize village and *gram panchayat* well-maintenance funds.

However, without this supervision by the project, lack of proper maintenance and repairs might well prove an important negative factor in the continued acceptance of village wells. A final situational factor has to do with the timing of the installation of wells and latrines. While the dry season, which is the most suitable time both from the point of view of other activities and in order to avoid cave-ins, is the time of most acute water shortage (i.e., mutual reinforcement), this season presents fewest problems which might be eased by the use of latrines. It is during the rainy season that people complain of the unpleasantness of going to the open fields at night over the muddy streets, and when the streets themselves tend to become muddy sewers. And it is then that the catchment tanks are filling up and all the new and accumulated debris is being washed down the banks.

While situational or environmental factors are generally not sufficient to ensure the acceptance of an innovation when it conflicts with aspects of the value system or with institutional patterns, this has been the case in the Barpali well programme. The strongest factor which had to be overcome initially by the well programme was involved in the policy of the project that wells (open type) should be a joint community effort and for the benefit of the whole community. This, of course, meant not only that members of the upper castes were expected to contribute manual labour along with Harijans (untouchables), but that the completed wells should be used by both the ritually pure and the ritually impure or untouchable. It is an indication of the acuteness of the water problem that at least half of the fifteen open wells completed were used by both these divisions of the community. However, after the pump wells were made available at one-third to one-half the price of an open well, and when Barpali Village Service dropped its demand that wells be used in common by the whole village, the practice of caste separation in the use of water sources was quickly re-established and now the general pattern is for a village to have one pump well in the Harijan section and one or more in the upper caste sections.

Concepts of ritual purity were considerably more important in inhibiting the latrine programme than they would have been in the case of the well programme even had there not been a scarcity of water. Contact with human excreta is considered extremely defiling; when necessary its removal is a task relegated to the lowest of the Harijan castes. Villagers interpret the flushing, cleaning, and even the use of latrines as defiling contact. It was considered extremely offensive to have a latrine located close to a dwelling house where a family not only lived, but prepared food and worshipped its deities. As a consequence of differing value systems of the villagers and the project technicians, it was impossible to translate the most significant reason for *initiating* these programmes as a reason for *accepting* them. Although it was attempted, it proved impossible to give the villagers an understanding of the germ theory of disease transmission. It was much more credible to them that diseases were caused, as they had always been, by minor deities and spirits who had in some way been displeased.[5]

It was usually the younger village men who were contacted by the project concerning latrines, and these men were most susceptible to purchasing them because of various types of pressure from project personnel and because of a degree of prestige in taking on an urban trait. However, it was among the wives of these men that resistance was perhaps the strongest. Being either the only adult woman in a small family or a junior wife in a large joint family, burdensome tasks such as hauling water for latrines fell to them. One of the few periods of relaxation and gossip with other young women available to them was the time of the morning and evening bath. These women felt that having a latrine near their homes would do away with much of the reason for these expeditions to the tank, and consequently they were strongly opposed to having and/or using latrines.

While the foregoing discussion has not touched upon all the factors involved in the acceptance of the well programme nor the rejection of the latrine programme, it has at least mentioned those which appear to be most important. Table 1 summarizes

---

[5]Compare the studies in north India by G. Morris Carstairs, "Medicine and Faith in Rural Rajasthan," in Paul, *op. cit.*, pp. 107-34, and McKim Marriott, "Western Medicine in a Village of Northern India," in Paul, *op. cit.*, pp. 239-68.

Socio-cultural Parameters in Directed Change

these factors, roughly indicating the weight or effectiveness of each. These are grouped according to the socio-cultural nodes discussed below.

PAIR 2—MORE AND BETTER VEGETABLES AND POULTRY

Although both the vegetable and poultry programmes of Barpali Village Service were given priority because of nutritional deficiencies in the area, both were also responsive to an explicit need in the villages: the need for more production in an expanding cash economy. Before the establishment of Barpali Village Service only very small quantities of such vegetables as chillies, edible greens, onions, garlic and small tomatoes were grown by members of the Mali caste, whose traditional occupation was gardening. Vegetable products, other than pulses grown by a few of the other cultivating castes, had hardly any place in the diet of the villagers except as seasoning. Highgrade protein intake was likewise extremely low. Many Harijan families kept a few diminutive, local chickens whose small and infrequent eggs were sold to wealthier village families. On special occasions the birds themselves might be sold at one of the weekly markets.

TABLE 1
FACTORS OPERATING FOR/ AGAINST WELLS AND LATRINES

Wells		Latrines	
For	*Against*	*For*	*Against*
SCARCITY OF WATER Subsidy Digging season	Maintenance	Low cost	*Inconvenience* *Digging season*
Separate caste pump wells	Caste purity Disease theory		CONTACT WITH EXCRETA 1. Near house 2. Near gods Disease theory
	Caste *Segregation*	Prestige	*Division of labour* Men approached

Note: Factors in capitals are considered DECISIVE; those merely italicized are important; those in plain type are of secondary importance.

While sporadic efforts to increase the quantity and quality of vegetables grown in the area were made by the project during its first two years, it was not until drought in 1954 threatened to destroy the rice crop completely that a serious programme to encourage vegetables in the area was undertaken. By that time cultivators had become aware of the success of vegetable growing in the project's demonstration garden and in the kitchen gardens of many of the village workers, and were themselves ready to attempt it in the face of potential crop failure and the concomitant hoarding of available supplies of rice. During the drought and in the ordinarily cool dry season following, many cultivators planted such vegetables as eggplant, cabbage, cauliflower, beans and beets. With the help and advice of project technicians a good yield was produced which the cultivators were able to market in order to purchase stocks of rice. During the following two years there was a slow increase in the number of cultivators planting vegetables and in the varieties planted as people realized the economic advantages of growing vegetables. With the coming of the first canal water in 1957, there was a tremendous increase in vegetable production, but because of insufficient preparation of the plots and lack of protective fencing, the yield that year was disappointing. However, since that time there has been a steady increase in variety, quantity, and quality of the vegetables grown in Barpali *thana*. The problem today is one of marketing the vegetables produced, because increasing quantities have greatly depressed local prices.

Among the earliest programmes of Barpali Village Service was the attempt to upbreed local poultry.[6] While the raising of chickens was carried on by many low-caste families as an adjunct to their customary occupation, the technicians hoped that some of these families might raise improved stock as a full-time occupation. Considerable emphasis was given to this

[6] In the village of Chiknipali where local cocks had been completely eliminated, a non-poultry raiser obtained a local cock for sacrifice. He brought the cock into the village the afternoon of the day on which the ceremony was scheduled. However, due to inauspicious circumstances the ceremony was postponed for four weeks. The cock was allowed to roam in the village, and by the time of the ceremony much of the upbreeding work had been undone.

programme. The first phase aimed at complete eradication of local cocks from several pilot villages, and later from a larger number, by the exchange of one purebred Leghorn cock for two local cocks. The second phase provided purebred eggs for hatching in the villages at minimal cost. In addition to these parts of the programme, village workers and technicians spent considerable time giving advice in the villages and helping with the care of the improved birds. During this intensive phase of the poultry programme there was apparently a fair degree of acceptance: during the first year of the programme over fifty men had joined in the improvement scheme. However, once it appeared that the programme had become established and the project technicians and village workers relaxed their intensive efforts in the villages, the villagers relaxed their own efforts with the result that the small local strain of poultry gradually reasserted itself. In spite of the fact that even first and second generation crosses were producing eggs almost double the size of those of the uncrossed local birds, and that the improved birds were significantly larger than their local ancestors, there seemed to be no concern on the part of the villagers to halt the rather rapid reversion to local type. By 1960, with the exception of two well-tended poultry farms maintained by *upper-castemen*, there was no trace of the improved poultry to be seen in the villages of Barpali *thana*.

Both the vegetable and poultry programmes of Barpali Village Service were conceived by the project with the double goals of increasing the nutritional standard of the villagers' diet and of affording villagers an additional source of cash income through the marketing of their increased production. Demand for both vegetables and poultry products was good, both locally and in the town of Sambalpur: the marketing at no cost by the local branch of the state animal husbandry department. Both programmes seemed to receive good initial acceptance. What are the factors which caused one programme to take firm hold in the area (to the point of creating a surplus problem) while the other programme withered away?

The success of the vegetable programme can be attributed to a relatively large number or moderately positive factors (see Table 2). Likewise, the poultry programme encountered a series of moderately negative factors, but also one significant conflict involving both the institutional and value systems of the local culture. In addition to the positive effect of the drought and of the coming of irrigation in 1957, the potential for increased cash income through vegetable growing was clearly perceived by most of the cultivators. In the case of poultry raising, the potential for increased profit was also present but it was far less certain. As the poultry programme aimed at *improving* village poultry populations it was directed at individuals already raising fowl. Thus direct comparison between the old poultry raising practices and the new was natural. It immediately became obvious that the improved birds required far more care and expense in every respect than had the small, local birds. For instance, the Leghorns required fencing, feeding of special diet, and inoculation, while the local birds wandered freely, scavenging for their own food and managing to protect themselves from predatory animals and birds and from diseases.

Vegetable growing and eating were in no way ritually trained, in fact the ritually purest diets were vegetarian. (The exceptions to this generalization, onions and garlic which are not eaten in some of the purest diets, were traditional vegetables of the Mali caste and did not form a part of the improved vegetable complex). On the other hand, the raising of poultry is considered an unclean occupation and is confined to Harijans. Chicken and eggs are eaten by many members of the clean castes, but there are also many non-vegetarians who will not eat poultry products. These facts were recognized by the technicians of Barpali Village Service when they instituted the poultry programme. However, the project felt that because untouchables were already raising local poultry, they would be receptive to improving their flocks. This assumption was not borne out. In this situation some of the processes described by Srinivas[7] as "Sanskritization" appear to have been operating. The majority of poultry-raising families belonged to an untouchable weaving caste. These people were aware of the fact that within the memory of most adults another similarly untouchable caste of weavers had elevated their status, through the

---

[7] M.N. Srinivas, 1956. "A Note on Sanskritization and Westernization," *Far Eastern Quarterly*, Vol. XV, August, pp. 481-96.

assumption of ritually pure behaviour, to that of a clean caste. While poultry raising was unclean in itself, it was carried on by these people as a sideline, simply as a convenient way to bring in a little bit of additional cash income but something which could be given up at any time. The intent of the Barpali Village Service poultry programme was to elevate poultry raising to a full-time, or at least systematized *occupation*. As members of a caste aware of the possibility of their own upward mobility these people were unwilling to formally assume an unclean occupation which would preclude such mobility. It is the assumption of the present analysis that, while the villagers were not consciously aware of this reasoning, these factors were (and are) of sufficient importance to assure the failure of poultry raising in any kind of *systematic* fashion among Harijans. It is significant in this report that within the *thana*, two individuals who have taken over the raising of improved poultry are not Harijans but both members of a higher cultivating caste. Their ritual status is assured and they have simply taken on a new, potentially profitable business which may even have for them a certain prestige value as a form of Westernization.[8]

In the acceptance of the vegetable programme by traditionally non-gardening castes there was the slightly negative, or perhaps only neutral, factor that there was already a caste of vegetable growers in the area. However, because there was no important overlap of varieties grown in the area, there was apparently no opposition from the Malis who might have had a vested interest in vegetable growing. On the other hand, the very possibility of poultry raising becoming a caste occupation for the Harijans already engaged in it as a sideline, was enough to defeat the programme. A further factor related to caste which has been found to operate in a large number of community development programmes all over India is that it is always the economically and socially more secure castes or groups that most readily accept innovative programmes. A final incentive to taking over vegetable growing was the fact that the yearly round of the cultivators created slack periods between the initial planting and cultivation of rice in the monsoon period and the

[8] *Ibid.*

harvest some months later in the middle of the dry season, and again after the rice harvest. The fact that the activities involved in vegetable growing fell neatly into these two slack periods further contributed to the success of the programme.

As in the preceding section, the factors discussed above are summarized in Table 2, and the attempt is made to indicate the significance of each.

PAIR 3—COOPERATIVES FOR LEATHERWORKERS AND WEAVERS

In working with both the weavers and leatherworkers, Barpali Village Service sought to accomplish two goals: more economical and efficient production and marketing operations and improvement of the quality standards of the products. These goals would help to increase the individual income of the artisan and lead to improvement in his living conditions. The situation of the Barpali weavers had been one of almost perpetual indebtedness to cloth merchants and middlemen in the area: the weavers received advances in cash and in kind, and were forced to contract their total output to the middlemen or merchants. Because of the desirability of the cloth woven in this area the merchants were able to realize large profits while the weaving families subsisted in substandard housing on an average wage (advance) of one rupee (about 21 cent) per day. While the situation of the local Chamars (Hindi: *camar*,) or leatherworkers, was in no sense as extreme as that of the weavers, they were finding that one of their most profitable occupations was becoming less and less profitable. This was the collection of dead animals in the villages of the *thana*. Whereas removal of carcasses had been a *duty* of the Chamars alone, other low castes in the villages were now competing for the dead animals, parts of which had a ready market in Sambalpur. Thus, Chamars were either deprived of these saleable commodities or were forced to pay for them. In addition, the sale of hides to Sambalpur and the subsequent repurchase of leather by the local Chamar shoemakers, funnelled a large portion of potential local profit into the hands of the Muslim hide dealers in Sambalpur.

Socio-cultural Parameters in Directed Change

TABLE 2
FACTORS OPERATING FOR/AGAINST VEGETABLES AND POULTRY

Vegetables		Poultry	
For	Against	For	Against
Income Drought Irrigation Slack season		Income 1. Large eggs	Maintenance
Neutral ritually 1. To grow 2. To eat Varieties not traditional		Unclean ritually 1. To grow 2. To eat SANSKRITIZATION	
High castes	Tradition of Malis	POTENTIAL OCCUPATION Low castes	

Encouraged by the cooperative department of the state government, Barpali Village Service began a programme aimed at organizing the shoemaking Chamars of Barpali and providing instruction in tanning and the preparation of their own shoe leather. Although this scheme threatened to cut into the business of some of the Barpali Chamars who acted as middlemen between the village hide-collecting Chamars and the hide dealers in Sambalpur, the organization took shape and gradually grew. This growth was, however, more apparent than real, as it represented mostly simple shareholders in the cooperative organization rather than actual shoemakers. By 1956, the third year of the organization, a transition occurred rather abruptly. One of the products traditionally salvaged by the Chamars was the bones of dead animals. During the past decade there has been a steadily increasing market for processed bones as a source of fertilizer. In view of this it was decided *by the Chamars* to devote the major efforts of the organization to the collection and processing of bone for fertilizer. The organization, now consisting of at least the family head of each Chamar family in Barpali village, was registered as a cooperative by the state; the cooperative has provided a pump well for the use of all Chamar families; and bone processing equipment has been purchased to replace crushers and digesters originally loaned by the government. While in the beginning some financial assistance on the part of Barpali Village Service was required, the cooperative has repaid all debts and is now operating entirely independently of the project.

The initial project work with the weavers of Barpali, while aimed at improving the quality of their goods and raising their economic standards, was not directed toward the goal of any sort of a permanent organization. The idea of a cooperative did not arise for some years after Barpali Village Service had been successfully handling several aspects of the weavers' production and marketing operation. Essentially, the role of Barpali Village Service during these first years was to purchase the entire output of a small group of weavers, selected on the basis of their weaving ability, at the rate of three rupees for each day of labour involved. This rate was determined by the weaver himself and represented three times the average rate of payment for other local weavers not working for Barpali Village Service. The project then undertook to market these materials either through outlets in Indian cities or through private orders from the United States. Cooperation between project technicians and Indian chemical companies resulted in fast dyes of standard colours which were jointly used by the weavers before taking their yarn home for weaving. In 1957, the initial group of weavers in addition to a few more members were registered as a cooperative under the laws of the state of Orissa. Barpali Village Service had been largely responsible for this step, hoping that it might lead the group of weavers to take aver all the functions of purchasing yarns and dyes, supervision of quality, and marketing, which were then being performed by the project. In addition, it was hoped that the cooperative might be able to repay the project for at least some of its financial assistance in the beginning. Not only did this repayment fail to materialize, but the cooperative was forced to contract even larger debts to the project. At the end of 1960, the outstanding debt amounted to over thirty thousand rupees (about $ 6,300.) However, more than this amount was tied up in the cooperative's inventory. The handling of both domestic and foreign sales by the cooperative was generally unsatisfactory and required more or less constant supervision by project technicians. And finally, no consistent policy, nor even the beginnings of one, could be agreed upon by the members of the cooperative. With the withdrawal of Barpali Village Service set for the autumn of 1962, it seems reasonably certain that the weavers' cooperative will be totally unable to maintain itself as a viable organization.

Both the weavers' cooperative and the Chamars' cooperative were outgrowths on the part of Barpali Village Service to improve the economic condition of these groups of artisans and secondarily to improve product quality. A subsequent goal was the establishment of a permanent organization owned and controlled by the producers to maintain procurement and marketing functions on a joint basis for the sake of efficiency and profit to the members. In both cases the economic standards were raised through the effort of the project; even weavers not belonging to the cooperative became able in time to demand a higher rate from their middlemen. Particularly in the case of the weavers, quality control has risen markedly: and this too is reflected in the work of weavers not belonging to the cooperative. However, in terms of organizational viability, one group has succeeded to the point of becoming totally independent of the project in both finance and supervision, while the other group is hopelessly in debt and will probably collapse entirely once the supervision and technical aid of the project is withdrawn. On the basis of what factors can such a difference be explained?

In terms of the situational factors alone there appears to be more reason to expect the weavers' cooperative to succeed than the Chamars' cooperative. For instance, the weavers, by working with Barpali Village Service and later by being members of the cooperative, were assured a reasonably steady flow of orders throughout the year, their marketing was undertaken by the organization, they were encouraged to improve and widen their repertoire of types and designs of material, and a cash wage was provided by the cooperative which was two or three times that prevailing in the *thana*. On the other hand, the original work and organization among the Chamars was confined to improvement in shoemaking techniques. Not only were there few Chamars actually engaged in shoemaking, but the reservation of hides for local processing was at least a potential threat to those Chamars whose business it was to collect local hides and sell them in Sambalpur. However, there were balancing factors in both cases. The fact that the activities with the weavers had been organized within the framework of the project itself, and that Barpali Village Service had not realistically accounted for the services of its technicians in developing markets and handling orders and books, has made it difficult for the locally based organization to assume responsibility and understanding of the established pattern of operations. Likewise, through the urban and overseas contacts of the project technicians, an extensive system of external relationships was set up with which it would be difficult at best for a rural organization to cope. The positive balancing factors in the case of the Chamars' cooperative were largely associated with the change of function from shoemaking to preparation of bone meal. In the first place, this was a programme developed by the internal leadership of the organization, and it coincided with the increasing demand for fertilizer in the area as a result of the efforts of Barpali Village Service and the local community development block. In effect the function of the Chamars' cooperative was satisfaction of local demand with processed local resources, while, the weavers' local production had become involved in a completely external pattern of demand.

In the case of both cooperatives the fact that their activities corresponded with the traditional caste occupations of the membership provided a strong positive factor, and in the case of the Chamars this was reinforced by a very marked sense of caste solidarity, more highly developed among the Barpali *thana* Chamars than in other castes of the area, to the point of members subordinating their own interests to those of the cooperative and caste. The decisive differential factor in these two programmes was the way in which the activities were related to the caste structure. In the case of the Chamars, the programme was directed at a single caste group, largely localized in Barpali Village, and already having a pronounced sense of caste solidarity. On the other hand the members of the weaving cooperative, and indeed the original group of weavers worked with Barpali Village Service, were largely from outlying villages of the *thana*, and represented two different castes whose interests were not identical. The initial intent of Barpali Village Service had been to work with weavers on the basis of their skill and ability regardless of their caste affiliation, and indeed, it had at least been an implicit goal to work toward the weakening of caste differences and barriers. For two reasons the two lowest weaving castes did not become involved in the organization. First, their output was confined to plain white or coloured garments with only the simplest border designs, and second, the higher-caste weavers would have refused to work in the same organization with the untouchable Ganda weavers or the recently Sanskritized but still very low Kuli weavers. Although the two castes making up the cooperative have been able to work together in relative harmony *under* the direction of Barpali Village Service, they have recently exhibited complete inability to function together as a decision-making body. Invariably, when there are two sides to an issue for decision, all members belonging to the Bhulia caste will take one position and all Kusta weavers will take the opposite side. Beyond this there is friction in the actual operation of the cooperative because the Kusta weavers, producing cloth of handspun *tussah* silk, would ordinarily be eligible for various government rebates on the production of *khadi* (handspun, handwoven cloth). However, because the Bhulia weavers use mill-made cotton yarn in their goods, the cooperative cannot be considered a *khadi* organization, and thus all rebates are denied.

As has been pointed out elsewhere,[9] the likelihood of a cooperative in India surviving, or even developing, in a form similar to Western cooperative organizations is negligible. The concept of member-owner is alien to the Indian villager. It appears that while even economically insecure villagers are often willing to go into business for themselves,[10] they are unwilling to enter into risk-taking situations where responsibility is *shared*. That is, if they cannot be in reasonable control

---

[9]Daniel Thorner, 1961. "Prospects for Cooperation in Indian Agriculture," MSS. Paris: Ecole des Hautes Etudes.
[10]See David C. McClelland, 1961. *The Achieving Society*. Princeton: Van Nostrand, Chapter 7.

themselves as entrepreneurs, they will relinquish all opportunity for responsibility in favour of the security of an employee status. This has certainly been the case among the Chamars and weavers of Barpali as well as in other cooperative ventures encouraged by Barpali Village Service. Among the Chamars this situation has in no way hindered the development of a viable organization (although not a true cooperative) as the caste structure itself provided a framework on which to add the functions of the cooperative. Decision-making and managerial authority was naturally assumed by the already strong and effective caste leadership, and support (financial and organizational) was given by the whole caste. Active members considered themselves employees of the cooperative/caste and followed the directives of their traditional leaders.

Among the weavers, however, no such structure existed. Not only were two distinct and independent castes involved in the cooperative, but neither one of them alone had the cohesion and centralized authority of the Chamars. There are at present several other weaving cooperatives in Barpali *thana*. However, these are quite simply private businesses of individual entrepreneurs, legally registered as cooperatives in order to benefit from the preferential regulations governing this type of organization. Weaving has traditionally been a family occupation carried on in relative isolation from other weaving families in many villages dispersed throughout the area. Consequently the structure of the weaving castes has been extremely loose and with no clear patterns of authority. This, coupled with the dominant management position of Barpali Village Service in the initial stages of organizing the weavers, has resulted in *all* the members of the cooperative looking on themselves as employees ready to follow orders but none ready to assume any sort of responsibility. In spite of the project's efforts to educate the members in cooperative management, no effective leadership either joint or individual has emerged, nor has any outside individual with management skills been willing to assume responsibility for the organization.

Table 3 presents a summary of the above discussion. As in the preceding tables, the attempt is made to weight the factors operating to assure the viability of the Chamars' organization and likewise to assure the failure of the weavers' cooperative.

Conclusion: Toward Developing a Predictive Methodology

From the foregoing analyses the fact emerges that factors decisive to the acceptance or rejection of programmes of directed change may lie at any point along the socio-cultural spectrum. However, the factors do tend to cluster about institutional and/or normative nodes which are important to the recipient culture. It hardly need be said that these nodes usually do not coincide with institutional and normative nodes of an alien donor culture (in this case Euro-American). The importance of these nodal points is that they serve as cultural foci or reference points for orienting normal behaviour as well as defining deviations from traditional practice (which is the condition of an innovative programme when it is first presented). Because of their function as foci of orientation, the pure nodes are connected by extensive linkages with many other aspects of the socio-cultural system. It has been seen that the caste structure, through its linkages with the economic, occupational, and power patterns in the villages, had a *direct*

Table 3
Factors Operating For/Against Chamars' and Weavers' Cooperatives

Chamars		Weavers	
For	Against	For	Against
Resource/ need—local increased demand *Self-developed programme*	Hide Dealers Few shoemakers	*Income Marketing Steady orders*	BVS *management* 1. Finances 2. External markets 3. Programmed by BVS
Traditional occupation STRUCTURE OF CASTE 1. Solidarity 2. Leadership 3. Totality *Employee security*	Member- owner	Traditional occupation	Member- owner MIXED CASTES *No caste leadership* Family pattern of weaving

effect on every programme discussed except latrines, and that in the case of three of them (poultry, weavers' and Chamars' cooperatives) this effect was decisive. Furthermore, through ideological linkages with ritual purity, this node has far wider effect, and at this point becomes a decisive influence on reaction to the latrine programme.

While the caste structure node is of tremendous importance in determining the response to potentialities for cultural change, the material presented may have exaggerated its significance. It is not the only such node operating to facilitate or hinder the acceptance of new practices or items. Although linked with caste, ritual purity can be justified as an independent node. Likewise, the seasonal and agricultural cycle appears to represent a nodal point, particularly when its linkages with the pattern of income and expenditure are considered. Factors stemming from the organization of the family and domestic division of labour have only been mentioned here twice, but these factors have been of considerable importance in other programmes undertaken by Barpali Village Service.[11] Another node which has been significant in many of the project's programmes is village factionalism. Village factions entered into the differential acceptance of the well programme, but the problem is too complex to be dealt with in an article of this length. The problem has been outlined by the author elsewhere, and is given full treatment in a forthcoming work.[12]

What implications can be drawn from the foregoing that will be of assistance in planning programmes of directed change and in predicting their outcome? Of course, no short-cut or formula will ever be devised which can substitute for complete and detailed knowledge of the recipient culture. However, it is often impossible to gain such knowledge before the initiation of a programme of change, either through fieldwork or even from existing literature. Consequently, the administrator or his anthropological advisor must be alert for clues to important areas of the recipient culture which may be expected to have

---

[11] See Fraser *op. cit.*, especially cases 4 and 11.

[12] Fraser, *op. cit.*, 1956. Cases 1, 6 and 11; and Fraser, 1961." Barpali Village Service: A Quaker Experiment in Community Development," *Journal of Human Relations*, Vol. IX, No. 3, Spring, pp. 285-99.

significant influences on the reactions of members of the society to the attempted innovations. This must be more than an intuitive feel for the culture, or an awareness that it is somehow different from Western culture. A cultural model composed of nodes and linkages could serve to provide such clues objectively to the programme planners. It could have the initial advantage of being immediately useful in an outline form, and capable of further elaboration as the innovating group became more familiar with the recipient culture.

The construction of such a model can be accomplished in numerous ways, depending on the recipient culture itself and on the perceptiveness, training, and amount of time at the disposal of the initial and subsequent investigators. The following outline suggests some of the steps which might be useful in the preliminary identification of nodes in rural Orissa. Needless to say, this would represent only a beginning; there are other equally valid first steps and, of course, a succession of subsequent steps of increasing specificity eventually leading to a virtually complete knowledge of the culture. The following steps, then, are presented as an example of how a planner might first approach a village in such an area as Barpali *thana*:

1. What is the largest building in the area? What is it used for? Who uses it? Answers to these queries could indicate important areas of ideological culture (temples), economic (factories, storehouses), social organization (segregated usage, landlordism), etc.

2. Are there significant differences in size and type of residential dwellings? Do there appear to be distinct living areas in the village for different groups? Investigation of the bases of such differences and their significance in the village would reveal factors related to social and economic stratification, and might ramify into areas of occupational distribution and land tenure, etc.

3. What is the relative proportion of men, women, and children engaged in different observable activities? Does this proportion vary from one group to another? Does it vary according to season? Such findings would point out information about family structure such as domestic division of labour, about social stratification and occupational distribution, and about the yearly cycle of economic activity.

4. What do the villagers feel to be the "real" objectives of the outsiders in establishing a project in their locality? What kinds of changes do they think the project plans to introduce? Answers to these questions in Barpali tended to cluster around (a) the caste system; (b) land tenure; and (c) religious beliefs, all significantly related to local cultural nodes.

5. Does one group respond in a markedly different manner to the project than do other groups? Can such groups or their differential behaviour be related to previous findings about stratification, landholding, etc.?. Or can they be identified as factions operating on another basis? If factionalism is identified, consideration should be given to the desirability and implications of trying to exploit it to further programme objectives.

6. What reactions can be observed among villagers, or different groups of villagers, toward (a) the project staff; (b) other villagers or groups; (c) natural objects; and (d) strange objects? Answers to any of this group of questions, hostility, fear, whether generalized or differentiated, can be of value in bringing to light aspects of the value system (e.g., the concept of ritual purity), supernatural beliefs, expectations from external relationships, etc.

Having begun the construction of the model by isolation of nodes, the next stage in programme planning would be a careful consideration of the ways in which proposed programmes might relate to the identified nodes. On the basis of the above outline, a considerable amount of predictive evidence would be available about the six programmes discussed earlier. It should be immediately evident that because of the strong patterns of group (caste) segregation probably identifiable in all six of the steps outlined, the formation of an organization involving the cooperation of members of different groups (i.e., the weavers' cooperative) would have little chance of success. Likewise, evidence of strong organization and solidarity within a group would indicate the probability of success in fostering an organization (i.e., the Chamars' cooperative) whose functions were related to a traditional occupation of the group. The yearly cycle of seasons and of agricultural and other activities would permit acceptance of wells and of vegetable growing. The technical feasibility of wells (i.e., a high water table) and their relatively low cost should tend to give weight to a prediction of success if no negative factors appeared in other nodes. In the case of vegetable growing, the existence of a traditional gardening caste should suggest caution at least in trying to introduce the programme to other cultivators. The fact that the range of vegetables promoted in the Barpali Village Service programme did not overlap the traditionally caste-tied vegetables could certainly be considered a positive factor. Given this situation, the specific drought conditions and the recognized potential for continued cash income would constitute evidence for a fairly bright prognosis. Once the concept of ritual purity had been identified by project planners, either through the sixth step, the caste structure, or through other evidence, the latrine programme could have been considered doomed to almost certain failure. With further information on domestic division of labour and occupational patterns, this prediction would have been confirmed. Of the programmes discussed, the only one which might have been misjudged on the basis of such preliminary investigations as outlined, is the poultry programme. While certain caution signs might have been present, such as the ritual impurity of poultry raising and its relegation to definitely secondary importance among the occupations of the raisers, probably the overriding evidence would have been that the group of people aimed at were *already raising poultry.* It is probable that sufficient refinement of the working model would not have been attained early enough to take into account mechanisms for caste mobility, and the difference between incidental and routinized association with unclean objects or jobs.

The conclusions presented here are by no means new or original. Furthermore, they are relatively limited in their ability to probe the deeper, often most important, areas of a cultural system. They do represent, however, examples of the kinds of first steps that can be taken in undertaking a programme of directed change. There is a real need, particularly in community development programmes, for even such a limited type of investigation systematically carried out toward a clearly conceived analytical end. All too often development programmes having neither the resources nor the time for full-scale socio-cultural research, abandon all attempts at this sort of analysis and guide their programmes "by the seat of their pants." Perhaps the point of view respresented in this paper will stimulate further consideration and research toward the development of a precise methodology for dealing with the process of directed culture change.

McKim Marriott

10 Technological Change in Overdeveloped Rural Areas

When in America, we think of "rural areas" in remote parts of the world we are inclined to imagine rugged, crude, partly developed spaces—in the official phrase, "underdeveloped areas." It is usual, too, to think of technology as something that can be added to a rural area to develop it. I want to suggest that we will come closer to understanding the real problems of technological change in most of the world if we reverse the emphasis. From the point of view of the people in them, many rural areas are not so much underdeveloped as they are overdeveloped.

The problems of technological change in an overdeveloped area are not the same as our familiar additive problems. Rarely does technological change merely add new things; more often, it alters the pattern and the structure of people's lives. It does not just add, but creates a new structure or pattern, and often destroys an old structure or pattern. In this fact lie some of the most serious practical problems of technical change. Some problems of technological change are involved in finding the appropriate new technique, others may be involved in teaching and explaining the technique once it has been found, but major problems always await us in the overdeveloped context into which the new technique is introduced.

What I mean by technologically "overdeveloped" is the pressing of techniques up to and beyond the point of an optimum relation between man and environment. In an overdeveloped area, too many techniques are too exhaustively applied by too many people to too little land.

This phenomenon of overdevelopment affects the spread of new techniques in several ways:

(1) Development in an overdeveloped area is an old story. Much development has occurred in the past, often too much development. Techniques have reached what seems to be a static equilibrium. A new technique has little room in which to spread.

(2) Overdevelopment leads generally to tight interconnections among techniques. Thus the introduction of additional new techniques may disrupt or require readjustments in many old techniques.

(3) Technology in an old overdeveloped area is likely to have become interconnected with many patterns of personal and social behaviour—groupings, ideas, beliefs. Introduction of a new technique may be followed by acceptance or rejection according to criteria which are not directly technical at all but social, cultural, and political.

(4) Finally, overdeveloped areas have technological problems and their people know that they have them. Technological change itself is likely to have become an institution with a regular social organization, national or even international. The spread of new techniques will therefore be affected not only by the local situation, but also by the culture, society, and politics of the people who introduce the new techniques. Those who introduce changes may have to deal personally with all of these four effects of technological overdevelopment.

I will discuss these four problems of technological change as they appear in one overdeveloped rural area of India. Problems in other places will not be identical, but Indian overdevelopment demonstrates, in extreme form, the kinds of problems which are likely to attend the introduction of technical changes anywhere.

The observations which follow were made in remote villages of the Ganges plain about one hundred miles from the capital at New Delhi. The immediate area had undergone no industrial development and there were no obvious signs of any programme for technological change. The rural population numbered six hundred per square mile, the people being jammed into tight little villages. Wheat, barley, and peas supplied most of subsistence by means of what appeared to be very primitive techniques. The area was so conservative, and my presence so frightening, that I was politely thrown out of three villages before I was finally allowed to settle in a fourth.

A Long History of Technological Development

Although this area had at first seemed to be very backward and unchanging, I was struck soon afterwards by evidence of a great amount of recent development. Indeed, the very existence of a population problem implied that there had been extensive technological expansion and change.

I was impressed by evidence of American influences—influences much older than those of Point IV. Farmers were cultivating potatoes, maize, tomatoes, and a strain of improved cotton all of them imported from America. I was surprised, too, to find many other crops in the village which I knew were not native to the Ganges valley. Carrots, originally from Central Asia, were being eaten in huge quantities by men and beasts instead of the native turnip. Mustard oilseed plants were crowding wheat and barley in the grain fields; villagers told me that there had been none two generations ago. Sugarcane of an improved variety was being cultivated in my village as a valuable small cash crop, while it had become the only crop in other villages beside the canal a few miles away.

I also noted that certain mechanical innovations were being used in this seemingly static agricultural village. A home-made seed drill was being used for sowing wheat in place of the broadcasting by hand which had once been traditional. Big hand-cranked, rotary iron chaff-cutters were cutting half the fodder fed to the village animals. A gasoline-powered flour mill was grinding one-third of the village grain and was beginning to replace the hand-operated stone querns formerly used in every house. There were also a few modern jim-cracks: flashlights, kerosene lanterns, a phonograph, a japanese banjo, a harmonium, European-style shoes and shirt-tails.

There was all this evidence of technological change both in crops and in machines, but it stood out against a background of poverty, malnutrition, poor health, and extreme inefficiency in most as the essential agricultural activities. Ploughing, for example, was done with great labour using a three-inch iron point set in a wooden share. Irrigation required drawing up one bucket at a time: a week's labour by three men and two oxen was needed to irrigate a single acre of wheat. Sickles the size of a man's hand were used for harvesting all the grain, and the grain was threshed under the slow treading of the hooves of oxen.

The change which had occurred had not penetrated very deeply, but had gone far enough to permit a slow growth of population in the village during the past century. There is now scarcely a spare square foot of land to be found. In the present generation, pastures and forest plots have all been cleared and sown with grain. While I was in the village, the last bits of interstitial land—roadways, cremation grounds, shade trees, gravel pits, and the like—were leased out for cultivation. This was clearly desperation. Agricultural development had now gone so far that every new organic element is completely extracted from the soil once, twice, or many times each year. Almost every plant is fully used. Grass and weeds are carefully dug up, roots and all, to be used as animal fodder. All useable leaves are stripped off the trees, systematically. The entire land lies absolutely bare and brown for three months of each year; the air, too, is brown, for it is full of the precious soil, dried and blown about as dust. I learned that one family of every ten had been compelled to leave the village in this generation in search of food. Yet many economists have represented this generation in northern India as one of relative "agricultural prosperity."

Despite obvious crises, there is great hope to be derived from knowledge of the history of technological development. Without anyone growing crops recommended by the grovernment, without anyone having seen movies or slides or listened to radio propaganda for higher food production, many changes and much expansion of food supply have actually come about. Through the centuries, quietly and without urging, the peasant has made many changes on his own. And the changes have stuck. Sticking is surely one criterion of effective technological change.

Technological Change in Overdeveloped Rural Areas

INTERCONNECTIONS OF TECHNIQUES

There is hope in this picture of past development, and yet there is also great difficulty in adding anything more to the total complex to technological equipment used by such a people. To make room for anything new, one would first have to uproot something old. To improve on something old, one would have at least to modify its older form. Every improvement requires a minimum of experimentation, but the technology of an overdeveloped area allows very little free room for experimentation. An overdeveloped village has room only to subsist. It has no room to try, and certainly none in which to err; the margin is too small.

What is more, each part of an overdeveloped technology is likely to have come to have positive connections with many other vital parts of the total technology. If one incautiously adds some new element, not just one old part but many connected parts of the old technology will be affected, sometimes for the worse as much as for the better.

New items and new techniques may succeed if they prove viable in the total context of interconnections. I have already noted several instances of successful additions to the village's repertory of crops. Potatoes and carrots, for example, replaced cotton and turnips. As human food, both potatoes and carrots proved to be popular substitutes for turnips, and were in time favoured far beyond them. Carrots found favour among the livestock and have become an important fodder crop. Potatoes can be preserved and sold for cash, making it possible for the peasant to buy much of the cotton which formerly occupied his potato fields. What had seemed to be mere additions to the technology were thus in fact replacements. Most additions of new crops must become replacements, for resources of land, labour, and water in an overdeveloped area are strictly limited.

Another more complex instance of successful replacement, this in the recent past, is the replacement of an old native variety of sugarcane by an improved new variety. The new variety, which yields much more sugar to the acre, is thin-stalked and very tough. It is so tough, in fact, that it cannot be properly crushed by the old wooden presses which were formerly used. Its successful replacement of the old cane depended upon the introduction of a new heavy iron cane crusher. Fortunately, iron crushers were introduced at the same time as the improved cane. The improved cane brought part of its context along with itself. Sugar yields were increased materially, enough to pay the increased cost of renting the iron crushers, and enough to provide slightly higher profits than before.

Carrots, potatoes, and improved sugarcane were successful because they fitted into the old contexts of the items which they replaced, or where they did not fit, they provided good, realizable, economical alternatives. Because they successfully met the criterion of total adaptation to the context of an overdeveloped technology, these successes were achieved without the intervention of any government officials, without consulting high-priced experts, without the necessity of anyone's travelling halfway around the world.

These successes point the way to further successful change, but in themselves they do not begin to touch some of the most desperate technological needs of the village. Despite the ready presence of what seem to be obviously better techniques, despite explicit study, despite energetic government propaganda, the desperate problem of making further increases in food production remains unsolved. To get more food, three necessary technical changes have been stressed above all others: more manure, better seed, and more water for irrigation. Technicians hold that food production in India could be increased as much as a hundred per cent if all three of these technical changes were made. But the peasants of my overdeveloped village, like the people of most Hindu villages, have not seen the light. Let us see why they must look upon the proposed improvement so darkly.

Manure, for instance. Farmers are urged to put more of it on their fields. The peasant farmer in my village knows the value of manure very well, all popular writing to the contrary notwithstanding. And here let me incidentally indicate the problem of obtaining reliable information about peasant life. There is a common belief among foreigners that the Chinese, like the Europeans, appreciate the value of manure and particularly of human night-soil, while the Hindus, for some religious reason, do not. Nothing could be further from the truth. Most of my farmers took special pains to defecate in their own fields, walking as far as a mile to do so. I was many times cordially requested by one or another Hindu farmer to please perform my natural functions in his field, so as to enrich it. The manure of the bovine is also treasured and is actually worshipped. Twice a year each farmer pays to have his household trash and his surplus animal dung carried to his distant fields. Knowledge of and belief in the value of manure are clearly present; no educational campaign is needed.

But remember that the elements of an overdeveloped technology are likely to be interconnected. Manure in this village is connected as one of a set of alternatives with many other possible uses of animal dung. Manure competes therefore with cooking, especially with the cooking of clarified butter (*ghee*), which requires slow-burning dung as fuel; it also competes with plastering a house, which requires a plaster made of dung, and even with smoking the hubble-bubble, which requires a sweet dung fire in the bowl of the pipe. The supply of manure has a direct connection with population and with the pressure of population on land. Because of pressure on the land for food, forest land and scrub jungle were cleared and turned into cultivated fields. Thirty years ago, those same lands had furnished free and ample fuel wood for cooking many families' meals on the village hearths. Now that the wood supply has been cut away, other sources of fuel must be found. Only dried leaves and the stalks of certain crops are left. And dung. More and more dung has had to be expanded to fill the gap in cooking needs left by the loss of wood as fuel. Less than half the dung remains to be used as manure for the fields which need it more desperately with each passing year.

One reformer about a generation ago discovered that the manure problem was connected with cooking needs. He tried to solve the problem by inventing a kind of insulated box that would keep milk almost at the simmering point for an hour or two after it had been brought to the boil on a quick fire of crop refuse. That device should have permitted housewives to manufacture clarified butter without burning precious dung cakes. The reformer worked hard to get some boxes made in a city and then showed many village housewives how to use the box. But village carpenters did not know how to make the box, and so the idea did not spread. When the first boxes broke they were not repaired, and housewives went back to burning dung cakes. The change failed because the technological problem was not solved in its full context.

Better seed is a second main road to greater food production. Why have so few hungry villagers travelled that road? The native wheat seed, used universally in my village, produces only half the yield that the available improved seed will produce, given good conditions. The improved varieties are hardy ones, carefully selected and tested over many years. They are "available" in the sense of being present in nearby government seed stores. Peasants know about the stores and know about the seed. Why then do they not rush to get and use the improved varieties? The replacement of an old, inefficient seed by an improved seed of the same plant would seem to be the simplest kind of technological change, a change so simple that one might easily ignore the complexities of the total context. How could there be elaborate technical repercussions from so simple a change? But we are discussing an intensely overdeveloped technology in which there is no waste, in which most organic elements are exploited to the last calorie. In such a tightly-knit technology there can be no change, not even the smallest, which does not have repercussions.

Let me list some of the objections which farmers in my village, and in other nearby villages, have raised against the improved wheat seed. It is true, they said, that if the Lord pleases, one will get a better weight of fat wheat from the field sown with the government's improved seed: the yield in weight is really very good. One or two farmers had tried it. However, they had no intention of doing so again. The operator of the seed store was an impossible man. He gave the seed at a low enough rate of interest but he demanded that it be paid back on a certain date, which might not be at all convenient if one had other debts to pay after the harvest. What was most unreasonable, the seed store operator demanded that the seed should be grown and returned pure, not mixed with the barley, peas, gram, and oil seeds that guaranteed against complete crop failure in a bad wheat season. Aside from these impossible conditions governing the loan and use of the seed, look at the resulting crop. The grain is indeed big—so big and tough that the women cannot grind it well in the old stone flour mills. Dough made from the new flour is difficult to knead and hard to bake into good bread. The new bread, which is all a poor farmer would have to eat, does not taste like the good old bread. It is flat and uninteresting (the explanation being in part, of course, that it does not contain that potpourri of barley, peas, gram and mustard seed that "wheat" contained in the old days). Next, look at the cows and bullocks! They do not like to eat the straw of the new wheat; they will die of hunger if we grow it. The straw is worthless, too, for thatching roofs. It does not even make a good fire to warm our hands in winter.

An improved wheat seed thus does not appear to the Hindu farmer as a simple addition, or a simple replacement or improvement on one item of his technology. The new seed brings along with it a whole new plant; the many parts of the plant and their many uses lead to an unknown series of threatening consequences. When techniques are so tightly interconnected we must admit the wisdom of the Hindu farmer's conservatism. He rightly feels that even small alterations in his precarious, overdeveloped technology may lead to catastrophe. Somehow, the peasant's legitimate technical fears must be answered by the innovator. Only by taking the larger technological context into account can the introducer of new techniques claim that he is acting responsibly. Only when he does so is he likely to be operating effectively—introducing changes that will not raise more problems than they solve, changes that will stick.

Social and Cultural Connections of Techniques

Considering how to get more water to irrigate the crops—the third main road to greater food production—brings us to another kind of observation about overdeveloped technologies: that the elements of technology tend to be tightly connected not only with one another, but also with other aspects of rural life which are not technological at all. Thus the sacred cow cannot be manipulated without regard for her position in

Hindu belief and social custom. Thus, techniques of agriculture, since they occupy so much time in the total lives of Hindu peasants, often have a direct and important effect on social groupings. People's developed attitudes towards each other and people's developed beliefs may be so deeply involved in technological matters that possible advantages of a new technique may be outweighed by the threat of personal and social disruption.

I shall cite only one example of this principle from the field of irrigation. Reformers of Indian agriculture, both private and governmental, have long attempted to stimulate wider use of a mechanical irrigation device known as the Persian wheel. The PW is a device for raising water from a dug well by means of an endless belt of pots on a rope, or more recently, steel buckets on a chain. Its gears are operated by a camel or an ox. It can raise about five times as much water in twenty-four hours as can an ordinary well which is operated by drawing up one leather bucketful of water at a time. The PW is common through most of Punjab, but its distribution stops rather suddenly about forty miles north of my village. A large number of PWs, which had been installed a few miles to the west twenty years ago by an agricultural reformer, now lie unused and broken. Why does use of the PW stop where it does? Why is it not used in every place where the water level in the well is sufficiently close to the surface of the ground? There are, of course, real technical problems of construction, finance, and provision of facilities for repair of the PWs. More than that, there are serious problems of social organization, law and supernatural belief. The PW is such a valuable and expensive investment, and has such power to affect a large plot of land, that it requires cooperation among several peasant families to make its use profitable. The cooperating families who have adjacent fields must agree on terms of investment, and later on terms for the use of the water, for sharing the costs of repairs, etc. In those western parts of Punjab where the PW is most at home, the system of land tenure has had to be reshaped, making the block of fields around each well rather than the lands surrounding a central residential site the unit of tax assessment. A new type of ownership of fractional shares in water rights, along with rules for buying and selling, borrowing and renting water, have had to be worked out so that all the scattered fields of a water owner will be irrigated. Over and beyond these legal problems of controlling the well that has a PW, there arise special social problems within the working group of people who will operate it. To bring real profit on the investment, PWs in many places have to be worked twenty-four hours a day. Someone has to sit up all night prodding the ox or camel around the towpath. Many Hindu villagers believe that the dark fields are populated by thieves, ancestral ghosts, and dangerous animals. To offset such fears, to provide for taking turns on the PW, and to organize some control over use of the precious water, it has been necessary for farmers in west Punjab to split up their houses and build them right beside their wells. This splitting-up of houses conflicts sharply with the scheme of village organization which is usual near my village in the upper Ganges plain. There all houses are crowded into the smallest possible space at one point in the centre of the village's fields. My villagers looked to their old, fortress-like plan as offering them maximum security in a threatening world. The old laws of house-building, too, have until recently discouraged the drastic rearrangement of dwellings that the PW would demand. If the PW were to be introduced effectively, provision would have to be made for solving the problems of law, social structure, and belief that are directly involved.

Such involvement of non-technical elements in the technology of an overdeveloped area may be stated as a general truth. Sometimes problems of social organization may retard the adoption of technical change, sometimes they may speed it, and occasionally they may be approximately neutral. But they are always likely to be involved. They demand to be considered before a large effort at introducing any specific technical change is launched.

Thus far I have suggested that (1) much technological change can occur and has occurred in the overdeveloped areas of the world that now appear to be static; (2) any one technical item tends to be connected with many other parts of the total technology; and (3) technical matters may have very important connections with wholly non-technical matters of social organization and the like.

Technological Change as a Political Institution

We move now to the fourth point, that in overdeveloped areas technological development itself has often already become something of an institution. Villagers and government people both have rather definite ideas about technological change in general and about specific new items of technology in particular. Development in such a nation as India has become a very well-developed institution: definite people are concerned with the business of development and villagers are coming to have definite expectations about such developers. The question of development has come to be mixed with questions of power and status.

When I sought out my remote village in 1951 and casually settled there, I had not heard anything of the American technical assistance programme later called Point IV. I was astonished at what my villagers told me. I simply said I was a student from America who had come to learn how they lived. They were not only convinced that something like Point IV was sure to happen, but seeing me in a jeep were further convinced that I was, personally, the first wave of the American Empire. Just as the British had begun their conquest of India by seizing the island of Bombay two hundred years ago, so I had begun my conquest with their village, some told me in all seriousness. The government of India had called me to solve the problems of change that the government could not solve by itself; or, conversely, Pandit Nehru had taken a big loan of grain from America, and I was here, in the conventional manner of village grain-lenders, to make a credit-rating of the debtor, perhaps to seize all grain from the coming harvest as repayment. Many villagers predicted what would happen next. Two hundred to five hundred Americans were already on the way or were in Delhi even now. I would take over the village houses, buy or seize (by virtue of my secret weapons) the best, or all of the village lands. I would then carry on all agricultural work of the village by machines, harvesting the crops and disposing of the grain. Families would cease to exist: everyone would now have to eat at a great cafeteria and sleep only in hotels, as they do in America. Many villagers thought that they might have more food to eat, but just what would the food be? Would it be those strange loaves of English bread? Would they be forced to eat the forbidden beef? All the children would, of course, be taken from their parents and raised apart in schools as in America—this they knew. Would I pay their wages, and how much? Incidentally, I would handle all law suits, dispense criminal justice, abolish all the old Hindu rites and ceremonies, and deliver moral lectures from time to time, for—and this phrase summed up matters pretty well for many villages—I was their Mother and Father.

Most persistently through the following months, villagers whispered among themselves that I was about to introduce a revolution in agriculture by means of machines. For instance, they hoped to have the secret device which had made American farmers so wealthy—four times the amount of surface land, to be achieved by digging a basement under the fields and by erecting two or three stories of artificial fields, supported on poles above the present ones. That is how Americans get such remarkable yields per acre. On a more credible and practical level, villagers often begged me for seeds of strange American plants and for the most minute descriptions of how the technology of agriculture, and all the other necessary works of like, were carried on in America. For them, these were tales of wonder and delight that had to be repeated hundreds of times. Such a response to the mere presence of one official-looking person might be understood in part as an expression of courtesy and respect. From their reactions, one might also easily conclude that villagers in the old, overdeveloped village of India are psychologically prepared for technological change on a grand scale, that they are ready for an accelerated programme of technical assistance.

Some are prepared for change in the sense that they have fantastic hopes and wild expectations. Others are prepared in the sense that they feel they are being attacked. Many are prepared in the sense that they know enough of the outside world to realize that their own technology might be changed for the better. But most see change as something that is to be handed down to them from above, as indeed has been often attempted in the past. Villagers in this overdeveloped area know that their technology is precarious and are therefore conservative; confronted with the enormous consequences of technological change, they can only throw themselves upon the paternalistic mercy of the innovator, making him totally responsible for the possible effects of his great power on them. These are the kinds of attitudes that may shape the innovator's role in villagers' eyes. For the introducer of change who is hoping that there will be some modest efforts on the part of the peasants themselves, such attitudes and such a role present both difficult obstacles and interesting opportunities.

Without discussing some of the possible ways of handling such attitudes towards change, I do want to point out that these are attitudes of dependency—attitudes which are justly famous in India as *ma-bap-ism*, the "mother and father" attitude. This *ma-bap* dependency is a source of continual distress to Indian workers on projects of technological change. Gandhi's philosophy of technological change by pure self-help is a direct challenge to the passive fantasies of *ma bap* attitudes. Gandhi knew, and his followers today know, that mother and fatherism not only reduces people to a rather undignified condition of apathy, but prevents effective mobilization of energies to put new techniques across in a practical sense. Gandhi's programme of change through self-help is one on which tens of thousands of social workers are operating in India today. They aim to develop agriculture not on a great industrialized scale but rather on a scale that will be within the technological competence, knowledge, and control of ordinary, poor, illiterate farmers. Since the country is poor in industrial resources, really effective changes in techniques must be those which are desired, understood, and willingly carried out by the masses of peasants without elaborate superior direction. In this connection, they have talked a good deal about "cottage industries," and worked to get them started.

Now whether or not one believes that the Gandhian programme can solve all the technological problems of raising production in overdeveloped areas, it is important to realize

Technological Change in Overdeveloped Rural Areas

that peasant feelings may be strongly in sympathy with certain parts of Gandhian doctrine. Peasants want to be in control of their technology, old or new. They react with passive mother and fatherism when they are threatened with the power of a new technology which is completely out of their control.

Let me illustrate this by describing villagers' attitudes towards certain technological changes which have been markedly outside their spheres of knowledge and control. Great mechanical changes have passed over their society, bringing ruin to many old ways and slight or no profit to the peasant. Irrigation is one of the most striking instances: canals and tube-wells are capable of bringing vast supplies of water to the thirsty crops, yet villagers of the upper Ganges plain often look on canals and tube-wells with deep distrust. In many places a sizeable proportion of villagers are not willing to use water from canals and tube-wells that stand at their very doors, or will use it only when their land taxes are increased to the point that they must grow a crop of sugarcane, which requires more irrigation than an old-fashioned well can produce. The canal, then, seems to them to be a coercive device by which the government can extract more work and more money from the peasants. The canal is bad, many villagers say, because all must pay higher taxes to support the canal which distributes its water very inequitably. There is usually fighting among the farmers who have to use water from the same canal distributary channel, the ones at the far end complaining that most water is taken by those at the near end. What is more, the canal agents are said universally to demand small bribes from the farmers, who are helpless to resist them. The farmers cannot send up complaints against the petty officials who are exploiting them without incurring great cost, and without perhaps suffering ultimate reprisals which may be far worse than the day-to-day costs and troubles suffered in the past. Tube-wells are even worse since entire control of the tube-well's water lies in the hands of one outsider who operates the electric pump machinery. He normally takes large personal fees for giving the water on time and in full quantity, which raises the cost of tube-well water to an amount more than double the government's rate. Operators of tube-wells are generally suspected of being criminals or of being in league with criminals, since they not only have power and take bribes, but move about the rural areas in trucks, sometimes at night, and associate with literate urban people of the landlord class.

What villagers often say about the new technology then is that it is operated by corrupt people who have come to prey upon them, the ignorant and helpless ones who are forbidden to open a canal lock and do not know how to run an electric pump. Villagers feel much the same way about tractors, gasoline-powered flour mills, and hospitals. All of these complicated devices are beyond the range of their social control. The mechanic, the canal agent, the clerk, and the doctor are able to exploit the peasant without check or redress and are therefore immoral. The range of activities within which the villager can exercise some moral control is, to be sure, a very narrow one; this range may not even be as large as the village itself. It is more likely to be the range of the family, or the clan, or the ward of the village. This, then, is one reason why in India Gandhi's programme of small-scale industry—industry on the scale of the family or small group of families—makes sense to villagers. If enthusiasm and self-acting energy are to be mobilized from villagers in programmes of technological change, then this problem must be considered: that large-scale centralized programmes are doomed to a minimal or negative response so long as they leave the villager dependent upon persons who are utterly beyond his familial type of group controls. Public health, medicine, improved seeds, more water, and fertilizers, must somehow be worked into the area of social control within the village where they will be handled morally and for the maximal good of all. Or, conversely, village organization must be trained upward to handle such new jobs; it is not now competent. What is clear is that the villager's dependency cannot be realized in fact. The outsider can never really bring prosperity to the village in the simple, one-directional way in which a mother and father feed and clothe a child.

Technological change in overdeveloped areas has stimulated not only latent dependent attitudes and several competing philosophies, but also regular social institutions with their own structures of rank and power. Such institutions have made deep inroads into the structure of government. Government is, of course, the biggest mother and father of them all, one principal source, in fact, of mother and fatherism—although my villagers were more apt to refer to government agencies obscenely as their "step-mothers" or their "mothers-in-law." Indian government officials especially deputed to create development and change are legion. Their agency is being extended downward so that many a village now falls within the sphere of a whole hierarchy of development officers, development inspectors, development leaders, development trainees, etc. Many of these developers were selected for their political work during the independence struggle. Few have yet been able to do much beyond the writing of programmes and slogans. Most lack any technical knowledge, and few are competent in the social and administrative techniques which would be essential to transcend the inherent handicaps of a government department in the rural countryside. Most serious of all, these developers have until recently lacked material resources. National planning and foreign aid will bring some of the material resources with which to carry out the programmes that the regular officialdom has been dreaming of for years. But new development projects in many lands such as India cannot and will not be operated entirely by the local persons who had formerly functioned as regular administrative officials. To the extent that development projects import outside experts and hire technicians, who are not regular officials, they will be setting up a development bureaucracy which rivals the regular bureaucracy. Cutting around the regular officials does not, however, abolish them; the regular administration will be there carrying on its work long after any temporary, special staff has gone. Diplomacy in this difficult competitive situation may have a large influence on the ultimate success and spread of the new techniques which are introduced. Potentially the situation is fraught with jealousy; either side may try to discredit the other's claim to be the real leader of successful change. I know of one great development project in India where rivalry between the temporary but effective development workers inside the project and the ineffective regular officials outside it has led to discontent and wrangling on a scale which has threatened to cripple the technical work. Solution of such intergroup problems of power is not just a matter to be settled by directives of higher policy, but one requiring administrative adjustment and day-to-day good politics on all levels.

Technological change in overdeveloped rural areas implies a redevelopment, a restructuring of patterns. The course of that redevelopment may be determined by the pre-existing technology of the rural people, by the way in which redevelopment is connected with the rest of rural social life and culture and by the way in which those who introduce new techniques manage the problems of their own peculiar structure of power.

Morris E. Opler

11 Cultural Context and Population Control Programmes in Village India

There has been a good deal of discussion, both within and outside India, of population growth, population control, and their relationship to India's economic development. Often opinions about the advisability of foreign aid or estimates of the possibility of industrialization and the time required for it hinge on judgements regarding India's ability to control demographic factors. It is well-known that the Indian government is concerned about overpopulation and that relatively large sums have been included in the present five-year plan to disseminate birth control information and to experiment with methods for achieving family limitation. Many of the proposals seem to assume that it is mainly ignorance and poverty which stand in the way of a solution and that if simple, direct educational techniques can be devised to bring knowledge to the local level and if a cheap, effective method of birth control can be taught, general acceptance and progress are assured.

It is true, of course, that ignorance and poverty are extremely important in the situation. With poverty and crowding goes a lack of privacy and facilities which make it very difficult to carry out the directions of a family planning adviser. The illiteracy which is usually linked with poverty prevents the use of written instructions and puts a premium on expensive and slow methods of personal contact. Yet, too often the analyses and the plans which see ignorance and poverty as the prime obstacles assume that there is a vacuum of need and receptivity which can be filled once these first barriers are overcome. Actually, there is no facet of Indian life where there are more profound and solid convictions than in the area of procreation and family life. It is only by taking into account this realm of practice and belief that those who are concerned with population control can appreciate the currents of thought and action which can aid or hinder them and which they will have to utilize, counter, bypass, or ignore.

Opinion varies concerning how important a knowledge of cultural factors is to the solution of practical problems. There are those who believe the involvement of administrators and planners with complicated social science data leads only to excessive timidity and postponement of decisive action. They argue that a technological or economic break-through or a firm directing hand forces whatever adjustment is necessary in ideology and customary usage. Others argue just as stoutly that the inability or reluctance of planners to take deeply rooted, traditional practices and convictions into account deprives them to sources of support for their programmes and blinds them to centres of resistance for which they could be prepared.

Without entering directly into the debate at this point, I should like to present material about family life and population control in a village of north central India. The village in question, which we shall call Madhopur, is located in the Jaunpur district of the state of Uttar Pradesh. The great majority of the residents of the village are Hindus. The Muslims number only seventy-nine. They are believed to be descendants of converts of Islam during Mohammedan rule. Whether or not this is true, they carry out Hindu practices in many of their activities, and even their religious behaviour is influenced by Hinduism. The material upon which this highly condensed resume is based was collected by me and by associates in the Cornell University India Programme from 1947 to 1957. From our own comparative work and from the literature, we know that many of the traits and views described are found throughout most of the rural sections of India. I leave it to the reader and, hopefully, to the planner to decide how much of this general picture is pertinent to the programmes which are now being initiated.

The particular community we are considering has a population of about two thousand people. The actual number in residence fluctuates. Most of the time approximately one hundred men of the village are involved in outside employment, primarily in urban centres. They seldom sever their village ties and often return seasonally to aid when agricultural work is heaviest. There is a movement of women in and out of the village, too, girls leave the village in marriage, and married daughters return to visit their parental homes. As this suggests, there is a village exogamy and patrilocal residence, girls are expected to leave the village at marriage and to become identified with their husbands' families. As we shall see, there is a strong accent on the importance of the male and of the male line. Traditionally, property has been inherited by males, and this practice persists in ignorance or defiance of recently enacted inheritance laws which entitle the widow and daughters to inherit equally with the sons.

Another prominent feature of the social organization is the joint family. Not only do sons remain in the village of the father after marriage but, if possible, they continue to share the same household. In fact, it is considered a serious affront to the father for a son to live separately from him. It is more common for brothers to separate after death of the father, but even here it is thought desirable that they remain together. In 1956, of 316 families in the village 211 were joint. Of these, 149 were composed of males of more than one generation and their families, and sixty-two were made up of brothers who had cast their lot together. The elementary, or nuclear, families of the village numbered 105. Not only was there a larger number of joint families than elementary families, but it must also be remembered that the joint families are on the average larger. Consequently well over two-thirds of the people live under the influence of a joint family system. Moreover, some elementary families exist by necessity rather than by choice. These are cases where a solitary individual is the sole representative of a line or where a line has shrunk as a result of deaths or the failure to produce male issue. In fact, the latter exigency is one of the gnawing fears in Indian thought. It should also be remembered that the term "joint family" indicates more than simply living under one roof. It connotes that land and property are held jointly and that a manager (*malik*) acts in business matters for the whole group. It means that a common kitchen and storeroom are maintained and that the women of the household share the domestic labour. It implies that the children of the household are entitled to the affection and support of all and can expect equivalent treatment and education according to sex. Because there is so much loose and unfounded talk about the disappearance of the joint family in India, one further observation may be in order. As a result of the death of the father who has been the nucleus of a joint family or because of disagreements between brothers or their wives, joint families are often dissolved. Yet, because of the marriage of sons and their continued residence with their fathers, it is just as common to find joint families becoming newly established. A quarrel which destroyed a joint family is more dramatic and conspicuous than a number of uneventful conventional cases of patrilocal residence. Consequently, observers, especially foreign observers are sharply conscious of such disruptions and have been predicting the imminent disappearance of the joint family for some seventy-five years.

Because the central and state governments of India have shown concern about excessive population growth and are providing funds and personnel for family limitation programmes, it is sometimes assumed that the people as a whole are worried about population size and are prepared to welcome birth control programmes for patriotic reasons. The thinking of national leaders and of a highly educated urban elite should not be confused with the outlook of the villager. India is a country of intense regionalism and local separatism. Until recently India was subject to foreign rule, and independence and national unity were realized only yesterday. Americans can identify prominent Indian national leaders more readily than can most Indian villagers. Even national elections are contested locally on village issues. Consequently, it is scarcely realistic to expect that population size will be thought of as a national problem or that the dimensions of the question will be anything but local or personal. In fact, perceptions, because they are so local and circumscribed, often belie statistics. For instance, despite the fact that the village population has greatly increased in the last fifty years, some villagers have actually told us that they think the population is decreasing. They claim that there are more deaths than there used to be and that families are smaller, and they point to certain lines that are dying out. A person who belonged to a large family which became segmented, who becomes more conscious of death as he grows older and his responsibilities in death rites multiply, and who hears continual lament about lines without male issue, is likely to form such an opinion. Pressure on land, which should have been a clue to population growth, was often explained instead as a consequence of the rapacity of the landowning caste or the failure of land reform programmes. Even when population growth was recognized as a problem, the blame was projected upon others. Members of one caste conveniently tended to see other castes growing too fast and acting incontinently. Seldom did caste fellows see themselves as the culprits or even see themselves involved. This inability to conceive of a national problem and the reluctance to accept responsibility or even to admit involvement on the local level increase the possibility that lip service to population control programmes is likely to outstrip genuine participation in them.

One of the factors which cannot be ignored in discussing family size or population growth in India is early marriage. Here a distinction must be made between marriage and the initiation of sexual relations between husband and wife. Prepubertal marriage in India is common; pre-pubertal cohabitation is rare. Also, there is considerable variation in the age of marriage according to caste. The general pattern is something like this: the marriage of children, especially of daughters, is a solemn and, indeed, a religious duty. So strong is this feeling that persons without daughters sometimes symbolically participate in the giving away of a girl in marriage. Parents and grandparents are apprehensive until this obligation is discharged. In a country where the span of life is short and where widespread sickness and disaster strike suddenly, they feel relieved if they have performed their function early. In addition, they are particularly anxious about the prospects of the daughters of the household. In a situation where marriage is an arrangement between families and where a woman's sphere is traditionally restricted to domestic work and to sharing the caste work of her husband, it is absolutely essential to arrange a secure future for her in a household to which she will go in marriage. In spite of the recent law which sets a minimum marriage age of fifteen years for girls and eighteen years for boys, most of the low-caste girls are married between the ages of five and ten, and most of the boys are wed when slightly older. Among the high-caste groups, which do not permit widow remarriage, the unions take place when the girls are twelve years old or a little older and when the boys are approximately fifteen years old. The marriage rite is held at the home of the bride; and if the girl is immature, the groom and his marriage party return to their homes without her. She may, however, come for a token visit to her husband's home and may come to his home to live and work for several years much as a daughter of the household without intimate relations or much contact with her husband. These practices take account of the fact that marriage means a totally new environment for the girl and affirm the belief that she can become best adjusted to it by coming to it when she is young and malleable. Whatever the arrangement, it is very likely that the young husband and wife will not be allowed to have intimate relations until the girl is mature. Even so, the young couple are very likely to begin living as man and wife somewhat earlier than their counterparts in Western cultures. There are various other rationalizations and sentiments which tend to justify and promote early marriage, such as that India has a hot climate in which young people mature quickly and that parents and grandparents have a natural wish to see their grandchildren before they die.

There is, however, especially in the contemporary setting, an important countercurrent to early marriage. Because of the esteem for the male, the dowry in marriage goes to the family of the groom. The amount is based on the status and prestige of the family of the boy and is increasingly becoming related to his degree of education. This, of course, is associated with his potential earning capacity, it is assumed that a more highly educated youth will command a better position and salary. But education takes time, and the more highly educated grooms are certain to be older on the average. Their brides will also be older, for there should not be too great an age difference between mates; and though the groom should be better educated as well as older than his bride, there should not be too great a discrepancy between the two in education either. Thus it is likely that the drive for education is doing more to advance the age of marriage than are legal enactments. Nevertheless, it is very difficult to depart too widely from the prevailing practices in regard to age of marriage. If relatives of some eligible girl have not asked for the hand of a boy in marriage by what is considered a reasonable time, it is assumed that the young man must have some defect or that the record of his family is wanting in some particular. If the marriage of a girl is not arranged by the time she is mature or shortly thereafter, her desirability may be suspect and, moreover, the list of males who are eligible and still available steadily shrinks. Recently the family of one young man who had reached the age of eighteen without marrying, instead of receiving a dowry, had to pay two hundred rupees to arrange a marriage.

It is all very well to talk about population control and the right of the husband and wife to determine whether they can afford to have children, but any careful study of village life impresses upon one the degree to which women are conditioned to see their success and their destiny in terms of procreation. An older woman meeting a younger one says: "May you be fruitful." "Get a good husband." "May you have sons." "May your family grow and increase." Even anger and curses point to the same values. One of the most baneful things one woman can say to another is: "May your children die." In interviews both men and women stated that the mark of a good wife was to bear children, especially boys, and to be faithful. Consequently, once marriage relations are initiated, the most fervent hope of the young woman is that she prove her worth to her husband's family by producing a healthy male child. She knows very well that she will have little standing in her husband's home until she bears him a son. Nothing is more frightening to her than the spectre of barrenness. The word of a barren woman is the same as the term used for a parasite on a tree. It is seldom that a young woman escapes emotional disturbance if she has not become pregnant within five years of marriage. On the other hand, we noted a number of cases of childless women who had constantly complained of chronic ill health or persecution by malignant spirits, who miraculously recovered health, poise, and confidence after giving birth to a son. The practical reasons for this attitude on the part of the young wife are not difficult to find. The birth of a son entitles a woman to respect and status and exempts her from much hard work. She and her baby are likely to be pampered for some time after parturition. Henceforth she is referred to through the name of her child; she becomes "the mother of so-and-so."

The woman who bears no children receives markedly different treatment and lives in a different atmosphere. Among the low castes, where divorce is permitted, barrenness usually terminates in divorce. Among the high-caste groups, which do not permit divorce, most cases of polygyny in the village of which we could learn occurred because the first wife had borne no sons. Information on the religious practices of women indicated clearly how important the desire and need for children, especially male children, loomed. The prominent *shamans* of the region acknowledged that much of their activity was based on the beliefs of women who desired sons. Many of the offerings made at the shrine of the goddess Kali in Madhopur were by women who were imploring the goddess to grant them a son. If appeals to local *shamans* and the goddess failed, the women of the village travelled even farther to obtain help. In the city of Banaras, twenty-five miles distant, is a well famous for bringing sons to the childless. Near the well is a shrine to Lolarak Baba, the presiding deity of the place. Madhopur women, often accompanied by their husbands, visit this place for a ceremony which they hope will result in pregnancy. So great is the general concern over a wife who does not have children that women outside the family have been known to make offerings on her behalf to the local gods. If many years pass and a woman does not become pregnant or if two or more children born to her have died in succession, she may vow that, if a certain deity will grant her a healthy baby, she will have its haircutting ceremony performed at a shrine or temple dedicated to the helpful god. Also, if a woman feels that the ceremonies of *shaman* have helped her achieve pregnancy or give birth to a son, she may have the haircutting ceremony of the child performed at the shrine of the deity to whom the *shaman* appeals.

When a young woman bears a first child who is a daughter, this is disappointing, but it at least proves that she is fecund. No matter how many girls she bears, she will probably attempt to have children until she has borne a son. Consequently, there is little use trying to determine from the number of children in the family whether the parents are likely to favour limitation of family size, it is the number of sons that counts. If one asks why sons are considered so important, the answer is that daughters marry, often very early, and are lost to the family. Moreover, their marriage entails great expense. It is the sons who bring the dowry, who are needed to inherit the land and continue the line, who are present to aid in the work and to take care of their aging parents, and who finally carry on the funeral rites for the repose of the souls of their parents.

The need for a son is considered so great that only one son is deemed an insufficient safeguard. Childhood diseases take such a toll that safety is sought in numbers. As a village proverb phrases it: "One eye is no eye, and one son is no son." And another proverb tells us: "No one is satisfied with the amount of milk and the number of sons." After the continuity of the line is assured by the presence of at least two sons, a daughter is desired. As was mentioned before, it is a religious duty to give a daughter in marriage. Even here the emphasis is on the welfare of the man. "Girl babies are wanted so men can marry," villagers told us. The very word for marriage means to give a daughter in religious alms. Therefore it is said that when a daughter is born, the womb of the mother becomes sacred. When interviewed concerning ideal family size, most informants, no matter how poor, asserted they would want at least two boys and a girl.

Next to being barren, the misfortune that a young woman dreads most is to lose children by still-birth, miscarriage, or in infancy. A woman who consistently loses children is either considered somehow remiss and therefore culpable or is thought to be persecuted by ghosts and malignant spirits. If a woman who has lost young children becomes involved in a heated argument, she may be charged by her opponent with having "eaten" (i.e., caused the death of) her children. In one instance, a young woman who suffered a miscarriage ordered away two unmarried girls who came to her assistance. She feared that her bad luck would be communicated to the girls if they touched her while she was in this unhappy and polluted condition. But an older married woman who was present also hesitated to become involved. She was afraid that any contamination she suffered would be projected on to the young, unmarried girls of her own household. Even a low-caste midwife, who was called to massage the abdomen of the sufferer, found excuses for avoiding this task until the period of pollution was over.

As might be expected in such an atmosphere of concern, women go to great lengths to insure a safe delivery and a healthy child. For instance, a midwife with "good hands" is chosen, one who has had no mishaps or failures in her work. Persons from other families are excluded from the room and area where the birth is taking place so that no possibility of unfriendly intentions will cause trouble. The low-caste woman who assists at the birth shakes her clothes over the protective fire that guards the door so that no evil forces will gain entrance. One woman who had several children die in her husband's village went to her parents' village to give birth in the hope of breaking the chain of bad luck.

There are still other means by which a woman who has been unable to raise boys seeks to preserve her new-born son. She may have his nose pierced, as is done for a girl, and thereby deceive malignant spirits into believing that a mere girl, whom they hardly need bother to persecute, has been born. Or, to divert the jealous supernaturals, an opprobrious name such as "He-who-has-been-thrown-away," "He-who-has-been-driven-away," "He-who-is worthless," He who-has-been-sold," etc., may be bestowed on the child. As one of the names suggests, a boy may be symbolically sold by a woman who has failed, in the past, to rear sons to maturity to a woman who has been conspicuously successful in this. The baby boy is weighed, and his weight in barley is given by the "purchaser." In return, the mother of the child gives the purchaser a sari. If the boy survives, the grateful mother continues to give gifts to the "purchaser" on various occasions until the boy marries. Still another practice is to make a stove of clay and place the baby boy on it for a few minutes. Then the stove, which of course has never been ignited, is broken.

Presumably the mischievous spirits are expected to believe that the child has been destroyed and that they need not seek him out for their unkind attentions.

It is quite evident that in these attempts to mitigate anxiety and to guarantee the birth of children it is the welfare and the perpetuation of the male which is emphasized. Despite the importance, for religious reasons, of having daughters, the feeling in regard to girls is reflected in the village saying: "If God gives daughters, he should be so kind as to make a man rich." The differential attitude toward boys and girls is noticeable in beliefs and practices that even antedate birth. For instance, it is considered a good omen if the fetus is carried directly in front of the woman; then a son is likely to be born. When the low-caste woman who is called to cut the umbilical cord is on her way to the room where a birth has occurred, she is escorted by one or two men who are considered a guard to repel evil influences. If the new-born child is a boy, two men accompany the woman; if a girl has been born, one man suffices. Needless to say, she receives more for her services if the infant is a boy. At the time of birth the midwife picks up the new-born baby and places it on a winnowing tray. The tray is covered with a new piece of cloth if the baby is a boy; an old piece of cloth suffices if the infant is a girl. If a son is born, the midwife is generally given a sari and some money; she receives nothing if the baby is a girl. As soon as the birth of a boy is announced, the women in the house immediately begin singing a *sohar*, a type of song associated with birth and infancy; if it is a girl who is born, there is no singing. If a boy has been born, an older woman of the household goes about the neighbourhood spreading the news. A band may be summoned to play. At the very least someone will beat a brass tray. A man of the household may discharge a gun. This clamour is partly in celebration and partly to discourage evil forces that may threaten the new-born child. These activities do not take place at the birth of a girl. When a woman gives birth to her first son, the barber who serves the family and who has ceremonial as well as practical functions is sent to inform her parents. If it is a daughter who is born, no messenger is sent; eventually a visitor to the woman's natal village or a letter will carry the news. If a woman gives birth to a son during a visit to her parental home, the barber is immediately sent to her husband's village to notify her in-laws. There is no haste if the newborn infant is a girl. Women of the neighbourhood gather in the evening for twelve days to sing *sohars* in the courtyard of a home where a son has been born. For a girl, they only appear on the sixth and twelfth evenings. Again, if an infant has been born in an unlucky sidereal period, an elaborate ceremony called *Mul Shanti* is performed to remove the curse, providing it is a boy. During the hair-cutting ceremony of boys, a rite that takes place during a child's first, third, or fifth year, the women present sing *sohars*; in the case of girls, they sit impassively and do not burst into song.

It is not only in ceremony and symbol that the male baby receives favoured treatment. One of the conclusions which was drawn from the work of a small dispensary which we maintained in the village for some time was that the illness of a male infant was likely to receive more prompt and anxious attention than that of a girl and that families were willing to spend considerably more on medicine and medical aid for a boy than for a girl. One can sense this attitude in the lecture of one of the older women of a joint family to a young mother. She climaxed her remarks by saying: "Because of your carelessness, you killed two daughters. Now be careful with this one. He is a boy and he needs proper care and attention. Boys need more care than girls. Don't you see, girls survive nicely, but if a little thing happens to a boy, he dies." Again the traditionally guided perception clashes with fact. Actually there are approximately fifty more males than females in the village population. Moreover, this superior survival record of males is duplicated throughout the region and the state. At the time of the 1951 Census, there were three million more males than females in the State of Uttar Pradesh. The greater concern for the health, nourishment, and safety of the male certainly has some bearing on these figures, although the confinement of *parda* (purdah) and the hazards of delivery in insanitary surroundings undoubtedly are contributing factors.

There are a number of calendrical rites which embody features associated with the preservation of the married state and with the health and longevity of husbands and sons.

These rites are extremely complex and cannot be described here in detail. A few of the practices especially germane to our topic may indicate the attitude they support, however. One called Chotka Basiaura, which occurs at the onset of the heat, is meant to ward off the epidemic diseases brought by a goddess. It is performed only by families which have requested the goddess to grant them a son. About two weeks later there is a companion ceremony, Barka Basiaura, which is observed by all families. This, too, is directed mainly toward protecting the children of the family against the diseases sent by the goddess Bhagavati Mai, especially smallpox and cholera. Again, the protective attitude toward males is conspicuous. Small figurines of silver, one for each male member of the family who has ever had smallpox or chickenpox or who has been vaccinated for smallpox, are used in the rite. Figurines of this kind are not made for girls. Yet it is the women of a household who conduct Basiaura.

Roughly similar concepts and practices are found in the worship of the goddess Bani which takes place in late summer. After a son is born, a family usually requests a goldsmith to make a ring of silver called a *thos*; these are never made for girls. If a son has been born in answer to a vow to the goddess Bani, the *thos* is square in shape with a human figure molded on it. If a *thos* is not made after a son's birth, two must be obtained at the time of his marriage. A *thos* made at a boy's birth is not kept by his family but is given by his kin to a Brahmin priest who serves them. The priest puts it with others in a container in his house, and the whole collection from the many families he serves represents or personifies Bani. On a Monday or Friday during the month of Savan (approximately July-August) following a son's birth, Bani is worshipped. For the occasion the Brahmin comes and brings his box of *thos* with him. Unmarried girls may not witness ceremonies to Bani or be connected with them in any way.

Soon afterwards Cauth, or Kajali Day, is celebrated by the women. This ceremony is connected with the worship of the elephant-headed god, Ganesh. On this day unmarried women fast until noon, but women who have sons fast the whole day. The women sing *kajali*, or songs with romantic themes. They take seedlings from barley they have planted some time before and tie one of these to the pigtail of each male member of the family. In the early afternoon the women gather at one of the houses and continue to sing *kajali*.

In early fall comes Tij, a women's fast and festival which honours the husband and acts as a supplication for the continuance for the married state. Parvati, the devoted consort of God Shiva, is worshipped on this day. Wives and unmarried pubescent girls keep the fast and carry on the ritual; widows are exempt from participation. Married women receive presents from the homes of their parents on this day. They go together to bathe at a tank, singing *kajali*. In one of the songs a woman mentions her husband by name, the only time of the year that this kind of reference to her husband is permitted to the wife.

Soon after Tij there are ritual observances in honour of Shashthi Devi, the goddess who presides over married women and children and who gives and protects sons. In this ceremony, Lalahi Chath, only married women with sons participate. One woman of each household keeps a strict fast. She collects certain foods and places them on a brass tray. The arrangement of food is somewhat different for households where a son has been born within a year. The women meet and go together to a tank near which a protective circle of buffalodung has been traced. In its centre a figure is molded of the dung to represent Shashthi Devi. Stalks of a sacred grass are fixed on the figure. Each family representative tries to tie a knot in a stalk of grass, using only the thumb and little finger of the right hand. To succeed is to add to the lives of the sons of the family. One of the women tells six stories. Most of these tales recount how a son's death was thwarted by faithful observance of this fast and ceremony. On the way home women sing *sohars*. A gesture of hospitality attends this rite; curds are offered to anyone who comes to a household in the morning.

A little later in autumn falls another important ritual occasion, Jiutia. The word is probably related to the term *jiu* (life). Jiut Baba, the god of this occasion, especially blesses sons. Again, it is the women of the household who are responsible for the events. A woman begins to observe the rite only after she has borne a son. If she has borne only daughters, she may

Population Control in Village India

keep the fast in the hope that Shitala Mai, another deity worshipped on this day, will grant her a son. At least one woman in each family keeps a total fast for twenty-four hours in connection with Jiutia. When a woman observes Jiutia for the first time, she keeps her fast a secret to everyone except women of the family. The female head of each family has in her keeping a necklace of small, elongated gold or silver beads strung on a red and yellow cotton thread. There is one bead for each male in the family. This necklace is called *fiutia*, and it is brought out and displayed at this ceremony. Toward evening on Jiutia the women go together to bathe at a tank, accompanied by a band. Nearby a large sacred circle has been prepared. At its centre a mound of cowdung representing Jiut Baba has been shaped. An alter is prepared at this spot and offerings are made. The women offer water to the ancestors, saying: "Old ones, this is for you." Some women hold baby sons over the altar of Jiut Baba to secure blessings for the infants. A Brahmin who is present tells stories appropriate to the occasion and kindles a sacrificial fire. It is expected at this time that women who have no sons will try to steal something, especially the *fiutia*, from more fortunate participants. Before she starts for home, each woman lights the wick of a little earthen lamp from the sacred fire and tries to reach her destination with the light still burning. The flame is associated with the life of the sons of the family. On the way the women talk to themselves in a stylized manner, saying: "Go tell God that the mother of (naming her son) has kept a very strict fast and therefore he should guard and protect my family." At dawn the women break their fast and worship the female ancestors of the family, because Jiutia falls within the half-month set aside for honouring the ancestors and is the day on which female ancestors are particularly remembered. These ancestors are, of course, the mothers of the male members of the line. Previously women have prepared foods which are especially associated with their sex, and they dine on these.

Godhana and Piria are two related ceremonies. The first occurs in early winter and the second a month later. They are entered upon by girls to lengthen the lives of male relatives, especially the brothers, and they involve an exchange of gifts between sisters and brothers.

Still later in winter comes Magh Cauth. This ritual is observed only by families in which a son has been born or married during the past year. In the ideology of this ritual, Ganesh, the elephant-headed god, is associated with the moon. Once more a woman of the family fasts all day. A place in the courtyard is purified and ritually designed. A figure of a lamb, made of sugar, is brought to the sanctified place. When the moon is rising, the younger brother of the father of the boy, or a Brahmin, sacrifices the lamb by decapitating it with a knife and offers the head to Ganesh. As he does so, he may pray silently, saying: "Oh God, we are offering you all this. Keep our children safe." The one who has made the sacrifice then rushes out of the house, taking with him the head of the lamb. The next morning the body of the lamb is distributed to family members and friends as sanctified food. The woman who fasts lights a lamp and circles it in the air five times as if moving it around the moon. It is believed that this observance will bring blessings and good luck to the boy in whose name it is carried out.

Finally, Shivaratri, another winter ceremonial occasion, may be mentioned. There are conflicting legendary explanations of the day, but most think of it as the anniversary of the marriage of Shiva and Parvati. Unmarried girls fast on this day in order to obtain good husbands. Women go to the shrines and temples of the vicinity, especially to those associated with Shiva, to pay their respects to this deity.

These are only a few details of some of the rituals carried on for the purpose of assuring a large and prosperous family. It is obvious that women are central in the conduct of these observances and that this aspect of the ceremonial pattern offers them an exceptional opportunity to identify themselves with the husband's line and to take responsibility for its welfare. It is evident, too, that this affirmation and identification are achieved largely through sons and that the contribution of the woman, both ritual and secular, depends greatly upon being the mother of sons. It is very likely that birth control propaganda picturing a national population crisis will have little effect until Indian women have some avenue of achieving status and security equivalent to the consideration they now receive from demonstrating their fecundity and ability to bear sons.

Thus far we have stressed the factors of status religion and tradition which support the desire for a large family. There are a number of less abstract and more earthy considerations that have a similar effect. In general it is assumed that it is desirable and advantageous to have a large family. In fact, prosperity and a large family are linked in the villager's mind. "As the harvest grows from the work of the farmer, so the family grows from the good *karma* (actions) of its members," runs the village proverb. "Who doesn't want children? People want as many as they can have," said one of the villagers. And there are reasons why this attitude has grown up and persists.

For one thing, rural and agricultural life tends to obscure overpopulation and underemployment. On an unmechanized farm there are always chores to occupy everyone. At times of preparation of the fields, irrigation, and harvest all hands are desperately needed. In fact, at these times women and children are pressed into service, and men return from urban employment to participate. It is the image of these peak work periods that lingers in the mind of the villager when he discusses population size.

In the second place, a good many villagers are sent by their families to work in cities and towns on a seasonal basis. These family members remit a good deal of their earnings to the village, and this supplies a cash income with which the families can undertake new projects, educate sons, buy land, and in general advance their status. Families with surplus members are in the best position to take advantage of the possibilities of both the village and urban centre. The wives of those who are working in the cities almost never accompany them, partly because of lack of facilities, partly because of their own timidity, and also because family members wish to be sure that the young men retain their ties with the village and will return.

Another practical advantage of a fairly sizeable family relates to involvement in the *jajmani* system, the network of hereditary work obligations and exchanges. A barber family, for instance, serves a number of families of other castes and occupations. The arrangement is one between families and not between specific individuals. Consequently, if one member of a barber family is ill on the day when certain *jajmans* are to be visited, his brother or his father can substitute for him. When there is only one person available to honour the traditional work obligations, sickness or some other emergency may be a great inconvenience.

In seeking credit, too, the larger family may have a decided advantage. Debts are considered a family obligation; and if a man has brothers, sons, and grandsons who can be approached in case he dies or defaults, he is much more likely to receive financial consideration.

Nor can the familism, the factionalism, and the rough-and-tumble of village life be ignored in interpreting the desire for a large kin group. Disputes over land and other issues are common. To be a member of a flourishing joint family gives security of poverty and person which is not enjoyed by those identified with a small or weak kin group.

The factors which have been reviewed to this point are mostly those which glorify parenthood and undermine the importance of a large and strong family. There are, however, traditional ideas and restraints which work in the opposite direction. Moreover, it is quite possible that Westernization, technological development, and new programmes are doing more to undermine these internal checks of the social system than to counteract the forces that have created enthusiasm for large families.

It will be remembered that the bride, especially if she is young, often does not go to her husband's house immediately after the marriage and that several years may elapse before she takes up regular residence with her in-laws. Even after she has come to her husband's village and home, the marriage most likely will not be consummated for some time. It is only in a wealthy family with a large house that the girl will have a room of her own. The wife and husband do not see each other alone and have a virtual avoidance relationship in the presence of other members of the household. In fact, their communication is conducted through older women, and the young man risks ridicule if he shows too much interest in his young wife or is seen too much in her company. The formality between the two is a measure of the respect owed to the older members of the house, and the young bride of a joint family is usually in *purdah*, or seclusion, and has a respect relationship with the elders of her husband's family. Consequently, at least for some time, meetings for intimate purposes are determined by family elders to suit the needs and convenience of the family. It is traditionally the wife of the husband's elder brother who makes the actual arrangements, who tells the younger woman where to go to receive her husband, and who directs or leads her younger brother-in-law to his wife's room. Later on the couple may take more initiative; when his wife is serving food to the men, the husband may whisper a request that she leave her door unlocked that night. But in many joint families arrangements through intermediaries continue for some time. Even if a man succeeds in indicating his desires, he may not be able to visit his wife. An unwilling woman can feign that she has not heard the message and bolt the door or send word pleading illness. Of course, in nuclear families husband and wife relations are necessarily much freer, and even in joint families the husband and wife feel less difference as they advance in age.

Even when the husband has reasonable access to the wife and where children and the continuation of the line are desired, there are strong philosophical and psychological restraints on sexuality. Hindu philosophy and doctrine have contrasted the intellectual with the physical and have encouraged asceticism. The average villager does not know too much about this in the abstract, but he has not been untouched by these currents of thought. He has heard many times that semen is highly purified blood and that it takes up to ten thousand drops of blood to form one drop of semen. Consequently, he takes a grim view of the debilitating effects of incontinence. It was pointed out to us that the best wrestlers and athletes were young, unmarried men. One respondent said to a field worker: "If I had reached your age without being married, I would be so strong that all I would have to do is touch a tree to make it fall down." A ninety-year old man solemnly attributed his longevity to the fact that he was thirty years old when his first child was born and that, although he became a widower in middle life, he never remarried. A well-known dance, a speciality of one of the castes, depicts weakness from sexual over-indulgence. One of the arguments frequently offered for vegetarianism is that meat stimulates sexual feelings. Sexual indulgence not only allegedly produces weakness but is accountable for serious sickness. The heat generated by sexual intercourse can supposedly lead to tuberculosis. Since sexual activity is so distracting and dangerous, it is considered incompatible with educational progress. The name for the Indian student who is receiving an orthodox Hindu education is *brahmachari*, a term that has come to be synonymous with "chaste" or "continent." As we have already mentioned, marriage is now often delayed in order to permit young people to complete their education. It was explained to us time and again that boys are not considered fully developed until they are twenty years of age or older and have to be careful and, if necessary, strictly controlled in matters of sex until then.

With this background of disparagement of unbridled sexuality, it is not unreasonable to expect that physical intimacy is felt by many to be only proper for procreation. The heroes and strong men of village tradition are those who visited their wives until the family had a son or the requisite number of children and then lived a life of continence thereafter. Even the gods do not indulge in sexual activity overmuch. There is a taboo against uttering the name of a Hindu month on the first day of that month. The explanation given is that this is the day of the month when Bhagavan Rama (the name by which the Supreme Deity is known in the village) visits his wife for sexual relations. The call attention to the day will remind people of this. Just as God keeps man's intimate secrets, so should man refrain from embarrassing God. This custom suggests the control, the shame-faced attitude, and the secrecy with which sex is attended for God and man in the eyes of the villager.

While it is admitted that few attain the ideal and it is lamented that "men go to their wives too often," the doctrine does have an effect. One family was severely censured because it was considered that a young bride became pregnant too soon after coming to her husband's home. The family elders were taken to task for allowing the young couple to come together for intimate relations so early in their married life. Yet to judge from the date of delivery, the girl must have been at her husband's home over six months before pregnancy occurred. Once a woman is pregnant, intimate relations should cease. One explanation for this is the fear of incest. It is said that if the fetus is that of a female, a man would be having relations with his own daughter. Possible injury to the fetus is another reason given for the post-pregnancy taboo. The head of the fetus is soft and vulnerable until birth, it is explained, and could be damaged during sexual intercourse. Properly, the abstinence should continue not only until childbirth but for two years beyond. Weaning is late, and it is felt that the health of the nursing child will be impaired if the mother becomes pregnant again. Therefore it is a disgrace if children are born too close together. In a case where a child was two and a half years old when a sibling arrived, the family was roundly criticized throughout the village. Another element in the situation, less a matter of constraint than of belief, is the notion that the period of greatest fertility immediately follows menstruation. Often, when a child is wanted, the young couple bathe and carry on ritual and are brought together at this time.

In the Hindu view a person's life is divided into four *ashrama*, or periods, and it is to the second of these that sexual activity is appropriate. The first is the period of studentship, *brahmacharya*, when chastity is strictly enjoined. A person enters the third *ashrama*, *vanaprastha*, when all his children are grown and he has a grandchild. It is the general feeling that sexual activity should cease by this time or, ideally, before this. One woman, who had conceived nine times and had six living children, told how embarrassed she was to breast-feed her youngest child in the presence of the oldest of his siblings. Another woman was the subject of much gossip and criticism because she bore a son even though her daughter and her daughter-in-law already had children. We were assured that a woman of thirty-five years of age, whose husband had died four years before, will probably never marry again, although she belongs to a caste which permits widow remarriage. She has two married daughters and therefore, as we were told, "is getting too old to marry."

It is the consensus of the villagers that remarriage must be entered upon cautiously. Divorce and widow remarriage are forbidden among the high caste, though separation does occur. Even separation is a grave blow to the high-caste woman, for her sons will undoubtedly remain in their father's house. A high-caste widower may remarry and will almost certainly do so if he is fairly young and if his first wife had borne only daughters. If he has sons and there is any kins-woman to help him care for them, he will be much less inclined to remarry. The harsh stereotype of the step-mother in Hindu lore is a sobering influence. In a second marriage the man is likely to be considerably older than his bride. Among the low castes divorce and remarriage are possible for both sexes. There is no bar against widow remarriage, either. However, a woman who seeks separation or divorce or a widow who remarries faces almost certain loss of her sons.

Another custom that separates married pairs and acts as an indirect check on population is the visits of the woman to her parental home. It is assumed that marriage will be a difficult transition point for a girl. After all, she has had no contact with the family with which she will become so closely associated. In fact, it is considered bad manners to discuss a girl's impending marriage in her presence. The expectation is that the girl will be lonely, frightened, and homesick when she takes up residence with her in-laws and will want her own kin to call her home for a visit. A girl who is not invited back to her parents' or her brother's home soon after marriage is likely to feel deserted and aggrieved. Actually her solicitous kin seldom disappoint her. These visits of the married woman to her former home and her return to her husband's family are often major undertakings. Ceremonious messages must pass between the two families; an escort must attend the woman; and expensive presents, upon which family status and honour rest, accompany her. Consequently, the visits are prolonged ones, seldom less than three months in duration and often lasting a year. During the first period of a woman's married life she may spend as much time in her natal village as in the home of her father-in-law. As she grows older, has children, and acquires greater status and responsibilities in her husband's family, the number and duration of the visits to her village of origin diminish. By this time, however, her period of childbearing may be over or drawing to a close.

Present economic practices and conditions also separate married couple for significant periods to some degree. It will be remembered that according to our census figures approximately one hundred male adults are engaged in work in urban centres at any one time. Although some of them return for a month or two every year and although few of them continue in their urban jobs permanently, many of them remain away for a continuous period of from one to two years. Not all of these migrants are married; but, because of early marriage practices, most of them are wed, and it is predominantly the younger married men who are to be found in urban employment.

It should also be recognized that the villager is not a complete stranger to population control measures; in fact, on occasions he has used rather drastic ones. Among the Kshatriya of the village, infanticide was practised until the last quarter of the nineteenth century because of the expense of arranging marriages for daughters and because of the humiliation in seeking mates of higher status for the girls of the household. Infanticide formerly existed and is rumoured to occur occasionally now in cases of illegitimacy, for the growing outside employment of men has resulted in an increasing amount of extramarital relations involving the wives who have been left behind. Abortion, too, takes place when a girl is faced with disgrace. There are a number of specifics in Ayurvedic medicine which are used to prevent conception by those who are engaged in unsanctioned liaisons or to induce abortion when an unwaranted pregnancy occurs. Mercury is obtained by the drop at high price from goldsmiths for these purposes and the root of a giant milkweed is used in a concoction with the same ends in view. A number of respondents have admitted to the withdrawal technique, and others have acknowledged that they use condoms, which they obtain in towns and cities. Condoms are probably more often used in connection with illicit relations than in ordinary married life. Most of those who attempt to prevent conception do so because their children are grown up or married and because they already have grandchildren and fear the embarrassment of now having additional children of their own. It was suggested to a number of village women who sought to avoid further pregnancies because of an already large family or poor health that they seek help from a birth control clinic in Banaras. The fear that they might have to undergo a physical examination was the chief deterrent in these cases.

It is often said that there is nothing in Hindu religion which would prevent the dissemination of birth control information and practice. In this connection the cooperation and affirmative stand of the Indian government is cited. But some cautions need to be observed here. After all, no less an Indian leader than Mahatma Gandhi urged, on religious grounds, that no method be used other than the self-restraint doctrine we have already discussed. The concept of non-injury to living creatures, *ahimsa*, is also strong. In discussing birth control, many respondents made it clear that they would want assurance that any practice they used would not destroy life. There is good reason to believe that a method that prevented fertilization would be much better received generally than one which destroys the fertilized ovum. One also has to take into consideration the large section of the population which is enthusiastic over naturism and which insists that the only medicines which should be taken by man are natural products and not chemical agents. In all plans for population control that are contemplated for the present period, the dependence and enforced modesty of the young girl in village India and her reluctance to contradict and lead her husband must also be kept in mind.

A thorough knowledge of the more subtle aspects of culture frequently reveals the weakness of opinions arrived at from more superficial observation. There are those, for instance, who assume rather easily that the replacement of the joint family by a smaller family unit would surely have a depressing effect on population growth. Usually such judgements are pronounced without an understanding of the internal controls on sexuality and childbearing that have developed in the joint family. A consideration of these factors suggests, instead, that a weakening of the joint family and of the restraints which the presence of adults of different generations in the same household mutually impose might well result in an initial rise in the birth rate.

A close look at Indian culture and at Indian rural life in particular impresses one with the degree to which thought and behaviour in intimate family matters are shaped today by early marriage, the dependence of women, the limited means at the disposal of women for achieving status, and the economic and social advantages of a large and strong kin group. It is certain that more education, the greater control of disease, further industrialization, and the implementation of laws now on the statute books will alter existing relationships and concepts. But programmes always begin in a present among determined people and not in a timeless expense populated by automatons obedient and responsive to the wishes of the technician. Consequently, any population control plan that does not take these cultural realities into account initially and does not respond to whatever changes occur in them as time goes on is adding psychological and cultural difficulties to the ordinary mechanical problems that confront any large-scale effort.

John F. Marshall

12 Topics and Networks in Intra-village Communication[1]

Intra-village communication is an important but inadequately understood element in programmes of planned change. A growing number of behavioural scientists are investigating what Rogers and Svenning (1969:126) label interpersonal localite communication and Niehoff (1967) just calls gossip. In "Bunkipur," a multi-caste village of 570 people in north India, the variations in these communication networks and the resulting differential effects on the success of programmes of induced change were striking. For example, information about a new variety of wheat spread rapidly and evenly among the villagers for whom it was relevant, but information about birth control diffused slowly and unevenly, and failed to reach many of the villagers for whom it was most obviously intended.

Some variation in communication pathways can result merely from chance. A child, for example, could overhear information not intended for his ears and disseminate it more or less randomly within the community. But in Bunkipur the variation in direction and extent of diffusion had some regularity. This regularity is partly a result of such things as the originator, timing, style and medium of the communication, and most important, the topic of the communication. The focus of

[1] The field research on which this paper is based was supported by a Fulbright-Hays Center fellowship (GFH7-70) and grants from the East-West Center and East-West Population Institute in Honolulu.

concern here will be on the last of these factors.

Communication pathways within a village are founded upon the social organization. "Standard" cultural norms regulate interpersonal behaviour, and thus provide for each role a basic body of rules for the transmission of information. The social organization of small multi-caste north Indian villages has been well documented, and there is no evidence to indicate that Bunkipur was culturally a typical of the village in the area. Briefly, the standard norms resulted in restricted social intercourse most obviously between the sexes, especially between a woman and men older than her husband; between the highest and lowest castes (*jatis*); and between widely separated age groups of men.

But for intra-village communication, "subject-specific" norms could either relax these standard norms or, more commonly, add further restrictions on communication. The topic of communication, like any stimulus, elicited associations for each individual and the thought of transmitting a given topic to another person evoked other associations. Some of these subject-specific associations—both those stimulated by the topic and those stimulated by the thought of communicating the topic to someone else—concerned "whatever it is one has to know or believe in order to operate in a manner acceptable to the society's members." Since this is part of Goodenough's definition of culture (1957:167-168), they might be called "cultural" associations or subject-specific norms. Other associations are purely individual, with little or no bearing on acceptable behaviour; these are "idiosyncratic" associations. Though both kinds affected communication networks, the cultural associations allow statements about patterns of information diffusion.

Norms elicited by the topic of a communication affected the diffusion process in three ways. Most important, subject-specific norms determined the appropriate audience for communication on a given topic. For example, the elderly shepherds of the Gardariya *jati*, about in the middle of the caste hierarchy, were more likely to talk about an infraction of caste rules with the younger men in their own *jati* than with men of their own age in slightly higher or lower *jatis*. On the other hand, when the topic concerned a murder in a neighbouring village, the men were less likely to talk with the younger men in their own *jati* than with men of the same age and fictive generation in the other *jatis*.

In the first instance, talking about infraction of caste rules evoked dominant associations concerning such things as fear that other castes would exploit the situation in their struggle for upward mobility, anxiety that public knowledge of the issue might adversely influence efforts to establish marriage ties, and a general feeling that such matters are private and to be handled internally if at all possible. The results of these associations were *jati*-based norms defining the appropriate audience. In the second instance, a murder in a neighbouring village evoked curiosity, perhaps pity, but no associations that superseded the standard norms of the village. As a result, to maintain status and respect, the men tended to talk with others in their age group, including those outside their own *jati*.

An attack by thieves, or some other calamitous and urgent event would elicit the fewest inhibiting rules, allowing the most spontaneous communication. A new bride might even scream for help from her father-in-law or husband's older brother, members of the society with whom she theoretically has no direct communication. Clearly, simple proximity plays the dominant role in such cases, with constraints regarding caste, age, sex and so forth regulated to insignificance.

At the other extreme, if the topic concerned methods of abortion for an unmarried girl—or male sterilization—a large number of associations involving modesty, fear and shame would exclude communication with all but a very few people.

A second way the topic affects the diffusion process is limiting the social settings in which communication about it could occur. For example, two women who talked about the sexual proclivities of a neighbour while cutting fodder in the fields together would be less likely to discuss such a topic while they performed a rite at a village shrine. Some topics, such as a community effort to improve a road, are generally discussed in group situations; others, such as sterilization, generally occur in didactic situations. If there are limited situations in which communication on a specific topic can occur, the pattern of diffusion on that topic is obviously affected.

The topic of communication influences diffusion in a third way, by affecting the degree of detail and degree of persuasion transmitted. Verbal communication can range from barely expressive grunts to elaborate pleas for action, and the kind of communication that occurs hinges on such things as the relevance, inherent appeal and cultural association evoked by the topic. If a landless goatherd hears about an improved breed of goats, he is more likely to provide a detailed and persuasive report about it to a caste brother than if he heard about a new chemical fertilizer or steel-tipped plough. Clearly, there is an interaction between the degree of detail and the degree of persuasion; strong positive or negative feelings about a topic result in more detailed discussion than neutral feelings on a topic.

A comparison in some detail of the effects of two topics— a new wheat variety and birth control—on communication networks in the village illustrates the variations. Both topics originated outside the village; both were brought to the village primarily by government workers; both were formally introduced to Bunkipur through meetings with village elders, both concerned ideas somewhat dissonant with existing ideas; and both were aimed ultimately at behaviour modification. But since the two topics had entirely different meanings to the villagers and elicited different norms, their spread within the village followed different patterns.

Though the village had not previously been exposed to a formal family planning programme, nearly all the adults had heard something about it. To the villagers, family planning generally meant sterilization and sterilization was frequently associated with castration, impotence or, at best, chronic pain and weakness. Other contraceptive techniques were vaguely and inaccurately known, but were considered dangerous, not only for their physical implications, but also because they loosened the morals of women, denied God's will by limiting the number of offspring, left a man forever shattered if his sons or wife died, and so forth.

But in terms of intra-village communication, the most important aspect of the topic was its indelicacy. Birth control for most of the villagers was *kharab bat*—a bad thing, a dirty issue, a vulgar topic. And within the village a deep-rooted value of modesty existed, manifest not only in *purdah* and separation of the sexes, but in speech. Great care was taken to avoid sexually indelicate topics with inappropriate people, and violations of the modesty code could result in loss of respect and status, hostility, and even physical beatings.

Talking about a new wheat seed, however, was neither threatening nor immodest. The only apparent subject-specific norm evoked by the topic of wheat was that concerning relevance: since they recognized that a new variety of wheat was not particularly important to a man with no land, the villagers were more likely to talk about it with people who owned or leased land.

Both subjects—the new wheat strain and birth control— evoked several associations that attend any topics leading ultimately to behaviour modification. First, in Bunkipur a villager who enthusiastically disseminated information and supported an innovation created suspicion about his motives. The other villagers asked themselves what he (or she) got out of it; has he sold out to the establishment? Is he conning us into something simply because he'll get favours from the village level worker or *panchayat* secretary? Second, a person who talked positively about an innovation to members of a group within which he had not established authority was accused of "trying to be a leader." In a society where leadership is still more often ascribed than achieved, that could be a damning accusation. Third, to tell someone about an innovation and to encourage him to adopt it was to assume some responsibility for it. If one's talk about the new wheat resulted in another's adoption, and if the crop failed, it wasn't only the gods and the weather who were blamed. To involve another in birth control was to assume even more responsibility, and repercussions could be far more severe. Every villager knew the possible implications of giving unsolicited information and advice, and was often reluctant to give a detailed or positively persuasive account of his knowledge. If a person did talk about an innovation, it was safer to condemn it and support the status quo; little harm could come from that. And this in turn contributed to the fact that negative reports about an innovation—sterilization more so than the new wheat—tended to travel more quickly and over a larger area than positive reports about them.

All these considerations interacted with the standard norms

of behaviour to produce the distinct diffusion patterns for each topic. In a normal landowning family, a member who had heard about the new variety of wheat could talk relatively freely about it. There were the standard exceptions, of course, regarding communication between a man and his sons' wives or younger brothers' wives, and between a young man and his own wife in the presence of his parents. But brothers talked among themselves and with their sons and fathers. If the new variety of wheat was a viable option for them, they frequently discussed the innovation in considerable detail and with some degree of persuasion. Since wheat had implications for the women in the family in terms of harvesting, cooking and cash profit if it were sold, they were generally involved too, for a man could and did talk freely about it with his wife, sisters, mother or daughters. Finally, in many landowning families, the women discussed among themselves the advantages and disadvantages of the new variety.

On the other hand, communication within the family about sterilization was somewhat different. Regardless of possible interest in limiting the number of births, men rarely talked with their fathers, sons or even brothers about the indelicate subject except for innocuous statements about the existence of family planning workers in the village or about a propaganda movie being shown. For a man to speak with his mother, sister or daughter about it was especially immodest and shameful for the woman. In several instances, men used the casual joking relationships with an older brother's wife to communicate about family planning, and in a few cases a man talked more with this woman than with his wife about the topic. Husband-wife communication varied widely, as Poffenberger (1969) has observed, with a tendency for younger, more educated couples to discuss it more than their elders. The women in a family were a little less inhibited than the men when talking among themselves about family planning; sisters and others of approximately the same age discussed the topic, and older women sometimes expressed their opinions—frequently negative—to their daughters-in-law.

Outside the family, discussions of the new wheat were usually held with other members of one's age group or with larger, more flexible interest groups. Discussions on birth control, however, rarely occurred in group situations and generally consisted of one man quietly talking with another from his age group. In most cases serious discussions of the topic occurred with one's *joridar*, an especially close friend of the same age, usually from the same *jati*. Communications among women outside the family were somewhat more relaxed; groups of women of several *jatis* and various ages discussed both the new wheat and family planning among themselves. To my knowledge, communication about family planning between men and women outside the family never occurred, but the new wheat was mentioned several times between the sexes.

The spread of birth control information from the old men who first heard the formal presentation by the government workers was very slow. Unlike the topic of wheat, where a young man could hear directly from an elder in his family or interest group, birth control was almost always spread only within a man's age group. But the youngest man in one age group was the eldest in a younger age group to whom he could speak about sterilization, and in this way the topic slowly diffused to the youngest men in the village. Since age was not as important for women, occasionally a woman heard the message of the family planning workers before her husband, but she was usually too shy to initiate discussions of it with him.

These observations seem to indicate several tentative generalizations.

First, contrary to the apparent assumptions of some agents of change, specifically the family planning workers who came to Bunkipur, there is not simply one communication network in a village. Many diffusion networks exist, in part as a function of the topic of communication (cf. Polgar 1963).

Second, though they are related, the diffusion of an innovation may have rather different dynamics than the diffusion of information about an innovation. Modesty, for example, is of only middling importance in an individual's decision to accept or reject a contraceptive device, but it is paramount in his decision to tell someone what he knows about it.

Third, knowledge of the social organization of a community is necessary, but not sufficient, to understand communication networks. It is also essential to know what the topic of communication means to the members of the community as well as the associations it elicits concerning cultural values, beliefs, goals, interests and so forth.

Finally, recognizing that there are subject-specific communication networks within a community, agents of change should attempt to identify the subgroups within which free communication on the topic can exist. Less emphasis might be placed on meeting with village elders (if the message concerns family planning, for example) and more with representative members of various age, sex, *jati*, and interest groups. An immediately apparent implication of this is that more women have to be employed in family planning programmes in India. Further, it might be profitable to try to avoid the communication barriers created by a highly restricting topic by linking it with a topic that allows freer communication. The effort in India to spread family planning through maternal and child care programmes was an experiment in this direction.

REFERENCES

Goodenough, W.H., 1957. "Cultural Anthropology and Linguistics," in P.L. Garvin, ed., *Report of the Seventh Annual Round Table Meeting on Linguistics and Language Study*. Washington, D.C.: Georgetown University Press, pp. 167-73.

Niehoff, A.H., 1967. Intra-group Communication and Induced Change." Paper presented at the annual meeting of the Society for Applied Anthropology, Washington, D.C.

Poffenberger, T., 1969. "Husband-wife Communication in an Indian Village." Central Family Planning Institute Monograph Series, No. 10, New Delhi, India.

Polgar, S., 1963. "Health Action in Cross-cultural Perspective," in H.E. Freeman, S. Levine, and L.G. Reeder, eds., *Handbook of Medical Sociology*. Englewood Cliffs, N.J.: Prentice-Hall, pp. 397-419.

Rogers, E.M., and L. Svenning, 1969. *Modernization Among Peasants*. New York: Holt, Rinehart and Winston.

Kusum Nair

13 Human Element in Indian Planning

In every part of rural India development programmes are being delayed, resisted or wasted because the new opportunities or the techniques they demand conflict with the attitudes or practices of the people. These usually have their roots in religious beliefs or social imperatives and the obstruction they offer to development cannot be dissolved by reason or even promise of profits or a better way of life.

Certain communities will cultivate only certain types of crops, not because they are unaware that other crops would be more rewarding or for lack of resources, but because of their dietetic habits and attitudes to surplus, or simply because it has been customary for them to do so. On such attitudes may depend the success or failure of irrigation projects costing millions of rupees. To add to the complexity, these attitudes and behaviour patterns vary from one community to the next, even within the same region and where they basically have equal resources and opportunities. Often they are rigid enough to prevent the villagers learning by example through the "demonstration" effect, on which economists so much rely for the spread of a new idea or technique. Even over a period of several decades the people may ignore example and resist change.

Thus, in certain districts of Assam the local peasants have been living alongside immigrant settlers from Mymensingh, now in Bangladesh, for three or four decades under identical conditions, often in the same village. They are all tenants or small land owners.[1] The Bengali immigrants, however, are not only more hardworking than the native Assamese, but they have varied and supplemented their work and income from the single-crop paddy fields of the area by cultivating vegetables. This has brought the immigrants prosperity and the Assamese see it, but they still refuse to turn their hands to vegetable growing and continue to eke out a bare subsistence from their single crop of paddy, which gives them work for only three months in the year.

Neither the example of their immediate neighbours over the decades nor the persuasions of the official extension agencies (part of the area has been covered by the community development programmes since 1953) have succeeded in persuading the local Assamese to diversify their crop and so improve their earnings. "For one thing, we have no experience—it depends on habit," they explain "Mymensingh people have it, we do not. Secondly, it requires more labour. Thirdly, the Mymensingh farmer will grow his vegetables and take them to the market in a basket on his head. That we cannot do. It is below our dignity. If we do not take it ourselves we will have to hire a servant to do so; that would be expensive and the servant might cheat."

In spite of acute poverty, dignity is more important to them than money and enough to eat. To put it another way, their desire for a higher standard of life, is not even strong enough to overcome their traditional attitudes to work and status. It is not even strong enough to make them circumvent such inhibitions, for it should not have been impossible for them to organize the marketing of their vegetables so that they would not have to carry them on their heads. These peasants are not only needlessly denying themselves a better income, they have slowed down the nation's effort to obtain more food production.

What does a government, anxious to press ahead with its programmes for a planned and speedy economic development, do in such a situation? In a democracy, as in India, it cannot resort to compulsion—simply order the peasants to cultivate the vegetables. It can only reason with them and if demonstration and persuasion fail, wait and hope, even though it may take

---

[1]The example is taken from the author's *Blossoms in the Dust*. Duckworth, 1961, p. 138.

a very long time, until the community's concept of dignity alters.

If it is decided that the urgency of Indian development does not permit such patience, the government could try to deliberately induce the necessary change. But that would necessitate a prior and detailed knowledge of the systems and values underlying the behaviour and attitudes of every community, so that the factors likely to nourish a community's growth and development, as well as those that might thwart or stunt it, could be understood and allowed for. The social factor, taken in its comprehensive sense, would have to be recognized as one of the primary determinants of underdevelopment and of the pace of development and made an integral part of economic analysis and planning.

That is far from the case at present. Economists, on the contrary, generally assume that a farmer anywhere must want to make as much as possible, and that in an underdeveloped economy he is unable to break through the vicious circle of poverty primarily because he lacks capital—the resources to invest in modern techniques which alone can improve production.

The process of development is therefore, mainly reduced to the mechanics of providing the initial capital, communicating knowledge of and training in new techniques, and creating an institutional framework that will enable them to work smoothly. Once initiated, it is expected to create its own pre-conditions, economic and non-economic.

Anyone who has firsthand experience in the field, however, knows that from these assumptions some vital factors are missing. A community's attitude to work, for example, can often be a more decisive factor in raising productivity than resources or technology.

"Yes, of course, I could earn more if I cultivated the land myself," a Brahmin landowner will admit. But he will not do so because it is taboo to him even to touch the plough. Members of other high castes may not be prevented by religion, but they also will normally not work on the land themselves because "it would be beneath our position."

Nor is the desire for more material wealth and profit—the so-called revolution of rising expectations—as dominant and universal a phenomenon among the rural communities as it is presumed to be. Whatever the reason—the hierarchical structure of society, limited horizons or the underlying socio-religious philosophy—my experience is that the aspirations of the Indian peasantry for higher living standards tend to be static, with a ceiling rather than a floor. The upper level a peasant is prepared to strive for is limited and so therefore is the range of his effort and investment. In some groups it is very much higher than in others, but generally the lower the community in the social strata the lower and more static its aspirations tend to be. As Ramulu, a young landless peasant in Andhra, said to me: "If I am given the choice I will ask only for as much land as will give me enough to feed my family. I have five children and a wife and my mother. I want only one acre."

This phenomenon of limited aspirations further invalidates some of the main generalizations underlying economic planning. Unless a man feels a constant and urgent desire for material wealth that is strong enough to make him work for it, he cannot be expected to have a continuing interest in higher production or new techniques, even if the necessary capital and knowhow be made available to him. He may and often does disdain to engage in activities yielding the highest net advantage. And where an extraneous factor like the introduction of irrigation or higher prices brings about an increase in his purchasing power, the increase may be wasted in non-essential forms of consumption instead of being invested to further increase production as postulated by economists. All of these characteristics are widely prevalent among the Indian peasant communities.

Moreover, whereas in industry a small elite can go a long way in initiating and sustaining rapid growth, in agriculture in a country like India, where production is the individual responsibility of over seventy million peasants distributed over some six lakhs villages, a much broader based revolution in their inner attitudes and motivations is an essential prerequisite. How exactly the revolution is to be achieved democratically, and within the short period of time that has been projected for economic development, has yet to be discovered and because of the growth of population the matter is urgent.

Tremendous faith is being placed in the spread of education as a certain cure for all backwardness, but this again is based on an assumption that is only partially true. Education does broaden the horizon and it equips and enables an individual to understand better the more complex techniques which, especially in industry, hold the ultimate key to higher production. It can also be expected to undermine to some extent traditional ways and thought, and to introduce new attitudes.

Mere change, however, is not enough, and it can even be a change for the worse. In India today, with negligible exceptions, the son of a farmer who has been to school for seven or eight years does not become a more efficient farmer than his illiterate father—he ceases to be a farmer altogether. This is not because there is always a more attractive job waiting for him in a town. On the contrary, the prospect is that he will simply join the ranks of the educated millions already unemployed. He would, however, rather remain idle—even if he owns enough land to give him more income than any white-collar job he could possibly hope to get with his limited qualifications—because, in his estimation of himself as an educated man, to work on the land would be beneath him. In effect, then, education among the peasantry is tending to create a new and functionless caste—unwilling to work with its hands, unable to find the simple clerical work that is all that education has fitted him for. Unless this status attitude associated with education is altered, therefore, there is little prospect that the spread of literacy among peasants will help to raise the exceedingly low level of agricultural efficiency and productivity in India.

The problem is essentially one of bringing about, within the framework of democratic planning and policy, the necessary changes in people's deeply held attitudes and values. It is not that there is no progress. In spite of inhibitory attitudes and practices among the peasantry, there has been development in the Indian agricultural sector, and in some regions like the Punjab it has been impressive; but it is patchy, it is not as rapid as it could be if the importance of the human element in planning were fully recognized and it is not enough for the needs of the Indian economy. It is doubtful if Indian agriculture can be fully developed until the braking effect of the peasants' attitude is understood and somehow lifted.

Part Three

Programme Administrators and the People

Joan P. Mencher

14 Change Agents and Villagers

Many studies of development have focused on traditional attitudes, superstitions, and lack of trust in new things, as deterrents to change. I should like to show that there are other forces at work which may be far more crucial to the success or failure of change programmes. Thus, a given social system may in some ways impede aspects of modernization because of the way in which the various strata within society relate to one another and to scarce resources; indeed, the interaction between different social systems (in this paper, the village social system and that of the administrative bureaucracies) is most complex and the nature of this interaction may tend to reinforce existing power relations.

It appears to date that most innovation programmes, while tending to encourage increased productivity, have discouraged changes which might seriously threaten ongoing power relations. This is not meant to imply that everything is as it was fifty years ago, but rather that there are profound forces at work within south Asian (as well as other) societies to hold in check some of the potential changes, and that it is often not the villager nor the man at the bottom with his "superstitions" who is fighting this type of change, but the change agent himself.

These comments are based primarily on my own five years of field experience in India, though I draw mostly from my work in 1966-67 in Tamil Nadu and during the summer of 1969 in Kerala and Tamil Nadu (when I was travelling around, meeting both government officials and villagers).

One of the questions that has often been raised by people in other disciplines is: what can a social anthropologist contribute to an understanding of the problems of modernization and socioeconomic change in the world today? If I look for relevant data on this question (not only for India, but for other parts of the Third World as well), I draw heavily on work in other disciplines, such as economics (including agricultural economics), extension education, political science, etc. Nonetheless, perhaps one function can be best served by making use of aspects of the anthropological approach. One thing which most anthropologists try to do, is to put themselves in the position of each of the people in the social nexus being studied (in this instance, villagers at all socioeconomic levels, the various change agents, government officers, etc.) and try to look at the forces at work on each of these people as they live their lives out under present conditions and as they try in one way or another to remake the world in which they live. Having looked at a situation from the pivotal point of each of the participants, the anthropologist can then get a different perspective on the way things are interrelated. To examine the question of development in India, as in any modernizing nation, one cannot ignore other dimensions such as the type of social class structure, relationship between politics and power, the role of bureaucracies and who are recruited to them, how they interdigitate with the rural social structure, and the nature of the village social structure. In other words, an understanding of the development process involves and understanding of these other crucial factors.

I should like to focus on two aspects of change currently going on in India, family planning and agricultural development, and to discuss their successes and failures in terms of their underlying dynamics. We know from studies in the United States that responses to change relate closely to the interaction between the change agent system and the local social structure.[1] This factor is of considerable importance in

---

[1] Estelle Fuchs' study, 1969. "How Teachers Learn to Help Children Fail," *Transactions*, pp. 45-49, shows how the structure of New York

analyzing these two programmes in south India.

My analysis starts from and includes certain fundamental assumptions about Indian society (some of which are generally agreed upon, others not so), and also some more general assumptions about socioeconomic change (though, again, these may be challenged by some of my colleagues). Certain of these assumptions about India are almost self-evident and many are not unique to India.

(1) Socioeconomic differentiation in India, as in many developing (and even some developed) countries, is extreme, and the clearly articulated social classes have their particular vested interests, methods of manipulation of the masses, and the like.

(2) In India, tensions of all sorts have, traditionally, been held in check by an array of sanctions which are now being challenged as people's horizons are expanding. Having worked intensively with low-caste people.[2] I would disagree with some of my colleagues who believe that the lower castes were (at least in the past) to some extent "contented with their lot." Possibly, the traditional system offered them some degree of security in exchange for the slave-like status, but I am convinced that there was considerable tension in that system, which was held in check by various power relations.

(3) In Indian society, caste has been used to keep and safeguard socioeconomic power. (Joseph[3] has shown for the Lebanon how the wealthier people of each religious sect have kept the poorer people of their own group from uniting with those of the other.) Similarly, wealthy leaders of dominant castes have traditionally kept the very poor of their own caste

---

slum schools makes failure inevitable for the vast majority of students. Likewise, research now in progress (Nina Glick, Columbia University) shows the way the structure of social agencies and the larger society in New York can keep Haitian migrants from improving their position within the society.

[2]For some of my comments see "Past and Present in an Ex-Untouchable Community of Chingleput District, Madras," in Mahar, ed., 1970. *The Untouchables in Contemporary India*. University of Arizona Press.

[3]Joseph, Suad, 1969. 'Pluralism as a Guise for Class Interests: The Lebanese Case," presented at the Middle East Studies Association, Toronto, November.

from uniting with other poor people by stressing caste loyalties, superiorities, etc. This has started to break down in recent times. In the Kuttanad area of Kerala, poor Nayar (high-caste) women and poor Pulaya (untouchable) women are now found uniting in agitations for higher wages.[4] In parts of Tamil Nadu today, I have observed landless caste Hindu men and Paraiyan (untouchable) men, under the age of thirty playing cards together and voting as a block vis-a-vis others in the village.

(4) Because of this extremely stratified social system, it is obvious that intergroup relations would have to play a role in the development process. Most of the people in key positions in the bureaucracy have come from wealthier social groups. Furthermore, in a situation like this the lower ranking "developers" come from the lower middle class.

The following are some more general assumptions relating to socioeconomic change:

(1) That in a highly stratified society, those people who are in power will (by and large) try to stay in power;

(2) That the man who has just moved out of a low-ranking position will often try to maintain his new status within the system, by creating as much distance as possible between himself and those below him;

(3) That the average villager has been wrongly and in many ways dangerously characterized as conservative, bound up by superstition and beliefs.[5] (I will go into the reasons behind this characterization shortly, but it suffices here to note that such a characterization has been, and continues to be, an extremely useful rationalization for government failures in programmes.) Similar characterizations of the

---

[4]Trade union activity is extremely active in Kuttanad with frequent conflicts between the workers in unions and landlords. The Nayar workers today are not only active members in the Pulaya dominated unions, but they also work under Pulaya leadership. (Personal communication, A.K.B. Pillai, Columbia University.)

[5]This is not to say that no villager is conservative or that no superstitious beliefs are ever held by villagers, but rather that there will always be enough poor people willing to try something new, to make it possible for programmes to get somewhere if people are convinced that some real benefit is possible.

poor in the United States have been shown to be invalid by some writers. Jaffe and Guttmacher[6] pointed out that most of the poor, though wanting smaller families, are unable to afford through private physicians, the efficient contraceptive methods used by non-poor couples. For many reasons—restrictive policies, inconvenient timing, overcrowding, inaccessible clinic facilities, lack of information, or impersonal treatment—adequate family planning services have been denied to them. They also note that, when convenient and dignified educational and contraceptive services are provided; the same poor respond positively. I return to this matter later on when dealing with the family planning programme in south India. For the moment, I merely want to make the point that certain characterizations of villagers are more related to the social system than to the reality of village life.

AGRICULTURAL DEVELOPMENT: BACKGROUND

Much has been said in recent years about the "green revolution" going on in the Indian countryside, and there is no question that a change has occurred in Indian agriculture. New high-yielding seed varieties, along with increased use of fertilizers, pesticides, and irrigation facilities, are now producing substantial increases in yields in at least some parts of the countryside. In fertile, well-irrigated areas, farming today has become very profitable for the middle-class man. A man with ten acres of land can live quite comfortably. As one young engineer (now earning over Rs 1,500 per month) put it to me:

> Today, with sixteen acres of pump-set irrigated land near Pondicherry (his native place), I could be better off than I am now, have all the modern conveniences, electricity, running hot and cold water, a much larger house than I have in Madras, a jeep to take me and my family to the

---

[6]Jaffe, Frederick S. and Alan F. Guttmacher, MD, 1969. "Family Planning Programmes in the United States," *Demography*, Vol. 5, pp. 910-23.

nearby town, send my children away to good schools etc. I sometimes feel torn about going back. Even intellectually, it could be challenging. If I don't get another promotion soon, then I definitely will. One of my brothers has done just that. And my father is doing very well in farming nowadays. A man can really have a good life this way.

What is the nature of this "green revolution"? What is behind it, and what is happening now? What kind of warnings were given, and what kind of repercussions are setting in? What populations have been reached, and with what effects in each case? We also need to learn something about the role played by the various change agencies of the government.

From the beginning, agricultural development has had most of its impact on farmers with medium or large holdings. It has been aimed to do this partly because it fits in with the outlook of India's elite, and partly because of pressures from outside advisers, who would only look to the Western cases for comparison. Yet, for a number of years, various individuals have predicted that this approach might have serious social (and ultimately economic) repercussions. For example, P.C. Joshi,[7] in an appraisal of the community development programme written in 1960, noted that:

> ... democratic processes will continue to be thwarted as long as wide disparities in the distribution of economic resources and benefits persist and leadership and influence in village society remain interlinked with economic and social status.

In 1965 (before the full impact of the "green revolution" had begun to be felt), Hanumantha Rao noted the following:

> The Farm Management Studies conducted in various parts of the country have shown that output per acre is generally

---

[7]Joshi, P.C., 1960. "Community Development Programme: A Reappraisal," *Enquiry*. No. 3. Reprinted in A.M. Khusro, ed., 1968. *Readings in Agricultural Development*. Bombay: Allied Publishers, p. 460.

higher among the smaller farms and that it shows a significant decline with the increase in farm size . . . . Output and productivity can be maximised if ceilings on landholders are imposed at a sufficiently low level and surplus lands redistributed among small farmers. . . if somehow ownership rights can be conferred on the tenants in India such as has happened in Japan after the Second World War, agriculture would become more dynamic.[8]

Nowadays, if one talks with landowners (or even agricultural officers), about raising the wages of day labourers, the usual comment is that it would reduce the profitability of agriculture. However, the definition of profitability depends on the orientation of the person talking, and may not bear a direct relationship to the amount of grain grown in a given acre of soil. What a well-to-do man with ten acres of well-irrigated paddy land calls profitable, and what a small landowner with one to two acres calls profitable, may differ considerably. The bigger operator, who is primarily concerned with selling his produce, has to figure many costs, and labour is a big item. For the small landowner, who does most of his work himself or with his family, labour involves no outlay of cash. Thus, in theory, a man can work to the point where food intake and energy output are close to equal.

According to Sen,[9] cultivation is carried out on the small farms right up to the point where the marginal product is zero (or at least below the ruling market wage), and stops on the capitalist farms at the point where the marginal product

---

[8]Rao, C.H. Hanumantha, 1965. "Agricultural Growth and Stagnation in India," *The Economic Weekly*, February, 27. More recently, Anthony, Koo, 1968. *The Role of Land Reform in Economic Development: A Case Study of Taiwan.* New York: F.A. Praeger Publishers, has shown for Taiwan that, with land reform agricultural productivity increased rapidly (though the increase could not be attributed only to land reform). There seems to be evidence that the former tenants "seemed to have put in more capital and labour per unit of land and to have been anxious to learn modern agricultural practices" (p. 77) after land reform was passed.

[9]Sen, A.K., 1964. "Size of Holdings and Productivity," *The Economic Weekly*, February, 16, pp. 320-26.

equals the market wage. Bhagwati and Chakravarthy,[10] commenting on this, point out that it can only hold insofar as we explicitly postulate that the peasant family labour cannot necessarily find alternative employment at the given wage. But it is important to note several facts here which I have documented for Tamil Nadu and Kerala (and others have found elsewhere). To begin with, at least for rice cultivation, wages are not uniform during the course of an agricultural year. Wages are certainly extremely high during harvest periods. Indeed, for many poor people this is the main time in the year when they earn their livelihood. At this time, people work round the clock, harvesting whatever is available, wherever it is available. Thus, in Chingleput district of Tamil Nadu, along with a free noon meal, men are paid $5\frac{1}{2}$ measures of paddy (a minimum of Rs 5) per day, and women about $4\frac{1}{2}$ measures of paddy per day. Harvest time, however, is not crucial for increasing the yield acre. What is crucial is ploughing, transplanting and weeding, applying fertilizers, checking on the water, watching for birds, etc. And these operations are paid at a very low wage rate (Re 1 to Rs 1.50 per day).

To my knowledge, no one has done an analysis to show whether Re 1 to Rs 1.50 would justify a man putting in more time on a landlord's land or on his own, but it is certainly clear that, if the man gets such a fixed wages regardless of the quality of work done, he is not likely to push himself beyond what seems reasonable to him. (Incidentally, such work is often done at times in the year when there may be a shortage of food, and landless labourers may have less physical energy.) Furthermore, landlords tend to give maximum employment at these times to few men rather than to give a little to everyone. Sometimes, this means having one or two permanent labourers apart from using day labour. One might postulate, as Rao has done,[11] that "where hired labour is used all year round,

---

[10] Bhagwati, Jagdish N. and Sukhamoy Chakravarthy, 1969. "Contributions to Indian Economic Analysis: A Survey," *The American Economic Review*, Vol. LIX, September, p. 41.

[11] Rao, C.H. Hanumantha, 1966. "Alternative Explanations of the Inverse Relationship between Farm Size and Output Per Acre in India," *The Indian Economic Review*, Vol. 1, October, p. 5.

the application of family labour could be within profitable range because some labour is hired at the margin throughout the year and a mere decline in the proportion of family labour input cannot explain the increase in profit per acre." However, it is clear that the "permanent farm labourer" gains little if anything by working hard on the landlord's land during the slack seasons. In some parts of Chingleput district, the one or two permanent *padiyals* are paid one-sixth of the produce. However, they know that they will probably be fired the following year (landlords are afraid of keeping the same *padiyal* too long), and, in any case, they do not see themselves getting enough to make a lot of work worthwhile.

In Chingleput district there are other times in the year when, for a brief period, there is work available for a man who goes out as a day labourer, but in general this work does not interfere with the yearly cycle of rice and lesser grains. It is clear, from the villages which I know best, that men will take most care of their own small piece of land—somewhat better care if it is land that they have on a fifty-fifty share-cropping basis (even though in this areas the landlords do not pay for any of the inputs)—but that their effort decreases when they work either on *alvaram* (one-sixth share, where the landlord provides all of the inputs), and even less as day labourers. Though I lack statistical verification of this, I can report case after case of men speaking frankly about it to me (when no land-lord was present). They will say that they are not going to kill themselves for the landlord's stomach. "What does he care how we feel? He would like to squeeze us dry."

Bhagwati and Chakravarthy[12] note that "small farms" not far from the bottom of the scale, themselves hire labour at the margin and even derive income from employment of family members in other occupations. . . ." However, the question here is when and for what purposes. Even a man with a small plot of land, say a quarter to a half acre in Chingleput district, must employ a group of women two times a year for five hours each time. This is because of the way in which paddy is transplanted. His wife will probably work with the women, and will then go off and work on other neighbours' fields, but I would

---

[12]Bhagwati and Chakravarthy, *op. cit.*, p. 42.

hardly call that anything more than a kind of local cooperative work (even if it is paid for in cash). Normally once a man decides to transplant his paddy from his tiny nursery, all of the work has to be completed in a few hours. Then he can let the water into the field at once. However, it is interesting that in a small-scale survey I ran in 1967, such small farmers reported that they hired labour. Only when probed intensively did they say for how long and for what kinds of work.

It is clear today, that the "green revolution" has considerably increased the wealth of the medium-sized and large landowners, without any proportionate change in the situation of the lower peasants (small landowners and landless labourers). As a result, the gap between the groups has increased and this increase has been, if anything, worsened by the acceleration of of food production. This situation has been greeted with a loud outcry by numerous Indians, such as Kusum Nair, a number of individuals in close contact with the Planning Commission, and friendly outside advisers. Recently, it has been the subject of a study and report by the Home Ministry,[13] and is beginning to be discussed by most foreign advisory groups who had previously ignored the possibility.

Farmers who have sufficient means to participate in the "green revolution" often claim to be caught in a difficult situation vis-a-vis their tenants and labourers; because of the costs of the new inputs and additional facilities, such as pumpsets, which are required to maximize their benefits, they claim to be unable to raise wages substantially. What this appears to mean is that they will only adopt measures which gives them a really large margin of profit. If the profit is cut down by paying higher wages, or by not being allowed to sell for a high enough price, then these middle-sized and large farmers are less motivated to adopt new measures. (This is strikingly illustrated in Kerala, where I was told by many different people during the summer of 1969 that many more middle and large landowners are taking to improved seeds in Trichur and other districts than in the package programme district of Palghat, where the government was holding down the price of

---

[13] *The Hindu*, Madras, 8 December 1969, and *The New York Times*, 19 January 1970, p. 69.

paddy in order to benefit the poorer peasants.) As far as the country's economy as a whole is concerned, any increase in productivity may be encouraging, but it offers little comfort to the landless labourer. Perhaps in a good year, he can buy a new shirt, or a pair of sandals, but this is a far cry from the kind of change of life-style that even a middle-sized farmer can envision for himself.

It has been generally stated that increasing production as fast as possible (which might even mean increasing inequality) is absolutely essential if India is to survive. Partly true! However, increasing productivity need not necessarily imply increasing inequality. It is correct that the small farmer often lacks capital, but in that case provision of adequate capital with some sort of risk insurance[14] might be a more reasonable strategy than ignoring him. It is not true everywhere that the small farmer lacks irrigation facilities, or that it would be impossible to provide them for him. In the villages I worked in Chingleput district, if one systematically examines landholdings, it is clear that many small farmers own land which is not reliably irrigated, but strikingly, many also own tiny plots of reliably irrigated land. On the other hand, many middle-class and wealthy men have their holdings divided between dry and wet land, and have recently dug tube-wells with government loans on their dry land. (Why hasn't the government dug tube-wells and sold that water to small landowners instead?) The idea that rationality demands that progress proceed from middle and upper classes down derives from, I would suggest, certain basic assumptions about Indian (or I would say also American) society. If change agents talk first with, and work only with, the middle or upper classes, naturally the men at the bottom can only get any thing by downward diffusion. But, that is talking after the fact from a higher status position. Back in 1963, I was practically begged by many small farmers for any information I could get them about new methods of rice growing, fertilizers, pesticides, etc. But the new programme which I observed in 1967, and again in 1969, did not reach

---

[14]Lipton, Michael, 1968. "Strategy for Agriculture: Urban Bias and Rural Planning," in Paul Streeten and Michael Lipton, eds., *The Crisis of Indian Planning*. London: Oxford University Press, pp. 111-12.

these men—not because of their attitudes, but because of the way the development programme was structured. In the spring of 1967, I ran a small open-ended survey in ninety-six villages, covering four community development blocks, in the southern part of Chingleput district. Certain results were striking. Of the informants owning under four acres of land, only eleven per cent were using new seeds, whereas for the informants owning over twenty acres (though the number was smaller) fifty per cent were using new seeds. Furthermore, as one might expect, there was a correlation at the 0.999 level between the size of landholding and village office.[15] Among these village offices, fifty-four per cent were using new seeds, whereas among the people not having any village office, only twenty-eight per cent were using new seeds. More striking, although not statistically significant—since we did not get enough responses—of the ones who did not have any village office, seventeen per cent report that they asked for new seeds but the government said no stocks were available.

Starting in the late spring of 1970 (for the southwest monsoon season), the central government has designed a new programme to focus on the small farmers. It is to be tried in one district in each state, and will attempt to provide credit facilities tractors on hire, etc., to help the small farmer. The small farmer is to be defined differently in each state; for Madras it is a man owning between two and five acres of paddy land. Even such a programme will face many problems. In Madras, it will leave out a large number of people, including most of the untouchables. Thus, the problems of the really small farmer cannot be touched with this kind of a programme. Secondly, there is no clear provision for preventing larger landowners from sabotaging it in various ways, if they should decide to do so. For one thing, it would be possible for a large landowner to obtain some of the benefits under this programme for small holdings registered in the name of an old grandmother, small child, etc. Furthermore,

---

[15]I have dealt with the question of the relationship between wealth, political power, and the modernization process elsewhere. Mencher, 1968. "Politics, Religion, and Caste in Madras Villages: An Analysis of their Interrelations and Implications for Development," American Anthropological Association Meeting, under revision for publication.

there is no clear way to offset the influence which the large landowner derives from mobility as well as his ability to bribe officials. Over and over again, in 1967 and again in 1969, farmers who were using new seed varieties or had managed to get loans for additional pump-sets, etc., reported that they had to make numerous trips to the development headquarters (at their own expense and on their own time) simply to get these things. This is not possible for a man with a small holding. In my survey, twenty-four per cent of those commenting on fertilizer use said that influence was important in order to get enough, especially at the right time. Possibly that is easing up in relation to fertilizer, but it is certainly still true with regard to the new seed varieties. It is clear that the structure of the bureaucracy itself, makes it virtually impossible to eliminate the way in which "influence" functions.[16]

The government is now talking about really enforcing land ceilings in rural areas, but it is clear from having worked with land records that a man of influence can manipulate these records very effectively. It would in effect take an administration willing to offend these people, for land reform to be really successful. In other words, it would require commitment to a fundamental change in the relationship of groups in society. This may be possible but certainly not easy.[17]

AGRICULTURAL CHANGE: AGENTS AND VILLAGERS

A common attitude among agricultural development workers is

---

[16] Thought not discussed in detail Heginbotham provides several examples of how influence functions in the development bureaucracy. (Heginbotham, Stanley J. 1970, "Patterns and Sources of Indian Bureaucratic Behaviour: Organisational Pressures and the Ethic of Duty in a Tamil Nadu Development Programme," Ph. D dissertation, MIT, pp. 75-94.)

[17] Dandekar, V.M., 1969. "Overpopulation and the Asian Drama," *Ceres* (FAO Review), Vol. 2, November-December, pp. 52-55, points out that if ceilings were to be put on the maximum size of owner-cultivator farms, then this must be supplemented by other organizations which make it possible for joint action for irrigation, etc. This again would involve, I believe, fundamental changes in the way relations are structured at present.

described by Prowl in the following terms:[18]

> According to generalisations which have developed into stereotypes, farmers are ultraconservative individuals steeped in tradition, hemmed in by customs, lacking motivation and incentive, captives of age-old methods, lacking in ability to make wise decisions. The educated, the elite, the administrators of agricultural development programmes and the general public have tended to accept stereotype generalisations of this kind. However, many development field workers confess that they find the farmers more receptive to change than the agents of change and the administrators with whom they work.

Today, many individuals who have had close contact with farmers will certainly agree that, by and large, they are eager to increase production and improve their situation if possible. Myren,[19] working in Latin America, noted in 1964 that even small farmers desire to produce more efficiently, and are eager for information on how to do this. Apart from the fact that it is the "convenient excuse for development workers to use when a programme appears to be failing," it is clear that there are a number of factors which prevent the workers from interacting effectively with farmers. Some of these are discussed here.

Who are the development workers in question? Even if one limits the discussions to those in the agricultural development programme, there is wide spectrum involved—from the *gram sevak* (or village-level workers) to high-level officials of the central and state governments. Obviously, they are from different backgrounds, have varied degrees of education, varied degrees of awareness of the total social world around them varied aspirations for themselves, and varied expectations of their work. Perhaps most critical to the villager are those people who are lowest in the system: the *gram sevak*, occasionally the AEO (agricultural extension officer) and also the BDO

---

[18]Prowl, W.L., 1969. "It is the Agents of Change Who Don't Like Change," *Ceres* (FAO Review), Vol. 2, July-August, p. 57.

[19]Myren, Delbert, 1964. "Training for Extension Work in Latin America," *America Latina*, Vol. 2.

(block development officer). If a villager is very rich and powerful, then of course he may have contact with higher level people, but the average farmer cannot expect to reach anyone higher than these, and in fact most of the time he will confine his contacts to officials on the lowest level. Now it is precisely these people whose position in the bureaucracy, and status in the society as a whole, is the shakiest.

Those who hold the position of *gramsevak* are generally people who have no hope of ever getting anything higher. Though the majority of them have passed their SSLC (equivalent of high school), this job represents for most of them the endpoint of their career. (Only a few can hope to earn another Rs 50 per month by becoming community developers, and only in exceptional circumstances can a *gramsevak* become a BDO. Indeed, only one or two such cases of the latter are reported in Chingleput district during the past ten years.) Thus a *gramsevak* is in a position comparable to that of a lower-level clerk in a government office, except that even the clerk can hope for some promotion eventually. However, the *gramsevak* can improve his position a little by associating with moderately well-to-do landowners in the village (not the largest farmers, since they would be less approachable); providing them with useful information and services in return for small favours, (and occasionally even small bribes). In addition, in this way he is able to maintain his status and his self-image as a middle-class government employee. The relationship can be mutually beneficial in a number of ways, since it allows the farmer to maintain good relations with the *gramsevak's* superiors, in addition to providing the *gramsevak* himself with an ally in the village.

Regarding the agricultural extension officers (AEOs), their work on the whole brings them into contact primarily with individuals from their own socioeconomic group or else from groups with which they would like to identify. It is easy for a middle-class person (which most of the AEOs are), or a person aspiring to middle-class status, to work with a middle-class farmer, since they think alike on many issues. Most of the AEOs would prefer to avoid actually going out and talking to farmers in the field; it is more convenient, as well as more prestigious, to set in one's office and talk to the farmers who come to visit. On the whole, of course, it is only the more well-to-do farmers who can take the time for such visits. If pushed sufficiently by the district agricultural officer, the AEO especially if he is very junior) will pay visits to the fields, but even then he would prefer to visit someone who can invite him into his house for a cup of tea. Working with poor, illiterate farmers is a very different matter, and there are relatively few AEOs who are dedicated enough or have enough time to pay much attention to the problems of such men. Indeed, there are factors in their job situation which make it very difficult to devote much time and energy to extension work. As Heginbotham[20] has noted, the bureaucratic set-up keeps most of the government officers, from the bottom up, busy with paper work a large percentage of their time.

In addition, and equally crucial, the change agents are caught in a system which provides no opportunity for feedback from villagers, let alone from change agents to those higher up. They are under various bureaucracies, either agriculture, or community development, or health, etc., and they are clearly made to feel that the only way they can survive and do well in the system is to accept the values of the bureaucracy they belong to and act out its mandate.[21] A government servant, after all, must keep quiet when it comes to politics, and must send in good reports. Indeed, I have been told that the code of conduct for civil servants in effect makes it very hard for a government servant to engage in any kind of opposition politics.[22] (It has been pointed out[23] that to some extent the

---

[20]Heginbotham, *op. cit.*, pp. 226-67.

[21]It should be pointed out here again that this is not unique to India. It tends to be Prevalent in most bureaucracies, or for that matter, in most large organizations, though there may be quantitative differences in the kinds of pressures exerted on those at the bottom in different systems.

[22]Before independence (in 1964) *the Government Servants' Conduct Rules* stated that "no Government Servant shall take part in, subscribe in aid of, or assist in any way, any political movement in Indian affairs" (p. 7). This rule was intended by the British government to keep Indian civil servants from engaging in any activity connected with the independence movement. It is striking that today, even though there have been some minor modifications in the rules for civil servants, government servants are still not permitted to participate in any politi-

reservation of seats for scheduled castes might have had a negative side effect in that untouchable protest groups have sometimes been deprived of educated leaders by the process of giving many of them jobs as clerks in government offices, or as school teachers, or in other kinds of civil service positions. This process serves to absorb them into the establishment if they should take the job, and may keep them in a situation of having to choose between being out of work and keeping their mouths shut.)

As the agricultural development programmes were set up, it has been very hard to reach the small farmer, the man with less than two acres of land. According to Joshi, back in 1960:[24]

> In areas where the farming population consists predominantly of small cultivators, and cultivating tenants, the general level of benefit derived from the programme [Community Development Programme] is bound to be low. . . . Technical improvement in millions of scattered, small land-holdings *under the present institutional framework* [italics added] would necessarily involve a colossal capital outlay.

Whether or not development personnel in general would agree with Joshi's comments, the point is that the bureaucracy as it is presently set up provides no scope for even examining the possibility of fundamental changes in approach. It is often easier to maintain a series of beliefs about poor farmers, the less educated men, than it is to challenge the prevailing viewpoint. If a man has come up from poor circumstances to a position of some power in the government, it is common for him to develop what M.N. Srinivas has referred to as a type of "amnesia"; that is, he will be prone to forget what things are really like at the

---

cal activity, to write pamphlets or any propaganda material for a political party, or to work for any party without the permission of the government. Action has been taken by the government against individuals who have broken these rules. It should also be noted that civil servants in other countries (e.g., in the United States during the Vietnam war moratorium in November 1969) have been prevented or discouraged from engaging in opposition political activities.

[23] Personal communication, T.N. Krishnan, United Nations.
[24] Joshi, *op. cit.*, p. 458

village level.[25] This is probably necessary if the man is to survive and function professionally in the bureaucratic environment. (This subject would make a most fascinating study in its own right, but cannot be gone into in more detail here.)

The Family Planning Programme

Today in India, a great deal of money and effort is being put into family planning programmes. There are some important questions involved in their implementation, which I feel need to be discussed. How are the change agents chosen, and who are they sociologically speaking? What are the stereotypes they hold of the people they have to reach? How do they function with people? How does the question of social class membership relate to this? It is clear that, in comparing a family planning programme with present agricultural programmes, special allowance has to be made for the fact that the former involves intimate contact with people at all social levels, whereas to date the agricultural programmes have not involved such interaction.

When I talk about change agents in the field of family planning, I am referring to two sets of people: (*i*) those working at primary health centres or hospitals or at community development offices involved directly in the implementation of programmes; and (*ii*) some (not all) of the people involved in planning programmes for these service people.

Sociologically speaking, just as in the United States the majority of people involved at various levels with the family planning programmes come from the middle classes, in India they come most commonly from the middle or upper castes; they are mostly educated people. Even the health visitors, the *gramsevaks*, etc., are mostly high school graduates. Among the lower level workers, one finds primarily people belonging to the lower middle classes who are most eager to assert their separateness from the riff-raff. This tends to colour their attitudes towards villagers and poor people in general. And these attitudes in turn are reinforced by the village leaders, to whom they normally go first. Some of the principal attitudes, as expressed by individuals I have talked to, are: (*i*) "These people really

[25]Personal conversation, New Delhi, September 1967.

don't care how many children they have. It doesn't make any difference. They can always use another hand to work in the fields." (*ii*) "They are too ignorant to really understand. The upper classes and the more educated people are coming forward for family planning programmes but not the low-caste and uneducated people."

Among higher level people, at the top of the development bureaucracy, one also often gets a stereotyped picture of the villagers as "simple people" who are "fatalistic" and "accept their lot philosophically." This attitude tends to breed a kind of paternalism, which may be at variance with the attitudes of the villagers themselves. A great effort has been and continues to be made on changing the attitudes of villagers, or in "motivating" them, but very little in listening to them and looking at the logic of what they say.

There is a tremendous mythology about the attitudes of village people towards family planning programmes. Though I have not conducted any kind of statistical survey, I have talked to a large number of village people over the years. I am convinced that there are enough (not all) village people interested in family planning, that if a programme were aimed at them, taking into account their needs, preferences, etc., even though present methods might not be the most suited to the Indian situation, appreciable results could be obtained.

A few specific examples, though anecdotal, might make these points clearer. In 1963, while doing a house-to-house census in one of the villages I have studied in Tamil Nadu, I came upon a woman belonging to the dominant agricultural caste doing some agricultural work near the road. She insisted that I talk to her there, since I was not likely to find her at home. In the course of collecting my data on household composition, it came out that she had had seven confinements and had five children living. I made some comment about it being a lot to feed and she added (in public), "I didn't want so many. During my last confinement, I even went to the health centre and asked for an operation. The people there said the doctor was away and would not be back for a week or two and if I wanted it, I should go by bus to Conjeevaram. How can one take a bus thirteen miles during labour? So now, I have to wait until I have another mouth to feed before they do something for me." Now, this is an example which illustrates another point; individuals like this woman, who are very outspoken about their desires for the services the government is trying to propagate, could be used effectively by change agents to spread propaganda among their neighbours and friends. In this instance, the woman was a poor but well-respected member of the dominant caste. If such a woman were helped to be the first to have her needs taken care of, she could certainly be counted on to spread the world.

Another case involves a young man in Kerala who married a girl of fifteen. Being unemployed and very poor, he wanted to postpone having any childern for a few years. When he went to the government hospital for information about family planning, he was politely told that he could come back after he had two children. Now then, this man may have been exceptional in wanting to delay the first pregnancy (actually I am not sure he is the only one in his village who feels this way, though he may be rare in acting on it). On the other hand, even such exceptional people can be effective spokesmen. It is certainly not a good idea to turn such a man away. Yet I personally know of many other cases where it was done. In some cases, it seems that when a particular type of programme is being pushed (e.g., vasectomy or IUDs), individuals who do not happen to need or want that particular method at that time are simply turned away. Admittedly, it is harder to provide all in a mass programme. But, also, one cannot expect that poor people will have no personal opinions or desires that merit consideration. Other comments by villagers suggest that change agents are often not aware of some of their problems and feelings.

Let me simply quote some comments from the untouchables in two villages in Chingleput district: (*i*) "They only do things to stop people from having babies. Look at X, he and his wife have been trying for so long. If they did something also to help people, why, may be then people would trust them more." (*ii*) "Now, I have two, they seem all right. But look at my neighbour Kalyani. She had seven and only two are alive now, the oldest and the youngest. If I stop forever, then what if a child dies? They don't do much to help a child. If you bring a child who is sick to the health centre or government clinic, if it isn't the right hour, it can die before they get to look at the baby. May be if you give *bakshish* it helps, but not always. They think we are not human beings, that we don't care what happens to our children. They don't really care." (*iii*) "Yes, we are knowing about all that, and we like to do some kind of family planning if we can do it secretly. We don't like to do it publicly. The rich people don't have to have all their neighbours know what they are doing. Do they expect us to be like cattle, to have no shame?" (*iv*) "Why don't they send a lady doctor, even once a week? I don't see why my wife should go to a male doctor; it isn't right, male doctors seeing females."

It is usually assumed that ignorant villagers are uninterested, and incapable of, making their own decisions. But twice in a good-sized gathering in two different untouchable hamlets, comments like the following were made to me: "Why don't they come and sit with us and answer our questions? True, we are not educated, none of us have been to high school, but they can send someone to explain slowly and carefully. Why can't they let us decide what method to use, instead of government people? You sit here and talk to us, no government worker has ever done this." In some cases, the questions asked are very specific, such as the following: "It is possible to stop and then have a baby later on? I have heard about that but no one will explain to us. Here they only do the operation." Or, "I heard about the loop, but everyone says it can be dangerous. I had a cousin in Madras who got a loop, but there she could go and check when she had a pain. Here, if I have pain, they will say, sorry the doctor is at some camp."

A very serious problem for the poorer people is the kind of treatment they receive in dealing with government personnel, and the feeling of hopelessness engendered by this. We know for the United States how a man in very shabby clothes, who cannot sign his name, is treated in a clinic (especially by the lower rungs of the hospital administration). As Polgar has noted: "For the medically indigent, the callous treatment not infrequently given them in public hospitals, combined with the timidity of the staff to become involved in a 'controversial' service, have not encouraged requests for contraceptive advice."[26] The same

---

[26]Polgar Steven, 1966. "Socio-cultural Research in Family Planning in the United States: Review and Prospects," *Human Organisation*. Vol. 25, Winter, p. 326.

certainly holds true in India. If a person is really seriously ill, then he or his relatives might go to the clinic or primary health centre, but at least some people will avoid such a situation if they can.

Villagers say that when people from the government come to the village to talk, they go to the high caste and/or wealthy people first. "That is only natural," one man said, "then they will send a lady to give a talk to the ladies' club. That is for women of good families, who have a new fancy sari to put on, and who can serve tea afterwards. Not for women who work in the fields. Sometimes we are able to stand outside and listen, sometimes they say we should go away."

Often surveys dealing with ideal family size, report that people state an ideal of three, while they actually have five or six. The normal conclusion to such a study is that the ideals are not firmly held. Is this true? Or is it that the difficulties in maintaining the ideal are too great? Often what appears to be resistance is more likely to be fear: to have a baby involves no contact with change personnel or higher caste or richer people. To avoid having a baby does. It is certainly true that the mortality rate is changing faster than people's ideas about it. But to the village couple, the next-door family is more significant than the statistics of the government. It is possible that people might be made more aware of the fact that a child born today has a better chance of living than a child born a few years ago, but it is not that easy to convince people when they see death strike next-door. In this connection, I think we cannot underestimate the importance of providing the villager, as well as the poor urban dweller, with adequate medical care and some assurance of longevity for their children.[27] I personally think that until this very simple fundamental fact of life is made more of a reality than it is at present, the family planning programme is going to be very much frustrated.

---

[27]Raulet, in a study in West Pakistan, has noted that since 1947 there has been a marked drop in infant and child mortality for the top income group and that this is the same group in which acceptance of family planning was markedly higher. (Raulet, Harry M., 1968. *Family Planning and Population Control in Developing Countries.* Institute of International Agriculture, Michigan State University, p. 36.

Village Social Structure and Family Planning Programmes

What are some of the ways in which the village social structure influences the direction of change by inhibiting certain types of innovation and reinforcing others? What are some of the things which motivate people's action? Certain of the dominating attitudes and values are directly influenced by the structure of village society, a type of society which places considerable stress on hierarchical principles. Let me list some of these first, then show their relevance to family planning programmes:

(1) *Prestige and status.* The need to maintain and enhance one's own and one's family's status vis-a-vis others in the village, within one's caste and between castes.

(2) *The fear of ostracism* and the need to avoid doing anything that will incur disapproval. To remain innocuous, or at least to avoid being the main subject of gossip unless one has so much money or support that one can risk it.

(3) A closely related factor, *the need to avoid punishment* by those with more power or prestige, including any encroachment on their position, unless one is certain that they can be defeated; and

(4) *Power*—and here I include two facets, both the bold desire for political power (similar to that of any small town political boss or wealthy factory owner in America) and all that this entails and, alternatively, the desire on the part of the small man who feels that everyone is over him to in turn have some power over some group or someone. I personally have seen several instances where both kinds of power-drives can be behind a strong opposition to many kinds of changes.

It is clear that any contact involving change agents with lower castes and/or poor people must occur in a context where these four things are recognized and that they cannot be separated from one another. Power and prestige come together in many contexts. A successful birth control programme must reach the poor and the low castes. On the other hand, such a programme (at least as presented in the areas I personally know well) has had little to offer to the local leaders themselves. A man of prestige will fight to get a fancy water system for his village, or a school, or something else which will get him greater patronage, but he will not support a programme whereby government personnel might be able to short-circuit the chain of command by dealing directly with the riff-raff. Important men have nothing to gain, and many think they have a lot to lose, by such contact. "It is better that they shouldn't get too many smart ideas and start challenging the local leaders." After all, why should a *panchayat* president care if there are more mouths to feed in a Harijan colony or even among the poor of his own caste? True, one might not want the Harijans to become so numerous that they out-vote the caste Hindus, but there are political means of keeping them divided and retaining power. It is striking how hard some of the *panchayat* presidents work to try to keep government personnel and others from having too much direct contact with the poor. They obviously have some, but the less the better. That is an additional reason why most higher-caste village Hindus are not exactly happy about lower-caste children being educated. Comments may be heard about how the Harijans nowadays, since they send their children to school and go to the government health centre, have started getting much too bold. ("Why, they even dare to wear shirts or shoes in the village streets.") If a man is feeling liberal, he might want something done for poor people or low-caste people, but he wants it to be clear that he is their patron and that they should be grateful to him and remain dependent on him.

One implication of the modernization process today is that the ability to control, or at least influence, outside agents has become an important means of gaining and maintaining power. Indeed, "the role of panchayat president has been increasing in importance as the benefits to the village from the government have become channeled through the panchayat. . . . The ability to control or at least to influence outside agents therefore... continues to increase in importance as a means of gaining and maintaining power."[28] Thus, leaders use innovations as a way of enhancing their own prestige. In this context, it may be

---

[28]Mencher, *op. cit.*

suggested that people involved with family planning programmes have often found that, as these programmes are presently constituted, important leaders will not give them their full support

In an excellent study conducted by the Demographic Research Centre at Kerala University in Trivandrum,[29] comparing various methods for spreading information about family planning, the conclusion was reached that ". . . the most effective means of reaching eligible couples is through house-to-house canvassing." However, discussion[30] with people involved in the study revealed that, though they accepted this conclusion they all agreed that "of course this method is impossible to apply. It would be far too costly." The question is, how does one measure cost? I am not sure that anyone has actually measured it, or compared it with the cost of the alternatives. I am frankly not convinced that it costs too much, when I see large sums being spent on programmes whose effectiveness has not been established by previous study, and which do not take into account the real desires or behaviour of villagers. For example, when written propaganda is prepared for distribution to villagers, it should be of a type which answers the questions they are already posing. Today, in many rural parts of India, people have heard about family planning. They want answers to very straightforward questions. What methods are available? Where can one go for each type of treatment? (e.g., Can one get an IUD inserted in the early morning at the local primary health centre, on Monday, Tuesday, and Friday? When can a woman have an operation? When and where can one find a nurse who will sit and talk to a husband and wife about alternative methods?) The language used should be the kind that is used in daily conversation in the village and can be understood by anyone who can read at all. If aimed at "opinion leaders," it would be important to know if people really listen to "opinion leaders" when it comes to such intimate matters. (Often the so-called "opinion leaders" are considered too rich and politically powerful to talk about personal matters of this kind.

---

[29]"Family Planning Communication and Action Research Project," Mimeo. Report. University of Kerala: Department of Statistics, p. 18.
[30]Discussion at Kerala University, August 1969.

Also, they are often not considered to have the interests of poor people at heart, except perhaps in the few regions where paternalism still prevails.)

One reason, I would suspect, that certain kinds of programmes have a greater appeal in the big cities is that, from the point of view of the urban bureaucracies, there is a need for programmes which create more urban jobs for lower middle-class workers in ways that do not involve direct contact with people. Most people (not only in India but all over the world) do not want to go out and talk to villagers, get worn out walking in the sun and rain, have trouble getting meals, etc., if they can avoid it. It is much nicer to have an office job. However one cannot simply blame the middle-class worker. There is a very important need to give him some incentive, something to make it really worthwhile (monetarily as well as in terms of prestige and personal satisfaction) if one really expects to see a change in his behaviour.[31] Simply changing his job specification is not enough.

The question of measurement of success and failure of a programme or of an individual worker depends on various criteria. To a superior within the system, the main measure of success is: "Were the targets met?" because if one meets targets, then one can avoid criticism from one's superiors. Heginbotham quotes one DAO as follows:[32]

> A good DAO... must be two things. He must be helpful to the farmers and he must complete the government schemes in a successful way.... My superiors judge me by my success in fulfilling my targets and in keeping my paper work up-to-date.

This problem relates to the total organization of the bureaucracy. It also means that even if a lower change agent (either in a health centre, or in agriculture) wants to spend much time helping people, he must do it mostly in his spare time because over eighty per cent of his time will be spent in attending to

---

[31] Beasley, Joseph D., 1969. "View from Louisiana," *Family Planning Perspectives*. Vol. I, Spring (especially pp. 11 and 15).
[32] Heginbotham, *op. cit.*, p. 75.

bureaucratic concerns. One result of this is that often people have to be bullied into doing things they don't like and a programme can backfire.

A clear example of this is the male sterilization programme in Tamil Nadu, which is now generally conceded to have been a failure. It started with the hiring of a number of canvassers, who were paid a given amount for every man they produced at a primary health centre. The patient himself was also to be paid for having the operation. A study done at Gandhigram population centre has shown that only 63.3 per cent of the vasectomized individuals had wives in the age group of fifteen to forty-four. Furthermore, the average age of the wife of vasectomized men was 39.5. In addition, the average period of time which had elapsed since the last live birth was 5.7 years.[33] Since the canvassers were concerned only about getting paid or fulfilling targets, such factors were of no concern to them; on the other hand, the programme certainly was of limited value for population control.

Again in the field of agriculture, if the *gramsevak* or AEO has to be primarily concerned with listing the number of acres of new seeds grown, he cannot (even if he should be motivated to) focus on a number of really small farmers. If he only needs six large farmers to give him an acreage of X amount and that is his target, then since nothing else matters, why should he waste time unnecessarily contacting the smaller men? It is true that fear of risk may impede the farmers, but that is not the whole picture, since clearly the smaller farmers have not been given a chance. Obviously, the measurement of success relates directly to the way in which the systems interdigitate with one another. When success is measured, it is always from the point of view of targets, not from the point of view of the people for whom the programme was designed. Thus, there is no self-correcting mechanism built into the system.

Conclusion

I have been trying to explore, in a preliminary way, some of the

[33] Srinivasan, K., and M. Kachirayan, 1968. "Vasectomy Follow-up Study: Findings and Implications," *Institute of Rural Health and Family Planning Bulletin*. Vol. III, No. 1, July, pp. 20-21.

sociological factors involved in aspects of current development programmes. I am primarily making use of data from the two areas I know best, Kerala and Tamil Nadu. Obviously there are significant differences from region to region within south Asia. Nonetheless, I should like to postulate that there are certain structural similarities, and that these may even go beyond the confine of south Asia.

First of all, the programmes under discussion are being introduced in bureaucratic structures that follow patterns set down long before the "development programmes" got going. Secondly, these structures are not calculated to break down barriers between people; indeed, in at least some cases, they were intended to create barriers. (Leeds[34] has shown from work in slums in Rio de Janeiro that programmes introduced along traditional paternalistic patterns cannot hope to have the impact conceived of by the planners.)

One of the things which I am suggesting is that we need to look more at the question of power relations insofar as they affect and are affected by the modernization process. We need to see how the attitudes of change agents (in this case, many of the traditional stereotypes perpetuated by a highly stratified society) can be changed. Can they be changed within the present structure or is that impossible? Heginbotham's study shows how completely the bureaucracy of development parallels the old pre-independence set-up.[35] On the basis of the research reported here, the conclusion seems to me inescapable that certain kinds of change cannot be carried out unless the planners and change agents themselves can be made aware of the importance of their

---

[34]Leeds, Anthony, 1970. "Paternalism vs Egalitarianism: Contradictions, Hence Failures, in Two Action Programmes in a Rio Favela," American Anthropological Association Meeting, December 1967. Leeds also noted that the lower class exploit the paternalism for their own ends which are different from those of the agency being paternalistic. Leeds also deals with this question in Leeds, Anthony and Elizabeth Leeds, "The Myth of Urban Rurality: Work, Experience and Values Among Squatter Settlement Residents of Rio and Lima," in A.J. Field, ed., 1970. *City and Country in the Third World*. Cambridge: Schenkman Press.

[35]Heginbotham, *op. cit.*, p. 135.

own position and attitudes, and the ways in which these affect the development process. They also have to be aware of what kind of a society they are trying to create, and the long-range implications of what they are doing.

F.G. Bailey

15 The Peasant View of Bad Life

This paper is concerned with why in which some poor peasants living in the hills and jungles of one of the less advanced states of the Indian Union—Orissa—think about themselves, about leaders, about the politicians and officials who govern them, and how they conceptualize time and the future.

I have chosen this restricted subject for several reasons. Firstly—and negatively—a presidental address need not always be a speech by the President on the state of the nation. The importance of sociology and the direction in which it should develop are subjects at once too easy and too difficult for this occasion. Of course, insofar as sociology is an underdeveloped subject, it may be that my discourse will not be wholly without interest for those concerned with the politics of the social sciences in this country, since it concerns closed minds and inflexible attitudes.

Secondly, although one cannot fail to be impressed with Niagara or writing by sociologists and political scientists on problems of development and modernization,[1] their work is heavily biased towards the elite. There are many reasons why this should be. Top people, we assume, are the people who shape

---

[1] There are many ways of defining "modernization": my training inclines towards a definition based upon role pattern—diffuse as against specific roles—and I make use of one such definition later. But I do not consider it necessary to discuss the question at length here since my argument applied to any kind of innovation into the peasant world whether or not we would want to class this innovation as modern.

history. Top people, too, behave in ways that the alien social scientist can understand: for example, many of them speak—and write books in—English or French. But the alien social scientist cannot so easily understand what the human majority of the developing nations—the mass, the non-elite—are thinking, or why they are thinking it: they are strange, remote, annoyingly diverse, unpredictable, a mystery even to their own elite, apathetic, afraid to take risks, improvident, parochial in their outlook, superstitious—and so on through a string of adjectives which range from the patronizing to the contemptuous. These attitudes no doubt reinforce the morale of the modernizing elite and convince them that they are right to fight for the good of the peasants against peasant ignorance and prejudice. But a conviction of one's own effortless superiority is no adequate substitute for knowledge, for intelligence, in the military sense of that word.

There is, in fact, an inverse relationship between the force which a modernizer must use in his war against traditional values and behaviour, and the knowledge which he must have of the enemy's dispositions. If he has overwhelming force—and this is not the case of the developing nations—then he can wipe the board clean and in one generation write upon it a new set of modern roles and values. But short of this hypothetical extreme, the modernizer cannot compel but must persuade: to do this he must know what values the people already hold; how they see the world and society around them; in short, he must know their cognitive maps.[2] In this situation knowledge is a substitute for—one might say a kind of—power; with an adequate map—an adequate understanding of the traditional way of life—the modernizer can most economically and effectively deploy his limited resources.

Here I shall talk about those peasants in India whom I happen to know, about certain concepts which they hold and which a modernizer should take into account. I shall also out-

---

[2]There are many near synonyms for "cognitive map," some more and some less inclusive: ethos, world-view, collective representations, beliefs and values, ideology and—most inclusive—culture. The metaphor of a map is appropriate because it suggests a guide for action. Cognitive maps consist of a set of value directives and existential propositions which together help to guide social interaction.

line a very broad strategy for those who wish to promote economic, social and political development. On another occasion I hope to make similar analyses of the cognitive maps of the elite themselves: of politicians, administrators, merchants, entrepreneurs, students and (one might add) city mobs.

For a number of reasons, tracing the cognitive map of a culture not one's own is difficult. In recent years linguistic anthropologists have developed a technique which may provide the scientific exactness so far lacking, but as yet these tools have been used to elicit the categories through which people perceive their kinsmen, or the types of food they eat or the way they think about the consumption of alcohol, or about disease, or about the land on which they grow their food. The more general moral categories with which I am here concerned—good and bad, success and failure, and the difficult idea of the moral community—remain beyond the reach of these techniques. My account, therefore, will be impressionistic and difficult to verify.[3]

Anthropologists begin by selecting native concepts and teasing out their meanings. A one-word translation is always inadequate. Often the concepts are presented in the native language: *mana, taboo, totem* are well-known examples, and they can be described only by specifying the contexts in which they may be correctly used. Sometimes the people themselves have no general term. For example, the concept of an "outsider" is my summary of a range of terms which peasants have for particular outsiders: *Sircar* (government); *Marwari* (a trader); *Gujarati* (another kind of trader); *Kotaki* (a man from the coastal plain); and so forth. In short, these are quite considerable problems of translation.

Thirdly, it is not easy to decide at what level of generality to make the translation. Perceptions of the world vary according to sex, to age, to caste status and so forth. In the context of modernization in peasant India it is usually appropriate to look at the cognitive maps of adult males, but this does not get round variations in caste and ethnic allegiances. I shall be talking of the hill peasants of Orissa who, in the area in which

---

[3] I am not competent to discuss psychological techniques for ascertaining peasant attitudes.

I lived, are either Oriyas or Konds.[4] The cognitive maps of both these peoples contain the same element of xenophobia, but they differ radically in their perceptions of human inequality. To average out these differences makes nonsense; there is nothing to do but make two cognitive maps, for ideas of rank are clearly relevant in the modernization process. In what follows I shall be talking mainly about the Oriyas who, being a caste society, see the social world in categories of rank. The other themes which I shall discuss are found at greater or lesser degree in many peasant societies: but I could not claim that they are universal.

Every society discriminates between different categories of persons, giving to the highest full status as members of the community, able to bear social responsibilities and commanding the corresponding social rights, and relegating the lowest into a category which is scarcely human at all. Those who are so marginal as to be considered outsiders can be used as if they were objects or instruments, providing the user has the power to do so: this is not regarded as a moral relationship but as one of exploitation. Standards of honesty, respect and consideration, insofar as they are moral imperatives, are diminished as the status of the person at the other end of the relationship becomes more marginal. Moreover, one expects him to reciprocate. One justifies cheating government agencies by saying that the officials concerned are cheating you. This perception is often so firm that even behaviour which is patently not exploitative but benevolent is interpreted as a hypocritical cover for some as yet undisclosed interest: by definition all horses are Trojan.

The steps by which categories of people are charted as marginal are not evenly spaced. For the villagers whom I knew the moral community[5] comprises their own family, the

---

[4]For a detailed account of Konds and Oriyas see Bailey (1960, pp. 121-93).

[5]The concept of a moral community is complex and difficult. In everyday language this is the distinction between "we" the moral community) and "they" (the outsiders). For those who follow Durkheim, the adjective "moral" is perhaps redundant, since the society (or community) is co-extensive with moral action. Nevertheless, I retain the adjective to emphasize the continuous judgement of right and wrong

members of their own caste in the same village, their fellow villagers (markedly graded according to their distance from ego in the caste system), their kinsmen in other villages and their caste fellows in other villages and, getting near to the limit, people of other castes in those same villages. Then, after a gap, come people who are villagers like oneself, with the same lifestyle and speaking the same dialect, but with whom, as yet, no connection can be traced: if they desire to be admitted to the moral community, the villagers use elaborate and rigorous techniques to test their cultural credentials.

Beyond this category are people whose culture—the way they speak, the way they dress, their deportment, the things they speak about as valuable and important—places them unambiguously beyond the moral community of the peasant; revenue inspectors, policemen, development officers, health inspectors, veterinary officials and so on, men in bush-shirts and trousers, men who are either arrogant and distant or who exhibit a camaraderie which if the villager reciprocates, is immediately switched off; men who come on bicycles and in jeeps, but never on their feet. These are the people to be outwitted: these are the people whose apparent gifts are by definition the bait for some hidden trap.

The significance of this for political modernization and for development is obvious. Suggestions are commands to assume modern political or economic roles come from outside the moral community: they are therefore automatically categorized as dangerous and sinful, and those villagers who adopt the new roles run the risk of being marked as deviants and punished. Equally, if any innovation does in fact turn out to be harmful (for example, the improved seed that fails), the villager does

---

which characterizes interactions within the community. Beyond the community such judgements do not apply: to cheat an outsider is neither right nor wrong: it is merely expedient or inexpedient.

It is also difficult to draw a boundary around a particular moral community, for each one varies according to the ego who is chosen as the point of reference. The Brahmin and the sweeper do not have the same moral community even within the one village. Nevertheless, for both of them, there are some common—and large—discontinuities, so that vis-a-vis for instant outsiders, it is possible to regard both Brahmin and sweeper as members of the one moral community.

not feel obliged to search for what he would regard as a rational scientific cause; he finds a perfectly satisfactory explanation in the fact that it came from outside; and he also finds confirmation of his perception that external things are evil and dangerous (cf. Bailey, 1959, pp. 252-54).

It is, therefore, something of a paradox that the way a peasant tries to exploit a politician or an official, or to avoid being exploited by him, is by transforming the modern specialized relationship which he has with that man into a multiplex relationship, a type which is characteristic of his own peasant world. The peasant dealing with a clerk finds a broker to help him establish personal relationship which will soften the rigorous unpleasantness of the official relationship. The politician seeking votes or the development official seeking peasant cooperation will call them "brothers and sisters." When the peasants want something out of the official they will address him as if he were a kinsman and therefore has the obligation to be generous, or perhaps by that opening to many Indian petitions "You are my mother and my father. . . . " The implication in all these cases is that the official relationship, which is single-interest and specialized, is not enough: it must be reinforced with other relationships.

Relationships within a peasant or tribal community are for the most part multiplex: that is to say, they are specialized to deal with a single activity. There is, of course, some division of labour as, for example, between the landowners and the landless; but even then this relationship, which I have described through its economic stand, will also carry political and ritual and possibly familial strands. This, indeed, is the characteristic pattern of the caste system as it works inside an Indian village.

It is to be noticed that whether the initiative comes from the official and politician or from the peasant, it is the supplicant who seeks to make the relationship diffuse: to make it a moral relationship. The dominant partner will usually play hard-to-get; if the official or politician is dominant he will try to retain the transactional character of the relationship and not have the sharp edge of the bargain blunted by moral considerations; if the peasant is dominant, he is likely to reject the proffered relationship, because it comes from an outsider, or to accept it simply as a transaction and get what he can out of it. I have ample evidence that this was overwhelmingly the attitude of villagers towards campaigning politicians in India.

When as a supplicant, the peasant tries to bribe a clerk or to establish a dependent relationship with an official in the idiom of a family relationship or of a courtier at the king's palace, he is in fact trying to coerce the clerk or the official by including him within his own moral community. He is trying to transform the transaction, which he knows is one of exploitation, into a moral relationship *because it is in his interest to do so*. In just the same way, when the campaigning politician addresses him a "brother," the peasant sees this as an act of hypocrisy, and looks behind the facade of symbolic friendliness for the hidden interest.

The watershed between traditional and modern society is exactly this distinction between single-interest and multiplex relationships. The hallmark of a modern society is the specialized role and the whole apparatus of its productive prosperity rests upon the division of labour between specialized roles. Of course we have diffuse institutions like the family, but the public official who finds job for his relatives or the fact that a large part of Macmillan's cabinets could be shown on a chart of kinship and affinity, is something which our modern culture condemns: or at least we feel uncomfortable about it.

This feeling of ethical disquiet may be the reason why planners in India resolutely close their eyes to the fact that the society they are attempting to modernize is founded upon multiplex relationships. No doubt there is bribery and nepotism; but it is loudly condemned. Even in situations which could be met without bruising the modernist conscience, the official gaze is resolutely averted: for example, when the *zamindari* holdings in Orissa were abolished, the *zamindar's* place was taken by an official specialized in the collection of revenue; but the *zamindar's* other functions—moneylending, dispute settling, and so forth—were not systematically provided for.

The attitude of the peasant towards single-interest relationships is not, I think, marked by ethical displeasure. Such relationships, being with outsiders, are not *im*moral so much as *a*moral: when one is dealing with an instrument, standards of what is just and unjust do not apply: one wants only to use the instruments most effectively.

The Peasant View of Bad Life

A second important theme in the peasants' cognitive map is what we would call hardship. Villagers recognize two kinds of big men: a secular leader whom we will call "chief" and a man of religious eminence whom the villagers call a *yogi* or a *guru* (teacher) but whom we will call a "saint." I will argue that the idea of disinterested service to the community is only a minor element in one of these categories and is altogether absent from the other.

A chief is a man who is able to take care of his honour (*mohoto*), and who regards honour as the supreme value in social life. Honour entails the notion of competition and conflict, for a man gets honour by demonstrating in various stylized ways that his rivals have less honour: that is to say, by shaming them. Heads of families, especially wealthy men of high caste, are all chiefs and they treat one another, when not in combat, with a dignified formality and restraint.

Insofar as a man is a chief he is expected to protect the interests *not* of the community at large, but the interests of his own followers against rival chiefs and their followers. Moreover, even within this relationship between chief and follower the notion of disinterested service is weakly developed: loyalty, except for the innermost circle of followers, is bought by the protection which the chief gives and by the largesse which he hands out to his own followers. If the chief cannot provide these things, then the follower is not expected to go through an agony of heart searching but to use and find a stronger and richer chief. There is an element here of the amorality found in the "outsider" relationship. Also notice that although the chief is expected to provide a service for others, the notion of this service is the very antithesis of what we mean by *"public service"*: as their equivalent in our civilization might say, "chiefs are not in business just for their health." The idea of service from a posture of humility is entirely absent.

Some of these chiefs, when they become old men, turn into "philanthropoids." They build temples, or resthouses for pilgrims, or plant trees to give shade, or excavate bathing pools where the devout may take purifying baths. Peasants certainly mark with approval wells and bathing *ghats* and shady trees: but the act of giving is considered cynically as a kind of conscience money. A man in a village close to where I lived had cheated and bullied his way to great eminence, but in middle age was still without a son. He then invested in a number of spectacular public works and in a new young wife: in due time she presented him with a son. This son lived to manhood but, as the man who told me noted with satisfaction, the old man outlived him and there were no grandchildren.

Villagers look more kindly on a man of religious eminence than upon a chief. But, like the chief, the saint too is looking after himself and his own soul, as we would say: his life is not spent in the service of others. Even if he is a *guru* (a teacher), he is a consultant helping individuals with their particular difficulties rather than a man active in the public service. The saint is respected—even loved in a special numinous sense of that word—not for what he does for the community, but simply for what he is—a holy man.

Some traditional ideas about secular leadership are relevant to political modernization and economic development. Notice that the appropriate relationship between a leader and a follower is not inconsistent with the attitude which one has towards an outsider. Leader-follower relationships within a moral community have a degree of hardness and calculation of self-interest: when the relationship crosses the boundary of the moral community, wariness hardens into suspicion and double-dealing. Within the moral community the peasant understands the range of possible action; within limits, he knows what his opponent will do because he and his opponent (whether leader or follower) share certain basic values: furthermore the relationship is seen to be regulated by councils or *panchayats* or superior leaders. But outside the moral community none of these controls apply: official action is unpredictable; values are not shared; and adjudicative institutions like courts of law, are not part of the peasant moral community but are regarded as instruments or weapons to be used in the contest. Within the moral community, one looks carefully to see if the leader is fulfilling his side of the bargain: outside the moral community, one knows that a bargain will not be fulfilled, and one must therefore insure oneself by anticipatory cheating.

Secondly, the language of cooperation is almost completely absent from the traditional leader-follower relationship. The language of cooperation is, of course, found in the village but it is a language used between equals and within the moral community. It is found in the formalized equality symbolized in the procedures of the village council or in the ceremonial meeting of the senior kin of a bride and groom; it is also found, with less formality, in cooperative work parties or in hunting when the men, after a rest, urge one another to resume the chase with those strange staccato cries of mutual encouragement that one hears coming out of a pack of rugby forwards. Everyone gives the orders to no one in particular. But leaders do not appeal to their followers to pull together as a matter of moral obligation: rather they offer them inducements (rewards or punishments) to do so.

Traditional leaders do not ask for cooperation. Outsiders *cannot* effectively ask for cooperation from the peasants. But they do so continually, and to the villagers this seems either a joke or something to be very worried about, as a football player would be if he heard himself being urged on and urged to cooperate by the captain of the opposing team.

The peasant looks upon outsiders (including officials) as his enemies. But within his conceptual world, there are also, a number of persons whom we might see as peace-making or mediating. How does the peasant see these persons? The men could be traitors; they could be enemy agents; or they could be accepted and given moral status as true mediators, thus widening the boundaries of the peasant moral community.

At first sight some chiefly roles—in India *rajas* or non-absentee *zamindars*—could span the gap between officials and the peasant world. These statuses combine in the one person general administrator, tax collector, justice of peace, welfare officer and moneylender, custodian of sacred symbols and organizer of collective rituals at harvest or sowing time or on other religious occasions.[6] All these people have now been

---

[6] Dr B.D. Graham has suggested to me that the political "bosses" of state Congress parties and their subordinates succeed partly because they play the same kind of multiplex role as did landowners and *rajas*. In Orissa, party politicians used to complain about the diversity of demands made by their own constitutents, (he wanted me to find a bride for his son), and mock their rivals by saying they held *durbars* for their constituents. Peasants find it hard to accept the idea of functional specialization in authority roles.

legally—but not always effectively—dethroned in India. They were to some extent a part of the moral community of their peasants. We anthropologists have made much of a relationship of this kind: emphasizing that the king, as the custodian of sacred objects and the performance of sacred rituals, symbolized the unity of his people and their values. I am sure we were right to do so, and not a few difficulties in enforced modernization arise from ignoring non-political components of traditional leadership roles and neglecting to make provision in modern institutions for these components.

But, for several reasons, it is hard to see *rajas* or landlords as mediators in the modernizing situation. Firstly, they were not allowed to do so because the cognitive map of the modernizing elite marked them as enemies identifying them correctly as an important part of the political system created by the British authoritarian administration. Secondly, since they are the very apogee of the chiefly role, their status as members of the peasant moral community was somewhat precarious. One Orissa ex-*raja*, who had been elected—almost unanimously—to the legislative assembly, told me that he did not bother to campaign and that if he had chosen to nominate his elephant his people would have returned it to the assembly. But, in the next election, he was defeated. His state had been abolished for ten years and the many roles that he had combined in his person were either not being performed or were being done by a scatter of administrators. I think he underestimated the transactional nature of his tie with his former subjects. The love of which he boasted, turned out to be cupboard-love (the contents of the cupboard being, of course, culturally defined). Thirdly—and the fate of the *raja* will serve to illustrate this too—once such men begin to behave like outsiders, then inevitably they take on the role of outsiders and lose their place in the moral community of the peasants. A few exceptional men—there were two striking examples in Orissa—built up a transactional following in the modern role of politician: no doubt they were helped by their loyal status to make a start, but this status alone would not carry them for very long. Incidentally, the modernizing elite was very reluctant to admit that these two men were in fact playing modern roles.

The second kind of potential mediator is the man who has

recently made the jump into the elite, and who still has close kinsmen who have remained peasants. In most parts of tropical Africa the indigenous elite are new boys: so too, in India, are many politicians at the state and even at the national level; but this is less true of the civil services. This happens because the children of the elite acquire education and the children of the poor do not. This has been the case for many generations in India. I suppose it will also become true of Africa, and one already hears reports from West Africa that the elite is hardening into a class (see Lloyd, 1966, intro.).

How do the peasants regard a kinsman who has become part of the elite? He is still part of their moral community and is expected to take the responsibilities and obligations of a kinsman. That these obligations may conflict with his modern roles is not countenanced. Such a man must take care what role-signs he displays: when he goes on leave, he discards the bush shirt and trousers for a *dhoti* before he enters his village. Indeed, those actions which the modern world stigmatizes as nepotism and corruption, are in fact often the fulfilling of a man's obligations in the traditional world. The conclusion must be—and it is something of a paradox—that the newly joined member of the elite can act neither as a mediator between the two worlds nor as a modernizing agent among his own people: he can in fact only retain the tie with his own people so long as he acts in accordance with their values.

The third category of brokers are those who use religious symbols which are valued by the peasants in order to seek membership of the peasant moral community: or (which perhaps more accurately describes the motives of the most famous of them), in order to disclaim membership of the modernizing elite. How do the villagers look upon such men and women?

The saintly figure is part of their known world. He stands for something—however vague—which they value: one might call it personal salvation. They do not bargain with or try to exploit a saint. For most people the relationship is distant and impersonal, one of respect and reverence symbolized by giving alms and receiving what we call blessing. Those who form a closer relationship as pupils or disciples choose to do so for ideological or moral reasons; the saint does not drum up a following in the way that a chief does.

But the politician who presents himself in the saintly style, clad in a *dhoti* and sandals and arriving on his feet, does not always behave in the manner which the villagers associate with his appearance. The visitor does not sit silently under the tree or give his advice only to those who ask for it; he makes speeches. Moreover, what he advocates must seem to the villagers very surprising, like sacred music sung to rock-and-roll. He talks about hygiene, or basic education, or why the poor should be given land—all topics which suggest to the villagers *Sircar*, the government. Vinoba Bhave's men came to the village where I lived and were rejected as completely as if they had been government agents—indeed, more completely, for it was known that they had no force to back up their requests. We talk easily of charismatic leaders, since Weber gave us the word, but I think we are often taken in by the propaganda of those who have ambitions to be charismatic leaders.

The remaining mediating role has probably been the most effective in spanning the gap between peasants and elite. This is the village broker: the man who makes a profession of helping officials or politicians and peasants to communicate with one another, and is paid either directly or indirectly for doing so. He knows how to get licences and remission of tax, he knows where to place bribes, he can get real medicines from the hospital dispensary: for the other side he recruits voters or agents or people to make a good showing when some superior visitor is coming down; he can do privately and discreetly all these jobs which the rulers of modern institutions forbid, but which modern people find must be done (see Bailey, 1963, pp. 55-67).

Although his stock in trade is the favours he has done for people, such a man is not honoured or even trusted by the villagers. He is renegade, a half-outsider, albeit necessary to temper the cold winds of bureaucracy. But no such man could possibly achieve moral status as a mediator between traditionalists and modernizers. Both sides place him in the category of outsider. In fact he does positive harm: for his makeshift activities perpetuate the gap in communication between peasants and elite.

From the point of view of those who wish to modernize, the picture which I draw is not encouraging. There are a few exceptional people who can become, so to speak, honorary members of the peasants' moral community and yet urge peasants to take on new and modern roles. But they can do this only to a very limited extent, for the peasants have a very low threshold of tolerance for those of their own members who connect too closely with the outside world.

The root of my argument is that building a modern society is not a routine process in which all the steps are known and all contingencies anticipated. On the contrary: it is a world of mistakes, frustrations, disappointments, anxiety and conflicts. On the quite rare occasions when peasants enter this world voluntarily, they do so because they think they are going to get something out of it: they are out to exploit. If their expectations are disappointed, they withdraw, as they would withdraw their allegiance from an unsuccessful leader. Only people who have a moral commitment to a modern society will persist in the face of disappointment and failure. I have been discussing a number of roles which, at first sight, might seem to provide this moral commitment by holding the trust of the peasants. But in virtually all cases this trust is withdrawn if the broker is seen to be a missionary for modernization.[7]

I have talked about the peasants' categories of outsiders, leaders and brokers: that is about persons. Now, at a more abstract level I shall ask what peasants think, not about politicians, but about policies. Much has been written about what particular peasants or tribesmen think about particular policies; but not so much about the idea of policy-making.

In this idea, there are two main components, neither of which forms part of peasant culture. The first is that man has a good chance of controlling his own destiny and his environ-

---

[7]There is an extensive literature on "hinge men": those who mediate between different cultures or between different levels in the same culture. A good example is Wolf (1956). The range of such roles extends from simple transactions (for example, the petition-writer at an Indian administrative headquarters) to highly developed patron roles which come near to attaining moral status, see Boissevain (1961). The roles considered in this essay are not those of *cultural* brokers" in the sense of providing a communication of ideas and a meeting of minds: on the contrary the village broker at least is a device which enables the peasants and the elite to avoid a meeting of minds. By providing pragmatic contracts they render unnecssary normative communion.

ment: no one would continue to formulate policies if he thought that he could never implement them. Indeed the essence of policy-making is that it is a plan for manipulating variables which we know we can control, in order to adapt ourselves to those variables which we know we cannot control: and so, in a paradoxical way to achieve some kind of control over the uncontrollable.

One of the components of our romantic view of rural life is its certainty and dependability. The four seasons follow one another: year after year life renews itself in the same way. This cycle of eternity, recorded and edited and abridged for us in poetry or at the cinema, gives us a sense of security. We do not doubt, when we go to sleep, but that the same world will be there when we wake up in the morning.

I do not know whether the peasants with whom I lived have this mystical sense of life's continuance: I doubt it since, unlike us, they know rural life in the raw, unexpurgated, unabridged, and uncleaned for dramatic presentation. Certainly, whatever the stability of nature's grand design, they see little security in their own life. No one can be sure whether the harvest will be good or bad: no one can be sure who will be alive this time next year, or even next week. In two or three years a rich man can become poor or a poor man rich. Women die in childbirth: there were women in Bisipara (a village where I lived) who had had five or eight or, in one case, ten children and raised not one beyond its second year. In circumstances like this, no one can feel that man is the master of his environment: nature may have a grand continuing design, but a man's life is filled with discontinuities. No peasant thinks in terms of five-year plans, and I would argue that the idea of planning can exist only in those cognitive maps which include the idea of man in control of predictable and controllable *impersonal* forces.

Even in our cognitive maps, persons seem less predictable and controllable than things. Sometimes we attribute our failures to other people's malevolent actions; we do this particularly when the undertaking is difficult and a gamble—if the five-year plan fails, that is because of the wicked internal opposition, the stupid peasants and the intrigues of the neo-colonialists: witch-hunting is found in everyone's culture. But we also stress and widely employ the idea that failures can be the result of our miscalculation of variables which are purely impersonal, which have no will of their own, and which cannot be held to be morally responsible. In such cases the idea of punishment or revenge or deterrence makes nonsense: it is the mistake that must be corrected, not the person. To the extent that a cognitive map does not include the idea of impersonal non-moral forces, it also cannot include their idea of planning. To a much greater extent than we do, peasants blame failure upon the malevolence of human agents.[8] It is true that in India and in some other cultures, fate is used as an explanation: but fate, although predictable, cannot be controlled. Success—spectacular success—is also attributed to human wickedness. The man who, as we say, makes a killing, is not reaping the rewards of hard work and correct calculation, but made his way through sorcery or magic or at least in some way which was harmful to his fellows. Judging from the stories I was told of how men in Bisipara first became wealthy the peasant mythology contains no category of honest riches. Notice the significance of this for innovation and modernization: any peasant who adopts new ways and becomes rich, must have cheated, must have exploited his fellows, and to that extent should be punished or put outside the moral community.

In brief, both the uncertainty of peasant life and the fact that they explain failure by blaming people rather than by supporting a miscalculation or impersonal forces means that policy-making and planning are not part of their cognitive map of the world and human society. They do not reject the idea of planning as wicked: they simply do not have the category.

At first sight such a statement seems wrong, for no peasant could survive unless he planned the use of his resources. They breed cattle; they save for marriages; nowadays they make wills; they plan with Machiavellian subtlety ways of doing one another down; and, to name the simplest and most fundamental act of planning, they keep seed for next year's sowing. But, I would argue, such activities are not to be considered planning in the way in which that word is used in, for example, the

---

[8] The best-known exposition of this outlook on life is Evans-Pritchard (1937).

phrase "five-year plan." This brings me to the second component in the idea of policy-making.

The second component in policy-making is innovation. The policy-maker sees a future which is different from the present not just because it is separated from the present by week or a year, but because life then will be of a different kind from what it is now. Let us separate these two kinds of thought about the future by calling the first "the round of time" and the second "time's arrow" (Bourdieu, 1963).

The peasant plans for the round of time. He allocates resources as if he held the assumptions that with minor variations and barring accidents, next year will be this year over again. Each resource is seen against a round of time: so many years before the son replaces the father; thatching every third or second year. In this world, too, people are not so ready to look for the witch behind every failure. A man whose crop is poor when all around have good crops cannot blame witches if he is known to be a slovenly cultivator: it is recognized that with luck (i.e., the absence of human malevolence and adverse fate) good crops are the result of hard work and skilled cultivation. But, as is perhaps also true in our society, few people think hard work and skill a means of changing a poor man into a rich man in twenty years' time: if changes like that happen, they come overnight by mystical means, by magic or fate or luck; by finding a crock of gold; in our culture by devious and anti-social property deals or by winning on the football pools.

Those who make five-year plans are thinking of time as an arrow. The work has a beginning and an end: there is a target to be reached. The end is a state of affairs quite different from the beginning, and itself is a starting point for further ventures. We have no difficulties with this notion. To plan a future state of affairs which is radically different from the present is to us quite rational. But those who think in terms of the round of time see such changes as coming from mystical forces like fate, or luck, or witchcraft or acts of God, and to plan for such events makes nonsense. The politician who promises a good life in store for everyone, if they help to implement the plan, is heard by the peasants as we would hear a man promising everyone a first dividend on the pools every week.[9]

These are cultural categories and, as with statistical norms, they allow that individuals can be found holding different ideas. Some peasants have learned to see time as an arrow: and most peasants, at least in countries like India, are from time to time compelled to behave as if they saw time that way. But when there is a failure, where accidents occur and the arrow misses the target, then they look for explanations and they take initiatives in the idiom of the round of time—in terms of human wickedness rather than of scientific error. Even those who make the plans, in whom the idea of time as an arrow is internalized, may react to failure by looking for the scapegoat rather than the cause.

This concludes my examination of a few basic cultural themes in the cognitive map of the Indian peasant. These themes hang together: the relationship with a leader is instrumental and exploitative: still more so is that with an outsider. Spectacular success is evil because your success means my failure is caused by your malevolence. Outsiders talk about spectacular change and spectacular success, but we peasants can only be instruments in their schemes: in any case, if their fantasies were realized, this could only be by anti-social means. How shall I conclude this discourse, which for a modernizer is certainly a jeremiad? I would insist that to look upon the bright side and simply deny what I have said, is to pretend that the enemy's bullets will turn to water and his tanks are made of cardboard.

Furthermore, it makes little sense to ask why people hold these values, in the hope that, discovering the causes, we can bring about change. At this level values and categories of thought are ultimate and given; they have no causes and they cannot be further reduced. Indeed it is as pointless as to ask *why* peasants think in the round of time, as it is to ask why the Oriya numeral for unity is "eko" while we say "one." We can explain values by relating them to one another, as one analyzes

---

[9]For peasants social life is a zero-sum game. One man's gain is, of necessity, another's loss. See Foster (1965).

the structure of a painting or a poem: but we cannot ask what is the cause of a set of values.

What we can do, however, is to show how a particular set of ideas such as those I have been discussing, and the experience of the people, validate one another. The connection is a functional one and the line of causation between ideas and experience points in both directions. Belief and action are connected with one another. My argument is that fundamental categories of thought (like those of time) and fundamental values (like those attached to leadership and authority) are impervious to direct ideological attack—at least in the short run and given the resources at the disposal of modernizing elites in most of the new nations. The sensible tactic, therefore, is to change the "action" element (which is another word for "experience"), in these sectors of action that are least connected with ideological convictions.[10]

The operational prospects are not in fact so bad. I have been talking about collective representations—about thought: and thought is not the same as action. People can be pressured by carrots or sticks into doing things which they consider are evil or foolish; and a long enough experience may convince them that in fact these things are neither evil nor foolish. Vaccination and DDT spraying and some agricultural innovations (especially some cash crops) have this kind of success. But parliamentary democracy of other kinds of political modernization and many economic innovations and social reforms do not and could not show such immediate and tangible returns: they may in fact seem to produce immediate and tangible disasters. The conclusion must be that, given peasant resistance, a radical policy of political and economic modernization can only be

---

[10] Peasants are generally distinguished from tribesmen by their contact with towns, markets and high cultures. Routine experiences in traditional towns are unlikely to modify the broad features of the map of peasant cognition sketched here, since these experiences are part of this same map. But the traumatic experience of migrant labour and factory work in "modern" towns is likely to bring change in peasant values and beliefs: so also is production largely for a market, which turns the peasant into a farmer. I cannot here discuss urban contacts, except to say that my argument applies to peasants and not to farmers or to industrial workers.

achieved by pressure and by continued success in material terms.

Short of this—but consistently—those resources which are available for modernization are wasted if they are used directly for propaganda about duty, service, self-sacrifice and so forth. Modernization is an end too vague and too complex to be readily symbolized and understood: even *swaraj* (independence) was a non-message so far as Indian peasants were concerned: they listened when Congress began to exploit agrarian discontents. "Democratic decentralization" is a non-message: remission of rent or the removal of a greedy landlord will be understood and accepted (with due suspicion). Any plan for modernization which is based on the assumption that peasants will feel an immediate moral commitment to modernity as such and will persist voluntarily in the face of failure and frustration because they are so committed, must be ineffective.

Let me repeat that my discourse is about collective representations—about the way peasants think. This is but one—indeed, the last of the variables with which the modernizer must operate it. If his plans fail, clearly his first question should be about physical and technical matters. Leaving aside human wishes, is it possible for anyone to carry out that particular plan? Perhaps there is something special about the soil of the demonstration farm, absent from most peasant farms? Perhaps the price of fertilizer is too high, so that even if the peasants want it, they cannot buy it? There are many factors of this kind, and their control is usually far easier than attempts to influence and control peasant values and categories of thought.

Secondly, there is a set of variables which belong to peasant social structure rather than to peasant values. The line between social structure and values is a difficult one to draw, but I have in mind a great variety of particular role constraints which affect the peasant's life. For a simple example, given a certain level of poverty, the contribution which children make to transplanting paddy can be crucial: where I lived in India the village schools were closed at planting time and this seemed to me a sensible recognition of the productive role of children in the peasant family. Again—an all too familiar example in many Indian villages—to give the vote to untouchables in elections for village *panchayats*, without the additional protections of a secret ballot, is to invite failure. In other words, innovations may have social costs which are unknown to or have been ignored by the modernizer.

Both the technical and the structural factors can only be discussed against the background of particular cases. What prospect there is of successful modernization in India and other developing nations, rests upon the willingness of the planning elite to continuously improve their manipulation of technical and structural variables—to make sure that the price of water from the canal is reasonable and is seen by the peasants to be reasonable, that improved seed developed on the demonstration farm will in fact grow on peasant plots, and to remember that the headman will come under great pressure from his kinsmen, and so forth. I suspect that there is a temptation to evade the drudgery of seeking technical—and I suppose we might say "structural"—efficacy by saying that the peasants need a change of heart and rushing out to make a speech. If all the technical and structural variables have been correctly handled and the project still fails, one might argue that there is no recourse but to bring about a voluntary change of heart in the peasants. To argue this is to argue that the task is impossible.

From this there emerges one broad strategic directive. If resources for modernization are limited, they are most effectively spent if they bring about a change in the physical environment, which the peasant must accept willy-nilly and which force him to adapt himself to the new conditions. When change has come about, at least in village India, it is generally because new methods of irrigation have been introduced, or a road has been built to the market, and so forth. Such measures, of course, do not always succeed; but I suspect that they succeed more often than does a direct onset upon peasant social structure, and still more often than an attack upon those generalized and internalized values and perceptions about which I have been talking here.

Cognitive maps do change: but for the most part they do so slowly as the result of experience. As the flow of water can change the course of a river, so experience can erode received ideas and allow others to settle in their place. With this most modernizers must be content. Occasionally force of circumstances or a massive expenditure of resources can produce a flood of new experiences that change the map overnight: but this is rare. For the most part modernizers must think small: and the least effective use of their resources is to plan directly that the peasants shall have a change of heart. The cultural themes which I have been discussing here are like swamps and rocky mountains: the modernizers should plan to make a detour.

Beyond that, one can make few recommendations. The gnarled oak of peasant alienation (as the modernizers would see it) is only one tree in the forest. It is a tree which takes many different forms, even in India, even within the one village from which I have drawn my material. One needs a much wider sample. One should also look at some of the other trees, at the many divisions within the elite. What view do they have of themselves, of each other, and of the peasants? Armed with all these maps and with a systematic knowledge of technical factors and of social structure, one might begin to understand some of the diverse changes which have occurred—or failed to occur—in the new nations.

REFERENCES

Bailey, F.G., 1959. *Caste and Economic Frontier: Village in Highland Orissa.* Manchester: Manchester University Press.

————, 1960. *Tribe, Caste and Nation.* Manchester: Manchester University Press.

————, 1963. *Politics and Social Change.* London: Oxford University Press.

Boissevain, J., 1961. "Patronage in Sicily," *Man.* Vol. 1, New Series, pp. 18-33.

Bourdieu, P., 1963. "The Attitude of the Algerian Peasant Towards Time," in J. Pitt-Rivers, ed., *Mediterranean Countrymen.* Mouton.

Evans-Pritchard, E.E., 1937. *Witchcraft, Oracles and Magic Among the Azande.* Clarendon Press.

Foster, G., 1965. "Peasant Society and the Image of Limited Good," *American Anthropologist.* Vol. 67, No. 2, pp. 293-315.

Lloyd, P.C., ed., 1966. *The New Elite of Tropical Africa.* London: Oxford University Press.

Wolf, E.R., 1956. "Aspects of Group Relations in a Complex Society," *American Anthropologist.* Vol. 58, No. 6, pp. 1065-78.

Adrian C. Mayer

16 Development Projects in an Indian Village

The programmes of rural community development in India form a vital part of the present attempts to change the economic and social conditions of the nation. The First Five Year Plan, ending in 1956, provides for the inclusion of 84,700 villages, with a population of fifty-six million, in the scope of the community projects administration and the national extension service;[1] the coverage will be further increased in the Second Plan. It is obviously important to evaluate the impact of these projects on the villagers themselves and both private and official accounts have provided a great deal of data. What follows will, it is hoped, add usefully to this material. The article falls into two parts. In the first are set down the author's impressions of development planning in a village in which he lived for a year,[2] with some reference to villages with which he had personal acquaintance. In the second part, this account is briefly related to other writings on the subject, and to some of the wider sociological aspects of these programmes of planned change.

The village studied lay in a national extension service block in southern Madhya Bharat—some four hundred miles

[1] India, 1955, Delhi: Government Press, p. 203
[2] Acknowledgement is due to the Australian National University, Canberra, whose research fellowship enabled the author to spend the year ending June 1955 in this village, and to the development officials, Government of Madhya Bharat, for their willing cooperation.

equidistant from Bombay and Delhi. The block was inaugurated on 2 October 1953. In the eighteen months of its operation, the villagers had received improved seed and artificial fertilizers; they had obtained loans for sinking and improving irrigation wells, for digging drainage trenches and for purchasing fencing wire; they had borrowed money from the State Cooperative Bank for their own purposes; and grants had been made for completion of a village hall and for construction of a three-quarter-mile approach road from the main highway. Finally, two plots were cultivated to show improved methods of paddy growing. All these activities meant that there had been many contacts with the development officials. Over the year their visits to the village probably averaged on a week, and many villagers made repeated journeys to the project office in the market town to see about their loans and make other enquiries.

The villagers' relations with officials connected with developments can best be described as "correct." In some cases they are cordial: that they are not so in more instances is largely because many villagers look on development officials (as, indeed, on all outsiders) with suspicion and cynicism. This attitude is little different from that held for the other types of officials; and, indeed, one could hardly expect that it could have been changed in a mere eighteen months into the desire to cooperate fully with development officials in nation-building activities.

This feeling of the villagers is traditional and is expressed in the often repeated statement that governments come and go (the Moghuls, the Mahrattas, the British) but the farmers have exactly the same privilege under them all—to pay the rent. The farmer feels precisely what the development schemes are designed to change—that he has always given to the town, in money and services, but has received little in return. In addition, there is now a further complication arising from the merger of twenty-five princely states into the Indian Union State of Madhya Bharat. Before 1948, because this village was in one of the smaller states, all knew their Maharajah by sight, or even personally; they knew where he lived, who were his nobles, and the personnel of the hierarchy below them. Now, few know the ministers in charge of affairs, or even how far the boundaries of Madhya Bharat extend. The officials with whom the villagers now deal may not be local men and are often transferred after a year or two. Villagers feel that any successful business must be carried on with an opposite number, or at least an intermediary, who "recognizes one," in whom one has trust through a previous history of transactions. But this condition, in many cases, no longer exists. Therefore, until the present administration has had time to become an established fact in the lives of the populace, there is bound to be an uneasiness about contacts with the government, which development officials must overcome. The general uncertainty can be seen in the comment of a villager after an evening filling out targets for the Second Five Year Plan. "It does not matter what we write," he said, "for '57 is soon upon us." There is a widespread belief among the people that India suffers a cataclysm every hundred years—the events of 1857 and of 1757 (Battle of Plassey) are cited to support this view, which might not, however, be so widely held were it not for the scope of the social changes which have been taking place and are yet to come.

It must be emphasized that the development officials are well aware of the need to change the feelings of the villagers toward them. It is often said that the official himself needs a change of role, to become the servant, rather than the ruler, of the people. This must remain a long-term aim: for in as much as the official has certain powers and certain desired goods to dispense, he inevitably dominates the relationship. For the present it is especially important that he should better understand the ways of thought of the villagers, particularly the way in which their considerable intelligence works to imagine what he himself gains from his actions. For example, five officials came to a village to announce that an important visitor would be arriving the next day. Their jeep stayed fifteen minutes and, after it had left, the main comments made were that one man could have come to the village on bicycle or by bus, to do the same work, but that there must be some advantage in it for the officials, probably travel allowance. The officials may have had no such motive but they might have avoided this rustic reaction if they had given further reasons for their coming. Again, the demonstration paddy plots in the village were made subjects for a competition; they were sampled, their yields calculated from the sample, and compared with other plots. The statistical basis of the size and position in the field of the sample was justified, when seen against the total number of plots sampled. But it could of course prove inaccurate in single cases. Thus, the yield forecast here was about twice the yield actually harvested—and this was clear at the time of sampling, which was made in part of the field which had a better growth. The villagers were pleased to be able to say "I told you so" for they had been sceptical over the new method from the start; later, in fact, it appeared that they refused to believe in genuinely high yields from other villages. And some imputed the high forecast to various interested motives of the officials.

Villagers do not accept all that they are told at its face value and are quick to look—with considerable ingenuity and sophistication—for the self-interest in any action. The officials, as long as they are comparative strangers in the village, must not underestimate this, as the less experienced townsmen among them tend to do. Only when they are more established can they act more freely, without thinking of the other possible interpretations of their actions. One way of creating this confidence is for officials to make longer visits to the village. It is hard, with the best will in the world, to make a rapport in a half-hour's or an hour's stay. Usually the official comes with a specific purpose and must necessarily do most of the talking to get this across. Longer visits would enable the villager to talk more. To sit leisurely, to talk sometimes about matters not connected with development, is to gain a fuller contact with the villagers, and this is seen on the occasions when officials spend an afternoon or stop overnight. The pace of discussion is that of the village meeting: nothing may be immediately achieved, but the general understanding gained may pay later dividends. At present, however, officials are expected to cover a large number of villages, and can hardly spare the time for extended visits if their targets for material distribution are to be reached. In discussion, they agree on the value of staying longer in villages, perhaps at the cost of this greater coverage. When more personnel becomes available, both may be possible.

What of the villager's attitude towards the development schemes? This village was primarily the recipient of aid for agricultural development, which is more easily appreciated. Objections raised are usually practical ones such as, government policy results in over-cultivating the land and allowing insufficient fallow time; or that greater production is offset by falling prices (major commodity prices fell by half in 1954-55). But people see the value of those agricultural schemes which do not call for a radical departure from traditional methods (as did the paddy cultivation scheme).

In certain welfare plans, however, there may be no clear indication of the benefit to the villagers and thus little incentive to work. In the village in question the major work of this kind was building the approach road. Though there was some feeling that the prestige of the village might rise with a direct road, few people saw the advantages to be gained. A direct bus service to town was a minor factor (the poor usually cannot afford to use a bus; the better-off tend to go in their own bullock carts). The advantage of having a good surface, instead of the perpetual mud and flood of the three months rainy season was not seen as being in proportion to the labour involved. There were some explicit objections too: there would be more frequent visits from government officials and the road would deprive some people of land.

Since the village has, from 1 April 1955, been included in a community project block (which lays more emphasis than the national extension scheme on non-agricultural development such as public health) there was an added need to stimulate some idea of the value of these activities. Partly, as noted, closer contact with the officials will lend weight to their persuasion. Another successful method is to educate the village leaders who are most likely to spread the new ideas. This has chiefly meant the head (*sarpanch*) of the elected village council (*panchayat*), which is the statutory local body through which development schemes are carried out. The *sarpanch* thus comes into close contact with the development officials, which in itself gives him a greater grasp of the programme. This experience has been supplemented with organized tours to other development blocks in Madhya Bharat, where schemes have been operating for longer periods.

During the year of observation, the *sarpanch*'s manner changed considerably. After his tour he talked much more, and with greater authority, about possible schemes for the village and was obviously impressed with the scale of the whole development programme, the number of villages involved and the amount of money authorized. Toward the end of the year, in fact, he was talking almost like a development officer himself. It is to be hoped that these tours to other areas can be made more frequent so that more villagers can see for themselves what development schemes can accomplish, and realize that this is a part of a larger movement already under way with solid backing and enthusiasm. Further, a larger representation would lessen the risk of taking members of only one faction on tour: and the scheme should particularly be extended to those farmers who say they do not have time for village affairs. Though these men may not be the actual leaders, they are, as substantial farmers, people of some influence and should not be overlooked because they do not come forward on public occasions.

It may happen that even *sarpanch* who is eager to work cannot get things started. Such was the case in this village, in connection with the road, partly because of differences about where the road should go (and thus over whose land) and partly because of lack of conviction about the need for such work. The policy of the development projects is against compulsory labour. It is felt that, since there is so much compulsion already inherent in official-villager relations, these programmes should take the opposite course, to ensure at least a modicum of voluntary effort, as well as an education in democratic processes. Some may feel that initial compulsion is necessary to break the connection between lack of interest and inaction. In Madhya Bharat, the law constituting the village *panchayats* specifies that all men between twenty and sixty years must do five days of annual work on development projects, under pain of a fine. In this village all avoided this labour as far as they could and worked only if it appeared likely that fines would actually be collected. The *sarpanch* was thus caught between the villagers who delayed giving their quota of work and the bureaucracy which pressed him to apply the rules. For two years or so he delayed, using persuasion, but in the end he had to send out warnings of fines if the work was not done in a specified period. Then he became discouraged over the difficulties, and said he wished to withdraw from the work. Too rigid a rule for compulsory work may thus defeat its own purpose in some villages, where a slower tempo seems necessary.

Another difficulty is that there may be more than one major leader in a village. If only one man is treated as intermediary, taken on tours and so forth, the others may try to obstruct his work. A distinction must be made, however, between the kinds of division in the village. In some villages in the area studied the individual leaders were at the head of distinct factions, whose membership was recognized by all, whereas in other villages there were no such well-defined groups. Instead, there might be several prominent men, rivals of varying degrees of bitterness and duration. Each might have his close supporters, but most inhabitants would not be committed to anyone and would change their support when expedient.

In the first type of village, development work may go forward faster than in a united village. Both factions may work at the same time and try to outdo each other. Lewis gives an example of this from north India.[3] Or one faction at the time will control the *panchayat* and will work hard to surpass its rival. A good authority maintained that of the four best villages in the development block studied, three were motivated by such rivalry. The danger is, of course, that the development work itself may be taken as the main issue of opposition, and may thus fall into disrepute.

Progress is harder in the second type of village. Here the alternate leaders may not be in the *panchayat* and so cannot be contacted officially; and no leader has enough influence to get a large group working well.

Are there other ways of stimulating work? Economic advantage is important and is, of caurse, paramount in all schemes for agricultural development. But it does not operate in "welfare" plans to nearly the same extent, and the fear of being fined for not contributing labour is a strictly limited—and negative—use of this incentive. There is also the desire for

---

[3]For an example of this from north India, see O. Lewis, "Group Dynamics in a North-Indian Village," *Economic Weekly*; VI, 18, p. 505.

prestige, especially for preservation of one's name for posterity. When making any gift, custom demands that as large a public as possible should know of it. A greater emphasis might well be made of this fact. A plaque at the head of the approach road or on a well, for example, bearing all the names of those who worked to build it, might provide an additional incentive for people to work. So far, events which incorporate this idea seem to have been few and at too high a level. For example, the paddy-growing competition was district-wide and had only one or two winners; the rest went without rewards for their participation or other public recognition of their efforts.

There is less objection to doing work which is of a traditional socio-religious kind, including the construction of large irrigation tanks, dams and wells (when for public use) and of resthouses for travellers. It is worth noting that the same people who had difficulty in completing a road had half built, from their own funds, a large village hall for public meetings and housing travellers and guests. Again, nobody was heard to grudge the time spent on improving one of the drinking wells. The writer was frequently told that the best gift he could make to the village would be a well by the roadside, not necessarily within the village limits. Not only would this be a work of public service and thus deserving of merit, but his name, and through it the village's name, would live on in the future. Such work, being more easily accomplished, might be used to start programmes in new areas rather than, say, approach roads or village sanitation schemes.

One's main impression after a year was that people realize things have changed and are to change still more. In some cases this makes for insecurity, in some for resistance, to which is added the traditionally cautious attitude to all outsiders and new things. But it is a step in the direction of making changes to have people prepared for them. In some villages a powerful leader, or a clear-cut factional division may spark off considerable activity. In other villages where divisions are shifting and leadership is weak the work may lag and depend more on the personal relations of officials to villagers. The hardest job of all seems to be to convince of the benefit of many of the innovations;[4] to show them another scheme already working seems to be the best method. It can be aided by bringing into play the incentives best appreciated in the village, until the worth of the projects themselves is established.

Can this report, of one village among the many thousands under such development schemes, be taken as valid for India's village development programme as a whole ? At the level of general application of policies, much of this account is confirmed from other sources, for other areas. The need for detailed visits by officials, and for the building of mutual trust and understanding between them and the public has often been stated,[5] as has the need to keep the same official in the area for several years.[6] Again, the Indian government has stressed the need to select activities which fulfil felt needs of the villagers, and which must therefore avoid any element of compulsion, of the danger of being "official" rather than "popular" programmes.[7] Hence, it considers its first task to be the creation of a new attitude among the people, a desire for progress and knowledge,[8] and sees dangers in the over-expansion of projects where these aims cannot be attained.[9] Finally, the point has also been made that villagers have more intelligence than is sometimes supposed and that they are often more aware of the social and technical implications of the innovations than is the official.[10]

[4] As a related example, concerning the initial reluctance of the landless to apply for land distributed under the Bhoodan programmes, see H. Tennyson, 1955. *Saint on the March.* London, pp. 154-57.

[5] See Mayer, Albert, "A Progress Report on Pilot Development Projects at Etawah and Gorakhpur, U.P., India," Report No. 573, Mimeograph Series 212. Agricultural Missions Inc. New York, p. 2; R.D. Singh, 1951. "The Village Level," in E.H. Spicer, ed., *Human Problems in Technological Change.* New York, p. 61; D.G. Mandelbaum, "Planning and Social Change in India," *Human Organization,* XII, 3, p. 12.

[6] Programme Evaluation Organisation, Evaluation Report on Second Year's Working of Community Projects, New Delhi: Government Press, 1955, p. 48.

[7] *Ibid.*, pp. 18, 22, etc.

[8] *Ibid.*, p.1.

[9] *Ibid.*, pp. 26-27.

[10] Srinivas, M.N., "Village Studies and Their Significance," *Eastern Anthropologist.* VIII, 3 and 4, p. 222.

These and many similar statements are the fruit of observations all over India. The suggestion made in this account of a specific locality (for more public recognition of work, etc.) appear not to have been so explicitly stated, as far as the author is aware, but might well find general agreement. There is evidence, for example, that a greater emphasis is to be placed on travel tours for the inhabitants of villages in development blocks.[11]

Though these observations are generally applicable, their force varies in particular villages. Partly, of course, this is because of the different personalities present on the village and the government sides. When these are mutually sympathetic, work will go well. The programmes depend greatly on such imponderables. Partly, also, this may be due to differences in the types of village.[12] It has already been suggested that various types of factional organization influence the implementation of development programmes. Again, some experienced officials maintain that in backward villages the traditional patterns of leadership, based on the authority of the headman and the weight of the elders' opinions, are strong. Hence, if a relatively few key men are convinced of the benefit of a project, the whole village will follow. In advanced villages, however, this type of authority is no longer the major factor. Younger, educated men feel that they are as knowledgeable as their often less formally educated elders. Any decision by one or two men, even though they may be buttressed by membership of the officially sponsored *panchayat*, is liable to be questioned by others, and so work may be hindered. Presumably, in even more "advanced" villages there is a general understanding of the programmes and an acceptance of the majority's authority, which produces a willingness to act parallel to that of the backward villages.

There does not seem to be any clear correlation between

---

[11] Information given to the writer by officials concerned. See also an account of a nationwide tour for 460 peasants of North Gujarat, in *Overseas Hindustan Times*, 29 September 1955, p. 3.

[12] See Opler, M.E., and R.D. Singh, "Villages of Eastern Uttar Pradesh, India," *American Anthropologist*. Vol. 54, pp. 179-90, for an example of the differential effects of certain outside policies on villages of different type.

the number of major castes in a village and the adoption of development projects. Internal village quarrels holding up work can just as easily take place between different lineages of the single major caste of a village, as they can between two or three major castes in a village of more complex caste composition. Externally, however, the caste composition of a village is significant in the influence it has over the pattern of linkages with other villages.

It is true that members of different castes all feel a unity as fellow villagers and may act together as such; but they may also have ritual and secular customs which differ from those of other castes in the village, and they are linked by marriage or blood to similar groups outside the village which caste endogamy makes exclusive to them. The horizontal solidarity, as Srinivas has called it,[13] is an important feature of village structure, and it may be that communication with other villages about development projects will tend to take place along the channels it provides, for kinsmen and caste-men tend to meet each other more than others, whether in village or market town. They may aid each other economically, will help each other in such social duties as matchmaking, and especially congregate at rituals of all kinds—notably wedding and funeral feasts. If a programme is a success in one village, then informal knowledge about it will tend to spread to villages where there are considerable members of similar castes. The development official can, in such cases, to some extent anticipate the reactions he will get from villages other than the ones to which he is devoting his main effort.

This is significant where, for economy's sake, there are interstitial villages left between the blocks of village included in a development programme.[14] It is expected that these villages will get information about the projects from the villages being developed and will seek aid from the government on the basis of the views expressed by the inhabitants of the latter, rather than as the result of direct demonstration and education. Mayer does not mention how the interstitial areas

---

[13]Srinivas, M.N., 1952. *Religion and Society Among the Coorgs of South India.* Oxford University Press, p. 31.
[14]Mayer, Albert, *op. cit.,* p. 3.

were demarcated in the project about which he writes but, if this hypothesis is correct, a survey of the villages' major caste compositions over the area to be developed would provide a general idea of the main channels of inter-village communication and so guide the definition of the interstitial areas, and of the selection of those villages in which most work should be done. More study could well be directed to the problem of inter-village communication in different situations-for example, where the major castes in adjacent villages very often differ, where there are usually the same major castes in all villages, where there is a general pattern of prohibiting marriages within the village, and finally where a large percentage of marriages take place within a single village or between no more than two or three nearby villages.

The community development projects are in their infancy. A most impressive amount has already been accomplished but much work lies ahead, and it is hoped that these comments prove of constructive value to those who are responsible for evaluating the work and for trying to further sharpen the techniques of planned change.

S.C. Dube

17 Communication, Innovation, and Planned Change in India

Although the administrative structure of British India was geared largely to law and order, it did include a number of nation-building departments. Some of these departments rendered useful service to the people, but their programmes were rarely pursued with any urgency or vigour. The general administrator, wielding vast powers for the maintenance of law and order, was unmistakably the central figure in the administrative set-up; the specialists and the technicians were relegated to secondary positions. Officials, both general administrators and technical experts, constituted a special class and functioned as a subcultural segment of the society. Those on the higher echelons of the bureaucracy consciously tried to maintain a distance from the masses. The life of the officials was one of relative ease, and the tempo of their activities was generally slow. Free from political pressures and economic compulsions, they continued practising the prescribed routines in their respective spheres.

Attainment of freedom changed all this. The emphasis in state activity shifted from maintenance of law and order to planned development. For the new tasks, both the politician and the bureaucrat were not quite prepared. The former came to positions of power with a rich background of agitational politics and of solidarity-building, but with little experience of problem solving; the latter, used to a sheltered existence and stereotyped ways, was by temperament and training inadequately fitted to assume the vastly enlarged role expected of him. Radical and purposeful changes in the norms of political as well as bureaucratic behaviour were indicated.

Two types of communication networks were well developed in India: the network of administrative communication and the network of political communication. The first consisted largely of an organization for gathering administrative intelligence—mainly information relating to the state of law and order, especially concerning the possible sources of trouble. The responsibilities of the nation-building departments were limited and precisely defined. Their field agencies, supported by the network of general administration, kept them well informed regarding situations requiring their attention: for example, they knew where they had to rush relief during famines or following serious fires, and where they had to enforce preventive measures, for instance at the outbreak of smallpox, plague, and cholera epidemics. The concept of working in association with the people was neither emphasized nor understood. If the people resisted persuasion, they had to be pushed.

The network of political communication, resting on the hatred of alien rule, was excellently developed for the flow of agitational information. It succeeded admirably in building certain patriotic images and in spreading the political ideology of the nationalist movement. But nation-building requires modification in existing norms and institutional arrangements, creation of new norms and institutions, and innovations for more effective communication. Traditional societies cannot be modernized by exhortation alone. For the additional communication functions required in nation-building, the existing network was not particularly suitable.

Viewed in the context of the requirements of nation-building, effective communication between several identifiable segments was necessary. This comprised:

1. Communication between the political sector and the bureaucracy;
2. Communication between the planner and the political decision-maker;
3. Communication between the planner and the research agencies;

4. Communication between the planner and the units of production;
5. Communication between the different departments and agencies of the government;
6. Communication between the different levels of administration;
7. Communication between the general administration and the technician;
8. Communication between the modernizers and the common people;
9. Communication between aid-giving and aid-receiving countries;
10. Communication between overseas consultants/advisers and their native counterparts.

Communication between the politician (the new political chief) and the bureaucracy (the old work horse) was difficult, especially in the earlier years of freedom. Although both were patriotically motivated, their orientations and ethos were different. There was considerable mutual distrust between the two. The politicians' image of bureaucracy, especially of the higher civil servants, identified it closely with alien rule (did not the civil servants lead a secure and comfortable life when the freedom fighters suffered hardships and made sacrifices to drive the British out?). They regarded the bureaucracy, by and large, as unimaginative, unworkable, and immobile and felt that as a group it was concerned more with power and perquisites than with the higher motivation of serving people. The civil servants, many of whom had more than a sneaking admiration and respect for the freedom fighters, resented this attitude. They found that in positions of power some of the patriots were not quite embodiments of service and sacrifice, and not without some of the failings for which they criticized the civil servants so vehemently. The bureaucracy, smug in its familiarity with the skills of administration, was perhaps convinced of its indispensability.

The experience of working together threw up some new problems, but in many ways it also brought the bureaucrats and the politicians closer together. Personalized politics and diffused expectations of the politician were now the major source of worry to the bureaucracy. Bureaucracy's concern for set procedure and established routine annoyed the politician and the former, in turn, was dismayed by the impatient ways of the political executive who did not want to go by precedent. The two broadly agreed on the aims of national policy, but they did not see eye to eye on the methods of implementing it. The roles of the political and permanent executives were not sharply distinguished, not at any rate by the politician. A curious consequence of this, in some instances, was the merging or transfer of the two roles. Good intentions and pious exhortations by themselves could not remedy the situation. Some political executives tried to set a good example by confining themselves only to the making of major policy decisions and to the exercising of general supervision over the work of the ministries or departments they controlled; they did not interfere in their detailed working and respected the bureaucracy's right of placing its views freely and fearlessly. The higher civil servants also modified their thought- and work-ways. In between those who adopted the path of abject surrender and those who continued to sulk resentfully, a sizeable section of civil servants learned to live with the politician. With a view to achieving speed and efficiency, they modified their procedures, but they also generally insisted on their right to present all aspects of a given case with their own advice. The ultimate decision was of course with the political executive, and this position was never in any serious doubt. Passage of time was expected to evolve the norms governing the relationship between the two.

On the intermediate and lower levels, modifications in the established institutional arrangements and creation of new institutional patterns were expected to establish proper communication between the civil servants and the politicians. Some innovations were also tried: for example, participation by the members of the two sectors in common orientation courses and seminars was expected to bring them closer.

Communication on the highest planning level was also not always easy. All major policies were to be determined by the political decision-makers, but the specialized job of preparing detailed blueprints had to be handled by the technocrats. Implementation of the plans and policies was largely left to the bureaucracy. All three, the politician, the bureaucrat, and the technocrat, continued to speak their respective dialects. There were significant differences in their approaches and ways of working. Unlike the technocrat, who tried to look at problems objectively from the point of view of his specialization, the politician could not be oblivious to ideological commitments, to parochial pulls, and to the possible political consequences of the policies suggested by the specialist. In respect of the priorities and the emphases in planning, the two often did not see eye to eye. Acting under pressures of different types and for a variety of reasons, the politician had to commit himself to positions that did not meet with the approval of the expert. The expert's computations and projections were often beyond the comprehension of a majority of the politicians. These factors created difficulties in the way of communication.

The structure of India's Planning Commission, though, is such that it includes politicians, administrators and technocrats —the three types of personnel most acutely needed in the process of planning for national development. The Prime Minister of India has been the chairman of Planning Commission from its inception. Its membership is varied and includes, besides some of the key ministers of the government of India, members drawn from the ranks of technocrats, administrators, and politicians. This diversity in its membership posed some problems of communication but, on the whole, the Commission has succeeded in working at a team without sharp cleavages and pronounced differences. The prestige of the late Prime Minister Nehru and the presence of some important members of the Union Cabinet added weight to the views of the Planning Commission and made them generally acceptable to the Parliament. Nevertheless, the dominating presence of the Planning Commission was occasionally resented by politicians both inside and outside the Parliament. It was particularly criticized for its tendency to override the ministries by scrutinizing their proposals and pronouncing judgements over them. For an extra-constitutional body like the Planning Commission to exercise such control over the ministries was regarded as unusual and objectionable. The Commission was sometimes described as a "parallel government" or even as a "super cabinet." The echoes of this criticism were also heard in the capitals of the various constituent states of the Union. Although some channels of communication between the Commission and political institutions have been created, many inadequacies still persist.

The planner (and also the administrator) has not been able to communicate effectively with the various research agencies which have important roles to play in the country's massive efforts for economic development and technological change. The Planning Commission and the various ministries concerned with the implementation of development policies have to use a great deal of research, both for formulating their policies and for more economical and efficient implementation of these policies. Besides utilizing the existing agencies, and impressive network of organization devoted to research, mostly of an applied nature, has had to be created. As a substantially large part of the funds for research is provided by the government, it can directly or indirectly exercise considerable influence on research policies and priorities. While it is true that in framing research policies, scholars and scientists are consulted, the control of research funds and the management of research organizations is largely vested in the bureaucracy which, despite some notable exceptions, has little insight into or understanding of the nature and problems of research. In consequence, little really useful work can be done inside the impressive buildings that are put up for the research organizations.

The structure of the research organizations also leaves much to be desired: modelled on stereotyped bureaucratic patterns, it is not conducive to smooth and effective communication within the research agencies themselves. They are run more as offices than as organizations intended to produce high quality research. In recent years, this problem has exercised the minds of both the scientists and the planners. The question of allowing a greater measure of autonomy to research institutions is being considered. They are to be restructured in such a way that intra-agency communication, conducive to greater productive efficiency, may be assured. So far only pious hopes have been expressed; steps to translate them into action have yet to be taken. It may be added that the research workers themselves have shown little initiative in trying to break the barriers to communication. Being preoccupied with fundamental problems they often fail to relate their research directly to the requirements of national planning and development. The scientists, especially the social scientists, speak and write in a jargon that is becoming less understandable to those outside their circle. Their findings cannot make the desired impact unless they translate themselves in a language that can be understood by the politician and the administrator.

India has a mixed economy. The growing public sector is under state control. This makes for relatively easy communication between the government and the public sector. But this sphere is also not without problems of communication. The public sector not only has to meet the requirements of planned development but also has to work for the fulfilment of some of the ideals of social justice adopted by the government. At the same time, it cannot be entirely oblivious to the operation of the laws of a market economy. At several points it has also to communicate with the private sector. The nature of its structure, aims, and control creates problems of communication. The problems of the private sector are of a different nature. Within the framework of an economy ideologically committed to develop along socialistic lines, state controls on the public sector are many. Licences, import permits, foreign exchange, state purchase, fiscal measures, and company law administration are some of the major instruments in the hands of the state to control the activities of this sector. In recent years, some innovations have been made to establish communication between the planner and the government, on the one hand, and the units of production—in both the private and the public sectors —on the other. The industrial policy resolutions set the direction for industrial development. A number of development councils for various industries, such as chemical and electrical industries, have been set up. The membership of these councils is drawn from both the sectors. The planning and administrative wings of the government are also represented. Common programmes of production are worked out by discussion and mutual exchange of views by these councils. Another example of such innovation is provided by the Export Promotion Council, which discusses all questions concerning production for the export market as well as those concerning incentives for exports and quality control.

India is not the only country whose government is characterized by interministry and interdepartmental rivalries. As elsewhere, ministries and departments of the government in this country also try to inflate their own importance and attempt to enlarge their spheres of influence. Planning is a complex and many-sided process that requires pooling and integration of the resources of these departments. The prevalence of rivalries and jealousies between different parts of the same government, especially among those who are engaged in the tasks of nation-building, creates serious problems. It is not difficult to imagine what happens to developmental activity when, for example, the ministry in change of irrigation or cooperation differs in its approach and operational strategy with the Ministry of Agriculture. Similarly, differences between the Ministries of Education, Health, and Community Development can also create awkward situations. These barriers to interministry and interdepartmental communication have been recognized. Interministerial and interdepartmental coordination committees have been set up to bring about a degree of harmony and unison in their planning. Ministries and departments working in allied fields are brought together in such committees.

Although India has a fairly stable and well-organized administrative structure, communication does not flow smoothly between the different levels of administration.

The wider national view and the narrower view of the constituent states, in regard to even, some of the more pressing problems, are not always in harmony. Local problems and pressures force the state governments to view the issues in a different perspective. The National Development Council and other similar bodies, which bring together representatives of the central and state governments, try to provide a forum to harmonize competing claims and evolve common acceptable policies. But communication mechanism still remains inadequate.

Communication from the centre and from the state headquarters to the district (the key unit of administration) and the block (the key unit of development) is also defective, although perhaps the best organized. Directives move from the higher to the lower units in the hierarchy, but the flow of information in the reverse direction is not equally well provided for. Within the bureaucracy, status structure is a strong barrier to the flow of information from the lower to the higher levels. Many officials on the upper echelons do not have sufficient tolerance for suggestions coming from those down below.

In the political hierarchy, the situation is different. The political executive, besides having the benefit of established channels, also obtains information through formal and informal political channels. A certain number of local problems reach the higher civil servants through the political executive, although these political channels mostly communicate only complaints and the more pressing needs.

Several innovations have been made to remedy these defects. Through repeated exhortation and organized training, an attempt has been made to break the class barriers between officials. These efforts have contributed to develop emotional awareness of the fact that development is a collaborative effort, but this awareness has not appreciably eased the process of communication. Under the scheme of democratic decentralization, an effort has been made to link the political and the administrative networks: democratic institutions, charged with the responsibilities of planning and development for their respective spheres, have been set up at the village, block, and district levels; and the administrative machinery of the government at these levels has been placed under these democratic bodies.

A third innovation in this field is the setting up of statutory and/or ad hoc advisory councils or committees. These bodies have a special focus; their terms of reference cover one central interest or a set of related interests. On them, representation is given to politicians and administrators, as well as to groups intimately connected with the particular interest the body represents.

Nation-building requires close collaboration between the general administrator and the technician. In India, as perhaps elsewhere, these two groups do not interact well and communication between them often becomes difficult. The traditional structure of administration in the country was highly compartmentalized: each department had a distinct line of command; interdepartmental links were few. Although the general administrator enjoyed a distinctly superior status, little direct and formal control was exercised by him on the technical departments. Integrated development programmes required a high degree of coordination. In the community development blocks the technicians were placed under dual control; the block development officer exercised administrative control over them, while higher officers of their respective departments continued to exercise technical control. This innovation, basically sound in conception, met with considerable resistance, and even today, twelve years after the inauguration of the community development programme, this modification in the traditional arrangement has not been emotionally accepted. The general administrator feels that the authority vested in him to control the technician is not adequate; the higher officials of the technical departments are resentful because they have lost a chunk of their empire. Orientation and training programmes, aimed at rectifying the breach, have not met with the required degree of success.

The eighth problem area in the communication process in nation-building—involving communication between the modernizer and the common people—will be discussed more fully in the rest of this contribution. The practical significance of this aspect of the problem is widely recognized. It has been approached in two different ways—almost from two opposite directions. An extension network has been created to take the message of modernization to the common people. At the same time, in order to articulate interest in the local communities, a network of decentralized democratic institutions has also been set up. This arrangement was intended to establish a two-way process of communication. In a limited way, it has succeeded in achieving its objective. However, as we shall see later, the two sets of institutions are hampered by blurred images, inner contradictions, and operational difficulties. Proper communication between the two has not yet been established.

India has had to depend upon foreign aid for many of her development projects. The policy of nonalignment with either of the two major power blocks necessitated her having to seek such aid without any political strings. For several years this policy was misunderstood, and it even aroused active hostility towards India in certain quarters. There was also misunderstanding in respect of some of the priorities in planning; several aspects of her national policy were not clearly understood. The new images, aspirations, and idiom of India were not adequately appreciated by either block. In consequence, relations between aid-giving nations and India continued to remain somewhat uneasy. India herself was partly to blame for this as she failed to project her programme and policy in a manner that could be easily understood by the aid-givers. On the other hand, little evidence exists to suggest that the more advanced nations, on their part, made any conscious and sustained effort to understand the Indian attitude and sentiments. This unhappy chapter in the history of India's relations with aid-giving nations indicates the necessity of a serious examination of the different aspects of the problem of international communication in the field of technical assistance.

Many of the overseas technicians, consultants, and advisers who came over to India were not sufficiently sensitized to the existing conditions and work-ways in the country, especially to its political culture and bureaucratic patterns. It was apparent that some of them were not chosen very carefully and that their preparation for the overseas assignment was obviously inadequate. Positive and forward-looking individuals, equipped with cross-cultural perspectives and empathy, constituted a minority. Though numerically small, this group was perhaps the most successful in interacting well with Indian co-workers. Others could not feel at home in the country and were generally impatient and critical of the ways of their Indian associates. While some of them developed antipathy and hostility to India and Indian things, others chose the line of least resistance by adopting an attitude of formal compliance to the minimum requirements of their jobs. On the other hand, Indian personnel chosen to work with foreign technicians and experts were also not carefully prepared for their new role. The dialogue between the two was on the whole unsatisfactory, and their collaboration could not become very productive.

The above outline is intended only to be suggestive of certain important areas in which there exists a need for effective communication. In a sketchy and somewhat perfunctory manner, an attempt has been made to list some of the innovations that have been made in India to fill the gaps in communication. Mention has been made of some efforts to modify existing norms and institutional arrangements, of some attempts at creation of new norms and institutions, and also of a few innovations for more effective communication. It may be emphasized that while many of the maladies have been recognized, their treatment has so far been largely symptomatic. Serious diagnostic studies of the nature and strength of the different types of barriers to communication in different areas of development planning and administration have yet to be made. In the absence of such scientific studies, covering every significant aspect of the problem, comprehensive planning for removal of inadequacies and defects in communication cannot be attempted.

INDIAN VILLAGE: INNOVATION IN COMMUNICATION

To carry the message of change to the rural masses, several types of innovations in communication have been attempted in India. They include: (1) creation of new channels of communication; (2) introduction of new methods of communication; and (3) utilization of traditional methods for new purposes.

The new channels of communication created for this purpose are:

(a) A network of extension services
(b) A network of local agents of communication
(c) A network of decentralized democratic institutions

In the past, the nation-building departments tried to introduce some changes in their respective jurisdictions but their efforts lacked coordination and integration, although in a limited way they did succeed in persuading the village people to adopt some progressive innovations. The benefits of these efforts were mostly confined to a few individuals or to small segments of the village communities. Inadequate support from other departments responsible for activities in allied fields resulted at best in half-hearted efforts to bring about change. The greatest weakness of this approach was that it did not take a total view of the problems of village development and did not make any effort to involve the community in the process. Field agents of different departments were trained essentially as technicians;

human skills required in successful extension did not form a part of their equipment.

Community development organization in India has made a conscious attempt to rectify these defects. Planned change is viewed by it as a unified and integrated process requiring a variable, multi-faceted, and multidimensional but coordinated approach. To achieve this, a number of specialities such as agriculture, cooperation, animal husbandry, public health, education, and rural engineering have been brought together under a single organizntion. The *development block* has emerged as the key unit of planning and development for the villages: its personnel is a multi-speciality team under unified control. This team is expected to work in close association with the people and their voluntary statutory organizations. Pre-and in-service training programmes, devised for the development personnel, aim at inculcating desirable attitudes and attributes in the action agents and at developing the required interactional and communicational skills in them.

Although not without weaknesses and defects, this approach has made a considerable impact. Today, there exists in the country an effective and organized network of extension workers able to communicate directly and more successfully with the rural masses.

Some of the inadequacies and drawbacks in the system are:

(1) Within the facade of unity imposed by the block organization, there are several inner contradictions. The acceptance of the unified pattern is more apparent than real. Interdepartmental jealousies and rivalries powerfully obstruct the emergence of the block organization as a unified multi-speciality team. The technicians still continue to speak their respective dialects.

(2) The extension agents continue to have a dual image of their roles and function; even their approach and methods are characterized by such split images. They are aware of the importance of educational *extension methods,* but for quick results they sometimes feel that the traditional *executive methods* would have been more effectivc. Official pressure from above for fulfilling targets often deters them from giving a real trial to the slow and time-consuming methods of extension.

(3) Although training programmes for development workers

include instruction on human skills and communication, much of this learning is by and large theoretical. Little effort is made to assess the backgrounds of individual participants and to relate the training to their specific needs. Significant typological differences between development workers are thus not recognized; and extremely limited, if any, attempts are made to offer individual counselling to them. On-the-job guidance on human skills is practically nonexistent. They are introduced to a number of audiovisual aids in communication, but even during their training they know that they will not have the time or occasion to use many of them. Utilization of these aids under actual field conditions is also not effectively explained to them.

(4) Failure to back the field agent with adequate and timely supplies and technical support results in his "loss of face." Handicapped by this lack of support, he cannot carry the communication process to completion. Village people soon lose faith in the extension worker and also in the innovations he seeks to promote.

An attempt has been made to create a network of local agents of communication. This problem has been approached from two angles: on the individual level, certain key persons are selected, trained and associated with specific programmes of village development; on the group level, associate organizations are created to help the communication process in relation to development.

The first approach is exemplified by the offices of *grama sahayak* (village helper) and *gramalakshmi* (village goddess of prosperity), both of whom are chosen from among the village people. They are given some training and then associated with development work. Associate organizations—*yuwak mandal* (youth club modelled on 4-H clubs) and *mahila mandali* (womens' club)—aim at creating new leadership, at articulating interest, and at involving organized groups in the tasks of development. A number of village leaders' training camps are also organized.

This effort has encountered some serious operational difficulties. Not many persons are willing to come forward for the offices of *grama sahayak* and *gramalakshmi*; recruitment to the latter is especially difficult because of the traditional definition of the woman's role and because of norms requiring her seclusion. In the absence of popular enthusiam for these positions, the question of selecting persons with the requisite aptitude and personality traits does not arise; the villagers have often to be coaxed and cajoled into accepting these assignments. Their training is poorly organized, and because of its short duration and unimaginative handling, it does not succeed in imparting either technical competence or human skills. And, finally, their role in development work is not properly defined. Apart from rendering some general assistance to extension agents, they do not appear to do anything in particular.

Associate organizations are also often set up in a hurry. They start with considerable enthusiasm but organizational difficulties, lack of guidance, and absence of support, soon reduce them to a languishing and lingering existence. The training of their leaders is also neither well organized nor particularly effective.

Reference has already been made to the creation of a hierarchy of democratic institutions on the village, block, and district levels. This has been a bold and significant step in the right direction. It has definitely helped in the articulation of interest and in the flow of communication from the village upwards. It has also enabled the less privileged to break the harsh ascriptive order of the Hindu social system by providing them an avenue to rise in the emerging power hierarchy. Democratic decentralization has been a powerful instrument in developing political articulation.

These advantages notwithstanding, the experiment is undergoing some teething troubles. The more important ones among them are the following:

(1) In general, these institutions have failed to comprehend their role in the process of development. They have either seen themselves in the role of traditional *panchayats*, with arbitration, mediation, and dispute-resolving as their main functions, or they seek political authority and control of the administrative machinery of the state without evincing much direct interest in programmes of development.

(2) The role of extension services under these institutions has not been closely defined. The resultant confusion has, in some parts of the country, slowed down the tempo of development activity.

(3) Arrangements to orient and train the political and

permanent executives of these institutions have rarely been adequate. Effective communication between the people's representatives and the officials still remains to be established.

Several new methods of communication have been pressed into service to transmit the message of development to the village people. Important innovations in this field are these:

(a) Intensive utilization of the group discussion method
(b) Use of "method" and "result" demonstrations
(c) Use of audio-visual aids like posters, filmstrips, films and radio
(d) Use of printed materials; especially newspapers and pamphlets

For arousing interest in innovation and for teaching the related skills, face-to-face communication is without doubt the most important instrument in underdeveloped societies. Field agencies of community development have done remarkably well in using this type of communication. In this context, it is necessary to remember that the extension agent has under him unmanageable areas with large populations; he had several competing pressures on his time; and he has to spend a great deal of his energies in complying with formal official routines. These handicaps notwithstanding, he has succeeded in reaching a fair proportion of village people and in stimulating them to try at least some innovations. The results could have been more encouraging had the extension worker been given a set of clear indicators for the choice of the most appropriate groups for such discussions and had he been able to find time to sustain their interest through repeated follow-up discussions. Timely support, in the shape of technical guidance and required supplies, would have also added to the effectiveness of communication.

The main focus in India's rural development programme is on agriculture. Use of demonstrations—both of method and of results—can be, and has been to a degree, a useful aid to the acceptance of innovations in agriculture. Routinization and ritualization of this method has, however, considerably restricted its utility.

The following conclusions emerged out of a series of case studies of method-and-result demonstrations carried out in different parts of the country:

(1) No definite criteria were adopted in the selection of sites for the demonstrations. A majority of the plots were unsuitable.

(2) Similarly, the agriculturalists were also not chosen with any discrimination. There was little evidence to suggest that they had any interest in the demonstration. What was worse, they could not be used as "agents" to further promote the item.

(3) Some of the demonstrations related to practices that had already gained wide acceptance. As such, they were unnecessary.

(4) Technical guidance and support to the programme was generally poor.

(5) Preparatory steps which vitally affect the demonstrations, such as advance publicity, were ignored in many cases.

(6) The various stages of the demonstrations were neither publicized nor were they properly explained. People were not given an opportunity to compare the results of the new practices with those of the old practices. Even at the time of harvesting, people were not taken to the demonstration sites.

(7) Proof of net gain was not calculated and explained to the people.

(8) Some of the demonstrations could not be given because of the lack of timely supply of fertilizers, seeds, or implements.

This picture is indeed disconcerting. It is often forgotten that bad demonstrations are an obstacle rather than an incentive to adoption of innovations.

Posters can carry simple messages effectively and can even arouse interest if their thematic presentation is imaginative and if they use a symbol system that can draw people to them. The possibilities of this medium have not been fully exploited. Often enough, the posters use images that are alien to the village people; their language is hard to understand, if not entirely foreign. There has been practically no use of irony and sarcasm even in the posters aimed at anti-social practices. Cartoons have also not been widely used.

The use of filmstrips has been nominal rather than widespread. This medium could be used to illustrate processes, but for a variety of reasons this has not been done.

The popular image of the film, in the rural mind, associates it with two attributes: (1) they provide entertainment; and (2) they have a corrupting and deruralizing influence. Only limited use has been made of this medium to teach detailed practices; their principle use so far has been to build certain images and to convey information regarding specific programmes and innovations. Most of the films have an urban bias. Where they seek to entertain as well as to educate, the emphasis on entertainment is so great that the educational part is wholly or partly missed. Or, alternatively, the instructional element is so heavy and drab that the film bores the village people. Choice of themes, mode of treatment, and use of language and symbols leave much to be desired.

Radio has been—at least indirectly—a powerful source of information to the village people. Innovative use of this medium is beginning to show some impressive results. Programmes aimed at the rural audiences, in the past and even today, are generally dull, statistics-ridden, and heavy, and yet they are not without a happier aspect. Some stations of All India Radio have given a personality to their rural programmes by building them around a central character who can arouse and maintain interest by adopting the folk idiom and by interpreting the more pedantic and dull speakers to the rural masses through well-timed interruptions. Radio farm forums, i.e., organized listening groups of agriculturalists, are also a useful innovation. It has been found that the message conveyed over the radio penetrates deeper if it is followed by a discussion between the village people and some of their opinion leaders. A two-way communication between the broadcasting station and the village people also stimulates interest.

In the case of radio, as in the case of the other media, the choice of idiom and themes and of manner of presentation is of critical importance. Evidence exists that they can be purposefully handled, but the limited number or successful experiments need to be duplicated on a wider scale. Production of inexpensive and trouble-free receiving sets and arrangements for repair to these instruments are two other important problems connected with the utilization of this medium.

In a country with a high rate of illiteracy, the use of the printed word of necessity will be limited. But the literate section of the village population cannot be ignored: in opinion-formation and in dissemination of ideas, it has a vital role. Useful literature for this section is not being produced. The situation in regard to the neo-literates is worse. In actual practice, anything printed on coarse paper and in big type passes as material suitable for rural readers. Periodicals produced especially for villages contain more news on VIPs than information relevant to development programmes. Pamphlets and books tend to be heavy and pedantic: in style and language they are often not suited for rural readers.

Utilization of the traditional media of communication for new purposes provided considerable scope for innovation. In their conventional form, these media are used primarily to entertain or to recreate the mythological and historical past. These traditional media have been successfully geared, in some parts of India, to the requirements of development communication. Folk forms of entertainment and drama, such as *Burra Katha* in Andhra Pradesh, *Katha Kalakshepam* in the south, especially in Madras, *Kavigan* in Bengal—to give only three examples—have lent themselves admirably to adaptation for such use. Here, the setting and the principal characters are familiar to rural audiences. The actors know the rural mind and have a firm grasp of their idiom. In the hands of talented and resourceful actors, the treatment of development themes, either as a main attraction or even as a side attraction, can be really forceful. Interpolations in the form of *bol* (words spoken at regular intervals) during the *Bhangara* dance in the Punjab, and in the form of dialogue during the singing of *Laoni* and *Powada* in Maharashtra, have been successfully used for conveying the message of development. Puppet shows have also been effectively used in some parts of the country.

Comment on Innovations

Thus, during the first decade of its existence, the Indian community development programme has made several significant experiments with the innovative use of communications. These pioneering efforts—through their successes and failures—have demonstrated the possibilities and limitations of the utilization of different communications strategies for national development.

The programme has rightly emphasized the use of face-to-face oral communication at the principal vehicle for the promotion of innovations in village India. Other media have also been pressed into service to supplement this effort, but their secondary role was never lost sight of.

A conscious effort was made to prepare the extension workers for their new and vital communications function. Experience suggests that the effectiveness of communication on the part of these change agents depended largely on their successful handling of three problems in the field—role definition, rapport, and impression management.

A lesson that is obvious, but one that needs to be emphasized nevertheless, is that to convey a message with effect it is essential to use the language, symbols, and styles familiar to the audience. A great deal of waste of effort can be avoided by approaching the village people through their own cultural frame of reference. The limited but successful use of traditional methods for new purposes, especially for attitude change, supports this approach. Urban bias in the handling of communications has perhaps been the most important single factor responsible for inadequate and faulty communication.

It is also evident that an oral message, by itself, is not enough to promote new practices and techniques. The effectiveness of the message increases manifold when it is supported by visual demonstration. A further step is equally necessary. As an instrument of development policy, communications should also be backed by a sound organization to provide technical guidance and required supplies. Nothing contributes more toward generating apathy, frustration, and lack of faith in the possibility of change in the village people than the failure on the part of change agents to actively assist them to experiment with the innovations for which interest has been aroused in them.

The effort to create a network of local agents of communication emanates from a basic principle adopted by the community development programme in India—the principle of actively involving the people with every phase and with all facets of the programme. Some significant steps have been taken in this direction, although they have not all been uniformly successful. The failures in this field need not cause despair. They only suggest what every policy-maker and change agent should know, that institution building is a slow process: doctrinaire idealism alone can never create the desired institutions. The process inevitably requires patient and sustained experimentation. Evaluation and adjustment are two other essential components of a successful strategy of institution building for communication and change.

Creative effort to introduce new methods of communication is both desirable and necessary. It calls for imagination, innovation, research and evaluation. India, like other underdeveloped countries, requires a body of specialists who can effectively handle the poster and the cartoon, the newspaper and the pamphlet, and the film and the radio for attitude change and for promotion of innovations.

And finally one other lesson that India and other developing countries can learn from some of the failures of this country's communications strategy is that bureaucratization, routinization, and ritualization of approach often make communication sterile. It is necessary to guard against these dangers. Time is an essential element in the process of change: to make a deep and lasting impact on the village people the message of innovation has to be repeated and demonstrated several times.

Summing Up

India has pursued her programme of modernization and national development with an exceptional sense of urgency. Recognizing the crucial role of communication for the success of these plans, she has made a series of noteworthy innovations in this field. Having to explore uncharted territories, she has had to proceed with caution and necessarily has had to encounter some failures in the process. The lessons that have been learned are valuable.

Even today the country lacks a positive, comprehensive, and long-range communications policy. This is understandable, for the country is still searching for an identity and has not yet been able to evolve a consensus on what it ultimately wants to be. There is a mounting desire for attaining increasingly higher standards of life, but the ultimate social and cultural goals still remain somewhat hazy. A considerable gap still persists between the elite and the masses. The country's small modernizing elite has to approach the problem cautiously for two important reasons: first, because the traditional elite is still a force to reckon with; and second, because the conservatism-ridden masses can react unpredictably if they are pushed too hard in the direction of modernization. In a democracy, the elite can only influence opinion; the ultimate decisions rest with the people. Until there is greater interest articulation and more political education the image of the future is bound to continue to remain blurred. And it may be added that even the elite is of two minds—if it is not confused—about the final choice: it is convinced of the desirability of modernization, but at the same time it cannot resist the pull of tradition.

In this context, an operational aspect of the communication process needs to be seriously taken note of. As the mass media are not relatively well developed, the modernizer cannot approach the rural population directly. He has to rely largely on traditional networks and on oral face-to-face communication through local intermediaries. The intermediary's logic of selectivity and interpretation often determine what part of the message will filter down to the masses and in what form. Bias and vested interests thus modify and distort the message considerably.

The communication policy also has been handicapped by the paucity of scientific research and evaluation and by the absence of a body of specialists who are adept in the innovative handling of communication for rural audiences. Problem areas of communication are beginning to be identified, but as yet there are no penetrating analyses of the range and dimensions of gaps, faults, and difficulties in these areas. An effective strategy for reaching the rural masses cannot be developed because so little is known about reference groups, opinion leaders, and decision-makers in the village communities. The reach and effectiveness of newspapers, books, radio, and film also have not been scientifically assessed. In the absence of this data the policy-maker has had to proceed largely on hunch and intuition. Carefully organized evaluation of these efforts could have suggested correctives, but unfortunately this has not been done on a wide enough scale. Inadequacy of innovative handling of communications for development is also explained by the woefully small number of persons who have training, experience, and desire to forge ahead in this field.

It is heartening to observe, however, that the importance of communications for programmes of planned change is being increasingly recognized. This recognition, it is hoped, will be followed by purposeful, imaginative, and concerted action. For the speedy and smooth realization of the objectives of development policy, the need for more inputs in research, in evaluation, and in the training of mass media experts in the general field of communication cannot be overemphasized.

Part Four

Rural
Communities
and Change

M. N. Srinivas

18 Village Studies and Their Significance

My aim in this essay is to assess the significance of anthropological studies of Indian village communities for other disciplines such as economics, comparative religion and history, and for the practical tasks of social and agricultural reconstruction. I have in view only the really intensive field-studies conducted by trained anthropologists who use the latest techniques and methods. Judged by this standard a good deal of what passes for fieldwork does not bear examination. I assume that the reader has a layman's acquaintance with social anthropology, and will, therefore, refrain from attempting to give him an idea of the way in which the social anthropologist sets about the task of making an intimate and firsthand study of a small community. However, it is necessary, to state that one of the aims of the social anthropologist in selecting a small community is that he wants to obtain an idea of the way in which all the parts of a society hang together. Even if he is studying only a single aspect of a society such as religion or law he tries to view it in relation to the total social system in which all the aspects are found to be constantly interacting. The fieldworker records practically everything he sees even when, for instance, his aim is only to make an analysis of the kinship system of the people he is studying. He will try to collect as much information as he can, in the twelve to eighteen months at his disposal, about the other activities of the people such as agriculture, house-building, commercial activities, manners, morals, law and religion. This is partly due to his overdeveloped sense of curiosity, and partly to his awareness that the various aspects of a society form a closely-woven mesh, and that the particular aspect he is studying might influence and be influenced by every other aspect of social life. The fieldworker will have obtained by the time he has completed his study, an intimate and allround knowledge of the village or tribe he has been with.

It may be argued that, on his own admission, the anthropologist has knowledge of only one tiny village or tribe, and in dealing with vast countries such knowledge cannot be a reliable guide. But then, systematic comparison is considered to be of the essence of the method of social anthropology. For instance, no anthropologist would dare to speak of Indian villages as a whole until a sufficient number of villages in the different cultural areas had been studied. Secondly, an anthropologist takes care to see that his village is either typical of an area, or that it is suitable for the study of a particular theoretical problem such as the nature of inter-caste relations, or the effects of irrigation on social and economic institutions, or the relation between religion and the caste structure. And it is necessary to point out that the study of a single village is productive of much more than knowledge about a single village. It is an attempt to answer a general theoretical question. In addition, it provides the anthropologist with some insight into rural social life all over the country. Of course, such insight is not knowledge, and once this distinction is clearly made, even a single village study enables the anthropologist to say a good deal about rural social life in India as a whole.

Intensive fieldwork experience is of critical importance in the career of an anthropologist. It forms the basis of his comprehension of all other societies, including societies differing greatly from the one of which he has firsthand knowledge. No amount of book-knowledge is a substitute for field-experience.

When the anthropologist reads an economist or political scientist or statistician on the country in which he has done an intensive field-study, he cannot help comparing his experience with the economist's or political scientist's or statistician's. The economist, political scientist and statistician usually deal with large areas, or with a great number of people, and their experience is of quite a different kind from that of the anthropologist. With the former, the collector of primary data is frequently different from the expert who interprets it. The "macrocosmic" studies of the economist and statistician make such a division of labour inevitable, but it is obvious that there are grave risks in making such a division. Firstly, it requires from the collectors of primary data a high level of integrity, intelligence and training, which they only too often do not possess. This is strikingly clear in an underdeveloped country such as ours where the government requires the hereditary village officials like the headman and accountant to collect a vast amount of information on a variety of topics. These officials do not as a rule have either the training or the interest to collect accurate information and besides, in a majority of cases, they have a vested interest in supplying wrong information. For instance, during prevalence of rationing the government was buying up all the surplus grown by peasants at a fixed rate. The surplus was calculated by the village accountant on the basis of the return declared by each peasant and deducting from it the grain necessary to feed the members of his family, servants and old labourers, and for seed grain. It is well known that the accountants winked at low returns, allowed the peasants to include casual guests as members of the family, and so on. The ill-paid accountant was not unwilling to oblige the peasant for a consideration, and the case of the powerful landlords, he was eager not to incur their wrath.

Even where graduates have been employed to collect answers to questionnaires devised by some expert in Delhi or beyond, the investigators are at best able to have only a partial grasp of the significance of the questionnaires, as they lack a sound training in social anthropology and sociology.

It is essential that in order to comprehend the significance of the information solicited, the investigators must have a full knowledge of the basic problem that is being investigated, even when it is not a problem in pure theory.

On the other hand, questionnaires can only be compiled after the expert has had some knowledge of the local conditions. The expert frequently lacks such knowledge. These drawbacks could be to some extent remedied where the investigators have been properly trained, and where the expert encourages them to express their opinions freely, but everyone will agree that this is not common.

In the case of anthropological field-studies of village communities, however, the anthropologist both devises the questionnaire as well as collects the answers, and even where he employs an assistant, he is both physically present in the village and also possesses enough local knowledge to exercise close supervision.

II

We have a government which is solicitous of the welfare of the peasantry and it is aware, as few governments are, of the need for accurate facts on a variety of matters affecting the peasant, such as the extent of subdivision and fragmentation of holdings, the nature of rural credit, the conditions under which the landless labourers work in different parts of the country, and the extent to which underemployment or disguised unemployment prevails in the rural areas. (Two reports, one on rural credit and another on agricultural labour, have already come out). It is understandable that the government's aim is severely practical in conducting these surveys. It is not, however, realized that the successful prosecution of that aim requires what may appear to be a departure from the strictly practical. The various aspects of rural social life are closely integrated with each other, and an analysis of any one aspect of social life may, and usually does, involve an analysis of one or more related aspects and their interactions. Thus, for instance, a survey of rural credit cannot ignore the existence of elaborate marriage and funeral rites, and ideas regarding how they ought to be performed. Statistics regarding cattle make no sense if considered without reference to the agricultural techniques and the peasant's economy, and also to the ethical and religious beliefs of the people. In short, a consideration of each rural problem as though it was detachable from others and from the total social and cultural matrix, will not lead to the formulation of a proper solution. I repeat that it is entirely understandable that the government should want to concern itself only with "practical research" and that it should aim at producing quick results, but what is not understandable is the failure of anthropologists and sociologists to point out that such aims are bound to defeat themselves. This is to some extent due to the utter poverty of university departments which are starved of funds for research and this makes them accept any conditions, however unreasonable, imposed by the government.

In short, only the social anthropologist attempts to study the village community as a whole, and his knowledge and approach provide an indispensable background for the proper interpretation of data on any single aspect of rural social life. His approach provides a much needed corrective to the partial approach of the economist, political scientist and social worker. Again, unlike the other social scientists, he tries hard to keep his value judgements to himself, and this gives him the necessary sympathy to grasp the rural or tribal situation.

An example will perhaps make clear what I am trying to say. We hear a great deal about India's cattle problem from economists and reformers. We are told that India has the largest cattle population with the smallest milk-yield, that the peasant does not take proper care of his cattle, and that his religious sentiments come in the way of a sensible cattle policy. What light does a study of a single village shed on this matter? The facts which I am about to relate are from the village of Rampura, about twenty-two miles to the southeast of Mysore city. It is likely that they also hold good of many other villages around Rampura. In this area, the cow is not as important as the buffalo from the point of view of milk. It is true that people prefer cow-milk for drinking, and in fact infants and patients use nothing else, but buffalo-milk is far more popular for making *ghee*, curd, buttermilk and coffee and tea. Those who sell milk find that it is easier to dilute buffalo-milk than cow-milk. This situation obtains in other parts of India too. Taking the country as a whole, it is very likely that the buffalo is at least as important as the cow as a producer of milk, though not as a draught-animal. But it is extremely strange that in discussions on the cattle problem the buffalo is conspicuous by its absence and that this fact has gone uncommented.

In Rampura—and this is true of a considerable part of India as a whole—the bull buffalo is not used for draught purpose. It is, however, a favourite for sacrifice to village goddesses. A cynic might say that people only choose to sacrifice an utterly useless animal which it would have cost fodder to keep. This may be contrasted with the popular view that Hindus refuse to kill off old and useless cattle because of religious sentiments. In this case, the same sentiments *require* the slaughter of one kind of cattle.

Bullocks are draught-animals in Rampura—and in a great part of India. Practically every cultivator in Rampura keeps a pair of bullocks, while only a few keep a cow or buffalo for milk and manure. This is primarily due to the shortage of pasture-land. It is difficult enough to find fodder for bullocks which *have* to be kept, for no landowner would like to engage a tenant without bullocks of his own and there is keen competition to obtain land to till. Owning a pair of bullocks is a strong qualification in the struggle to obtain land. But the poverty of the peasant forces him to buy the cheapest bullocks available—in 1948 the lowest price for a pair of small bullocks was about Rs 550. Small bullocks were about Rs 250 each. Small bullocks cost less to feed than big ones. The death of a bullock seriously upsets the peasant's economy, and it may be recalled here that the life of a bullock was precarious before veterinary hospitals became common. An epidemic of rinderpest used to wipe out hundreds of cattle. The peasant is aware that he may be suddenly called upon to replace one or both of his bullocks during the middle of the agricultural season. Secondly, ploughs in this area are light, being made of wood, and big bullocks are not needed to draw them. Thirdly, rice is cultivated in small, ridged-up plots, and bullocks must be small enough to turn in them. Big bullocks confer prestige on the owner. One man in Rampura kept two pairs of very big bullocks, magnificent beasts, but he kept them more for show than for draught purposes. The villagers envied him, but also thought him silly, for bullocks are meant for use and not to bring glory to their master. This man was a spendthrift, drank toddy, smoked *bhang*, kept mistresses, and his going in for huge bullocks was of a piece with the rest of his thriftless life.

Contrary to the impression obtaining among the urban intelligentsia, the peasants take as much care of their cattle as their resources permit. Bullocks are made to work hard during the monsoon months of June-August, and the peasant feels grateful to them. During September and October, when there is not much work to be done in the fields, the peasant gets up sometime after midnight to hand-feed his sleepy bullocks with green rice shoots. This feeding goes on for a few hours every night. Once I saw a peasant thrusting paddy sheaves into the mouth of a bullock and I asked him why, when there was an acute rice shortage in the cities, he was giving it stuff which could keep human beings alive. He replied, "Didn't it help me in sowing and transplanting? Why shouldn't it eat a little of what it helps me to grow?" Gratitude is to be shown not only to human beings, but also to cattle. The peasant's world-view, in some respects or contexts, is not anthropocentric. The bull is after all Basava, the son of Shiva, the animal on which the great god Shiva rides. No bullocks may be yoked to the plough on Monday, for Monday is sacred to Shiva, and Shiva's son should be given rest on that day.

A few rich landlords in Rampura kept a few small cows each, for the sake of manure. There is a great shortage of manure and the rich lanlords try to obtain additional manure by keeping cows. A small boy drives them every morning to some pasture-land two miles from the village, and he returns in the evening with the animals. The pasture is poor, but fodder is so scarce that it is worthwhile to collect what is available. The droppings of the cows are collected in a basket and brought home. Cattle-shed manure is emptied on to the manure heap. A boy costs only about thirty rupees a year plus food and clothing. Each cow is a mobile Sindri, converting the sparse tufts of poor grass into valuable manure. It may be added here that in Rampura cowdung is not burnt for fuel in spite of the great shortage of fuel. This is due to a rule enforced by the village elders sometime ago—not by the official *panchayat*, however.

It is commonly believed that the peasant's religious attitude to cattle comes in the way of the disposal of useless cattle. Here again, my experience of Rampura makes me sceptical of the general belief. I am not denying that cattle are regarded as in some sense sacred, but I doubt whether the belief is as powerful as it is claimed to be. I have already mentioned that bull-buffaloes are sacrificed to village goddesses. And in the case of the cow, while the peasant does not want to kill the cow or bull himself, he does not seem to mind very much someone else killing it elsewhere. There are, in this area, itinerant Muslim traders who go from village to village exchanging cattle. The trader exchanges one of the calves in his possession for another in the peasant's possession. Peasants say that the trader always gets an animal and a few rupees in exchange for the animal that he parts with. The cattle which are finally with the trader end in a butcher's yard in Hogur or Mysore city.

I hope I have said enough to indicate how complex the cattle problem really is and how some of the opinions current about it are a little less than the whole truth.

III

Over the last hundred years or more, the peasant has been represented as extremely conservative, pigheaded, ignorant and superstitious. And this picture of him seems to have gained greater currency these days as a result of the many organized efforts, official as well as non-official, to change his agriculture and way of life. The anthropologist who has made an intensive study of a village community is unable to subscribe to the current views regarding the peasant.

In a paper entitled, "Technological Change in Over-developed Rural Areas" (*Economic Development and Cultural Change*, 1952, pp. 261-72), McKim Marriott shows that villagers in Kishen Garhi in Uttar Pradesh have not opposed all change but, on the contrary, have accepted new crops and new techniques of cultivation. What is even more important, he shows that the technology of the peasant is not the simple thing that it is popularly believed to be, but really a complex and interrelated whole, and a change in any single item of it produces repercussions in the entire system. The technological system is closely related to the economic, social and religious systems, and this partly explains the peasant's opposition to change. Change is much more serious and pervasive in small and stable societies where the same people are involved with each other in a number of relationships, than in huge, industrial societies where the different aspects of social life do not form as a closely-knit whole, and where relationships between individuals are specialized and disparate. A desperate shortage characterizes the peasant's economy. He is in need of a few things for sheer survival, and each of these multipurpose goods is in acute shortage. To give an example: the peasant has several uses for each leaf and twig growing in his area. The cactus is excellent for hedging, it is burnt as fuel when dry, and if it is buried underground when green, makes good manure. The fruit of some varieties of cactus are eaten in some parts of the country. Similarly, agave is good for hedging, its leaves are used to protect new mud walls during the monsoon, and to wall in nurseries, and it provides fibre for rope. Its central shoot is burnt as fuel. Every part of the ubiquitous *babul*, including the two-inch thorns, are put to use. Its twigs are used for hedging, its leaves and pods are eaten by the omnivorous goat, its wood, is used as timber and fuel, short lengths of *babul* twigs are used as toothbrushes, its thorns as pins, and its fragrant flowers to adorn women's hair and to make garlands. The popularity of the goat is a measure of the shortage of fodder. Its omnivorousness enables it to survive even in our overstocked countryside, and its survival makes arboriculture extremely difficult if not impossible.

The peasant uses cowdung as fuel not because he does not know that it is valuable manure, but because he is desperately short of fuel. His plough is wooden and light because his bullocks are small, and he has frequently to grow his livelihood on a few inches of topsoil above hard rock. He spends money at weddings and funerals because if he does not do so he loses face with his relatives, friends and neighbours. It is not fair to hold him responsible for institutions which have existed for many centuries. He can only be blamed for not having the courage to break them, and going against custom is much more difficult in the small, face-to-face and stable village community than in the heterogeneous and huge city. His poverty places him in the obligation of people and this in turn forces him to behave in such a way that he does not displease others.

The conservatism of the peasant is not without reason. His agricultural techniques are a prized possession embodying as they do the experience of centuries. His social and cultural institutions give him a sense of security and permanence and he is naturally loath to change them. It may be added here that conservatism is not peculiar to the peasantry—nobody likes change, especially when he is past his youth. It is the experience of fieldworkers that in every village there are a few young men who like to alter their traditional ways, but they are in the grip of the authority of the elders. Nowadays, in many villages, sharp conflict is visible between the elders and youths. The youths have not made much headway in capturing power because respect for elders is strongly emphasized in their tradition, and the institution of joint family and village *panchayat* tend to protract the dependence, economic and otherwise, of the young men on the old. Thus, changing an item of agricultural technique is not merely a technological matter, but one affecting social relation between father and son, and between elders and youths, and in a sense, the integrity of the entire culture which emphasizes respect for the old as a primary value.

His conservatism makes him sceptical of new ways and techniques. He is unconvinced by the success of a variety of rice on a government farm because he knows that his own resources are pitiful while the government's are enormous. Not infrequently is he a jump ahead of the expert for he has already calculated the effect of a new idea or tool on the power-structure in the village. Thus while the expert is elaborating the advantages of a new tool or process, the peasant is thinking of the power it will place in the hands of the headman or elders. If he then opposes the tool or process, it is not because of his stupidity but because of his intelligence. I have seen with my own eyes how the gift by the government of a superior breed of bull-calf to a village was used by the headman to exercise tyrannical authority over a poor and unfortunate kinsman to whom he gave the calf. Every new tool or technique means changes in social relationships and part of the opposition of villagers to new tools and techniques is due to their perception of the social implications of the innovations. Thus the headman of Rampura wanted bulldozers and electricity but not a school. Bulldozers would level his land, electricity would brighten up the home and village and make possible starting small industries, while schools would make labour even scarcer and make the poor people lose the respect they have for the rich. Everyone who has had any experience of our villages knows that in each village there are a few keymen whose position in the structure and whose intelligence will enable them to exploit every change to their benefit. This fact has to be taken note of while introducing every measure of reform.

IV

A vast body of written literature, sacred as well as secular, is available to the student of Indian social institutions, and the existence of this literature has exercised a decisive influence on the analysis of Indian sociological problems. For instance, references to caste and kin relations in literature have been treated as historical data, and conditions obtaining today have been compared and contrasted with conditions alleged to prevail in historical times. The law books (*Dharma Sutras and Dharma Shashtras*) have been assumed to refer to laws which were actually in force among the people and it has not been asked whether the laws did not refer to merely what a particular lawyer considered desirable or good. Even for the major lawyers it is not known when exactly they lived, it being not uncommon for one scholar's estimate to differ from another's by as much as three centuries. This is especially so in the case of the earlier lawyers. Dr I.P. Desai writes, "A further difficulty in the development of Hindu law is the lack of agreement among scholars regarding the dates of various works. ... There is no agreement regarding the time sequence (of the various authors). Buhler considers Gautama as the earliest Dharmasastrakar and Apastamba as the latest, while Jayaswal reverses the order, considering Apastamba as the earliest and Gautama as the latest Dharmasastrakar" ("Punishment and Penance in Manusmriti," *Journal of the University of Bombay*, XV, Part I, July 1946, p. 42). The provenance of a lawyer, and the sanction behind the rules enunciated by him are frequently far from clear if not unknown.

It is pertinent to mention in this connection that there is, among our educated people, an unstated but nonetheless real and deep-seated assumption that what is written is true, and the older a manuscript, the more true its contents. Learning is almost synonymous with poring over palm leaf manuscripts. This bias in favour of literary material is most clearly seen in the syllabuses of Indological studies in our universities. Indology has come to be regarded as knowledge about India's past. Any suggestion that Indology should include the study of tribes and villages which are in existence today would be regarded as too absurd to merit consideration. Caste in the Vedas and in

Manu ought to be studied but caste as a powerful force in modern Indian life ought not to be. Such a separation between the past and present is not healthy.

The observation of social behaviour is everywhere a difficult undertaking and, in certain respects, observing one's own society is far more difficult than observing an alien society. In the case of Indians, there is the additional difficulty that ideas which are carried over from literary material, and from the caste to which one belongs by birth, vitiate the observation of field-behaviour. An example of such a failure to understand the factual situation is provided by the way in which the idea of *varna* vitiated the understanding of caste. I have discussed this point elsewhere (*A.R. Wadia, Essays in Philosophy Presented in his Honour*, Bangalore, 1954, pp. 357-64), but I will briefly summarize it here. According to the *varna* scheme, there are only four castes and a few other groups, while as a matter of actual fact there are, in each linguistic area, several hundred castes, each of which is a homogeneous group, with a common culture, with a common occupation or occupations, practising endogamy and commensality. The castes of a local area form a hierarchy. There are several features of this hierarchy which run counter to the hierarchy as it is conceptualized in the idea of *varna*. Firstly, in the *varna* scheme there are only four all-India castes each of which occupies a definite and immutable place, while in caste at the existential level, the only definite thing is that all the local castes form a hierarchy. Everything else is far from certain. For one thing, the hierarchy is characterized by uncertainty, especially in the middle region which spans an enormous structural gulf. Each caste tries to argue that it occupies a higher place than the one allotted to it by its neighbours. This argument has an important function because it makes mobility possible, and castes are mobile over a period of time. There is occasional leapfrogging inside the system, a caste jumping over its neighbours to achieve a high position. Another important point is that the hierarchy is local, varying from one small local area to another, if not from one village to another. Two groups bearing the same name and living in the same linguistic region often occupy different positions in their respective local hierarchies and differ from each other in some customs and rites. The Kolis of Gujarat are a case in point.

It is clear that the idea of *varna* is far too rigid and simple to cover the immensely complex facts of caste. But the idea of *varna* helps to make the facts of caste in one region intelligible all over India by providing a conceptual frame that is simple, clear-cut, stable, and which, it is imagined, holds good everywhere. And it helps mobility too, for ambitious castes find it less difficult to take on high-sounding Sanskritic names with the name of one of the *varnas* as a suffix, than to take on the name of a local higher caste. But all this is lost sight of because *varna* is treated as describing caste accurately and fully. But this would not have happened if we Indians had not taken it for granted that the idea of *varna*, derived from literary material, adequately explained the facts of the caste system. The only cure for this literary bias lies in doing field research. The fieldworker, confronted by the bewildering variety and complexity of facts as they actually are, is forced to relate what he sees to what he has assumed it to be, and the lack of correspondence betweeen the two, results in his attempting to reassess the written material.

V

In every part of India only a few castes at the top enjoyed a literary tradition while the bulk of the people did not. Under British rule the top castes supplied the intelligentsia which acted as the link between the new masters and the bulk of the people. And the new intelligentsia saw the social reality through the written literature, regarding the deviations from the latter as aberrations. This group also perpetrated an upper-caste view of the Hindu social system on the new masters and through them, the outside world. Conditions prevalent among the upper castes were generalized to include all Hindus. For instance, women are treated much more severely among the higher castes than among the lower, but this distinction was ignored by the early reformers. They talked about the plight of the Hindu widow, the absence of divorce, the harshness of the sex code towards her and so on, but on all these matters the institutions of the lower differ in important respects from those of the higher castes. The point I am trying to make is that the observation of Hindu social life has been, and still is, vitiated by the book view and the upper-caste view. A sociological study of Indian sociologists would yield interesting results.

An emphasis on religious behaviour as such, as distinguished from what is written in the religious books and the opinions of the upper castes, would have provided us with a view of Hinduism substantially different from that of the philosophers, Sanskritists and reformers. I shall try to explain what I mean by example. In the summer of 1948, I went along with the elders of Rampura village to the temple of the deity Basava to watch them consult the deity about rain. The priest performed *puja*, chanting *mantras* in Sanskrit, and then the elders began to ask the deity to let them know whether it was going to rain or not in the next few days. I was expecting them to behave as I have seen devotees behave in the temples of the upper castes, viz., stand with bowed head and folded palms, shut eyes, and utter words showing great respect for, and fear of, and dependence upon, the deity. I was completely taken aback to find them using words which they used to an equal, and a somewhat unreasonable equal at that. They became angry, shouted at the deity, taunted him, and went so far as to say that they considered even the government more worthy of confidence than him. And they were deadly serious all the time. Nothing could have been further from an urban Hindu's ideas of what the proper relationship was between man and God.

It is frequently said by apologists and reformers that Hinduism is not a proselytizing religion like Christianity and Islam. This again is not strictly true. Besides the Buddhists and Jains, the Lingayats, who began as a militant reformist sect in the south in the twelfth century, A.D., secured converts from all the castes from the Brahmin to the untouchable in the early days of their history. The Lingayats are a well-organized sect, and they have monasteries scattered all over Karnataka. In southern Karnataka, for instance, the monasteries have a following not only among Lingayats but among a number of middle-range non-Brahminical castes with whom they are in continuous contact, and over whose life they exercise some kind of direction. The head of each monastery collects a levy from each of his followers through a hierarchy of agents. It is important to note that this is not confined to the Lingayats though they are the best-organized of the sects. The Brahmin followers of the great theologian and reformer, Sri Ramanujacharya, have a monastery at Melkote, about twenty-six miles from Mysore city, and the monastery has a following among the people in the surrounding towns and villages. Thus, both Brahmin and non-Brahmin sects have deeply influenced the people at large through organizations which have existed for hundreds of years. Still one frequently reads in books on Hindu religion and philosophy that Hinduism is unique in that it is not a proselytizing religion. It is true that Hindus do not try to convert Christians or Muslims, but in a sense conversion is going on all the time within Hindusim. The lower castes and tribal people have been undergoing Sanskritization all the time, and sects, Brahminical and non-Brahminical, and Vaishnavite and Shaivite, have actively sought converts. Persecution for religious views and practices has not been unknown.

VI

The studies of village communities which are currently being carried out in the different parts of the country provide the future historian with a vast body of facts about rural social life, facts collected not by travellers in a hurry, but by men who are trained to observe keenly and accurately. These studies therefore constitute valuable contributions to the social, political, economic and religious history of our country. Their value is further enhanced when it is realized that the changes which are being ushered in independent and plan-conscious India herald a complete revolution in our social life. It is true that in historic times India has been subject to invasions by diverse peoples including the Mughals and British, and that British rule inaugurated changes the fulfilment of which we are observing now, but the break with the past was never as complete and thoroughgoing as it is today. We have, at the most, another ten years in which to record facts about a type of society which is changing fundamentally and with great rapidity.

Historians have stated that a knowledge of the past is helpful in the understanding of the present if not in forecasting the future. It is not, however, realized that a thorough understanding of the present frequently sheds light on the past. To put it in other words the intimate knowledge which results from the intensive field-survey of extant social institutions does enable us to better interpret data about past social institutions. Historical data are neither as accurate nor as rich and detailed as the data collected by field-anthropologist, and the study of certain existing processes increases our understanding of similar processes in the past. It is necessary to add here that great caution has to be exercised in such a task, for otherwise history will be twisted out of all recognition. But once the need for extereme caution is recognized, there is no doubt that our knowledge of the working of historical processes will be enhanced by this method. For instance, the study of the extant institution of feud in certain African societies has enabled anthropologists to conclude that the classical view of the feud as it obtained among the ancient Anglo-Saxons perhaps needs to be changed in important respects (see M. Gluckman's essay on "Political Institutions" in *The Institutions of Primitive Society*, edited by E.E. Evans-Pritchard, Oxford, 1954, pp. 74-75). It is probable that the study of factions as it obtains in an Indian village today will shed light on local political history.

Enough has been said, I hope, to indicate the importance of the intensive study of villages which are at present being made in different parts of India. To the anthropologist, the villages are invaluable observation—centres where he can study in detail social processes and problems to be found occurring in great parts of India, if not in a great part of the world. An anthropologist goes to live in a village for a year or even two not because he wants to collect information about curious and dying customs and beliefs, but to study a theoretical sociological problem, and his most important aim is to contribute to the growing body of theoretical knowledge about the nature of human societies. The success of welfare work is considerably helped, indirectly, by the growth of this theoretical knowledge. The universities are the proper organizations to conduct this research, and the government can help by giving money to the establishment of teaching and research posts in social anthropology and sociology. Too much stress on utilitarian research will defeat itself, and will further lower intellectual standards.

I may now mention a few of the problems that are either being studied, or have just been studied, by anthropologists in the last ten years. One anthropologist is making a study of the effects of the introduction of irrigation, and commercial crops, on what was formerly a predominantly "dry" village. A sugar factory was put up in this area in the thirties, and the village in question grows some sugarcane for the factory. A study of this village should also help to throw some light on the effects of the introduction of a cash economy and urbanization on rural social institutions. Another anthropologist has made a study of the effects of peasant social institutions on peasant economy in Orissa. A third has made a study of the impact of urbanization and Westernization on intercaste relations in a Tanjore village. One of the students in the M.S. University, Baroda, is about to begin the study of a multicaste village in Gujarat in which genealogical records, going back to about two hundred years at least, are available for each of the principal castes. Here the aim is to study the effects, if any, of the presence of a written or historical tradition on the institutions and beliefs of a peasant community. My own aim in making a study of Rampura was to a get a detailed description of the way in which each of the nineteen caste groups behaved towards the others. I must confess I was a bit tired of reading about caste in general, and it may come as a surprise to some to know that in spite of the great interest in the institution of caste, no one had seen it fit to go and live in a multicaste village and record in detail the interactions between the various castes. I also wanted to find out the relation which the caste system bore to the pattern of landownership in the village. My study has convinced me of the enormous value of studying all Indian sociological problems in single villages. I do not say all sociological problems can be studied in the village, but only many of the most important ones.

Mildred Stroop Luschinsky

19 Problems of Culture Change in the Indian Village

A village woman of the Noniya caste[1] squatted near the door rubbing her jaw. She said that she knew why her teeth were aching. An evil spirit was troubling her. The village *shaman* had told her so and she was performing ceremonies to placate the spirit under the *shaman's* direction. An American research worker had tried to persuade her to go to a dentist in Banaras but she had refused, asking, "What would such a man know about evil spirits?"

The pain continued in spite of her ritual acts and she finally agreed to accompany the research worker to Banaras. She entered the strange office and endured the novocain needle and the dental treatment without flinching. It was only when the novocain wore off that she complained bitterly about the dentist. During the next few days she did not comment on her condition. Finally, on the fourth day, she said, "I have no pain in my teeth." The writer replied that the dentist must have helped her. "Yes," she said, without much conviction.

"But the *shaman* said that an evil spirit was causing the tooth trouble."

She replied quickly and firmly, "It was an evil spirit."

---

[1] In the area where this village woman lives, Noniyas are earth-workers and have a caste status which is relatively high among clean Sudras. Clean Sudras rank above untouchables, who are sometimes called unclean Sudras, but below Vaishyas, Kshatriyas, and Brahmins.

"But if it were an evil spirit, how was it possible for the dentist to help you?"

"The dentist didn't do much. A day or two before that, I went to L," she named a *shaman* of another village. "He made a little offering and told the spirit to leave. After that there was less pain. When I went to Banaras, there was just a little pain. The dentist finished the job, that's all."

"Then you believe that the *shaman* drove away the spirit?"

"Yes."

"But how can you be sure? Perhaps it was the dentist who really helped you and not the *shaman* at all."

"No, if the evil spirit were still here, it would be causing pain in another tooth, or in my back, or in my legs."

As she said this, she rubbed her jaws, back, and legs. She had a pained expression on her face as she imagined what the evil spirit might do to her.

This story of the Noniya woman and the dentist is only one small example of the difficulty which an extension worker—or in a wider frame, the Indian government itself—encounters in the attempt to introduce changes for the benefit of the rural population. The *shaman*, the evil spirit, and other aspects of local tradition are powerful forces. Their full strength is not always felt in the city agencies where the plans are made. This article will describe a few innovations in the fields of public health, education, land reform, and village government. It will explore the cultural factors influencing their acceptance by the population and compare the intent of the planners and legislators with the actual impact of the plans at the village level.[2]

Public Hygiene

Successful rural extension work requires not only a basic knowledge of village culture but also an insight into the mechanisms of culture change. One government worker of the

[2]This article is based on village research undertaken by the author from 1954 to 1957. The village of Senapur has a population of about two thousand. It is located twenty-five miles north of Banaras in the state of Uttar Pradesh and was selected for a research project by the Indian programme of Cornell University under the direction of Dr M.E. Opler.

Senapur area had both of these assets. She taught a midwifery course in a town three miles from the village. A low-caste woman of Senapur decided to take advantage of the course. She had served as a midwife in Senapur for a number of years but thought she might increase her earnings if she successfully completed the course. In one of the classes, the instructor told the midwives that villagers should not be permitted to cut the umbilical cord with an unsterilized sickle. She explained that this may result in tetanus. Tetanus is a disease attributed by Senapur village women to an invisible flying insect called Jam. Villagers believe that the touch of Jam causes a baby's death. The instructor taught the midwife trainees that tetanus results from unhygienic conditions but advised them to associate tetanus with Jam. She said:

> Explain that Jam may touch the sickle and other things which are used. Since no one can see Jam when he touches objects in the room, everything should be put in boiling water before use. In this way, the impurities caused by Jam will be destroyed.

This instructor undoubtedly believed that villagers would not bother to sterilize their equipment unless the association were made between tetanus and Jam, and that eventually as tetanus ceased to be a threat, the belief in Jam would disappear.

Sometimes innovations are accepted because villagers themselves incorporate the changes into their existing beliefs. This occurred in Senapur when government officers introduced smallpox vaccination. Senapur villagers believe that smallpox is caused by a disease goddess called Bhagauti Mai. They have great fear of Bhagauti Mai because many men, women, and children have died in smallpox epidemics. There are numerous traditional methods of propitiating this goddess, but villagers had discovered that Bhagauti Mai was not fully satisfied with their efforts to please her. In spite of their offerings, smallpox persisted. As a result, a few villagers were cooperative when government inoculation officers first appeared in Senapur. Because of their fear of the disease, they were willing to do anything which might protect their children from illness or death.

After the goverment officer left the village, the parents of the vaccinated children watched with concern to see what the effect might be. There is a widespread belief that pox marks and fever are signs that Bhagauti Mai is residing within the person who is affected. When the boys and girls who were vaccinated became feverish, the parents exclaimed that Bhagauti Mai was possessing their children and they performed ceremonies in her honour. After this, they discovered, the goddess did not bother the children. Other villagers watched and were impressed. Now many children of Senapur are inoculated when the government officer appears in the early spring, although adults seldom bother to receive booster inoculations themselves. Had the public health workers told the villagers that Bhagauti Mai does not exist and that smallpox is caused by a virus, the villagers would probably have assumed that such blasphemy would so offend the goddess as to make useless everything these outsiders had to offer.

Some Western observes have expressed the opinion that it is wrong for extension workers to introduce improved medical techniques, such as asepsis at childbirth and vaccination, without challenging traditional beliefs. The fact is, however, that as tetanus, smallpox, and other diseases are brought under control[3], villagers will be less fearful of Jam and Bhagauti Mai and will eventually cease to believe in them.

In the examples given above, the influence of traditional beliefs on the acceptance of innovations has been described. The following is an illustration of a social need preventing a sanitary improvement. Two extension workers employed by Cornell University tried to persuade villagers of Senapur to build indoor borehole latrines instead of using the fields as their latrine. Village women agreed that there were many reasons why such latrines should be built, but they admitted that there was one reason why they did not favour the change. They used these daily trips to the fields as occasions to meet and chat with friends whom they would not otherwise see. Young women of high caste who are strictly confined to their home during daylight hours voiced unequivocal disapproval of

---

[3]Cholera is another disease which villagers attribute to Bhagauti Mai.

indoor latrines when the woman extension worker talked to them alone.

It was outside the scope of the university extension programme to provide women with greater opportunities for socializing and recreation. To do this would challenge the custom of purdah (seclusion of women) which is deeply rooted. Any changes in this custom will come slowly. As long as high-caste women of Senapur are in seclusion, they will welcome the night hours and the one excuse that they have for moving about at this time. Without the excuse, they are afraid that they might even be denied this amount of freedom. Because the high-caste families of Senapur are the only ones who can afford the expense of innovations of this kind, it goes without saying that the borehole latrine project was a failure.

Education

Since Indian independence, the educational facilities of many rural schools have been improved and new schools have been built. In Uttar Pradesh, Primary education has been free since July 1957, although it is not yet compulsory. Before July 1957, it was free for girls of all castes and boys of untouchable status. The villagers of Senapur have not taken full advantage of these expanded facilities and increased opportunities, although there are many reasons why they value education.

Most villagers would like their sons to have a formal education because they regard education as a means of attaining status. High-caste parents are especially eager for their sons to enjoy the prestige of a grammar school and high school education. How would it look, they ask, if the sons of their servants went to school for a longer period than their own sons?

Low-caste families, in turn, are often status conscious in another sense. They want to improve the position of their caste group in the caste hierarchy. In Senapur, this is particularly true of Lohars, Camars, and Noniyas.[4] The older men of these

---

[4]Lohars are carpenters who rank high in the clean Sudra category. Camars are untouchables whose caste occupations are leather-work and midwifery. In Senapur, Camar women do serve as midwives but Camar men have abandoned leather-work in an effort to improve the

groups want the younger men to be able to read and write so that they cannot be tricked or fooled by those who may wish to exploit them and so that they can inform their caste brothers of state or national events, of legislative acts, and of any other matters pertinent to caste group activity. It is interesting to note that Senapur Camars welcomed the government offer of free primary education for their children. In 1956-1957, fifty per cent of the boys attending the first grade of Senapur school were boys of depressed castes, mostly Camars, and the same was true of twenty-three per cent of grade two, eighty-nine per cent of grade three, eighty-five per cent of grade four, and twenty-five per cent of grade five.

Other villagers who favour education for boys are those who know what litigation entails. An illiterate man is at a great disadvantage at court, and villagers are well aware of this.

Finally, and perhaps of greatest importance, is the yearning of all parents to have their sons hold white-collar jobs. They no longer assume that a young man who completes college is certain to secure a good job, but they think that the chances are sufficiently great to make a college education very desirable for men. As one villager said:

People think that education is the best form of investment. If your wealth is in land and money, you may have to share it with others. But your education can never be taken away from you.

In spite of the high regard villagers have for college education, few families of Senapur can afford to send their sons to college. At present there are four postgraduates and seven graduates in the village. Twelve have completed twelfth grade and a few of these are now in colleges. At the other end of the scale, many villagers (fifty-two per cent of all males aged eleven years or above) have had no schooling at all.

---

caste standing of their group. They earn a living chiefly by working in fields as agricultural labourers. Camar women also work for wages in the fields of Thakurs. The Camars of Senapur comprise the largest caste group in the village. There are 701 Camars, while the dominant Kshatriyas number only 527. Noniyas have already been identified (footnote 1).

Education for girls is a more controversial subject. For many years villagers could see no reason for educating girls beyond the second, third, or fourth grades. Even today, many men and women argue against education for girls in the same way that their grandparents argued before them:

> Why should girls have many years of education? They go to their in-laws' homes where they do housework and bear children. Whatever they learn in school they soon forget because they have no use for it. Only reading and writing is useful. It's good if they can write letters to their parents after marriage and if they can read the letters they receive.[5]

Girls who have had more than two or three years of education are greatly respected, however. One young married girl of Camar caste had completed six years of education when she made her home in one of the Camar hamlets of Senapur. All of the women in her hamlet called her *masterain* (feminine form of master) and treated her with great respect. In the presence of the girl, one woman said:

> But in spite of this education, she is willing to do any kind of work when she is told to do it. She is a sweet girl. Her husband has had only three years of education. His family had to take him out of school to do fieldwork. Sometimes I find her crying in her home. She feels bad that her parents didn't find an educated boy for her so that she could live a different kind of life and wouldn't have to do such heavy work in the fields and in the house. She isn't accustomed to this kind of work.

Both a girl and her family enjoy enhanced status as a result of the girl's education. It is not surprising, therefore, that many high-caste families took advantage of the government's offer of free grammar school education for girls. But many lower-caste families did not do so, either because they were not attracted by the incentive of increased status or because they needed the girls' help in the homes.

[5]Girls marry out of their paternal villages.

There is another factor which prompts high-caste families to modify their previous attitudes toward education for girls. There is now the view that educated boys want to marry educated girls, or at least that their families want to arrange such matches. If parents of high caste want to place their daughters in families which have high status and which enjoy some degree of economic security, it is felt that they should send the girls through grammar school and, if possible, through junior high school.

In spite of these factors, only eight village women have completed six or more years of education. Fifty-one have studied in grades three, four, or five.

There are, therefore, many reasons why villagers want their boys and girls to have formal schooling. But they are not ready for compulsory education, which government officers mention as a goal of the future. Many villagers say that they are too poor to send their children to school. They say that they cannot afford to buy books and supplies for them. They claim they cannot get along without the help of their sons in the fields or in caste occupational work, or the help of their daughters in the home. If compulsory education legislation is passed before the general standard of living is raised, Senapur villager will be among those who defy the law. As one villager answered when asked why he did not send his daughter to school:

> When there is worry about how to fill the stomach, the mind doesn't turn to other things of life.

Before any programme for compulsory education is enacted, government planners would also benefit by a careful appraisal of the quality of teaching in government supported schools. In the Senapur primary school, teachers physically punish the children on occasion for errors in classroom recitation as well as for misbehaviour, and the punishment is sometimes so severe that children either refuse to return to school or beg their parents to let them remain home. Thirty-five men or women were asked why they did not send their sons to school. Forty per cent of these villagers replied that their sons were afraid of being beaten in school so they did not insist that they go. If teachers would use interest rather than fear as the means of control, enrollment in the school would be greater than it is now. A system of compulsory education will be met by considerable resistance unless children as well as adults are committed to it.

Birth Control

A major concern of the government is the limitation of the Indian population by birth control. Although education in birth control has not yet reached Senapur, it can be anticipated that it will not be wholly successful. There are many reasons for this.

Every man and woman of the village wants children, and in this androcentric culture, they are particularly eager to have sons. They ask:

What will happen to my lineage if I have no sons?

Concern for lineage perpetuation is very strong in village India. They also ask:

If I have no sons, who will care for me in later years? Daughters go off to other villages to live. I may be ill and feeble in old age. I want the security of sons.

But they are concerned for the life hereafter as well as for their old age. According to Hindu religion, a man's son must perform certain functions at his funeral if his soul is to have successful passage to the next life.

Other reasons why couples want sons are readily apparent from their statements. At certain periods of the agricultural cycle, many hands are needed in the fields. Sometimes the crops must be irrigated very quickly if they are to be saved. The seeds of the summer crops must be planted immediately after the first monsoon rainfall. In such emergencies, hired hands are not always available. A man is considered fortunate if he has sons. Political emergencies also disrupt village life from time to time. Individuals or factions sometimes express their ill will toward one another by crop cutting, crop burning, or threats of one kind or another. Disputes over land rights, loans, insubordination, etc., are not uncommon. No man trusts his good nature alone to keep him out of trouble. He wants the security of friends who will stand by him in times of need, and if he heads a large family with a number of sons, his wishes are more likely to be considered on the village political scene.

Women have another reason for desiring sons. They enjoy enhanced status when they give birth to sons. Older family members treat them with greater respect and are more respectful to their demands after the young women have given sons to the family.

For all of these reasons, a woman who has only daughters will not be interested in birth control measures. In all likelihood, she will welcome further pregnancies in the hope of getting a son. And infant mortality being as high as it is, she may want to try for a second and third son.

One might expect that villagers would welcome family planning programmes because of the rising cost of living in village India, the increasing degree of land fragmentation, and the financial burden of daughters' marriages. These factors will undoubtedly facilitate family planning work to some extent. But Senapur men are more often heard complaining of the paucity of sons in times of agricultural need or the danger of lineage extinction than they are heard commenting on the cost of living or land fragmentation. Educators in birth control will have to take all these factors into consideration. Birth control programmes are likely to be only partially successful until industrial development gives the people of India greater economic security and until improvements in public health and sanitation bring about a lower infant mortality rate. Even then the androcentric nature of the society, emphasis on the perpetuation of the male line, and religious beliefs may continue to deter many villagers from a ready acceptance of family planning.[6]

---

[6]For a detailed discussion of population problems in rural India, see M.E. Opler, "Cultural Context and Population Control Programmes in Village India," in the volume in honour of Douglas Haring edited by Earl Count, *Fact Theory and Social Science*, Syracuse University Press.

Land Reform

While the birth control programmes in India attack the problem of poverty by trying to limit the population, the land reform sponsored by various states seeks to effect a more equitable distribution of the agricultural wealth. In Uttar Pradesh, land reform was instituted by the Zamindari Abolition Act of 1950. *Zamindars* were persons who were either designated by British administrators as owners of large tracts of land or whose prior control over land was endorsed by the British. They were responsible for collecting rent from the peasants who cultivated the land and for transmitting a certain share of this rent to the British government as land revenue. In this way, the British obtained revenue with minimum effort. The system appeared to be simple, but in some areas a high degree of subinfeudation developed. Some tenants subleased their land to others, who in turn did the same, until there were many intermediaries between the cultivator and the government, which was previously British and then Indian. In a sense, the Zamindari Abolition Act of Uttar Pradesh is inadequately named. It seeks not only to abolish the position of the *zamindar* as such, but to prevent the existence of intermediaries. One aim of the Act is to make the cultivator directly accountable to the state.

For an understanding of the consequences of the Zamindari Abolition Act in village such as Senapur, it is necessary to have knowledge of traditional landlord-tenant relations in the village. In the sixteenth century, Kshatriyas migrated to the Senapur area from Sultanpur district, Uttar Pradesh, and made themselves full owners of the land which they found. The present descendants of the Kshatriya invaders believe that the original inhabitants fled from the area, leaving the new masters with more land than they could easily cultivate themselves. For this reason the Kshatriyas are said to have encouraged families of low caste from nearby regions to move to the villages which they were founding and to serve them as artisans and agricultural labourers. These families became the tenants of the Kshatriya landlords whom they called their "Thakurs."[7]

---

[7] *Thakur* means landlord or master in this area.

Problems of Culture Change

Some tenants acquired occupancy and hereditary rights to the land which they were cultivating. Others obtained only the right to work land for specified periods of time or even for indefinite periods which could be terminated by will of the owner. In this way, there developed different classes of tenancy.

According to Senapur informants of low castes, the landlord-tenant relationship was in most cases a satisfying one to both parties in earlier years. Landlords supported their tenants in village disputes and in litigation, provided agricultural credit, let them borrow bullocks and farm implements, gave them work in preference to other villagers and paid them adequately for their labour, gave them old clothes, gave them food in times of need, and advised them about personal and family problems. In return, tenants helped their landlords when they were asked to do so, loaned their bullocks and equipment if necessary, and supported their landlords in village disputes.

As the village population increased and landholdings became more and more fragmented, however, landlords could no longer afford to give as much food or clothing as they used to give. Tenants, in turn, were not willing to serve their Thakurs as freely as they did in the past. At this time, when landlord-tenant relationships were already strained, rumours of the proposed *zamindari* abolition legislation reached the landlords of rural Uttar Pradesh. Many *zamindars* responded to the rumours by evicting tenant from their land. Some Thakurs of Senapur, with the help of the local land revenue officer, were able to get the names of tenants with permanent tenancy rights crossed off the land records and their own names entered instead. In this way, before *zamindari* abolition legislation ever came into being, some tenants found themselves robbed of the few land rights which they did have. Even after 1950, a number of village Thakurs succeeded in getting the land records altered in their favour. The unscrupulousness of these landlords and the corruptibility of the government agents concerned caused tenants to react with fear to the words *zamindari* abolition.

State leaders have said that the ultimate aims of the Zamindari Abolition Act are to alleviate the poverty of agricultural tenants by removing intermediaries who have profited at the expense of the cultivators, and to make the tenants' economic position more secure by giving them the opportunity to purchase the land which they have worked. Low-caste villagers of Senapur, in turn, have only one comment to make about the Act:

It has not helped us in any way.

In order to understand the reasons for villagers' reaction, it will be necessary to consider a few main provisions of the Act.

Framers of the Uttar Pradesh Zamindari Act created four classes of agriculturalists: *bhumidhars* who have absolute security of tenure and full resale rights, *sirdars* who cannot sell, mortgage, or bequeath their land by will but who normally have both occupancy and hereditary rights in the land, *asamis* who have short-lived tenancy rights, and *adhivasis* who were former tenants-at-will on the home farmlands of smaller *zamindars*. By an amendment in 1954, all *adhivasis* were reclassified as *sirdars*.

Zamindars automatically became *bhumidhars* or full owners of all their unlet farmland, provided they qualified as "cultivators" of this land.[8] *Sirdars* could become full owners by depositing with the state a sum equal to ten times the rent they had paid their landlord annually. If their landlord did not take the land away from them, *asamis* could also become full owners but the state required them to pay a sum equal to fifteen times their annual rent if they wished to purchase the land. Only after becoming full owners have former tenants been granted a tax reduction amounting to fifty per cent of their former rent. Tenants who have not become full owners of their land are required to pay the same rent which they paid before the legislation. Villagers with hereditary and occupancy rights in land pay this amount as a tax to the state; tenants with short-lived tenancy rights pay it as rent to their landlords.[9] Similarly;

---

[8]See Daniel Thorner, 1956. *The Agrarian Prospect in India*. Delhi, University of Delhi Press, pp. 20-21.

[9]The category of *asami* (tenants with short-lived tenancy rights) is regarded as temporary. After the death of the farmers now classified as *asamis*, tenancy will be permitted only on the land of persons who are unable to work the land themselves, such as unmarried women, widows, minors, lunatics, idiots, blind persons, young students, members of the armed forces, and persons who are in prison. (See Section 156 of the U.P. Zamindari Abolition Act of 1950.)

ex-landlords pay the same rent to the government which they were paying when the legislation was enacted.

There are two reasons why these provisions of the Zamindari Abolition Act have not provided relief for the majority of low-caste families of Senapur. Most of the tenant families of the village are too poor to purchase any land at the specified rate. To do so, they would have to go into substantial debt, and they are not willing to do this. In the second place, their land taxes have not been reduced. Many of them had been paying much higher rent to their landlords than their landlords, in turn, were required to pass on to the government in taxes. An informant of Thakur caste said that some landlords had exacted from their tenants rental fees equal to ten times the amount which they were paying in taxes to the government. The Zamindari Abolition Act did not alter the tax rates and the disparity continues even now, to the decided advantage of the ex-landlords. This is explained by the government decision to compensate the *zamindars* for their loss of land. Government planners had decided that the state could not raise sufficient money to compensate the landlords unless the tenant families continued to be taxed at a high rate. As a result, the poorest families of the state are now paying for the land reform programme by their taxes and by land purchase.[10]

Better days may be ahead for ex-tenants. There is reason to believe that the state will reduce their taxes of the *zamindars* have been compensated for their losses. Meanwhile, however, many poor families perceive landlord abolition as a government programme which fails to alleviate their poverty.

If this were all that there is to tell about land reform in Uttar Pradesh, the story would not be of great interest to students of directed culture change. Unlike the other innovations already discussed in this article, in *zamindari* abolition there was no question of villagers' needs, beliefs, or values preventing or limiting their practical acceptance of the programme. The people had no choice in the matter. The programme was rigidly structured and was enforced by the government. But there are other aspects of the problem of directed culture change which must be considered. Programmes

---

[10]Daniel Thorner, *op. cit.*, p. 24.

which are imposed on people by an outside agency are often accompanied by consequences which are not foreseen by the planners because they lack adequate knowledge of the culture they are trying to change.

Tenant families of Senapur complain that they are actually suffering from the land reform programme in several ways. Some of them say, in effect, that if they had benefited from the main provisions of the Act, they would have accepted the secondary disadvantages without complaint, but they feel they have not been helped at all, either directly or indirectly. One of the indirect consequences of the programme has been mentioned. Some tenants lost their land rights at the hands of unscrupulous landlords who had the land records altered before the Act was enforced. The provisions which had been made for securing the land records against such falsification were not adequate, and secrecy was not maintained during the planning stages.

Senapur tenants who did not lose any rights to land in the early years of *zamindari* abolition have other reasons to complain about the programme. Most of the tenants and ex-tenants are marginal farmers. They have to borrow seed for planting and return it with interest at harvest. When they need new implements, they have to borrow money in order to pay for them. *Zamindars* readily extended credit to their tenants. They did not hesitate to do so because they could demand that a tenant repay his debt with labour if he could not return grain or money. If the tenant refused, he could be evicted. After many tenants became *sirdars* and *begari* (forced labour without remuneration) was forbidden, however, Thakurs of Senapur were reluctant to extend as much credit to former tenants as they did before. There were no other local agencies to whom the ex-tenants could turn for assistance. If the state had provided other sources of credit for tenants at the same time it instituted the *zamindari* abolition programme, one of the most serious side effects of the legislation would have been avoided.

Ex-tenants have another complaint against the *zamindari* abolition programme. They object to the rigidity of the rent collection schedule. Government agents appear at regular times to collect rent and they demand that the rent be paid at that time. One man of Khatik caste could not pay his rent on time and the government collector took the Khatik's bullock to the cattle pound where it remained until the rent was paid. Cultivators explain that crop failures, marriages or deaths in the family, illness, and other factors of this kind sometimes make it impossible for them to pay their rent at specified times. They remember the leniency of village *zamindars* who would often wait several months or more for their rent, if necessary. The ex-tenants say:

> Our landlord knew when we were in trouble because everyone who lives in the village knows what is happening here. But the government agents live outside the village. They don't know what happens here and they don't care. This new system of rent collection doesn't help us in any way. It adds to our difficulties.

Poor families of Senapur also complain that village Thakurs have reduced the amount of land which they are willing to lease on short term. Some realize that this is the case because a clause of the Zamindari Abolition Act forbids new leasing of land, but those who have scarcely any land to call their own are not happy to be denied the opportunity to cultivate additional land. They beg village Thakurs for small plots of land which they can cultivate as they choose for a given rent. Such land gives them the sense of security which they crave. The Thakurs, in turn, are reluctant to disobey the law, but they are afraid that their tenants and former tenants will stop working for them if they refuse each request for land. The result is a compromise between the demands of law and the demands of the lower-caste villagers. Thakurs do give some land on lease, but not as much as before. The low-caste villagers say that they earn considerably more by working on leased land than working as labourers in the fields of Thakurs. They mention this as one more reason why they have been adversely affected by the *zamindari* abolition legislation.

It is not difficult to understand why the tenant families have reacted negatively to the state land reform programme. They have been adversely affected in several ways, and they do not understand that benefits may accrue to them from the programme in later years. Had policy-makers given more careful attention to the functions of the landlord-tenant relationship, some of the undesirable consequences might have been obviated. But in fairness to the policy-makers, the land reform programme should be viewed in broader perspective. Even if *zamindars* had not been able to get the land records changed in their favour, if adequate credit facilities had been made available to ex-tenants, and if arrangements for rent collection were less rigid, the average ex-tenant would still be poor. Ultimately, the only solution to the poverty of rural India is the development of industry. There are too many people working the soil and their landholdings are too small. In Senapur, only eight per cent of all families have more than ten acres of land, and since ten acres has been designated an "economic unit" by the Uttar Pradesh Abolition Committee, the landholdings of ninety-two per cent of Senapur village families can be regarded as uneconomic. Most of the holdings are, in fact, very small. Seventy-three per cent of village families have less than three acres or no land at all. Only the successful development of rural industries as planned by the government of India will relieve the suffering of the tenant class.

Local Government

The government of Uttar Pradesh has instituted a major programme in local self government as well as in land reform, but the two programmes are very different. *Zamindari* abolition is an example of a highly structured programme which the people could not modify and which has been received critically by tenants because of its adverse consequences. The local government programme, on the other hand, is less rigidly structured. The people have given it shape and substance and the critics this time would be the government planners if they were to become fully aware of what has happened.

Formerly, village leaders were older men who were respected and trusted by all. When two or more villagers quarrelled and could not reach an agreement, they called together several of these leaders to arbitrate their dispute. An assemblage of such men was known as a *panchayat*, literally "council of five," although the number was never restricted to five.

After the introduction of the English court system, traditional rural *panchayats* began to decline. Villagers took their cases to court where they gradually learned how favours are obtained through bribery and corruption. When poor families of Senapur speak of the court system today, they have only this to say:

There is no justice.

Even before India attained independence, government leaders were urging the revival of village *panchayats,* but no practical action was taken. The matter was again brought to public attention when the framers of the Constitution wrote:

... the state shall take steps to organize village *panchayats* and endow them with such powers and authority as may be necessary to enable them to function as units of self government (Article 40).

This intent of the framers of the Constitution took form in 1947 in Uttar Pradesh when the Panchayat Raj Act was passed. The act provides for the establishment of three organs of local self government: The *gaon panchayat* (loosely corresponding to a board of administration but usually referred to as a village *panchayat*) consisting of elected individuals representing every village or group of villages with a population of a thousand or above; the *gaon sabha* (village assembly) consisting of all men and women over twenty-one years of age who live in the area served by the *gaon panchayat*; and the *adalti panchayat (panchayat* court) comprising individuals from three to five village *panchayat* areas, each area sending five representatives.

A village *panchayat* is charged with assisting state and district officials in fulfilling their administrative responsibilities (the enforcement of zamindari abolition, for example) and with village development in agriculture, health, education, transport, and communication, etc. This body does not have any judicial function. For a population of a thousand, thirty *panchayat* members are elected; for an area comprising one thousand to two thousand people, thirty-six members; for two thousand to three thousand people, thirty-nine members; for three thousand to four thousand, forty-five members; and for more than four thousand, fifty-one members.

The functions of a village assembly are to elect the members of its village *panchayat* and the *panchayat* court of the area, and also to supervise the village *panchayat* in three respects: by ratifying the budgets, by examining the accounts, and by approving biennial reports of operation.

A *panchayat* court has limited judicial functions. Its members can hear cases involving minor disputes of civil or criminal nature, and although they do not have the power to imprison, they can levy fines up to one hundred rupees. Actually, state leaders have urged the members of rural courts to settle disputes whenever possible by effecting compromises according to the methods of the ancient village *panchayats*.

According to the Panchayat Raj Act, *panchayats* are to be financed by district board grants, fees paid by individuals filing suits with *panchayat* courts, taxes levied by the *panchayats*, and voluntary contributions.

This new *panchayat* programme is very different from the earlier system of village self government. Formerly villagers of exceptional ability and moral stature took the initiative in village affairs or other villagers called on them for assistance as it was needed. In this way, offices developed around the personalities of specific men. New villagers must elect men to designated offices for given periods of time. They have not been guided in appropriate campaign or election technique, nor were they told what mutual rights and obligations should characterize their relationship to the men whom they have elected. As a consequence, the villagers of Senapur have perceived and implemented the *panchayat* programme in their own manner, with results which differ considerably from the intent of the Panchayat Raj Act. This act was meant to give more efficient local administration and a more accessible form of local justice based on compromise and practical solutions. In practice, neither of these aims has been fulfilled because Senapur villagers do not expect the *panchayat* members to be impartial, which in fact they are not, because the high-caste men wielding power in the village do not feel obligated to support any administration which they have not helped to elect, and because the elections have not been secret nor have they been conducted in a democratic manner.

In traditional village government, impartiality characterized the position of the *panchayat* members. Although it is doubtful if villagers trusted the impartiality of any man in all situations and at all times, they did believe that certain men would be honest and just in given circumstances. Where the interests of two caste groups were at stake, *panch* (arbiters) from disinterested caste groups were selected. The villagers' desire for impartiality determined their choice of leaders.

The present system, however, is inelastic. Neither the *panchayat* leader nor its members can be changed as new problems arise. These men remain at their posts until they are replaced at later elections. Villagers conceive of the election campaign as a struggle for power by men who represent certain limited interests, including the interests of their own caste groups. They do not expect the elected members of either the *panchayat* court or the village *panchayat* to be impartial, except in instances where they do not stand to lose by their impartiality. Even then, they assume that these leaders will not be fully impartial because they will remember those who voted for them and those who voted against them. As a result, they have not taken their disputes to the *panchayat* court members and they show little enthusiasm for the village *panchayat*. They assume that the head of the village *panchayat* will favour members of his own caste when the government aids in village development, and since they expect their leaders to show favours, the leaders do not feel any qualms about doing so as appropriate occasions arise. This new village concept of the positions of *panchayat* leader and member is one reason why the present system of village self government may fail to ease much of the tension that exists in villages, and thereby fail to mobilize villagers in creative group effort.

For the *panchayat* system to be successful, villagers must develop commitment to the principle of majority rule. For this they are in no way prepared. They are committed to the system only if it serves their individual interests. In 1947, a *praja* (tenants) party was formed under the leadership of an

Ahir, a Noniya, and a Brahmin.[11] The aim of party members was to win the first *panchayat* election, and they were successful in this because they represented a majority of villagers and because Thakurs took little interest in the event. But after the election, *panchayat* members discovered that they were powerless to effect any significant changes in village life. They had impressive titles but Thakurs retained their power. It was clear to villagers of all castes that the new *panchayat* systems would be ineffective unless Thakurs took control of it. They were unaware of any alternative, and if anyone had suggested that men and women might be helped to develop commitment to the democratic principles of self government and had explained what they meant by this, the average villager would undoubtedly have shaken his head sadly and said, "Impossible." But no attempt was made in the Senapur area to educate villagers in the broader meanings of the new *panchayat* system. This was a second failing.

In accord with their idea of the election campaign as a power struggle, villagers used several means of winning votes in the two *panchayat* elections about which information was gathered. One of these methods was persuasion, but villagers have little faith in campaign promises. Another method was intimidation. Some landlords warned that they would evict any tenant who did not vote as they were instructed. Some employers threatened to discharge their labourers. No voice was raised against this method. Those who were threatened showed fear but not indignation. Another method was bribery. Many votes were bought, but some villagers indicated afterwards that they were

---

[11]Ahirs are cattleherds and farmers, and enjoy a status somewhat higher than Noniyas in the Senapur area. Noniyas have beeen identified (footnote 1). Brahmins are priests and farmers, and rank at the top of the caste hierarchy. This Brahmin had been outcasted, however, and was noted for behaviour which his caste brothers considered degrading for a man of his birth. Within Senapur itself, there are only two Brahmin families: the family to which this Brahmin belongs, and a widow who lives alone. As a result, there is little immediate castpressure brought upon him to reform. Thakurs of the village are oute spokenly critical of his behaviour, however. His political aid to persons of low-caste in 1947 was undoubtedly his means of expressing his resentment toward his critics as well as means of drawing attention to himself.

ashamed of this. Occasionally, supporters of opposing candidates also tried to weaken each other by cutting or burning each other's crops. If government planners had observed these practices, they might have written in less glowing terms about the birth or rejuvenation of democratic institutions in village India. Government officers who acquainted Senapur villagers with the new *panchayat* system did not attempt to educate them in democratic methods appropriate to the aims of the new Government of India.

In the second *panchayat* election of Senapur in 1955, two Thakurs contested for the position of *panchayat* leader. Although the younger of the Thakurs called himself a socialist and friend of the poor, most persons of low-caste did not believe that either candidate would serve their interests. All villagers were emotionally involved, however, as a result of the intensive campaigning, threats, bribery, and crop cutting incidents. Women who observed the strained relationships of many men were whispering about the possibility of murder. Some of the poorer families were so frightened by economic threats that they decided to split their votes in order to prevent reprisal by the successful candidate in later months. One young man of Barai caste was so disturbed by the campaign that he ran away from the village. He was talking irrationally when he was found several days later. There is no doubt that state legislators were thinking of secret elections when they framed the Panchayat Raj Act, and if the elections had been secret, the extreme tension that characterized the election period might have been avoided. But assembled villagers voted by raising their hands. Every person knew in advance that his vote would be public.[12] If a man voted for the candidate whom he really preferred, it was only because he felt sure that he did not take any risk by doing so.

It is of course not possible for a new nation such as India to sponsor extensive educational programmes in rural areas prior to the enforcement of major legislative Acts. India does

---

[12]This was not the case in the national and state elections where ballots were secret. For a description of this election period in Senapur, see M.E. Opler, W. Rowe, and M. Stroop, 1959. "Indian National and State Elections in a Village Context," *Human Organization*, Vol. XVIII, No. 1, Spring, pp. 30-34.

not yet have sufficient financial resources for such programmes. But the government officers who work with villagers often fail to appreciate the significance of the plans which they are introducing and the legislators seldom have village experience. It is to be hoped that a greater effort will be made in the future to close the gap between the planners and the villagers who can make or break a plan as they shape it according to their needs, values, and goals.

Summary and Conclusion

This article has described a number of innovations which were planned and imposed by an outside agency on the people of a north Indian village and has discussed various cultural factors influencing the people's acceptance of the innovations, the consequences of the innovations, and the correspondence between these consequences and the objectives of the men who conceived the changes. It has shown how a government educator made asepsis in childbirth acceptable to the people by associating it with their belief in a spirit called Jam, and how the people accepted smallpox vaccination after making the same type of association themselves, this time with the goddess Bhagauti Mai. It has described how women in *parda* rejected a hygienic improvement because it would have conflicted with their desire to socialize. It has appraised the relative influence of such factors as poverty, the traditional view of women, the desire for status, and the desire for economic security in villagers' reaction to educational opportunities. It has predicted that methods of birth control will not be wholeheartedly accepted by villagers whose desire for lineage perpetuation, for status, and for economic and political security prompt them to try for many sons in this androcentric culture. Finally, the article has described in detail the government programmes of land reform and local government, showing that the rigidly structured land reform programme has had a number of undesirable consequences which were not taken into account by programme planners, and that the more loosely structured programme of local self government has been given an undemocratic shape by the villagers upon whom it was imposed.

These examples have indicated how essential it is for

villagers, on the one hand, to understand the intent of government planners, and for the planners and extension workers, on the other, to be intimately acquainted with the cultures which they hope to change so that the innovations will not be blocked by conflicting cultural factors and detrimental side effects will be avoided.

Joan P. Mencher

20 Conflicts and Contradictions in the "Green Revolution"

It has commonly been argued in the literature of economics that "development" and "redistribution" (or "distributive justice") are incompatible. Thus it is claimed, by those of this persuasion, that because of the severity of India's food crises in the mid-1960s, it was essential to opt for growth even if it meant an increase in inequalities: this has in fact led to a situation where, despite the availability of more food, for at least part of the year the poor cannot afford to eat enough to maintain adequate nutrition (see Dandekar and Rath, 1971: 25-48). A number of economists in India and elsewhere (see Seers, 1972: 2-6, and Joshi, 1972: 33-36), are opposed to this proposition. In considering their view it would be useful to clarify some of the basic concepts employed.

Uphoff and Ilchman (1972: 86-92) make a sharp distinction between the concepts of growth and development, identifying growth with production and development with productivity. In their formulation, growth is a simple quantitative term, whereas to achieve development, one has to change the structure so as to raise productive capacity (89). Thus, mere increases in scale, e.g., growing more rice, would be considered as "growth without development," whereas an increase that included some sort of change in the structure of production would be called development. "The British political economist Dudley Seers points to the classical argument that inequality is necessary to generate savings and incentives and thus promote growth (1972:123-38). He notes that there has been very serious questioning of that argument, simply because we know that the rich (and even the upper middle class) by no means invest all or even half of their earnings in future production but spend large amounts on consumption for themselves (125). He also notes that there are many serious reasons for questioning the traditional notion that equality and economic growth are incompatible. He suggests that the questions which arise from all of these matters point to a set of "internal contradictions" in development process as severe as those to which Marx drew attention (126). Taking the same definition of development as Uphoff and Ilchman, Seers considers that the important questions to ask about a country's development are: "What has been happening to poverty? What has been happening to unemployment? What has been happening to inequality? ... If one or two of these central problems have been growing worse... it would be strange to call the result 'development' even if per capita income doubled" (124). He further notes that economic systems with a large percentage of people who are poor, undernourished, and under (or un-) employed, can never provide a firm basis for growth.

In this paper,[1] I do not wish to become involved in the debate about what is meant by the term "green revolution." I am using it quite simply to refer to a striking quantitative increase in foodgrains production. I am not arguing that it has occurred in all areas, nor that even where it has occurred it has been nearly as successful as one might wish. However, it is clear that there has been a striking increase in rice production in Tamil Nadu. From having been a deficit state in the production of rice in the 1950s, Madras state emerged as an exporter of rice in the late 1960s. This has been the result of three factors operating at once: (1) the early and continued

[1]This paper is primarily based on research in Chingleput district, especially in 1967 and in 1970-71. The latter research was part of a joint Columbia University/Delhi School of Planning and Architecture project (sponsored by the National Science Foundation) comparing Tamil Nadu and Kerala. Intensive data were collected from eight villages in each state, as well as broad-scale materials on the block and district level.

use of hybrid seeds: (2) the massive increase in tube-well irrigation in Chingleput, South Arcot, and North Arcot districts, and irrigation facilities that allow for a second crop in Tanjore: and (3) the blessings of good rain for the year 1970 onwards.

In considering the effect of the green revolution in Tamil Nadu, one must clearly confront head-on the issues raised by Uphoff and Ilchman as well as by Seers. It has been the main focus of the Tamil Nadu government (as opposed to that of the government of Kerala) to place greatest emphasis on growth with only some token nods towards distributive justice. Indeed, an examination of performance shows that the latter has been seen as a kind of secondary appendage, despite the lip-service given to it at many official talks.

Although Tamil Nadu has emerged as a rice-exporting state, the programmes for increasing rice production have not been as successful as programmes for increasing wheat production. As recently as January 1973, M.S. Swaminathan has noted:

> High-yielding varieties of rice, unlike their counterparts in wheat, are yet to make a marked impact on yield, although in the All-India Coordination Trials and National Demonstrations the new dwarf varieties of rice have given even greater increase in yield over the tall strains, as compared to the relative performance of dwarf and tall wheat strains.

Swaminathan points to a number of reasons for this happening. These include such physical factors as low per hectare utilization of fertilizer for rice, pest and disease problems, and water management problems during the monsoon and in the event of too variable rains—all of which make the risks associated with rice much greater than those in wheat. Countries like Taiwan, which have made a success of increasing their yields of rice under conditions of small farmholdings, have done so mainly through co-operative action by whole villages and or by watershed farming communities. What Swaminathan neglects to mention is that Taiwan, believing that the main reason for the success of the Communists on the mainland of China was their emphasis on land to the tiller, had instituted a fairly far-reaching land reform measure in the

1950s, which was largely responsible for making co-operative action feasible and effective. Not only were tenants made secure and rents sharply reduced, but all absentee landlords had to sell their land at fixed government prices and resident landlords were compelled to sell their land in excess of the permissible ceiling which itself was quite low and the price paid by the government not excessively high. Furthermore, the acreage allowed was fixed retroactively on the basis of the amount of land owned per household—not per individual (see Hadejinsky, 1965, pp. 2-4). Within India, it has been clear that the only state (Kerala) to seriously push for land reform measures has had a long uphill struggle, and has had to concentrate all of its efforts on that alone. In most states, apart from lip-service, there has been relatively little attention given to effective land reform.

In Tamil Nadu, until recently, the ceiling was fixed at thirty standard acres (which comes to much more in terms of actual acreage). It has been lowered to fifteen standard acres now, though there is a lot of confusion about how and whether it can be enforced. Officially, a record of tenancy is being drawn up by the revenue department; however, one of our student assistants, spot-checking in 1972 in villages where we had worked in 1970-71, noted that none of the tenants had been given any permanent rights to cultivate any plots of land. How could they have been given any? Most farmers of size in the area of our project had been worried about the possibility of some sort of tenancy regulations for years. Thus, most people giving land out for tenant cultivation made a practice of changing their tenants regularly. Only a few tenant families (often those working for widows or elderly people) could say that they had been cultivating a particular piece of land for a particular landlord for even four or five years. A considerable number of landlords changed their tenants yearly, or at least moved them from plot to plot. Occasionally, tenants changed even with the seasons. As far as land ceilings are concerned, while on paper few people could be found to possess more than fifteen acres, if one checked carefully on households (instead of individuals), a significant number had over thirty acres of paddy land.[2] It is striking that even radical critiques of the government's policy in India generally accept the equation of development with growth and the opposition between development and "distributive justice." Thus they argue that the government is making the wrong choice, and that it should accept a curtailed level of development for the sake of greater equality of distribution. While this may seem plausible in a static, short-term frame of reference, the formulation by Uphoff and Ilchman makes more sense in a longer term, more dynamic framework. They point out, for example, that a programme which increases the production of three hundred small farmers may be preferable to one benefiting one hundred larger farmers, even if the private short-run cost-benefit ratio is less in the farmer (1972:496). This is true not only because the smaller farmers get a proportionately greater boost in their standard of living, but more importantly because improved distribution at one period is linked to still greater production in the next. For these reasons, the social benefit ratio will be larger both in the short and the long run.

In this paper, I would like to show that equating growth with development, and setting them up in opposition to distributive justice, has offered an excuse to avoid even the consideration of other possibilities for development. The continued emphasis on the growth-development equation also appears to suit the ideology of those introducing the programmes in Tamil Nadu as well as their earlier American advisers. Moreover, because in Tamil Nadu the medium to large landowners have till now had sufficient influence over the political apparatus and the poor have been very divided (see Mencher, 1968;

---

[2] In collecting data on household landownership, one finds a surprising number of ways in which people have managed to conceal their actual landholdings. Some are listed in the names of relatives far and wide (sometimes even dead), some in the names of loyal illiterate servants in debt to the landowner, some in different villages so that all their land does not appear on the same register. Often the name will be listed just slightly differently so that it is hard to keep it straight which man in another village actually owns the land. Some land is simply missing from the register (i.e., the Chitta, the book which lists land by Pattadar). I plan to deal with this in detail in a forthcoming book.

TABLE 1
POPULATION STATISTICS

	1961*	1971**
Percentage of total rural workers listed as cultivators	40.5	32.2
Percentage of total male rural workers listed as cultivators	43.9	32
Percentage of total rural workers listed as agricultural labourers	30.4	39.6
Percentage of total male rural workers listed as agricultural labourers	22.7	43

NOTE: At the 1961 census. . . every individual was compulsorily asked if he was engaged in (*i*) cultivation; (*ii*) in agricultural labour; (*iii*) at household industry; and (*iv*) in any other work in the above order. A person who is basically an agricultural labourer, even if he cultivated just a couple of cents of land in his backyard, declared himself first as cultivator and then as an agricultural labourer. . .the participation rate in cultivation at the 1961 Census obviously got inflated. There was also a possibility that during the period when there was much talk of land reforms, several agricultural labourers were tempted to declare themselves as cultivators of land rather than as agricultural labourers with the hope of establishing a right as cultivator. . . This was corrected in the 1971 Census. (Census of India 1971, paper 1, p 27, Supplement Provisional Population Totals.)

SOURCES: *From Census of India, 1961, Volume IX, Madras Pt IIPA, General Population Tables, pp. 332-33.
**Census of India, 1971, p. 143.

and in press), there has not been the kind of pressure that is found in Kerala to force a redirection of the programme. On the contrary, the numerous delays in implementing land reform in Kerala which have resulted in delays reaching the development programmes to the different segments of the agricultural population, has merely served to make it easy for Tamil Nadu to de-emphasize land reform. Agriculture administrators could always say, "They have not even become self-sufficient in rice, so why take their lead?" However, the lag in increasing rice production in Kerala is not due to land reform per se, but is the result of a number of complex factors, including (*a*) the numerous obstacles created by former landlords, using the cumbersome mechanism of the Supreme Court (see

Mencher in press); (*b*) the need for constitutional amendments and other legislative or judicial action to effectively implement the land reform measures; (*c*) the numerous other difficulties involved in developing the social organization required to capitalize on the new technology; and (*d*) a variety of physical factors, including the failure thus far to develop new varieties of rice which can withstand waterlogging for considerable periods of time.

It is undeniable that, at least in the rice regions, the "green revolution," along with increasing agricultural production, has increased economic class differences, and (at least covert) intergroup tension. But this is not the whole story. If long-term increases in food production are to occur, certain other key developments must also be understood. Only then can we clearly visualize the alternatives available. Because of the severity of the food crisis during 1966, there was an overriding concern in New Delhi to grow more food; this concern was passed on to the states. However, the approach to be taken was determined by the states in question. Tamil Nadu opted clearly for a strategy aimed at growing more food regardless of all else and with the least disturbance of the status quo. Thus, there emerged a focus on the middle and larger landowners. There is no question that the programme has partially succeeded and that more rice is being produced; but there are signs that other factors are beginning to cloud the horizon. Before discussing these, I should like to describe the area of our project research.

Chingleput District

Chingleput district was designated by the government of Tamil Nadu as an IAAP district, even before the advent of the new miracle rice varieties normally considered the sine qua non of the "green revolution." Though receiving less assistance than the IADP districts (such as Thanjavur), the IAAP districts received more assistance from the government than did the ordinary district. As early as in the mid-1960s, efforts were being made there to get farmers to use more fertilizers, etc. When the miracle rice varieties began to arrive on the market, there was administrative machinery available to start pushing them in this area. The programme was being pushed even before the arrival of the IR-8 and later varieties from the Philippines or the variants developed in north India. The main variety in the early days was ADT-27, a local hybrid. (First results with this hybrid were extremely encouraging, and it was pushed in a big way for several years. But, by 1971, it was being replaced by IR-8, in part because IR-8 was said to be a bigger yielder, in part because some farmers claimed that ADT-27 had lost its hybrid vigour and was no longer producing yields greater than the traditional varieties.) The really big push in 1967 for ADT-27 was political in origin. The DMK in their election campaign of that year had promised the urban poor rice at a rupee a measure. The only way they could obtain this was to push for massive production. Because rice prices had been relatively high, they did manage to get an impressive number of farmers to grow ADT-27 during the second planting season (January-April) of 1967, and they were able to buy a good part of it so as to provide some sort of rice at a rupee a measure in the fair-price shops in the urban areas.

Chingleput district of Tamil Nadu, where my own research was conducted, ranks second only to Thanjavur in rice production. It has been described by several writers as an area of "peasant proprietorship" (e.g. Dupuis, 1960). This description, however, is questionable for a number of reasons.

According to the preliminary tabulations of the 1971 Census, in rural areas of this district forty-three per cent of all working males are agricultural labourers. And there seems to be some indication that this is not a new phenomenon (for discussion see Kumar, 1965; Mencher, 1972; Mencher in press)—though certainly, in absolute terms, there are more agricultural labourers than there were even ten years ago. (It should be noted that the massive increase between the censuses of 1961 and 1971 is partly the result of a change in the way households and people were classified. In 1961, a man who owned one quarter of an acre, but earned most of his family income as a landless labourer, would have been classified as a landowner. In 1971, people were classified according to their main source of support.)

Apart from the existence of this large segment of landless

TABLE 2
CHINGLEPUT DISTRICT, TAMIL NADU (1970-71); ECONOMICS OF IR-8 VERSUS TRADITIONAL VARIETIES

Type of seed	Average yield per acre	Cost of inputs per acre (Rs)	Selling price per bag (Rs)	Profit per acre** (Rs)
IR-8	32 Bags*	550-600	40	680-730
Traditional best varieties like Vaikuntam and Kichili	20 Bags*	250	60	950
Traditional rough varieties for second season, e.g. Kar, Kulakar	16 Bags	200 (maximum)	45-50	560 (approximately)

NOTES: *Some farmers are known to have got as much as sixty-six bags per acre of IR-8, but according to the agriculture officers consulted, the average for Chingleput district was thirty-two bags. This means that some people got considerably less than thirty-two bags. Indeed, in our sample villages some villagers reported getting only twenty bags, others as much as forty-five bags. This seems to depend on the use of fertilizers and other inputs, possibilities of water control, and details of agricultural practice. There is also variation in the yield per acre for standard varieties, though the range is far less than for the new seeds like IR-8. It should be noted that hardly any of the farmers used IR-8 during the first season when the traditional choice varieties are grown. Thus, the main use is during the second season where it competes with *Kar* and *Kulakar*. However, the traditional varieties can be left alone during most of the growing season. They do not require extensive weeding, nor pesticides, nor much fertilizer. Furthermore, they survive even when the amount of water available is less than ideal.

**According to informants, the expected profit for an acre of sugarcane, after deducting all expenses and the loan from the cooperative, comes to approximately Rs 2,000.

labourers, even in villages described to me by people in the agriculture department or in the block development offices as typical "peasant" villages, one finds—if one takes the household (instead of the individual) as the unit—a far greater concentration of landholdings than is suggested by the official figures. Thus, in a survey of five villages conducted in 1967, six per cent of the households owned forty-six per cent of the land. Even if we exclude those owning one acre of land or less, we find that fifteen per cent of the remaining households own forty-eight per cent of the remaining land. The holdings of this fifteen per cent range from about ten acres to over forty acres per household. Since most of this is fertile paddy land, which if irrigated could produce two or even three crops in a single year (or at least a second crop of groundnuts and/or millets or pulses), ten acres here can provide a family with quite a luxurious standard of living, with a good reserve of jewellery and the like.

Because there has been relatively little stress on effective land ceilings, or redistribution, or on helping the smaller farmers (those who own less than three acres of land), it was primarily the medium or large landowners who were encouraged to grow the new rice varieties (at first ADT-27, after 1968 IR-8, and more recently a number of other varieties). However, these better-off farmers were not interested in consuming IR-8 themselves. In Chingleput district, IR-8 has been mostly eaten either by the poor, purchased by the government, or exported to other states. By 1971, many of the better-off who had switched over to IR-8 found that, even if they grew more than they did with traditional varieties, they could not earn as much per bag. In early 1971, while a bag of IR-8 sold for Rs 40 or a bit less, the better or fancier varieties of rice sold for Rs 60 or even more. Even the traditional rough variety, usually grown in the second season (*kar*), sold for Rs 45 to 50 a bag. While it was true that the increase in the number of bags, especially for farmers who grew more than the average, did bring an increase in profits during the second *navari* (see Table 2), a sizeable number of middle-size farmers were beginning to talk of switching over to cash crops, especially groundnuts or sugarcane, and occasionally pulses or millets. In a few areas, some were even reported by agriculture officers to be switching to casuarina trees—a source of firewood—in order to save the expense on labour or on other inputs. This was partly due to actual increases in wage rates (see Mencher in press), partly due to anticipated increases, and partly in order to minimize the need for interaction with labourers. (It is striking in this regard that, for sugarcane cultivation, the landowner is responsible for ploughing and preparing the land, for planting, weeding, and applying fertilizers, but not for having the cane cut. That is done by the sugar mills when they come for the cane. Thus, the landowner avoids having to deal with labourers during the harvest season. Furthermore, sugarcane is harvested only once in the year; whereas paddy if it is irrigated might be harvested twice or, under the best circumstances three times in the year. Thus, a switch to sugarcane means a decrease in work for labourers, and less interaction between workers and landowners.)

The decrease in the acreage of land under paddy was first reported in 1969-70. At that time, it might have been partly due to drought conditions in some parts of the state; but the continued decrease in 1970-71 cannot have been due to drought as much as to switching of paddy land to other crops by the middle- and large-size farmers. A few of the middle or large-size farmers have also switched back to the traditional varieties which require little or no artificial inputs and which do not require such careful supervision in the fields during the growing season.

According to one of the agriculture officers:

Unfortunately, in 1970-71, because of bumper yield, prices came down. In my division, we exceeded our target for production. Here the average production was 32 bags for IR-8 per acre. If getting 32 bags had meant that it sold at the old rate of Rs 60 per bag, it would have been good, but now it sells for only Rs 40. We want more production. . . we want to be self-sufficient for rice, but the problem is only that we want some stabilized floor price. Nowadays the rate depends on dealers and business people, on the market. Some of the big ryots are switching to commercial crops.

This was not a unique case. Consistently in interviews with agriculture officers, the impression came across that what they thought was needed to sustain the "green revolution" was to forget about people with "uneconomic holdings"—because these small farmers really could not contribute to increased production. This was not always stated explicitly (though at times it was), but it was clearly implied both by what was said and what was left unsaid.

What was striking was that they never asked what size holding would be viable for a family with, let us say, three children. Yet our data indicate that, among families of this size, those with holdings of over two acres rarely have to go out and work as day labourers. Indeed, if the land is irrigated and produces two or three crops in a year, even one to one and a half acres seem to be the dividing line. Even among families with one or two older sons, it is unusual to find people in three-acre families with time to work for others. It has been stated that an efficient farm must: (a) be so large that it fully employs the labour of the family without the need to work outside the farm, (b) fully employ a pair of bullocks; and (c) provide a minimum norm for a civilized life for a family. (Khusro, 1973: xix). On these bases, in this area criteria 1 and 3 may be satisfied by less than two acres of double cropped paddy land, though undoubtedly a pair of bullocks can work more land than this.

In any case, such considerations rarely, if ever, came up in discussions with officials. When instances were mentioned of "progressive farmers," they invariably turned out to be fairly well-off, whereas in our field investigations we often found some of the smaller farmers to be quite interested in trying out new inputs and being innovative in general. Little enthusiasm was shown for land reform. On occasion, when government *poromboke* land was given to the poor, the tendency was not to give it to the landless but rather to those who already owned a few acres—often relatives or political cronies of influential villagers. The explicit rationale was that the landless do not have the wherewithal to use the land effectively anyhow (see below). The consensus was that a "floor price" was needed for paddy so that better-off farmers would not hesitate to grow the high-yielding varieties. (In many discussions of this type, the clear impression came across that they were quoting straight from texts from the United States, or from ones written by thoroughly Westernized Indians. Many even made a point of telling me about "floor prices" in the United

States, though few were aware of the fate of poor farmers in the United States (see Hightower, 1972, pp. 10-22). It is clear that the family farm as a way of life in the United States is on the way out with the extreme consolidation of farms into agrobusiness, over three million migrant workers living a precarious close-to-starvation existence, and most middle-class farmers being forced to move to urban areas).

It is clear that, in the present context in Tamil Nadu, floor prices without redistribution would only serve to make paddy cultivation even more profitable for the better-off. Even if they were matched by some sort of government subsidy so that the price of rice for the poor stayed low, it would mean paying the better-off sector out of government funds to be able to feed the poor. Certainly, it would not make the larger landowners any more willing to submit to land reform. After all, why not hold onto the land, if it pays well? It appears that the central government has now decided to accept, at least in part, the principle of price support by increasing the *kharif* procurement prices for rice and coarse grains. This increased burden is being passed on to the consumers, as on 1 November 1973, by increases of twenty-five to thirty-three per cent in the cost of these grains in ration shops. It seems clear that the reason for this is that not much could be done to keep the black marketeers from enticing the better-off farmers, so that procurement has become difficult.

In Tamil Nadu, what has perhaps made greater difference to the use of new "miracle seeds" has been the effect of other changes introduced at the same time. Perhaps more than anything else, the focus on multiple cropping has begun to revolutionize agriculture in this area. Even traditionally, some land was always planted a second time in Chingleput district. Apart from the few acres that were irrigated by man-driven lifts from local wells (never more than a few acres), the only second crop areas were those irrigated by tank water. In a good year, a substantial proportion of the village lands would be irrigated by water from the tank during the second season; but in a bad year, the amount of second crop land was quite small. (Thus, in one of the villages studied, for which we have full records, the acreage cultivated once a year between 1935 and 1962 ranged from a minimum of 999.34 in 1949-50 to a maximum of 1085.92 in 1962-63. However, the acreage cultivated twice a year ranged from 8.78 in 1936-37—or more recently 60.79 in 1968-69—to 629.54 in 1960-61.) In only a few villages close to major sources of water did one ever find third crops being grown.

Now all that has changed. In Chingleput district, the most miraculous aspect of the "green revolution" has been the widespread introduction of tube-well irrigation which guarantees the owner a secure second crop,[3] and often a third crop if the ground water is good. Because of the way the government allotted loans for tube-wells and/or pump-sets, it was primarily those who owned over ten acres of land who benefited. If a man with ten acres manages to grow two or three crops in his land with even traditional varieties, he is better off than he was before. True, there is also more demand for agricultural labour if more crops are being grown; but, from the viewpoint of the labourer, who sees landowners obtaining substantial increases in their incomes, things do not look that much better. However, for those who work as sharecroppers, there has been a decrease in their own share. In this district, at least for the past twenty-five to thirty years, if a man worked as a sharecropper on tank-fed land, he usually kept fifty per cent of the grown harvest. However, on tube-well irrigated land, he normally gets one-third, another one-third going to the owner, and the remaining one-third being said to go to the tube-well (i.e., ostensibly to pay off the cost of the well, pumpset, etc.). Furthermore, land irrigated by tube-wells, even if it gets enough

---

[3]K.N. Raj, in discussing Mexico, Taiwan, the Punjab, and Madras notes "there was an extension in the irrigated area during the period in which high growth rates were recorded. . . . Such extension. . .was responsible to a significant degree for the increases in output" (1970: 193-98). For Madras, his materials were based on studiesing using data for 1960-1962. However, there was actually much bigger increase in tubewell irrigation in districts such as Chingleput and the Arcots between 1962 and the early 1970s. It is certainly true that the percentage area that can be provided with assured water is limited. This makes it a matter of greater concern that only the better-off have been enabled to obtain tubewells, and that it is possible when the government finally does got around to digging wells on a cooperative basis, or else for selling water to the poor, the ground water level might go down and they might decide to stop digging wells.

water to permit three crops, continues on the books to be listed as dry land, so that the landowner pays hardly any taxes on it.

Is There Social Tension?

The obvious question which arises in looking at all of this, is what types of tension have developed in this area between the landless, the tenants, and the landed. It is certainly true that there is a great deal of resentment and hostility on the part of the landless and poorer tenants; but only rarely in this region has it burst into any sort of overt conflict. In 1970, in one area in the southern part of the district, a strike was conducted by agricultural labourers, in order to get their harvest wage raised. Because it was just before the elections, one DMK member of the state legislature supported the strikers and they were successful in gaining higher wages (see Mencher, in press). There have been other strikes in nearby areas but most of them have not been successful.

What is striking on the whole is the relative lack of overt tension. There are a number of reasons for this. To begin with, the landless crosscut caste, and this includes Harijans as well as Naickers (who each account for over twenty-five per cent of the total population in the region) and a few smaller low-ranking castes which are found in scattered villages. These caste differences have been exploited by wealthy or middle-class leaders to keep the poor Naickers (who are sizeable in number), as well as the other poor low-ranking Hindus, from uniting with Harijans on the basis of common class interest (see Mencher, 1968). Furthermore, considerable energy has been siphoned off into local populist politics. In addition, there is often a conflict of interest among the landless. Thus, in a given year a particular family might be holding land as a tenant. At that time, they might temporarily be employers of landless labourers themselves. In another year; they might not be given land to cultivate on a sharecropper basis. This yearly rotation, which started as fears of tenancy legislation mounted in the late 1950s and early 1960s, has also served to keep the landless competing with one another for sharecropping rights. (In one of our project villages, where Harijans did occasionally manage to get land as sharecroppers, they tended to pay labourers of their own community a higher wage than others paid them.)

Apart from the shifts between the landless and sharecropper category, we found tenants who were also landowners. Though a clear distinction can usually be made between the well-to-do landowner who leases in some land to further increase his holding, and the poor man with say one and a half acres (or even up to three acres) who leases in another acre or two, it is also true that this does serve the function of slightly blurring class lines. It is clear that the reasons for the lack of consistent overt conflict are complex and cannot be given a single factor explanation. Beteille (1972: 122-51) has noted that in the eastern half of the old delta in Tanjore, where most of the landless are Harijans, class polarization has occurred more and overt conflict has become endemic (see also Gough, 1973 and Shivaraman, 1973). However, it seems to me that the other reason why class conflict there has assumed clearer lines, as in the Kuttanad part of Kerala, is that in these areas tenants are less often drawn from the landless category. Furthermore, for a number of reasons populist politics has been less highly developed than in Chingleput or the Arcots.

Why Produce More?

A number of writers seem to agree with Francine Frankel's statement, that an excessive emphasis on redistribution may destroy the incentive and means to increase production (1971: 202). This implies that the only incentive that would lead a man to produce more is the prospect of making a big profit and not the chance of feeding his family better, or being able to provide better in other ways for his immediate family needs.

Possibly an emphasis on redistribution would destroy the incentive of the larger landholders. who would then have to spend more time worrying about how to keep their land, or how to hide their exact amount of land from the government. This would not be the case with the smaller landholders, however, who have nothing to fear, and certainly not with the man who becomes a landholder as a result of redistribution. Furthermore, the former large landholder will not necessarily have all of his incentive destroyed. I am personally acquainted with one formerly large landholder in north Kerala who has recently lost a lot of his land. This man at least has been stimulated into trying out new crops (such as rubber), which increase the profitability of his now reduced acreage.

Though the computer analysis of the data from our project has not yet been completed, examining by hand the data from one of our villages provides some intriguing material. In this village, there are, three really large landowners. Of the three, two have put only three acres under high-yielding varieties, whereas the other man, a radical by everyone's standards, has put about half of his land under IR-8. But, among the medium to small landholders (those owning between two and six acres), there are also people with anywhere from one to three acres under high-yielding varieties. Many of these people actually got their seed from the black market or from friends, and not from the government. Many more say that they would like to use IR-8 but have not got the resources, either water or money, for fertilizers and pesticides. This also holds true for the one-acre farmers.

In 1967 (when ADT-27 was the only new type of seed available), a survey of every household in five villages in this area produced some interesting results. Of those owning between ten and twenty-five acres of land, close to one-third were using ADT-27 on some of their land. Of those owning over twenty-five acres, only twenty-two per cent were using ADT-27. On the other hand of those owning between one and three acres of land, ten per cent were already using ADT-27, and even among those having less than one acres of land, 6.7 per cent were using the new variety. And this was in a region where it had been automatically assumed that the small landowners would not use new seeds, and no effort was therefore being made to reach them. In talking to the farmers, the investigators found that a considerable number of the smaller landowners would have used the new varieties if they had been helped to do so. What was striking, however, was that the large landowners—those with more than ten acres of land-had not by any means put all of their land under the new seed. Rather, plots seemed to vary between half an acre to three acres.

Both the above pieces of data are suggestive: If a great deal of attention and propaganda from agricultural extension workers results in only three acres of land being put under high-yielding varieties by a landowner of over thirty acres (the case of our 1970 village noted above) or even by farmers owning over ten acres, then it must make one question the official stress on larger farmers for increased production—quite apart from the question of redistribution.

It has been argued that giving land to poor farmers will not do them any good because they do not have the capital to invest in agriculture, whereas the better-off farmers have the capital to invest and are thus a better risk from the point of view of rapid growth of paddy production.

Certainly, redistribution alone would not be the answer. As has been noted by one of the ministers in the present Kerala government, where there has been an increasing stress on redistribution (and certainly greater stress on it than in Tamil Nadu), increased agricultural production can only be achieved if after the redistribution of lands something is done to help the new landholders—by creating cooperatives and providing "immense financial and organisational support and guidance to those who secure lands by distribution under the various land reform measures" (see John, 1973: 51). These immense resources can only be found indirectly, through financial institutions such as the nationalized banks. Others (Khusro, 1973: xxv) have also noted the need for cooperatives of small farmers whose farms are below a certain fixed limit.[4]

In this connection, looking in detail at data from one small area in Tamil Nadu, it is strikingly evident that as things are presently set up, those with over ten to fifteen acres of double-crop paddy land have tied up government money that could have been used to finance new landholders or small landholders.

---

[4] A great deal has been written about the failures of cooperatives in India, but it is clear that the greatest reason for failures has related to the fact that people with different sized holdings were in the same cooperatives. Thus, there is no reason to expect a cooperative to fail with people who all own under three acres. Indeed, in such an organization, one would expect that even the one-half acre or one-quarter acre farmer would benefit from the advantage of scale and of steady employment.

Thus, in a survey run in 1967 in four *panchayat* unions in Chingleput district, we found that almost all of the agricultural banks reported themselves to be badly in arrears. Most of the arrears were from loans to well-to-do landholders (who are often office-holders in the cooperative banks). Likewise, in 1970-71, we found in our sample villages that a significant number of the larger landowners had large longstanding debts to the government, and these the larger landowners were not exactly rushing to pay off. Most of the tube-wells built by better-off landholders were on government loan. Some certainly have been repaid, but many have been in arrears for a long time. This is generally known to most agriculture officers in the region. (They hope that with loans now coming mostly from the nationalized banks, it will be easier to make the better-off farmers pay back, but I am sceptical.)

If the government had built the wells and then sold water giving preference on reduced rates for those owning under two acres, I wonder if they would have been any worse off in the long run. In 1970, there was a start in Chingleput district to set up small farmers' lift irrigation societies. When I left in August of 1971, some were functioning (one fully, two just getting going), but the government was clearly giving it only half-hearted attention. The majority of agricultural officers whom I questioned about it were quite sceptical. Perhaps more to the point, however, was the fact that it was actually made extremely difficult for the small farmers to manage. They were expected to form a society, get a loan, and dig a well without any assurance that there would be water, instead of the government taking the risk. Obviously, many were and are afraid to take a chance. Thus, the programme lags.

If agricultural programmes (the spread of high-yielding varieties, increased irrigation for multiple cropping, etc.) had been aimed first at the smaller landowners (those having under three or four acres of land), I suspect that they would have been as successful as the present programme has been in increasing production; even more, they would have laid a much firmer foundation for the future—especially if it had all been accompanied by really meaningful land reform. Such a strategy would have ensured a more dedicated group of people who really cared about success, not as an abstraction but because growing more meant primarily feeding their children adequately and having a little surplus for other essential things. A family that traditionally eats all or most of what they grow would certainly be more amenable to growing a variety which would feed them all and provide an excess for the market.

Obviously, such a focus would have involved major differences in approach because the poor cannot afford to take risks, and it is known that the high-yielding varieties are more susceptible to pests and rats than traditional varieties. The government would have had to provide them with some sort of risk insurance. On the other hand, it is far more likely that a man who has at long last grown enough food to feed his family, or one who finally has something to sell instead of consuming almost all of his rice, would continue using a new type of seed longer than the person solely geared to profit.

My main point here is that the thought process which automatically assumes it to be impossible for growth to occur along with development is, indeed fuzzy. The real question is, what is the purpose of growth? Is it to feed people better, or is it to fill the shops with food that many people cannot afford to buy? As noted above with the present system the only way to keep the better-off farmers growing the high-yielding varieties would be to have a floor price for paddy and to subsidize the price of rice to the poorer consumers. But if the same amount of money that is being requested for subsidies were to go into helping the poorer farmers and the new farmers (i.e., who would get land from effective redistribution), building the infrastructure for greater production (such as cooperative tube-wells, long-term loans for fertilizers and pesticides or even free fertilizers and pesticides) for the first two or three seasons, etc., then I submit that the goal of increased production would be met far better, and without violating the principle of distributive justice.

It has been said that the next steps in the "green revolution" in India are to be: (1) the introduction of dairy farming with improved breeds on a large scale; (2) the extension into pulses, oilseeds, and dry cropping all over India, including Tamil Nadu; (3) market gardening and poultry farming in suburban areas; and (4) developing suitable marketing and credit facilites to sustain all these activities. All of these could focus primarily on the small farmers; indeed they are programmes especially suited to them. This would be especially true if they are tied to some sort of cooperative marketing set-up or, even more ideally, to genuine cooperative undertakings. Whether it will be taken up in this manner or not will, I suspect, depend far more on politics and power relations than on the actual feasibility of programmes. Seers has noted: "Practically every decision taken by government officials has implications for the degree of equality—to lend to big farmers or small... to build roads for private motor cars or for goods vehicles.... It would not be a bad thing to put up in every civil service office a sign: 'will it reduce inequality?' " (1972: 126). In deciding how the new programmes are to be implemented, it is questionable whether Seers' question will enter anyone's mind.

It is so easy for the better-off sections to convince officials (who, after all, belong to the same social class) that only they can make things work, can do what is necessary to sustain growth. Whether effective land reform measures will ever be effectively enforced in Tamil Nadu remains to be seen. It is equally problematical whether the major focus for new programmes will ever be carried out in a way that is beneficial to the small and marginal farmers.

Conclusion

In 1961, Balogh, in commenting on the Third Five Year Plan, noted:

> The Government can either fully back the successful owners of viable type and hope for a bourgeois-entrepreneurial type of revolution on the land or it can energetically push the risk of new cooperative rural organisation, through determined leadership. ...

It is clear that, at least in Tamil Nadu, the government made the first choice. Yet, it is by no means clear that this is the only way to increase production. This paper argues that the professed goal of maximizing production is actually more compatible with small farmer cultivation (and/or cooperative cultivation) than with the present stress on the capitalist farmer.

Maximized production is only compatible with capitalist farming if profits are high. But if profits are not high enough, then the capitalist farmer will turn away from basic food production into more lucrative and less troublesome crops. This is borne out by data from Chingleput district. It is true that in most divisions of the district, the targets were met; but the data suggests that they would have been far surpassed if the programme had been preceded by effective land reform with meaningful ceilings, and had focused on helping the small farmers and developing cooperatives that have a good chance of working. Not only that, such a strategy (which is still possible) would lay the framework for ever-increasing production, since it would resolve the inherent contradictions of tenant and coolie cultivation. Such a strategy would involve a great commitment to, and more faith and trust in, the common man.

REFERENCES

A.M., 1972. "Calcutta Diary," *Economic and Political Weekly*, 21 October, pp. 2137-2139.

Balogh, Thomas, 1961. "Economic Strategy for the Third Plan," *The Economic Weekly*, 3 February.

Bernstein, Henry, 1971. "Modernisation Theory and the Sociological Study of Development," *Journal of Development Studies*, pp. 141-60.

Beteille, Andre, 1972. "Agrarian Relations in Tanjore District, South India," *Sociological Bulletin*, Vol. 21, pp. 122-51.

Census of India, 1971. Supplement Provisional Population Totals. Delhi: Government of India Press.

Dandekar, V.M., and N. Rath, 1971. "Poverty in India—I," *Economic and Political Weekly*, 2 January, pp. 25-48.

Dupuis, J., 1960. "Madras et le Nord du Coromandel. Paris: Librarie D' Amerique et D' Orient, A Maison-neuve.

Gough, Kathleen, 1973. "Harijans in Thanjavur," in K. Gough and Hari Sharma, eds., *Imperialism and Revolution in South Asia*. New York: Monthly Review Press.

Hightower, Jim, 1972. "Hard Tomatoes, Hard Times: Failure of the Land Grant College Complex," *Society* (formerly *Transanctions*), Volume 10, November/December, pp. 10-22.

Jodha, N.S., 1973. "Special Programmes for the Rural Poor," *Economic and Political Weekly*, March.

John, Baby, 1973. "Land Revolution in Action," *Link*, 7 January, pp. 47-51.

Joshi, P.C., 1972. "Structural Change," *Seminar*, pp. 33-36.

Kumar D., 1965. *Land and Caste in South India*. Cambridge: Cambridge University Press.

Ladejinsky, Wolf, 1965. "Study on Tenurial Conditions in Package Districts," Report of Ford Foundation Consultant. New Delhi: Planning Commission.

Mencher, J.P., 1968. "Politics, Religion, and Caste in Madras Villages: An Analysis of Their Interrelations and Implications for Development," American Anthropological Association Meeting. (Under revision for publication.)

———, 1970. "Change Agents and Villagers: An Analysis of Their Relationships and the Role of Class Values," *Economic and Political Weekly*, Vol. 5, July.

———, 1972. "Continuity and Change in an Ex-Untouchable Community of South India," in Mahar, ed., *The Untouchables in Contemporary India*. pp. 37-56.

———, (in press). "Agricultural Labour Movements in their Socio-Political and Ecological Context," to appear in B.N. Nair, ed., *A Feitschrift in Honour of Professor Aiyappan*.

———, (in press). "Limitations of Flexibility and Their Implications for the Creation of Socialist State: The Case of Kerala," to appear in S. Devandas Pillai, ed., *Changing India: Studies in Honour of Ghurye*. Bombay: Popular Prakashan.

———, (in press). "Agricultural Labour Unions: Some Socio-Economic and Political Considerations," for IX International Congress of Anthropological and Ethnological Sciences in vol. edited by K. Dabid. Mouton Publications.

———, (in press). "The Caste System Upside Down or the Not-so-Mysterious East," *Current Anthropology*.

———, (in press). "Group and Self-Identification: The View From the Bottom," *Research Abstracts*. New Delhi: ICSSR.

"Modernising Indian Agriculture," Fourth Report on the Intensive Agriculture District Programme (1960-1968). Vol. II. Delhi: Ministry of Food and Agriculture, Community Development and Cooperation.

Raj, K.N., 1970. "Some Questions Concerning Growth, Transformation, and Planning of Agriculture in the Developing Countries," in E.A.G. Robinson and Michael Kidron, eds., *Economic Development in South Asia*. London: Macmillan, pp. 102-26, discussion on pp. 193-98.

Rao, C.H. Hanumantha, 1965. "Agricultural Growth and Stagnation in India," *The Economic Weekly*. February 27.

Rao, C.H. Hanumantha, 1966. "Alternative Explanations of the Inverse Relationship between Farm Size and Output per Acre in India," *The Indian Economic Review*, Vol. 1, October, p. 5.

Seers, Dudley, 1972. "The Meaning of Development," in Uphoff and Ilchman, eds., *The Political Economy of Development*. Berkeley: University of California Press. pp. 123-38. Originally published in *International Development Review*, December 1969, pp. 2-6.

Shivaraman, Mythily, 1973. "Thanjavur: Rumblings of Class Struggle in Tamil Nadu," in Kathleen Gough aud Hari Sharma, eds., *Imperialism and Revolution in South Asia*. New York: Monthly Review Press.

Shourie, Arun, 1972. "The 'Garibi-Hatao' Debate," *Economic and Political Weekly*, December 30, pp. 2517-19.
Swaminathan, M.S., 1973. "Perspectives in Agriculture," *Seminar*, Annual number, pp. 63-66.
Tamil Nadu Reforms (Reduction of Land Ceiling) Act adopted 10 April 1970. Madras: Government Press.
Thorner, Daniel and Alice Thorner, 1962. *Land and Labour in India*. Bombay: Asia Publishing House.
Uphoff, Norman T. and Warren F. Ilchman, 1972. *The Political Economy of Development*. Berkeley: University of California Press.

G. Morris Carstairs

21 Medicine and Faith in Rural Rajasthan

The Problem: The Gulf of Misunderstanding Between the Western Doctor and the Indian Villager

In one of his many Indian short stories, Rudyard Kipling describes how a young district officer persuaded a frightened village community to submit to vaccination by reminding the people that its effectiveness derived from the sacred cow, and then by getting one or two of the leading men to be the first to undergo it. No doubt this story was founded on observation. Certainly it illustrated one way to make such a measure acceptable. Another method, adopted in the early years of this century by the chief health officer of Jodhpur state, turned upon a judicious use of showmanship. This doctor, an Irishman and a famous athlete, included in his retinue one of those emaciated beggars, blind and pock-marked, who are still all too common a sight in India. When he came to a village he would summon everyone with his stentorian voice. "Take a good look at him," he would bellow, "that is what Mataji [the goddess of smallpox] does for you." He would then strip to the waist and display not only his vaccination scars but also his muscular torso. The demonstration was convincing.

In contrast, during my recent stay in the village of Delwara I witnessed a conspicuously less successful technique. The public vaccinator came to pay his annual visit of a few days. He was a supercilious young man from Udaipur city, who had passed a course in this speciality, and he regarded villagers as an inferior and stupid lot—especially when they refused to accept his scarifications. During his four-day stay in Delwara, the task degenerated into a hunt. I would see a herd of children and young mothers come bolting out of an alley-way with hilarity and panic mingled in their shrieks, while the vaccinator pursued them, brandishing the weapons of his trade.

It is not enough to bring new medical techniques to a community. No matter how well established these may be in Europe or America, they must be presented afresh to each new social group in a way that will command conviction and acceptance. In order to do this effectively, one has to understand the climate of ideas into which these new elements are to be introduced. A practitioner from another culture may find himself faced with situations that appear incomprehensible to him at first sight.

For example, when I first practiced medicine in India, I found that in a case where I did nothing at all, except diagnose pregnancy, I was given great credit; in another where the patient died of diphtheria despite my treatment, I was lauded; and in a third, where I made an accurate diagnosis, I was held to blame. As a Westerner, I was puzzled by these reactions. It was only gradually that I came to realize that they all made sense in the context of the villagers' own beliefs about sickness and its cure, and of their concept of the role of a physician. It was only after many months had passed and after numerous contretemps, that I began to appreciate the reason for the misunderstandings between us. This process of learning can best be illustrated by describing some of the incidents during my apprenticeship as a country doctor in india.

THE SITUATION: LOCAL CONCEPTS OF DISEASE AND MODES OF TREATMENT

Village life in Rajastan

In 1950 and 1951 I had the opportunity to spend a number of months in two different villages in Rajasthan, where until recently the maharajahs ruled with medieval splendour and unrestrained autocracy. It is a lovely country, although harsh to the eye like the Bad Lands of Wyoming, and the people are handsome in their bearing and in their bright peasant costumes; but still, I was rather disappointed at first that my sociological research should be carried out here. I had hoped to go and live among really primitive peoples—Sea Dayaks, perhaps, or Melanesians—whereas to my mind the people of Rajasthan were not at all primitive.

To begin with, I had been brought up among them. My earliest memories were of playing field hockey, marbles, and other local games with a pack of little Hindu boys; of riding through dusty villages on my shaggy country-bred pony; and of special occasions when we toured the countryside by bullock-cart, living under canvas. My father was a missionary, and there was nothing he liked better than these excursions away from the beaten track. At dusk or before sunrise, he and I would scour the surrounding jungle for quail or duck or partridge for our next day's dinner. I well remember one such occasion when we saw from our bullock-cart a cavalcade of Rajput horsemen, lance in hand, galloping in chase of a wild boar. That night we camped beside the mud-walled fortress of the chief who had led the hunt and listened to his minstrels extemporizing songs in honour of the day's sport.

The Rajputs are far from being the only inhabitants of this region, but they do constitute its aristocracy and set standards of valour, self-respect, and pride of bearing to which many of the lowlier castes also aspire. The great historian of Rajasthan, Colonel James Tod (who was himself a Scot), was the first of many who have pointed out similarities between the clans of Scotland and the thirty-six principal lineages of the Rajputs, and in my first experience of life in a Rajput village I had many occasions to remember this. The village is called Sujarupa, and it is situated on the fringe of the jungle-covered slopes of the Aravali Mountains in the extreme north of Udaipur state.

Sujarupa is a compact little hamlet of stone-walled cottages, each surrounded by a thorn fence that serves as a corral for the family herd of goats and one or two heads of cattle. The people are all farmers, cultivating fields that they or their immediate forebears have cleared from the jungle. Men and women work hard in these fields, the women covering their faces with a head cloth if a stranger approaches. The children work too; from the age of eight or nine they learn to drive the village flocks through the dry foothills. Like David, each carries a sling and practices throwing jagged stones that roar as they fly through the air, to scare off jackals, hyenas, and an occasional wolf. It is a hard-working community, accustomed to a minimum of comfort; and yet the people are usually sure of a meal twice a day. Except for years in which the rains fail—and this happens on an average every fourth year in Rajasthan—they are able to raise enough wheat to sell some for cash.

Nearly everything in the village is homemade. The ploughs and sickles that the villagers use are manufactured by artisans in the nearest large village, as are their cooking pots, their shoes, and their clothes. Their houses and their wells are made with their own hands. They are all Hindus, and on feast days some of them may visit a distant temple of Mahadev or Sri Krishna, but throughout the year they are more concerned with the local gods whom they regard as intermediaries between them and the remote Great Gods whom the Brahmins worship. It took me many weeks to distinguish the numerous stones and trees that were severally consecrated to these gods.

Almost all the farmers in Sujarupa, as well as those of the surrounding district, are Rawat Rajputs; and when we sat and talked together, or walked through their fields, or set off in a party to visit the nearest small township, I often thought how similar they were in many ways to the only other farming community that I knew at all well—my own kinsfolk, living in Western Highlands of Scotland. Sometimes I used to think of those small clusters of houses, the hamlets of Clachan or Glenbreckire, and wonder how those Highland farmers would react if a stranger with a different coloured skin were to settle among them for a few months and presume to analyze their way of life. It was a profoundly discouraging reflection.

What prognosis meant to the villagers

Fortunately, the farmers of Sujarupa were comparatively forthcoming. The very day after I had pitched my tent on some level ground near the village, a young man called Govind Singh came to summon me to his house. He had heard that I was a "Daktar Sahib" and he begged me to do something for his young wife, who was possessed by a devil and in great pain.

I found myself bitterly regretting the shortcomings of my training at Edinburgh University, which was all too light on exorcism; but bearing my stethoscope like a talisman, I followed him to his hut. Inside, a girl of seventeen was rolling about on the floor, wailing loudly. I examined her nervously at first but with more confidence as it dawned on me what was going on; and then I told Govind Singh that hers was a very healthy little devil, as he would soon see for himself. In fact, her first baby was born that evening, a lively boy. Govind Singh himself came to my tent with a present of milk and rich pudding to tell me the news. Afterwards, he pretended that he had known all along what was the matter: "But these young women, you know, Sahib, they get frightened over nothing."

From that moment the people of Sujarupa were very cordial toward me. They said it must be drafty and uncomfortable out there in the tent, which was true, and invited me to live in the large *paul* or guestroom of their hamlet; and I received numerous requests to treat their children for sore eyes and their old people for chronic bronchitis. I was agreeable surprised at this welcome, but a little puzzled. It was only much later that I realized that although I had done nothing for the young mother, I had spoken the magic words: "She will be all right. She will have a healthy baby." And events had proved me right. In their opinion, pronouncing a prognosis is one of the most important functions of a healer, but with this difference: when their healers say, "He will recover," they are not expressing a personal opinion but are speaking with the authority of the supernatural power, which is the real agent of their cure.

Cures and treatment in Sujarupa

Throughout my five months' stay in Sujarupa, I carried on a small and intermittent dispensary practice; but I soon realized that my remedies were only one of several sorts of healing, and by no means the most popular. My village friends were not narrow-minded; they were willing to give my sort of medicine a trial, but they did expect immediate results. This did not mean that they always demanded immediate results from their own form of cure—but that was a different matter because they already had faith in these, and so once the condition was diagnosed and the prescription given, they felt assured that the correct steps had been taken and recovery was bound to follow. My sort of medicine carried on such aura of conviction, and therefore it was required to justify itself dramatically, and without delay.

I was naturally curious to hear about my rival practitioners, and to see their work; I did not have long to wait. Within a week of my settling in Sujarupa village, my neighbours called me out one night to attend an open-air celebration of worship. A throng of men and boys sat around a great log fire beside a hilltop shrine and sang the praises of the god of that place, one Kagal-Devji, a black snake-god. Sometime after midnight, when the singing had worked up a high pitch of excitement, an elderly man sitting at the side of the fire gave a loud cry and began to dance and shake convulsively. It was whispered in my ear: "Look, he's begun to 'play.' The breath of Devji has come into him." Then the possessed individual, who was the priest of the shrine, ran indoors and saluted the idols; he then appeared in front of us still twitching and gasping for breath and called out a number of rather cryptic prophecies about the coming year. After this he sat trembling before the image, and people came before him one by one. They poured out small offerings of grain and begged the god to tell them the cause of their own, or their children's or their cattle's illness; and what they must do to be well.

At this stage I knew too little of the local dialect to understand what was going on; one or other of my new friends had to keep prompting me in Hindustani. Several weeks later, however, I went with two families of Sujarupa to attend the weekly "possession" at a shrine which lay some seven miles off in the jungle. This was the shrine of Danaji, a local demon-god, who had acquired a special fame as a healer of all sorts of ills. It was generally conceded that it was better to go instead to Devji if one were bitten by a snake (cobras and kraits being the common local venomous varieties) because after all he was a snake-god himself. In such an emergency, the priest would invariably become possessed and then throw himself upon the patient, noisily sucking at the wound and supposedly drawing out the poison. For all other troubles, however, Danaji was regarded as the more reliable authority.

The importance of Danaji was brought home to me by an event in the hut next to the one which I came to occupy in Sujarupa. This was the home of Nol Singh, his wife, and two sons, one of whom was a sturdy boy of twelve years, the other a sickly baby named Lum Singh. The father had served in the Indian Army, and hence was one of the three men in the village who had travelled far afield and who were literate. In keeping with his knowledge of the world, he professed to have great faith in "Sahibs' medicines" and called me in twice to attend to Lum Singh, first for acute conjunctivitis and next for dysentery. But Lum Singh fell sick again, and this time his father did not consult me but went to Danaji. Some days later, when there was a small waning moon, I saw Nol Singh enter the village carrying an all-black goat, which he had bought.

Two nights later, at the blackest of the moonless period, he came to ask for the loan of my sharp *kukri* knife. I was now sure that some curative rice was in progress, but he was very reluctant to talk about it, promising to tell me everything in due course. Next day he returned the knife and explained that the Danaji had diagnosed that a witch was eating Lum Singh's liver. In order to appease her, a black goat had to be killed at midnight, five men each putting a hand to the knife, and then the head and entrails were to be set in a broken pot at a place where three paths crossed. This was a striking demonstration of the parallels between folk beliefs about witchcraft in medieval Europe—the goat, the midnight sacrifice, the offering in the broken pot, and the place where three paths cross are all to be found in accounts of European witchcraft—but it had a tragic sequel.

Late one night a few days after the sacrifice, Nol Singh called me to his house. He was very anxious about his child's health, and with good reason, for I found him in a state of profound toxemia, suffering from diphtheria. There was nothing in my box of medicines that could meet the case, but I knew there was a government dispensary and a doctor in the village a few miles off. So I set off by bicycle in the starlight and woke up the doctor. Unfortunately, he had no anti-diphtheritic serum in his stock, not even any penicillin. I cycled back and gave the child an injection of tropine, simply in order to let the distracted parents feel that something was being done. The boy died in a few hours, and I went with all the men of the village to his hurried burial, piling thorn branches and stones over the grave so that the hyenas could not dig up the body. Then we all went to bathe and wash our clothes at the well, to cleanse ourselves of the pollution of contact with death.

I thought that perhaps this time I would be blamed, because, I had given Lum Singh an injection and he had shortly died; but I was wrong. Throughout the rest of my stay I had to listen again and again to Nol Singh's graphic account of my heroic ride on his son's behalf, braving countless ghosts, and twice crossing a stretch of the road which was known to be frequented by leopards. At the time, I was not aware that there were leopards about; and I am sure that I would not have enjoyed my ride so well had I known. In fact, neither I nor the Danaji was blamed. After the first outburst of grief, the family repeated the traditional formula: it was his fate; his day had come; he was a loan from God, to whom he had retured.

After this, I was curious to see the celebrated priest of Danaji at work. Accordingly, one Sunday night when two families of the village announced that they were going to his shrine to consult the oracle, I set out with them. The moon was big once more, and we enjoyed our seven-mile walk under the brilliant Indian night sky. The shrine was in an out-of-the-way little valley, and from some distance off we could see the flickering glow of a fire, then as we drew nearer we could hear occasional loud cries from the priest, who was already in a state of possession. We removed our shoes and laid aside our swords and staves a little way from the sacred place, where many other visitors had already done the same, and then sat near the priest, who crouched trembling violently, and now and again gave a sudden wild shout. The Spirit had come to him strongly this night.

There was something particularly dramatic in the way he summoned certain of his supplicants. He would interrupt the series of patients who came before him with a cry: "A man and a woman of Kachabli," "Three brothers from Tragarh." and these would press forward from the waiting crowd. One of his summonses was for "Two men from Mandawar road," and my companion of the walk nudged me, saying, "That means us, Sahib; we came by that road." He sat before the priest first and consulted him about his little boy, whom the Danaji had saved from witchcraft. He was told to perform certain offerings, and then to carry the child three times around the shrine. Then it was my turn. The priest gave me a pinch of grain. "How many?" he said. "Four grains." He gave me one more, to bring it up to the auspicious number, looked to the shrine for inspiration, and then shouted out his prophecies: "The British will return to rule again. You will get a promotion—a new post, with great power and much pay. When this happens, come back and honour the Danaji." With this he gave me a small dried lemon; telling me to guard it carefully. Then he continued to attend a series of sick people and anxious parents, presenting their whimpering children for his advice. I watched about thirty of these consultations and noted his remedies, which all involved soliciting the help of the Danaji and other gods.

Late in the night the session came to an end. The priest raised his arms with a loud cry, and then became an ordinary villager once more as the Spirit left him. He came to talk with us, professing to recognize me for the first time. "I saw you once before, Shaib," he said. "Don't you remember I was lying sick in the government hospital, and you came and examined my chest with those tubes and said, It is all right; you will get well."

I did remember having seen him a month or so before, when he was acutely ill with pneumonia. Again I was reminded of the magic power ascribed to a confident prognosis. I replied "You and I do the same work, helping the sick get well." But the priest replied at once, "It is not I, Sahib; God alone can do that"—and I was reminded, as every practitioner must often be reminded, that our individual skill is only one part of the complex business of healing.

Village concepts of illness

It might be argued, by those who are accustomed to our

pragmatic tests of the efficacy of treatment, that surely these magic prophecies must become discredited over and over again and in time lose their efficacy. The answer to this is that these villagers do not, as we tend to do, believe that one can influence the course of events simply by the exercise of a technical skill. To them, the supernatural is everywhere immanent, and events can be influenced only by enlisting supernatural aid. They naturally assume that there is a magic quality in the prescriptions of Western medicine as well; and this is one reason why the administration of intramuscular injections, with its ritual of aseptic precautions and the dramatic quality of the act of acupuncture, is especially highly valued among those who have had some contact with allopathic doctors.

There was one young man in Sujarupa who, when he came home on leave from his work as a labourer in the distant city of Ahmedabad, used to beg me to give him just one very powerful "objection" in order to make him strong. He knew only two or three words of English, and this was one of them. I remember him particularly because he was a singularly robust man, and I used to tease him when he insisted that he felt weak, as though he were wasting away. During my few months' practice in this region, I frequently encountered patients who simply complained of weakness; and my head was so filled with anticipation of vitamin deficiency, of malnutrition, chronic malaria, dysentery, anaemia, tuberculosis, and so on, that I sought and fancied that I had found one or another of these conditions in every case. It was not until the following year, in Delwara village, that I came to realize the true significance of this complaint.

In the meantime I gradually widened my circle of acquaintances in the nearby hamlets and encouraged some of the divinely inspired healers to share some of their secrets with me. One old man, who had recovered from an acute attack of dysentery after taking a course of sulfa drugs which I had sent him, was kind enough to explain to me how he could tell that a sick person was possessed by a witch or a demon, by feeling his pulse. What the old man actually did was to lay his forefinger gently across the patient's wrist and wait to see whether he could feel a tremour in one of the flexor tendons of the fingers. There was, however, no consistency in his interpretation of the sign; it served, rather, as the cue for an immediate intuition, as a clairvoyant will hold an object belonging to an absent person and then claim to have a direct awareness of details of his appearance and personality. The most important aspect of this procedure is that the patient and all the onlookers know what the healer expects to find. If there is deception, to our way of thinking it is one in which they all participate; and one in which the Western doctor can find himself unwittingly caught up. We take the act of feeling the pulse so much for granted that we can easily overlook the fact that this may have a quite different significance to the patient and to us.

Every practitioner is familiar with the misunderstandings that so readily occur in everyday practice. Patients and relatives, when keyed up with anxious fears, often place a wrong interpretation on their physician's smallest gesture or his misheard remark. This is naturally still more likely to happen when patient and physician approach the illness with totally dissimilar systems of ideas. It is, of course, not only oriental peoples who have a non-scientific conception of their own bodily processes; one can find abundant instances much nearer home.

Elementary instruction in the physiology of reproduction is now recognized to be an essential part of prenatal care; and the experienced practitioner learns to elicit from his patients something of their own (often fantastic) beliefs about what is happening inside them to make them feel ill. Where the general level of formal education is low, an understanding of physiology can only grow slowly, in relation to what most intimately concerns the health of each particular community. For example, there are already many parts of India where the relationship between malaria, mosquitoes, and quinine has become part of everyday knowledge, whereas in less heavily endemic areas the onset of a malarial rigour is still believed to be the possession of the patient's body by a god. There is no propaganda agent so effective as a demonstrable cure; but it may take many years before conservative villagers are convinced that it is the Western drug which has in fact effected the cure.

I remember one night when I was working with a neighbour (one of the priests of Devji) by the light of my pressure-lantern.

we were interrupted by a young farmer who lived about a mile and a half away on the fringe of the jungle. He said that his wife was struck by a fierce witch, or so it seemed to him, and he came to ask the priest for help. They both invited me to accompany them, and so we set off in single file along a series of field paths. When we approached the house, we could hear loud moans and shrieks. The young woman crouched in the yard, giving full expression to the pain and terror she was suffering. A string bed was drawn forward to serve as a seat for the priest and myself, and then there followed a polite altercation: he urged me to attend to the patient, while I insisted that it was his help the family desired. Accordingly, he felt her pulse and confirmed the husband's diagnosis, then spoke a charm over a small brass pot of water and gave the woman a few drops of this sanctified water to drink. The pot was then placed on the rooftop, so that no one's shadow might fall across it and thus impair its virtue.

As soon as this was done, I was told that now it was my turn. With some difficulty, I managed to persuade the patient to calm down long enough to allow her to explain that she suffered from a severe pain in the chest, which had begun the day before; now it was much severe, and she felt sure that her destruction was imminent. At the thought, she began to cry out once more. In the presence of her husband and strangers, it was impossible for her to unveil her face, but she was persuaded to reveal the side of her chest, where I found vesicles of herpes zoster. The husband led me back to Sujarupa, and I entrusted him with codeine tablets and with spirit for local application. He returned the next day for more, saying that his wife was very much better already.

In that instance, everything was done so politely and with the exchange of so many flattering speeches that both the priest and I felt assured that we had made the significant contribution to the patient's recovery. The same was not the case, however, with another patient to whom I was summoned a few nights later. He was a merchant from a large village twenty miles away and lay on the bullock-cart on which he had made the journey. I examined him on the roadside by the light of my lantern and found him very ill indeed. He had had typhoid fever six weeks previously and now his heart was grossly enlarged and his pulse very rapid. On auscultation I could hear a gallop rhythm. He was extremely agitated and begged me to save his life. I felt doubtful of my ability to do this but encouraged him as best as I could; and gave a heroic dose of digitalis. The cart took him to the nearest large village, where he stayed at a kinsman's house, and there I visited him daily. For the first two days he still looked and felt acutely ill, and his pulse did not fall below 120/minute; but on the third day there was a remarkable change. The pulse was ninety-six, the patient sat up and talked cheerfully, and for the first time showed some desire to eat. I wondered if this was attributable to my therapy, and soon found that it was not. What he had omitted to tell me until then was the reason for his state of panic; he had become convinced that some enemy had caused fatal sorcery to be placed on him. Against this belief, neither my medicine nor my reassurances had been effective. He knew that Sahibs tend to make light of sorcery, and so he had not liked to discuss it with me. Instead, he had obtained the services of a local man who possessed a powerful charm, and on the previous night this man had brought it into play with a dramatic peformance, at the end of which he branded the back of the patient's neck with a red-hot iron. This drove out the evil spell; and it was the relief that the patient experienced at his feeling of escape from mortal danger which had brought his pulse-rate down.

What is expected of a healer

This case, and many others of my village cases, served to impress upon me that the expectation of my patients here was different from that to which I had been accustomed. There was not the same attribution of personal responsibility to the physician for the success or failure of his treatment, because a sovereign fatalism determined the patients' attitude to events; whatever happened was coming to one anyway. What was expected from the healer was reassurance. So long as the illness was nameless, patients felt desperately afraid, but once its magic origin had been defined and the appropriate measures taken, they could face the outcome calmly. The parallel with our own clinical experience is obvious.

The few months I had spend in Sujarupa gave me a little insight into local preconceptions about sickness and cure, and this proved invaluable next year when my wife and I made a ten months' stay in the larger, more sophisticated village of Delwara, which lay only eighteen miles from Udaipur, the capital and indeed the only large town of this state. Delwara was almost a small town in itself, having 2,500 inhabitants and a row of merchants' shops in its central street. Unlike Sujarupa, but like most other large villages in India, it included households belonging to a wide variety of castes, both the upper crust of the "twice-born" (the landlord, priest and merchant castes) and no fewer than thirty-six different groups of hereditary artisans; all interrelated in a complex pattern of traditional obligations and rewards. Besides their varied occupations, almost every family had a stake, however small, in the land. Until the recent change of government in India, Delwara had been the seat of authority of one of the powerful feudal landlords, the Raj Rana of Delwara. The former ruler's vast fortress-palace still towered above the village; and at a high window the Raj Rana himself sat every day, brooding over the slightest occurrences in the bazaar below. He generously put a section of his palace at our disposal for our kitchen and sleeping quarters, but in order to carry out my work I had to hire a room in the centre of the village.

During my stay in Delwara I learned much more about village ideas concerning medicine; and some things I learned only slowly and painfully. In this category I should put my long and unsuccessful struggle to plan my day on Western lines, by the clock. I tried to adhere to the rule that I would see patients only the first thing in the morning (this was at 6.30 a.m. in the hot weather) and again in the late afternoon, but it simply did not work. The villagers themselves preferred to wait until they saw me coming down their lane, and then would call me in with every sign of desperate urgency to see a patient who had been sick for days; and peasants from the surrounding countryside would just walk into my "office" and sit patiently on the floor until I attended to them. Often they would beg me to go with them to their hamlets to see a close relative who lay very sick, but after one or two such excursions I learned to harden my heart and stick to my rule of refusing these requests, the majority of which proved to be cases of advanced phthisis.

One day, however, during the first month of my stay, a powerfully built young farmer appealed to me with great earnestness to help his brother, who lay ill in a hamlet two miles off. He had a high fever and had coughed up blood-stained sputum, which sounded ominous; but his brother insisted that the whole illness was of only a few days' duration. No doubt what finally persuaded me to go was that the young farmer had borrowed a horse from the palace and held it saddled for me to make the journey. I was very glad in the end that I did go, for the patient was suffering from double pneumonia and was acutely ill. I gave him a massive injection of penicillin and followed it up with sulfa merazine, and as I entered home I wondered what his chances of survival were. He gave me the answer two weeks later by walking into my office with a *thali* (a ceremonial tray of gifts) of sweet corn and other produce of his fields.

At the time I thought that this might lead to my dispensary practice growing to uncomfortable proportions, but such was not the case. Throughout my stay both villagers and country folk remained very sceptical of the quality of my medicine. They had three grounds for distrusting it. First, I did not describe their illnesses in the terms they had come to expect from their own healers. Second, I failed to prescribe elaborate dietary restrictions as did the practitioners of classical Hindu medicine. Again and again my patients would pause after receiving their pills and say, "Kattay parhez" which is the customary opening formula: "No bitter condiments, avoid this and this. . . ." In the end, I adopted a simple and familiar list which would do them no harm and seemed to make my treatment at once more comprehensible. Finally, they were dismayed to find that I did not invariably, and in dogmatic terms, assure them that my medicine would immediately cure them. In their eyes, my failure to do so amounted to malpractice. As many of them pointed out to me, it is not so much the ingredients of the prescription which effect the cure as the patient's unhesitating belief in its efficacy. For this reason, every homely recipe (of which everyone knew two or three) ended with the peroration: "Take that and you will certainly be cured of your fever within a day."

Near the end of my stay in Delwara I was called to a house

to treat a merchant who seemed to be suffering from a cancer that obstructed the portal vein and gave rise to ascites. After we had tapped several pints of fluid from his abdomen, his son asked me how ill his father really was, and I told him the prognosis. That same evening a friend who had been present reminded me of this, with a smile; he found it simply incomprehensible that one could say a thing like that. "You know," he said, "our custom here is that even if a man is sure to die, we never say so. We always say something like 'If it is God's will, he will get better'."

I realized that just as in the past I had been given credit for a decisive intervention simply because I had uttered a hopeful prognosis, now the reverse was the case. I had committed a serious impropriety in stating that the patient would not recover.

In Delwara I was able to keep a record of at least some of the new cases which I saw in my office. They are summarized below.

DIAGNOSES IN ORDER OF FREQUENCY

Malaria	44	Gonorrhea	10
Diarrhea	36	Severe anemia	7
"Spermatorrhea" as		Acute respiratory infections	6
presenting symptom	17	Syphilis	6
Scabies	16	Typhoid or paratyphoid	6
Chronic bronchitis	16	Cataract	5
Eye infections	15	Leukorrhea	3
Dermatitis (including		Chronic otitis media	2
leishmaniasis)	15	Chronic sinusitis	2
Tuberculosis	15	Rickets	2
Major involvement		Acute appendicitis	1
Chest	9	Leprosy	1
Other	6	Madura foot	1
Dyspepsia	13	Undiagnosed	5

Total new attendances recorded: 244

The list fails to include many patients whose arrival interrupted an interview with an informant and who were therefore seen and sent away as quickly as possible. It also omits a large number whom I was called in to see when I chanced to pass their doors; these were mostly cases of malaria, scabies, cutaneous leishmaniasis, septic eyes, and cataract.

A cultural body-image

In Delwara, as previously in Sujarupa, I was frequently asked by apparently robust men to give them medicine—or better, an injection—to make them strong. At first, I continued to regard them as cases of anemia or malnutrition until my eyes were opened one day to the real condition by interpolations of a bystander, who was watching me examine one of these patients: "Of course he's weak," he said, "He was such a libertine when he was a young man that his semen got spoiled, and it's been leaving him ever since."

The patient seemed relieved to have it stated for him in this blunt manner. What he really wanted, he explained, was some medicine that would remedy this condition and cause his semen to stay inside his body instead of leaking away and making him feel weak. From that day on, whenever a man asked me for strength-giving medicine. I urged him to tell me more about his trouble, and once he realized that he and I "talked the same language" in terms of symptomatology, a similar story always came out. Perhaps it is important to mention that this preoccupation was quite independent of the recognition of venereal disease and the fear of having contracted it. Gonorrhea was specifically mentioned as being only one of many ways in which "spoiled semen" might leave the body.

I found that a consistent belief about the nature and functions of the semen was held by all these patients, in different degrees of complexity according to their education. They were all able to describe how blood is made by the digestion of good food in a sort of low fire contained in the stomach, from which comes the warmth of the body; and that from every forty drops of blood one drop of semen is laboriously formed. This semen, in which lies the source of a man's strength and of his subjective sense of well-being, is stored in a reservoir in his skull, which has a capacity of about twenty fluid ounces. The amount of well-formed semen which a man carries in this hidden store is not merely an indication of his state of health; it is also a measure of his moral and religious status. This is made clear when one learns what factors are conducive to the increase of semen, and what detrimental. In the former category come "cool" foods, such as dairy products, wheat flour, sugar, some fruits, and a number of the milder spices; in the latter, the cheaper and heavier cereals, unrefined sugar, vegetable oil, strong spices, and some of the commonest fruits. An especial anathema is placed upon eating meat and eggs, and drinking all forms of alcohol.

The striking thing about these food preferences is that all the foods in the approved class are the more expensive ones, which only the wealthier members of the high castes can afford to eat regularly. The mass of low-caste peasants and artisans eat meat and cheap cereals and drink wine; it is only on feast days that they treat themselves to wheat cakes and pure sugar and dishes made with milk.

Even more important than these dietary restrictions, however, is the belief that the quality and amount of one's stored semen can be diminished by a failure to observe "right behaviour." Obviously, it will be dissipated by an excessive indulgence in sex; but it will be lost more quickly and irretrievably if this indulgence is extramarital, and the bad effect will be intensified if the sex partner is of a low-caste community. Indeed, any act that incurs the condemnation of the elders of one's caste is believed to militate against the formation of the "Royal Principle." For example, many people told me that the reason the present generation of young men is so puny is this: it is a consequence of the growing habit of sitting in tea-shops, drinking "English tea," (known in England as Indian tea). This habit is condemned, first because it implies a disregard for the serious, ritualistic practice of eating the two meals of the day; second, because it is a frivolous extravagance; and most important of all, because it exposes one to the ritual pollution of sitting to drink in company with others of lower caste. In general, it can be said that any violation of the many strict rules of behaviour which concern the orthodox Hindu is regarded as detrimental to his store of semen, and thus to his mental and physical well-being.

Now at last these reiterated complaints of weakness began to make sense. They were the expression of chronic anxiety engendered by feeling of guilt. Small wonder, therefore, that my iron tonics and vitamin concentrates had little effect; what these people really wanted was a release from their burden of guilt, and this release they could only find in their own traditional way, by making a pilgrimage and bathing in one of the many sacred lakes or rivers which have the property of washing away one's sins, or by one of the elaborate and costly ceremonies of purification at which the Brahmin priest is always ready to preside. Actually, these drastic measures are seldom taken; for the most part, they seem content to go on worrying and resolving to do something about it one day. There are even some who appear to derive a certain pleasure in describing their impending physical decay, like Calvinists who dwell lugubriously upon the prospect of hell-fire.

I have emphasized the element of guilt in this "general weakness" syndrome because there it was etiologically important. In time, however, I came to realize that it entered to some extent into every form of illness. The patient and his extended family always had the feeling that they were temporarily on a state of ill favour with some divine agency. One is reminded of the description of depression which is put forward by psychoanalysts of the Melanie Klein school as a fantasy of ingesting "bad objects" so that the whole self feels bad. Be that as it may, the village patient did not feel relieved of his illness unless he had the subjective assurance that the divine had been placated at the same time as his physical symptoms were relieved.

Sacred and secular diseases

This was dramatically shown in their treatment of snake bites. All snakes, but especially the black cobras, were believed to be the embodiment of powerful godlings. For example, every plot of cultivated fields had a protector-god, known have as Radaji, and in the form of a black snake the Radaji often patrolled the fields entrusted to his care. Should anyone trespass or otherwise offend the god, he would get bitten. Here, as in Sujarupa, there were priests of the snake-god whom the sufferer might consult. They would become "possessed," suck out the poison, and be placated with an offering.

There was, however, another and more popular remedy. This was to consult one of the four elderly men in the village who were known to possess powerful charms against just such an occurrence. One of these, a handsome bearded Brahmin called Nathu Lal, told me about an instance that occurred two years previously. A blacksmith called Pratab had cut across a neighbour's cornfield and was bitten on the foot. One of the other healers was summoned, and a great crowd gathered in the yard of the blacksmith's house, Nathu Lal among them. It soon became clear to him that the other healer's charms were not strong enough to meet the case because this was evidently the work of a more than usually powerfull god—probably the very Radaji whose shrine was set up to protect the main entrance of the village. At last, Nathu Lal himself decided to intervene. He took a pinch of dust between his fingers, whispered his strongest charm over it, and blew it toward the patient. "The dust did not touch him, Sahib, but the air of it was enough."

At once, compelled by the charm, the god entered the body of his victim, who shrieked with rage and flew at Nathu Lal, but, he had anticipated this and dodged into a room, closing the door behind him, and calling out to the bystanders to tie Partab securely to a pillar. There then followed a heated discussion between him and the god speaking in the body of the patient. In the end, the Radaji promised to spare him if he made certain sacrifices before his shrine, and the "possession" came to an end. The case was not yet closed, however, because when Pratab came to his senses, he maintained that the offering was more than he could afford and refused to make it. The onlookers were scandalized, but after he had had his face well slapped he did as he was told.

It was, of course, common knowledge that such possession might occur. Every adult villager has seen it happen many times; indeed, his familiarity with the expected behaviour is presumably what causes the patient's trance-like state of dissociation to take this particular form. One patient of mine recalled how when he was a boy of five or six, both he and his mother were bitten by a snake. They went to an old man famous for his charms, and he took the precaution of tying them to a tree before magically summoning the snake's spirit. "My mother became possessed," said this young man, "I remember seeing her shake all over and cry out and struggle as she tried to attack the healer, but the Spirit did not come to me."

In later years, after he had seen two or three dramatic instances of possession and cure, suggestion would have told, and he too would be possessed—or so one might think. But actually the situation was quite different. This youth, whose name was Prithwi Singh, became a devoted worshipper of the Goddess Vijayshan-Mata, whose shrine stands just outside of Delwara. Like his soldier uncle before him, Prithwi Singh attended all occasions of worship of this goddess, and it was he who performed the sacrifice of goats and sometimes young buffaloes in her name, decapitating them each with a single cut of his sword.

In the summer of 1950, Prithwi Singh was bitten on the finger by a cobra one afternoon as he was returning from his fields. This happened about a mile and a half from the village, and by the time he reached home, the poison was working in him. He felt thick-headed and confused, and could hardly drag his legs along.

"Sahib," he said, "at that time I really thought that I was about to die. But I managed to make my way to the shrine of Mataji, and I prayed to Her that if it was Her will, She should make me well. Then I went back to my house to an inner room where I have a little brass image of the Goddess, and I lay down below it on the floor, and at once I became unconscious. I lay there for some hours in a fever, and they said that I groaned in my sleep; and then I had a dream. In my dream I saw the Goddess come into the room and stand beside me. She lifted up my hand and sucked the poison from my finger, and then She turned and went away. I woke up, wet with perspiration and quite weak; but from that moment I began to get well."

Among my stock of medicines was a set of dried polyvalent antivenine serums for intravenous injection in cases of snake bite. I let it be known that this was available, but although I heard in due course of several such cases, two of which were fatal, no one asked for this treatment. I believe now that this was on account of the close association of the illness and the god. A physician who was previously insensible to the all-important divine agent could not inspire confidence in treating this condition.

In the same way there was bitter opposition to the efforts of governmental authorities to promote universal vaccination against smallpox. Here, as all over India, this disease is believed to be due to the wrath of the demon-goddess, locally known as Sitala-Mata. Epidemics always occur in the hot weather, when flies are most abundant. High fever is taken as a sign that the goddess is hot. She is angry. She devours children in her rage. For this reason, at the begnning of the very hot season, there is a placatory ceremony at the goddess' shrine, and this is repeated should there be a spell of especially hot weather or should smallpox break out in the vicinity. On such occasions, the image of Sitala-Mata is bathed with cool water, and garlands and fruits are laid before her. "We are cooling her down," say the women.

In contrast, there were some afflictions that were less decidedly associated with divine intervention. For example, there was no talk of "possession" when one was stung by a scorpion, although every practitioner who had charms against snake bite seemed also to know one of the lesser charms against such a sting. My local-analgesic oily preparation was in great demand during the hot weather nights, when stings were most frequent. On one occasion I came upon a group squatting in the dusty village lane. A young man had received a severe sting. His leg was swollen and very painful. My old friend Nathu Lal was engaged in exorcizing the poison, stroking the leg over and over again with a neem twig and whispering the appropriate charm. When he saw me squat beside him, he paused and suggested that I should apply my medicine, but I knew that at this stage it could do nothing to relieve his pain, so I persuaded Nathu Lal to continue his good work.

The role of faith in curing

There were so many lesser healers and magicians at work in Delwara that one tended to overlook the fact that there was also a government dispensary, with a doctor trained in Ayurvedic medicine, and a dispenser. Their services and their medicaments were available free; and yet strangely enough they found very few clients. In all the many conversations I had with them in their sparsely equipped premises, I can remember only thrice being interrupted by the arrival of a patient. This state of idleness, it must be confessed, was not uncongenial to the doctor's temperament; indeed, he tended to encourage it by maintaining that these free medicines provided by the government were not very good anyway—let people come to his house privately, and he would let them have others, which would cost a good deal and which were correspondingly effective. In this way, he carried on a desultory sort of practice among the better-off families but earned the resentment of the poorer majority.

In Delwara, as in Sujarupa, the chief resort of families afflicted with sickness (or indeed any other trouble) was to the priests of a number of shrines in the vicinity; and here, too, there was one shrine that enjoyed an outstanding reputation in this respect. It was the shrine of Vijayshan-Mata, of which Prithwi Singh was one of the attendants. Every Sunday night without fail the priest became possessed and sat quivering on the floor in front of the image of the goddess, while a long succession of patients and supplicants came before him to be diagnosed and treated. In time I got to know the priest quite well, and I could see that sometimes he seemed genuinely in trance, while at others he was wide awake and made only a pretense at still being "possessed." In fact, this was evident the first time I attended his ceremony, a few months after my wife and I had settled in the village. When the priest had worshipped Vijayshan-Mata to an accompaniment of gongs and conch-shell music, her spirit came to him and he flayed himself ecstatically with an iron chain, and then began to utter his divinations. At this point I found myself thrust forward to the door of the temple and voices said, "Go on, ask Mataji anything you want to know, and she will tell you the true answer."

After racking my brain for a moment, I asked a question which in fact had been exercising my wife and me for several weeks: "Mataji, this baby that we are going to have shortly, will it be a boy or a girl." The quivering priest forgot himself for one moment and nearly burst out laughing. To conceal this, he turned toward the image as if seeking guidance, and then cried out, "Choro vaygo," (village dialect for "It'll be a boy"). And for days everyone in the village made us repeat this prophecy and then congratulated us upon our coming good fortune; but the baby proved to be a girl after all.

I sat beside this priest for many hours watching villagers and peasants present their sickly children or themselves for the blessing of the goddess' treatment, and I became familiar with the small range of common complaints: fever, dysentery, tuberculosis, childlessness, and, above all, witchcraft, which covered a multitude of women's and children's illnesses. One thing impressed me especially: these patients did not give a history of their complaint in the way to which we are accustomed. They took it for granted that the divine healer would know at once what was wrong. (Here, as many times in these villages, one was reminded of analogies to the Gospel stories.) This observation reminded me of the many occasions when country people had come up to me and silently extended a hand for me to take their pulse. And when, after doing so, I asked, "What is troubling you?" they would answer, "Sahib, that is for you to say. We are only poor ignorant people; how should we know."

This attitude bepoke their ready trust. It meant that, having once decided to believe in a certain healer, they would uncritically accept whatever he told them. It was also an indication of their faith in the physician's cure. And that faith was always absolute; they knew no half measure. My village informants were quite explicit on this point. "Medicines are all very well," they would say to me, "But really, Sahib, it is *tasalli* (faith) that makes a sick man well. No matter how rare a medicine you give a patient, unless both you and he have faith in it, he never will be cured."

In the case of the priest's therapy, this was certainly true, because he seldom applied any physical treatment at all. Watching the scores of peasants who passed before him, I came to realize that what they asked from him (or rather, from the goddess) were two things: that the affliction should be given a name and so become less terrible, and that the priest should utter his prediction, "He will get well." It mattered not that this formula was repeated to every other patient, every night. To each one it was like a personal communication from the goddess herself and put new heart into him.

At first, I must confess, I was filled with scorn and hostility toward this charlatan; but in time I came to realize that he was no less convinced than all his patients of the worthwhileness of his work. After all, he was simply performing what is one of the most important functions of the general medical practitioner, by letting these sick people feel that they were not alone and helpless but part of a succouring community, both real and supernatural. In my boyhood in Scotland I knew an eccentric old country physician who was remarkable for two things: for his detestation of internal combustion engines ("Damn these motors!" he would cry when an early Model-T Ford made him skip to the side of the road) and for his habit of falling to his knees and "putting up a prayer" whenever one of his patients chanced to die. Unkind critics pointed out that he had more scope for this exercise than had his younger competitors, but his practice remained a large one to the end of his days. Our Presbyterian neighbours felt that in him they had a guide through life and the hereafter.

IMPLICATIONS

Nowadays simple piety is at a discount in the Western world. In its place we offer the assurance of a securely based scientific training, which enables us to treat our patients and utter our prognosis with a sincere, if measured, confidence. It will be a long time before the scientific approach to the understanding and treatment of disease reaches remoter villages such as Sujarupa and Delwara. Until the material resources and the educational level of the public permit us to give them something demonstrably better, it would be a disservice to these people to try to undermine the chief solace they have in time of trouble.

By this I do not mean that we are justified in adopting a defeatist attitude toward the problem, but simply that we have to work from below upward. There were evidences of such new ideas in Delwara in 1951. Young men who had left the village to work in the city or to serve in the army came home with a smattering of new ideas about hygiene and sanitation. They spoke up at the village council in favour of cleaning up the lanes and building proper city-style latrines. A young Congress party worker read in the newspaper about infections spread by water and persuaded the council to disinfect the main well of drinking water during the fly-infested season. It was here, I felt, at the village level itself, that the new ideas must take root if they were ever to command the confidence, the all-important *tasalli* of the village people, which alone could make them work.

Perhaps the most significant lesson of my stay in these two villages was the realization that it was not enough to bring good medicines and efficient hygienic techniques to these country people. Before they can take effect, they must be accepted, and this will never come about so long as a wide gulf separates the thinking and experience of Western doctors from that of their village patients. There are three ways in which this gulf can be bridged: by the slow diffusion of information about sepsis and infection; by a better understanding of the expectations with which the people approach the doctor; and by presenting new techniques in a way which will link them up with what they are expected to supersede. Just as the earliest "horseless carriages" evolved only slowly and as if reluctantly toward the streamlined efficiency of a modern roadster, so we must expect new ideas in medicine to take root, at first by emphasizing their continuity with old traditions. To confront the village with radically new departures from all that is familiar in the domain of health and sickness will only alarm and bewilder him and forfeit his co-operation, as has so frequently happened.

Summary

This paper has been devoted to the recording of a number of lessons that I learned in the course of my attempts to practice medicine in two country villages of northern India. I was forced to recognize the seriousness of certain obstacles to the acceptance of Western medicine, obstacles whose true nature could be understood only when I had learned a good deal about the villagers' own beliefs concerning sickness and cure. Misunderstandings were found to arise from false expectations on both sides, based on different conceptions of the role of the physician.

After a period of practical experience, I realized that one can scarcely expect village people to change their whole cosmology simply to accord with the outlook of a Western-trained doctor. Scientific knowledge seems likely to be disseminated throughout India as education becomes widespread and the products of Western technology become a part of everyone's environment—but one cannot afford to wait for this to happen. In the immediate future, it devolves upon those who are introducing western techniques in public health and medicine to study how best they can adapt the roles of the doctor, the pharmacist, and the public hygienist to fit into the existing cultural expectations. In the process, they may have to consent to assume the mantle of the priest or the magician. This does not mean, of course, that they will themselves subscribe to non-rational beliefs, but simply that they will accept the inevitable fact that their own techniques of healing will be accepted "irrationally," as indeed they are for the most part in the West. Western health personnel can, however, turn this fact to advantage by dramatizing the concepts of infection, sterilization, and chemotherapy for all they are worth and by accepting as an asset the quite unscientific awe which the ritual of even minor surgery can inspire.

Public health workers will have to formulate their measures so that they can be linked with the old teachings, and above all must aim to enlist the support of the leaders of village opinion. These considerations may sound devious and Machiavellian, but so long as Western-trained workers remain clear in their own minds about the worth of the contribution they have to make to the community's well-being, they will be able to play their roles with that conviction and assurance of ultimate success which the villagers themselves recognize as the hallmark of truly potent therapy.

McKim Marriott

22 Western Medicine in a Village of Northern India

THE PROBLEM: THE MARGINAL POSITION OF WESTERN MEDICINE

"Western medicines are best," I was told by an old carpenter in the remote village of Kishan Garhi, "but doctors never cure anybody." The old carpenter had worked in a large town for many years and knew what doctors were like, but to people who have never lived outside Kishan Garhi, the carpenter's dilemma is equally real. In this village of 850 persons, more than twenty have sought treatment from Western doctors,[1] but only two of these—a man saved from hydrophobia by a course of injections and a youth whose crushed and gangrenous arm had been amputated—believed that the doctors' treatments had effected their cure.

The villages of western Uttar Pradesh (United Provinces) are considered to be among the most healthful of India, and Kishan Garhi, a mainly Hindu community in Aligarh district, is representative of the more conservative agricultural villages of that region. Kishan Garhi lies several miles from any road or town and in 1952 was still far away from any of India's

[1] The term "Western" is used for convenience and should be understood as meaning Western in type or tradition. Thus, the designation "Western" would apply not only to a European or American medical practitioner, but also to an Indian practitioner trained in the Western type of medical institution.

energetic new community development projects. Its 165 families live in houses of mud, crammed wall upon wall around the base of a landlord's fortress. The farmers of Kishan Garhi grow ample amounts of wheat and barley by dint of hard manual labour in the encircling fields. They subsist ordinarily on bread, crude sugar, and little buttermilk, supplemented rarely by seasonal vegetables and fruits. They quench their thirst on water drunk from open, muddy wells. Villagers pride themselves on their simple life, the purity of their food, and on what they believe to be their exceptional toughness and good health.

But a trained observer might perceive much room for improvement in the general health of Kishan Garhi. The great majority of villagers suffer chronically from dysentery and from trachoma. Dysentery is readily communicated to the mouth either directly by hands soiled with fecal matter, or indirectly by perpetual clouds of flies from the feces which lie exposed in the village lanes. The first of a life-long series of eye infections is passed on to each new infant before his eyes are fully open. The vision of many adults is seriously impaired. In addition, nearly one in five villagers suffers from malaria. Epidemics of cholera and smallpox have taken a large toll of lives, while typhoid, gonorrhea, and tuberculosis still flourish endemically. Deficiencies in the standard village diet are evidenced in the high frequency of boils, skin and eye ailments, lack of a appetite, general fatigue, and in the slow healing of simple injuries, even under medication.

In seeking treatment for these and other diseases, the residents of Kishan Garhi have at their disposal both traditional methods of treatment and the services of western medical practitioners. Western facilities have been provided by the government, by Christian missions, and by a few private practitioners, and have existed in all large towns and cities of the Ganges Valley for more than fifty years. Yet they have hardly touched most of the villages. In the lives of most villagers, clinics serve as momentary stopping places on the sick man's pilgrimage from one indigenous practitioner to another, and hospitals serve all too frequently as the last resorts of the dying. Many elaborate scientific facilities in the area are unused today or are used in bits and fragments which rarely effect cure, and tend rather to vitiate faith in the techniques themselves. Even assuming that an increase in clinics and dispensaries of the present type would have some value—an assumption that seems contrary to fact—the cost of such an increase would be far more than any government or charitable organization could support.

The facilities of Western medicine are largely ignored by the inhabitants of Kishan Garhi, but indigenous folk-medicine— magical, sacred, and secular—flourishes in every village of northern India. In terms of numbers of patients, amount of expenditure, and frequency of use, patronage of indigenous medicine surpasses that of Western medicine one hundredfold. Although the customs and tenets of indigenous medicine are generally at variance with those of Western medicine, some indigenous practitioners working in cities appropriate certain palliatives or paraphernalia from Western medicine and live well on their trade. Villagers will cheerfully pay a rural wizard for the utterance of a spell and give high reward to an urban practitioner who promises extravagant results from the hypodermic injection of what is actually plain water. However, the same villagers seem unwilling to take pills from a Western-type dispensary unless the pills are given free. Western medicine sits outside the door of the village, dependent upon governmental subsidy and foreign alms for its slim existence.

The Situation: Organization of the Village and Medical Practice

For a period of fourteen months during 1950-52, the writer lived in Kishan Garhi, making an anthropological study of village social organization.[2] Experiences with the villagers during the course of this study made me vividly aware that there was both a need and an active demand for more effective means of dealing with disease. Hindu peasants

[2]Field study was supported by an Area Research Training Fellowship granted by the Social Science Research Council. The writer is directly indebted to Dr John B. Wyon for proposing the medical exploration and for carrying it out with great zeal. For comments and suggestions on this paper, thanks are due to Mrs Gitel P. Steed, to Mr Albert Mayer, and to many other helpful readers.

brought written reports on their own blood counts, urine analyses, chest X-ray plates, and numerous unfilled prescriptions for foreign medicines; they begged me to help them to decide what they should do next. Many villagers were surprised and disappointed when they discovered that I would not perform surgical operations, that my first-aid medical kit contained none of those prized Western machines—the stethoscope, the ophthalmoscope, and especially the hypodermic needle. These and many more devices of scientific medicine are known and desired.

An exploratory effort

After six months in Kishan Garhi, I was able to enlist the cooperation of a young English physician who was then in the area. To see at first hand what happens when Western medicine is brought directly to the village, we set up a small clinic to run for one week. We publicized our project in advance. We then tried to present western medicine in its most favourable light: patients were dealt with carefully as individuals of equal worth; accurate diagnostic techniques were made available; medicines were offered at cost rates far below those prevailing on the open market; examination, diagnosis, and dressings were given free. The people of the village were encouraged to see how the doctor worked. They were helped to understand the doctor's diagnoses both through immediate explanations and through illustrated talks given later by the writer. Beyond his clinical hours, the doctor participated in many informal gatherings throughout the village. Villagers expressed their liking for his personal manner and their praise for the excellence of his skill.

Yet the results of this brief exploration in Kishan Garhi differed little from the response to western medicine which has been so familiar in other clinics in rural India. Persons soon flocked into the clinic to receive simple palliatives for such complaints as headache, toothache, and inflamed eyes. But out of 150 sick persons examined, barely a dozen were willing to pay in advance for even sample doses of the effective medicines which the doctor had prescribed to cure the causes of their ailments. The doctor was obliged to spend nearly half of his clinical hours in coaxing the patients to pay the tiny amounts charged for medicines in order that the clinic might support itself. Most of the patients pleaded false poverty and begged to be given medicines free. On the other hand, some poor patients put substantial amount of money into the doctor's hand, demanding that he give them only the finest medicines along with a money-back guarantee of certain cure.

At many points, too, the doctor was impeded in his work because of having to disengage the patients, for purposes of individual examination, from the many anxious family members who accompanied them. Frustrating situations frequently arose in which people begged for medicine which then went unused. One Brahmin girl, for example, was suffering the chills and fevers of acute malaria during the doctor's visit. The girl's father and her father's brothers came repeatedly to beg that the doctor give her quinine. The doctor sold a full course of quinine pills to the men but discovered three days later that none of the quinine had been permitted to reach the girl. An old widowed aunt who ruled the women of that family had voiced objections, and the whole matter of Western treatment was dropped.

A follow-up study of the clinic's patients was even more discouraging. After the doctor's departure, nearly all of those few persons who had begun his treatments soon fell back upon their indigenous practices and practitioners. The only wage-earning son of one poor labourer, a neighbour of the writer, was diagnosed by the doctor as tubercular. Calcium lactate and shark liver oil were prescribed, and a supply was arranged for the boy at nominal cost. A few days after the doctor's departure, the labourer went deeply into debt in order to buy for the boy a preparation of honey and gold which had been made and guaranteed by an indigenous specialist. Among the others, only two villagers ever sought to obtain any of the more extensive treatments which the doctor had advised them to seek from urban hospitals; those two did so only after receiving repeated reassurances and specific help from the writer.

We had brought Western medicine to the village and the village was full of sick people, but Western medicine did not reach the sick. Why did villagers not accept the doctor's instructions? Why did they not seem to trust him? Why wouldn't villagers shoulder even slight financial responsibility for their own cures? Why did they ultimately prefer treatment by less effective means? Here again was the old carpenter's paradox: "Western medicines are best, but doctors never cure anybody."

The villagers' apathetic responses to the exploratory clinic sharpened the challenge, but in themselves suggest only negative ways out of the dilemma. The exploration had at least narrowed the issues and eliminated some of the presumed difficulties. Difficulties evidently did not lie merely in the physical distance of Western facilities from the village, nor in any personal aloofness on the part of the doctor. They did not lie simply in peasant fears of something unknown, nor in objections to scientific techniques, nor in careless diagnosis, nor in high costs—faults which are commonly cited to explain the failure of Western medicine to take hold in rural regions of India. While the brevity of the exploratory clinic at Kishan Garhi cannot be discounted as influencing the outcome, it seems clear that other and more powerful factors were at work. Even allowing for the impossibility of demonstrating many cures in so short a time, the significant difficulties encountered by this clinic were identical with those which continue to trouble many long-established centres of Western medicine in India. These difficulties require explanation.

Answers to the dilemma seemed to lie not in gross technical matters, but rather in the system of interpersonal relations. Trust, responsibility, charity, power, respect—these are the issues on which failure turned. These are not technical issues but issues which concern the cultural definition of medical roles. The solution of the dilemma and the keys to greater success seemed to consist in developing an acceptable social place in the village for Western medicine.

To discover the reasons behind the difficulties met by the exploratory clinic at Kishan Garhi—and behind the failure of Western medicine to take hold in rural India generally—we must understand the nature of the existing social and medical institutions of the village and how these institutions influence the manner in which the villager perceives the Western medical practitioner.

The social world of the Indian village

Kinship. Village society in India, like most non-European societies of the world today, is very largely a familial society. The groups within which people can always trust each other and cooperate are limited to groups such as the household, the lineage of common descent and, in northern India, the network of families in different villages that are related by marriage. Fellow members of such familial groupings must help each other by extensive gifts, by loans often without interest, and by first preference in all economic dealings. They must give absolute mutual support in case of trouble. Members of the different lineages that have existed together for centuries in the village of Kishan Garhi tend to regard each other as quasi-kinsmen and may address each other politely as "father's brother," "brother's son," and the like. But such extended relationships are never really so certain, never so free from the fear of treachery as are genuine family relationships.

Beyond the circle of his own true family, the individual must assume the world to be indifferent to his welfare, for it is made up of other closed kin groups, each constituted like his own and each furthering the interests of none but its own members. A villager does not ordinarily dare to venture out of his village for any important purpose unless he knows where he will find a bed and who will give him bread, unless he knows that he will be able to achieve his purpose through his own relatives or through people of his own village with whom he has some strong, dependent tie.

Some special characteristics of the northern Hindu village are that its kinship groups, with all the loyalties they command, are so small and so numerous, and that they so frequently lack any single leader. Families are themselves sharply divided for almost all activities into separate male and female worlds, each having its separate structure of power. Inside the village of Kishan Garhi, a man can count an average of fewer than twenty persons, both male and female, within the widest limits of his lineage group. A village of average size will contain at least ten—Kishan Garhi contains forty-six such ultimate familial groupings. Each lineage group is totally unconnected by marriage or descent with any other lineage in the village, and each is wholly distinct in responsibility. Each gives almost limitless rewards to its members and makes almost limitless demands upon them.

Such extreme subdivision of the people of a single village into a large number of discrete kinship groups puts great obstructions in the way of wider cooperation. Individuals cannot easily form new relationships. If villagers who are not kinsmen try to band together out of friendship or even out of vital interest in some common task, they often risk suspicion of being disloyal to their own familial group. "The village is full of dishonest people, full of thieves," villagers frequently warned me. When a new financial agreement requiring cooperation and trust is proposed, even if its weight is trivial, any safeguards are likely to be felt necessary: witnesses may be called to listen to repetitions of the terms; a single coin may be given, binding giver and receiver in a sacred contract to fulfil all the terms of their agreement. Outside the family, all things must be made doubly sure.

Caste. A second special characteristic of Hindu village society provides a partial answer to the problems raised by the first. This is the use of ranking, or hierarchy, as a major element in relationships among persons and kinship groups. In Kishan Garhi the multiplicity of forty-six closed and autonomous lineages is appreciably reduced by a ranked ordering into twenty-four castes. Each kinship group in Kishan Garhi is merged into one of the local caste groups, and each local caste group is part of a larger regional caste.

Each local caste group in the village holds an approximate caste rank, and holds a stable place in one of the four still larger ranked blocs of castes—Brahmin, high, low, and untouchable. The local ranking of the castes and blocs of castes correlates in a general way with differences of wealth and power but more precisely with certain observances between the castes. Ways in which people can eat together, sit together, or address one another serve continually to reaffirm the order of caste ranking which is generally recognized in Kishan Garhi. Thus, a member of the highest Brahmin or priestly caste must be greeted by a person of lower-caste rank with the sentence, "We should touch your feet, honourable learned man." A Brahmin when so addressed must reply with a blessing, "Live happily." A Brahmin must always be seated at the head of any cot when other castes are present, and only members of the high castes may share the cot with him. A Brahmin can eat only those foods that have been prepared in certain ways by members of certain other high or "clean" castes. Each caste below the Brahmin also has its special position in the system of ritual and etiquette. Each has its honorific title, the main landlord caste being called by a title that is identical with one name of God, while the lowest sweeper of latrines has the title "headman" or "sergeant."

Most families are obliged to give honorific service to certain families of higher castes and are privileged to demand honorific service from certain families of lower castes. The nature of these honorific services is fixed in tradition for each caste. Some castes have the traditional duty of following certain menial occupations, some of practicing particular crafts. Other castes traditionally grow food; others engage in trade; others conduct religious rituals; and still others wield power and govern. From each of its servant families of lower caste, the patron household may demand some essential, unique service; from each of its patron families of higher caste, the servant may claim a dole of bread upon the performance of the service, a fixed quantity of grain twice during the year and many other kinds of assistance whenever necessity arises. "The point of the whole system," villagers told me, "is to make sure that there will always be someone whom you can depend upon." Without the caste system of honorific rituals and services which arranges everyone in higher and lower ranks, many villagers fear that their society would have no order at all.

Individuals are born into families that occupy particular caste and service positions. Differences in individual achievement of wealth, power, and ability may be acknowledged, but such achievements remain irrelevant to caste; the ritualized caste position into which an individual is born always continues to affect most of his relationships with his fellow villagers. Regardless of a villager's personal qualities, regardless of his learning to practise some new or educated profession, he will continue to receive the formal treatment required by etiquette for all members of his caste. The poorest man of the village, if he is a Brahmin by caste, will still be asked to sit at the head of the cot; the wealthiest man of the village, if he is a lowly leather-worker by caste, still sits on the floor or stands respectfully at a distance; and the cleverest man of the village, if he is a sweeper by caste, still lingers below in the street.

Such extreme stability of caste and kinship leaves individuals fairly free to think and to believe as they please. Thus, within one family there may be devotees of as many different gods as there are members; one member of the family may know nothing and care nothing about the gods worshipped by another member. But the requirements of active loyalty to family welfare and observance of intercaste etiquette place severe limits on an individual's social scope. An individual is not free to form friendships or to develop any personal alliances which conflict with the interests of his own caste and kinship group. Beyond the large family and its caste, the only approved and reliable relationships are the formal cross-caste ties between high patrons and low servants.

Outside the village. When villagers must deal with strangers, they have their choice of including the stranger either in a family or in an intercaste type of relationship. If strangers are thrown together anonymously as in a bus or in an urban shop and if their common activities are casual ones, then they may classify each other by relative age as pseudokinsmen. Ultimately they may trace more specific kin-like connections through villages with which they share real family relationships.

But when villagers must deal in important ways with outsiders who are more powerful than themselves—with lawyers, officials, urban creditors, and the like—then they generally attempt to extend upward a caste-like form of relationship. Whenever possible, intermediaries are used who have some genuine, stable tie both with the villager and with the powerful outsider. When intermediaries cannot be found, then direct flattery and courtesy may be used to simulate obligations between persons of high and low castes where such obligations have not actually existed before. When intermediary negotiations, flattery, and hospitality are rejected or prove insufficient —a situation that often arises in relations with outside government officials—then payment of money remains almost the only way in which the villager can ensure his own interests.

But outside the family and village, monetary gifts cannot

create immutable, sacred obligations as they do inside. Bribes have only temporary effects which fluctuate with the amount given and with the expectation of more. The poor villager is rarely in a position to give enough money to guarantee more than momentary favour from an official or poor goods from an urban shopkeeper. He gives petty amounts, despises the taker, and suspects the worst of what he gets in return.

The people of Kishan Garhi thus recognize three great social realms; that of kinship and family, which is an area controlled by limitless demands and mutual trust; that of the village and caste, which is an area in part controlled by particular obligations and formal respect; and that of the outside world, of government and the market place, which is an area controllable only by money and power—things which the villager scarcely possesses.

For the people of Kishan Garhi, Western medicine has existed up to now only in the third or outer realm beyond family and beyond caste and village. It has remained, therefore, in the realm of contrived dependency and fundamental distrust. Until the day when the relations of the inner and outer social realms may be differently defined and perceived, Western medicine seems doomed to languish. If Western medicine is to be established not merely in, but as a part of, the middle or inner realms of village society, it must be made to fit the organizational forms of that society. To illuminate these problems of social adaptation in more specific terms it is instructive to examine the indigenous medical services of the village. Their problems are not dissimilar to those confronting Western medicine, and they have solved these problems of social adaptation with noted success.

Indigenous medical practice

Indigenous village medical services are overwhelmingly preferred to Western medicine. Their strength is due in large part to their successful adaptation to the fundamentals of village social organization. The social roles of an indigenous practitioner embody certain elements which no practitioner in rural India can afford to ignore. Some of these elements present incompatible contrasts, while others present rather close parallels with the position and behaviour of the physician in Western society. Whether these role elements are similar or dissimilar, villagers have specific expectations based on their life-long experiences with relationships between therapist and patient. These expectations affect their comprehension of Western medicine and their initial reaction to it.

Indigenous medical specialists in an Indian village such as Kishan Garhi are extremely varied. They include priests, exorcists, magicians, and secular physicians, as well as numberless minor technicians such as bone-setters, charm-sellers, cuppers, cultists, surgeons, and thorn-pullers. Like all other persons in traditional Indian society, specialists must occupy relatively higher or lower positions in the village hierarchy of caste and power. Despite great diversity of content among the medical theories and practices of the many specialists, the principle of hierarchical ranking imparts a certain similarity to the whole array of specialized roles.

The family and medicine. Specialized medical services are always rendered within the context of the family, and each family tends to occupy a definite position in the village hierarchy. Village families do not isolate an ailing member, as is often the case in the Western world, but rather envelop him. Few villagers would think of seeking medical treatment of any consequence without taking family members along with them. Reciprocally, the writer has seen indigenous medical specialists demand that family members be present. The duties of the attending family members are to protect and gain attention for the weakened person, to help the specialist in his work (since ritual rules of intercaste pollution would sometimes hinder a specialist's treatment), to remember directions for home treatment, and to stand security as a group for the costs of the treatment. The larger family in the village thus does what in Western society would be done respectively by receptionist, lawyer, nurse, orderly, secretary, and bondsman. It is difficult to see how the Western type of medical practitioners in Indian villages could manage to do without such essential family contributions. To use them, of course, is to abandon certain occidental conceptions of privacy and individual responsibility in favour of group responsibility.

Lines of power within village families also affect the utilization of medical treatment. Whatever the treatment may be that is suggested by a specialist, it will be mediated and enforced, or perhaps modified or rejected, according to who is most influential in that particular family. The exploratory clinic in Kishan Garhi encountered this problem directly when courses of treatment were thoroughly "sold" to some members of a family but were later rejected by others who had controlling voices in the family. Since families in villages of northern India frequently lack lines of authority that are obvious to nonmembers, and since the social worlds of men and women are sharply divided, authoritative communication by the medical specialist must aim to include all important family members of both sexes, if it is to be effective. As will be seen, the techniques of diagnosis and treatment used by certain religious exorcists in Kishan Garhi do in fact encourage many members of the family to participate in the cure under the direct guidance of the exorcist.

Resulting in part from this diffusion of power within most village groups is the fact that individuals of the same village—even of the same family—often hold highly varied medical beliefs and follow widely divergent practices. To the same sort of cut or boil, one man will apply a hot mango leaf; his neighbour will apply a paste of wheat flour; his father will apply a poultice of cow dung, while his wife continues to believe firmly in the efficacy of plain butter. If the wife is under the thumb of her husband's mother, then that matriarch's proposal for a magical sweeping and blowing may be added to the other treatments. In case of conflicting ideas, all advisers' suggestions for treatment may be applied in succession, or even all at once. Butter, dung, flour, and leaf may be simply laid on in successive layers—a typical solution to the problem of insistent but varied individual beliefs. Standardized medical treatments scarcely exist, while the internal divisions present in village and family structure are of no help in developing such treatments. Since some kinds of Western medicine need to be applied alone and exclusively the problem of finding an authoritative role for such treatment becomes all the more acute. Until such a role is found, Western medicine must reconcile itself to existing in dilution along with its many competitors.

Magical medicine. In Kishan Garhi and other villages, magical medicine comprises a body of mechanical techniques that can be directed against invading spirits. Its techniques include the wearing of protective strings and amulets and the expulsion of invading spirits by rituals of exorcism. Most young children wear two or three charms purchased from magicians —silver moon pendants, small red beads, capsules containing written spells, tiny bags containing iron, grain, and so on— tied around their necks or wrists. Adults may also wear charms designed for specific ailments which they fear may strike them, or from which they already suffer. When acute infections require that a spirit be exorcized, the magician blows on the infected part through a tube and sweeps it with a broom made of certain leaves, at the same time whispering his secret verbal formula until the spirit departs. In contrast to the mere writing of a prescription by the Western doctor, the charm or the performance given by the village magician has an objective existence. Its effect is inherent, and villagers say that they can feel immediate improvement. The magical exorcist is therefore paid a few coins at once for his service, according to his standard low rates.

Blowing, sweeping, and the wearing of charms are appreciated by many villagers because such techniques are painless, quick, and safe. Magical exorcism has the special advantage that if the infection has been caused by a spiritual invasion, the spirit can simply be invited to depart without creating any further trouble. The same spirit is likely to become angered if direct medication is applied to his abode in the body. Only if medication can be understood as cleaning a wound rather than as killing the infection, can it remain theoretically compatible with magical exorcism. Thus, one priest of Kishan Garhi vigorously "cleaned" his son's dog-bite wound with potassium permanganate which I had given him; on alternate days, without conflict, he had it swept and blown by a magician.

But smallpox, a disease that is thought to result from an invasion by the goddess Mata, must be treated circumspectly through magical and religious techniques alone. If vaccination

or medication of the skin were applied to any child of the
village at a time when Mata was also present in his body, the
touchy goddess would be angered and would surely kill or
maim those victims whom she had already seized. Government
vaccinators ordinarily succeed in inoculating a high proportion
of new infants on their visits to Kishan Garhi. However, once
during my stay the vaccinator arrived there on his regular
circuit when two or three children were sick with chickenpox.
The parents of the unvaccinated new babies mistook chickenpox for smallpox, were greatly alarmed, and paid the vaccinator to go away without inoculating anyone.

Despite such obvious differences and conflicts between
magical belief and Western medical theory, the social role of
the medical magician in Kishan Garhi has a good deal in
common with the social role of the druggist in Western society.
The techniques purveyed by both kinds of specialists are, in
their respective societies, popular, mechanical, and impersonal.
Magic treatments in this Hindu village society, like patent
medicines in Western society, can be dispensed by persons of
almost any social rank and can be applied with little deference
to hierarchical differences. Both can be bought and sold much
as are other commodities on the market.

But these very similarities lead us to take note of a great
contrast between the Western world and rural India in attitudes towards technical activities. In the Indian village merely
technical and petty commercial activities are of distinctly low
rank; in no case do they impart any elevation to those who
practice them. In Western society, elaborate technical competence in the performance of his professional role actually
becomes one chief basis of the doctor's high professional prestige and authority. If the prestige of Western medicine in a
village such as Kishan Garhi had to depend on its techniques
alone, its prestige would be no greater than that of barbering
or shopkeeping—no greater than that of magic itself, which is
a relatively low craft commanding little respect. Such low
prestige would be incompatible with the authority and confidence required for the more complex and serious kinds of
medical therapy. Western medicine clearly cannot establish its
full worth in an Indian village through technical performance
alone.

Religious exorcism. Certain religious exorcists in Kishan Garhi stand a notch above the technicians of magical medicine. Their wizardry comprises a rather more difficult art, an art that is inspired and actuated through religious devotion and that is often symbolized by the artist's slightly wild appearance or peculiar manner of dress. As professionals who trade on their intangible talents and on their ability to impress their clients, these specialists have something in common not only with modern faith healers in the West, but also with many Western medical doctors of an older time.

Would-be practitioners of religious exorcism must first become "devotees" of a suitable god or goddess whom they will later be able to control by singing special hymns. Devotees may be recruited from many different castes above untouchable rank, although exorcists of higher caste tend to be most successful in developing a large clientele. Learning of the particular arts of exorcism usually descends within particular castes and lineages. In Kishan Garhi certain families of the priestly, weaving, and leather-working castes carry on the traditions of exorcism, and each controls distinct gods and goddesses. An initiated exorcist is called "wise man." As a sideline, he often practices certain complex magical crafts, such as divining the names of thieves and locating stolen property.

A villager may call on a religious exorcist when he suffers from certain bodily ailments or psychic aberrations, or from any unusually suspicious series of external calamities affecting himself or his animals. The patient visits, or summons to his home, from one to a whole team of performers, who often reside at a great distance. The patient's entire family may be required to assist in the cure over a long period of time, preparing altars, sacrifices, or feasts, and giving clues to the exorcist that may help him identify the troublesome ghost or godling. The exorcists invoke their deity to drive other infesting spirits away. During the treatment the patient demonstrates his condition and its spiritual cause by one of several forms of emotional agitation or trance. The effectiveness of cure is believed to depend on the disposition of the spirits, the devotion of the performer, and the intensity of the performance. Its result is quickly known.

Payment to these religious exorcists works by an explicit

principle quite different from that by which magicians are paid in the village and from that by which legitimate physicians are ordinarily paid in Western society. The more the exorcist is paid, the better his curing is expected to be. Naturally, a large fee is promised in advance. Gifts of food are sometimes required to precede the treatment and continue at intervals throughout its course. Ultimately, however, depending on the results, a final cash price may be modified by negotiation. By contrast, legitimate medicine practiced according to Western customs usually aims to standardize its techniques and to reduce costs as much as possible.

Carrying over the "more-the-better" principle of payment to their contacts with physicians trained in Western medicine, villagers of my acquaintance often felt disappointed and distrustful when they learned how cheap and simple such physicians' treatments were. Thus, the doctor at the government dispensary nearest Kishan Garhi was considered unhelpful by the villagers because he usually ordered his pharmacist to dispense the inexpensive remedies subsidized by government funds. A persistent rumour held that the doctor would give better, more costly medicines and more energetic treatment if he were approached and tipped privately after hours. There was no direct evidence to support the rumour; indeed, the doctor was ready at any time to provide such a service as injections of penicillin for all patients who needed them and who were able to pay the costs. It appeared that his efficiency and thrift were perceived as unhelpfulness and had also served to brand the doctor as corrupt.

Western medicine might gain much and lose little if the asking prices of aspirin and bicarbonate of soda, for example, were adjusted upward to create an aura of quality that would engender confidence in the curative value of these useful products. It is true that the enhanced fee is a device that is well-known to charlatans both in India and the West, but it also has its legitimate applications.

Sacerdotal medicine. Domestic priests, who are recruited only from among the highest of Brahmin caste, engage in a purely religious medical practice as a part of the profession of priesthood. Priests advise their cients to perform certain religious rituals as means of obtaining good health, prosperity, and children. They prescribe similar rituals as cures for illness that are believed to have been caused by religious laxity or immorality. Priestly prescriptions combine a limited number of fixed ritual elements; making pilgrimages, bathing in the Ganges pouring water at the roots of sacred trees, praying, conducting sacrifices, offering charitable contributions to priests and beggars. Priests in Kishan Garhi, along with their domestic ritual duties, also give astrological advice, which helps their clients time their activities according to astral omens so as to avoid illness and other misfortunes.

Such priestly medical practice is regarded as ancient and sacred, as notably more dignified than the acquired arts of the religious exorcist. Unlike the Western doctor however, the priest only has authority to advise ritual treatment and to enunciate unintelligible Sanskrit formulas. He possesses no reputation for wisdom in solving a diffuse range of problems, and through his practice he gains no individual authority. Priestly emphasis on fixed formulas conflicts strongly, furthermore, with an inquiring, pragmatic approach to health problems.

The ambiguity of the priest's medical role is brought out clearly by the manner in which he extracts a living from it. In each medical prescription he includes a redundant charitable gift—food, money, or a cow—for himself. For giving astrological advice, as for performing domestic rituals, he demands piece payments. A few of his pious clients may voluntarily send him food stuffs each month on the day of the full or the dark of the moon, but much of his remuneration is in the form of fixed grain dues, paid after the spring harvest. To collect his dues of unthreshed grain, the priest must hurry to his client's threshing floor whenever he is called and must carry the bundle of grain on his head. For such servile dependence on the farmers' charity the priest is mildly despised. While piece payments or the familiar fixed levy in kind might seem useful devices for financing a village doctor in India, the low prestige that results from such financing would be likely to undermine the authority necessary for the effective practice of modern medicine. And as will be seen below, the highest kinds of village curing require no such debasing devices for their maintenance.

Snake-bite curing. The two snake-bite curers of Kishan Garhi are not professional specialists, but they are among the most respected and trusted of all the local medical practitioners. They are respected because of their high ethics, their self-sacrifice, and their devotion to philanthropic duty. Anyone who is considered sincere and fit—usually a person of fairly high caste and wealth—may apprentice himself to a teacher who knows one of the secret spells that neutralize snake poison To prove his fitness, the apprentice must cook his own food, fast, and sleep on the floor for a year. Then, after the performance of many rites, he may be admitted to knowledge of the sacred spell. He is henceforth bound to give free treatment to anyone who sends for his help. He must drop his plough in the middle of his field, or rise swiftly in the middle of the night to go at once, no matter when or to what distance he is called. From the moment he is called he may eat or drink nothing until a cure has been effected. By no means are all of the bites which he treats inflicted by poisonous snakes; and many of his patients do, of course, recover. The curer is not allowed to accept food, water, or anything else by way of payment. His only earthly rewards are the praise and respect and token gifts which are later given him. There are religious rewards, too, and the patient's grateful family assures the curer that he has earned great merit for himself, to be reaped both in this life and in the next.

"Your doctors," a villager told me after watching an arduous snake-bite cure which had taken the whole of the previous night, "can never do anything like that." The Hindu snake-bite curer's great prestige resembles the prestige accorded medicine, ethically the highest profession in Western society. But while the Western doctor often lays his Hippocratic oath aside, the Hindu snake-bite curer acts out his dedication in every treatment. The Hindu curer's prestige depends, be it noted, not upon his skill as such but upon his spiritual power gained through piety. This piety consists both in his austerities and in his giving service without tangible reward. Psychologically, one might say, it consists in creating a sense of immeasurable gratitude on the part of his clients. Practitioners of Western medicine might wish to hold a place in the village that would grant their work the prestige and authority of the snake-bite curer, but they would have literally to fast and sleep on the floor to attain such a place, according to the social logics of the villagers.

Secular medicine. The indigenous secular physicians of India share some of the snake-bite curer's piety but operate on a more self-supporting basis. They are the most highly trained of all the indigenous specialists. "You needn't worry about medical care here," a man of Kishan Garhi told me early in my stay. "We have many clever country physicians—*hakims* and *vaids*—in all the villagers here about. We villagers go to them, not to doctors." The *hakim* and *vaid* share many things with the Western doctor—a learned tradition, relative lack of limitation by religious and magical formulas, high respect, and economic solvency. Interestingly enough, the indigenous Hindu physician, like the Western doctor, often has the status of an outsider to the villages in which he practices. But, as will be apparent, the indigenous physician's relationships to his clients, which are the key to his success, differ sharply in certain other ways from the relationships typical of most scientific medical practice in the West.

Persons who become *hakims* and *vaids* carry on their practice as a kind of noblesse oblige. Recruits to country medicine in the villages around Kishan Garhi come from the highest castes and higher economic classes of rural society. By origin they are often the people who reside in the high fortress or in the great brick house above the ordinary clutter of mud huts. For the most part they are landlords, big tenants, or wealthy priests, or merchants. Their medical training sets them still farther apart from ordinary people, since most of them study outside the village for at least a year in order to earn the certificate of a school and the government's licence to practice simple medicine. These Hindu physicians study medical texts, those who study in the unani system being called *hakims* and those who study in the ayurvedic system being called *vaids*. In practice, the two systems differ little. The ayurvedic and Unani texts are respected; neither is in itself regarded as especially sacred. Still, the high original status of the *hakim* or *vaid*, coupled with his literacy and urbanization, creates a gulf between him and his patient which requires explicit handling.

The first device that the *hakim* or *vaid* uses to bridge the gulf of status between him and his patient is to cultivate a reputation for having a superior and penetrating—almost magical—knowledge of the body. This inspires the patient's confidence. The first thing that such a physician does by way of diagnosis is to grasp the patient's wrist. From the pulse—and from other astute observations which often go unnoticed—he tells everything. He asks no questions, or only indirect ones, for he is expected to know. One *hakim* in a village near Kishan Garhi had the reputation of being able to tell the contents of the stomach by feeling the pulse. He would take the patient's hand and inform him whether he had eaten wheat, barley, or millet bread at his last meal, and whether he had eaten the bread together with sweet milk or with curd. Another *vaid* was credited with being able to predict anyone's life-span to the day and hour. On one occasion, he felt a very old woman's pulse and said she would die at noon that same day, all treatment being futile. Villagers swear that the woman died on the hour, as if by command. Of course, a Western doctor's diagnostic skills and devices would occasionally permit him to play out much the sort of drama if he chose to do so and similarly to create a reputation of power. Villagers' fascination with the diagnostic and predictive powers of thermometers and stethoscopes has already forced many indigenous physicians to add these to their kits, even though they may understand little about the actual use of such instruments.

A second special device which helps the *hakim* or *vaid* create confidence—to make himself a dependable man—is the theory, similar to the theory which surrounds the snake-bite curer, to the effect that he is practising medicine for piety, for the sake of enhancing his own religious merit. The indigenous physician often seems to charge nothing for his skilled services. Indeed, he is felt to be giving his services as charity. Ragged villagers must therefore approach the lordly, white-clothed physician in a manner of worship. It is usual for the *hakim* or *vaid* to hold free clinic each morning at which he advises supplicants as to the diet and regime that may be proper for their ailments and the season. The poor most often seek attention at these early clinics, weaker persons being carried to the physician's house on the back of stronger family members. For the physical labour of walking to a wealthier patient's home, the *hakim* or *vaid* charges a substantial fee amounting to a sum two or three times the daily wage of a labourer. One well-known *hakim* came from two miles away to call on a lone and injured landless labourer of Kishan Garhi; his refusal to accept payment from the lame labourer added a great deal to that *hakim's* reputation for selfless piety. It is believed safe for a poor patient to deal with a rich physician who is also pious, for then the physician will not exploit the poor man.

The pharmaceutical arrangements of the *hakim* or *vaid* are a third device which, perhaps even more than piety and skill, contributes to the financial and social strength of his practice. Since such a physician does not charge directly for his treatment, he must obtain most of his income through the sale of medicines. He himself travels to distant markets to purchase what are believed to be rare materials. He himself grinds and mixes the materials. Then when he wraps his powders in small packets and retails them at high prices, he creates an illusion of value and a feeling of confidence in the treatment, here exploiting a logic much like that used by the religious exorcist.

But the *hakim* goes still farther and guarantees his medicines. If a medicine is very expensive, the *hakim* may ask for its cost in advance, or may take a small initial payment so as to seal a contract for full later payment by the patient. Such guarantees constitute acceptance of the patient's dependency, and at the same time give the patient a sense of control over the high physician. Any suspicion that the physician is making some economic gain by exploiting the patient's illness is removed from the therapeutic situation by such a contract or guarantee. The physician assumes full responsibility; the patient is reassured; and the two parties are united in a set of mutual obligations, recognizing their respective positions of dominance and subordination.

Such a method of charging only for proven results does require that prices be high and that the physician make a certain capital investment in his patients at the start. In other words, such finances are speculative. To collect his bills after the cure, the *hakim* or *vaid* needs to have intimate knowledge of relationships among the families and caste groups in the neighbourhood where he practises. A satisfied local patient who may desire treatment for his family members in the future may usually be depended on to pay ultimately. When the patient is unknown or comes from far away, he usually guarantees his good faith by approaching the physician through an intermediary from among the physician's own kinsmen or from among the physician's servants of other castes. The *hakim's* effective reliance on the particular group connections of his patients contrasts strongly once again with the Western doctor's characteristic habit of dealing with his patients as responsible individuals.

Some *hakims* and *vaids* pursue philanthropy almost as far as the snake-bite curer, and treat patients entirely without discussing charges. A villager explained the finances of one such philanthropic *hakim* as follows: "He never takes money from anyone. If you want to, you can give him something, but he never asks. He is concerned only with curing people. People who are cured just put money into his pocket or go to his house and give the money there. He is like a saint." Thus, the patient can also gain the merits of charity by gifts which help to further the physician's pious work. Unsolicited gifts made to the *hakim* or *vaid* are thought to assure his goodwill and careful attention to the patient; they are considered to be more effective than payment of charges. Several young men told me that they longed to have enough money to be able to establish themselves in the virtuous and often remunerative profession of indigenous medicine.

The obvious prosperity of the *hakims* and *vaids* near Kishan Garhi and the enthusiasm of their patients testify that the system of spontaneous giving can be a profitable one. There is nothing in the techniques of Western medicine that would make a similar set of mutual obligations between a Western-trained doctor and his village patients impossible, or financially and therapeutically less effective.

The five type of village medical specializations described above do not by any means exhaust the variety of medical resources that can be found in an average village of the Upper Ganges Valley. Kishan Garhi is served by at least twice that number of medical specialists. The roles of the others are governed by principles only slightly different from those thus far cited. Each specialist has his approximate place in the hierarchy of caste and individual power, and each has his appropriate means for solving the problems of that place. Without detailing other varieties, let us take one more look at the Western type of doctor as he is seen through village eyes.

The Western type of doctor and village society

The doctor, even more than the *hakim* or *vaid*, has always been an outsider who stands far above village society. He has had no part in the common understandings of the life in any village, but is rather a participant in Europeanized culture. Whether he is Indian or European, he must speak English for he must have received his medical training through the medium of English. He would never have learned his profession were he not a member of the wealthiest class of people in the district, were his own family not one of wealthy landlords, moneylenders, or government officials. In village language, the doctor is always a sahib—a "gentleman." Persons of the "gentlemanly" class are often respected as being above the village and, therefore, as being above the petty, corrupting influences of village society. But they are never looked upon as people with whom and ordinary villager dares to establish a relationship of intimacy or mutual trust. The "gentlemanly" class as whole is believed to exploit villagers by means of its technical superiority and by its possession of special political power. There is little in the usual role assumed by the Western doctor which would tend to disassociate him, in the eyes of the villagers, from that class.

In Western society any differences of social standing that may exist between the doctor and his patient are generally considered irrelevant to the therapeutic relationship. The doctor strives to discuss the medical problem with a maximum of rationality, inquiring confidentially and arriving at a diagnosis dictated in that particular situation by the doctor's technical knowledge and authority. The relationship may be brief, often coming to an end with the doctor's writing a prescription and the patient's paying the bill, sometimes in advance of cure. Such arrangements are workable and may even be necessary within the mobile structure of modern Western society. They are not necessary parts of medicine as such, nor are they appropriate to the social organization of the Indian village. They are not easily understood by the villager.

In the exploratory clinic in Kishan Garhi, Western doctor

attempted to ignore the general inequality of power and rank which separated him from his village patient, as democratic foreigners often do. Since the villagers regarded the doctor as a person immeasurably higher than themselves and unalterably beyond their control, it is not surprising that many found the doctor's friendly equalitarian bedside manner threatening rather than reassuring.

"No small man would have a mighty friend if the two were not up to some mischief," a wise villager told me. The Western doctor's equalitarianism, even when it is accepted as concealing no sinister motive, denies to the villager that subordinate, dependent relationship in which alone he is accustomed to find emotional security when confronted with figures of authority. So long as the doctor denies the relevance of differences of social standing, he forfeits his opportunity to profit from the *hakim's* best device for creating confidence. When the doctor denies his own general superiority, he compromises his role as a reliable, compassionate person.

Furthermore, the doctor's "confidential" interview cuts out the possibility of negotiation with crucial members of the patient's family, members whose relations with the doctor may determine whether the treatment will be carried on or not, whether it will succeed or fail, and whether the bill will be paid. Next, the doctor's inquiring approach shatters faith in his competence, for the villager rather expects to be told what is wrong with him, as the *hakim* or *vaid* tells him by feeling his pulse.

Implicit in the role of the Western type of doctor is the assumption that his own known technical competence will itself carry a large part of the burden of establishing therapeutic trust. As noted above, technical competence is the chief basis of authority and trust in the lower forms of village magico-medical treatment, but is not the only basis for establishing interpersonal security in the higher forms of secular and religious therapy. If an outside doctor's great technical competence were in fact demonstrated to the satisfaction of the Indian villager, as it is already accepted by the Western patient, the villager would have all the more reason to feel uneasy about the possibility of the doctor's exploiting him, since the doctor, as a mere technician, will be bound by none of the usual bonds and sentiments that ordinarily operate to control persons at the top level of village society.

The Western doctor, like the doctor at the government dispensary nearest Kishan Garhi, usually deals in few medicines himself. He expresses his diagnosis in a written prescription which the village patient cannot read, and which the patient must have filled by a pharmacist in an urban shop or by a compounder attached to the clinic. In the eyes of the villager, who is used to the elaborate caste-defined division of labour, the doctor's prescription to the pharmacist suggests that the doctor has only limited skill, that he does not know himself how to make medicines, or that he considers such work trivial and beneath him. The village patient may then feel doubly exposed to cheating by the urban pharmacist, another technically superior urban person over whom the villager has no adequate means of social control. Village patients in the exploratory clinic often begged the doctor to treat them himself, however crudely, to give them medicine which he had prepared himself in preference to any other. In my own first-aid work, I found that a villager suffering chronically from toothache would wait weeks for me to bring him "with my own hand" aspirin tablets from a market place which he himself often visited, rather than risk a bargain with an unfamiliar shopkeeper over my written prescription.

Finally destroying the patient's confidence is the Western doctor's usual method of presenting a bill simply for his advice or for his treatment in advance of therapeutic results. Here is none of the faith-inspiring dedication of the village snake-bite curer or of the philanthropic *hakim*. Even looking at the matter technically, villagers argued, if the doctor is sure of his diagnosis and his prescription, then why should he object to payment after the success of the cure has been proved? If, on the other hand, the doctor is not sure, then how can the patient be sure? The doctor's demands to be paid for a mere technical performance are like the petty demands of the magician and the priest. At the same time, the doctor's diagnosis has none of the objective therapeutic value that inheres in the expressive treatment conducted by the magical and religious practitioners. One trusting patient at the exploratory clinic in Kishan Garhi loudly affirmed that the pain in his chest had been quite drawn out when the doctor applied his stethoscope; he was dismayed to learn that stethoscopy was only intended to discover, not to extract, the cause of the pain. Many other patients had to be told when to leave the clinic after receiving medicines, for they had experienced no immediate outward sign of cure. The patient who is required to pay the doctor before he has been cured is left with a sense of financial loss, suspicion of the doctor's moral integrity, and doubt about ever being cured.

In the clinic at Kishan Garhi, the doctor had tried to solve the problems of supply and payment by dispensing medicines himself at the lowest possible wholesale rates. "What kind of gentleman is this doctor?" asked one labourer. "He is not a gentleman, he is a sort of shopkeeper" was another villager's reply. When there was discussion of the possibility that the writer might set up a regular dispensary on the same basis, a village friend objected. "Surely you are not going to charge those little bits of money," he said. "That would be beneath your dignity." When sick people came to me from distant villages, promising me money if they were cured, people of Kishan Garhi frequently bid up their offers, insisting that the amount offered must be commensurate with my status and with what was felt to be the enormous probable value of my own unpriced, simple medicines.

IMPLICATIONS

Difficulties evident in the social and cultural conditions described above have in the past demoralized many workers trained in Western medicine. "You see," one skilled surgeon at a half empty city hospital said to me, "these villagers do not really want to be cured." More recently, among the more constructive medical workers, the persistent defeat of their efforts has forced them to conclude that Western medicine, if it is to be effective, must be brought directly to the villages. Only if Western medicine is established within the village, close to medical needs at their source, can it prove its worth on equal terms with indigenous medicine. Only then, these workers argue, can understanding of "scientific" practices and knowledge of "rational" preventive procedures have a chance to spread along with the curative techniques. Only when it is established within the village, will Western medicine have a chance of paying its own way.

But beyond this, it is important to note that a distinction can be made between "Western" and "scientific" medicine. Westerners conceive of Western medicine as a system of curing based on "rational" techniques, and "scientific" concepts of cause aud effect. But this characteristic, which forms the basis for the technical practices used by Western medical specialists, only partly determines the total range of practices involved in treatment and cure. Treatment is bedded in a social as well as a scientific matrix, and many practices of the Western doctor are based on cultural values and on ideas of personal relationships that are peculiar to Western society. Without the slightest detriment to the technical effectiveness of Western medicine, there seems much scope for divesting it of its Western cultural accretions, for fitting the practice of medicine into a role that is appropriate to the social organization of the village and to the therapeutic situation in which Indian villagers live.

Western ideas of personal privacy, of individual responsibility, of the dignity of certain techniques, and of the democratic nature of interpersonal trust are not intrinsic parts of scientific medical practice but are cultural accretions upon it. These ideas are not compatible with the traditional social organization of such an Indian village as Kishan Garhi. Not being supported by the social experience of villagers, such ideas tend to weaken or disrupt any medical approach that attempts to base itself upon them.

In the light of this analysis, it would appear that if Western medicine is to find a firm place in the village under present conditions, its role must be defined according to village concepts and practices. The doctor may define his role as that of a philanthropist, a saint. He cannot maintain therapeutic confidence merely as a personal friend who has achieved mastery of advanced techniques. Medical work can be supported by guaranteed charges for medicines, or by the spontaneous charity of the patients. It cannot be supported if it is presented to villagers on the one hand as a low, menial service, or on the other hand as a system designed to exploit them financially.

Study of village social organization in Kishan Garhi as a whole, and study of the indigenous medical specialists' roles in particular, suggest many ways in which Western medicine can be fitted into the scheme of traditional village culture. To bring this about effectively, the methods chosen need only be consistent with each other, with the purposes of therapy, and with the larger organization of village society. Testing of some of these alternative methods in the village may well be made an early subject of scientific medical experimentation.

SUMMARY

This study of medical practice and practitioners in the Indian village of Kishan Garhi has attempted an analysis of the social and cultural problems involved in introducing more effective medical techniques to a conservative Indian village. It describes the overall social organization of the village of Kishan Garhi, then analyzes the village medical institutions in particular, and finally re-examines the role of the Western doctor as it appears to villagers in the context of their own social organization and their own medical institutions. Analysis reveals several contrasts and conflicts that have existed in the past between the roles assumed by indigenous and by Western medical practitioners, conflicts that have acted as obstacles to the spread of Western medicine. Analysis also points to certain resemblances between the roles of indigenous and Western medical practitioners and suggests how some of these resemblances might be exploited in establishing scientific bridgeheads. The successful establishment of effective medicine here appears to depend largely on the degree to which scientific medical practice can divest itself of certain Western cultural accretions and clothe itself in the social homespun of the Indian village.

REFERENCES

Mandelbaum, David G., 1953. "Planning and Social Change in India," *Human Organization.* Vol. 12, Fall, pp. 4-12. Surveys a variety of efforts to effect specific changes in peasant life in India. Emphasizes the need for thorough social and cultural knowledge in order to avoid unforeseen obstacles and repercussions. Includes examples from medicine, administration, and agricultural technology.

Marriott, McKim, 1952. "Technological Change in Overdeveloped Rural Areas," *Economic Development and Cultural Change.* Vol. I, December, pp. 261-72. Describes problems of introducing better seed, more manure, and more irrigation water to improve the agriculture of Kishan Garhi village. Stresses the importance of taking into account the interconnections of each new technique to be added and each old technique to be replaced.

Marriott, McKim, ed., 1955. *Village India: Studies in the Little Community.* Chicago: University of Chicago Press. Describes the culture and social life of eight villages in different parts of India. Contains an analysis of the external relationships of Kishan Garhi village, with special attention to political organization, caste, and religion.

Opler, Morris E. and Rudra Datt Singh, 1948. "The Division of Labor in an Indian Village," in C. S. Coon, ed., *A Reader General Anthropology.* New York: Henry Holt and Co., pp. 464-96. A fuller, formal description of intercaste relations in Senapur, another village in Uttar Pradesh, India, whose social organization is much like that of Kishan Garhi.

Wiser, William H., 1936. *The Hindu Jajmani System.* Lucknow: Lucknow Publishing House. Describes in detail the socioeconomic system which interrelates members of a Hindu village in services, some of them medical services. The village described is not far from Kishan Garhi. See also Charlotte and William H. Wister, 1930. *Behind Mud Walls* New York: Richard R. Smith Inc., Chapter 6. Also published in New York: Friendship Press, 1946.

John F. Marshall

23 Some "Meanings" of Family Planning to an Indian Villager

The production of children in rural India is not simply an accident by which ignorant or irresponsible parents burden an already hungry family with additional mouths to feed. The fact that rural women maintain high fertility even after contraceptives are physically available demonstrates that the production of children has meaning to the people of Indian villages. Conversely, efforts to restrict the production of children—through the government programme encouraging contraception —also has meaning to the people of Indian villages.

Bunkipur, a small multi-caste village in Western Uttar Pradesh, is one such village. In 1968-69 I lived with the 570 residents of Bunkipur before, during, and after their first exposure to a formal family planning programme. The purpose of the investigation was to understand the villagers' decision-making processes—that is, to be able to describe *why* they reacted as they did to the family planning programme. In large part, it became a study of the "meanings" of family planning to the people.

These "meanings" can be defined as the total of beliefs and knowledge—all the cognitions—that relate to the individual's decision to adopt or not to adopt modern contraception. As such, meaning consists of cognitions relating to exposure to sources of information about contraception, to the assimilation and processing of the information, and to the possible implementation of the decision. Thus for each individual the "meaning" of family planning is a massive, and inconsistent, body of cognitions, most of which are rooted in culture; that is, much of the meaning of family planning includes knowledge and beliefs that are necessary for an individual to operate in an acceptable manner in his society.[1] Though the meanings vary for each individual, generalizations are possible for groups by defined sex, age, caste, parity, landownership, and other attributes.

It is clearly impossible in a brief paper to discuss in detail the array of "meanings" of family planning for even a single resident of Bunkipur. It is possible, though, to illustrate the breadth of "meaning" by identifying a few of the clusters of cognitions that are related to the villagers' responses to the family planning programme. It is also possible to try to illustrate the depth of this "meaning" by briefly discussing the cultural matrix in which these cognitions are produced.

As examples, several of the less conspicuous "meaning" will be described, on the assumption that most readers are familiar with the fact that to an Indian villager contraception could mean such things as a marginal risk of losing economic security in old age, a marginal loss of power and status that would result from a smaller family, or a delay in justifying a woman's place in the family if a son were postponed.

Government Workers

In Bunkipur the family planning programme involved, first of all, exposure to government workers—and this contributed to a vague but pervasive belief that the entire family planning effort was untrustworthy and probably exploitative. The male landowners, who comprised only one-sixth of the adult men and consisted almost exclusively of dominant caste Thakurs, saw village-level government workers as, at best, infrequent acquaintances who could relate the most recent gossip from neighbouring villages. More frequently the landowners perceived these

---

[1]The model underlying the observations in this paper is presented in an article by John F. Marshall, 1972. "A Conceptual Framework for Viewing Responses to Family Planning Programmes," *Journal of Cross-Cultural Psychology*. Vol. 3, No. 1, March, pp. 1-21.

workers as somewhat lazy and ineffectual, to be manipulated so that new seeds, fertilizers, pesticides, loans, and low taxes would result. Few perceived any other meaningful benefits from government sources.

The landless, comprising the bulk of the population of Bunkipur, had little contact with the two government servants who were most familiar with the village—the village level worker and the *panchayat* secretary. Among the Chamars—the ex-untouchable caste that made up nearly a third of the population—half the men and nearly all the women were unaware of the existence of the VLW or his position. The lower castes normally expected governmental neglect, a feeling justified by such things as the recently erected electric lines that conspicuously missed their sections of the village. And when they did have direct contact with government employees, they expected to be exploited and harassed. The milk-sellers of the Gardariya caste had recently seen one of their brothers jailed for six months, allegedly for selling watered-down milk. In fact, they insisted, he had simply dared to refuse to pay the weekly bribe to the government milk inspector, who had retaliated by adding water to the milk and taking him to the police. All the lower-caste villagers knew that the *panchayat* secretary, the government worker assigned to supervise the village councils in the area, effectively pressured six low-caste men (five of them over sixty old) into getting vasectomy operations so he would meet his quota; he had not tried to exert pressure on the upper-caste men. Though the lower-caste villagers operated with a kind of obsequious respect in the presence of nearly any government worker, most of them— especially the young—harboured a deep distrust of these men and their programmes. And, of course, the family planning workers were seen as government workers, whose sudden interest in the lower-caste villagers was met with great suspicion. That the family planning workers were high-caste Hindus did nothing to relieve the anxiety among the Muslims and lower caste. Thus family planning meant to many of the villagers—especially the lower castes—the possibility that some governmental skulduggery was afoot.

Pregnancy

To skip somewhat arbitrarily to another sphere, the meaning of family planning also involved what can be called "anticipated consequences." These included cognitions relating to expected physiological, sexual, and social effects of contraceptive use, and those relating to the implications of not having another or delaying a child. One of these anticipated consequences—that is, a "meaning" of family planning—was that adoption of the innovation would result in avoiding, or at least postponing, pregnancy. And pregnancy, independent of the optimal outcome of a healthy male offspring, was an inherently desirable state for village women. Though they recognized that it caused occasional sickness and that intercourse must be avoided during the last weeks, there were significant perceived benefits, especially for a newly married woman. In the upper castes, a pregnant woman's workload was lightened in the final months, and in all castes—if the family could afford it—she was allowed to eat special foods. For a childless woman, and to lesser degrees for women who already had living sons, the relationship to the husband and his family improved markedly when it first appeared she was pregnant. A sample of twenty village women were shown two pictures—a silhouettes of a pregnant woman was seen as well as of an unpregnant woman who was not pregnant—and without exception the pregnant woman was seen as happier, younger, healthier, better fed, more secure, more influential, and more respected. Frequently, then, family planning meant to the woman the absence of this desirable state.

Village Growth

In a discussion of what family planning means to the villagers, it may also be important to note what family planning does NOT mean. For example, to none of the people of Bunkipur did personal use of contraception mean that population pressure on limited land and other resources could be slowed. Only the landowners—and there were exceptions among them—and a handful of the landless maintained any concepts about the maintenance of the economic or ecological status quo through aggregate population control. And even those concerned villagers felt continued village growth was beyond their individual control.

It is interesting that the workers in the family planning programme in Bunkipur urged the villagers to consider the effects of continued population growth in the village, apparently oblivious of the fact that most of the people saw little connection between the size of their families and the size of the Thakurs' fields. More interesting is the fact that when ninety villagers were confronted—usually for the first time—with questions about optimal village size, eighty-five per cent of them responded that continued growth was highly desirable—beyond their control, but desirable. In several cases, village growth seemed to be considered good simply because it was growth; as a young man of the lowest caste explained, "when a person grows we say it is good, and if he loses weight we say it is bad. So, too, with our village."

More frequently, population increase was seen as a harbinger of economic growth and conveniences. Were Bunkipur to expand, it was argued, there would be new buildings, shops, tea-stalls, and eventually even a cinema hall. Jobs would then be easily available, and no longer would landless labourers have to travel to other villages and towns for employment. Several also felt that a larger village would be given more attention and assistance by the government and would have more power and prestige among the settlements in the region.

Women frequently mentioned that a larger village would have more social life: there would be more people to talk with, more visitors, more weddings to attend. Among the landless there seemed to be an equation of the previous population growth and the rise in their per capita food consumption; logically, then, continued growth would result in even more food. Few of the landless residents, including even those who had lost jobs as agricultural labourers in the fields of Bunkipur, were aware of the farmer's fears of overcrowding the land. The predominantly Thakur landowning men saw many of the alleged advantages of population growth, including a larger market for their surplus produce, but also recognized the inherent problems if their own numbers continued to increase. Though the need for a limited population in the *village* was clear to the Thakur farmers, several insisted that the population of the *nation* had to be increased so that attacks from China or Pakistan could be repelled. The women in the landowning families usually looked forward to continued growth in the village and seemed much less aware than their husbands of the economic implications.

Although for low-caste landless men the relationship between aggregate population growth and the economic situation played essentially no role in their decision to adopt contraception, the perceived relationship of aggregate population growth to the *political* situation did play a role—though indirect—in the response to contraception. The Chamars, for example—the numerically largest, but economically and politically weak caste of ex-untouchables—felt strongly that growing numbers (coupled with such things as increasing job opportunities and a more democratic village council) would lead to growing power in the village. Though as far as I can tell, this belief did not impinge directly on any individual's decision about adopting contraception, it had important indirect consequences by affecting the kind and amount of information to which the Chamars were exposed. For example, some of the Chamar leaders who worked in the nearest city rarely disclosed accurately or positively what they learned about contraception—in part because to them family planning meant a method of reducing the numbers and power of their caste.

Infant Mortality

Village parents lived with the knowledge that their children had only a tenuous grasp on life. The residents did not know specifically that the infant mortality rate for Bunkipur during the year was 321 (i.e., nearly a third of the children died within their first year of life)—more than twice that alleged for India as a nation, and sixteen times that of the United States. The people did recognize, though, that a disconcertingly large number of their infants and children died, and that death struck in an apparently random fashion. Some parents watched helplessly while all their offspring died one by one; other parents were spared entirely.

Unable to explain or control the high mortality, the villagers felt the need to compensate for it by having many children.

Women between the ages of twenty and twenty-four averaged 1.6 births but only 0.8 surviving children; women thirty to thirty-four averaged 6.6 births with 3.6 living children. But individual women could not be assured of being "average." To be protected against the possibility that their offspring would die at more than an average rate, it is probable that many parents tried to overcompensate, or stockpile, children.

Contraception in such a situation becomes an unattractive innovation. Permanent methods—male or female sterilization—eliminated the possibility of ever replacing children who die; temporary methods slowed the process of stockpiling. Family planning, then, meant a reduction in the certainty that one would have an "adequate" number of children.

That reactions to contraception were in part a function of perceived mortality rates is demonstrated by a comparison of villagers whose attitudes regarding family planning had changed positively with those who had changed negatively after exposure to the family planning programme. The two groups were similar in age, socioeconomic condition, degree of exposure to the family planning programme, and number of living sons and daughters. A large difference, however, appeared in the number of deaths of offspring: the positive-change group averaged only 1.1, the negative-change group 2.8. During the six months between the interviews assessing attitudes, the seven parents in the positive-change group had experienced an average of .29 live births and no child deaths. The twelve parents in the negative-change group, however, had experienced an average of .17 live births and .33 child deaths.

Conclusion

The approach sketched here—that is, the identification of the "meanings" of family planning and the description of the cultural context in which each meaning occurs—has implications for both policy development and programme implementation.

Obviously, implementation of family planning programmes is easier if the agents of change are aware of the extent of information and misinformation in their target population, and gear their communications appropriately. It is not necessary to elaborate on this, though it is worth asking whether or not it is appropriate for an anthropologist (or any other social scientist) to provide information to be used to persuade people to adopt an innovation that is, given the situations of many individual villagers, of arguable merit. Large, not small, families are a necessary and integral part of the life style considered desirable by the people of Bunkipur.

And this question leads into the implication of the approach for policy development. In a way, the introduction of the family planning programme into Bunkipur was like a plebiscite, in which the people were asked: "Is your life style in the village such that you *can* accept this innovation that we feel is for the good of the nation?" The answer was a resounding "No." During the six months of observation after the intensive programme, not a single individual adopted a contraceptive method as a result of exposure to the family planning programme. And a study of the "meaning" of the innovation reveals why this was the case. It suggests that the people *CANNOT* accept the ideal, until, for example, (*a*) government workers become credible sources; (*b*) status, recognition, and feelings of competence for women are achievable in ways other than getting pregnant; (*c*) village life contains amenities or adequate transpotration to cities so that it is attractive as a small community; and (*d*) infant mortality is lowered; and so forth. The government must consider policies dealing with these other realms as part of a genuinely effective population planning programme.

Part Five

Development
Administration
in Tribal Areas

Jawaharlal Nehru

24 An Approach to Tribal Problems

Mr Chairman and friends, this audience is more or less a select one since it consists largely of experts. I am not an expert and I am afraid I shall not be able to contribute much if we were to sit down and discuss your problems.

I suppose you have invited me here because I happen to occupy the office of Prime Minister, but I think I have another, and possibly greater, claim to participate in this conference. The claim is that I have always—long before I became Prime Minister—felt very strongly attracted to the tribal people of this country. This feeling was not the curiosity an idle observer has for strange customs; nor was it the attraction of the charitably disposed who want to do good to other people. I was attracted to them simply because I felt happy and at home with them. I liked them without any desire to do them good or to have good done to me. To do good to others is, I think, a very laudable desire but it often leads to great excesses which do not result in good to either the doer or the recipient.

In the tribal people I have found many qualities which I miss in the people of the plains, cities, and other parts of India. It was these very qualities that attracted me.

The tribal people of India are a virile people who naturally went astray sometimes. They quarrelled and occasionally cut off each other's heads. These were deplorable occurrences and should have been checked. Even so, it struck me that some of their practices were perhaps less evil than those that prevail in our cities. It is often better to cut off a hand or a head than

to crush and trample on a heart. Perhaps I also felt happy
with these simple folk, because the nomad in me found congenial soil in their company. I approached them in a spirit of
comradeship and not like someone aloof who had come to look
at them, examine them, weigh them, measure them and report
about them or to try and make them conform to another way
of life.

I am alarmed when I see—not only in this country but in
other great countries too—how anxious people are to shape
others according to their own image or likeness, and to impose
on them their particular way of living. We are welcome to
our way of living but why impose it on others? This applies
equally to national and international fields. In fact, there would
be more peace in the world if people were to desist from
imposing their way of living on other people and countries.

I am not at all sure which is a better way of living. In
some respects I am quite certain theirs is better. Therefore, it
is grossly presumptuous on our part to approach them with an
air of superiority or to tell them when to do or not to do.
There is no point in trying to make of them a second rate
copy of ourselves.

Now, who are these tribal folk? A way of describing them
is that they are the people of the frontiers or those who
live away from the interior of this country. Just as the hills
breed a somewhat different type of people from those who
inhabit the plains, so also the frontier breeds a different type
of people from those who live away from the frontier. My own
predilection is for the mountains than for the plains, for the
hill folk rather than the plains people. So also I prefer the
frontier, not only in a physical sense but because the idea of
living near a frontier appeals to me intellectually. I feel that
it would prevent me from becoming complacent, and complacency is a very grave danger, especially in a great country like
India, where the nearest frontier may be a thousand miles
away.

We should have a receptive attitude to the tribal people.
There is a great deal we can learn from them, particularly in
the frontier areas, and having learnt, we must try to help and
cooperate. They are an extremely disciplined people, often a
great deal more democratic than most others in India. Even

An Approach to Tribal Problems

though they have no Constitution, they are able to function democratically and carry out the decisions made by elders or representatives. Above all, they are a people who sing and dance and try to enjoy life; not people who sit in stock exchanges, shout at each other and think themselves civilized.

I would prefer being a nomad in the hills to being a member of the stock exchange, where one is made to sit and listen to noises that are ugly to a degree. Is that the civilization we want the tribal people to have? I hope not. I am quite sure that the tribal folk, with their civilization of song and dance, will last until long after stock exchanges have ceased to exist.

It is a very great pity that we in the cities have drifted so far away from the aesthetic side of life. We still have a good many folk-songs and dances when we go to the villages, because modern civilization has more or less left them untouched. The progress of modern civilization in India involves both good things and bad. One of the things we have lost is the spirit of song and dance and the capacity for enjoyment and this is what the tribal people so abundantly have. We seem to pay too much attention to the cinema. It is undoubtedly an excellent medium for many good things, but unfortunately it has not proved to be particularly inspiring. We must imbibe something of the spirit of the tribal folk instead of damping it with our long faces and black gowns.

For half a century or more, we have struggled for freedom and ultimately achieved it. That struggle, apart from anything else, was a great liberating force. It raised us above ourselves, it improved us and hid for the moment some of our weaknesses. We must remember that this experience of hundreds of millions of Indian people was not shared by the tribal folk. Our struggle for freedom did influence the tribes in Central India to some extent but the frontier areas of Assam, for instance, remained almost unaffected by it. This was partly due to the inadequacy of the means of communication available to us in the old days. Of course, there were other reasons too.

One of the reasons was that the city people were a little afraid to leave their familiar haunts and go into the mountains. The Christian missionaries went to various tribal areas and some of them spent practically all their lives there. I do not find many instances of people from the plains going to the tribal areas to settle down. Apart from our lack of initiative, we were not allowed to go there by the British authorities then in power. That is why our freedom movement reached these people only in the shape of occasional rumours. Sometimes they reacted rightly and sometimes wrongly, but that is beside the point.

The essence of our struggle for freedom was the unleashing of liberating forces in India. This force did not even affect the frontier people in one of the most important tribal areas. The result is that while we have had several decades in which to prepare ourselves psychologically for basic changes, the tribal people have had no such opportunity. On the contrary, they were prepared the other way round through the efforts of the British officials and sometimes the missionaries.

The missionaries did very good work there and I am all praise for them but, politically speaking, they did not particularly like the changes in India. In fact, just when a new political awareness dawned on India, there was a movement in northeastern India to encourage the people of the northeast to form separate and independent states. Many foreigners resident in the area supported this movement. I do not understand how it could be considered practical or feasible from any point of view. My point is that the people of the northeast frontier had been conditioned differently during the past generation and even in more recent years. The fault lay partly with us and partly with circumstances. These factors have an important bearing on any genuine understanding of the tribal folk.

They are our own people and our work does not end with the opening of so many schools and so many dispensaries and hospitals. Of course, we want schools and hospitals and dispensaries and roads and all that but to stop there is rather a dead way of looking at things. What we ought to do is to develop a sense of oneness with these people, a sense of unity and understanding. That involves a psychological approach.

You may talk day after day about development programmes in regard to schools and other matters but you will fail completely if you do not touch the real core of the problem. The need, today is to understand these people, make them understand us and thus create a bond of affection and understanding. After the achievement of independence, the basic problem of India, taken as a whole, is one of integration and consolidation. Political integration is now complete but that is not enough. We must bring about changes much more basic and intimate than mere political integration. That will take time, because it is not merely a matter of law. All we can do is to nurture it and create conditions where it finds congenial soil. So the greatest problem of India today is not so much political as psychological integration and consolidation. India must build up for herself a unity which will do away with provincialism, communalism, and the various other "isms" which disrupt and separate.

As I said, we must approach the tribal people with affection and friendliness and come to them as a liberating force. We must let them feel that we come to give and not to take something away from them. That is the kind of psychological integration India needs. If on the other hand, they feel you have come to impose yourselves upon them or that we go to them in order to try and change their methods of living, to take away their land and to encourage our businessmen to exploit them, then the fault is ours, for it only means that our approach to the tribal people is wholly wrong. The less we hear of this type of integration and consolidation of the tribal areas, the better it will be.

We ought to be careful about appointing officers anywhere, but we must be doubly so when we appoint them in tribal areas. An officer in the tribal areas should not merely be a man who has passed an examination or gained experience of routine work. He must be a man with enthusiasm, whose mind, and, even more so, whose heart understands the problem it is his duty to deal with. He must not go there just to sit in an office for a few hours a day and for the rest curse his fate at being sent to an out of the way place. That type of man is completely useless. It is far better to send a totally uneducated man who has passed no examination, so long as he goes to these people with friendship and affection and lives as one of them. Such a man will produce better results than the brilliant intellectual who has no human understanding of the problem. The man who goes there as an officer must be prepared to share his life with the tribal folk. He must be prepared to enter their huts, talk to them, eat and smoke with them, live their lives and not consider himself superior or apart. Then only can he gain confidence and respect, and thus be in a position to advise them.

The language problem is almost always exceedingly important from the psychological point of view. The best of solutions can come to nought if misunderstood or misinterpreted by the party concerned. It is absolutely clear to me that the government must encourage the tribal languages. It is not enough simply to allow them to prevail. They must be given all possible support and the conditions in which they can flourish must be safeguarded. We must go out of our way to achieve this.

In the Soviet Republic we have the example of a country that has adopted such a policy with success. Lenin and other leaders in his time were exceedingly wise in this respect. Regardless of their ultimate objective, they wanted to win the goodwill of the people, and they won it largely by their policy of encouraging their languages, by going out of their way to help hundreds of dialects, by preparing dictionaries and vocabularies and sometimes even by evolving new scripts where there were none. They wanted their people to feel that they were free to live their own lives and they succeeded in producing that impression.

In the matter of languages there must be no compulsion whatever. I have no doubt at all that the West Bengal government must have built special schools in places like Darjeeling and Kalimpong for the Tibetan-speaking people. If the tribal people have a script we must, of course, use it. But normally they do not have a script and the only script they have thus far learnt, to some extent, is the Roman script. It is a good script no doubt; and because many people have learnt it, I would not discourage it.

But if we are to evolve a script—here I do not speak with any assurance but am merely saying something that has occurred to me—it might be better, for the future, if we were to use the Devanagari script. It is a relatively easy script, apart from the fact that it can put the tribal folk more in touch with the rest of India than any other script. In areas where a majority of the people know the Roman script, I would not suddenly force them to abandon it because I do not want them to feel compelled in any way.

I find that so far we have approached the tribal people in one of two ways. One might be called the anthropological approach in which we treat them as museum specimens to be observed and written about. To treat them as specimens for anthropological examination and analysis—except in the sense that everybody is more or less an anthropological specimen—is to insult them. We do not think of them as living human beings with whom it is possible to work and play. The other approach is one of ignoring the fact that they are something different, requiring special treatment, and of attempting forcibly to absorb them into the normal pattern of social life. The way of forcible assimilation or of assimilation through the operation of normal factors would be equally wrong.

In fact, I have no doubt that if normal factors were allowed to operate, unscrupulous people from outside would take possession of tribal lands. They would take possession of the forests and interfere with the life of the tribal people. We must give them a measure of protection in their areas so that no outsider can take possession of their lands or forests or interfere with them in any way except with their consent and goodwill. The first priority in tribal areas, as well as elsewhere in the country, must be given to roads and communications. Without that, nothing we may do will be effective. Obviously, there is need for schools, for health relief, for cottage industries and so on. One must always remember, however, that we do not mean to interfere with their way of life but want to help them live it.

Verrier Elwin

25 Growth of a "Philosophy"

When Shamrao and I first settled in the Maikal hills we were singularly ill-equipped to be of use to anyone. Shamrao knew something about medicine. I knew a little about gardening but our knowledge, say, of chicken-breeding, which was based on P.G. Wodehouse's *Love among the Chickens*, was typical of our experience of practical realities. At that time, of course, there were no five-year plans, no great schemes for the all-round development of India. Even the handful of social workers who specialized in tribal matters thought mainly in terms of opening small schools and dispensaries.

Our original idea was a mystical rather than a material one, though we hoped to express it in practical terms. We thought that simply by living among the tribes, sharing their life as far as possible and, to some extent, suffering with them, we would make reparation for their long neglect and their treatment by a hard-hearted world. It was a way of becoming part of "the whole human condition." It was not, of course, possible for us to really identify ourselves on the physical plane with the poorest Gonds. Even the possession of a wrist-watch or a fountain pen put us far away from them. On the other hand, we did live, not as a temporary gesture but for a very long time, in houses like their own very simply indeed, suffered from the same anxieties, were bullied, as they were, by government officials, and were tormented in typical village fashion by malaria. We felt that even this small attempt towards identification would mean something and I think that there is no doubt that it did touch the hearts of many thousands of tribesmen who realized that, impractical as we were, we were thinking about them and showing them affection.

Psychologically at least, I think we were able to bring them a new spirit and a new hope, for they were very crushed when we first settled among them.

We were not, of course, content with this. We opened schools and started a dispensary where Shamrao in time became famous, people coming fifty, even a hundred, miles to consult him. We were able to help a large number of individuals by acting as peace-makers in their disputes, assisting them when they got into trouble with officials and by our advice when they were dragged to court. We did what little we could, and slowly began to learn the practical needs of village life.

One of the things that meant a great deal to us was the opening of our refuge for lepers, small as it was. At that time the chaulmogra medicines available for the treatment of leprosy were not very effective, but we thought that at least we could make a place where these unfortunate people could live fairly comfortably and in security, and at the same time we might check the spread of the disease by containing it in one colony. Even at this time leprosy was regarded with something of the horror that it inherited from the Dark Ages, and the opening of this home was for us ourselves a special symbol of concern and love. We kept it going for about a quarter of a century and, as time went on, learnt the new method of sulphone treatment.

In those first years our policy, if we can dignify it by that term, was partly to encourage the people by simple everyday acts of kindness, but also to rouse them to a sense of their rights—for we early saw that any real progress was in their own hands. We fought many battles with the police, forest officials, merchants and others on their behalf, and so taught them in time to fight for themselves. This made us very unpopular with most of the non-tribals, who did not hesitate to spread every sort of scandal about us and, what was even more dangerous, told the villagers that our medicines were diluted with water drawn by untouchables, that we were planning to convert them to Christianity and that we would send their boys and girls away to institutions in the cities. It was only when, fortunately, a sub-inspector of police got gonorrhoea and Shamrao cured him, that the officials began to come round.

At this time we were mainly concerned with problems of economics and as early as 1934, in an article on the Baigas in the *Modern Review*, the first that I ever wrote on the tribal problem, I pointed out "the appalling poverty, destitution and ignorance of this heroic and fascinating people." "You are certain to be enchanted by them," I wrote, "but you are equally certain to lie awake at night—and for many nights— haunted by the scenes of suffering that you have witnessed, and wondering what judgement must be passed on a society that can calmly allow such things to continue from generation to generation."

Poverty and disease were the fundamental problems, but the need for protection against every kind of exploitation was also constantly before us. I wanted to save what was beautiful, what was free: I have always opposed those who try to inject a sense of guilt into love, especially the love and happiness of simple people: I wanted to save them from anxiety—about their land, their forests, their next meal. I was absurdly misunderstood, but the poets and artists were always with me. W.C. Archer, for example, in his book of poems *The Plains of the Sun*, addressed one of his pieces (written during the war) to me and I put it in here, not just because I was flattered by it, but because it expresses exactly what I was trying to do.

> Among you burning hills, the lonely jungle
> Roars in the summer. The sterile land
> Rests; and news comes up like clouds
> While you are active in the needs of peace
> Saving the gestures of the happy lovers
> The poems vivid as the tiger
> Faced with destruction from the septic plains
> And with you love and art delay
> The crawling agony and the death of the tribes.

The Chinese invasion of NEFA set everyone thinking about the frontier but, instead of acclaiming our policy which had ensured a loyal and even enthusiastic local population to support the defence forces, a number of critics made it the

Growth of a "Philosophy"

subject of bitter and extravagant attack. For weeks it was impossible to open the newspapers without finding some denunciation of the "philosophy" of NEFA or even of myself.

Not one in a hundred of the people who so readily denounced *A Philosophy for NEFA* appeared to have ever read it. The main reason why it was believed to have failed was that I was supposed to have advocated a policy of isolation, to have urged the separation of NEFA from the people of Assam, and naturally the old cry of keeping the tribes as museum specimens was raised again, though no one could point out how any of this had affected the course of the military operations. Generally my critics attributed to me views which were the exact opposite of what I had advocated. In actual fact, I had not supported any policy of isolation of the NEFA people but had devoted several pages of this book to condemning it. The Inner Line, as it was called, by which the frontier is kept as a restricted area only to be entered by authorized persons, was established eighty-five years before my book was written and though I realize I am getting on, I am not as old as that. As for the Assamese people, for whom I have great affection and respect, I had included in my book the suggestion that every scheme of development, progress or welfare in NEFA should be submitted to the test whether it would help to integrate the tribal people with Assam and, of course, with India as a whole.

At the same time there were many supporters of our policy and Christoph von Furer-Haimendorf, for example, wrote enthusiastically after a very recent vist to NEFA:

> The 19th and early 20th century policy of laissez faire of provincial and state governments favoured exploiters and land-grabbers and the voices of the few devoted civil servants who spoke for the rights of the aboriginals remained largely unheard. There is only one region where a really bold and sympathetic approach to the problem of tribal development has saved the tribesmen from exploitation and the domination of outsiders. In the North-East Frontier Agency an administration has been instituted which develops the country solely for the benefit of its tribal inhabitants, and all those who have had an opportunity to visit this area in

recent years must have been impressed by the skilful combination of a modernization of external living conditions with the retention of tribal traditions and values. Here the tribesmen have lost neither their dignity nor their *joie de vivre*, and they know that they themselves and their children are going to profit from the economic development of their country. The lessons learnt from the decline of many of the tribal communities in other parts of India have here been applied, and it is an encouraging thought that the *Philosophy for NEFA* has borne such splendid fruit.

I

Let me then summarize my ideas for the tribal people as a whole, all twenty-five million of them (of whom the NEFA tribes are a small but significant part). To my mind, the five most important needs, in the context of the many-sided schemes of development of agriculture, communications, medical facilities, education, and so on common to the whole of India, are these:

1. That their land should be guaranteed to them and that any further alienation of it to outsiders should be stopped.
2. That their rights in forest should be respected and that an entirely new attitude should be taken towards them by the forest authorities throughout India.
3. That the problem of indebtedness should be solved without delay, partly by legislation and partly by a great intensification of the cooperative movement and the availability of easy credit from official sources.
4. That the problem of the industrialization of the tribal areas must be regarded much more seriously and that where the tribal people are dispossessed of their lands and settled elsewhere, intelligent and generous measures should be taken to compensate them.
5. That the long isolation of the tribes should come to an end, that they should be welcomed everywhere with warm affection and on equal terms, and that they should be given every opportunity of public service.

Growth of a "Philosophy"

I stress these points because they have been badly neglected in the last ten years, because they are simple and obvious, and can be solved if there is a real will to solution in the central and state government.

But there are five other points which are more complex:

1. We must help the tribes to come to terms with their own past so that their present and future will not be a denial of it but a natural evolution from it.

2. We must fight the danger of pauperization, the creation of a special class called "tribal," who will want to be labelled "backward" in order to get material benefits from the government. Unintelligent benevolence can be as great a danger as intelligent exploitation.

3. It is essential to avoid creating a sense of inferiority in the tribal people. This means that we must not impose our own ideas upon them. We must not create a sense of guilt by forcing on them laws and customs they do not understand and cannot observe. We must not make them anxious and afraid: we must not make them feel ashamed, of their own natural ways.

4. We should lay much greater stress on the possibility of the tribal people helping us. At present all the emphasis is on our helping them. Let us teach them that their own culture, their own arts, are precious things that we respect and need. When they feel they can make a contribution to their country, they will feel part of it: this is therefore an important aspect of their integration.

5. We must try to ensure that the people do not lose their freedom and their zest for living. I have put at the head of this chapter words that to me are the heart of the matter.

> What more felicity can fall to creatures
> Than to enjoy delight with liberty?

Although my final conclusions were present in my thinking thirty years ago, the emphasis changed as I gained experience and as conditions changed in the country as a whole. At first my ideas were limited but intense, and I saw the problem as basically a spiritual one, investing every act of kindness with symbolic value. Gradually the harsh realities of the time caused me to emphasize the need for protection. It was only much later that I became concerned about the preservation and development of tribal culture. In northeastern India protection was already assured and the important problem was how to give the tribes the good things of our life without destroying the good things of theirs. Internal political issues and international affairs generally have recently turned our thoughts to the importance of integration, although many of us had been thinking of this ever since independence. And finally, I see a large, difficult, almost majestic, plan which includes on one side schemes for food, health, mobility and knowledge and on the other, respect for an encouragement of tribal culture in the widest sense—religion, language, self-governing village institutions, social polity. To reconcile these two aims, to develop, yet not to destroy, is not easy but I believe it can be done.

Another very important aspect of what I was trying to do was to make the tribal people known. At that time in India, in spite of the work of a few anthropological pioneers who were seldom read, the tribal people were regarded either as tiresome savages who caused trouble or as a colourful and picturesque fold engaging themselves in sexual orgies, human sacrifice and head-hunting. As a result, although a few people tended to sentimentalize them, the general idea was to regard them as a different kind of human being, who might excite our condescending pity but could hardly arouse any kind of admiration.

I felt that if the tribes were to make any progress, it was essential that the rest of the country should treat them properly and regard them with affection and respect.

II

My views on the protection of the tribes caused a regular flutter, and for many years, indeed right up to the present time, I have been accused of wanting "to keep them as they are," to hold up their development, to preserve them as museum specimens for the benefit of anthropologists. This is, and always has been, nonsense.

Growth of a "Philosophy"

Some of the attacks upon me have been the result of deliberate misrepresentation, and generally my critics have not bothered to read what I have actually written. For in fact there was nothing very extraordinary about my policy. I thought the tribes had discovered secrets of living under hard conditions that the rest of us needed, and that their development should be a matter of careful timing. I wanted to ensure that they should only be "civilized" (for it was obviously inevitable that they would be) when they could be civilized properly and I wanted to give them a breathing-space to build up pride in their own life and become economically self-sufficient so that they would not be completely overwhelmed when the outside world came upon them. I wanted them to make terms with their past and go forward in a natural evolution from it.

In the early years, however, I was greatly impressed by the urgent need of protection and in my book *The Baiga*, published in 1939, I advocated some sort of National Park in a "wild and largely inaccessible" part of the country, under the direct control of a tribes commissioner. But this did not mean that nothing was to be done.

Inside this area, the administration was to allow the tribesmen to live their lives with the "utmost possible happiness and freedom." Wide powers were to be given to the traditional tribal councils and the headmen of the villages would have their old authority re-established. Non-tribals settling in the area would be required to take out licences. No missionaries of any religion would be permitted to break up tribal life. Everything possible would be done for the progress of the people within the area, provided that the quality of tribal life was not impaired, tribal culture was not destroyed and tribal freedom was restored or maintained. Economic development would be given high priority and schools should be on the lines of what is now called basis education, simplified and adapted to local needs. Fishing and hunting were to be freely permitted. The dictatorship of subordinate officials was to come to an end.

As I wrote a little later, we should, even for the wildest and most isolated groups, "fight for the three freedoms—freedom from fear, freedom from want, freedom from interference. We may see that the aboriginals get a square deal economically. We may see that they are freed from cheats and imposters, from oppressive landlords and moneylenders, from corrupt and rapacious officials. We may see that they get medical aid . . . . We may guard them against adventurers who would rob them of their songs, their dances, their festivals, their laughter." This was not a policy for the isolation of the tribes: what I wanted was planned and controlled contact—which is a very different matter.

My suggestion in *The Baiga* was badly put and I should have realized the unfortunate connotations of the expression "National Park." But in 1939, what on earth was one to do? It was not a question of preserving Baiga culture—for the Baigas had very little culture: it was a question of keeping them alive, saving them from oppression and exploitation, giving them a simple form of development. In actual fact, the government of India has now appointed a tribes commissioner and established tribal welfare departments in several states, as well as scheduled and tribal areas, which in practice are not unlike what I suggested so long ago.

III

During the years preceding independence there was not much scope for working out policies or philosophies, though there was a good deal of rather unrealistic academic discussion on the future of the tribes. The reason was that plans for the tribal people obviously had to keep pace with plans for the country as a whole. At this time *everybody* was neglected. The great majority of Indian villagers were still illiterate; they were still attached to antiquated and economically injurious social, religious and agricultural habits. They had little medical assistance, meagre educational facilities, bad communications; they were exploited and oppressed just as the tribal people were. The latter, however, were even more neglected than the rest and their lot was complicated by the anxiety of the British government to prevent the independence movement from spreading among them. Congress workers were often not allowed to go into their hills, and when I myself first began work for the tribes I was kept under police surveillance for several years, perhaps

Growth of a "Philosophy"

naturally, for I certainly had a "programme of discontent." I was not allowed to open schools for the Baigas. Visits to forest villages were carefully supervised, if not prevented. There were hardly any roads, hospitals or dispensaries; there was little interest in the improvement of agriculture and there was no real protection against those who then preyed on and impoverished the tribal people.

This did not mean that nothing could be done but we had to be content to work at specific cases and within restricted limits. I used to draw the attention of the authorities to any outstanding abuses which I discovered, made suggestions for improvements in detail and studied such special subjects as the conditions of the tribal people in jail, the problem of shifting-cultivation and so on. At the same time, I and others continued to keep the tribal people in the public eye.

But then came independence and with it a great awakening throughout the country. The tribal people found their place on the map; they became news; great schemes of development were proposed. It quickly became clear that the timid and grudging programmes of British days were entirely unsuitable in free India. Although things still moved slowly, there came a new stress on the need to bring the tribes out of their long isolation and integrate them with the rest of India. Although before independence I myself had accepted the position that some of the smaller and remotest tribes would have to remain out of the picture for the time being, this was never what might be called a "philosophical" position: it was due to the necessities of the situation. Later, even for so remote an area as NEFA, made it sufficiently plain in, for example, the second edition of *A Philosophy for NEFA*, that even there our policy was neither to isolate the tribes nor to freeze their culture and way of life as it was. During the five-year plans large sums of money have been and will be spent on the tribal people throughout India, and I have been one of those who have advocated spending a great deal more than was originally proposed. You do not keep people "as they are" or as a picturesque enclave by building roads into the very heart of their territory and by taking up very widespread schemes of development. I want change. Even in 1932 I wanted change. But what I want, and what those who think with me want, is change for the better and not degradation and decay.

There is endless talk nowadays about tribal development: if even a quarter of it were translated into action the position would be transformed. And in every conference, at every committee, in every speech, people feel it their duty to discuss over and over again the old controversy of Isolation, Assimilation or Integration, forgetting, that it has been put completely out of date as a result of one major circumstance—that the whole of India, including tribal India, will be covered by community development blocks in a year or two's time. This is a decision, this is going to happen, and it is therefore meaningless to discuss whether it is desirable to bring the tribes into the stream of modern civilization or whether it is good or bad to open up their country. Whether we like it or not, whether they like it or not, they are going to be "civilized"; their territory will be opened up. There is, of course, still plenty to discuss, but such discussions must henceforth concern themselves with the details of programmes: the fundamental policy is settled. The conclusion of my committee appointed by the Home Ministry to study how these plans could be implemented, and my own view, was that, in the context of modern India, development in the tribal areas must be much more intensive than elsewhere to enable them to catch up with their neighbours, that special emphasis must be laid on economic programmes and on health, and that very large sums of money must be spent on roads to make the people accessible. "The unit of the hills and plains," I wrote, "is as essential to the general national interest as it is to that of the hill and forest people themselves. We may indeed look forward to an enriching process of mutual fertilization: we have much to give the tribes and they have much to give us."

IV

With the coming of independence and the birth of the community development movement I felt more and more that my own task was to emphasize attitudes and methods rather than to draw up programmes at which I could only be an amateur, and in the first five years after independence I wrote and spoke

Growth of a "Philosophy"

mainly about the attitude that should be taken towards the tribal people and the psychological and social adjustments that had to be made both in ourselves and in them. I also pointed out the need for caution, the danger of overwhelming the people with too many schemes, of depressing them by our technological superiority and of creating an inferiority complex and anxiety about their land by importing too many outsiders into their villages.

It was also clear that, with the great schemes of development coming into being, a two-fold policy was necessary. One was to ensure that the people were not culturally emasculated in a way that would rob them of their identity and character. India's is a rich and varied tapestry, as Mr Nehru has said, and the tribes had to be encouraged to maintain their own personality, their own culture and their own language. But although in the earlier years I had thought in terms of *preserving* tribal culture, I came later to think in a less static way. Culture obviously must be a living, moving thing always subject to change, and Mr Nehru's formula of developing the tribal people along the lines of their own tradition and genius seemed to put what was needed in a nutshell.

At the same time I emphasized, writing in 1944, that "it would be deplorable if yet another minority community which would claim special representation, weightage and a percentage of Government posts were to be created." I wrote again five years later in the *Statesman* that "the special care and protection given to the tribesmen must not cast any shadow on the unity of India. They must be educated to feel that they are full citizens of the Republic, with real rights and still more urgent duties."

In most of tribal India the problems were comparatively simple. The people needed protection, development and social justice. But in a few places the problems were more complex. In the Saora hills and among the Murias, for example, there was still a strong, vigorous and very happy tribal life, and when I come to NEFA I found that here and in other parts of the frontier the tribes had retained their ancient culture and were developing their arts in a way that was rare elsewhere in India. Tribal life was still vigorous. It still meant something. It was not a question of reviving anything: it was more a problem of introducing change without being destructive of the best values of the old life.

Nari Rustomji had been thinking about these problems for a number of years and his ideas were already being put into practice on the frontier, though unfortunately I did not get copies of his notes until much later, and as a result did not do him justice when I wrote *A Philosophy for NEFA*.

As long ago as 1948, for example, we find him advocating very sound policies which would apply to the advance of civilization anywhere in the world. He condemns "reckless" talk of "uplifting and civilizing" the tribes. Officials or social workers must go to the people not as "masters who dictate but as elder brothers who have suffered themselves and wish through their experience to spare others the pains they have had to endure." They must not try to impose a uniform machinery of administration everywhere and certainly not try to bring the traditional judicial system of the hills into line with that elsewhere. They should not dream of "imposing a system, notorious for its abuses and its delays, over areas where a sense of justice is, one might almost say, inherent amongst the people, and where the law operates both speedily and effectively."

And a later note, which Rustomji wrote in 1953, anticipated so exactly what I was to think and say later that I will quote it in full:

Much of the beauty of living still survives in these remote and distant hills, where dance and song are a vital part of everyday living, where people speak and think freely, without fear or restraint. Our workers must ensure, therefore, that the good that is inherent in the institutions of the hill people is not tainted or substituted by practices that may be "modern" and "advanced," but are totally unsuited to their economy and way of thinking. The hillman has, essentially, a clean, direct and healthy outlook; he is free, happily, from the morbid complexes induced by the unnatural life of the city folk.

The greatest disservice will be done, therefore, if in an excess of missionary zeal, our workers destroy the fresh creative urge that lives, strong and vital, within the denizens of the hills. For if we wish to serve, we must show that we have respect for the hillmen and their institutions, their language and their song; and, in showing such respect, we shall secure their confidence in the work that lies ahead. For this reason, everyone should make it his first task to familiarize himself with the local language, take an interest and come to understand the customs and usages of the people and share fully in their life, not as a stranger from without but as one of themselves.

V

My first contribution to a philosophy of tribal change and development in NEFA was contained in a report (unfortunately marked "Secret") that I submitted to the governor, who sent it up to the Prime Minister, after a seven-week tour in Tuensang. Almost everything that I later elaborated was contained, at least in germ, in this report, on which Mr Nehru wrote a long note giving his general support to what I had proposed.

After this I worked with my colleagues in the NEFA Secretariat for two or three very interesting years thinking out in great detail all sorts of problems and policies. Sometimes we met in Raj Bhavan to discuss tribal religion with the governor. More often we met in my own house. The very first seminar we held was on the subject of tribal dress, and this was followed by a good many others. The administration embodied our conclusions in a series of directives and later asked me to prepare a book which I called *A Philosophy for NEFA*. The first edition was short and plain but it earned an encouraging foreword from Mr Nehru and aroused sufficient interest for me to rewrite it entirely; I doubled its length, inserted plenty of illustrations and republished it in 1957. Mr Nehru gave a new foreword to this edition in which he laid down his famous Panch Shila (Five Principles) for the tribal people. The book was reprinted two years later, and has now been translated into Hindi and Assamese.

The fundamental basis of this philosophy goes back to the attitude of my Oxford days; even then I had a dislike of imposing things on people and this naturally developed into an aversion in the religious sphere to proselytizing and converting people or, in the social sphere, to forcing one type of civilization on another. So in this tribal policy, nothing was to be forced or imposed on the people, who were to be encouraged to develop (the key word is "develop") along the path of their own traditions. They should come to terms with their past and grow from it by a natural evolution. This, of course, imposed considerable restraint on officials who, in all countries, are apt to feel superior to so-called primitive folk and to think that they have a God-given right to teach them better and do them good. But Mr Nehru said:

> The problem of the tribal areas is to make the people feel that they have perfect freedom to live their own lives and to develop according to their wishes and genius. India to them should signify not only a protecting force but a liberating one. Any conception that India is ruling them and that they are the ruled, that customs and habits with which they are unfamiliar are going to be imposed upon them, will alienate them.

There is no room here to summarize the closely-packed argument of *A Philosophy for NEFA* which dealt with tribal problems under the heading of material needs, psychological adaptations, and social, religious and cultural problems. Perhaps the most fundamental aspect of this idealistic policy was actually a material one—that, as Mr Nehru said, "tribal rights in land and forest should be respected." Another was we should build up and train a team of the tribal people themselves to do the work of administration and development. Indigenous social and cultural institutions should be regarded as allies and not as rivals. Many tribes have very old youth clubs or dormitories which provide an excellent foundation for building up educational training institutions. The development of tribal councils, to which in NEFA very wide powers have been given, has proved of great importance in establishing the people in their own self-respect.

Then we were anxious to preserve the good taste of the tribes. Businessmen were not permitted to settle in NEFA; instead, the people themselves were encouraged to go in for trade, a policy which has proved very successful. The arts—the beautiful textiles, the music and the dance—were not to be corrupted but encouraged. There was no idea of keeping anything static and, in actual fact, there is continual creative development in all these fields. In architecture the idea was that even official buildings should be built so that they would grow out of the landscape and not appear as strangers in the rural scene, though unfortunately this has not proved very successful. Above all, the attitude of the official or social worker, whoever he might be, was to be based on a feeling of complete equality and friendship.

The ideas of this book were in the first place evolved in the NEFA context, but many of them can be, and have been, also adapted to other tribal areas. Some of these have very different problems—indebtedness, for example, on the impact of industrialization—but the essential attitude is needed for them all.

My own policy is expressed, perhaps most clearly, in *A Philosophy for NEFA*. But it also appears in two other works. The first is in the report of the committee for Multipurpose Tribal Blocks, of which I was chairman and for the writing of which I was largely responsible. The second is in the report of the Scheduled Tribes Commission, generally known as the Dhebar Commission, of which I was a member. I was asked by the Dhebar Commission to prepare a shortened version of this rather formidable report (which ran to over 750 pages) and the little book that I did, *A New Deal for Tribal India*, should be read along with *A Philosophy for NEFA* by anyone sufficiently interested to know my wider ideas about what could be done for the tribal people throughout India.

In the Scheduled Tribes Commission Report, Dhebar's emphasis on social justice led us to stress protection side by side with development. In essence, the report of this Commission, which was exhaustively debated in Parliament and accepted by it, is justification of the stand I have made for thirty years and shows that the attacks upon me for stressing the importance of the war against exploitation have hardly been justified.

VI

My "philosophy" has had its critics. At a conference in

Ranchi one of the development commissioners present got up and asked plaintively, "How can we develop the tribes along the lines of their own genius when they haven't got any genius?" It is true that many of the more sophisticated tribes have lost nearly all their culture and individuality, but there are others which have retained a great deal that is good and they all reveal to the sympathetic and intelligent observer certain things on which to build.

Another criticism is made in the interest of integration. It is said that if we allow the tribal people to retain their languages, dress or social institutions, we keep them separate from the rest of India, and if we want to integrate them properly we should assimilate them as quickly as possible and smooth them out, as it were, so that they will be exactly like everybody else. The fallacy in this is that the people of India as a whole are marked by great variety and that there is no standard of culture, religion or language to which we can adapt the tribes. In practice, too it is just those tribesmen who have smoothed themselves out and adopted a way of life that is indistinguishable from that of their neighbours who have been most clamorous for separation from the rest of the population. They have realized that they are losing their identity and are desperately anxious to preserve it. Many of the Naga rebels have taken to a Western way of life and dress in Western clothes. The hill people of Assam proper who want a separate state are just those who have been most completely assimilated. It may well be that in the long run all the tribes will lose their distinctiveness and sink into a drab uniformity possibly dominated by the overpowering American civilization that is so rapidly spreading across the world. But it seems to me foolish to try to accelerate this process in the interest of integration, for this does not and will not work.

Report of the Scheduled Areas
and Scheduled Tribes Commission

26 A New Deal for Tribal India

We have come to the end of our long survey. It is now time to look back and summarize the philosophy that has inspired us and the fundamental ideas from which our recommendations have stemmed. Our aim has been that of India's Constitution itself, to secure for the tribal people, along with all the people of India, a social order based upon justice in all fields of life, liberty of person and property, equality of status and opportunity and a fraternity assuring the dignity of the individual and the unity of the nation.

The most important fact that we have to face is the effect of changes of every kind that are sweeping across the hills and forests in India—changes initiated by people, by the government and by the tribals themselves. Tribal people today are faced by an unprecedented evolutionary crisis in their history. The commission has gone into this aspect very carefully, basing its thinking on Gandhiji's famous quotation:

> I do not want my house to be walled in on all sides and my windows to be stuffed. I want the cultures of all lands to be blown about my house as freely as possible. But I refuse to be blown off my feet by any.

The tribal people have been awakened from their centuries-old slumber. The urgent needs of border defence are affecting even the most secluded villages of the sub-Himalayan mountains. Great schemes for development are bringing and, by the end of the Third Plan, will have brought to every tribal village new ideas, new techniques and new contacts. Roads are everywhere surging their way into places which have hitherto been virtually inaccessible. Education, as it spreads, is revolutionizing even the social and economic conditions of the tribal villages and is creating new demands as it generates new skills. In many of the hills and forests where the tribals live, there are vast resources of minerals, industrial raw materials and hydraulic power. The demands of the industrial age cannot be refused. At the same time they must not be permitted to push out the tribal or allow him to be overwhelmed. In other tribal areas great changes are taking place as a result of industrial development. The short-term and the long-term consequences of the industrial invasion of the tribal areas, at any rate in the central belt, have, of course, an enormous significance. They raise the issue of rehabilitation, land possession, education, training and equipment. If the tribals are to be absorbed, it must be at a proper level. They may be poor, but they are persons of dignity and self-respect: each has his place in his own society. We must fulfil the ideal of the Constitution in ensuring him continued dignity with equality of opportunity. Other aspects of industrialization will affect the aims and standards of the people who will now be residing in the tribal areas along with the tribals.

All this will make demands for extensive psychological and physiological adjustments. They will affect the code of tribal life, and specially social discipline, the integrity of the family, the integrity of the village community and may even in some places cause the disappearance of the village community, the general culture and spiritual and aesthetic values. The new way of life may also lead to the spread of certain social vices which generally accompany urbanization.

We must accept these changes and bear the burden of the perplexities they bring. The tribals themselves are not afraid of them. Indeed many demand a speedy entrance into the modern world. The doors and windows can no longer be kept shut. Change is generally inevitable, whether among tribals or nontribals as in the rest of the world. But whatever the demands of the changes, we have come to the conclusion that the moral and cultural foundations of the society must be safeguarded if the society has not to be rootless. A tribal's home and family is the precious and fundamental basis on which the future edifice of his welfare is to be built. A freedom that does not guarantee him the freedom to decide how he will mould his destiny, official programmes that do not give him the choice of how he will organize his own development and to what end, will be sad impositions on him, materially poor but spiritually rich and independent as he is.

We have quoted Gandhiji's great conception of the winds of the whole world going freely about a house with a strong and secure foundation. This seems to be the view of the trible people themselves, whose own desires for the future, in these days of democracy, must obviously have the supreme consideration. Happily we find that their emphasis on the preservation of the best in their way of life is not inconsistent with a desire for change. Change and adjustment are in fact the two indispensable conditions of human survival. It is a challenge to the leadership engaged in this great sociological process, to ensure that the best of the old does not vanish in the excitement of the new. The instrument of democracy is also a guarantee that nothing will happen which is not acceptable to a substantial section of the tribals. What is best and worth preserving in the final analysis can be determined only by themselves.

We must, side by side, also ensure to him all the facilities of life to which as a citizen and human being he is entitled, and provide him with everything necessary to successfully fight against the privations of poverty and ignorance, unemployment and disease, exploitation and neglect. We must also ensure that the tribal people are not overwhelmed by the technological superiority of the invaders of their hills and forests and do not lose their moorings in the industrial age.

As we have suggested, in this ferment of new ideals and new possibilities of life there is a danger that the foundations of the tribal house may be impaired. This has happened in other countries. We should do all we can to ensure that it does not happen here. Mere economic advance will have little value if the discipline and standards of society are destroyed and the spiritual ideas of life are lost. In other words, we should strike a balance between stability and change. In any balance that we strike, the most important way of safe-guarding even the spiritual and psychological stability of the people in the background that the tribals possess, is through land. It is for this reason that throughout our report we have laid the utmost stress on the subject of protection of the rights of the tribals in land. The tribals will never feel fully integrated with India unless they have a stake in the land to which they belong. Many of them, under the impact of change, may leave their villages and go in search of other ways of life; many may feel lost and bewildered. But so long as they have their own land at home there will always be something at their back to reassure them and to which they can return. We have proposed legislative and administrative measures to put a halt to the widespread and tragic diversion of land out of tribal hands throughout the country. What we need now are officials and social workers who will make it their mission and responsibility to see that these plans are implemented, who will be inspired with a passion for economic justice. It will mean an enormous amount of rather dull and tedious labour in offices and courts. But the result will be the smiling faces of the poorest of the poor enjoying a new life on land that is really theirs. We have to reconcile our duty to the new age and to the tribal people and in some cases the tribesmen will have to move from their ancestral lands in the interest of great national projects. Men with a sense of mission and inspired by love will have to ensure that they are given other lands instead.

Almost equally important is the establishment of the tribal councils in every tribal village. It is through these councils that for centuries the people have maintained their moral and social standards and their religious ideas. If these weaken, the whole fabric of tribal life may weaken and decay. They must not, and need not, be swept away by the new statutory *panchayats* but should coexist with them. Here again men and women with a sense of mission are needed to build up afresh what has been lost in some places and has declined in many.

There will, of course, be a great many tribals who for years to come will be unaffected by industrialization and will continue to live in the hills and forests. Lest anyone may think that such habitation does not contribute to the strength of the country, we would like to be clear that it is important that these interior and border lands of our country continue to remain inhabited. It is only then that it would be possible for their wealth to be developed in the interest of the country. It is only then we shall be able to assure permanent vigil on our frontiers. Only the hardy tribals will be willing to live in them. It is necessary that they should be considered to be the essential part of the forests and it is essential therefore that the forest rights of these people should be preserved. Indeed we have suggested a policy of friendship and alliance between forest officials and forest dwellers which would be to the advantage of both.

A third matter of great importance is the attitude of the official or social worker, indeed of every kind of non-tribal, to the tribal people, for their attitude will influence the attitude of the tribals themselves towards their own foundations. All changing and developing societies must come to terms with their past. It is common for very simple peoples who have always lived in isolation, when they come in contact with the modern world, to throw away everything in their old life and to despise their past, however good and valuable it may have been. The important thing, of course, is to build on the past and to grow out of it by a natural process of evolution. By their correct attitude, non-tribals can greatly assist in this. If they approach tribal institutions with humility and respect, the tribals themselves will be less inclined to forget them; they will not develop a sense of inferiority: they will retain their self-respect and dignity.

We are not alone in our views and we will quote three fine statements of the kind of approach that should be made. The Prime Minister, Shri Jawaharlal Nehru, has said of the tribals that:

> They are our own people and our work does not end with the opening of so many schools and so many dispensaries and hospitals. Of course, we want schools and hospitals and dispensaries and roads and all that, but to stop there is rather a dead way of looking at things. What we ought to do is to develop a sense of oneness with these people, a sense of unity and understanding. That involves a psychological approach.

As I have said, we must approach the tribal people with affection and friendliness and come to them as a liberating force. We must let them feel that we come to give and not to take something away from them. That is the kind of psychological integration India needs. If, on the other hand, they feel you have come to impose yourselves upon them or that we go to them in order to try and change their methods of living, to take away their land and to encourage our businessmen to exploit them, then the fault is ours, for it only means that our approach to the tribal people is wholly wrong.

Elsewhere he has said:

Avenues of development should be pursued within the broad framework of the following five fundamental principles:

(1) People should develop along the lines of their own genius and we should avoid imposing anything on them. We should try to encourage in every way their own traditional arts and culture.

(2) Tribal rights in land and forests should be respected.

(3) We should try to train and build up a team of their own people to do the work of administration and development. Some technical personnel from outside will, no doubt, be needed, especially in the beginning. But we should avoid introducing too many outsiders into tribal territory.

(4) We should not over-administer these or overwhelm them with a multiplicity of schemes. We should rather work through, and not in rivalry to, their own social and cultural institutions.

(5) We should judge results not by statistics or the amount of money spent, but by the quality of human character that is evolved.

The President, Dr Rajendra Prasad, said:

There can be, and should be, no idea or intention of forcing anything on them either by way of religion, language or even mode of living and customs. Even where we feel that the religion or the life that is offered is better than theirs there is no justification for forcing it upon them against their will. My own idea is that facilities for education and for general improvement in their economic life should be provided for them and it should be left to them to choose whether they would like to maintain their own separate tribal existence.

And a third statement of policy, which stresses the part which must be played by the tribals themselves in schemes for their own development, comes from the report which sets out the proposals of the Planning Commission for the Second Plan:

> Welfare programmes for tribal people have to be based on respect and understanding of their culture and traditions and an appreciation of the social, psychological and economic problems with which they are faced. The welfare and development programmes in tribal areas inevitably involve a measure of disturbance in relation to traditional beliefs and practices. In their implementation, therefore, the confidence of the people and, in particular, the understanding and goodwill of the elders of tribal communities are of the highest importance. It is, therefore, necessary that welfare extension workers of all kinds should be found as far as possible from amongst the educated youth in tribal communities. In commending the adoption of new techniques, tribal leadership should have a major role and any suggestions of imposition from without should be avoided, and for each step the ground should be carefully prepared in advance. The anthropologist, the administrator, the specialist and the social worker have to work together as a team, approaching the problems of the tribal people with sympathy, understanding and knowledge of the social psychology and needs of tribal communities. Tribal people have to be assisted largely through their own institutions. Details of development programmes should be formulated in consultation with members of advisory councils, leaders of tribal opinion and institutes engaged in the study of tribal problems. The tribal people should feel that these programmes are, in a real sense, a response to their own urge for better standards of living and the development of their culture. If the programmes are

implemented with popular support, they will give the tribal people in all parts of the country, a sense of partnership and integration with the Nations as a whole.

Translated into practical terminology this approach means:

(i) The tribal should be made to feel confident that no one will tamper with his way of life or his beliefs and customs. It is for him to decide how he will adjust himself in the future set-up.

(ii) He should be assured that his rights in land are safe. If, for the requirements of the nation he has to be dispossessed, the state will, as a part of the scheme which leads to his shifting, see to it that he is fully rehabilitated.

(iii) He should also be assured that his rights in forests are equally safe. If there is any change in the forest policy leading to any curtailment of his rights, he will be given satisfaction in other ways. It will be better still if forest development is integrated with his own economic betterment.

(iv) He should be assured that government and society are there to protect him from all forms of exploitation.

(v) He should recognize that changes are indispensable, without which no development is possible. The development is intended to secure for him and his family greater opportunities of life along with the rest of the country of which he is an inseparable part.

(vi) As a part of this process of change which is implied in any development activity, while we should ensure that all help in rehabilitation, education, training and equipment is given, he should be prepared for the necessary adjustment.

(vii) It is understandable that he would wish that the very process of change should be accompanied by schemes for rehabilitation, education, training and equipment. This is undeniably an obligation which the society has to fulfill.

(viii) Till this happens, he should not be disturbed from the moorings of his agricultural-cum-forest economy.

(ix) All this demands research and sympathetic study.

This side of the problem has so far received scanty attention at the hands of government and social organizations. The state governments should begin thinking about these problems without delay. The main responsibility for this will rest upon the centre.

Last but not least there is the problem of healthy, cooperative and fruitful contact with the rest of the country. This cannot be left to chance. It can be achieved partly through education, partly by care in the selection of officials and others sent into tribal territory. The whole approach to the tribal problem should be to promote integration.

These are the problems attendant on the question of approach. They cannot all be tackled simultaneously. The time concept is fundamental in the development of all human beings, whether they are tribals or others. These problems can only be tackled gradually. Gradualness is not the enemy of progress if it is purposeful and does not lead to complacency. Therefore, the progress may appear slow but it is only a scientific rational approach to the question of progress that can pave the way for a speed that would astound even the planners.

We have outlined our idea of a correct approach to the tribal problem and the philosophy that should inspire us. We would, however, like to briefly summarize a few of our practical suggestions which, in our opinion, form the kernel of our recommendations for the solution of this problem and on which we would like to lay the strongest emphasis.

THE CRITERIA

One of our terms of reference requires us to suggest criteria for declaring any new area as a scheduled area. We have come to the conclusion that four factors are essential for this purpose:

(1) That there should be a preponderance of tribals in the population;
(2) That the area should be compact and of a reasonable size;
(3) That it should be undeveloped; and
(4) That there should be a marked disparity in the econo-

mic standards of the people in the area as compared to those of their neighbours.

The Alternative Approach

As we have said in the body of the report, we believe that the application of these criteria will involve much labour and time and will result in diverting the minds of the people from the main task of expediting the processes of development which are still comparatively slow. We have, therefore, evolved an alternative programme. If the arguments given by us in support of this programme are not acceptable to the government or if it is otherwise considered unsuitable, or constitutional difficulties are likely to arise in giving effect to it, then the only course will be to declare those areas which fulfil our criteria as scheduled areas. For the purposes of declaring areas as scheduled areas we have not considered it advisable or proper to draw any distinction between the states and the Union territories. On our part we feel that there is no constitutional difficulty in giving effect to the alternative programme suggested by us which we regard as simpler and more practicable.

The formula of scheduled areas was conceived by the framers of the Constitution from the awareness of the need for special care and welfare of the scheduled tribes. Since the Constitution was adopted there has been increasing consciousness in the country and as a result of that consciousness concentrated efforts are being made for the development of the country as a whole on the basis of a planned approach. We have seen the functioning of the Fifth Schedule and while some progress has certainly been made, we have found that the object with which the scheduled areas were formed has been only partially realized. With the change in the approach of the people and the government and with the increase in the consciousness in the country, we feel it is possible, without losing time in ascertaining which areas fulfil the criteria, to go forward with the main task of development.

For the purpose, we have divided the problem of the scheduled tribes into two parts, namely, protection and development. In both the cases, we have suggested specific programmes specifying the targets to be achieved and suggesting a time limit within which they should be achieved. We have also suggested a change in the institutional set-up to see that this is done. In our opinion if this scheme is accepted the need for the creation of more scheduled areas or expansion of their existing boundaries would not arrise.

Protection

The framers of the Constitution, while they were clear that the scheduled tribes should be brought out from the age-old isolation and intensive efforts should be undertaken for their development, were also clear that in the process their existing right, customs and way of life should not be jeopardized. The first aim, therefore, of the Constitution has been to give the tribals protection against exploitation in general and particularly in regard to their interests in land and forests and to save them from exploitation by moneylenders. We have in the preceding paragraphs in this chapter explained our approach in that connection. The rapid changes that are coming about in the tribal areas cast a responsibility upon the people and the government to see that tribal interests in these vital matters are not jeopardized nor are they subjected to any kind of exploitation. Since the powers given the governor under the Fifth Schedule to make regulations for this purpose have not been fully utilized, we suggest that this should be done without further loss of time and early steps also be taken to implement them. We consider it necessary to specify a time limit within which such regulations should be passed and we have suggested that this should be done at the latest by the end of 1962.

The constituent assembly sub-committee had also felt that some sort of protection was required by the tribals residing in other parts not declared as scheduled areas which had a concentration of scheduled tribes population. Our reading of the constitution is also that it is the aim and the intention of the Constitution to offer to them such protection. The demand for declaration of additional areas as scheduled is really the outcome of this desire on the part of the tribals to secure protection. We think that protection should be uniformly extended to all the members of the scheduled tribes through general legislation. Where regulations have been issued the protective provisions of the regulations can be embodied in the general legislation to extend the benefit of these provisions to tribal people residing outside the scheduled areas. This will eliminate the suspicion that the protection is possible only within the scheduled areas. It will have the additional advantage of facilitating the process of de-scheduling when the time is ripe for it and thus facilitating the process of integration.

Legislation or regulation for the protection of the interest of the tribal in land should include and provide for grants of land, land tenure, land reforms, tenancy rights, records of rights, survey and settlement and special conditions for acquisition of land belonging to the tribals. Legislation or regulations relating to the protection of rights of the tribals in forests, if it cannot be done through executive instructions, should include and provide for grants of land for horticulture, agriculture, and grazing and also for participation in forest activities including exploitation of major and minor forest produce and the processing, of such produce. Legislation or regulations for the protection of tribals from exploitation of moneylenders should include and provide for:

(1) Prohibition of bonded labour of any kind;

(2) Automatic discharge from agreements in the nature of bonded labour without compensation;

(3) Scaling down of the past debts—application of the principle of Damdupat, placing an obligation on the creditors of filing their claims within a period and producing all their books and documents along with the claims, declaring usufructuary mortgages beyond a certain period to be automatically discharged and for restoration of the lands to the original owner; and

(4) Adequate alternative credit through simple procedures.

Development

In regard to the second aim of development of the scheduled tribes and administration of the scheduled areas, we have suggested that programme of tribal development blocks should cover all the scheduled areas and all other areas with a concentration of tribal population exceeding fifty per cent.

This will need regrouping of the areas and the delimitation of the boundaries of the tribal development blocks whether they are in the scheduled areas or outside. Our purpose is that the bulk of the tribal population should be brought under the scheme of community development so that it would be possible to concentrate on their development.

The blocks should concentrate upon the following four activities:

(1) Economic development
(2) Education
(3) Health
(4) Communications

Other activities may also be undertaken but precedence in the matter of time and expenditure should be given to these. That will avoid multiplicity of schemes, conserve resources and avoid crowding the areas with unnecessary personnel from outside.

The tribal development blocks should lay down specific targets to be achieved under these programmes; the broad objective should be that the tribal people in these blocks should attain by the end of the Fourth Plan at least the stage of development reached by the people in the neighbouring areas by the end the Third Plan. Even in relation to tribals, the programmes should be so organized that the benefits flow first to the most needy.

Economic development

In the field of economic development, the objective should be to ensure employment for everyone seeking it for three hundred days. We have suggested a scheme of integrated development by coordinating the activities of agriculture, forest, animal husbandry and cottage and small-scale industries. It should be possible to link other programmes of development under other departments of the government as well. A time schedule can be framed and tribals who want work should be intimated about it in advance so that whoever is willing to work can take advantage of it.

The machinery for economic development should consist of

two agencies—one to promote cooperation in the various activities relating to agriculture, animal husbandry, forest and cottage industries including credit, marketing and processing modelled on the lines of Andhra Scheduled Tribes Cooperative Finance and Development Corporation Limited and the other to mobilize and organize labour on the lines of the forest labourers' cooperative societies of Gujarat and Maharashtra.

The programmes of agriculture should emphasize measures for soil conservation, irrigation and improvement in techniques of cultivation. The programmes of cooperation should stress the ultimate realization of the objective of farming-cum-dairying, poultry and piggery included. The programmes of work through forests should include employment to the tribals at all stages of forest activities beginning from protection to exploitation. The middle men should be eliminated. The forest department and the tribal community should both develop a partnership approach. The programmes of rural industries should lead to the maximum utilization of all available agricultural, forest and animal husbandry resources for conversion into processed materials. The guiding principle of economic development should be work, credit and market and not charity, subsidy and waste.

Education

In the field of education the programme should aim at (*i*) vocational or craft-based education; (*ii*) bringing up the level of girls' education on a par with the neighbouring areas in the plains; (*iii*) reduction of the percentage of wastage and stagnation; and (*iv*) followup programme for those receiving technical education to secure employment for them. The block agencies should also prepare conditions for the introduction of compulsory primary education in the Fourth Plan period.

Health and housing

In the field of health, the programme should aim at having facilities for drinking water within a half a mile range for all villages and a maternity service centre at least within a radius of ten to fifteen miles from every village by the end of the Fourth Plan. The Public Health Department should undertake campaigns to combat TB, yaws, leprosy, VD and goitre and make provision for medical facilities up to the standard of medical facilities available in the neighbouring areas. In the matter of distributing house sites and houses, preference should invariably be given to the weaker sections amongst the tribals.

Communications

The block agencies should aim at all the year round tracks from village to market, village to forest and village to school, with foot bridges wherever necessary, within a period of ten years. The administrative links up to the *tehsil* level and with the development centres should also be completed.

TARGET AND TIME LIMIT

The accomplishment of targets laid down above both in regard to protection and development within a period of ten years should justify the de-scheduling of the areas where the targets have been achieved. On the fulfilment of the targets in the tribal development blocks and on the completion of the implementation of the regulatory or legislative measures for protection, the Fifth Schedule of the Constitution could conveniently be abrogated. The problem of the development of the tribal thereafter can be dealt with as a part of the general scheme of development of the people of India. There shall be need for continuous emphasis, even thereafter, lest remoteness may lead to complacency. The state governments and the centre can be trusted to do it.

CONSTITUTIONAL SET-UP

On the institutional side we have also made certain important recommendations. In the first instance, we consider it necessary to have a separate Commissioner for the Scheduled Tribes, for the problems of scheduled tribes stands on its own footing. We have also suggested that he should be a person of sufficient stature, so that he could deal directly with the Ministers at the centre and in the states, guide and inspire the officials, the public and non-official agencies and bring to bear upon the subject an independent and a direct approach. His functions should include among other things, making suggestions for the reorientation of the machinery at the centre and in the states for the purpose of fulfilling the targets mentioned above. His work will be completed on the de-scheduling of three quarters of the tribal development blocks. Thereafter the normal machinery of the government can attend to the problem without much difficulty.

At the ministerial level at the centre, scheduled tribes should continue to be the concern of the Ministry of Home Affairs as at present. But we consider it necessary that for a period of ten years there should be a separate minister under the home minister who should be exclusively in charge of the tribal programme and responsible for its implementation. We have no doubt that there will be a minister from the scheduled tribes at the centre. Along with other considerations, the governing consideration, however, in the case of allocation of this portfolio should be the capacity for the fulfilment of the task and not the fold to which he belongs.

There should be a separate department in the Ministry of Home Affairs in charge of the scheduled tribes. This department should attend to the constitutional functions devolving upon the Union government under the Constitution and also attend to the administrative, technical and financial needs of the states as well as the organization of surveys, research, coordination and evaluation. The Central Advisory Board for Tribal Welfare should be enabled to function more effectively than at present.

At the state level, we have suggested similar reorganization. There should be a separate minister in charge of the portfolio of scheduled tribes, not necessarily a tribal, wherever the tribal population exceeds a million. Such a minister should be responsible for effective execution of the programmes undertaken by the state. There should be a separate department for tribal welfare at the secretariat level wherever the tribal population exceeds a million and a separate director. The portfolio of scheduled tribes should be separated from welfare for a period of ten years. The state should have well organized research sections with sufficient funds to undertake surveys.

In our opinion the district and the field organization requires to be tightened up more than anything else. At the district and the field level the executive agencies for protection, and for economic development, education, health as well as communications should be under the direct charge of the deputy commissioner or the collector, who should be held responsible for the fulfilment of the objectives and targets. Necessary financial and supervisory and controlling powers should be delegated to the deputy commissioner or the collector for this purpose. We have suggested in the chapter on education that it is the responsibility of the state to lay down a regular policy for education, prescribe curriculum and texts. This is very vital from the point of view of integration. The deputy commissioner should also be responsible for enforcing the policies of the government in relation to education.

There should be tribes advisory councils in all the states so long as special representation for the scheduled tribes lasts. These councils should be made more effective and should have supervisory functions.

The governors' reports should not be merely formal documents. They should give information about the progress achieved in the various fields in the light of the targets and also give an idea of the impact upon the tribal people of the various programmes.

Non-official agencies should be encouraged to take over a share of the responsibility wherever they show the capacity and it is felt they can do the work better. It should not be forgotten that after the abrogation of the Fifth Schedule and the termination of the programmes of tribal development blocks, they will be the only agencies functioning in the midst of the tribals in the non-scheduled areas. Non-official agencies have a distinct role to play as the conditions of the tribals are sometimes more difficult in the non-scheduled areas than in the scheduled areas.

Thus ends our long quest for the solution of one of the most important and vexed problems that confronts the country. As we have said in the earlier portion of the report, the problem emanates from centuries of isolation. Only to this extent is it different from the problems facing the other sections of Indian society. Nevertheless or because of this very reason, it has its specialities. The great hopeful feature is that the tribal himself has awakened to the need for finding a solution and is responding. The aim of the country is to secure the advancement of the tribals without disturbing the essential harmony of their life and securing their integration without imposition. We have viewed the tribal problem from this wider angle of the interest of the tribals, need for maintaining harmony and of integration. We hope and trust that our recommendations conform to that objective and will be helpful in fulfilling it.

Christoph von Furer-Haimendorf

27 The Position of Tribal Populations in Modern India

The coexistence of fundamentally different culture patterns and styles of living has always been a characteristic feature of the Indian stage. While in most other parts of the world rising civilizations replaced those that had preceded them, and conquering populations either eliminated or absorbed earlier inhabitants of the land, in India the arrival of new immigrants and the spread of their way of life did not necessarily cause the disappearance of earlier and materially less advanced ethnic groups. The old and the new persisted side by side, and this phenomenon of cultural and ethnic heterogeneity was only partly due to the great size of the subcontinent and the dearth of communications. There are certainly many comparatively inaccessible hill-regions where primitive tribes were sheltered from the pressure of more advanced populations, but the persistence of the tribes in a state of material and social development such as elsewhere hardly survived the end of the Neolithic age. It was not only due to the nature of their physical environment. More important than this was an attitude basic to Indian ideology which accepted the variety of cultural forms as natural and immutable, and did not consider their assimilation to one dominant pattern in any way desirable. A social philosophy based on the idea of the permanency and inevitability of caste distinctions saw nothing incongruous in the continuance of primitive ways of life in close proximity to centres of the highest and most sophisticated civilization. Even at times of the greatest efflorescence of Hindu culture there were no organized attempts to draw the aboriginal tribes into the orbit of Hindu caste society, for the idea of missionary activity was foreign to Hindu thinking. This does not mean, however, that none of the tribes ever became incorporated in the systems of hierarchically ranked castes. Where economic necessity or the invasion of their habitat by advanced communities led to continued interaction between aboriginals and Hindus, cultural distinctions were blurred, and what had once been self-contained and more or less independent tribes gradually acquired the status of castes. In many cases they entered the caste system on the lowest rung of the ladder. Some of the untouchable castes of southern India, such as the Cherumans and the Panyers of Kerala, were undoubtedly at one time independent tribes, and in their physical characteristics they still resemble neighbouring tribal groups which have remained outside Hindu society.

There are some exceptions, however, and tribes such as the Meitheis of Assam achieved a position comparable to that of Kshatriyas. Aboriginals who retained their tribal identity and resisted inclusion within the Hindu fold fared on the whole better than the assimilated groups and were not treated as untouchables, even if they indulged in such low-caste practices as the eating of beef. Thus the Raj Gonds of middle India, whose rulers vied in power with Rajput princes, used to sacrifice and eat cows without debasing thereby their status in the eyes of their Hindu neighbours, who recognized their social and cultural separateness and did not insist on conformity to Hindu patterns of behaviour. This respect for the tribal way of life prevailed as long as contacts between the aboriginals and the Hindu populations of the open plains were of a casual nature. The tribal people, though considered strange and dangerous, were taken for granted as part of the world of hills and forests, and a more or less frictionless coexistence as possible because there was no population pressure, and the advanced communities did not feel any urge to impose their own values on people placed patently outside the sphere of Hindu civilization.

This position remained unchanged during the whole of the Muslim period. Now and then a military campaign extending for a short spell into the wilds of tribal country would bring the inhabitants temporarily to the notice of princes and chroniclers, but for long periods the hillmen and forest-dwellers were left to themselves. Under British rule, however, a new situation arose. The extension of a centralized administration over areas which had previously lain outside the effective control of princely rulers deprived many of the aboriginal tribes of their autonomy, and though British administrators had no intention of interfering with the tribesmen's rights and traditional manner of living, the very process of the establishment of law and order in outlying areas exposed the aboriginals to the pressure of more advanced populations. In areas which had previously been virtually unadministered, and hence unsafe for outsiders who did not enjoy the confidence and goodwill of the aboriginal inhabitants, traders and moneylenders could now establish themselves under the protection of the British administration, and in many cases they were followed by settlers, who succeeded in acquiring large stretches of the aboriginals' land. Administrative officers who did not understand the tribal system of land tenure introduced uniform methods of revenue collection, and these had the unintended effect of facilitating the alienation of tribal land to members of advanced populations. Though it is unlikely that British officials actively favoured the latter at the expense of the primitive tribesmen, little was done to stem the rapid erosion of tribal rights to the land.

In many areas the aboriginals were unable to resist the gradual alienation of their ancestral land and either gave way by withdrawing further into hills and tracts of marginal land, or accepted the economic status of tenants or agricultural labourers on the land their forefathers had owned. There were some tribes, however, who rebelled against an administration which allowed outsiders to deprive them of their land, and as early as the end of the eighteenth century there were tribal revolts, the suppression of which necessitated prolonged military operations. In Chotanagpur and the Santhal Parganas such rebellions of desperate tribesmen reoccurred throughout the nineteenth century, and there were minor risings in the agency tracts of Madras and in some of the districts of Bombay inhabited by Bhils. In some of the fighting the aboriginals, who were determined but badly armed, suffered heavy casualties. Thus the Santhals are believed to have lost about ten thousand dead in the rebellion of 1855. None of these insurrections were aimed primarily at the British administration, but they were the reaction to the exploitation and oppression of the aboriginals by Hindu landlords and moneylenders who had established themselves in tribal areas, and were sheltered by a government which had instituted a system of land settlement and administration of justice favouring the advanced communities at the expense of the simple, illiterate aboriginals.

In some cases these rebellions led to official inquiries and to legislation aimed at protecting the aboriginals' rights to their land. The effect of such legislation varied from province to province and district to district, but seen in historical perspective it appears that land alienation laws had, on the whole, only a palliative effect. In most areas encroachments on the land held by aboriginals continued even in the face of protective legislation. It is one of the ironies of history that before, and even after 1947, Indian nationalist opinion blamed British policy and British officials for unduly favouring the aboriginal tribes, and isolating them as a protected and sheltered minority from the main body of the Indian people. In fact, the deterioration of the aboriginals' position was largely due to the effects of the system of administration introduced by the British, even though this result was certainly not intended. It is true that many British officials sympathized with the tribesmen, to whose character and way of life they were greatly attracted, and some of the most fervent advocates of tribals were certainly found among officers of the Indian Civil Service. Yet their recommendations contained in numerous reports of commissions of inquiry were only seldom implemented in full, and even where they were incorporated in legislation they did not often prove very effective.

There was only one part of British India where a policy of non-interference and protection enabled the tribal populations to persist to a considerable extent within the framework of their traditional culture. In the hill-tracts of Assam, both to the south and to the north of the Brahmaputra Valley, the situation was different from that prevailing in peninsular India. Tribes such as the Nagas, Abors, and Daflas were the sole inhabitants of a vast region of rugged and largely wooded hills into which the population settled in the plains of Assam had never penetrated.

A small volume of barter trade between hills and plains was carried on by tribesmen from the foothills visiting some villages on the edge of the plains, but most of the hill-people never set foot in the Brahmaputra Valley. When in the second half of the nineteenth century and during the first decades of the twentieth century the British extended their administrative control over part of the hill-regions, they did not encourage the entry of plainsmen, but devised a system of administration which allowed the hillmen to run their affairs along traditional lines and left the government of the villages in the hands of their own tribal dignitaries. Apart from such superior offices as the deputy commissioners and subdivisional officers, a few clerks to do the office work, and a small force of Assam Rifles, no outsiders were posted in such areas as the Naga Hills district, and the settlement of traders and shopkeepers was strictly controlled. No plainsman was allowed to acquire land in the hills, and the indigenous system of land-tenure was retained virtually unchanged. The one major intervention in tribal affairs was the prohibition of head-hunting and the suppression of intervillage warfare. But even this limited interference extended only to the fully administered areas. Both on the Assam-Burma frontier and along the Assam-Tibet frontier there remained regions over which the government of India exercised no administrative control, and where the old tribal life continued without any outside interference.

As a result of this policy the hill-people of Assam suffered none of the exploitation and loss of land which so many of the aboriginals of peninsular India had experienced. This did not mean, however, that the hill-tribes of Assam remained totally isolated from developments in other parts of India. The establishment of schools, partly maintained by the government and partly by Christian missions, brought a measure of education to the hillmen, and for the past fifty years there have been Nagas who had been sent outside the Naga Hills for further education, and had then returned to work as doctors, schoolteachers, or clerks. No such development had occurred in the hill-tracts north of the Brahmaputra, where a loose system of political control did not include any substantial educational or development work.

During the last years of British rule in India the policy to be adopted vis-a-vis the aboriginal tribes became a matter of passionate controversy. Certain anthropologically minded administrators, such as J.H. Hutton, J.P. Mills, and W.V. Grigson, advocated a policy of protection, which in some specific cases involved even a measure of seclusion, and this policy was ably defended by the well-known anthropologist and social worker Verrier Elwin. Indian nationalists and Congress leaders, on the other hand, attacked the idea of segregation and seclusion on the ground that it threatened to perpetuate a division within the Indian nation, and delayed the integration of the aboriginals with the rest of the Indian population. Advocates of this view saw in any measure designed to prevent a tribal community from being swamped by more advanced Hindu population, a British plot to create new minorities, and one of the critics of the protectionist policy invented the slogan of the "anthropological zoo" in which the aboriginals were supposedly to be kept. This controversy had mainly been sparked off by the creation of the so-called "excluded areas," backward regions inhabited by tribal populations to which, according to the Government of India Act 1935 (para 91, 92), Acts of the Dominion Legislature or of the Provincial Legislatures were to apply only if the governor of the province so directed. The intention of this provision had been to prevent the extension of legislation designed for advanced areas to backward areas where primitive inhabitants might be adversely affected by laws unsuitable to their special condition, but Indian nationalists saw in it a device to retain British control over selected areas, some of which were of strategic and some of special economic importance. We shall see, however, that after the attainment of independence the government of India adopted a somewhat similar policy. The North-East Frontier Agency (generally referred to as NEFA) was established as an area excluded from the State of Assam, and placed under a special administration responsible to the President through the Ministry of External Affairs, and within several state regions inhabited mainly by aboriginal tribes were notified as scheduled areas, for which the governor of the state had a special responsibility.

Thus in 1947 a "tribal problem" had already crystallized, and this was acknowledged by the architects of the Indian Constitution, who provided for the notification of "scheduled tribes" and their protection by special legislation. But before we review the policy adopted by the government of India and the individual states vis-a-vis the tribal populations, it is necessary to set out the details of the problem in greater detail.

According to the Census of 1961 the total population of scheduled tribes was 29,446,300, and this represented an increase of over seven million compared with the figure for 1951. Thus nearly thirty million people were officially recognized as standing outside the Hindu caste system and forming a minority deserving of special treatment. Though compared with the total population of the Indian Union of 437,313,115, thirty million more or less primitive people spread unevenly over most of the states are numerically not a very important element, they nevertheless add appreciably to the heterogeneity of the Indian nation, and demographic developments over the past fifteen years do not suggest that there is any immediate prospect of their absorption within any of the larger sections of the population. The greatest concentrations of scheduled tribes are in the states of Andhra Pradesh (1.3 million), Assam (2 million), Bihar (4.2 million), Gujarat (2.7 million), Madhya Pradesh (6.6 million), Maharashtra (2.4 million), Orissa (4.2 million), Rajasthan (2.3 million) and West Bengal (2 million). The compact tribal population of the North-East Frontier Agency was only partly included in the Census operations of 1961, and those not enumerated would have to be added to the total figure for scheduled tribes.

Though set apart from the great mass of the Hindu population, the aboriginals are themselves divided into numerous ethnic groups differing in race, language, and culture. As the most ancient population element in the subcontinents, the aboriginals clearly belong to very archaic racial strata. The oldest of these is formed by the Veddoids, so called after the Veddas of Ceylon. They represent a racial type which extends from South Arabia eastwards across India, and as far as parts of the southeast Asian mainland and Indonesia. The Veddoids are dark-skinned, and often curlyhaired; their faces are roundish or heart-shaped, with broad and depressed noses, low foreheads, and pronounced superorbital ridges. Intermixed with more progressive racial types, the Veddoid element is found in nearly all the tribes of southern and middle India, but is virtually absent among the hill-tribes of Assam and the North-East Frontier Agency. These tribes belong to a racial stratum usually described as Palaeo-Mongoloid, which extends over wide areas of southeast Asia. Not only the hill-tribes of Burma, such as Chins and Kachins, but even the Dayaks of Borneo and the Ifugaos of the Philippines have close racial affinities with some of the tribal people of northeast India. A slight Mongoloid element is also discernible among some of the hill-tribes of Bihar and Orissa, such as the Saoras and Bondos, and it is not unlikely that in prehistoric times, before the invasion of India by waves of peoples of Europoid race, there was some marginal contact between the Veddoids inhabiting middle and southern India and the Mongoloids who occupied the Himalayan region and the northeast.

In the discussion of the prospects for the integration of the aboriginals within the majority of the Indian population, these racial factors are often overlooked. Many of the aboriginals, whether they are of Veddoid or of Mongoloid type, diverge in appearance considerably from the dominant population of their respective regions, and even complete cultural and linguistic assimilation cannot remove the fact that a Naga looks very different from the member of an Assamese Hindu caste, and a Kadar stands out from the general Hindu population of Cochin. It is all the more remarkable that despite racial differences no less fundamental than those found in countries with acute race problems, there have never been any cases of racial tension in India. While religion and language have frequently been factors in political discussion and controversy, distinctions in physical makeup have never been of any political significance. One of the causes of this racial harmony may be inherent in the ideology of Hindu caste society, which accepts that humanity is divided into totally and intrinsically distinct groups. As E.R. Leach has pointed out, in Hindu eyes "people of different caste are, as it were, of different species,"[1] and racial differences are

---

[1] Leach E.R., (ed,) 1960. "Aspects of Caste in South India, Ceylon, and North-West Pakistan," *Cambridge Papers in Social Anthropology*. No. 2, p. 7.

therefore accepted as natural. Since the endogamy and social exclusiveness of Hindu castes are by themselves a bar to close intergroup relations, there is no need to place social distance between racially distinguished groups. The normal operation of the caste system is quite sufficient to prevent intermarriage, commensality, and intimate social intercourse between members of different tribes, and prejudices against racial mixture such as exist in South Africa or America do not arise in a situation where even castes of identical racial characteristics abstain from intermarriage. Indeed, in the present state of Indian society there is very little likelihood of any substantial miscegenation involving people of basically different racial groups, and whatever progress in the cultural assimilation of tribal communities may be made, there can be no doubt that for a long time to come most tribes will persist as groups of distinct racial characteristics.

The fact that despite its great racial diversity India has been free of racial tensions does not signify an indifference to racial characteristics. Certain features, such as lightness of skin colour, are socially highly valued, and the folk-image of the man or woman of high social status is associated with a specific physical type in which Europoid features predominate. It would be unrealistic to assume that the aboriginals' divergence from this ideal type will not be to the disadvantage of individuals whose educational and personal qualifications should enable them to compete for positions of prominence and social prestige.

Another factor which separates many of the aboriginal tribes from the majority of the Hindu population of their respective states is that of linguistic diversity. The Census of India, 1961, lists a total of 1,549 languages spoken by Indians as their mother-tongues, and the majority of these are unwritten languages spoken by tribal communities. Among the tribal languages, sixty-five belong to the Austro-Asiatic group, and are spoken by 6,192,495 persons. While in India there are only 377,993 speakers of Mon-Khmer languages, those of the Munda group are spoken by 5,814,496 persons, and among these there are 3,247,058 speakers of Santhal, 736,524 of Mundari, and 648,066 of Ho. The greatest number of speakers of Tibeto-Burman languages is only 3,183,505, of which some 200,000 speak various Tibetan dialects. Most of the languages of these groups are unwritten tribal tongues, such as the languages of the various Naga tribes, and it is among them that we find the greatest diversity. While some languages, as, for instance, Garo, are spoken by as many as 300,000 persons others are current only in very limited areas consisting perhaps of three or four villages.

The Dravidian language family contains, besides languages possessing a great literature, such as Tamil, Telugu, Kannada, and Malayalam, a number of unwritten tongues spoken by tribal communities. The number of speakers of these tribal tongues varies between figures of over $1\frac{1}{2}$ million, in the case of the Gonds, and a few hundred in that of the 765 Todas and 862 Kotas, small tribes of the Nilgiris, each speaking a language of its own. Even among the Aryan languages there are some which are scheduled as tribal, Bhili with 2,439,611 speakers being the most important.

Language, however, is not an immutable feature, and while a tribal community cannot change its racial makeup in order to conform to the characteristics of the caste groups dominant in the region, it can become proficient in the main regional language. The first step in such a process of assimilation is usually bilingualism, and many aboriginals in contact with advanced populations are fluent in one, and sometimes even in two languages other than their mother-tongue. Sometimes bilingualism is only a transitional phase followed by the decline, and ultimate extinction, of the tribal tongue. A process of linguistic assimilation has gone on for hundreds and probably thousands of years, and many tribal communities have lost their original tongues and today speak one of the main languages of India. Thus more than half of the Gonds of middle India do not even know Gondi any longer, but speak Hindi, Marathi, or Telugu, according to the region in which they are settled.

The smaller a tribal community, the greater is the likelihood that it will lose its original language and adopt the language of economically stronger and culturally more advanced neighbours. Examples of the displacement of one language by another are numerous. Telugu, one of the written Dravidian languages, is steadily gaining ground at the cost of minor unwritten tribal tongues, which also belong to the Dravidian language group. This process can be observed in the Telengana district of

Andhra Pradesh. The Koyas of some groups of villages still speak their tribal Gondi dialect, but use Telugu as a second language of communication with their Telugu-speaking neighbours. The majority of Koyas, however, have given up Gondi altogether and also speak Telugu, among themselves. In the Adilabad district the Kolams living on the plains have similarly lost their tribal language and speak only Telugu, while in the hills there are still flourishing Kolam communities speaking Kolami. In the western part of the Adilabad district, which after the breakup of Hyderabad state was incorporated in Maharashtra, Kolams have come in contact with Marathi-speaking populations, and these same groups no longer speak Kolami but only Marathi. The result in this case is a fragmentation of the Kolam tribe into a Kolami-speaking, a Telugu-speaking, and a Marathi-speaking section. Members of the two latter are no longer able to communicate with each other, and the two sections have hence become endogamous subdivisions of the tribe. Both the Telugu- and the Marathi-speaking Hindu castes form in their respective areas the politically, economically, and socially superior populations, and the loss of the Kolams' tribal language is followed by a rapid acculturation to the locally dominant culture pattern.

The contact zones between tribal and non-tribal populations provide instructive examples of the manner in which a new language may infiltrate into the speech of small communities. The Bondos of the Orissa highlands, for instance, speak a Munda language, but in communications with their lowland Hindu neighbours they employ Oriya. As such contact is mainly in the sphere of commerce, it is not surprising that the Oriya terms for the higher numerals, for weights and measures, and other concepts connected with trade, have been incorporated into the Bondo speech. It is more remarkable, on the other hand, that many prayers and magical formulae are always spoken in Oriya, because the Bondos think it proper that such superior beings as deities and spirits should be addressed in a "superior" language. The Oriya is fast becoming the ritual and not only the trade language of the Bondos. One can easily foresee that with the introduction of primary school education imparted through the medium of Oriya the original Munda language of the Bondos will increasingly lose importance, and that the 2,500 Bondos will ultimately become entirely Oriya-speaking.

What happens if the language of a tribal community is displaced by that of a dominant neighbouring population? The language of the latter may not have terms for certain key concepts of the tribal culture. It is possible that some of the terms will be retained and incorporated in the adopted language, and by analyzing such terms linguists can identify a substratum. But more frequently terms for specific culturally significant concepts are lost, together with the rest of the language, and in that case the ideas which they reflect may be transformed in the process of being clothed in a new linguistic medium. To take an example, the Gondi word *pen* has the meaning "supernatural being, god, spirit." Among the different categories of supernatural beings described by this term, there are benevolent deities as spirits which are potentially both benevolent and malignant, according to the manner in which man approaches them. If for such an inherently neutral spirit the Hindi and Marathi term *bhut* or the Telugu term *dayam* is used, there is at once a change in attitude, for *bhut* and *dayam* signify malevolent spirits invariably hostile to man, and not spirits of an ambivalent nature such as Gonds describe as *pen*. Conversely the Hindi term *deo* means a divinity rather more exalted than a Gondi *pen*, and by applying the terms *deo* and *bhut* to the various figures of the Gond spirit world, as it is done by the Hindi-speaking Gonds of such areas as Chattisgarh, a division into two contrasting categories originally foreign to Gond thinking is brought into a tribe's religious system.

Whereas in this case linguistic change has led to a modification of concepts, the adoption of a new language may also involve the acquisition of entirely new concepts. If the members of a primitive tribe lacking pronounced pollution concepts change over to the use of a language possessing an elaborate vocabulary for distinct grades of ritual status, ranging from extreme pollution to a high degree of ritual purity, they will necessarily adopt some of the corresponding concepts and become, so to say, pollution-conscious. In such a case the spread of a language is accompanied by a diffusion of ideas and also, resulting from their acceptance, by a diffusion of behaviour patterns.

Whatever the results of linguistic change for the development of tribal cultures may be, there can be no doubt that in an age of rapidly improving communications extreme diversity of languages cannot persist unmodified. In some parts of the Naga Hills one could, even when travelling on foot, pass through three different language areas in a single day's march, and this state of affairs could only prevail because villages were isolated from each other by longstanding feuds, and there was no real need for any common language to enable people from distant areas to converse with each other. The pacification and opening up of tribal areas has put an end to the isolation of tiny communities, and there is now a need for a common language. In most cases the regional dominant language can fulfil the role of a lingua franca, and in Assam and the adjoining hill-tracts, for instance, Assamese is used not only for communications between the hill-men and the plains people, but also often for communication between members of different tribes.

Yet not everywhere is the situation as simple as in Assam, where only one language can possibly qualify as a suitable medium of intertribal communication. In other regions the position is far more complicated for several languages may at one time or other have been in competition with each other. A concrete example may elucidate this point. When I began to work in the Adilabad district of Hyderabad, no less than seven languages were spoken within that district, and it was not unusual for aboriginals to be fluent in as many as four. There were, first of all, three tribal languages, namely, Gondi, Kolami, and Naikpodi, all Dravidian tongues listed as separate languages in the Census of India. Of these three, Gondi was the most important and most widely spoken. Most Kolams and many Naikpods were also proficient in Gondi, but it was rare for a Gond to know either Kolami or Naikpodi. In the southern and eastern parts of the district Telugu was spoken by the Hindu peasantry, by itinerant merchants and some minor government employees, whereas in the northern and western parts Marathi held a comparable position. Throughout the district, village records were kept in Marathi, for most of village accountants (*patwari*) were Marathi Brahmins. The official language, however, in which the *taluq* and district administration was carried on was Urdu, and many of the officers of the government knew no other language. It was not unusual, therefore, for a Gond to speak Gondi at home, Telugu to his moneylender, Marathi when dealing with the village accountant and many traders, and Urdu to government officials. That a good many Gonds were able to do this is a measure of the intelligence and resourcefulness of aboriginals pitchforked between the conflicting influences of different advanced populations. Today the former Adilabad district is divided between Andhra Pradesh and Maharashtra, and Telugu and Marathi have been gaining in importance while Urdu, the previous state language, is of less relevance, though still used for communications between aboriginals and many of the older government servants.

The attitude of the government of India and the various state governments to the tribal languages is ambivalent. In Andhra Pradesh the use of Gondi as the medium of instruction in primary schools for tribal children, which the Nizam's government introduced in 1944, has been virtually abandoned and no more school books in Gondi have been printed since the breakup of Hyderabad state. The avowed policy of the government is clearly to educate all children through the medium of Telugu, and though the use of Gondi in the initial phases of primary education has not been officially banned and Gond teachers still speak to Gond children in Gondi, there has been no encouragement for the use of tribal languages, and as soon as stocks of Gondi school books are exhausted Gondi will presumably become extinct as a written language.

Though educational experts in most Indian states are unanimous in advocating education in the mother-tongue, at least up to high school level, this principle is not applied to tribal children, even in the case of such large tribal groups as Santhals or Hos, who speak languages not even remotely related to the dominant language of the state. Only in the North-East Frontier Agency have determined efforts been made to produce books and educational material in tribal languages and to begin instruction in the pupils' mother-tongue, though changing over to Assamese in the later stages.

The Scheduled Areas and Scheduled Tribes Commission set up by the government of India in 1960 under Article 339 of the Constitution severely criticised the reluctance of state governments to satisfy the tribes' demand for primary education in their own language. Under Article 350 A of the Constitution it has to be the endeavour of every state to provide adequate facilities for instruction in the mother-tongue at the primary stage of education to children belonging to linguistic minority groups, but the Commission pointed out that some of the states have taken this matter very casually, and failed to provide textbooks even in the major tribal languages. The Commission argued that:

> ...if it has been possible for the NEFA. Administration to produce in five years well over a hundred textbooks in thirteen different languages, it should certainly be possible to have textbooks in Saora, Kui and Gondi. In Assam several of the many tribal languages are recognised for examination purposes by the University of Gauhati which has also recognized the Abor language used in NEFA.[2]

Despite the progress achieved in Assam and some efforts of tribal leaders in Bihar, where there is a popular movement aiming at the creation of a literature in tribal languages, the prospects for the future tribal languages are poor, and it does not seem that the admonitions of the Commission have moved state governments to change their policy. Indeed, it can be foreseen that in most states, though probably not in Assam, the will gradually give way to the literate languages spoken by the dominant advanced communities which control the cultural, economic, amd political life of the states in which the tribal populations are living.

In any context other than that of India the predictable disappearance of languages spoken by well over twelve million people would be considered a tragedy, and it is indeed tragic that not only these languages but much of the poetry and oral epic literature existing in these languages seem doomed to

---

[2]Report of the Scheduled Areas and Scheduled Tribes Commission, Vol. I, 1960-61, p. 226.

extinction. Yet, in comparison with the total population of of India, the aboriginal tribes appear only as insignificant splinter groups, and there is very little public concern about the fate of their linguistic heritage. The voluminous publications issued by the Office of the Commissioner for Scheduled Castes and Scheduled Tribes, and other agencies concerned with the welfare of the aboriginals, contain very little information on the problem of tribal languages, and it is difficult to avoid the conclusion that politicians and officials alike regard their ultimate disappearance as inevitable and even desirable in the interest of the integration of the tribes with the majority communities. It may be argued that the Census figures do not support the assumption that the tribal languages are bound to become extinct. The number of speakers of some of the major tribal tongues has not declined, and may even have risen on account of the general population increase. Thus there were about 4,601,000 speakers of Munda languages in 1931, and 5,814,496 were enumerated in 1961, while during the same period the number of Gondi-speakers fell from 1,865,000 to 1,501,431. Neither of these figures indicates dramatic changes in the position of the tribal languages, and the former indicates indeed the vitality of what is probably the most ancient language group in the subcontinent. But in the period to which they refer the tribal people were not yet affected by the programme of mass education which now brings the respective state languages to many of the remotest villages, nor, by that time, had the improvement of communications opened the areas of tribal populations to the incursions of outsiders who nowadays penetrate many of the last refuge areas of tribal culture.

Languages spoken by many hundreds of thousands of aboriginals inhabitating compact areas and the languages of the hill-people of Assam and NEFA, where contact with non-tribal populations is relatively superficial, will probably survive for several generations. Other tribal languages were already in a state of rapid disintegration at the time of the Census of 1931, when several Census superintendents, among them those of the United Provinces, Mysore, and Baroda, commented on the displacement of tribal tongues by the languages of advanced communities. Under present conditions bilingualism will undoubtedly rapidly increase, for whenever school education is imparted in a language other than the children's mother-tongue a second language is soon acquired. Where the growth of political consciousness has led to a conscious evaluation of tribal identity, and hence the attachment to a tribal language, bilingualism would seem to be a solution which enables a tribal commodity to participate in the wider national life without losing touch with its own cultural heritage.

Besides the differences of race and language, there are various cultural factors which set the aboriginals apart from the bulk of Hindu society. Some of these are intangible and do not lend themselves to statistical assessment, but for many years the factor of religion was used as a criterion by which the tribes were distinguished from such communities as Hindus and Muslims. In the Census of 1931 about 8.2 million people were returned as adherents of tribal religions, but in more recent census reports tribal religions were not separately listed but were included under the head "others." The reasons for the discontinuation of the heading "tribal religions" are partly of a practical and partly of a political nature. Tribal religions are clearly not as easily definable as Islam or Christianity, and whereas usually no doubt exists whether a person is a Muslim or an adherent of a tribal religion, it is not equally easy to distinguish between some tribal cults and certain types of popular Hinduism. The political objections to the separate listing religions are based on the argument that Census statistics on religion tend to perpetuate communal divisions. In the 1931 Census the Commissioner had pointed out that "the Census cannot hide its head in the sand like the proverbial ostrich, but must record as accurately as possible facts as they exist,"[3] but his successors may have felt that the political arguments against the separate listing of tribal religions were too powerful to be disregarded, and the heading "tribal religions" was removed from the Census reports.

The tables of the 1961 Census contain separate statistics only for Buddhism, Christianity, Hinduism, Islam, and Sikhism. All minor religions, including those previously classified as "tribal," were collectively presented under the heading of

---

[3]*Census of India.* 1931, Vol. I: India, Part I: Report, p. 379.

"others," but from the figures for states and districts with a strong tribal element it is clear that many persons previously returned as adherents of tribal religions were now classified as Hindus. Thus in Andhra Pradesh, which contains a considerable population of aboriginals practising tribal cults, only 1,340 persons were classified under "others" in 1961, while in 1951 this figure was still 27,257. The fact that adherents of tribal religions were nearly all included among Hindus can be deduced from the figures for such districts as Adilabad, Mahbubnagar, and Warangal. The number of Gonds enumerated in Adilabad district in 1941 was 71,874, and virtually all of them professed a tribal religion and considered themselves entirely separate from Hindus. In my book *The Raj Gonds of Adilabad*[4] I have described the cult of the tribal deities of the Gonds, and recent visits to Adilabad have convinced me that there is no change in Gond religion which would justify their classification as Hindus. Yet, in 1961 only two persons were returned under the head "other religions" and there can be no doubt that all the Gonds were classified as Hindus. The same procedure must have been followed in regard to the Koyas of Warangal district, who in 1941 numbered 22,481 and in regard to the small tribe of Chenchus; primitive food-gatherers of Mahbubnagar district, for in Warangal only twenty-six members of "other religions" were listed and in Mahbubnagar this category is represented by one single individual.

In West Bengal the number of persons classified under "other religions" fell from 116,629 in 1951 to 39,727 in 1961, and in Bihar it dropped in the same period from 874,408 to 755,838. Detailed figures for Bihar are contained in the special tables for Scheduled Castes and Scheduled Tribes published as Part VA of the *Census of India* 1961, Volume IV. In these tables the tribal religions of the Hos and the Santhals are listed separately, and it is thus apparent how many Hos and Santhals were returned as Hindus and how many as adherents of their original tribal religion. In the whole of Bihar 185,951 Hos were classified as professing the Ho religion, whereas 118,909 were returned as Hindus. But only 89,751 Santhals were returned as adherents of their tribal religion, while 1,409,899 were listed as

---

[4]London: Macmillan, 1948.

Hindus. Of the 735,025 Oraons of Bihar, on the other hand, 428,868 were classified as Hindus, 173,245 as Christians and the rest as members of "other religions." The tendency to include the aboriginals among the Hindus is here clearly noticeable, and it becomes even more obvious in the returns for some of the districts of other states. Thus in the Koraput district of Orissa, which is the home of such well-known tribes as the Gadabas and Bondos, no single person was classified under "other religions," and—with the exception of a few members of tribes who may have been converted to Christianity—all aboriginals must have been included among Hindus. Even in Nagaland, where Hinduism had long been unable to gain a foothold, of a total population of 369,700 persons only 137,484 were classified under "other religions," which in this case certainly means the tribal religion, while there were 34,677 Hindus, as well as 195,598 Christians, representing the large group of Nagas converted to Christianity.

The officially inspired tendency to classify members of aboriginal tribes as Hindus and to play down the distinctions between tribal religions and popular Hinduism must not be taken as indicative cf an organized movement for the conversion of the aboriginals to Brahminical Hinduism. Apart from the discouragement of such customs as cow sacrifice and the use of intoxicating liquor as an offering to tribal gods, there is on the part of the local Hindu communities little desire to make the aboriginals change their beliefs and religious practices. Though in areas where aboriginals and Hindus stand in close contact Hindu ideas and customs are gradually spreading to tribal communities, they usually find acceptance as an addition to tribal beliefs rather than as their replacement. "Conversions" of tribesmen to Hinduism in a sense similar to conversions to Christianity or Islam are comparatively rare, even though in recent years Hindu missions have been active in some tribal regions of middle India. Their efforts have been concentrated more on the modification of social customs than on the propagation of a new doctrine. As some of the more puritanical Christian missionaries, such as the American Baptists operating in the Naga Hills, set out to wean the Nagas from alcohol and introduced new types of dress, so have some of these Hindu missionaries interfered in matters of diet and clothing, and have thus brought about changes in cultural matters unconnected with religion. Even where there are no such agencies for the propagation of the Hindu way of life, school teachers and minor government officials, who are almost invariably non-tribals, tend to discourage tribal customs which appear objectionable to Hindu sentiment, and although India is officially a secular state and great care is taken not to interfere with the practices of such major religions as Islam and Christianity, there have been instances of official interference with such tribal religious practices as animal sacrifices.

It would seem that in this respect there are certain discrepancies between the policies advocated by the central government and those pursued by individual states. The official policy of the government of India is one of tolerance towards the beliefs, customs, and way of life of the tribal people, whereas some of the state governments have shown themselves less sensitive to the rights of tribal communities to follow their traditional pattern of life even in matters not affecting the interests of other sections of the population.

The conditions under which aboriginal tribes have to adjust themselves to contact with other communities vary so greatly that generalizations applying to the whole of India cannot be valid. I propose therefore to discuss the present situation of the tribes in three specific areas with which I am familiar, and each of which presents certain problems of its own. The three selected areas are the hills of Travancore, the Telengana region of Andhra Pradesh, and the North-East Frontier Agency.

The forested hills of the part of Kerala which constituted the princely state of Travancore are the home of a number of tribes, some of whom are traditionally food-gatherers (for instance, the Malapantarams), while others are primitive shifting cultivators. Under the government of Travancore they enjoyed special rights and privileges in the state forests, and the forest department was invested with wide power to prevent the exploitation of aboriginals by outsiders. Today the situation has radically changed, for soon after 1947 the hills were invaded by large numbers of land-hungry plains people, who cleared the forests and settled on state land in defiance of the forest laws. With the consequent virtual disappearance of forest in many of the hill-regions which constituted the aboriginals' ancestral homeland, the protection which the tribes used to enjoy became largely illusory. Tribes which had persisted in their traditional way of life in the shelter of dense forests and of hills accessible only by footpaths find themselves today face to face with colonists from the lowlands who have denuded the forests and established their villages in valleys which, even ten years ago, were the haunts of elephant and bison. Against these settlers, hungry for cultivable land and indifferent to the far older rights of the tribesmen, the forest rules do not afford effective protection.

The type of shifting cultivation practised by most of the aboriginal tribes is dependent on the existence of large forest tracts, and the small patches on which the tribesmen used to cultivate millet and hill-rice made no appreciable inroads on the large forests reserves of the state. For they tilled every plot for only one or, at most, two years; as they did not remove the stumps of felled trees, little erosion took place, and when they abandoned a plot the forest quickly closed in on the fallow fields.

Today the areas still open for this type of shifting cultivation are few, and the destruction of forest through the more intensive cultivation of immigrants from the plains has deprived many aboriginals of their traditional means of livelihood. The establishment of tea, rubber, and cardamom estates in the last century resulted in an exodus of many aboriginals from large areas in the high ranges, but until some years ago there was still sufficient untouched forest in which they could find refuge. Now, however, the aboriginals are being squeezed out between the pressure of the old established commercial estates and the uncontrolled waves of agricultural immigrants from the plains.

Incapable of competing with these new settlers on equal terms, the aboriginals are bound to lose in the scramble for land, and unless urgent and drastic measures for their protection are taken, they will be deprived of even the small areas of land which they now occupy. Their difficulties lie not so much in an inability to develop more efficient agricultural methods, but in their inability to preserve for their own use any land which they have made suitable for permanent cultivation.

Whether we investigate the economic position of the Mukkuvans, the Mannans, the Uralis, or the Ulladans, we find that it is just in those localities in which the aboriginals had succeeded in constructing irrigated paddy fields, terraced garden plots, or cardamom lands that they lost the fruits of their labours to members of more advanced communities.

At this stage the prime need is therefore protection against the alienation of land still held by aboriginals, and the demarcation of areas from which they cannot be ousted. All other measures devised for the benefit of the tribals depend on the effectiveness of such a policy.

In Kerala there are no linguistic barriers between the tribes and other sections of the population. The aboriginals speak either Malayalam, or, in the case of tribes living close to the Madras border, a dialect of Tamil. There is consequently no difficulty in extending normal primary education to tribal children except for the distance of small isolated settlements from villages where a school can economically be maintained. In the whole of Kerala, includes not only the former states of Travancore and Cochin, but also the Malayalam-speaking parts of Madras Presidency, there were in 1961 a total of eighty-four primary schools and nineteen basic schools specially for tribals. The state government has opened a number of ashram schools, which are residential and have a craft bias, and these meet the problem of providing education for aboriginal children from widely dispersed settlements.

As the exploitation of the forests plays an important part in the economy of Kerala, and the aboriginals have an unrivalled familiarity with forest life, there are good prospects for their continued employment as forest labourers. With the progress of education the more skilled and responsible positions in the forest service should gradually come within their reach, but it would be unrealistic to assume that within a space of one or two generations people who until a few years ago lived in an economic style hardly superior to that of Neolithic man could adjust themselves by their own efforts to the complex economic and social system of Kerala. Protection and the continuation of special privileges will be required for many years to come if the former free forest-dwellers are not to sink even below the level of landless proletariat of untouchable caste.

The greatest danger facing the aboriginals of southern India is loss of the self-confidence which has enabled them to live fearlessly in forests inhabited by wild beasts. The distinguished Indian anthropologist Dr A. Aiyappan describes how "frustration and a feeling of inadequacy seem to make members of the small tribal communities in the South suffer from a severe inferiority complex," and how "bold heroes of the jungle who for sport net and spear tiger, quake with fear in the presence of revenue inspectors." This timidity is a result of the attitude of the Hindu plainsmen, who use any means to denigrate the tribes. Dr Aiyappan tells how the Aranadans of the Nilambur forests, though ruthlessly exploited by Muslim forest contractors, prefer to work for these employers, because the Hindus treat the Aranadans as impure and keep them at a distance. The same author describes the plight of the Mudugas of the Attapady Valley, who until recently had a fair degree of economic security as slash-and-burn cultivators, but are now being deprived of their ancestral lands as the hills where they used to live are being opened up by the construction of roads, and severe restrictions have been imposed on their traditional right to clear and cultivate the hill-slopes. The subsistence and survival of these and other tribes have been made problematic by the vacillations in government policy towards shifting cultivation. "The matter has been discussed threadbare by national and international bodies of experts, and the discussions seem endless, but meanwhile the distress of the tribesmen is welling up."[5]

While in Kerala the population of scheduled tribes is only 134,000, representing less than one per cent of the total population, the tribes of Andhra Pradesh number approximately 1,500,000 persons and constitute 3.68 per cent of the state's total population. The Andhra districts of the state, which are part of the former Madras Presidency, have a history of tribal development and administration different from that of the Telengana districts of the former Hyderabad state. The following more detailed account of the fortunes of tribal communities relates to parts of Hyderabad state where until the beginning of the century aboriginals were in undisputed possession of large tracts of land. In the district of Adilabad, for instance,

[5]Aiyappan, A., 1960, "In the South," in *Tribal India*. Seminar 14, Bombay, pp. 32-33.

the highlands between the valleys of the Godavari and the Penganga were almost exclusively inhabited by aboriginals. Gond rajas exercised judicial powers over groups of villages, and some tracts of land were recognized as the estates of such tribal chiefs. But the then prevailing system of land tenure did not provide for individual rights to cultivate land, and as the population was sparse and land plentiful, Gond cultivators were free to clear and occupy any piece of fallow land they fancied. It was only when agricultural populations from neighbouring, and more developed, areas began to infiltrate into Adilabad district that competition for land became a serious problem.

With the gradual improvement of communications and the influx of experienced non-tribal cultivators, the land gained in value and began to attract persons of landlord class who acquired whole villages to be managed on a commercial basis. As few of the tribals had title-deeds to the land they cultivated, the new settlers found it easy to oust them from all the best areas, and within a period of thirty or forty years much of the land in the more fertile lowlands fell into the hands of non-aboriginals, while more and more of the Gonds withdrew into the hills, where, for some time, they remained comparatively unmolested. By the early 1940s this refuge area too had also ceased to be safe for the tribals, for a policy of forest reservation deprived them of the possibility of extending the area of cultivation, and there were even cases of expulsions of whole village communities from areas notified as reserved forest without sufficient consideration to the needs of the local tribesmen. If this state of affairs had continued for another decade, the majority of the Adilabad Gonds, as well as the members of several minor tribes, would have become landless and unrooted.

In 1945, however, the Nizam's government decided on a bold policy of tribal rehabilitation. Large parts of the districts of Adilabad and Warangal were notified as tribal areas, in which non-aboriginals were banned from acquiring any more land. A staff of special officers was appointed to safeguard the aboriginals' interests, and regularize their right to the land. Within four years over eighty-five per cent of the tribals of Adilabad were given title-deeds to economic holdings of cultivable land, and the economic future of the Gonds appeared thus secure.

Simultaneously with the assignment of land, other measures for the rehabilitation of the aboriginals were enacted. The most important of them was an education scheme, which provided for the training of Gonds and other tribesmen as teachers and village officers. School books were composed and printed in the Gondi language written in Devanagari script, and as soon as teachers were trained to a modest standard primary schools for tribal children were opened in numerous tribal villages.

In order to protect the Gonds and other tribes from interference by outsiders likely to exploit them, tribal *panchayats* were instituted and invested with judiciary powers in civil as well as in minor criminal cases. All these measures were successful in raising the self-confidence of the aboriginals, and enabling them to recover their economic independence. The establishment of cooperative societies and grain-banks removed the need to rely on moneylenders, and within few years many tribal villages were almost entirely free from indebtedness to outsiders.

All these welfare activities were made possible by the creation of a special department initially attached to the revenue department. Some of the officers of this department, then known as social service, and now incorporated in a social welfare department, had received anthropological training, and many of them learned to speak tribal languages. There was no abrupt change of policy vis-a-vis the tribal populations when after the so-called "police action" of 1948 the government of India placed the state of Hyderabad under a military administration. The subsequent democratically elected governments of the state pursued the development of tribal areas in a similar manner, and with some modifications this policy was continued even after the merger of the Telugu-speaking districts of Hyderabad state with Andhra Pradesh.

Today the aboriginals of the Telengana districts of Andhra Pradesh are in a much better position to defend their rights and protect themselves from exploitation than they were twenty years ago. But some of the special privileges have been withdrawn and the Tribal Areas Regulation of 1950, under which the tribals were removed from the jurisdiction of the normal courts, has been suspended. It is too early to say how much these developments will affect the status of the aboriginals, but when I visited Adilabad in 1964 I learnt that pressure on land owned by tribals was again increasing, and already two years earlier I found that land alloted to Koyas in Warangal district in 1947 had been alienated to non-aboriginal settlers from some of the Andhra districts. Thus it appears that the position of the tribals, though much better than in 1940, is by no means secure, and that any diminishment of vigilance on the part of those responsible for tribal welfare might well result in a new erosion of tribal rights.

The spread of literacy and education, however, has enabled the aboriginals to make use of the democratic machinery of the recently established *panchayati raj*, and some members of the old chiefly families have come back to prominence by being elected as chairman of the new local councils. It thus seems that despite all the changes in the Gonds' fortunes, they still have confidence in their hereditary leaders, and are by no means on the way to losing their tribal identity. While in outward appearance and style of living the wealthier Gonds, as well those who have attained to political positions or employment in government service, do not greatly differ from Hindus of comparable material status, such assimilation is, as yet, very superficial, and there are no signs of any breaking-up of the very tightly organized structure of tribal society. Contact with Hindus remains confined to economic and official relations, and Gonds continue to consider themselves as standing outside the Hindu caste system.

Totally different from the position of the aboriginals in Andhra Pradesh is the situation of the hill-tribes of Nagaland and the North-East Frontier Agency. In Andhra Pradesh, as indeed in most states, the tribes form a minority which is neither politically nor economically of much importance, and which civil servants as well as politicians can disregard with impunity. Indeed, many state governments seem to react to the frequent proddings of the central government and the Commissioner for Scheduled Castes and Scheduled Tribes with some impatience, and are often slow in spending the very considerable funds voted by the Union of Parliament for tribal welfare. In Nagaland and NEFA, on the other hand, the tribes stand in the centre of interest, and the whole administrative machinery is geared to the various schemes for the development of the tribes.

The course of events in the Naga Hills since 1947 has been so bedevilled by political conflict and propaganda that no one without firsthand experience of the underlying causes of the Nagas' rebellion against the government of India can assess the situation with any measure of accuracy. Here we are clearly not concerned with the rights and wrongs of a movement which has placed the government of India in the embarrassing position of having to crush by superior military force a nationalistic upsurge which its leaders consider a war of national liberation. Without access to official records it is impossible to discover what went wrong in the Naga Hills immediately after the British withdrawal. The Japanese invasion of 1944 had certainly disrupted the previous administration, but the Nagas had, on the whole, proved loyal to the government of India and the British district officers. In the past they had always enjoyed a special status and there had been very little interference with their internal affairs. Taxation had been light and the villages had been allowed complete self-government. Neither police subordinates nor forest and excise officials, who in other tribal areas have so often been a source of irritation, had ever disturbed the harmony of village life in the Naga Hills, and except for the ban on head-hunting and inter-village feuds, the administration did not concern itself with the way in which the various Naga tribes governed themselves.

After 1947 the government of India pursued a policy which aimed at bringing all parts of its territory under a uniform administration. The Naga Hills were to be integrated into the state of Assam, and in order to achieve this the regular district administration, involving numerous officials of many different departments, was extended to the previously only lightly administered hill-tracts. While Assamese and other Indian officials posted in the Naga Hills saw themselves as the bringers of an altogether superior civilization and the benefits as schools and dispensaries, the Nagas saw in these newcomers novel rulers intent on depriving them of the virtual self-government the tribesmen had enjoyed in British days. This prospect they resented all the more as none of the Naga tribes had ever been conquered by the Assamese, who had lived in awe of the fierce hill-men. Indeed many Nagas felt that after the withdrawal of the British, who had imposed their rule over the hills, they should be allowed to run their own affairs. After protracted and fruitless negotiations between the government of India and the leaders of the Nagas, hostilities broke out when in 1956 tribal extremists kidnapped and later murdered a pro-Indian Naga politician. A division of troops was dispatched to the Naga Hills to restore order, but many of the Naga leaders went underground, and ever since there has been a state of war between the regular Indian army and Naga guerillas. Unable to suppress the rebellion, the government of India placed in 1957 the Naga Hills district and the Tuensang frontier division of NEFA under the Ministry of External Affairs, and in 1960 established a Naga state to be known as Nagaland within the framework of the Indian Union. This state was to have an administrative secretariat, a council of ministers, and a legislative assembly, but for an interim period responsibility for law and order was vested in the governor of Assam, who acted as governor of Nagaland.

The curtain of secrecy which screens events in Nagaland from the outside world prevents outside observers from understanding why the leaders of the Naga rebellion have felt unable to accept the limited autonomy granted by this arrangement, and are continuing to demand full independence and sovereignty. However unrealistic this demand may be, it is symptomatic of the desire of the tribal people to retain their cultural and national identity, even at the expense of having to forego many developments in the material sphere. The demand is unrealistic, because material change has already gone beyond the point of no return, and only substantial financial support from the Union government can assure continuation of existing services, such as roads, schools, and hospitals. But it is obvious that the Naga rebels, and with them a large section of the Naga population, are convinced that political integration within the Indian Union is incompatible with the retention of their cultural characteristics and their own way of life. That they have come to this conclusion is not the fault of the government of India, which has gone a long way in an attempt to reach a compromise, or even of the military officers trying to establish law and order, but it is the direct result of a certain arrogance found among many of the less-educated high-caste Hindus who look down upon aboriginals as savages and impure beef-eaters, and cannot see anything valuable or worth preserving in the tribal dress, art, social customs, and religion.

This attitude, often adopted by schoolteachers, medical personnel, and minor government officials, must have deeply offended the Nagas, who are a proud and independent people, used to being treated as equals by British officers such as J.H. Hutton and J.P. Mills, who had spent a lifetime learning about Naga culture. Considering the efforts made by successive Indian governments to come to terms with the Nagas and the large sums provided for development—during the Third Five-Year Plan alone, a total of 71,500,000 million rupees— the continued resistance of the Nagas cannot be explained other than by the assumption of such a sense of grievance and deep-seated distrust. More information on the early course of the rebellion may prove this diagnosis wrong, but until Nagaland is opened to impartial observers, we have no alternative to guesswork, based on our knowledge of the Naga character and the fate of aboriginals in other areas where they were exposed to the influence of caste Hindus.

The tragic events in the Naga Hills have made the government of India aware of the danger of disregarding the sensibilities of tribal populations, and in setting up the administration of NEFA special care was taken to avoid the mistakes made in the relations with the Nagas. Here it was possible to start with a clean slate, for of the 35,000 square miles of NEFA only a few hundred square miles had been under regular administration before 1947. At present NEFA is administered by the President of India through the governor of Assam as his agent. The governor is assisted by an adviser who is the head of the NEFA administration. Each of the five divisions (Kameng, Subansiri, Siang, Lohit, and Tirap) is administered by a political officer, who is in full control of all the entire staff of all departments, and responsible for the execution of all development schemes. The one-line administration has proved successful in coordinating a uniform attitude to the local tribesmen.

This attitude was largely shaped by Dr Verrier Elwin, who until his death in 1964 held the appointment of tribal adviser to the administration of NEFA, and spent the last years of his life in inspiring the members of the Indian Administrative Frontier Service, as well as a group of young research officers and many officials of other departments, with his tolerant and appreciative approach to the culture and way of life of the hill-tribes. The effectiveness of his influence was partly due to the wholehearted backing which the Prime Minister Jawaharlal Nehru gave to this policy of trying to preserve as much as possible of the tribesmen's cultural heritage, and to prevent the forcible imposition of Hindu values on people whose roots lay outside the sphere of Hinduism. This policy has not remained without critics, and many Indian politicians levelled against the administration of NEFA the charge that it kept the tribals in isolation and forbade other Indians to settle, or even to trade, in the hills.

Yet from the point of view of the welfare of the tribesmen, the policy pursued during the first ten years of the existence of NEFA must be considered a great success. My assessment is based not on published accounts, which are usually rather rose-coloured, but on observations during a visit to the Subansiri and Triap divisions in 1962. When I first travelled in the Subansiri region in 1944, the local tribes, the Apa Tanis and Daflas, had virtually no contact with the government. The greater part of the area was unexplored and the political officer, stationed in the plains, had no control over the inhabitants of the hills except for the prevention of raids on the plains of Assam. By 1962 there was an administrative centre in the Apa Tanis valley linked by a motorable road with the Brahmaputra Valley, and attached to it were a hospital, schools, cooperative stores, and various other amenities open to the tribesmen. More impressive than these developments, however, was the fact that the local tribesmen seemed to be deriving considerable economic advantages from the activities of the administration without suffering any apparent damage to their cultural and social life. As no outsiders were allowed to settle permanently in the hills, they were secure in the ownership of their land, and improved facilities for trade greatly benefited the Apa Tanis, who had always been keen traders. Their adoption of new methods and commodities was selective. Thus there was no interest in bullock-drawn carts or the use of animals for ploughing, but Apa Tanis were quick to learn to drive trucks, and the more enterprising traders used motor transport for bringing up goods from the plains. Schools were well attended and many boys had ambitions to enter government service. Indeed, some of the officials expressed apprehension about the possibility of finding suitable employment for the many young men who were receiving education, and imagined that the newly learnt skills would enable them to attain a standard of living far superior to that of the ordinary villagers.

Whatever problems might lie ahead, the administration of NEFA has certainly succeeded in preserving the tribesman's self-confidence. Contact with other populations being slight, the tribesmen do not feel themselves to be a minority less privileged than other communities, and as long as they are secure in the rights to their ancestral land, the prospects for their future appear to be good. There is certainly a world of difference between the depressed status of many tribes of middle and southern India, and the material prosperity and vitality which strikes one so forcibly among a tribe such as the Apa Tanis of NEFA. A measure of isolation combined with a sympathetic and imaginative policy of a progressive administration has here created a situation unparalleled in other parts of India.

This brief survey of the situation of the aboriginal tribes in three specific regions demonstrates the complexity of the problem of their integration within the wider Indian society. The conditions under which the tribes live in different parts of India are so varied that generalizations regarding their relations with other communities can have only a very limited validity, yet the populations notified as scheduled tribes all share special protection guaranteed them under Article 46 of the Constitution, which reads:

> The States shall promote with special care the educational and economic interests of the weaker sections of the people, and in particular of the Scheduled Castes and the Scheduled Tribes, and shall protect them from social injustice and all forms of exploitation.

Under Article 244 and the Fifth Schedule providing for the

Administration and control of scheduled areas and scheduled tribes, it is within the powers of the President to declare any tribal area as a Scheduled Area and to make administrative arrangements to give effect to the provisions of Article 46. The tribal areas notified as scheduled areas extend over 99,693 square miles, and though they are administered as part of the states in which they are situated, the respective governors are given powers to modify central and state laws in their application to them, and to frame regulations for their peace and good government and, in particular, for the protection of the rights of tribals to land, the allotment of wasteland and their protection from moneylenders. The Fifth Schedule also provides for the setting up of tribes advisory councils in all states containing scheduled areas, and it is the duty of such councils to advise on matters concerning the welfare of the scheduled tribes. Although such tribes advisory councils were set up in eleven states, their effectiveness has not been impressive, and the Scheduled Areas and Scheduled Tribes Commission of 1960-61 found that these councils met only once or twice a year, and that important items of legislation were not referred to them for discussion.

More important than the establishment of the tribes advisory councils was the appointment by the President of a Commissioner for Scheduled Castes and Scheduled Tribes whose duty it is to investigate all matters relating to the safeguards provided for these castes and tribes. The Commissioner reports annually on the position of the tribes in the various states, and on the progress of the schemes initiated for their benefit. His annual reports are published and constitute a valuable source of information on all activities of the state governments concerned with backward classes and tribes. The fact, however, that the Commissioner and his assistants are concerned only with the gathering of information severely restricts the effectiveness of his office. Though he may tender informal advice to state governments and embody his views in reports to the President, he is not in a position to initiate any scheme or decide on the utilization of the vast funds which the government of India provides for the betterment of the tribes.

At the centre the work relating to the scheduled tribes is attended to by the Ministry of Home Affairs, in which there are five sections specifically concerned with the scheduled caste and scheduled tribes. Moreover, the Planning Commissioner has a social welfare division, which deals with the development aspect of tribal affairs, and the publications on the five-year plans contain many data relating to the tribes.

It would appear that the provisions for the welfare of the tribes are strong on the constitutional and planning sides, but weak on the executive side. The concern of the government of India and of Parliament for the rights and progress of the tribes is admirable, but by the time measures decided upon at the centre have filtered down to state and district levels their impact is often weakened or outright lost. In all the reports of the Commissioner for Scheduled Castes and Scheduled Tribes, the Planning Commission and other bodies concerned with tribal affairs, there is the repeated complaint that the staff and administrative machinery provided by the state is not adequate to carry out the policy of the centre, even if the necessary funds are voted by Parliament. The welfare programme has been divided into "state sector schemes" and "centrally sponsored schemes." The latter comprise the schemes of tribal development blocks, cooperation, including forest cooperatives, tribal research institutes, and training scholarships. The state sector schemes, on the other hand, deal with the development of agriculture and cottage industries, education, housing, water supply, and public health.

Despite elaborate plans it appears, however, that in most states there is no clear policy for dealing with the problems of the tribal population. While it is generally accepted that departments responsible for forests, agriculture, fisheries, and health must have a staff of highly trained experts, there is little recognition of the necessity for experts in tribal welfare work. Other activities are given priority and therefore offer better promotion prospects, with the effect that officers who have proved efficient in tribal development are often diverted to other tasks which state governments consider more important.

One of the results of inefficiency on the executive level is the inability of states to spend the funds allocated by the Centre for Tribal Development. During the period 1950-61 no less than 493.5 million rupees were provided for the welfare of the scheduled areas, but the actual expenditure by the states fell very much short of this figure. In Madhya Pradesh, for instance, the Second Five-Year Plan made provision for close on fifty million rupees for tribal welfare, but less than twenty million were spent under the Plan.

A large part of the funds voted for the Second Five-Year Plan were to be spent on community development projects, and it was planned to undertake an intensive development of compact areas having large tribal populations. Forty-three special multi-purpose tribal blocks, covering 23,540 square miles and containing a population of 1,685,000 were opened under this programme, and the Third Five-Year Plan envisages opening 450 such blocks, which have been renamed tribal development blocks. In some of the blocks, however, the percentage of tribals was lower than that of non-tribals, with the result that funds sanctioned for the advancement of tribals were spent largely on non-tribals. The Commissioner for Scheduled Castes and Scheduled Tribes suggested, therefore, that in future only areas with a tribal population of not less than sixty-six per cent should be established as tribal department blocks.

The hopes set on the community development projects have only partially been fulfilled, and many Indian observers with firsthand experience of some of the tribal blocks take a pessimistic view of their usefulness. They point out that community development is basically a programme for directed and deliberate change, and that the people supposed to benefit have not been mentally prepared to accept changes. The tribesmen, like other Indian villagers, were used to looking to government officials for orders, and not for advice; though prepared to oblige the officers by paying lip-service to the development programme, they did not understand its implications and lacked the will for active cooperation. The government's insistence on the fulfilment of specific physical targets laid down by planners without any knowledge of local conditions, led to the expenditure of funds on projects of little utility. Thus houses were built, but people would not live in them, roads were built only to be washed away in the rainy seasons, basketry centres started where there were no bamboos, and beekeeping established where there were no flowers. Often all agricultural development was concentrated on the land of a few influential non-tribals, with the result that the aboriginals lost the little interest they had shown for the programme.[6]

The sort of difficulties into which community development could run in tribal areas can be gauged from an account of the situation in one such block in Bihar given by Dr Sachchidananda, the director of the Tribal Research Institute at Ranchi. He describes how the project officer and extension staff, who were all new to their jobs, found it difficult to comprehend their roles:

> Hitherto they had been accustomed to carry out orders, but now they were called upon to secure the cooperation of the people. Added to this was the difficulty of having to work in a totally unfamiliar area where the frame of reference to which they were used was inapplicable. Tribal culture had to be kept in the background of all development, but for them the pattern of work dictated from above was sacrosanct. They did not like to take upon themselves the responsibility of altering the programme to suit the peculiar needs of the area...there were also a number of administrative difficulties. The staff posted in tribal areas felt unhappy...some of them went even so far as to say that they regarded it as penal posting. Some others regarded it as a golden opportunity of serving themselves rather than the people. It is they who continued the tradition of exploiting the poor and simple tribals who had some work to be done at the block level.... For some time there was great resentment against Project authorities. People complained that the latter did not do anything with the consent of the villages and that they had done nothing to improve the conditions in Mandar. In some villages which were inhabited by influential non-tribals, much of the money has been spent. The general feeling everywhere was that the Project had benefited the non-tribals more than the tribals.[7]

---

[6]Sachchidananda, 1964. "Commuuity Development and the Tribals," *Journal of Social Research*, Vol. II, Nos. 1-2, pp. 70-78.
[7]Sachchidananda, 1964. *Culture Change in Tribal Bihar*. Calcutta, pp. 114-16.

I have recently observed similar situations in some areas of Andhra Pradesh, and if it is the non-tribals who profit most from aid provided by the government, one must assume that even in the tribal blocks the gap between the economic standards of the tribals and those of the rest is widening rather than closing. The root of much of these difficulties lies in the lack of communication between the development staff and the local aboriginals, and this is hardly surprising as long as officials are untrained and often recruited from castes which have a deep-seated prejudice against the tribal people.

The Planning Commission has clearly recognized the problem of finding suitable personnel for tribal development work, and in the Third Five-Year Plan the suggestion has been put forward that the central government and state government should cooperate in forming a special cadre comprising technical and other personnel for work in scheduled areas. The most significant aspect of such a policy would be that a body of trained persons would spend their entire period of service among the tribal people, so that their knowledge, experience, and sense of identification would become a vital factor in assuring rapid and uninterrupted service.[8]

This foresight and realistic assessment of the basic needs of an effective tribal policy are all the more remarkable as there is, even among educated Indians, a widespread unwillingness to face the fact that the thirty millions of aboriginals will for a long time to come form a separate and unassimilated element within the Indian nation. This became evident in a tribal symposium held in 1964 in Hyderabad, attended by anthropologists, administrators, and politicians. While the need for special protection was conceded by many of the participants, there was a general feeling that any privileges enjoyed by tribes were required only for a brief period of transition, and that within a span of about ten years the integration of the tribes within the rest of the population should be completed, whereupon there would be no more need for scheduled areas and the protection of scheduled tribes.

Most factual accounts of the situation in tribal areas and, above all, the Report of the Scheduled Areas and Scheduled

---

[8]Third Five-Year Plan, Delhi. 1961, p. 711.

Tribes Commission, belie these facile assumptions, and make it clear that for a long time to come tribal communities will persist as minorities, distinct in culture, language, and way of life from the neighbouring majority communities. Rapid progress in the field of education, which is perhaps the most striking development in recent years, does not directly solve the problem of the aboriginals' economic backwardness. For the core of the tribal problem lies in the discrepancy between their economic potentialities and the growing wants stimulated by contacts with more advanced populations. Barring a few notable exceptions, the aboriginals of today have no greater economic capacity than had their fathers and grandfathers. Their agricultural methods have largely remained the same, and such crafts as they traditionally possessed have declined rather than developed, partly on account of the spread of cheap industrially produced commodities, and partly because contact with Hindu ideas of caste have made certain occupations appear socially undesirable.

It is paradoxical that in many areas where aboriginals are exposed to the influence of caste Hindus, just those features of society which modern India strives to discard are newly introduced among populations to whom they had hitherto been foreign. Thus not only the prejudice against certain occupations, but also dietary taboos, child-marriage, and restrictions on the remarriage of widows and *divorcees* are gaining a foothold among the hill- and jungle-folk at a time when they are losing ground in the larger urban centres. This development is almost inevitable as long as throughout rural India compliance with the more puritanical percepts of Hindu morality remains the principal criterion of social respectability.

Acceptance or denial of the necessity for assimilation with Hindu society is ultimately a question of values. Are the aboriginals to be allowed to follow their own inclination in emulating or rejecting the cultural pattern represented by their Hindu neighbours, or are they to be compelled or coaxed to abandon their own cultural tradition and values? In the past, Hindu society has been tolerant of groups that would not conform to the standards set by the higher castes. True, such groups were denied equal ritual status, but no efforts were made to deflect them from their chosen style of living. In recent years this attitude has changed. Perhaps it is the influence of the Western belief in universal values which has encouraged a spirit of intolerance vis-a-vis cultural and social divergences. Yet India is not only a multilingual and a multiracial country, but is also multicultural, and as long as Muslims, Christians, and Parsees are free to follow their traditional way of life, it would seem only fair that the culture and social order of the aboriginals, however distinct from that of the majority community, should also be respected. No doubt assimilation will occur automatically and inevitably where small tribal groups are enclosed within numerically stronger Hindu populations. In other areas, however, and particularly all along India's northern and northeastern frontier, live vigorous tribal populations which may well follow the path of the American Pueblo Indians and resist assimilation as well as inclusion within the Hindu caste system. Many of those who know these hill-tribes intimately are confident that, if encouraged to develop on the lines of their traditional culture, they can make a distinct contribution to the overall pattern of Indian civilization.

With the introduction of a system of a democratic decentralization to take the place of the paternalism characteristic of the traditional form of Indian government, a new element has entered the relations between the tribes and the more advanced majority communities. The ability to vote in general elections for the Parliament in Delhi and the legislative assembly of their state did not make much difference to the tribals, because they did not understand the implication of the franchise, but the local elections aroused their interest to a much greater extent. The very fact that some of the most powerful people of the district approached the poorest villagers for their votes, and tried to gain their confidence, convinced them of a fundamental change. The very idea that they could choose their representatives was novel. At first, tribals only voted, for very few were sufficiently educated to stand for election. Even in areas with a preponderance of tribals, the elected representatives were often non-aboriginals and abused their powers by exploiting those who had voted for them. But as time passes and the aboriginals are gaining experience, they become more shrewd in the choice of their representatives, and tribal leaders

The Position of Tribal Populations in Modern India

have the opportunity of rising to positions of influence through the process of democractic elections.

Decentralization, however, has also its danger for the tribes, and the Commissioner for Scheduled Castes and Scheduled Tribes has expressed the fear that due to the existing pattern of concentration of social and economic power in the hands of a dominant section of the population, the democratic decentralization may lead to more extensive exploitation of the scheduled tribes. Moreover, the *panchayat samities* and *zila parishads*, which is some states have already taken over many of the functions of the former district officers, may be disinclined to support the implementations of tribal welfare schemes, for the simple reason that their leading members belong to the very classes which traditionally profited from the exploitation of the tribes. In his report for the year 1962-63 (pp. 9-10) the Commissioner proposed, therefore, that in order that the system of democratic decentralization might be smoothly introduced without endangering the interests of the tribals, "the State Governments concerned should ensure that in the *panchayats* constituted in the predominantly tribal areas the Sarpanches (chairmen) should invariably be elected/nominated from amongst the tribals only."

A problem almost as important as the revolution of the district administrations by the introduction of *panchayati raj*, is the impact of industrialization on the tribes in areas rich in mineral resources. Certain areas within the tribal belt of middle India, and particularly Orissa, West Bengal, Bihar, and Madhya Pradesh, have been found to contain rich deposits of minerals, their exploitation and the establishment of great steel-works in the very centre of the aboriginals' homeland, threaten to lead to a large-scale displacement of tribal populations. The Scheduled Areas and Scheduled Tribes Commission expressed grave concern regarding the ultimate fate of the aboriginals, whose last refuge areas in hills and forests are now being turned into industrial regions. While the Commission accepts their "substantial displacement" as inevitable, its report reveals (p. 271) that out of 14,461 tribal families displaced from an area of 62,494 acres, only 3,479 have been allotted alternative land:

The tribals were dislodged from their traditional sources of livelihood and places of habitation. Not conversant with the details of acquisition proceedings they accepted whatever cash compensation was given to them and became emigrants. With cash in hand many attractions in the nearby industrial towns, their funds were rapidly depleted and in course of time they were without money as well as without land. They joined the ranks of landless labourers but without any training, equipment or aptitude for any skilled or semi-skilled job.

The Commission recommends that the government, as trustee of the scheduled tribes, should not allow the tribes to go under in the process of industrialization, but should see that rehabilitation and training schemes enable tribesmen to find employment in the industry growing up on the land from which they have been forcibly displaced. Judging from the situation in places such as Rourkela, Ranchi, and Jamshedpur, one cannot escape the conclusion, however, that the prospects for the tribesmen deprived of their land and virtually expelled from their ancestral home is by no means good, and that a real proletarianization of the tribesmen of these areas appears unavoidable.

Nirad C. Chaudhuri, the frank and provocative analyst of the present-day Indian social scene, has expressed a similar assessment of the tribesmen's probable fate under the impact of industrialization in strong and colourful language:

In an industrialized India the destruction of the aboriginal's life is as inevitable as the submergence of the Egyptian temples caused by the dams of the Nile.... As things are going, there can be no grandeur in the primitive's end. It will not be even simple extinction, which is not the worst of human destinies. It is to be feared that the aboriginal's last act will be squalid, instead of being tragic. What will be seen with most regret will be, not his disappearance, but his enslavement and degradation.[9]

[9] *The Continent of Circe*, London. 1965, p. 77.

It is to be hoped that this gloomy forecast will prove unduly pessimistic, but unless the detailed recommendations of the Scheduled Areas and Scheduled Tribes Commission are acted upon, large numbers of displaced aboriginals from the new industrial areas may indeed become homeless vagrants unable to obtain any suitable employment which could compensate them for the land they had to give up as a sacrifice on the altar of India's modernization. The establishment of vast industrial enterprises in tribal zones lends urgency to the extension of protective measures to all tribals whose rights and way of life have been placed in jeopardy. The framers of the Indian Constitution were clear that while scheduled tribes were to be brought out from their age-old isolation, they should be saved from exploitation and from the erosion of their rights to their ancestral land. This aim can be achieved only by special legislation, and the Scheduled Areas and Scheduled Tribes Commission ended its long report with the plea to "secure the advancement of the tribals without disturbing the essential harmony of their life and secure their integration without imposition" (p. 499). The manner of integration of the tribals within the wider Indian society will ultimately depend on political decisions and these will be made on the basis of moral evaluations. Unless the advanced sections of the Indian population develop a spirit of cultural tolerance and an appreciation of tribal values, even the most elaborate schemes for the economic settlement of the tribals are likely to prove abortive. It is for this reason that the late Jawaharlal Nehru formulated the following five principles for the policy to be pursued vis-a-vis the tribals:

(1) People should develop along the lines of their own genius, and the imposition of alien values should be avoided.

(2) Tribal rights in land and forest should be respected.

(3) Teams of tribals should be trained in the work of administration and development.

(4) Tribal areas should not be overadministered or overwhelmed with a multiplicity of schemes.

(5) Results should be judged not by statistics or the amount of money spent, but by the human character that is evolved.

Except in a few areas, such as NEFA, these principles have seldom been put fully into practice. There are, moreover, indications that Nehru's extremely liberal ideas regarding the rights of the tribals and the preservation of their cultural heritage may not be shared by all of the present leaders of the Congress party, and it is likely that pressure for a speedier and more complete assimilation of the aboriginals will gradually increase and lead to changes even in tribal areas such as NEFA. The existence of a number of special agencies responsible for the protection of tribal rights, on the other hand, justifies, the expectation that despite occasional attacks on these rights our tribals will continue to enjoy at least some of the privileges provided for them by the Indian Constitution.

Bibliography

Adelman, Irma and George Dalton, 1971. "A Factor Analysis of Modernization in Village India," *Economic Anthropology and Development: Essays on Tribal and Peasant Economics.* New York: Basic Books Inc.

Altas, S.H., 1976. *The Myths of the Lazy Native.* London: Frank Cass.

American Friends Service Committee, 1957. "Selected Findings and Queries," *Community Development Review,* IV, pp. 4-35.

Atal, Yogesh, 1961. "Rural Studies: Indian Village," *Eastern Anthropologist.* Vol. 14, pp. 249-57.

———, 1976. *Social Sciences: The Indian Scene.* New Delhi: Abhinav Publications.

Atal, Yogesh and Ralph Pieris, 1976. *Asian Thinking on Development.* New Delhi: Abhinav Publications.

Bailey, F.G., 1966. "The Peasant View of the Bad Life," *Journal of British Association for the Advancement of Science,* vol. 23, pp. 399-409, December 1966.

Bastide, Roger. 1973. *Applied Anthropology.* London: Croom Helm.

Beals, Ralph L. and Harry Hoijer, 1971. *An Introduction to Anthropology.* Fourth edition. New York: Macmillan (Chapter 20).

Belshaw, Cyril S. 1972. "Anthropology," (Disciplinary Contributions to Development Studies), *International Social Science Journal,* vol. 24, no. 1, pp. 80-94.

———, 1976. *The Sorcerer's Apprentice: An Anthropology of Public Policy.* New York: Pergamon Press Inc.

Bernard, H.R. and P.J. Pelto, eds., 1972. *Technology and Social Change.* New York: Macmillan.

Betéllé, André, 1971. "Implementing Land Reforms," *The Times of India,* 9 September 1970.

———, 1971. "Social Framework of Agriculture" in L. Lefeber and M. Datta Chaudhri, eds., *Regional Development: Experience and Prospects in South and South-east Asia.* The Hague: Mouton.

———, 1972. *Inequality and Social Change.* Delhi: Oxford University Press.

―――, 1974. *Studies in Agrarian Social Structure.* Delhi: Oxford University Press, p. 206.

Bhagat, M.G. and Subhachari Das Gupta, 1975. *Developing Adivasis and Small Farmers.* Bombay: National Institute of Bank Management.

Bharati, Agehananda, 1963. "Cultural Hurdles in Development Administration" in Irving Swerdlow, ed., *Development Administration: Concepts and Problems.* Syracuse, N.Y.: Syracuse University Press, pp. 68-84.

Bodley, John H., 1976. *Anthropology and Contemporary Human Problems.* Menlo Park: Cummings Publishing Company.

Bose, Nirmal K., 1961. "Impact of Changing Technology on Society," *Economic Weekly,* vol. 13, pp. 473-74, 18 March 1961.

―――, 1972. *Anthropology and Some Indian Problems.* Calcutta: Institute of Social Research and Applied Anthropology.

Burling, Robbins, 1967. "Tribesmen and Lowlanders of Assam" in Peter Kunstadter, ed., *Southeast Asian Tribes, Minorities and Nations,* vol. 1. Princeton, New Jersey: Princeton University Press.

Carstairs, G. Morris, 1955. "Medicine and Faith in Rural Rajasthan" in Benjamin D. Paul, ed., *Health, Culture and Community.* New York: Russell Sage Foundation.

Chandra, Vimal, 1968. *Handbook on Scheduled Castes and Scheduled Tribes.* New Delhi: Office of the Commissioner for Scheduled Castes and Scheduled Tribes, Government of India.

Cliffton, J.A. ed., 1969. *Applied Anthropology: Readings in the Uses of the Science of Man.* Boston: Houghton Mifflin Company.

Cochrane, Glynn, 1971. *Development Anthropology.* New York: Oxford University Press.

―――, 1974. "What Can Anthropology Do For Development?" *Finance and Development,* vol. 11, no. 2, June, pp. 20-23.

Cochrane, Willard et al., 1968. *Development and Change in Traditional Agriculture: Focus on South Asia.* East Lansing: Michigan State University, Asian Studies Centre, Occasional Papers, no. 7.

Dalton, George, 1971. *Economic Anthropology and Development.* New York: Basic Books.

Dasgupta, Satadal and G.R. Madan, 1975. *Rural Social Structure and Agricultural Development.* Calcutta: Anthropological Survey of India.

De Gregori, Thomas R. and Oriol Pi-Sunyer, 1969. *Economic Development: The Cultural Context,* New York: John Wiley & Sons Inc.

Djurfeldt, Goran and Staffan Linderg, 1975. *Behind Poverty: The Social Formation in a Tamil Village.* Lund: Studentlitteratur.

Dube, S.C., 1956. "Cultural Factors in Rural Community Development," *The Journal of Asian Studies,* vol. 16, no. 1, November 1956, pp. 19-30.

―――, 1958. *India's Changing Villages: Human Factors in Community Development.* London: Routledge and Kegan Paul Ltd.

―――, 1961. "Human Element in Indian Development," *Kurukshetra,* vol. 10, no. 1, 2 October 1961, pp. 37-38.

―――, 1964. "Tradition, Social Structure and Agricultural Development," *Kurukshetra*, vol. 13, no. 1, October 1964, pp. 14-19.
―――, 1965. "Cultural Problems in the Economic Development of India" in Robert N. Ballabh, ed., *Religion and Progress in Modern Asia*. New York: The Free Press.
―――, 1967. "A Note on Communication in Economic Development" in Daniel Lerner and Wilbur Schramn, eds., *Communication and Change in the Developing Countries*. Honolulu: East-west Center Press.
―――, 1968. "Strategies of Influencing Change," *Anthropologist*, vol. 2, (special volume), pp. 1-14.
―――, 1971. *Explanation and Management of Change*. New Delhi: Tata McGraw-Hill.
―――, 1974. *Contemporary India and its Modernization*. Delhi: Vikas Publishing House Pvt. Ltd.
Dutta, Ratna, 1968. "Values and Economic Development," *Economic and Political Weekly*, vol. 3, nos. 1 and 2, (annual number), pp. 109-16.
Elwin, Verrier, 1959. *A Philosophy for NEFA*. Shillong: Government of Assam.
―――, 1964. *The Tribal World of Verrier Elwin*. Bombay: Oxford University Press.
Epstein, T. Scarlett, 1962. *Economic Development and Social Change in South India*. Manchester: Manchester University Press.
―――, 1972. "The Dimensions of Rural Development" in T. Scarlett Epstein and D.H. Penny, eds., *Opportunity and Response: Case Studies in Economic Development*. London: C Hurst & Co., pp. 241-51.
―――, 1973. *The Role of Social Anthropology in Development Studies*. Paper presented at the 1973 Annual Meeting of the Association of Social Anthropologists at Oxford.
―――, 1973. *South India: Yesterday, Today and Tomorrow*. London: Macmillan.
―――, 1975. "The Ideal Marriage Between the Economist's Macroapproach and the Social Anthropologist's Microapproch to Development Studies," *Economic Development and Cultural Change*, vol. 24, no. 1, October.
―――, ed., 1976. *The Paradox of Poverty: Socioeconomic Aspects of Population Growth*. Delhi: Macmillan.
Etienne, Gilbert, 1968. *Studies in Indian Agriculture: The Art of the Possible*. Berkeley: University of California Press.
Foster, G.M., 1969. *Applied Anthropology*. Boston: Little, Brown and Company.
―――, 1973. *Traditional Societies and Technological Change*. New York: Harper & Row.
Fraser Jr. Thomas M., 1963. "Socio-cultural Parameters in Directed Change," *Human Organization*, vol. 22, no. 1, pp. 95-104.
―――, 1968. *Culture and Change in India: The Barpali Experiment*. Amherst: University of Massachusetts Press.

Fürer-Haimendorf, Christoph von, 1958. "The West in the 'Underdeveloped' Countries," *Swiss Review of World Affairs*, December, pp. 16-18.
———, 1967. "The Position of Tribal Populations in Modern India," in Phillip Mason, ed., *India and Ceylon: Unity and Diversity*. London: Oxford University Press.
———, 1975. "Pattern of Development for Tribal Societies," *Development Policy and Administration Review*, vol. 1, no. 3, July/December, pp. 87-92.
Gaikward, V.R., 1971. *Small Farmers: State Policy and Programme Implementation*. Hyderabad: National Institute of Community Development.
Gillette, Cynthia and Norman Uphoff, 1973. *Cultural and Social Factors Affecting Small Farmer Participation in Formal Credit Programs*. Ithaca: Cornell University Rural Development Committee Occasional Papers, no. 3. (Mimeographed).
Goldthorpe, J.E. 1975. *The Sociology of the Third World: Disparity and Involvement*. Cambridge: Cambridge University Press.
Greenwood, Davydd J. 1973. *The Political Economy of Peasant Family Farming: Some Anthropological Perspectives on Rationality and Adoption*. Ithaca: Cornell University Rural Development Committee Occasional Monographs, no. 2. (Mimeographed).
Gould, Harold A., 1965. "Modern Medicine and Folk Cognition in Rural India," *Human Organization*, vol. 24, no. 3.
Government of India, 1955. *The Adivasis*. New Delhi: Publications Division, Ministry of Information and Broadcasting.
Hasan, Khwaja Arif, 1967. *The Cultural Frontier of Health in Village India*. Bombay: Manaktalas.
Haswell, M.R., 1967. *Economic of Development in Village India*. London: Routledge and Kegan Paul Ltd.
Hill, R., E.D. Driver and Moni Nag, 1968. *Needed Social Science Research in Population and Family Planning*. New Delhi: The Ford Foundation.
Hodgdon, L.L. and H. Singh, 1964. *Adoption of Agricultural Practices in Madhya Pradesh*. Hyderabad: National Institute of Community Development.
Hunt, Chester L., 1966. *Social Aspects of Economic Development*. New York: McGraw-Hill Book Co.
Hunter, Guy, 1966. *Modernising Peasant Societies*. London: Oxford University Press.
ICSSR, 1974. *A Survey of Research in Sociology and Social Anthropology*, vol. 2. Bombay: Popular Prakashan. (See Chapter 1 "Sociology of Economic Development: A Trend Report" by S.C. Dube.)
Jay, Edward, J., 1958. "The Anthropologist and Tribal Welfare," *Journal of Social Research*, pp. 82-89.
Kapp, K.W., 1963. *Hindu Culture, Economic Development and Economic Planning*. Bombay: Asia Publishing House.
Kivlin, Joseph, Frederick C. Fliegel, Prodipto Roy and Lalit K. Sen,

Bibliography

1971. *Innovation in Rural India.* Bowling Green, Ohio 13403: Bowling Green State University Press.
Leeds, Anthony, 1964. "Cultural Factors in Education: India, Brazil, the United States, the Soviet Union: Some Problems of Applied Anthropology" in Baidya Nath Varma, ed., *Contemporary India.* Bombay: Asia Publishing House.
Lengyel, Peter, ed., 1971. *Approaches to the Science of Socio-economic Development.* Paris: Unesco.
Lewis, Oscar, assisted by Victor Barnouw and Harvant Dhillon, 1956. "Aspects of Land Tenure and Economics in a North Indian Village," *Economic Development and Cultural Change.*
Lipton, Michael, 1968. "A Game Against Nature: Strategies of Security," *The Listener,* 4 April, pp. 437-39.
———, 1969. "A Game Against Nature: Theories of Peasants Decision Making," *The Listener,* 28 March, pp. 401-3.
Luschinsky, Mildred Stroop, 1963. "Problems of Culture Change in the Indian Village," *Human Organization,* vol. 22, no. 1, pp. 66-74.
Madan, T.N., 1968. "Caste and Development," *Economic and Political Weekly,* vol. 4, no. 4, pp. 285-90.
Majumdar, D.N. ed., 1955. *Rural Profile.* Lucknow: Ethnographic and Folk Culture Society.
Maloney, Clarence, 1974. *Peoples of South Asia.* New York: Holt, Rinehart and Winston, Inc. (See Chapter 16 "Rural Change and Development.")
Mandelbaum, David G., 1952. "Technology, Credit and Culture in an Indian Village," *Human Organization,* vol. 11, nos. 4-6.
———, 1853. "Planning and Social Change in India," *Human Organization,* vol. 12, no. 3.
———, 1972. "Curing and Religion in South Asia" in Surjit Sinha, ed., *Aspects of Indian Culture and Society: Essays in Felicitation of Professor Nirmal Kumar Bose.* Calcutta: The Indian Anthropological Society.
———, 1973. "Social Components of Indian Fertility," *Economic and Political Weekly,* vol. 8, no. 4, pp. 4-6.
———, 1974. *Human Fertility in India: Social Components and Policy Perspectives.* Berkeley: University of California Press.
———, 1975. "Some Effects of Population Growth in India on Social Interaction and Religion," in Marcus F. Franda, ed., *Responses to Population Growth in India: Changes in Social, Political, and Economic Behaviour.* New York: Praeger Publishers.
Marriott, McKim, 1952a. "Social Structure and Change in a U.P. Village," *The Economic Weekly,* 25 August, pp. 869-74.
———, 1952b. "Technological Change in Overdeveloped Rural Areas," *Economic Development and Cultural Change,* vol. 1, December, pp. 261-72.
———, 1955. "Western Medicine in a Village of Northern India," in Benjamin D. Paul, ed., *Health, Culture, and Community.* New York: Russell Sage Foundation.

Marshall, John F., 1920. "Some 'Meanings' of Family Planning to an Indian Villager," *Research Previews*, vol. 19, no. 1, pp. 24-29.

———, 1972b. "Topics and Network in Intra-Village Communication" in Steven Polger, ed., *Culture and Population: A Collection of Current Studies*. Chapel Hill, N C: Carolina Population Center, pp. 1-21.

Mathur, Hari Mohan, 1965. "Modernizing Traditional Agriculture," *Kurukshetra*, vol. 15, no. 1, 2 October, (annual number).

———, 1968. "Technological Change in Developing Countries," *Quest*, April/June, 57, pp. 48-51.

———, 1971. "Changing Contours in Village India," *Indian and Foreign Review*, vol. 8, no. 18, 1 July, pp. 13-18.

———, 1972a. "Putting Anthropology to Practical Uses," *The Indian Journal of Social Work*, vol. 22, no. 1, January, pp. 445-51.

———, 1972b. "Social Aspects of Administering Technical Aid Programmes," *Indian Journal of Public Administration*, vol. 18, no. 2, April/June.

———, 1972c. "Anthropology and Public Administration," *Indian Anthropologist* vol. 2, no. 2, pp. 71-78.

———, 1974. "India's Tribal Minorities: Bringing Them into the Mainstream of National Life," *Plural Societies*, vol. 5, no. 2, Summer, pp. 25-41.

———, 1975a. "Controlling Population Growth: An Anthropological View," *Asian Profile*, vol. 3, no. 2, April, pp. 217-24.

———, 1975b. "The Place of Anthropology in Population Control Programmes in India," *Eastern Anthropologist*, vol. 28, no. 3, July-September, pp. 281-90.

———, 1975c. "Ending Poverty, Unemployment and Inequality: Experience and Strategy," *Development Policy and Administration Review*, vol. 1, no. 2.

———, 1976a. "Anthropology, Government, and Development Planning in India" in David C. Pitt, ed., *Development From Below: Anthropologists Development Situations*. The Hague: Mouton.

———. 1976b. *Development Administration in Tribal Areas*. Jaipur: The HCM State Institute of Public Administration.

Mathur, K.S. *et al.*, eds., 1973. *Studies in Social Change*. Lucknow Ethnographic and Folk Culture Society.

May, D.A. and D.M. Heer, 1968. "Son Survivorship, Motivation and Family Size in India: A Computer Simulation," *Population Studies*, vol. 22, no. 2.

Mayer, Adrian C., 1956. "Development Projects in an Indian Village," *Pacific Affairs*, vol. 30, no. 1.

———, 1957. "An Indian Community Development Block Revisited," *Pacific Affairs*, vol. 30, no. 1.

Mayer, Albert *et al.* 1958. *Pilot Project, India*. Berkely: University of California Press.

McCormack, William C., 1957. Mysore Villager's View of Change," *Economic Development and Cultural Change*, vol. 5, pp. 257-62.

Bibliography

McNamara, Robert S., 1973. *One Hundred Countries, Two Billion People: The Dimensions of Development.* London: The Pall Mall Press.

Mellor, John W. et. al. 1968. *Developing Rural India: Plan and Practice.* Ithaca, N.Y.: Cornell University Press.

Mencher, Joan P., 1970a. "Family Planning in India: The Role of Class Values," *Family Planning Perspectives,* vol. 2, March.

———, 1970b. "Change Agents and Villagers," *Economic and Political Weekly,* vol. 29-31, July.

———, 1974. "Conflicts and Contradiction in the 'Green Revolution,'" *Economic and Political Weekly,* vol. 9, nos. 6, 7 & 8, February.

Michie, Barry H., "Variations in Economic Behaviour and the Green Revolution: An Anthropological Perspective," *Economic and Political Weekly,* vol. 8, no. 26, *Review of Agriculture,* 30 June 1973, pp. A67-75.

Misra, R.P. et al. 1974. "*Regional Development Planning in India: A New Strategy.* Delhi: Vikas Publishing House Pvt Ltd. (See Chapter IX, "Planning for a Tribal Region.")

Myrdal, Gunnar, 1968. *Asian Drama: An Inquiry into the Poverty of Nations.* Harmondsworth: Allen Lane, The Penguin Press.

Naik, T.B. 1972. "Applied Anthropology in India: A Trend Report," in ICSSR, *A Survey of Research in Sociology and Social Anthropology,* vol. 3, Bombay: Popular Prakashan.

Nair, Kusum, 1962a. *Blossoms in the Dust.* London: Gerald Duckworth & Co. Ltd.

———, 1962b. "The Problem of Limited Aspiration," *Yojana,* vol. 6, no. 2, February.

———, 1962c. "Democratic Planning Helps to Break Down Ancient Taboos," *India: A Survey compiled from the Times.* 26 January, London: Times Publishing Co. Ltd.

Nash, Manning and Robert Chin, 1963. "Psychocultural Factors in Asian Economic Growth," *Journal of Social Sciences,* vol. 19, no. 1, January, pp. 1-87.

Nehru, Jawaharlal, 1955. "The Tribal Folk," in Government of India, *The Adivasis.* New Delhi: The Publications Division, Ministry of Information and Broadcasting.

———, 1957. "Foreword" in Verrier Elwin," *A Philosophy for NEFA,* Shillong: Government of Assam.

Niehoff, Arthur M., 1959. *Factory Workers in India.* Milwaukee: Milwaukee Public Museum Publications in Anthropology, no. 5.

Opler, Morris E., 1952. "The Problem of Selective Culture Change" in B.F. Hoselitz, ed., *The Problems of Underdeveloped Areas.* Chicago: University of Chicago Press.

———, 1964. "Cultural Context of Population Control Problems in India" in Earl Count and Gordon T. Bowles, eds., *Fact and Theory in Social Science.* Syracuse, N.Y.: Syracuse University Press.

Orenstein, Henry, 1960. "Irrigation, Settlement Pattern and Social Organisation," in F.C. Wallace, ed., *Selected Papers in the Fourth*

International Congress of Anthropological and Ethnological Sciences. Philadelphia: University of Pennsylvania Press.

Pitt, David., ed., 1976. *Development From Below: Anthropologists and Development Situations.* The Hague: Mouton.

Pocock, D.F., 1968. "Social Anthropology: Its Contribution to Planning" in Paul Streeten and Michael Lipton, eds., *The Crisis of Indian Planning.* London: Oxford University Press.

Potter, Jack M. 1971. "Modernization Process and Rural Development in Developing Countries" in Raanan Weitz, ed., *Rural Development in a Changing World.* Cambridge, Ma.: The MIT Press.

Prasad, Narmadeshwar, 1970. *Change Strategy in a Developing Society: India.* Meerut: Meenakshi Prakashan.

Rao, D.V. Raghava, 1974. "Institutional Framework for Agricultural Development in Tribal Areas" in Guy Hunter and Anthony F. Bottrall, eds., *Serving the Small Farmer: Policy Choices in Indian Agricultural Development.* London: Croom Helm.

Rao, V.K.R.V., 1965. "Some Problems Confronting Traditional Societies in the Process of Development" in Raymond Aron and Bert F. Hoselitz, eds., *Social Development.* Paris: Unesco and the Hague: Mouton.

———, 1969. "Social Change and the Tribal Culture" in L.P. Vidyarthi, ed., *Conflict Tension and Cultural Trend in India.* Calcutta: Punthi Pustak.

Rao, Y.V. Lakshmana, 1966. *Communication and Development: A Study of Two Indian Villages.* Minneapolis: University of Minnesota.

Rogers, Everett M., 1973. *Communication Strategies for Family Planning,* p. 451, New York: Free Press.

Rose, Arnold M., 1968. "Sociological Factors Affecting Economic Development in India," *Studies in Comparative International Development,* vol. 1, no. 9.

Roy, Prodipto, 1967. *The Impact of Communications in Rural Development.* Hyderabad: National Institute of Community Development.

Roy, Prodipto et al. 1968. *Patterns of Agricultural Diffusion in Rural India.* Hyderabad: National Institute of Community Development.

Rowe, William L. ed., 1966. *Contours of Culture Change in South Asia.* (Reprint of *Human Organization,* vol. 22, no. 1.) Lexington, Kentucky: The Society for Applied Anthropology.

Saberwal, Satish, 1967. "Fallacies in the Development of Tribal Areas," *Quest,* April-June (53), pp. 76-78.

Sachchidananda, 1972. "Planning, Development and Applied Anthropology in India," *Journal of the Indian Anthropological Society,* vol. 7, no. 1, April.

———, 1972. *Social Dimensions of Agricultural Development.* Delhi: National Publishing House.

Sadie, J.L., 1960. "Social Anthropology of Economic Development," *The Economic Journal,* vol. 30, June, pp. 294-303.

Sahay, B.N., 1969. *Pragmatism in Development: Application of Anthropology.* New Delhi: Bookhive.

Bibliography

Sanday, Peggy Reeves, ed., 1976. *Anthropology and the Public Interest: Fieldwork and Theory.* New York: Academic Press.

Schneider, Harold K., 1974. *Economic Man: The Anthropology of Economics.* New York: Free Press.

———, 1975. "Economic Development and Anthropology" in Bernard J. Siegal, ed., *Annual Review of Anthropology,* vol. 4, Palo Alto, California: Annual Reviews, Inc.

Sen, S.C., 1955. "Problems of Medical Practice in India," *New England Journal of Medicine,* vol. CCL II, p. 18.

Singh, K. Suresh, ed., 1972. *Tribal Situation in India.* Simla: Indian Institute of Advanced Study.

Singh, Rudra Dutt, 1952. "The Village Level: An Introduction of Green Manuring in Rural India" in Edward H. Spicer, ed., *Human Problems in Technological Change.* New York: Russell Sage Foundation.

Singer, Milton, 1956. "Cultural Values in India's Economic Development," *Annals of the American Academy of Political and Social Science.* no. 305, May 1956, pp. 81-91.

Singleton, John, 1973. "Schools and Rural Development: An Anthropological Approach," in Phillip Foster and James R. Sheffield, eds., *Education and Rural Development.* The World Yearbook of Education, London: Evans Brothers Limited.

Sperling, Jan Bodo, 1967. "Human Problems in Technical Assistance: Rourkela, India," *Asian Studies,* vol. 5, no. 2, August (Philippines).

Srinivas, M.N., ed., 1960. *India's Villages.* Bombay: Asia Publishing House.

Srinivas, M.N. 1961a. "Sociological Aspects of Indian Diets," *Agricultural Situation in India,* vol. 16, June, pp. 246-48.

———, 1961b. "Changing Attitudes in India Today," *Yojana,* 1 October 1961, vol. 5, no. 19, pp. 25-28.

———, 1967. *Social Change in Modern India.* Berkeley: California University Press.

———, 1975a. *Social Environment and Management's Responsibility.* Paper presented at the National Management Convention, New Delhi, 30-31 January.

———, 1975b. "Village Studies, Participant Observation and Social Science Research in India," *Economic and Political Weekly,* special number, August, pp. 1387-94.

Taylor, Carl C. et al., 1965. *India's Roots of Democracy.* Bombay: Orient Longman.

Unesco, 1961. *Social and Cultural Factors Affecting Productivity of Industrial Workers in India.* Delhi: Unesco Research Centre on Social and Economic Development in Southern Asia.

Uphoff, Norman T. and Warren F. Illchman, 1972. *The Political Economy of Development.* Berkeley: University of California Press.

Vidyarthi, L.P., ed., 1968. *Applied Anthropology in India.* Allahabad: Kitab Mahal.

Zimmerman, Carle C. and Richard E. Durwors, eds., 1976. *Sociology of Underdevelopment.* Jaipur: Rawat Publications (Asian Edition).

Index

Abstinence, practice of, 219-21
Administrative communication, network of, 305; see also Communication process
Agricultural credit, problems of, 388
Agricultural development, and social tensions, 384,385; need of feedback from villagers for, 256
Agricultural minimum wages, suggestion on, 101
Agricultural modernization, 84,85; experiment on, 60-62; sociological survey on, 95
Agricultural operations, cooperative work in, 249,250
Agricultural productivity, maximization of, 390,391
Agricultural wages, question of, 248
Anthropological Survey of India, role of, 124
Archaeology, relevance of, 27

Badagas, social change experiment with, 73
Baigas, Verrier Elwin's proposal for, 127
Bani worship, ritual of, 213
Barpali village service, reactions to, 161-65, 167-70, 173-76; for sanitary lines, 160,161; programmes for water supplies, 159,160; setting of, 157-59; vegetable and poultry programmes of, 165-67, 171; weavers' and chamars' cooperatives, 170-73, 177
Barka Basiaura, ceremony of, 213
Birth control programme and cultural factors, 354,355
Brazil, development lessons from, 1
Bureaucracy and people, communication gap between, 85,86

Caste and kinship structure as a cultural hurdle, 108,109
Caste status and economic standing, link between, 50
Caste system, 177,178 428-30; and casteism, distinction between, 59-60; and response to directed change, 146,147; resistance to innovations, 106,107; vested interests in, 243,244
Census of India, role of, 123,124
Central Advisory Board for Tribal Affairs, anthropologists' association with, 126
Chingleput District, agricultural survey on, 376-84
Chotka Basiaura, ceremony of, 213
Cognitive map, modernizing elites, 280; peasants', 275-77; synonyms

for, 271; tracing of, 272
Communication, anthropologists' study of, 140-42
Communication process, analysis of, 322-26; innovations in, 315-22; segments of, 305-22
Community habits and tastes, influence on innovations, 140-42
Community development, 35
Community orchards programme, cultural hurdles in, 144
Congress of Americanists, suggested role for, 46
Constructive anthropologists, suggested cadre of, 68,69
Cross-cultural education, challenge of, 36,37
Cultural hurdles, concept of, 104; in India, 105-10; development administrators' evaluation of, 114-20
Cultural model, construction of, 177-80
Cultural policy, anthropologists' contribution to, 42-44
Culture, analysis of, 27,28; definition of, 27; idiosyncratic associations, rural and communication networks, 227: cognitive map of, 272

Development, and crash programmes, 34; definition of, 90,91; impact on family organization, 98,99; short- and long-term impacts of, 33; socio-economic variables in, 95
Development advisers, suggested cadre of, 47
Development anthropology, role of, 98-100
Development block, emergence of, 316
Development models, anthropologists' role in framing, 98,99
Development myths, example of, 92-94
Development personnel and people, relations between, 86, 87; evaluation of cultural hurdles by, 114-20; factors restraining dedication of, 254-56; peasants' relation with, 294,295; power influences on, 264; training of, 132; villagers' reaction to, 296-98
Development policy, anthropologists' advice on, 101; anthropologists' role in framing, 127, 128; propositions relating to, 33-35
Development programmes, and village factionalism, 298; planning predictive methodology for, 177-82; selective and differential acceptance of, 154,155; stimulation for, 298-300
Dharma Sutras, 339
Diseases, sacred and secular, 412-14
Divorce, 22
Dominant caste, concept of, 52

Early marriage, and population growth, 206: impact of education on, 206, 207
Economic growth, and economic development, 88, 89; impact on joint family, 96
Education, diverse impacts of, 237, 238
Educational development and culture change, 350-54
Educational policy, anthropologists' contribution to, 36-38
Educational programmes, influence of social practices on, 143-44
Elwin, Verrier, 127, 128; on tribal policy for India, 472-84, 531, 532
Environmental change, social implications of, 39,40
Ethnocentrism, 34,38

Factionalism, and response to directed change, 146, 148,149; and village unity, 80,81; study

Index

on, 344
Faith healing, 415-17, 434,435;
  practice of, 399, 400, 403, 404
Family planning programmes,
  background of change agents
  in, 258,259; deficiencies in, 245;
  information on, 265-66; people's mobilization, 259-62;
  suggestions for, 458; villagers'
  attitude to, 259
Family size, traditional factors
  influencing, 217,218
First development decade (UN),
  failure of, 89
Food preferences, notions on, 411

Gandhi, Mahatma, stress on self-
  help by, 196
Godhana and Piria, ceremonies of,
  215, 216
Government inter-department administration, segments of, 311-
  13
Green revolution, 89; extension of,
  319, 320; impact of, 250; nature
  of, 246
Growth performance and development, implications of, 30-32
Group dynamics and response to
  directed change, 146

High-yielding seeds, 386,388,389
Hill, Polly, on peasants' attitudes
  to social change, 82
Hindu Code Bill, adverse side
  effects of, 78
Hindu cyclical cosmology, impact
  on Muslims, 108, 108n
Hindu life cycle, *ashramas*, 221

Improved wheat seed, resistance to,
  190,191
India, cultural hurdles to innovations in, 105-10; development
  objectives of, 2, 2n; 20-point
  programme for, 2n; institutions
  promoting social research in,
  123-25; policy towards tribals,

127,128; religious tradition in,
  105, 106; utilization of anthropology in, 121, 122, 125, 126
Indian Council of Social Science
  Research, role of, 125
Indian development administration,
  suitable cadre for, 130-32; utilization of anthropology by,
  125
Indian family organization, flexibility and adaptability of, 98
Indian National Commission on
  Agriculture, anthropologists'
  association with, 126
Indian planning, anthropological
  analysis on, 48-67;urban bias in,
  7n, 48, 48n, 54
Indigenous medicine, acceptability
  of, 431-34, 440-45
Indological studies, suggestion on,
  339
Industrial decentralization, social
  variables in, 50,51
Industrial development, policy
  resolutions on, 310
Infant mortality and attitude to
  family planning, 456,457
Infanticide, 223
Innovations, cultural hurdles to,
  106-9; peasants' receptivity for;
  251,252, 254, 338; secondary and
  tertiary effects of, 153, 154
International Anthropological and
  Ethnological Union, suggested
  role for, 46
Interpersonal behaviour, cultural
  norms to regulate, 227
Irrigation development, problems
  of, 388,389

Jajmani system, 52, 217,218
Jiutia, ritual of, 214,215
Joint family system, decline of,
  96,97; undermining of, 78; impact
  on population size, 225

Kajali Day, 213,214
Kinship, in rural society, 427, 428

Kotas, social change experiment with, 71,72, 73

Land ceilings, implementation of, 253
Land reform, and cultural factors, 356-62; undermining of, 253
Land Reform legislation, adverse side effects of, 78; analysis on, 387; beneficiaries of, 82
Leader-follower relationship, 278, 279
Limited aspirations, phenomenon of, 237
Lingayats, religious sect of, 342,343
Lipton, Michael, on Indian planning, 65; on urban bias in Indian planning, 7n, 48, 48n
Literacy, relevance of, 72
Local government institutions and cultural factors, 362-68
Lokahitartha, Hindu concept of, 113

McLuhan School of thought, 50
McNamara, Robert, 89; on World Bank's new development strategy, 1,2, 2n
Magh Cauth, ceremony of, 216
Malinowski, Bronislaw, study of Trobriand islands by, 17, 26
Manure, problem of, 188, 189, 337
Mechanical irrigation, problems in introducing, 192,193
Magical medicine, 434; *see also* Faith healing
Modern anthropology, 29, 30
Modernization, and cultural change, 83-84; cognitive map of, 280; compulsion vs persuasion for, 271; definition of, 270n; impact of power relations on, 268; potential mediators for, 279-83; technical and social structural factors in, 289,290
Moral community, concept of, 273, 273n, 274
Multiple configuration expectancy,
principle of, 118,119
Mysore Land Grant Rules (1969), undermining the objective of, 92

Naga insurgency, background of, 529-31
National Institute of Community Development (India), role of, 124, 125, 132
Nationalism, reactions to, 33
Nehru, Jawaharlal, approach to tribal problems, 461-67; on Verrier Elwin's impact, 128; on tribal policy, 543,544
Non-literate economies, 29
Noronha, Raymond, analysis of World Bank projects by, 20

Okhamandal development, social change experiment of, 56-64
Optimizing peasant, concept of, 61, 61n
Ostracism, fear of, 263
Outsiders, peasants' view of, 279; villagers' attitudes to, 430

Pacific Science Association, suggested role for, 46
Panchayati Raj Act, 363
Panchayati Raj, and factionalism, ideal of, 65; impact of, 152; implementation of, 74-78; 79, 80; power play in, 65-66; power structure in, 52
Pearson Report, deficiency of, 23
Peasant conservation, myth of, 336
Peasants and tribals, distinction between, 288
Physical anthropology, relevance of, 27
Planners, and people, communication gap between, 85; bias of, 73,74; and development, anthropologists' concern with, 9, 10
Planning and development, anthropologists' evaluation of, 21,22; anthropologists' relevance in,132-35; anthropologists' role in, 2-6,

18; anthropologists' utility in, 13, 25,26, 45, 67-69, 121,122, 332,333; cultural and attitudinal hurdles to, 234-38; human factor in, 71; implementation, gap between, 68; social variable involved in, 24, 25, 72

Planning Commission, structure of, of, 308

Political Communication, network of, 305

Population growth, and attitude to male/female issue, 211, 212; attitude to procreation, 207, 208; and early marriage, 205, 206; and education, 206, 207; national vs local dimensions of, 204,205; traditional restraints on, 218-22, 223,224; villagers' image of, 217

Population control, traditional factors promoting, 218-22, 223, 224

Prawl, Warren L., on peasants' attitude to social change, 8n

Procreation, respectability attached to, 207, 208

Problem projects, anthropologists' analysis of, 22-24

Programme Evaluation Organization (Planning Commission, India), anthropologists' association with, 126

Protest movements, anti-developmental element in, 32

Public hygiene programmes, acceptability of, 418, 419; and cultural factors, 347-50

Rational economic man model, description of, 94; replacement by socio-economic model, 100

Religious behaviour, study of, 342

Religious exorcism, practice of, 436, 437; *see also* Faith healing

Religious tradition, and cultural hurdles, 105, 106; as aid to modernization, 110; securing the sanction of, 110-13

Research Programmes Committee (Planning Commission, India), 125

Role differentiation and response to directed change, 146

Rural communication networks, understanding of, 232, 233

Sacerdotal medicine, 437,438; *see also* Faith healing

Scheduled Areas and Scheduled Tribes Commission, anthropologists' association with, 126

Scheduled castes, changing status of, 65,66; constitutional protection for, 92; myth of, 92-94

Scheduled Tribes Commission Report (Dhebar Commission), 483, 485-502, 541-43; on tribal education, 517

Secular medicine, indigenous, 440, 445

Scientific and technological policies, anthropology's contribution to, 39, 40

Sexual indulgence, restraints on, 219-21

Shadow prices, techniques of, 21, 22

Share family, emergence of, 97,98

Shashthi Day, worship of, 214

Shramdan programmes, 143

Sivaratri, 216

Small farms, and agricultural productivity, 390,391

Small farmers, acceptability of innovations by, 251,252; and agricultural productivity, 246, 247

Small-scale industry development, social variables involved in, 55, 56

Social action, valuation and, 28

Social attitudes and response to directed change, 149-51

Social behaviour, study of, 340

Social beliefs, as hurdles to development, 145,146

Social change, experiments with, 71-73; traditional societies' attitude to, 21; trends of, 100, 101
Social exchange, transactional feature of, 41
Social practices, as hurdles to development, 142-44
Social relations, transactional feature of, 41; study of, 28, 29
Social segmentation and stratification, and response to directed change, 146
Socio-economic differentiation, vested interests in, 243
Subjective configuration pattern, example of, 117, 118, 118n
Symbol systems, studies on, 41

Technological gap, and development personnel, 198, 199; peasants' attitudes to, 194-98
Thailand, attitude to development in, 105; egalitarian tradition in, 111
Third World, development of, 3; new development strategy for, 1,2, 2n, 89
Time cycle, Hindu view of 149, 149n
Todas, social change experiment with, 73
Traditional hierarchy, modernization of, 56-64
Tribal Areas Regulation of 1950, 527
Tribal development, 532, 533, 535-39, 541; constitutional set-up for, 499-504; communications, 499; economy, 497,498; educational, 498; health and housing, 498, 499
Tribal education, 516, 528
Tribal integration, 533
Tribal languages, 511-14, 516
Tribal policy, Elwin's views on, 472-84, 531, 532

Tribal population, data on, 525, 526; ethnic links of, 509, 510 exploitation of, 507; languages of, 511-14; linguistic change, 514-16; under British rule, 505, 506; under Muslim rule, 504,505
Tribal problems, Nehru's approach to, 461-67
Tribal rehabilitation, policy of, 526, 527
Tribal rebellion, causes of, 505,506, 529; data on, 519,520
Tribal Research Institute in India, role of, 124, 132
Tribal welfare, 534,535
Tribals and Hindus, intereaction between, 504

Underemployment, villagers' idea of, 217
Untouchability, roots in caste hierarchy, 50; constitutional ban on, 152; impact of development on, 57, 59
Uttar Pradesh Abolition Committee, 362

Values and response to directed change, 151, 152
Village social structure, 263, 302
Villagers' conservation, myth of, 244, 245

Western medicine, acceptability of, 419,420, 448,449; indifference to, 423, 425,426
World Bank, 17; new development strategy of, 1,2, 2n; use of anthropologists' by, 4, 18,19
World Bank projects, anthropological analysis of, 20,21
World tribalism, notion of, 40

Zamindari abolition, impact of, 152, 362
Zamindari Abolition Act, impact of, 78, 356

LIBRARY OF DAVIDSON COLLEGE